D0204265

Criminal Behavior:
A Systems Approach

Criminal Behavior:
A Systems Approach

Bruce A. Arrigo
The University of North Carolina at Charlotte

PEARSON
Prentice
Hall

Upper Saddle River, New Jersey 07458

Library of Congress Cataloging-in-Publication Data

Arrigo, Bruce A.
  Criminal behavior: a systems approach / Bruce A. Arrigo.
        p. cm.
  Includes bibliographical references and index.
  ISBN 0-13-191521-5
  1. Criminology. 2. Criminal behavior. I. Title.

  HV6025.A675 2006
  364.3–dc22

                                    2004028706

Executive Editor: Frank Mortimer, Jr.
Associate Editor: Sarah Holle
Managing Editor: Mary Carnis
Director of Production and Manufacturing: Bruce Johnson
Production Liaison: Brian Hyland
Design Director: Cheryl Asherman
Senior Design Coordinator: Miguel Ortiz
Cover Designer: DePinho Graphics Design
Cover Image: Shuji Kobayashi/Getty Images/STONE
Cover Printer: Coral Graphics
Composition: *The GTS Companies*/York, PA Campus
Bindery: Courier Westford

Pearson Education Ltd.
Pearson Education Singapore Pte. Ltd.
Pearson Education, Canada, Ltd.
Pearson Education–Japan

Pearson Education Australia Pty, Limited
Pearson Education North Asia Ltd.
Pearson Educación de Mexico, S.A. de C.V.
Pearson Education Malaysia, Pte. Ltd.

10 9 8 7 6 5 4 3 2 1
ISBN 0-13-191521-5

For My Family

Contents

Contents

Part III
Justice System Approaches to Criminals and Criminal Behavior   217

Acknowledgments

Every book relies on the assistance of others to bring a project to completion. *Criminal Behavior: A Systems Approach* is no exception to this well-established practice. Several of my doctoral students (past and present) were instrumental in making this textbook possible and I would like to gratefully acknowledge them. Sheree Gallagher, PsyD, carefully and thoughtfully read drafts of every chapter and commented on the substantive, organizational, and stylistic soundness of the material. As senior review editor, she helped make the overall prose more compelling and the individual chapter sections more complete. Laura Brownmiller also helped organize the textbook. As senior copy editor, she made certain that key terms, discussion questions, and references were meticulously prepared. Corey Vitello, C. Draven Godwin, Stephanie Neumann, and Scott Winstanley all skillfully researched the contents of this book. As senior contributors, they each prepared preliminary drafts on a number of the sections, ensuring that high scholarly standards were balanced against student accessibility for an upper-division undergraduate audience. Charlotte A. Dudley worked tirelessly to prepare a detailed and accessible Glossary. Her assistance in these endeavors was invaluable.

I also want to thank the reviewers of this textbook: Michael Lilly and Travis Langley. Their insights and attention to detail, accuracy, and thoroughness helped fashion not only a first-class textbook but also a sound piece of scholarship. The nature of textbooks is that they strive to give their readership a worthwhile perspective and, hopefully, to foster integrative knowledge. The sensitive and probing observations of the reviewers meaningfully accomplished both of these important goals.

Finally, I want to thank the folks at Prentice Hall and Pearson Education. In particular, I draw attention to my acquisitions editor, Frank I. Mortimer, Jr., and his editorial team. Their commitment to and enthusiasm for this project was unwavering. You recognized in this textbook something unique, and you supportively worked with me to shape it into something worth sharing with students, teachers, and other professionals.

About the Author

BRUCE A. ARRIGO, PhD, is Professor of Crime, Law, and Society at the University of North Carolina—Charlotte, with additional faculty appointments in the Psychology Department, the Public Policy Program, and the Center for Applied and Professional Ethics. He served as Chair of the Department of Criminal Justice at UNC-Charlotte (2001–2004) and as Director of the Institute of Psychology, Law, and Public Policy at the California School of Professional Psychology—Fresno (1996–2001). Dr. Arrigo began his professional career as a community organizer and social activist for the homeless, the mentally ill, the working poor, the frail elderly, the decarcerated, and the chemically addicted. He received his PhD from Pennsylvania State University in the Administration of Justice and he holds a master's degree in psychology and in sociology. He is an internationally recognized scholar, having authored more than 125 journal articles, chapters in books, and scholarly essays. In addition, he is the author, coauthor, or editor of 20 books. Recent volumes include *Psychological Jurisprudence: Critical Explorations in Law, Crime, and Society* (2004), *Police Corruption and Psychological Testing* (with Natalie Claussen, 2004), *The French Connection in Criminology: Rediscovering Crime, Law, and Social Change* (with Dragan Milovanovic and Robert Schehr, 2005), and *Philosophy, Crime, and Theoretical Criminology* (with Christopher R. Williams, 2005). Dr. Arrigo was the Editor-in-Chief of *Humanity & Society* (1996–2000) and is founding and current Editor-in-Chief of the peer-reviewed quarterly, *Journal of Forensic Psychology Practice* (2001–Present). He is the Book Series Editor for *Criminal Justice and Psychology* (Carolina Academic Press) and *Critical Perspectives in Criminology* (University of Illinois Press). Professor Arrigo is a past recipient of the Critical Criminologist of the Year Award (2000), sponsored by the Division of Critical Criminology of the American Society of Criminology. He is also a Fellow of the American Psychological Association (APA) through the Law–Psychology Division (Div. 41) of the APA. He has been a (co)principal investigator for a number of public, private, and corporate grants and contracts totaling approximately $3,000,000. He lives in Concord, North Carolina, with his wife and two children.

Introduction

Criminal behavior is vast and multifaceted. Complicating both of these matters is the general lack of agreement on how best to identify and classify what it encompasses. To be sure, academicians, practitioners, and policy analysts remain uncertain about what is and what is not within the scope of this subspecialty area. This is because the study of it is evolving rapidly. Indeed, offenders are inventing novel forms of illicit conduct, victims are subjected to new forms of harm, and communities are left to respond to both, sometimes with only modest direction from the scientific and legal establishments.

The study of crime, behavior, and their relationship can occur in many ways. One way to appreciate this relationship is to investigate how the disciplines of criminal justice and psychology approach those crime and delinquency issues that straddle both fields of study. To do this effectively, the unique values and insights of these two fields of inquiry must guide the overall analysis. Moreover, a balance must be struck between explaining crime and interpreting behavior. Embracing this logic is challenging, especially because most practitioners, scholars, and teachers typically work from within one, but not both, of these frames of reference. Yet, this equilibrium is precisely what is needed if the problems posed by that behavior society defines as criminal are to be meaningfully addressed.

In this first edition of *Criminal Behavior: A Systems Approach,* the broad and thorny challenges confronting the domains of crime and delinquency are examined. These are the principal areas where the disciplines of criminal justice and psychology intersect. In order to facilitate this investigation, these challenges are interpreted systemically; that is, they are assessed within the confines of relevant theoretical models, realistic concerns, and institutional solutions. This "systems approach" is a useful organizational device for teachers, students, researchers, and lay professionals interested in established crime and delinquency problems as well as emerging trends in criminal behavior studies.

Aside from emphasizing the importance of criminal justice and psychology in the assessment of criminal behavior, another way to appreciate what this subspecialty area encompasses is to describe what it is not. Interestingly, there are several related fields that can eclipse this domain of intellectual and practical inquiry. Several of these corollary areas include deviant behavior, abnormal psychology, criminology, forensic psychology, and victimology. The manner in which this textbook differs from or is related to these worthwhile academic fields is briefly presented here.

The study of criminal behavior is not about understanding deviant conduct per se. This is because there are many forms of deviance that are not expressions of crime. For example, homelessness and mental illness are not clear and undisputed representations of criminality. However, under certain conditions, they may be criminal actions. If an urban street dweller remains visible to the public for a sustained period of time, the individual may be violating a vagrancy statute. If a psychiatrically disordered citizen engages in behavior that endangers the lives of others, the person may be criminally prosecuted and convicted. In these illustrations, we see how the crime and deviance relationship is somewhat fuzzy.

There are also expressions of crime that are not simultaneous representations of deviance. Arson, rape, and murder are classified in the Uniform Crime Report (UCR) as felonies. However, in specified circumstances, each of these behaviors may involve some substantial deviance-related activities. For example, when profiling arsonists, rapists, and murderers, the use of paraphilias (i.e., deviant sexual acts) may be essential for the crime's commission. As such, the link between the offender's conduct and the deviant forces giving rise to it are very much intertwined. Again, the crime–deviance association remains somewhat uncertain, somewhat fluid.

Investigating criminal behavior is not synonymous with research on abnormal psychology. Admittedly, abnormal psychology does examine mental illness. Moreover, under certain conditions, mental illness and crime are connected (e.g., insanity defense and mentally disordered prisoners); however, for the most part, abnormal psychology studies various forms of non-normative behavior (e.g., depression, sleep disorders, and eating disorders) that can be assessed, diagnosed, treated, and prevented. In these instances, the skills of clinical psychologists and related mental health professionals are called on to address the life problems caused by psychiatric illness. Criminal behavior represents only one type of problem that some persons with mental illness confront. Thus, where abnormal psychology represents a broad field and examines the spectrum of psychiatric disorders, criminal behavior represents a narrower subfield and investigates only certain forms of mental illness germane to the commission of only some crimes.

Exploring criminal behavior is not the same as learning about criminology. Criminology is the study of crime and delinquency based on the relevant biological, sociological, and psychological theories and empirical research. Research on criminal behavior is interested in these matters. It uniquely focuses on those offender (and victim) profiles and personality characteristics that account for the commission of crime. Moreover, investigations of criminal behavior seek to explain wrongful *behavior* rather than attempt to explain *crime* acts. In this regard, studying criminal behavior is about the conduct of a person that rises to the level of criminality and not about the criminality itself. This distinction is somewhat subtle; however, it goes to the core of what distinguishes these two areas of inquiry.

For example, rape is a crime. Criminologists study rape. They develop theories of rape and sexual assault more generally and seek to predict, control, and prevent these criminal acts. However, the student of criminal behavior is interested in those actions that constitute the rape event. What does the crime scene look like? Were sexual fetishes or props employed during the sexual assault? What can be said about the degree and type of violence the perpetrator used? Are there any victim characteristics that might enable law enforcement to apprehend the felon? These and similar questions are about comprehending the behavior that established the event as a crime.

Researching criminal behavior is not identical to the work of forensic psychologists. The latter use the tools of the law and psychology to investigate issues and controversies impacting the justice and mental health systems. Child custody evaluations, competency to stand trial determinations, and dangerous predictions are examples of what forensic psychologists do. Central to their professional practice work is the role of assessment, diagnosis, treatment, prevention, and courtroom testimony. Research on criminal behavior explores the topical areas listed previously; however, the mostly clinical core of forensic psychology is somewhat less central to the study of offender conduct and violence. Indeed, the subspecialty area of criminal behavior relies on a wide array of academic disciplines to inform its regard for crime and delinquency. In this way, criminal behavior studies is similar to criminology.

Investigating criminal behavior is not synonymous with what victimology encompasses. Victimology emphasizes how the insights and values of psychology, criminology, sociology, and the law help inform our understanding of personal harm and group victimization. In this respect, then, victimology is interested in human social behavior. However, its largely targeted focus on violence against victims is obscured by the focus of criminal behavior studies that includes victims *and* offenders. In other words, the study of criminal behavior includes many of the concerns raised by scholars, students, and practitioners of victimology, but it also includes nonvictimolgical issues specifically related to offenders and delinquents.

Based on the preceding assessment, we understand that criminal behavior studies share some affinities with the fields of deviance, abnormal psychology, criminology, forensic psychology, and victimology. However, we also recognize that research on criminal behavior is sufficiently distinct that it is not completely synonymous with any one of these intellectual and practical domains of inquiry. Thus, there is considerable room to examine a host of issues at the intersection of crime, violence, and behavior. This is precisely what this textbook endeavors to do.

One way to investigate these issues is to use a systems approach. Earlier it was suggested that this work is systemically organized, although, little explanation on this point was provided. To be clear, this textbook does not intend to offer an integrated assessment of theory, practice, and law. Thus, for example, *Criminal Behavior: A Systems Approach* does not systematically discuss how theory affects the behavior of police, court, and correctional agencies (and personnel) in dealing with specific offender types. Although certainly a worthwhile enterprise, this level of synthesis would necessarily entail the development of several volumes well beyond the scope of what this project intends.

Instead, the systemic approach entertained throughout this text is more modest and can be divided into three specific areas: theoretical, practical, and institutional. Part 1 includes four chapters. Each chapter relies on a particular conceptual frame of reference by which to study criminal behavior. Thus, chapter 1 emphasizes biological theories of crime; chapter 2 emphasizes psychological theories of crime; chapter 3 emphasizes sociological theories of crime; and chapter 4 emphasizes social–psychological theories of crime. Part 2 also includes four chapters, reflecting a systemic analysis of practical crime and delinquency problems. Each chapter focuses on a unique group of offenders and explores how these groups behave. Accordingly, chapter 5 addresses violent crimes and criminals; chapter 6 examines nonviolent crimes and criminals; chapter 7 explores juvenile delinquency; and chapter 8 investigates mental illness and crime. Part 3 completes this systemic assessment of criminal behavior. It singularly focuses on institutional or organizational responses to crime and criminal behavior. As such, chapter 9 considers the role of the police; chapter 10 reviews the role of the courts; and chapter 11 describes the role of prisons and jails. Chapter 12 completes Part 3 of this textbook. This chapter systematically identifies emerging areas in education, theory, and practice, where the study of crime, behavior, and public policy are evolving considerably. Future-directed research attention in these areas might be warranted, especially if the problems posed by criminal behavior are to be meaningfully addressed.

Mindful of this subspecialty field's relationship to other academic disciplines, and given the manner in which this text is organized, *Criminal Behavior: A Systems Approach* provides a unique (and much needed) orientation to the study of crime and delinquency. This first edition stresses the importance of relevant conceptual analysis, detailed practical problems, and thoughtful institutional interventions as the best overall strategy by which to explain crime and interpret behavior. Guided by the need to balance student interests in topical issues with what readers must know, important and useful information on offender profiles, victim characteristics, and crime statistics are provided throughout this volume. In addition, many well-publicized cases are described and several controversial problems are highlighted. These pedagogical tools are conveniently placed as inserts throughout each chapter for easy access and referencing. In this way, the reader can come to appreciate the scope and complexity of investigating crime and delinquency in relation to the concepts and issues explored in the body of the textbook. Finally, key terms and discussion questions are located at the end of each chapter. These items will facilitate the classroom learning as students and teachers alike explore, discuss, and debate the study of criminal behavior and society's fascination with and concern for it.

Bruce A. Arrigo

part I

Theories of Criminal Behavior

Biological Theories of Crime and Criminal Behavior

OVERVIEW

It is difficult to say whether biological theories offer any greater explanatory or predictive capability than any other conceptual approach for the origin of crime and **criminal behavior.** However, the earliest of studies on delinquent and criminal conduct sought to explain the presence of criminal behavior based on insights derived from the biological sciences. This chapter explores many of those models and perspectives that have received scientific attention during the past 200 years. Broadly speaking, the biocriminological, the genetic, and the diathesis-stress orientations tell us something profound about the nature or constitution of people. This is not to suggest that biological theories are disinterested in social, psychological, or environmental correlates; rather, the organic approach to delinquency and crime believes that the physical, neuropsychological, and chemical components of human nature offer more persuasive evidence than do all other alternatives. This chapter explores why and how proponents of the biological approach to criminal behavior come to this conclusion.

KEY TERMS

Acute stress disorder	Genetic theory
Aggression	Heredity
Binge drinking	Hypoglycemia
Biocriminology	Mesomorphic physique
Biological risk factors	Personality
Biosocial model	Posttraumatic stress disorder
Biosocial theories	Predisposition
Birth complications	Prefrontal lobe dysfunction
Criminal behavior	Psychopathology
Criminology	Reactive depressive disorder
Depression	Schizophrenia
Diathesis	Stress
Diathesis–stress model	Trait theories
Ectomorphic physique	Tryptophan
Endomorphic physique	Underarousal
General Adaptive Syndrome	Violence
Genetic mutations or defects	Vulnerability
Genetic risk	XYY chromosome

BIOCRIMINOLOGY

Introduction

Many schools of thought exist regarding the origins of criminal behavior. Scarpa and Raine (1997, p. 627) sum up the value of a holistic perspective toward the understanding of criminal conduct as "All human behavior involves a complex interplay of biologic, cognitive, social, and emotional forces. Antisocial behavior is no exception." In an effort to understand the root causes of criminal transgression, during the past 30 years researchers have provided new (and provocative) findings pertaining to biological factors that may predispose a person to antisocial, aggressive, and violent actions. Given the importance of these scientific data, investigators in the field of **criminology** are looking for useful and practical avenues by which to integrate these biological findings with psychological and sociological theories of criminal behavior. These sorts of undertakings reveal a more integrated and comprehensive explanation for the origins of criminal behavior.

As described in chapters 2 and 3, humanistic psychology, clinical psychology, and applied sociology subscribe to the model that the environment interacts with the mind to develop attitudes, values, and norms that, in turn, cause behavior. As described in chapter 4, learning theory, behavioral theory, and behavior modification programs subscribe to the stimulus–response model. This approach is based on punishment and reinforcement from the environment. However, both of the aforementioned orientations neglect or minimize the impact of biological variables. Indeed, a combination of these approaches would consider how biological variables interact with the environment through the brain and central nervous system. This is an approach that combines the nature and nurture controversy (e.g., Jeffrey, 1989). C. Ray Jeffrey, a pioneer in making criminology an interdisciplinary science, calls this approach an "interdisciplinary theory of criminal behavior" (p. 69). He advocates integrating scientific aspects of human behavior (including biology and brain functioning) with criminal law, social philosophy, psychology, and learning theory. Thus, the interdisciplinary or synthetic approach to the development of human behavior, specifically criminal behavior, places emphasis on the interaction of biology, psychology, and sociology. This area of research is often referred to as **biocriminology**, a **biosocial model**, or a bioenvironmental model of criminal behavior.

In this section, several important dimensions of biocriminological research are discussed and emphasized. These research domains demonstrate how violent crime is being linked currently with biochemistry, brain abnormalities, **prefrontal lobe dysfunction, birth complications,** hormonal issues, and biological predispositions. To be clear, these factors do not excuse criminal behavior and this is not the intent of the biocriminology approach to criminal behavior. However, it is important and useful to understand how advances in the biological correlates of crime, **violence,** and **aggression** deepen and improve our explanatory rationales, methods of prevention, and approaches to treating criminal behavior.

For example, consider the case of Timothy McVeigh, the man responsible for the Oklahoma City bombings. His behavior raises serious questions about why (and how) a person could commit such heinous and devastating acts of violence. According to Michel and Herbeck (2001), McVeigh suffered from three mild head injuries during his youth; however, it is unknown whether or not McVeigh's brain was assessed to determine if his head injuries could have shed any additional light on his criminal behavior. Further, there are countless illustrations of individuals on death row who experienced severe brain abnormalities earlier in their lives, subsequently identified as a result of neuropsychological evaluations conducted during the course of their trials. Again, findings such as these do not per se excuse illicit behavior; however, the value of this information must not be overlooked. Neuropsychological assessments have the potential to prevent nonoffending individuals with the same biological deficits from engaging in criminal acts in the future, and to establish appropriate and effective intervention and treatment techniques designed to rehabilitate persistent offenders with these deficits.

Even though the relationship between genetics and criminal behavior has been well established (Ellis, 1982), the theory of biocriminology does not subscribe to the notion that there is a gene that causes criminal behavior. Instead, biocriminology recognizes that the individual is a product of the interaction between his or her genetics and the environment. The link between the individual's genetics and his or her behavior occurs in the physical structure of the brain, the neurotransmitter system, and the hormones. This interaction forms a structure unique to each individual, determining the type of behavior the individual is capable of producing (Jeffrey, 1989).

Biological Risk Factors for Crime

There are a variety of **biological risk factors** that have been associated with criminal behavior. Some evidence from twin and adoption studies suggests that criminal behavior may be inherited, indicating a genetic component to such behavior (Ellis, 1982). The next section focuses on crime and genetics specifically and, as such, explores these matters in detail.

However, other studies examine biochemical influences on violence and have found a consistent relationship between crime and the neurotransmitter serotonin. Research reveals that persons with low levels of serotonin are more likely to be aggressive and that the neurotransmitters dopamine and norepinephrine may facilitate aggression. Fishbein (1992) studied aggression among women. Although studies of this sort are limited, the results suggest that women in particular are more vulnerable to cyclical changes in hormone levels, causing them to be hostile during the menstrual cycle. Another risk factor involving neurotransmitters is diet. Food intake has a profound influence on neurotransmitters. For example, acetylcholine is derived from choline, which is found in eggs, liver, and butter. Serotonin is a product of **tryptophan,** an amino acid that is derived from food products. Given that violence has been linked to low levels of serotonin, one possible intervention for an individual predisposed to such violence would be to increase the person's amount of food intake containing tryptophan (Jeffrey, 1989).

Hypoglycemia is also related to diet. Hypoglycemia is a condition caused by the body's inability to use sugar effectively, causing low blood sugar. The major symptoms of hypoglycemia are mental confusion, low energy, and emotional instability that are often accompanied by neurotic or psychotic behavior. This condition has been shown to cause emotional distress, significantly higher anxiety, somatization, **depression,** and obsessive–compulsive reactions. Hypoglycemia was used in the defense of Tracy Housel, a convict sentenced to death in Georgia for the murder of a woman he allegedly picked up at a truck stop. Attorneys for Housel brought out Tracy's medical history showing that, as a child, he had sustained severe head injuries and had a hypoglycemic medical condition that left him prone to blackouts (http://www.geocities.com/tracyhousel/hypoglycemia4.html).

Many serious instances of violence involve alcohol, including individuals who engage in **binge drinking.** Binge drinkers tend to neglect their nutrition, and lack of nutrition is known to lead to hypoglycemia, irritability, and a heightened risk of conflict and aggression (Pernanen, 1998). During an episode of low blood sugar, individuals have been found to experience marital and family conflicts, have more accidents, and even commit suicide.

Other researchers have assessed the level of arousal in offenders and found that **underarousal** may be involved in the development of antisocial and criminal behavior. For example, Raine, Venables, and Williams (1990) conducted a study on 15-year-old adolescent males by testing their heart rate, skin conductance, and EEG activity. Raine et al. followed the males until the age of 24 and found that those who had engaged in both violent and nonviolent crimes had a significantly lower resting heart rate, reduced skin conductance activity, and EEG activity that was slower than that of noncriminals. Subsequent studies have found many of these same physiological responses and have concluded that they are risk factors for antisocial conduct (e.g., Raine & Liu, 1998). In this particular study, the researchers were the first to show that all three response systems were linked to criminal behavior.

The Case of John
What is the practical relevance of this arousal research for purposes of explaining criminal behavior? Consider the following vignette. John is an 18-year-old male, recently arrested for burglarizing a home. Further investigation of John's past reveals that he joined a gang at 16 years of age. He has a prior criminal record, including assault and robbing a store. John's behavior may be the result of arousal deficiencies. These low arousal rates could cause him to engage in conduct or participate in events that increase his stimulation level. Another possible explanation is that individuals with low levels of arousal are less fearful. Lower levels of fear increase the likelihood that a person would participate in violence or other forms of aggressive behavior (e.g., fighting). Conduct of this sort would occur because the individual would not be concerned about the consequences for his or her actions. (For more on the practicality of arousal research for explaining criminal behavior, see Raine, 1997.)

Another biological risk factor for criminal behavior is prefrontal dysfunction in the brain. The frontal lobe in the brain facilitates complex mental processes, such as controlling judgment, social functioning, and ethical behaviors. Damage to the frontal lobe may lead to chaotic, disorganized, asocial, and criminal behavior (Goldberg, 2001). Arousal is also regulated by the frontal lobe; therefore, damage to the frontal lobe may explain underarousal. Studies conducted with murderers show that frontal dysfunction in violent offenders is a risk factor for criminal behavior: the greater the prefrontal dysfunction, the greater the risk of serious violence (Raine & Liu, 1998).

There are several ways that prefrontal dysfunction could lead to criminal conduct. For example, damage to the prefrontal cortex may result in behavioral changes. These changes manifest themselves in behaviors such as risk taking, emotional and aggressive outbursts, and argumentativeness. Frontal damage has also been shown to impact **personality**, resulting in a loss of control, impulsive behavior, poor social judgment, and an inability to modify or shape behavior to social norms (Eysenck, 1967). On a social level, the loss of intellectual flexibility and problem solving, and an inability to use information provided by verbal cues, may contribute to aggressive solutions to interpersonal encounters (Eysenck, 1977). Cognitively, a person with prefrontal dysfunction may suffer from poor concentration, conflicted thinking, and an inability to reason. These cognitive deficits may lead to school and employment failure, resulting in economic deprivation. All these risk factors may predispose an individual to violence. Other factors such as the environment, social conditions, and psychological factors will enhance or diminish this **predisposition** (Raine & Liu, 1998).

Some researchers have suggested that birth complications may be a predisposition for future violence (e.g., Reiss & Roth, 1993). Birth complications may lead to brain dysfunction resulting in neuropsychological deficits. These deficits may predispose an individual to violence. For example, birth complications may produce cognitive deficiencies, resulting in school failure or a loss of self-control. These tendencies can cause aggressive, impulsive behavior (Raine, 1993). Further, investigators have demonstrated that if an individual has a history of birth complications and experiences maternal rejection in the early years of his or her psychosocial development, this combination of risk factors can be linked to violent crime in adulthood (Raine & Liu, 1998). In this research, the interactive effect of birthing problems and an absence of maternal bonding were significant for determining which individuals were most at risk for violent offending. The finding that there is an interaction between biological factors and social predispositions highlights the importance of biocriminology, especially when attempting to explain the origin and prevention of criminal behavior. However, the research findings noted here are not definitive and require further replication to validate their efficacy.

Implications for Prevention and Treatment

One of the most important outcomes of research concerning risk correlates related to violence and its biological origins is the discovery of factors that actually protect individuals predisposed to crime. For example, biosocial research in the area of antisocial behavior generally reports that certain biological variables may safeguard against antisocial conduct for persons living in poverty, and that some social variables (e.g., family support) may protect against antisocial behavior in biologically vulnerable individuals (Brennan & Raine, 1997). Protective factors are factors that help an individual compensate for high levels of **stress** or risk factors. Individuals who have risks for violence may also have enhanced qualities of strength, facilitating positive life outcomes (Brennan, Raine, Schulsinger, & Kirkegaard-Sorensen, 1997). To illustrate, antisocial and violent individuals often have cognitive deficits; however, they also have superior information-processing skills, such as selective attention and visual–spatial constructive abilities (Raine & Venables, 1988). Thus, if school curricula are tailored to provide exciting and stimulating classroom activities for adolescents experiencing such cognitive impairments, these interventions could prevent them from engaging in delinquent activities that, if not addressed, might result in more serious crimes in adulthood.

Biocriminologists maintain that prefrontal dysfunction and impulsivity contribute to violent behavior. As such, studies on cognitive remediation therapy may be effective in reducing rates of violence. In addition, there are also several treatment implications for individuals who suffer from birth complications. Interventions aimed at better prenatal and antenatal health care for women who are underserved or are more vulnerable (e.g., teenage mothers) may help reduce the rate of violence. Also, efforts to develop appropriate education strategies and other interventions designed to lessen early maternal rejection appear useful. Indeed, children with birth complications may be susceptible to poorer mother–infant attachment and abuse. Required parenting classes for these new mothers and interventions that teach caregiving skills may have some impact on unwanted pregnancies and early maternal rejection of the child (Raine & Liu, 1998).

GENETIC THEORY

Introduction

Genetic theory proposes that an individual's chromosomal characteristics result from the genes received by the person from his or her parents during conception. However, other traits develop from genetic mutations during one's fetal development. Characteristics that are a result of genetic mutations are biological; however, they are not inherited. This section discusses the relationship between genetic composition and criminal behavior.

Trait Theories

The original attempts to explain criminal behavior and crime were based on biological traits present at birth. Researchers hypothesized that individuals with specific biological traits would ultimately lead a criminal lifestyle. The establishment of the biological trait theory has been credited to Cesare Lombroso (1835–1909), the father of modern criminology. Lombroso (1889) developed the theory of criminal atavism, which posits that delinquents possess irregular physical characteristics that make them more similar to primitive humans, for example, monkeys and chimpanzees. The similarities between delinquents and our more primitive ancestors are biological and physiological. Some characteristics that are thought to be held in common are enlarged jaw size, stronger canine teeth, a flatter nose, excess teeth, differences in head size and shape, unusually sized and shaped ears, long arms, or asymmetrical brain structure (Lombroso, 1889; Savitz, 1972). Overall, Lombroso felt that the trained eye could distinguish between born criminals and normal individuals. Critics

Sheldon's Body Types and Corresponding Temperaments

	Physique		Temperament
Endomorphic	Tends to gain weight; is soft and round; small boned; short limbs	*Viscerotonic*	Loves to eat; extroverted; relaxed body; sociable; relaxed
Mesomorphic	Muscular; lean body; heavy chest, wrists, and hands; large trunk	*Somatonic*	Dynamic, adventurous, energetic; enjoys walking and talking; is assertive
Ectomorphic	Lean body; fragile and thin; small boned; sagging shoulders delicate body	*Cerebrotonic*	Introverted; sensitive to noise and other stimuli; bodily complaints; fatigue

of Lombroso argued that it was impossible to accurately distinguish among individuals who were born criminals, those who had criminal traits, and those who were normal (Vold, Bernard, & Snipes, 1998).

Another trait theory was derived from the somatotype school of thought. This approach hypothesized that delinquents displayed distinctive body physiques or "types" that increased their susceptibility to certain kinds of criminal behavior. According to Vold et al., "The body type theorists argue that there is a high degree of correspondence between the physical appearance of the body and the temperament of the mind" (p. 46). The main proponent of the somatotype theory in the United States was William Sheldon (Sheldon & Stevens, 1942; Sheldon, Hartl, & McDermott, 1949). Building on the work of the German psychiatrist, Ernst Kretschmer (1925–1999; see also, Hall & Lindzey, 1970), Sheldon defined a physical and mental typology that is consistent with the three different types of tissue layers in the human body. The three body types and corresponding temperaments are the **endomorphic physique** and the viscerotonic temperament, the **mesomorphic physique** and the somotonic temperament, and the **ectomorphic physique** and the cerebrotonic temperament (Sheldon, Hartl, & McDermott, 1970).

The endomorphic physique has more developed digestive organs or viscera, increasing the individual's ability to put on weight. The endomorphic individual's tendency to gain weight is accompanied by a round-shaped body, short limbs, small bones, and smooth skin. Accompanying the endomorphic physique is the viscerotonic temperament. Individuals with a viscerotonic temperament tend to be extroverted and comfortable in social situations. This type of individual also enjoys luxurious activity such as relaxation (Sheldon et al., 1970).

Muscles, bone, and motor organs dominate the mesomorphic physique. Mesomorphic individuals tend to have large and heavy chests, wrists, and hands. The overall shape of the mesomorphic individual is generally triangular. The accompanying temperament type, the somotonic, is generally an active and energetic individual. The somotonic individual enjoys activities such as walking and talking. This individual often engages in assertive gesturing, which can be a result of aggressive behavior (Sheldon et al., 1970). Numerous studies have found significant positive correlations between the mesomorphic physique and delinquency (e.g., Cortes, 1972; Glueck & Glueck, 1956; Sheldon et al., 1970).

The ectomorphic physique presents with the skin, appendages, and nervous system as the main features. The ectomorphic individual has a lean body, is small-boned, has sagging shoulders, and has a small face. Ectomorphic individuals have a greater surface area than other body types; however, they tend to weigh less than the other body types. The ectomorphic individual often has a cerebrotonic temperament. Individuals with a cerebrotonic temperament are generally introverted, sensitive to noise, and avoid crowds. These individuals experience many physical complaints such as allergies, problematic dermatological conditions, fatigue, and insomnia (Hartl, Monnelly & Elderkin, 1982; Sheldon et al., 1970).

Sheldon et al. (1970) found that individuals often have characteristics of more than one physique and temperament type. Therefore, he developed a continuum on which these types existed. Sheldon used a number scale between 1 and 7 to indicate the extent to which the somatotype (including the corresponding temperament) was present in any one individual. For example, if a person were ranked as a 1–4–7, he or she would have few endomorphic characteristics, an average amount of mesomorphic characteristics, and many ectomorphic characteristics.

Individuals who promote **trait theories** tend to reject the notion of equipotentiality or "the view that all people are equal at birth and are thereafter influenced by their environment" (Siegel & Senna, 2000, p. 92). Despite much controversy, trait theories still provide one of many explanations for crime, delinquency, and criminal behavior in society today. For example, in their controversial work, *Crime and Human Nature,* Wilson and Herrnstein (1985) suggested that the link between body type and criminal conduct "leaves no doubt that constitutional traits correlate with criminal behavior (p. 90)." Admittedly, some research is consistent with this conclusion; however, the bulk of empirical testing does not support this finding (e.g., Rutter & Giller, 1984; Sampson & Laub, 1997). Notwithstanding these debates, empirical research continues to show some evidence for the association between criminal behavior and biological differences.

Heredity

A theorist who significantly challenged the perspective of Lombroso was Charles Goring (1972). Goring conducted a study comparing groups of convicted individuals with groups of nonconvicted individuals. Goring did not subscribe to the idea that individuals could be identified as born criminals, individuals with criminal traits, or normal individuals. Instead, in his research, Goring found that criminals, when compared to other criminals or noncriminals, did not have physically significant differences. Goring did note one exception to his conclusion: There were significant differences in stature and weight between criminals and noncriminals. Indeed, criminals were understood to have a smaller body stature than did their noncriminal counterparts. Goring generalized his findings and concluded that criminals were inferior with respect to **heredity.** As a result of this conclusion, Goring suggested that criminal behavior, similar to physical traits and features, was an inherited trait (Goring; Vold et al., 1998).

In his research on 3,000 English convicts and 3,000 nonconvicts, Goring (1972) measured the seriousness of criminality through the length of the imposed criminal sanction. He found that individuals with longer prison sentences were physically and mentally inferior to other individuals. Thus, he surmised that more serious criminals were physically smaller and were lacking in mental ability. Goring also explained that these two factors, physical size and mental ability, were inherited; therefore, Goring concluded that these inherited factors were positively correlated with criminality.

Goring's extensive research included additional facets of crime, criminal behavior, and heredity. For example, he examined the relationship between the duration of prison sentences and the rate of recidivism for the two parents, between the parents and the children, and between and among the siblings. Goring found no significant differences between these correlations and claimed that the lack of significance was a result of confounding variables from social and environmental conditions. Further, Goring maintained that despite his inability to ascertain the specific relationships between criminality and inherited traits, criminal behavior had no relationship with the environment. Therefore, he concluded that in order to decrease the crime rate, individuals carrying genes with criminal traits and characteristics would have to cease procreation (Driver, 1972; Goring, 1972).

Critics of Goring's conclusions have argued that his research was biased. The absence of accurate measurements for all the environmental characteristics involved significantly compromised his findings. Without such statistical precision, opponents assert that Goring could not eliminate the effects of the environment in his results (Vold et al., 1998). By eliminating the environmental effects without adequately measuring or accounting for them, Goring clearly demonstrated his preference for the significance of heredity and its ability to explain (and predict) criminal behavior. Notwithstanding the limits of Goring's research, his assessment on the link between criminality and heredity is significant. Indeed, this association remains a valid argument in the study of criminal behavior today. Moreover, he is credited with disproving the viability of the Lombrosian explanation. Indeed, as Bartol (2002) notes, "Goring's findings . . . put the genetics and crime issue to rest, [and] many criminologists quickly wrote the born criminal's obituary (p. 60)."

Biosocial Theories

Individuals who advocate social theories tend to embrace the notion that the environment can alter an individual's tendency to engage in criminal behavior. Therefore, **biosocial theories** of criminal behavior integrate biological and social premises into one school of thought. Biosocial theories tend to focus on four different views of antisocial behaviors: (a) biochemical reactions, (b) neurological dysfunction, (c) genetic influences, and (d) evolutionary theory (Siegel & Senna, 2000). Because this section generally focuses on genetic theories, the genetic influences emphasized by the biosocial theories are examined in slightly more depth than are the other three perspectives.

Biochemical reaction theorists are concerned with the relationship between an individual's biochemical makeup and his or her antisocial behavior. For example, Raine (1993) found that the overconsumption of minerals such as magnesium, copper, cadmium, and zinc can be linked with aggressive behaviors. Similarly, extreme exposure to lead can result in factors that place an individual at risk for delinquency and criminal behavior (Denno, 1988). In addition, researches have found that individuals who present with antisocial tendencies have poor nutrition with diets high in sugar and fat and low in protein (Farrington, 2001; Hickey, 1997; Patterson, 1996).

A second area of biochemical research deals with hormones and hormonal levels. Investigators argue that testosterone in male adolescents is a factor that contributes significantly to the extreme levels of violence in teenage males. Mood and behavior changes, as a result of the increased secretion of male harmones (e.g., androgen, testosterone), are leading causes of antisocial behavior in adolescent males (Buchanan, Eccles, & Becker, 1992). Overaggressive behavioral responses exhibited by males are often a result of hormonal sensitivity that can begin in the fetal stages, especially if the prenatal child is exposed to high levels of testosterone while in the uterus (Martens, 2000).

Despite empirical studies confirming the link between antisocial behavior and hormones, there is a major problem with this research. Investigators have shown that higher testosterone levels may not cause aggressive behavior; instead, aggressive behavior may result in the production of more testosterone (Vold et al., 1998). Additionally, a study conducted by Booth and Osgood (1993) found that increased testosterone levels in individuals might cause them to be more socially inhibited. Social inhibition is significantly correlated with delinquency. As Vold et al. (1998) state, "testosterone is associated with juvenile delinquency, and when controlling for delinquency, the relationship between testosterone and adult deviance diminishes further (p. 79)." As such, more empirical research is needed in order to establish more clearly what the link is between criminal behavior and testosterone.

Another area of interest within biosocial theory and criminal or aggressive conduct is neurological dysfunction. Biosocial theorists explore what the relationship is between the brain, the central nervous system, and antisocial behaviors. Studies examining neurological dysfunction encompass abnormalities within areas of the brain and the nervous system, such as "brain waves, heart rate, arousal level, skin conductance, and attention span, cognitive ability, and spatial learning" (Siegel & Senna, 2000, p. 94). Individuals who present with behavioral problems caused by neurological damage are often considered to have minimal brain dysfunction (MBD). One main type of MBD is learning disability. MBD is a "neurological dysfunction that prevents an individual from learning to his or her potential"

(Siegel & Senna, p. 95). Investigators hypothesize that MBD universally results in antisocial behavior, given one's inability to appropriately deal with negative emotions such as anger and hostility (Lewis, Pincus, Feldman, Jackson, & Bard, 1986; Seguin, Pihl, Harden, Tremblay, & Boulerice, 1995).

Another group of theorists who endorse the hypothesis of neurological dysfunction as a cause of criminal behavior are the arousal theorists. Arousal theorists state that delinquents engage in criminal behavior for the thrill of the crime. The thrill of committing the criminal offense motivates the individual to recidivate. Factors that contribute to an individual's arousal are not fully developed. Investigators speculate, however, that brain chemistry, such as serotonin levels, contributes to arousal levels. Another perspective is that stimulation is pursued by individuals who lack normal arousal levels. This hypothesis states that in order for one to attain normal arousal levels, the person seeks out stimulating activity, such as crime and criminal behavior. Pursuing such illicit activity elevates their arousal level to a normal state. A more detailed assessment of the perspective on arousal and antisocial behavior was previously described under the section Biological Risk Factors for Crime.

Neurotransmitters within the brain have been examined closely in recent studies of neurological dysfunction. For example, Cravchik and Goldman (2000) studied the link between the neurotransmitters dopamine and serotonin and human behavior. Another recent research project investigated the link between neurotransmitters and attention deficit hyperactivity disorder (ADHD). ADHD can be a predisposing factor for conduct disorder and antisocial personality disorder (Anonymous, 2000b). Neurotransmitters are "chemicals that allow for the transmission of electrical impulses within the brain and are the basis for the brain's processing of information" (Vold et al., 1998, p. 76). Three neurotransmitters have been identified in association with antisocial behavior. These neurotransmitters are serotonin, dopamine, and norepinephrine. Neurotransmitters are genetically determined; however, they can be manipulated through the use of drugs such as lithium carbonate, reserpine, and antipsychotics (Brizer, 1988). Therefore, researchers hypothesize that it is possible to decrease levels of antisocial behavior in an individual through the use of drugs. Neurotransmitters can also be manipulated through changes in the environment. For example, diet and stress can alter the levels of neurotransmitter production, resulting in an increased likelihood for one to engage in criminal behavior (Vold et al., 1998).

Genetic influences also play a significant role in the development of biosocial theories. Some biosocial theorists ascribe to the hypothesis that individuals are exposed to genes that predispose them to aggressive and violent behaviors. A recent development in theories of heredity illustrates that one main predisposition for violent and criminal behaviors is the possession of the **XYY chromosome** in males (Anderson, 2001; Anonymous, 2000a). When conducting studies examining genetic influences, it is difficult to distinguish between genetics and environment; therefore, twin studies and adoption studies are conducted to differentiate between environmental and hereditary effects and influences on criminal behavior (e.g., Jarvik, Klodin, & Matsuyama, 1973; Price & Whatmore, 1967).

Twin studies are conducted in an attempt to hold heredity constant. If heredity is held constant, conclusions can be made with respect to environmental influences. *Monozygotic* twins are the product of only one egg; however *dizygotic* twins are the product of two separate eggs. Because monozygotic twins are the result of only one fertilized egg, the genetic makeup of the twins is the same. Therefore, it is possible to hold heredity constant only with monozygotic twins (Vold et al., 1998). One of the earliest twin studies was conducted by the Munich physiologist Johannes Lange (Lange, Haldane, & Löhrke, 1929). Lange et al. examined imprisonment patterns in monozygotic twins. They found that when one twin was imprisoned, the other twin was imprisoned 77% of the time. On the other hand, in the examination of dizygotic twins and their imprisonment patterns, Lange et al. found that only 12% of dizygotic twins had the same imprisonment patterns as each other. Last, when conducting the same analysis between nontwin siblings, Lange and his research team found that only 8% of the siblings had similar imprisonment patterns (Lange et al., 1929; see also Legras, 1932).

Despite the results of Lange et al.'s (1929) study and those of similar investigations that followed (e.g., Claridge, 1973; Hetherington & Parke, 1975; Rosenthal, 1971), the aforementioned twin studies may have been the result of environmental influences. Indeed, there is no absolute way to distinguish between heredity and environment in twin studies, unless the twins are separated at birth and reared apart from each other throughout their respective lives. Three studies examined the antisocial patterns of twins after their separation at birth (Christiansen, 1977; Grove et al., 1990; Walters, 1992). Christiansen, Grove et al., and Walters' research found significant evidence of heredity in the determination of criminal and antisocial behavior.

Another useful method for determining the effects of heredity and environment on antisocial and criminal behavior is the adoption study technique. Schulsinger (1972) conducted one of the first adoption studies. He examined the similarities and differences in psychopathic traits in psychopathic adopted children and nonpsychopathic adopted children. When reviewing hospital records, Schulsinger found that a greater percentage (i.e., 4.4% of psychopathic adopted children) had biological relatives who suffered from psychopathic illnesses. In comparison, only 6.7% of nonpsychopathic adopted children had biological relatives who suffered from psychopathic illnesses.

A later series of studies conducted by Hutchings and Mednick (1977) examined adopted males and their similarities in criminal behavior patterns with their biological fathers and their adopted fathers. Hutchings and Mednick found in their first of three studies that adopted children were more likely to commit criminal acts when their biological fathers were imprisoned for criminal behavior. The second of these studies indicated that the criminality of the adopted father did not have as significant an impact on the criminality of the adopted child; however, when both the biological and adopted fathers were imprisoned, the effect of imprisonment on the adopted child was significantly greater. In their third study, Hutchings and Mednick matched criminal and noncriminal adopted children and compared the criminality of their adopted and biological parents. They found that adopted children who exhibited criminal behaviors had significantly more criminal adopted fathers, criminal biological fathers, and criminal biological mothers. Since the completion of the studies conducted by Hutchings and Mednick, other researchers have engaged in studies examining adopted children and their biological and adopted parents (e.g., Blackburn, 1993; Mednick, Gabrielli, & Hutchings, 1984, 1987). The overall consensus of these studies is that the effects of heredity are seen more frequently in individuals who commit less serious offenses. Serious and violent offenders who infrequently commit crimes often fall outside of the norms for adoption studies of less serious offenders (Vold et al., 1998). However, as Gabrielli and Mednick (1983) explained, "It is reasonable . . . to conclude that some people inherit biological characteristics which permit them to be antisocial more readily than others (p. 63)."

A final area that is examined by biosocial theorists is evolutionary theory. Evolutionary theory explains "the existence of aggression and violent behavior as positive adaptive behaviors in human evolution; these traits allowed their bearers to reproduce disproportionately, which has had an effect on the human gene pool" (Siegel & Senna, 2000, p. 100). The disproportionate rates of violence between the sexes are explained by evolutionary theory. Competition among individuals is perceived to be the way to survive and produce offspring in society. Therefore, males become violent and aggressive in order to compete with other males. The offspring of these males are often overly aggressive and considerably influenced by their heredity. These aggressive individuals account for the growing proportion of aggressive, violent, and criminal males in society today. Despite the prevalence of literature focusing on crimes committed by males, few theories speculate on the crime rate of females.

Genetic Mutations or Defects and Antisocial Behavior

Researchers have attempted to uncover a link between genetics and antisocial behavior. Investigators have found that some antisocial behaviors, such as violence and drug abuse, have a connection to genetic defects in the neurotransmitters, serotonin and dopamine.

Subsequent research has found that participation in criminal or delinquent behavior provides a chemical balance in the brain of the antisocial individual. Another genetic defect can be noted in hormones. Some scientists suggest that fetal exposure to an abnormal level of testosterone may lead the child to become more aggressive during adolescence. Repeated exposure to high rates of testosterone during fetal stages may cause the individual to have an elevated sensitivity to testosterone increases later on in his or her life. The central nervous system and the autonomic nervous system are two additional areas that can cause increased tendencies for antisocial behavior, if defective or mutated. The findings in these areas are very broad and inconclusive. Although several empirical studies have been conducted in both areas, there are no definitive conclusions. Several findings support the notion that the central nervous system and the autonomic nervous system play a role in antisocial behavior; however, what that role is remains uncertain.

DIATHESIS–STRESS MODEL OF CRIMINAL BEHAVIOR

Introduction

Kara, a 14-year-old female, was arrested for assault and attempted murder of a classmate. The question asked by the school was "Why would this young girl assault a classmate to the point of almost killing her?" There are many individual-based theories that attempt to explain the causes of criminal behavior. Thus far, I have paid a lot of attention to the genetic and biological factors that may predispose individuals to commit criminal acts. Other theories look at the interaction between the environment and the psychological traits of the individual that may work in concert to foster antisocial or violent conduct. When considering the many factors that contribute to criminal behavior, one biocriminological theory that often is used to explain it is the **diathesis–stress model.** The basic premise of this model is that stress activates a **diathesis,** transforming one's predisposition for violent or aggressive action into the presence of criminal behavior or **psychopathology.** This theory assumes that a delinquent or criminal act may be explained as the product of two independent processes, diathesis and stress. In what follows, I define these concepts.

Diathesis

Diathesis refers to those biological or genetic conditions that make an individual vulnerable to stress. Therefore, the diathesis is a necessary precursor for any disorder. In the diathesis–stress model, the diathesis is the necessary condition for the development of the pathology, whether it is mental illness or criminal behavior. The diathesis, then, may make a person vulnerable to stress. It includes such conditions as biological or genetic predispositions, negative thought patterns, or biochemical stress that occurs as a result of changes in hormone levels associated with pregnancy or drug use (Zuckerman, 1999).

The diathesis is often regarded as a biological or genetic predisposition. However, it is not necessarily genetic or biological in nature. Indeed, it may involve pessimistic habits of thought, or biochemical stress that occurs as a result of changes in hormone levels associated with pregnancy or drugs. When biological changes, like those just mentioned, are interpreted through the filter of cognitive distortions or negative thought patterns, they may be considered the diathesis that interacts with the stressful situation, giving rise to criminal behavior.

A person with a diathesis may be described as responding to ordinary conditions of life with an abnormal reaction. For example, a person might be predisposed to engage in criminal behavior due to their family history (e.g., the mother or father participates in a criminal lifestyle, or the individual is part of a gang). In a benign environment, the person may generally perform well, but when pressured by stressful events, he or she may get involved in illicit conduct due to a previous **vulnerability** and as a reaction to the stressors.

As a result of the interaction between the diathesis and the stressor, the person becomes involved in criminal behavior.

In the example of Kara noted earlier, the diathesis–stress model may be useful in explaining what led her to act violently or criminally. A closer look at the recent events in Kara's life reveals the death of her mother approximately 1 month previously. This death was caused by a drug overdose. The loss of her mother would be considered the stress that precipitated Kara's criminal actions. School counselors noted behavioral problems over the last 2 weeks that seemed to be getting worse (e.g., truancy, frequent crying spells, inability to concentrate, withdrawal, and irritability). The school counselor stated that Kara had had behavioral and emotional problems in the past, but noted an increase in the severity of these problems since the death of her mother. According to the diathesis–stress model, the stress is not sufficient to explain Kara's behavior. Kara's mother had a history of criminal activity and had been in and out of prison for most of her daughter's life. Given Kara's family history (including her mother's involvement in illicit conduct), she had a biological predisposition to engage in criminal behavior. When Kara's diathesis (i.e., her biological predisposition) interacted with her environmental stressors (i.e., the loss of Kara's mother), the predisposition was activated. Thus, the combinatory effect of diathesis and stress caused Kara to engage in criminal behavior.

According to the diathesis–stress model, the diathesis and the stressor are both necessary elements to produce the criminal behavior. For example, if an individual has a very small predisposition to engage in criminal behavior, major levels of stress may not contribute to a person engaging in crime at all. However, in a vulnerable person, such as one with a family history of criminal activity, it may take very little stress or environmental provocation to precipitate a delinquent or criminal act.

Diathesis–Stress and Mental Illness

Historically, in an attempt to understand psychopathology, theorists have stated that persons with a mental illness differ genetically or biologically from those who do not have a psychiatric disorder. The diathesis–stress model has frequently been used to explain mental illnesses such as depression, **schizophrenia,** and other psychiatric disorders. In the 1960s, Meehl hypothesized that the diathesis–stress model could help explain the etiology of schizophrenia. For example, according to Meehl (1990), research on schizophrenia indicates that an individual with this condition has a low threshold for stress provocation. Furthermore, Meehl suggests that unlucky events can precipitate schizophrenia in a genetically vulnerable person. The genetic vulnerability is the diathesis, and the stress is the unlucky event(s). These misfortunate circumstances precipitate the episode that characterizes schizophrenia. For example, Meehl reports that major traumas that occur during one's (pre)adolescent period (e.g., losing a parent before the age of 15) or minor traumas (e.g., continuous verbal rejections) could increase the risk for schizophrenia later on in one's life, particularly in a genetically vulnerable child.

Theories of depression have also used the diathesis–stress model. Depression fits the model of diathesis–stress because there is evidence that the first and subsequent episodes of major depression are triggered by stressful events in the social environment. For example, chronic economic stress and family difficulties play a role in the onset of depression. Social support and personality strengths and weaknesses are important in determining the reactions to stress. More recent studies investigating depression support Meehl's (1990) hypothesis and find that the risk for a severe stressor in producing depression is 2.4 times greater for those at the highest **genetic risk** than for those at the lowest genetic risk (Kendler et al., 1995). In this research, the diathesis was the genetic factor that influenced the susceptibility of persons to the depressive effects of stressful events. Additional research also indicates that other disorders, such as bipolar disorder, are associated with a greater risk for relapse of manic or depressive symptoms even in patients receiving appropriate psychotropic medication (Balon, 1997).

The link between the diathesis–stress model, mental illness, and criminal behavior indicates that abuse and neglect during childhood are stressors that make the manifestation of psychopathology in general more likely. The diathesis, or the person's preexisting vulnerabilities, will dictate the particular form that the illness will take (Ruggerio, Bernstein, & Handelsman, 1999). Returning to the case of Kara, evidence shows that she was neglected. This may have been associated with the stress that she experienced. Given her biological vulnerability to criminal behavior, the diathesis interacted with the precipitating stress of her mother's death, resulting in the criminal behavior of assault on a classmate.

What Is Stress?

The concept of stress refers to both external sources of negative feelings and to the physiological arousal that often accompanies stress (Seyle, 1976). Examples of arousal include an increase in heart rate, as well as other internal reactions (Monroe & Simons, 1991). Stress has been implicated in the development of psychopathology (Monroe & Simons, 1991). Biological or environmental stressors may contribute to the development of a disorder or may be the proximal trigger for the episodes of the disorder.

According to the stress–diathesis model, stress activates the diathesis, which in turn brings about the onset of a disorder. A criticism of the diathesis–stress model concerns the definition of "stress." Diathesis theories often do not specify a particular type of stress to interact with the diathesis in creating criminal behavior or psychopathology. The stress referred to in diathesis–stress theories is that which occurs just prior to the manifestation of a disorder. One explanation for stress comes from Hans Seyle (1976) and his **General Adaptive Syndrome.** In this biological and neurophysiological account, a sequence of events occurs giving rise to the body's "fight-or-flight" response (i.e., stress reaction).

Stress is often defined as the event or events occurring in close proximity to the appearance of psychopathology. For example, if a person lost a spouse 1 year or more ago and if there were no obvious, persisting effects after the death, then it is assumed that the loss is not the stressor. However, the effects of stress may be cumulative. Indeed, a series of milder stressors occurring in a short amount of time may be equivalent to a single, severe stressor such as the death of a loved one. Stress does not have the same effect on all individuals. In fact, it varies by the number and type of personal and contextual factors, including the individual's cognitive interpretation of the stressful event, the context in which the stress is experienced, and the coping behaviors one develops in response to the stress (Monroe & Simons, 1991).

Moreover, despite high levels of stress, such as the loss of a loved one, only a certain percentage of people experience depression, live with schizophrenia, or engage in a criminal lifestyle (American Psychiatric Association [APA], *Diagnostic and Statistical Manual of Mental Disorders*, 4th ed., text revision [*DSM–IV–TR*], 2000). One explanation for this is that a person's perception of stress will differ depending on multiple factors. For example, for a biologically predisposed vulnerable person, a pathological episode or a crime may be provoked by relatively minor stress. Alternatively, for a nonbiological predisposed vulnerable individual, only a major catastrophe could provoke the same. The concept of stress suggests a liability factor that makes some persons more susceptible to varying degrees of stress. For example, persons with a diathesis, such as a personality disorder, often suffer from cognitive distortions or negative thoughts. These distortions disqualify positive thoughts, leading them to interpret events around them in a negative fashion. Therefore, persons with cognitive distortions often associated with personality disorders and depression may interpret minor everyday hassles as major stressors (*DSM–IV–TR*, APA, 2000).

There are a variety of potential forms of stress that may bring about illness or criminal behavior. The diathesis–stress model gives biological factors stronger priority regarding risk factors in the development of personality disorders. The diathesis–stress model states that psychosocial stressors such as divorce, abuse, and neglect precipitate disorders; however, biology determines the form of the disorder. Therefore, heritable traits, or the diathesis, determine whether individuals are vulnerable to specific disorders. The cumulative effects of psychological and social factors determine to what extent psychopathology or criminal behavior develops (Paris, 1999).

People who have a predisposition to mental illness—which would be considered the diathesis—may be more vulnerable to stress. There are several disorders in the *DSM–IV–TR* (APA, 2000), including **reactive depressive disorder,** brief reactive psychosis, **acute stress disorder,** and **posttraumatic stress disorder.** In these instances, stress is assumed to be the major cause and, in some cases, the sole cause for the disorder. In addition, Meehl (1990) explains that among people with schizophrenia, stress may be the impetus for a schizophrenic episode, especially for those who have not been treated with medication. This makes them highly susceptible to even minor stress disturbances. Severe and prolonged types of stress can increase one's vulnerability to schizophrenia. However, in contrast, minor stress irritants may not be considered to be as troubling, especially for people who do not suffer from mental illness or some form of personality disorder. This information is intended to illustrate that the definition of what constitutes stress, within the diathesis–stress model, stretches across a broad-ranging continuum. Indeed, stress may be the result of cumulative minor disturbances, or it may be the result of one catastrophic event interacting with the individual's diathesis to produce criminal behavior or mental illness.

According to the diathesis–stress model, diathesis and stress are complementary. Neither the diathesis nor the stress is sufficient on its own to produce schizophrenia, depression, or criminal behavior. In fact, someone with relatively little predisposition for criminal behavior or mental illness may endure even catastrophic levels of stress without developing a psychiatric disorder or engaging in violent conduct. Other factors such as the environment affect the outcome of the diathesis and stress interaction. For example, individuals who have recovered from schizophrenia are less likely to relapse if they are discharged to a home environment with a positive and accepting emotional atmosphere as opposed to a stressful one. In the case of criminal behavior, juveniles with a diathesis toward criminality sent to a group home or to another community placement may experience a more positive, nurturing environment that promotes a lifestyle that does not include criminal behavior. However, when a juvenile returns to a home environment, experiences chaos and a stressful living arrangement, and has a diathesis (e.g., a biological parent involved in criminal behavior), the youth may be more inclined to relapse into a life of crime. This outcome is the result of the interaction between the child's diathesis and the stress invoked by the youth's environment.

Research

Research on the biological and psychological factors on the origin of mental illness uses the diathesis–stress model to explain the complex origins of psychopathology. Paris (1999) states that some individuals have genes that shape a predisposition to medical and psychiatric illnesses that interact with environmental stress to precipitate mental disorders. Other studies have found a significant relationship between the biological parents' criminal convictions and those found in their adopted children. This association supports the hypothesis that having wayward parents increases the likelihood that the children of these parents will engage in delinquent behavior (Mednick et al., 1984). Other studies support the diathesis–stress model as an explanation for criminal conduct. Cadoret, Yates, Troughton, and Woodworth (1995) examined adults who were adopted and who experienced a stressful home environment. Those adoptees who had biological parents with a history of antisocial personality disorder and alcoholism exhibited higher levels of aggression and conduct disorders than adoptees whose biological parents had no history of antisocial behavior or alcoholism. Empirical findings such as these support the diathesis–stress model as a viable explanation for the onset of criminal behavior. Again, in this instance the diathesis is the genetic predisposition (i.e., antisocial personality and alcoholic vulnerability). It interacts with the stressor (i.e., chaotic living arrangements). The combinatory effect creates delinquent or criminal conduct.

DISCUSSION QUESTIONS

1. What are some of the similarities and differences among biocriminology, genetic explanations for criminal behavior, and the diathesis–stress model?
2. There are several biological risk factors linked to delinquent or criminal conduct. Name several of them.
3. From your perspective, is criminal behavior genetic? Is it inherited? What are the differences?
4. In trait theory, one explanation for criminal or violent conduct indicates that there are different body types with corresponding temperaments. Describe this approach to criminal behavior. Can you think of any recent examples of offenders that support this theory's explanation?
5. What is the relationship between and among hormones, antisocial behavior, and crime? Does biochemical research prove that violence or aggression is the product of levels of testosterone?
6. What is the relationship between and among neurological dysfunction, serotonin, and criminal conduct? How does one's chromosomal makeup impact one's likelihood for committing crime or for engaging in delinquent conduct?
7. Explain the historical research on twin and adoption studies. What makes either of these approaches plausible explanations for current criminal behavior?
8. What is a diathesis? What is stress? How do the two interact to cause criminal conduct? Give an example of how this theory operates in practice.

REFERENCES

American Psychiatric Association. (2000). *Diagnostic and statistical manual for mental disorders* (4th ed., text rev.). Washington DC: Author.

Anderson, W. R. (2001). Biological predisposition of aggressive and violent behavior. *Futurics, 25*(1/2), 72–76.

Anonymous. (2000a). Current thinking of XYY syndrome. *Psychiatric Annals, 30*(2), 91–95.

Anonymous. (2000b). Impulsive, addictive, and compulsive behaviors: Predisposing factors. *Journal of Psychoactive Drugs, 32*(1), 27–38.

Balon, R. (1997). Does stress cause psychiatric illness? *Journal of Psychiatry, 154,* 1617–1618.

Bartol, C. B. (2002). *Criminal behavior: A psychosocial perspective* (6th ed.). Upper Saddle River, NJ: Prentice Hall.

Blackburn, R. (1993). *The psychology of criminal conduct: Theory, research, and practice.* Chichester, England: Wiley.

Booth, A., & Osgood, D. W. (1993). The influence of testosterone on deviance in adulthood: Assessing and explaining the relationship. *Criminology, 31*(1), 93–117.

Brennan, P., & Raine, A. (1997). Biosocial bases of antisocial behavior: Psychophysiological, neurological, and cognitive factors. *Clinical Psychology Review, 17,* 589–604.

Brennan, P., Raine, A., Schulsinger, F., & Kirkegaard-Sorensen, L. (1997). Psychophysiological protective factors for male subjects at high risk for criminal behavior. *American Journal of Psychiatry, 154,* 853–855.

Brizer, D. A. (1988). Psychopharmacology and the management of violent patients. *Psychiatric Clinics of North America, 11,* 551–568.

Buchanan, C. M., Eccles, J., & Becker, J. (1992). Are adolescents the victims of raging hormones: Evidence for activational effects of hormones on moods and behavior at adolescence. *Psychological Bulletin, 111,* 62–107.

Cadoret, R., Yates, W., Troughton, E., & Woodworth, G. (1995). Genetic-environmental interaction in the genesis of aggressivity and conduct disorders. *Archives of General Psychiatry, 52,* 916–924.

Christiansen, K. O. (1977). A review of criminality among twins. In S. A. Mednick & K. O. Christiansen (Eds.), *Biosocial bases of criminal behavior* (pp. 89–108). New York: Gardner.

Claridge, G. (1973). Final remarks. In G. Claridge, S. Canter, & W. I. Hume (Eds.), *Personality differences and biological variations.* Oxford, England: Pergamon.

Cortes, J. B. (1972). *Delinquency and crime.* New York: Seminar Press.

Cravchik, A., & Goldman, D. (2000). Neurochemical individuality: Genetic diversity among human dopamine and serotonin receptors and transporters. *Archives of General Psychiatry, 57*(12), 1105–1114.

Denno, D. (1988). Human biology and criminal responsibility: Free will or free ride? *University of Pennsylvania Law Review, 137,* 615–671.

Driver, E. D. (1972). Charles Buckman Goring. In H. Mannheim (Ed.), *Pioneers in criminology* (pp. 429–442). Montclair, NJ: Patterson Smith.

Ellis, L. (1982). Genetics and criminal behavior. *Criminology, 20,* 43–66.

Eysenck, H. J. (1967). *The biological basis of personality.* Springfield, IL: Thomas.

Eysenck, H. J. (1977). *Crime and personality* (2nd ed.). London: Routledge & Kegan Paul.

Farrington, D. P. (2001). Crime prevention. *Psychologist, 14*(4), 182–184.

Fishbein, D. (1992). The psychobiology of female aggression. *Criminal Justice and Behavior, 19,* 99–128.

Gabrielli, W. F., & Mednick, S. A. (1983). Genetic correlates of criminal behavior. *American Behavioral Scientist, 27,* 59–74.

Glueck, S., & Glueck, E. (1956). *Physique and delinquency.* New York: Harper.

Goring, C. (1972). The English convict: A statistical study. Montclair, NJ: Patterson Smith. (Original work published 1913.)

Goldberg, E. (2001). *The executive brain: Frontal lobes and the civilized mind.* Oxford: Oxford University Press.

Goring, C. (1972). *The English convict: A statistical study.* Glen Ridge, NJ: Patterson Smith.

Grove, W. M., Eckert, E. D., Heston, L., Bouchard, T. J., Segal, N., & Lyken, D. T. (1990). Heritability of substance abuse and antisocial behavior: A study of monozygotic twins reared apart. *Biological Psychiatry, 27,* 1293–1304.

Hall, C. S., & Lindzey, G. (1970). *Theories of personality* (2nd ed.). New York: Wiley.

Hartl, E. M., Monnelly, E. P., & Elderkin, R. D. (1982). *Physique and delinquent behavior.* New York: Academic Press.

Hetherington, E. M., & Parke, R. D. (1975). *Child psychology: A contemporary viewpoint.* New York: McGraw-Hill.

Hickey, E. W. (1997). *Serial murderers and their victims* (2nd ed.). Belmont, CA: Wadsworth.

http://www.geocities.com/tracyhousel/hypoglycemia4.html

Hutchings, B., & Mednick, S. A. (1977). Criminality in adoptees and their adoptive and biological parents: A pilot study. In S. A. Mednick & K. O. Christiansen (Eds.), *Biosocial bases of criminal behavior* (pp. 127–141). New York: Gardner.

Jarvik, L. F., Klodin, V., & Matsuyama, S. S. (1973). Human aggression and the extra Y chromosome. *American Psychologist, 28,* 674–682.

Jeffrey, R. C. (1989). An interdisciplinary theory of criminal behavior. In W. Laufer & F. Adler. (Eds.). *Advances in criminological theory* (pp. 69–87). New Brunswick, NJ: Transaction Publishers.

Jeffrey, R. C. (1991). Criminology: 2010 A.D. In R. Kelly & D. MacNamara (Eds.). *Perspectives on deviance: Dominance, degradation, and denigration* (pp. 63–75). Cincinnati, OH: Anderson Publishing Co.

Kendler, K., Kessler, R., Walters, E., MacLean, C., Neale, M., Heath, A., et al. (1995). Stressful life events, genetic liability, and onset of an episode of major depression in women. *American Journal of Psychiatry, 152,* 833–842.

Krestschmer, E. (1999). *Physique and character* (2nd ed.). New York: Routledge.

Lange, J., Haldane, C. F., & Löhrke, E. W. (1929). *Crime and destiny.* New York: Charles Boni.

Legras, A. M. (1932). *Psychese en Criminaliteit bij Twellingen.* Utrecht, The Netherlands: Keminken ZOON N.V.

Lewis, D. O., Pincus, J., Feldman, M., Jackson, L., & Bard, B. (1986). Psychiatric, neurological, and psychoeducational characteristics of 15 death row inmates in the United States. *American Journal of Psychiatry, 143*(7), 838–845.

Lombroso, C. (1889). *The criminal man* (4th ed.). Torino: Bocca.

Martens, W. H. J. (2000). Antisocial and psychopathic personality disorders: Causes, course, and remission—A review article. *International Journal of Offender Therapy and Comparative Criminology, 44*(4), 406–430.

Mednick, S. A., Gabrielli, W. F., & Hutchings, B. (1984). Genetic influences in criminal convictions: Evidence from an adoption cohort. *Science, 224,* 891–894.

Mednick, S. A., Gabrielli, W. F., & Hutchings, B. (1987). Genetic factors in the etiology of criminal behavior. In S. A. Mednick, T. F. Moffitt, & S. A. Stack (Eds.), *The cause of crime: New biological approaches.* Cambridge, England: Cambridge University Press.

Meehl, P. (1990). Toward an integrated theory of schizotaxia, schizotypy, and schizophrenia. *Journal of Personality Disorders, 4,* 1–99.

Michel, L., & Herbeck, D. (2001). *American Terrorist: Timothy McVeigh and the Oklahoma City Bombing*. New York: Regan Books.

Monroe, S., & Simons, A. (1991). Diathesis-stress theories in the context of life stress research: Implications for the depressive disorders. *Psychological Bulletin, 110,* 406–425.

Paris, J. (1999). A diathesis-stress model of personality disorders. *Psychiatric Annals, 29,* 692–699.

Patterson, G. R. (1996). Characteristics of a developmental theory for early onset delinquency. In M. F. Lenzenweger & J. J. Haugaard (Eds.), *Frontiers of developmental psychopathology* (pp. 81–124). New York: Oxford University Press.

Pernanen, K. (1998). Prevention of alcohol-related violence. *Contemporary Drug Problems, 25,* 477–509.

Price, W. H., & Whatmore, P. B. (1967). Behaviour disorders and patterns of crime among XYY males identified at a maximum security hospital. *British Medical Journal, 1,* 533–536.

Raine, A. (1993). *The psychopathology of crime: Criminal behavior as a clinical disorder*. San Diego, CA: Academic Press.

Raine, A. (1997). *The psychopathology of crime: Criminal behavior as a clinical disorder* (2nd ed.). San Diego, CA: Academic Press.

Raine, A., & Liu, J. (1998). Biological predispositions to violence and their implications for biosocial treatment and prevention. *Psychology, Crime, and Law, 4,* 107–125.

Raine, A., & Venables, P. (1988). Enhanced P3 evoked potentials during a continuous performance task in psychopaths. *Psychophysiology, 25,* 30–38.

Raine, A., Venables, P., & Williams, M. (1990). Relationships between CNS and ANS measures of arousal at age 15 and criminality at age 24. *Archives of General Psychiatry, 47,* 1003–1007.

Reiss, A., & Roth, J. (1993). *Understanding and preventing violence*. Washington DC: National Academy Press.

Rosenthal, D. (1971). *Genetics and psychopathology*. New York: McGraw-Hill.

Ruggerio, J., Bernstein, D., & Handelsman, L. (1999). Traumatic stress in childhood and later personality disorders: A retrospective study of male patients with substance dependence. *Psychiatric Annals, 29,* 713–720.

Rutter, M., & Giller, H. (1984). *Juvenile delinquency: Trends and perspectives*. New York: Guilford.

Sampson, R. J., & Laub, J. H. (1997). Unraveling the social context of physique and delinquency: A new long-term look at the Gluecks' classic study. In A. Raine, P. A. Brennan, D. P. Farrington, & S. A. Mednick (Eds.), *Biosocial bases of violence*. New York: Plenum.

Savitz, L. D. (1972). Introduction. In G. Lombroso-Ferrero (Ed.), *Criminal man*. Montclair, NJ: Patterson Smith.

Scarpa, A., & Raine, A. (1997). Biology of wickedness. *Psychiatric Annals, 27,* 624–629.

Schulsinger, F. (1972). Psychopathy: Heredity and environment. In S. A. Mednick & K. O. Christiansen (Eds.), *Biosocial bases of criminal behavior* (pp. 109–125). New York: Gardner.

Seguin, J., Pihl, R., Harden, P., Tremblay, R., & Boulerice, B. (1995). Cognitive and neuropsychological characteristics of physically aggressive boys. *Journal of Abnormal Psychology, 104*(4), 614–624.

Sheldon, W. H., Hartl, E. M., & McDermott, E. (1949). *Varieties of delinquent youth: An introduction to constitutional psychiatry*. New York: Harper.

Sheldon, W. H., Hartl, E. M., & McDermott, E. (1970). *Varieties of delinquent youth*. Darien, CT: Hafner.

Sheldon, W. H., & Stevens, S. S. (1942). *The varieties of temperament*. New York: Harper.

Siegel, L. J., & Senna, J. J. (Eds.). (2000). *Juvenile delinquency: Theory, practice, and law* (7th ed.). Belmont, CA: Wadsworth/Thomson Learning.

Seyle, H. (1976). *The stress of life*. New York: McGraw-Hill.

Vold, G. B., Bernard, T. J., & Snipes, J. B. (1998). *Theoretical criminology* (4th ed.). New York: Oxford University Press.

Walters, G. D. (1992). A meta-analysis of the gene-crime relationship. *Criminology, 30*(4), 595–613.

Wilson, J. Q., & Herrnstein, R. J. (1985). *Crime and human nature*. New York: Simon & Schuster.

Zuckerman, M. (1999). *Vulnerability to psychopathology*. Washington DC: American Psychological Association.

Psychological Theories of Crime and Criminal Behavior

Overview

There are many psychological approaches to the study of human behavior. However, those that are most relevant to a proper understanding of criminal conduct are a bit more limited. This chapter explores the most well documented and controversial of these perspectives. In particular, **personality theory, psychoanalytic theory,** and the theory of **criminal thinking patterns** are described. What is perhaps most significant about each of these accounts is that the origins of human action—including aggressive, violent, and even criminal behavior—reside within the personality structure or cognitive processes of the individual. In this way, delinquency and crime are not reducible to chemical states, physiological conditions, or biological predispositions. Instead, the mind of the offender is the inevitable source of crime. This chapter explores how various theorists and researchers reach this provocative conclusion.

Key Terms

Antisocial personality disorder
Antisocial personality traits
Anxiety (objective, neurotic, and moral)
Brain electrical activity
California Psychology Inventory (CPI)
Cardiovascular activity
Criminal thinking error
Criminal thinking patterns
Dangerousness
Defense mechanisms
Denial
Developmental theory
Displacement
DSM–IV–TR
Ego
Electrodermal activity
Empathy–dehumanization continuum
Free association
Humanistic psychology
Id
Impulsivity
Inferiority complex
Latent delinquency

Libido
Life-course-persistent theory
Motivation
Negative emotionality
Neurosis
Oedipus or Electra complex
Personality
Personality theory
Projection
Psychoanalysis
Psychoanalytic theory
Psychopathy
Psychosexual stages of personality
   development
Psychosis
Rationalization
Reaction formation
Repression
Self-analysis
Sociocultural and biosocial approaches
Sublimation
Superego
Thinking errors

PERSONALITY THEORY

Introduction

Personality theory is one of three psychological perspectives examined in this chapter. **Personality** "refers to the complex set of emotional and behavioral attributes that tend to remain relatively constant as the individual moves from situation to situation" (Vold, Bernard, & Snipes, 1998, p. 88). Personality theory assumes that criminal behavior originates in the complex web of emotional and behavioral characteristics of the individual rather than in biological factors or environmental conditions. Admittedly, personality theory encompasses research on the unconscious components of emotion and behavior. However, this material will be discussed in greater detail under the section addressing the psychoanalytic perspective. Personality theory also locates and anchors the basis for criminal behavior in its assessment of antisocial personalities and impulsive traits. Accordingly, in this section, criminal conduct is described as a result of personality defect (including **antisocial personality disorder**), the conscious or overt dimensions of personality, and the link between **impulsivity**, antisocial tendencies, and criminal behavior.

The study of personality can be approached from numerous viewpoints. The main theories of personality include biological, developmental, and environmental orientations. These perspectives address the debate surrounding the nature versus nurture distinction; that is, they consider whether people are born or made to act the way that they do. Another facet in the study of personality is whether a link exists between one's emotional and behavioral characteristics and one's motives (Derelega, Winstead, & Jones, 1991). These four approaches in the study of personality (biology, development, environment, and motives) are discussed in the Theories of Personality subsection.

Theories of Personality

The biological understanding of personality is based on three unique approaches: (a) the application of biology and biological methods used in conjunction with other measures to make hypotheses about personality, (b) the examination of individual differences among people from a biological perspective as a response to the presence of similar personality constructs, and (c) the analysis of independent biological variables used to classify different individuals. Biological personality theorists also utilize physiological variables as an indicator of personality types. Common physiological measures employed in personality research include **electrodermal activity**, **cardiovascular activity**, and **brain electrical activity.**

Electrodermal measures examine the electrical activity of the skin. Electrical activity is most frequently observed in the variations of the amount of perspiration in the sweat glands on the skin's surface (Davidson, 1991). Researchers have noted individual differences in electrical activity in extroverted and introverted individuals, depressed and non-depressed participants, and individuals with higher levels of anxiety and neuroticism (Coles, Gale, & Kline, 1971). Cardiovascular activity measures analyze an individual's heart rate and link the findings to personality differences. Investigators have reported differences in heart rates in shy and inhibited children, participants with depression, and individuals who exhibited a conditioned fear (Henriques & Davidson, 1989; Hodes, Cook, & Lang, 1985; Kagan, Reznick, & Snidman, 1988). Measures of brain electrical activity investigate the link between the central nervous system and the personality. The main area of the central nervous system that scientists study is the individual's ability to augment or reduce the effect of sensory stimulation (Petrie, 1978).

There are four approaches to the study of personality informed by **developmental theory.** These approaches include the psychoanalytic, behavioral, humanistic, sociocultural, and biosocial perspectives. Each of these perspectives is summarily described in the following section.

The psychoanalytic approach maintains that unconscious and repressed forces along with unexamined feelings and situations impact how one's personality is formed. Sigmund Freud (1856–1939) originally worked on his psychoanalytic interpretations in order to develop theories of personality and patterns of attachment. The behaviorist approach views the environment as a main determinant of personality. B. F. Skinner (1904–1990), a principal architect of behaviorism, argued that personality was shaped through one's ongoing reinforcement patterns (i.e., punishment–reward system). **Humanistic psychology** asserts that an individual's personality develops as a result of parent–child interactions. Carl Rogers (1902–1987), a leading exponent of this approach, suggested that a fully functioning person receives unconditional positive regard in parent–child relations and throughout the course of one's life. The **sociocultural and biosocial approaches** stress the significance of societal and cultural influences outside the individual on the development of personality. This theory also acknowledges the importance of cultural rules, social context, group dynamics, family values, and so forth, and how these factors affect individual attitudes and behavior. Overall, research on personality using developmental theory indicates that patterns of hostility and violence can be traced to people who experience problems with internal inhibitions or desires, environmental stimuli, interpersonal self-worth, and cultural influences. These patterns tend to persist throughout an individual's life and may contribute to the onset of criminal behavior in adulthood (Walters & Cheek, 1991).

Personality theory also examines whether emotional and behavioral traits exist uniquely for and within people or whether these expressions of individuality are a product of the environment. Researchers who reject the notion of personality traits believe that the environment or external situations operate as determinants for behavior. There are six hypotheses that address this "person–situation" debate. These hypotheses include the following: (a) Personality is a perception rather than a trait; (b) two individuals who judge a situation similarly do not necessarily have the same personality traits; (c) personality types are assigned based on stereotypes; (d) personality traits are based on a "social reputation"; (e) behavioral consistencies among individuals are a result of the external situation; and (f) an individual's behaviors across situations are not consistent; therefore, similar behaviors across situations are not significant (Kenrick & Funder, 1991).

Each of these hypotheses has a critical assumption. Kenrick and Funder (1991, p. 153) examined these assumptions at some length. The following observations are based on their insights. The supposition of hypothesis (a) is that people cannot agree in assigning traits to others. The assumption of hypothesis (b) is that people can agree, but do not distinguish among the people being rated. The supposition of hypothesis (c) is that people can distinguish among those being rated, but they cannot really observe behavior. The assumption of hypothesis (d) is identical to that of hypothesis (c). Hypothesis (e) presumes that people base trait ratings on behavioral observations, but that the behavioral consistencies are not due to traits. Hypothesis (f) assumes that there are traitlike consistencies in behavior, but that they are irrelevant. Each of these hypotheses and their corresponding assumptions have led some researchers to argue for a strong relationship between personality and social psychology and for an interaction between genes and the environment (Kenrick & Funder; Plomin et al., 2001).

Another facet to the study of personality is human **motivation.** Human motivation can be viewed from four different perspectives that examine the organization, direction, and purpose of an individual's life. These four perspectives are summarily described in the following section.

> (1) Human beings are motivated by reason to attain the "good" and the "rational"; (2) human beings are motivated by "bad" internal forces that ultimately bring pain and misery; (3) motives are determined solely by environmental learning; or (4) there exists an indeterminate number of different motives upon which individuals vary widely. (McAdams, 1991, p. 200)

These four perspectives of motivation focus on the biological, psychological, and cognitive bases of behavior. Biological and cognitive bases have been combined to allow for a more contemporary method of assessing motivation. This method focuses on the social motives of achievement, power, and intimacy (Dweck, 1992; Elliot & Sheldon, 1998). Investigators have identified several aspects of these motives and have demonstrated how they reflect significant differences in individuals' social conduct (criminal vs. noncriminal behavior), career goals, leadership abilities, intimate relationships, adjustment abilities, and personal health (Deci & Ryan, 1985; Kasser & Ryan, 2001; McAdams, 1991). One psychological assessment instrument used in the assessment of these personality structures is the Thematic Apperception Test (TAT) (Lilienfeld, Wood, & Garb, 2000).

The various approaches to the study of personality delineated previously can be applied to an analysis of crime and to certain types of criminal behavior. For example, explanations for the commission of violent acts such as murder, sexual abuse and assault, and arson can be offered by linking one's motives to one's personal relationships. In addition, an assessment of nonviolent criminal behavior can proceed based on an analysis of the situational and environmental variables impacting personality. Then, too, juvenile delinquency can be interpreted from the perspective of developmental theory (e.g., **psychoanalysis**) and the way unconscious and unexamined forces inform the emotional and behavioral characteristics of the adolescent. Finally, crimes committed by persons suffering from mental illness can be studied through the lens of biology and the perspective of developmental theory (e.g., sociocultural and biosocial). What is important to remember in each of these instances is that studying personality entails the application of varied conceptual approaches. These approaches attempt to assess whether, and to what extent, emotional and behavioral characteristics are a product of the person, are a product of society, or are a unique and complex product of both.

Antisocial Personality Disorder

According to the *Diagnostic and Statistical Manual* (4th ed., text revision [*DSM–IV–TR*], American Psychiatric Association [APA], 2000), antisocial personality disorder is defined as "a pervasive pattern of disregard for, and violation of, the rights of others that begins in childhood or early adolescence and continues into adulthood" (p. 701). An individual meets this pattern through an indication of at least three of the following criteria:

> . . . (1) failure to conform to social norms with respect to lawful behaviors as indicated by repeatedly performing acts that are grounds for arrest; (2) deceitfulness, as indicated by repeated lying, use of aliases, or conning others for personal profit or pleasure; (3) impulsivity or failure to plan ahead; (4) irritability and aggressiveness, as indicated by repeated physical fights or assaults; (5) reckless disregard for safety of self or others; (6) consistent irresponsibility, as indicated by repeated failure to sustain consistent work behavior or honor financial obligations; (7) lack of remorse, as indicated by being indifferent to or rationalizing having hurt, mistreated, or stolen from another. (APA, 2000, p. 706)

There are additional criteria that must be met in order for the diagnosis of antisocial personality disorder to occur. These include the following: (a) The individual must be at least 18 years of age, (b) the individual was diagnosed with or there was evidence of conduct disorder before the age of 15, and (c) the antisocial behaviors are present outside of episodes of mania or the course of schizophrenia (APA, 2000). The diagnosis of antisocial behavior in adults is often equated with criminality. Interestingly, however, antisocial personality disorder also can be compared to **psychopathy**, not just criminality (Arrigo & Shipley, 2001). According to some investigators, the former is regarded as an extreme or acute manifestation of antisocial personal disorder (e.g., Hare, 1996; Martens, 2000; Toch, 1998).

According to the **DSM–IV–TR** (APA, 2000), antisocial personality disorder is positively correlated with socioeconomic status and urban settings. Indeed, individuals of lower socioeconomic status groups tend to be diagnosed more frequently with antisocial personality disorder than are other groups. Additionally, antisocial personality disorder appears to be more prevalent in males than in females. This underrepresentation of females identified with the disorder can be interpreted as an underdiagnosis. One explanation for the underdiagnosis stems from the difference in aggression levels between males and females (cf. Aronson, Wilson, & Akert, 2002). Because males tend to be more aggressive, they are diagnosed more frequently with the disorder. In a sample of the community, the APA found that approximately 3% of males and 1% of females were diagnosed with antisocial personality disorder. The prevalence of the disorder in clinical settings was significantly greater, ranging from 3% to 30%. Further, even greater prevalence rates were seen in forensic settings and substance abuse treatment centers (APA, 2000).

When antisocial behaviors originate from the personality of an individual, there is no known effective method for the treatment. As a result, individuals who are diagnosed with antisocial personality disorders often remain in psychiatric facilities for the majority of their lives. If a criminal is diagnosed with antisocial personality disorder, it is assumed that the individual will continue to commit illegal acts if permitted to live freely in society (Hare, 1993; Martens, 2000). Therefore, the individual remains in a correctional facility to protect against antisocial behavior and prospects for illicit and lethal conduct (Shipley & Arrigo, 2001).

However, some researchers question whether this is an effective way to deal with individuals who have a mental illness or a personality disorder. In a study conducted to contradict popular beliefs that antisocial and psychopathic individuals should remain in a lockdown facility, McCord (1982) found that juvenile psychopaths tended to have recidivism rates almost equivalent to that of other delinquent nonpsychopathic juveniles. McCord also found a significant similarity in the rates of recidivism several years after liberation from an institution. Indeed, the recidivism rates were identical (McCord, 1982; see also Millon, Simonsen, Birket-Smith, & Davis, 1998).

Antisocial characteristics and traits are often detected in individuals through the use of personality tests. Personality tests include measures such as the Rorschach Inkblot Test, the Minnesota Multiphasic Personality Inventory-Second Edition (MMPI-2), the Millon Clinical Multiaxial Inventory-III (MCMI-III), and the TAT. These instruments assess levels of antisocial behavior in addition to a multitude of other factors. According to Vold et al. (1998), "psychological tests to measure personality differences have been developed more or less parallel to intelligence tests. Inevitably, delinquents and criminals have been tested with these 'personality inventories' to discover how their personalities differ from those of nondelinquents and noncriminals" (p. 96). Studies examining the use of personality tests in the detection of **antisocial personality traits** are discussed in the Studies Examining the Link Between Personality and Crime subsection.

Studies Examining the Link Between Personality and Crime

Various studies have been conducted in order to provide a broader understanding of the link between personality, antisocial behaviors, and crime. The first study to publish results on the personality differences between offenders and nonoffenders was authored by Schuessler and Cressey (1950). In their research, Schuessler and Cressey found that there was no statistical significance between the personalities of offenders and those of nonoffenders. As such, they concluded that it was not possible to establish an association between personality and one's propensity for criminal behavior.

In contrast to the conclusions reached by these investigators, Glueck and Glueck (1950) argued that the interrelatedness of personality characteristics within individuals differentiates the personalities of offenders from those of their nonoffending counterparts. In their comparative study of 500 delinquents and 500 nondelinquents, the Gluecks demonstrated that determining the association between personality characteristics and delinquency required the use of three prediction tables: (a) social background, (b) character traits based on the Rorschach test, and (c) personality traits formulated from the clinical interview. The Gluecks found these tables to be statistically significant. For example, only 10% of individuals in the best-scoring category were predicted to be delinquent; whereas

90% of individuals were predicted to be delinquent in the worst-scoring category. The Gluecks also found numerous personality traits that characterized delinquents. These traits included self-assertiveness, defiance, impulsiveness, narcissism, suspicion, destructiveness, sadism, lack of concern for others, extraversion, ambivalence, feeling unappreciated, distrust of authority, poor personal skills, mental instability, hostility, and resentment.

Considerable research exploring the associations among personality, antisocial behavior, and crime was conducted during the 1950s and 1960s. Many of these investigations attempted to extend or refine the insights of Schuessler and Cressey (1950). For example, reviewing the studies conducted between 1950 and 1965, Waldo and Dinitz (1967) found that 80% of them reported significant differences between the personalities of offenders and those of nonoffenders. However, perhaps the most important results generated by Waldo and Dinitz dealt with those studies that examined an individual's scores on specific sections of the MMPI. They noted that the published research repeatedly indicated that scores on scale 4 of this assessment instrument were considerably higher for offenders than for nonoffenders. As subsequent investigators have explained, scale 4 (or the psychopathic deviate scale) is the most significant scale on the MMPI when assessing criminality (Graham, 2000).

Antisocial Personality Disorder and Future Dangerousness

Current research in the area of predicting future **dangerousness** no longer focuses on the propensity of specific individuals to commit a crime. This was how antisocial personality disorder historically had been linked to delinquency or criminality. Currently, investigations on future dangerousness focus on identifying those factors associated with the increased or decreased likelihood for an individual to act violently (Monahan, 1996; Silver, 2000). In addition, present-day research focuses on juvenile delinquency and mild forms of criminality. This is because these offenses are easier to predict as compared to adult or serious types of criminal wrongdoing (Vold et al., 1998).

Researchers have identified numerous predictors for adolescent crime. For example, early indicators of future delinquency include (a) disruptive school behavior, (b) aggressive behavior, (c) lying, and (d) dishonesty (Loeber & Dishion, 1983). Other factors linked to juvenile delinquency include poor child rearing, criminal behavior by parental figures and siblings, low levels of intelligence, less education, and separation from parents (Loeber & Dishion). Investigations of this sort have lead researchers to examine theories of personality that relate crime and criminal behavior to impulsive characteristics.

Crime and Impulsive Personality Characteristics

Increasingly, social scientists believe that impulsivity is the one basic personality feature associated with antisocial conduct (Gorenstein & Newman, 1980; Gray, 1977; Walters, 2002; Zuckerman, 1989). There are four theories that have attempted to explain crime and criminal behavior in the context of impulsivity. These theories have been proposed by Wilson and Hernstein (1985), Walters (1990), Moffitt (1993), and Caspi, Moffitt, Silva, Stouthamer-Loeber, Krueger, and Schmutte (1994). The four perspectives on crime and impulsive personality characteristics are explained in the following section.

Wilson and Hernstein (1985) articulated the first theory on impulsivity and its relationship to crime. As they explained, the most significant individual personality factor linked to criminal behavior is the ability to think in terms of short-term goals and consequences rather than of long-term goals and consequences. The inability to think in terms of long-term consequences is most frequently associated with high levels of impulsivity and low levels of intelligence. Wilson and Hernstein also identified five factors that increase an individual's potential to engage in criminal activity. These include the following: (a) poor family life; (b) engagement in subcultures, such as gangs; (c) the media's positive portrayal of violence and aggression; (d) an individual's economic standing; and (e) the influence of schools.

The next theory on impulsivity is based on the work of Walters (1990). He argued that there are eight cognitive patterns that allow an individual to act impulsively. These patterns are mollification, cutoff, entitlement, power orientation, sentimentality, superoptimism, cognitive indolence, and discontinuity. These cognitive patterns tend to predispose an individual toward irresponsibility. Irresponsibility is part of the definition of a criminal lifestyle (Walters, 1990).

Another theory that focuses on impulsivity is the **life-course-persistent theory** of offenders, developed by Moffitt (1993). Moffitt proposed that life-course-persistent offenders engage in some form of antisocial behavior at every stage of their development. Moffitt concluded that these behaviors begin as a result of early neuropsychological damage caused by early-life shortcomings and prenatal deficiencies. In childhood, these deficiencies interfere with school success. Thus, antisocial behaviors are pursued and maintained as a replacement for rewards.

Criminal Behavior and Personality Defects

To better illustrate how personality affects an individual and one's susceptibility to crime and criminal behavior, two case examples are presented. The first vignette examines an adult male imprisoned for a 2-year sentence. The second scenario describes an adult female imprisoned for life. Both case examples are analyzed using the *DSM–IV–TR* diagnosis of antisocial personality disorder (APA, 2000). Recommendations for treatment are also presented.

The Case of Thomas

Thomas is a 28-year-old man who is serving a 2-year sentence for armed robbery. Although psychological tests revealed some psychotic thinking, his behavior initially appeared calm and controlled. Correctional psychologists believed he was faking the psychotic symptoms. However, shortly after the testing, he began to cause trouble and became very aggressive. He flooded the entire unit of the prison, spat on staff members, and threw fecal matter and urine at other convicts. He was then transferred to a maximum-security prison and put in solitary confinement. But even though he had neither clothes nor a bed to sleep on, he continued to cause problems. For example, he managed to strip his cell of its surface and make a knife out of these materials. He engaged in these behaviors just a day after his session with the ward psychiatrist. At that time, he seemed remorseful, controlled, and contrite. He blamed the guards for his violent behavior, rather than himself. His psychiatric history indicated that he had a record of repeatedly trying to act "crazy" and to get transferred to a psychiatric unit, from where he would ultimately escape. Thomas managed to convince all mental health professionals that he had psychiatric problems; although, no one could describe exactly what they were. These "problems" kept him from being severely punished for his aggression. The eventual treatment given to Thomas was anti-psychotic medication. However, individuals with antisocial personality disorder cannot be regulated through the use of medicines. Subsequently, Thomas entered a forensic unit of a psychiatric hospital, where he received care for a good portion of his life (Alloy, Jacobson, & Acocella, 1999, p. 497).

Questions regarding the possible recidivism of this offender can be assessed by using the *DSM–IV–TR* criteria for antisocial personality disorder (ASPD). One can anticipate that Thomas will recidivate because of the enduring nature of his personality disorder. Individuals with ASPD are often calm and conniving, and can deceive mental health professionals. Indeed, this is how they target the victims of their crimes; this is why they must receive treatment in order to reduce their criminal behavior.

The second vignette examines a female offender by the name of Margaret. She is diagnosed with ASPD. Although women are less frequently diagnosed with this condition, it does not mean that they fail to experience it, and it does not mean that they do not express or embody ASPD traits (APA, 2000).

The Case of Margaret

Margaret is a 25-year-old female in prison for a life sentence under the supervision of a psychologist. The psychologist believes that Margaret is not in need of mental health services, because Margaret is calm, collected, and of a quiet nature. However, she does not show remorse for her murderous crime. Additionally, Margaret poses a danger to others because of her consistent aggressive behavior and her lack of respect for prison rules and regulations. Margaret has been taking antipsychotic medications to reduce this type of conduct; however, it has not been effective. Again, Margaret is being considered for termination of mental health services. Do you think that the supervision of this imprisoned individual should be terminated?

Considering the diagnosis of ASPD and the DSM–IV–TR's predicted course for such individuals, Margaret's supervision should not be terminated. Prospect for alleviating the disorder are not in her favor. Indeed, the dangerousness posed by Margaret will continue and may worsen without sustained psychological treatment.

Caspi et al. (1994) proposed the fourth theory linking impulsivity and criminal behavior. In their research, the investigators found that proneness to engage in criminal behavior was dependent on impulsivity and negative emotionality. **Negative emotionality** refers to an increased likelihood of experiencing such feelings as anger and irritability. Individuals with greater levels of negative emotionality have more difficulty modulating or regulating their impulses. They also tend to convert negative feelings into emotional actions and reactions. These behaviors can include criminal conduct.

Summary

Overall, the role that personality plays in criminal behavior is not clear, despite the lengthy research conducted in this area. Through ongoing and direct observation, it is evident that some individuals have an increased likelihood for participating in criminal behavior, regardless of the situation in which they find themselves. However, the opposite viewpoint is also valid. In short, apart from the person's involvement in criminal behavior, there are situations that elicit delinquent and criminal behavior more frequently than do others. Therefore, some transgressors can be analyzed in the context of personality theories; however, it is not sufficient to focus only on this line of inquiry. Indeed, some research supports the perspective that the situation in which one is immersed is more indicative of whether the individual will behave criminally.

PSYCHOANALYTIC THEORIES OF CRIMINAL BEHAVIOR

Introduction

"Psychoanalysis is the most extensive, inclusive, and comprehensive system of psychology" (Arlow, 1995, p. 16). To examine the roots of psychoanalytic and psychodynamic theories is, arguably, to document the very birth of psychology itself. The field of psychoanalysis was established by a very brilliant and controversial psychiatrist in Vienna by the name of Sigmund Freud. The psychoanalytic approach to studying behavior forever changed the way the world viewed the human psyche and created a template by which to examine the human condition. To this day, many academic and clinical psychologists use the insights of psychoanalysis in their efforts to understand the conduct of people and the reasons for their actions. This section briefly examines the history of psychoanalytic thought and the basis on which this theoretical approach explains all facets of human behavior in general. In addition, this section explores how the early pioneers and the next wave of psychoanalytic researchers applied the insights of the field to an investigation of criminal behavior. The chapter concludes by identifying and assessing the influence of psychoanalytic thought on contemporary scholars, and how, through their guidance, the theory continues to provide useful and practical insights regarding the causes of criminal conduct.

History and Tenets of Psychoanalytic and Psychodynamic Theories

Psychoanalysis was conceived in the late 19th century by an aspiring neurologist named Sigmund Freud. Over a period of several decades, Freud explained and revised many of his notions, attempting to establish an elegant model for why people act the way that they do. In order to appreciate the historical evolution of psychoanalytic thought and its present-day ability to account for criminal behavior, several of Freud's major papers are summarily described. The first of these includes his observations on the patient, Anna O., published in *Studies on Hysteria* (1895).

Arguably, the birth of psychoanalytic theory can be traced to Freud's commentary on the infamous case of Anna O. Anna was a patient of Freud's colleague, Josef Breuer. Anna possessed the ability to self-correct her hysterical condition by verbalizing what appeared to be causing her strain under hypnosis. Under these hypnotic sessions, Anna would talk of some severely emotional episode in her life. Freud reasoned that if after talking about this emotionally volatile event her pathology was quelled, then the event was the impetus behind the **neurosis.** Freud's insights on unconscious neurosis (i.e., fear and anxiety) became one of the leading treatises establishing the theory of psychoanalysis.

In his work, *The Interpretation of Dreams* (1900), Freud explored the relationship between one's dreams and one's physical and mental symptoms. Indeed, while treating his patients, Freud detected a strong correlation between the pathology of his patients and their dreams. In part, he uncovered this interesting but unexplainable association through his work on self-analysis and **free association.** The latter concept refers to a process in which the patient says whatever comes to his or her mind in relation to the person's fantasies, memories, dreams, or conflicts. Freud maintained that through free association, the patient was able to analyze the thoughts, feelings, attitudes, and beliefs, that one experienced as troubling or distressing.

Another important dimension to *The Interpretation of Dreams* (1990) was Freud's theorization on the unconscious or the unconscious mind. Again, based on his many sessions with patients and relying on **self-analysis** and free association, Freud noticed that several subjects experienced profound discomfort surrounding sexuality. He eventually described this discomfort as a constant battle waged between the instinctual, aggressive impulses of the unconscious and the mediating, logical actions of the conscious. In subsequent works, Freud developed labels for, and expanded on, these complex forces.

As his theory of psychoanalysis evolved, so, too, did Freud's assessment of various psychological states or conditions. One of the most significant of these was his understanding of **psychosis.** The term *psychosis* can be distinguished from the term *neurosis*. Neurosis was "a term first used by Freud to include all but the most severe psychological syndromes; currently narrowly defined as an emotional disorder in which psychic functioning is relatively intact and contact with reality is sound" (Corsini & Wedding, 1995, p. 439). However, people who are psychotic or are identified as suffering from psychosis are "unable to maintain a stable integration of the concept of self or others" (Lerner, 1999, p. 75). Thus, psychotic individuals are dominated by primitive desires called "id" impulses. These impulses are employed as **defense mechanisms** that further debilitate or undermine their **ego** or sense of self. As Freud himself described the difference, "neurosis is the result of a conflict between the ego and its id, whereas psychosis is the analogous outcome of a similar disturbance in the relations between the ego and the external world" (Freud, 1923, p. 149). One interesting feature to the psychosis–neurosis distinction is the personality structure called Borderline Personality Disorder. This personality structure continues to be a *DSM–IV–TR* diagnosis (APA, 2000) and was named for patients who were "borderline," that is, somewhere between neurotic and psychotic.

In his work titled *On Narcissism* (1914), Freud further developed his theory of psychoanalysis. He argued that neurosis or mental anguish was a result of unresolved tension between the **libido** (the sex drive) and the ego (the drives for self-preservation). In addition, however, Freud described a more expansive theoretical model focusing on the aspects of the libido itself (Arlow, 1995). In particular, Freud detailed how the sex drive manifested itself in representations of external objects (e.g., Are sports cars, rocket ships, and cigars completely what they appear to be?) and in people's self-characterizations (e.g., Think about the image conveyed by contemporary singers such as Madonna and Britney Spears; Vaillant, 1992).

Freud's essay, "Beyond the Pleasure Principle" (1920), was an attempt to integrate the notion of aggression and the role it played in unconscious, instinctual drives. Again, through his work with patients, Freud noticed that aggression assumed a pivotal role in the pathological behavior of others. Freud's work on aggression and libido was very influential in several of his later papers where he reformulated and revised many of his original insights. Subsequent researchers appropriated these reformulated insights, believing that they furthered our understanding of the criminal behavior that people commit.

In 1923, with the publication of his paper, "The Ego and the Id," Freud retooled his psychoanalytic model and provided a more structured theory of the mind. This is the point at which he introduced the role of the conscious mind and how it interacts with the unconscious, especially in terms of the ego, **id,** and **superego** (Arlow, 1995). These constructs are described in the following section, in relation to the structure of personality.

Psychoanalytic Personality Theory: Id, Ego, Superego

In Freud's psychoanalytic scheme, personality is the result of three interactive systems: the id, the ego, and the superego. The way a person balances the unconscious operation of these systems determines how the individual will behave. In addition, every difficulty we confront in life is linked to the balance we strike among these different systems.

The id is present at birth. It represents unconscious, instinctual desires. These desires entail the pursuit of pleasure and the avoidance of pain. The id contains within it two competing drives: the life or sex instinct (energized by the libido) and the death or aggressive instinct.

The ego is the next mechanism of personality to appear. It mediates between one's primal needs and society's demands. The ego is sensitive to the realities of life. It holds in check the id's unbridled pursuit of sex and aggression.

The superego is the last system to emerge. The superego is the moral regulator or the conscience overseeing our behaviors and our choices. The superego functions much like parents who tell us "no," remind us to "be careful," or encourage us to think before we act. In this respect, the superego evaluates the various inclinations of the id. When we achieve a success, such as making the varsity basketball team or scoring a high grade on a difficult exam, the superego is responsible for our feeling satisfied or proud. When we experience a disappointment, such as failing to attend a religious service or missing the wedding of our best friend, the superego is responsible for our feeling guilt or shame.

Freud (1926) elaborated on the operation of the id, ego, and superego in his paper, "Inhibitions, Symptoms and Anxiety." He also explained how the three systems interact. For example, in this work, Freud discussed the importance of anxiety as it came to represent the telling signs of psychoneurosis. He described three types of anxiety. These included (a) **objective anxiety,** produced out of an awareness of an obvious conscious threat such as impending physical harm; (b) **neurotic anxiety,** produced when the ego feels it is being taken over by the id and feels these id-like impulses are beyond the ego's control; and (c) **moral anxiety,** produced when an inherent moral code or value is about to be violated (Hergenhahn, 1997). The threat of crime that one experiences is an example of objective anxiety. Overwhelming urges for food, sex, and fun are examples of neurotic anxiety. The death penalty, and one's religious commitment to the sanctity of life, is an illustration of moral anxiety. Feelings of anxiety act as a warning mechanism for the ego to utilize its defense mechanisms. Defense mechanisms operate on an unconscious level and distort reality to protect the person (Hergenhahn, 1997). A brief discussion of these defense mechanisms is presented in the following sections.

Repression is the ego defense mechanism involved in all other defenses. Repression occurs when a person is unable to bring to consciousness threatening (often disturbing and painful) thoughts, feelings, ideas, or memories. A good illustration of repression in the field of criminal behavior is the phenomenon of repressed memory syndrome. For example, consider how repression operates when an adult is unable to recall his or her childhood sexual victimization (e.g., molestation or rape; Nash, 1994). The critical memories, ideas, and feelings associated with the experience of sexual trauma are only able to enter consciousness if they are experienced as harmless (i.e., nonthreatening) so as to not arouse any anxiety (Hergenhahn, 1997). According to Freudian psychoanalysis, one's repressed thoughts or ideas surface in dreams, during free association, or through parapraxes (a slip of the tongue).

Displacement entails substituting an anxiety-producing goal with one that does not produce anxiety. When an employee is frustrated by the anxiety-producing behavior of a supervisor, the employee may vent these feelings onto family members. A more specific form of displacement is **sublimation.** Sublimation entails identifying and utilizing socially acceptable outlets for one's otherwise nonsocially acceptable thoughts, feelings, impulses, and ideas. Persons who are prone to or enjoy violence can express their aggressive tendencies through socially appropriate outlets (e.g., engaging in sports or taking a job as a police or correctional officer). One's involvement in violent crime is not an example of sublimation.

Projection occurs when an alternative way to deal with possible anxiety-producing thoughts is attributed to another person. For example, if you feel inadequate about or uncomfortable with your intelligence, appearance, or personality, you may talk critically about other people, saying things like, "she's not very bright," "he's ugly," "she always wears horrible outfits," or "he's mean spirited."

Rationalization occurs when a person relies on excessive logic to account for one's anxiety-producing situation. For example, victims of a burglary (a family) may indicate that had they better secured their home with multiple alarm systems or had they remained in their home, rather than visiting friends, they would not have been vandalized. In this instance, the family's rationalizations enable them to quell the objective anxiety they would otherwise confront.

Reaction formation takes place when the person does the direct opposite of what is indicated by the anxiety-inducing thought, feeling, or impulse. For example, a person who is gay may date many people and eventually marry a person of the opposite sex. The behavior is an attempt to override the deep-seated homosexual impulses the person experiences.

Denial occurs when a person refuses to accept the fact that something unpleasant or troubling has happened. When a parent adamantly refuses to accept that their missing child is dead, notwithstanding the mountain of evidence laid before that parent, the individual is in denial. Denial masks the harshness and brutality of the life event, keeping one's anxiety at least at arm's length.

Psychosexual Stages of Development

Freud's psychoanalytic theorizations also included an identification of various **psychosexual stages of personality development.** Freud (1926) noted that each stage included some amount of frustration, anxiety and conflict; however, if during the maturation process the individual successfully progressed through the difficulties of each phase, then appropriate and normal personality development would occur. If the person were unable to resolve the difficulties of a particular stage, being "stuck" in that psychosexual phase would produce unhealthy, dysfunctional personality development.

Summary

Many people have criticized Freud's theories, arguing that they are needlessly and excessively focused on sexual desires, and that these desires play a far too significant role in human development and personality structure. Additionally, critics dismiss Freud's theories because there does not appear to be a way to empirically validate or falsify his observations. Notwithstanding these apparent shortcomings, Freud's psychoanalytic concepts have been the basis for much speculation and debate in the behavioral and social sciences. One area of applied research that has seized on his insights is the field of criminology. In the following subsection, the contributions of Freudian psychoanalysis to the study of criminal behavior are presented. Although certainly not exhaustive, the research described demonstrates the long-standing appeal of this controversial approach to understanding the human tendency to commit crime.

Freud's Psychosexual Stages of Development

Freud identified five stages of psychosexual development. The first of these is the Oral Phase. It occurs from birth until the first year to 18 months of the child's life. In this stage, the center of sexual stimulation and gratification is the mouth. Consider how babies enjoy such behaviors as sucking, licking, chewing, and swallowing. According to Freud, during this stage sexual pleasures come through the lips, tongue, and mouth. If the infant experiences minimal or excessive oral gratification, fixation can occur. For example, as an adult the individual may eat, drink, or smoke too much. For some orally fixated individuals, they develop an oral–sadistic character, generally behaving in a pessimistic and aggressive manner.

The second stage of development is called the Anal Phase. It immediately follows the Oral Stage and continues up until the second or third year of the child's life. In this phase, the sexual pleasure zones include the anus and buttocks region. During the early part of this stage there is a focus on touching and smelling feces. When a person becomes stuck in this phase (e.g., fixated in the fecal exploring aspect of this stage), the individual may become anal–expulsive and grow up to be messy and disorganized. However, during toilet training, the child may, through reaction formation, become extremely neat and organized to avoid fecal and urinary expulsion. In adolescence and adulthood, this fixation may result in anal-retentive behavior. Examples of this include excessive neatness, extreme meticulousness, obsessive cleanliness.

The third stage is called the Phallic Phase. It begins roughly after the third year of life and continues until the end of the fifth year. Sexual gratification is situated in the genital area. The penis is the focus for both boys and girls; however, during this stage girls are also able to appreciate sexual stimulation in their vagina. It is during this stage that boys and girls develop the Oedipal or Electra complex. During this stage, the child develops strong sexual feelings toward the parent of the opposite sex and hostile intentions toward the parent of the same sex. This is perhaps best expressed by boys who say that they will grow up to marry their moms and by girls who say that they will grow up to marry their dads.

Freud admitted that boys and girls go through the Phallic Stage differently. Boys take pride in knowing that they have a penis and are startled to see or learn that girls do not. Upon discovering this, the boy wonders how this could have happened. The boy realizes that the strong and powerful father did this to the girl and that, more importantly, could also do it to the boy. The boy conceals (represses) his sexual feelings for his mother and accepts the authority of his father. The father's morality, conscience, belief system, and values are adopted by the boy. It is at this point that the boy's superego emerges.

The experience of the Phallic Stage for girls is quite different, according to Freud. Initially, the girl will have strong feelings for the mother; however, when the girl realizes that she does not have a penis, she harbors anger toward the mother whom she blames for this perceived deficiency. In fact, the girl realizes that the father has what she wants and develops "penis envy." Eventually, the girl develops feelings of ambivalence toward her father: She is both attracted to and envious of her dad. The coping mechanism employed by the girl at this stage is to repress sexual feelings toward the father and to emote hostile, ill will toward the mother.

The next psychosexual stage is called the Latency Phase. Freud believed that the conflict inherent in the Phallic Phase should be resolved by age 5 or 6. This is the point at which the child's personality is essentially formed. During the course of one's life, the conflicts and struggles dealt with during the Oral, Anal, and Phallic Phases manifest themselves in varying contexts. However, during the Latency Phase the child is mostly nonsexual. This period of rest and adjustment is important in that it facilitates the transition to the Genital Phase. During the Latency Phase, one's efforts are directed toward other external aspects of the world, such as friends, sports, school, and other hobbies. During this stage, there is a lot of conflict that takes place between the id and the superego, especially in relation to the external world. If not appropriately resolved, these conflicts can lead to sexual perversion, severe and persistent psychopathology, and other personality disorders or character deficits.

The final stage is called the Genital Phase. The genital stage begins at the onset of puberty and continues throughout the life of the individual. During this stage, latent sexual desires become far too overpowering to be subdued or repressed any longer. In fact, this is the time when the adolescent or adult acts on them. Sexual gratification is targeted toward members of the opposite sex. Assuming that normal development has occurred in the preceding stages, the individual will develop healthy dating relationships that may eventually result in marriage. If the person is stuck or fixated in a previous psychosexual stage, then dysfunctional dating patterns or sexual practices will occur.

Psychoanalytic and Psychodynamic Theories and Criminal Behavior

Sigmund Freud did not spend a great deal of time applying his psychoanalytic insights to criminal behavior. However, he did postulate that wayward conduct was linked to unconscious feelings of guilt, the result of an overdeveloped superego and the effect of unresolved emotion surrounding one's **Oedipus or Electra complex.** Closely associated with these repressed forces is the desire to be punished for harboring such ideas or impulses. Given these conditions, Freud (1923) suggested that people cope by engaging in criminal behavior. Moreover, he surmised that transgressors unknowingly would commit careless acts, facilitating their apprehension and their desire for punishment. In these instances, one's unconscious motivations compel the person to behave criminally, driven by a primal need to receive some sort of sanction. In chapter 5, the example of serial murderers is used to illustrate how some of these offenders harbor guilt and then leave clues at the crime scene so that they can be apprehended by the police and punished for their actions.

August Aichhorn (1878–1949) was a pioneer in the field of psychodynamic criminal theory. Freudian psychoanalysis was psychodynamic because it stressed the movement of "psychological energy within the person, in the form of attachments, conflicts, and motivations" (Wade & Tavris, 2003, p. 486). By relying on Freudian psychoanalysis, Aichhorn was able to formulate a psychodynamic theory of juvenile delinquency.

Aichhorn (1935) identified three types of youthful offenders. The first of these criminals possessed *underdeveloped* superegos. Thus, he reasoned that these adolescents had a psychological predisposition toward criminal behavior. Aichhorn called this predisposition **"latent delinquency."** During this period of latent delinquency, the id goes unchecked. As such, the youth seeks gratification impulsively, engages in pleasure-seeking conduct without regard for others or without concern for the consequences of one's actions, and experiences an absence of guilt or remorse for one's behavior, irrespective of personal costs or penalties. Aichhorn explained that these id-like impulses flourished because the adolescent's underdeveloped superego could not mediate the youth's unconscious desires, instincts regulated in an otherwise normally functioning human being. The notion of latent delinquency still operates somewhat today. Indeed, it is closely aligned with the *DSM–IV–TR* criteria of conduct disorder for adolescents and antisocial personality disorder for adults (APA, 2000). Aichhorn posited that the behavior of these delinquent youths was attributable to their parents, especially those who were either callous toward their children or who neglected them altogether. According to his psychodynamic theory, children needed to develop loving attachments early in life if proper development of the superego was to occur.

Aichhorn (1935) also described juvenile delinquency in the context of parents who loved their children too much, permitting them to do anything they pleased while they grew up and who experienced little to no discipline during the developmental periods of childhood and adolescence. Aichhorn indicated that these wayward youths were fewer in number as compared to their latent delinquency counterparts. In addition, Aichhorn observed what he believed were children with adequately developed superegos, but who related to or identified with their criminal parents. As such, these children emulated the deviant behaviors of their parental role models. Consistent with Aichhorn's observations, the psychoanalytic work of Friedlander (1949) and that of Redl and Wineman (1951) argued that some adolescents develop delinquent egos, resulting in hostile attitudes and aggressive impulses directed toward authority figures.

Another explanation for criminal behavior based on psychodynamic insights was proposed by Healy and Bronner (1931). Their research was consistent with and lent empirical validity to the threefold typology developed by Aichhorn (1935). In their study of 105 pairs of brothers, half of whom were delinquent youths, Healy and Bronner found that the delinquent brothers did not establish and maintain important emotional ties to their parents in the same manner that the nondelinquent brothers did. Research conducted by Bowlby (1953) also indicated that delinquency was caused by an absence of significant emotional attachments established early in childhood with a loving, nurturing figure.

Some psychoanalytic investigators have linked criminal conduct to the presence of an **"inferiority complex."** Alfred Adler, the father of individual psychology, proposed that abnormal, deviant behavior is a result of a person suffering from severe and profound feelings of inadequacy or worthlessness. In order to cope with these unconscious feelings, and in order to avoid the emotional anguish that would otherwise follow from acknowledging these sentiments, the individual conveys a superior attitude, dominates conversations, and craves control (Mosak, 1995). In the extreme, an inferiority complex can lead to aggressive, even violent, conduct. For example, one possible explanation for the repeated terrorist actions and human rights violations of Saddam Hussein, the former leader of Iraq, can be attributed to his own deep-seated feelings of inadequacy, worthlessness, and incompetency. A more conventional illustration would be the bully in the playground. Some kids are mean, hostile, and hurtful to others kids because they simply do not like themselves or feel good about who they are.

The inherent nature of psychodynamic theory focuses on unconscious aggressive impulses to explain human behavior in general. Thus, it should come as no surprise that more contemporary psychodynamic accounts of criminal behavior address more extreme forms of violent conduct. Psychoanalytic scholars acknowledge that the offender's interaction with and relationship to his or her victim is very important in explaining the etiology of the crime itself (Lerner, 1999; Palermo, 2002; Palermo & Farkas, 2001). Some of the leading research on violent criminal behavior using the insights of psychodynamic theory was conducted by Kennedy (as cited in Lerner, 1999). Kennedy developed a theory called the **"empathy–dehumanization continuum."** He argued that empathy could deter violent–aggressive acting-out behavior; however, he reasoned that if this empathetic structure was hindered, then the likelihood of that person causing harm to another increased. Thus, accessing the empathic, compassionate dimension of one's humanity was the best therapeutic response to avoiding, minimizing, or eliminating violent conduct.

One example of how the empathy–dehumanization continuum operates comes from research on victim impact statements presented during the penalty phase of a capital trial (Bandes, 1996). Some investigators argue that the use of these statements serves no purpose other than to foster vengeance, inflame hatreds, and administer retribution. These sentiments undermine the victim's ability to embrace their natural inclinations to show compassion, forgiveness, and mercy to others (Arrigo & Williams, 2003). Moreover, maintaining such dehumanizing feelings (i.e., regarding the offender as less than or other than human) inhibits the person harmed from coping with the pain, anguish, and sadness that follow in the wake of criminal victimization.

The most recent efforts to apply the insights of psychoanalysis to an understanding of criminal behavior come from those identified as Freudian revisionists. Perhaps the most well known of revisionists was Jacque Lacan (1901–1981). Lacan believed that the unconscious was structured much like a language. Learning how this language or grammar operated in different social settings or interpersonal exchanges was key to discovering the basis of human thought, knowledge, and action. Lacan's (1977) work principally focused on explaining the relationship between our thoughts and feelings, and our identity and subjectivity. Similar to Freud, he was interested in desire. However, unlike Freud, Lacan recognized that desire was always expressed through written or spoken words, and that these words did not necessarily represent or embody our individuality or unique identity. For example, a legal code, an employee handbook, and an instructional manual convey meaning; however, whose "voice" or whose personality is embedded in the written or spoken words? In some cases, it really does not matter whose voice or identity is lodged within the words. However, in other instances, it does. Lacan maintained that comprehending the subtleties of language and the way it potentially invalidates or dismisses one's own being was very important to understanding all human behavior, including criminal conduct.

Criminological researchers have appropriated the psychoanalytic contributions of Lacan (1977) and have applied them to various criminal justice and mental health concerns. Selected examples include insanity defense reform (Arrigo, 1997); civil commitment (Williams, 1998); police–citizen interactions (Shon, 2000); the guilty but mentally ill verdict (Arrigo, 1996); criminal responsibility (Voruz, 2000); and law, psychiatry, and punishment (Arrigo, 2002). This applied scholarship considerably advances our understanding of criminal behavior.

For example, by analyzing how criminologists and psychologists talk about, write about, and investigate such phenomena as "dangerousness," "competency to be executed," "psychiatric disorders," "confinement," and "mental health treatment," Arrigo (2002) explains how only system-supporting interpretations for these notions find their way into criminological and psychological discourse and decision making. However, by reducing the meaning of these phenomena to what the "experts" report, important opportunities for expanding and deepening our comprehension of these constructs (especially from those subjected to such institutional or professional decisions) are missed, ignored, or discounted. In short, studies such as this demonstrate that what we say and how we speak about crime and criminal behavior matter. Indeed, from a Lacanian perspective, by focusing on language and the analysis of discourse we learn a great deal more about the nature of our identities and the knowledge that we manufacture.

CRIMINAL THINKING ERRORS OR PATTERNS

Dr. Samuel Yochelson, former Director of the Program for the Investigation of Criminal Behavior at Saint Elizabeth's Hospital in Washington DC, developed a unique and controversial perspective to account for criminal and violent conduct. In conjunction with his research assistant, Dr. Stanton Samenow, Yochelson created what would become a three-volume anthology, titled *The Criminal Personality* (1976). What made Yochelson's (and Samenow's, 1984) perspective on criminality so unique was their complete abandonment of popular sociological and psychological explanations. Central to their theory was the belief that criminals simply think differently. Yochelson and Samenow argued that at one point the criminal begins to adopt thinking and reasoning patterns that are contrary to how a law-abiding citizen thinks and reasons (Samenow). These different thought processes result in criminal behavior and are termed **thinking errors.**

Yochelson and Samenow did not build their own perspective from former theories. In addition, they did not reformulate or modify aspects of other criminological models that came before them. Instead, they drew attention to an entirely different world in which criminals live, including a focus on the etiology (or origins) of wrongful conduct (Sharp, 2000).

The world of thinking errors is all-inclusive. Religion, employment, schooling, sexuality, recreation, and health are just some examples (Samenow, 1984; Yochelson, 1976). The same can therefore be said of thinking errors and crime. The creation of this overall criminal being is foreign to the life experiences of noncriminals. However, one way to appreciate how the criminal emerges is to examine and dispel what are called the myths of criminal behavior (Samenow).

Myths of Criminal Behavior

Yochelson and Samenow claimed that previous attempts to identify causal factors for illicit conduct and previous attempts to explain the criminal personality structure were nothing more than futile exercises. Thus, the first myth regarding crime relates to these beliefs. According to the school of "criminal thinking patterns," the deviant child is not a victim of poor parenting or questionable parental role models (Samenow, 1984; Sharp, 2000). As

Samenow asserted, "The parents become the first in the criminal's string of victims" (p. 26). Of course, this begs the question, How do children then acquire the criminal (thinking error) persona? In response, Samenow (1984) offered this explanation:

> [B]eginning as early as the preschool years, *patterns* evolve that become part of a criminal lifestyle. As a child, the criminal is a dynamo of energy, a being with an iron will, insistent upon taking charge, expecting others to indulge his every whim. His appetite for adventure is voracious. He takes risks, becomes embroiled in difficulties, and then demands to be bailed out and forgiven. No matter how his parents try to understand and guide him, they are thwarted at every turn . . . The parents' interminable struggle to cope with this wayward youngster saps their energy, drains their finances, weakens their marriage, and harms their other children. But the criminal child remains unaffected. (p. 26)

The delinquent youth asserts and embodies his wayward tendencies irrespective of a healthy, two-parent home environment or a dysfunctional, broken-home setting. Whether the child is from affluent surroundings or from those that are poverty stricken, these factors are all arbitrary and irrelevant. This is because *choice* is the sole determinant for one's (criminal) actions (Samenow, 1984).

The second myth addressed by Yochelson (1976) and Samenow (1984) was the effect that the deviant peer group had on the behavior of the juvenile. In chapter 4, this theory, known as differential association, is examined more closely. However, according to these investigators, delinquency is not the result of one's association with criminal peer groups. Yochelson and Samenow argued that to adopt this point of view would require that one dismiss or ignore the commonly held conviction that criminal conduct emerges from free will and purposeful behavior (Yochelson, 1976). As Yochelson and Samenow explained, beginning at a very young age, the well-adjusted child chooses to associate with whomever the youth wishes, but does not associate with others the child regards as trouble, bad, or deviant. In the **criminal thinking error** perspective, peer influence is not entirely ignored; however, it does not transcend independent choice making. To put it bluntly, a child's deviant path is not a result of falling in with the wrong crowd of people (Yochelson, 1976).

The third myth refuted by Yochelson (1976) and Samenow (1984) relates to employment and education. Some criminologists assert that poor schooling, inadequate infrastructure, and incompetent teachers contribute to the evolution of a deviant person. However, the criminal thinking error perspective argues that these are arbitrary variables used to account for delinquent behavior (Samenow, 1984). Indeed, the criminal is not affected by these external influences; that is, one's deviant or delinquent personality structure is formed independent of such outside factors. Samenow argued that this position finds support in the fact that there are many children exposed to such debilitating conditions, yet only a small fraction of these adolescents become criminals. Simply stated, ". . . criminals reject school long before it rejects them" (p. 68).

Moreover, Samenow (1984) believed that the school and the teachers that worked within them were unwitting victims of the youth's wayward and pleasure-seeking escapades. The juvenile delinquent rejects and isolates him or herself from the well-behaved and socially appropriate student, and attempts to become stronger by exploiting and preying on the weaknesses of others. The criminal child's persistent acts of deviance are attempts to eliminate boredom, as his peers work to make the most of their educational experience. Samenow offered the following additional observations to summarily portray the criminal child:

> What others find acceptable or even fascinating, he disdains. He stirs up excitement through a series of power plays designed not only to relieve tedium but also to call attention to him and establish a reputation. What others consider getting in trouble, he perceives as a boost to his self image. (p. 69)

Breakdown of Total Hours Spent with People at St. Elizabeth's Hospital

5,000 hours or more	12 people	50–100 hours	28 people
1,000 hours or more	17 people	10–50 hours	72 people
500–1,000 hours	7 people	Fewer than 10 hours	93 people
100–500 hours	23 people		

(Yochelson, 1976, p. 118)

Criminal Thinking Errors

The research compiled by Yochelson (1976) and Samenow (1984) took place over 14 years at Saint Elizabeth's Hospital in Washington DC. They spent a considerable amount of time with a number of individuals at the facility. The sample reportedly included all males, with the exception of three cases.

In volume 1 of *The Criminal Personality,* Yochelson (1976) outlined what he termed *general thinking patterns of the criminal.* A list and description of the most prominent thinking patterns are examined shortly. However, before examining these specific thinking patterns, Yochelson posited that there is a continuum of criminality. On one end of the spectrum there is the responsible "noncriminal." At the other end of the continuum there is the irresponsible "extreme criminal."

On this continuum the responsible person is honest, hard working, considerate, and constantly achieving goals. This individual shows respect toward others and, in turn, is respected and appreciated by other people. The responsible person rarely has deviant, criminal thought patterns and is nonarrestable. If criminal thoughts do materialize, they are discarded or ignored immediately.

On the other end of the continuum is the irresponsible person. This individual is deceitful, lazy, inconsiderate, and fails to achieve desired goals. The irresponsible person does not show respect toward others and does not experience respect or admiration from conforming peers. The irresponsible person harbors deviant, criminal thoughts. These tendencies can consume the individual's behavior.

According to Yochelson (1976), there are two types of irresponsible persons in relation to criminal behavior: the nonarrestable criminal and the arrestable criminal. The nonarrestable criminal is an irresponsible person whose actions do not necessarily violate the law. Nonarrestable criminals default on loans, run traffic lights, and regularly lie. They do not take responsibility for their conduct. Additionally, nonarrestable criminals go to work late, leave early, and are not terribly productive on the job. In fact, they may hold a series of positions as a result of constantly being fired for poor work performance. Nonarrestable criminals are not very dependable or trustworthy. However, their actions do not result in criminal prosecution.

Yochelson's Continuum of Criminality

Responsible	*Irresponsible*
Noncriminal	Extreme criminal
(Nonarrestable)	(Nonarrestable criminal to arrestable criminal)

(Yochelson, 1976, p. 253)

According to Yochelson (1976), "[A]rrestable criminals have all the thinking patterns of the extreme or hard core criminal, but their crime patterns are less extensive and serious" (p. 254). This type of offender steals small amounts of supplies from work and commits numerous other minor infractions that go undetected (e.g., shoplifting, petty theft, and driving under the influence of alcohol). For the most part, arrestable criminals have not achieved much in life; in fact, in the broad scheme of things they are what we would commonly refer to as the "failures" in life. Arrestable criminals succeed in situations where there is minimal risk (e.g., lax security at a department store) and where privacy, secrecy, and anonymity are highly likely (e.g., large metropolitan cities).

As Yochelson (1976) explains it, extreme criminals are a unique group. Their cognitive processes and behavioral patterns represent a person who thinks and behaves differently from law-abiding citizens. Although extreme criminals make up a relatively small percentage of the population, their commitment to offender behavior and the severity of their criminal conduct creates the most personal harm or property damage to society.

The cognitive processes unique to the criminal personality are what Yochelson (1976) and Samenow (1984) termed criminal thinking patterns. These patterns are located in the person's unique identity. Again, following the work of Yochelson and Samenow, these patterns indicate that criminals think differently from their noncriminal counterparts. As such, these cognitive processes produce thinking errors. Yochelson and Samenow originally identified 52 thinking errors (Yochelson, 1976). A brief description of the more important criminal patterns are outlined in the following sections.

Energy Level

The criminal is described as possessing an abnormally low attention span and an abnormally high level of energy, illustrated specifically in motor activities. The child displays a very great deal of hyperactivity in his or her recreational patterns and thought processes. The child's physical activity can be so energized that teachers may rely on bodily restraints to subdue or control the individual. High amounts of energy are channeled to those activities that keep the child's interest. This includes deviant conduct. This high level of energy, both mental and physical, is one of the most observable features among those who engage in criminal thinking patterns.

Fear

Contrary to popular characterizations in the media, the criminal is not an individual without fear. As Yochelson (1976) explained,

> Some of the criminal's fears can be traced to a traumatic experience or to specific teachings . . . [b]ut most of the criminal's fears are not traceable to a prototypic experience. His fearfulness is so pervasive from an early age that it almost seems independent of experience. If one were to survey the criminal child's various fears in terms of "minutes of fear per day" the greatest number would be related to being apprehended for some infraction or violation. (p. 259)

What the criminal fears is bodily injury or personal illness. However, what is most profoundly feared is the loss of one's life. As Yochelson (1976) observed,

> The fear of death is very strong, persistent and pervasive in the criminal's mental life. He lives every day as though it were his last. . . . The criminal is so afraid of losing his life that he perceives threats emanating from many sources. He may be afraid of heights, water, lightning, insects, and closed spaces. Later in life, some are afraid to drive. These fears do not appear to be linked with an early traumatic experience. (p. 259)

Another common fear harbored by the criminal is the fear of public ridicule or group humiliation. These "putdowns" can take many forms. For example, they can include a direct attack on the person's character or being ordered to do something by another. As Yochelson (1976) described it, "The criminal is putdown by any adverse event over which he does not have control. Indeed almost anything that does not give him a buildup is a putdown" (p. 261). Popular gangster movies typically illustrate the "macho" image that criminals embody.

Although fearful, the criminal does not openly admit to harboring these feelings. In fact, the offender generally professes not to be afraid of anything. Yochelson (1976) indicated that these fears were neurotic in nature, persisted from childhood, and could even be external to the person's deviant actions.

Anger

Similar to their energy level, the emotion of anger is highly pronounced in criminals as opposed to their nonoffender counterparts. As Yochelson (1976) aptly depicted it, "Anger is as basic to his personality as the iris is to the eye (p. 265)." In some instances, the criminal acts violently in response to feelings of anger or rage. On other occasions, the offender keeps anger bottled up inside until these feelings erupt, leading to aggressive, violent, and criminal behaviors. These acts may include verbal or physical abuse directed toward another. Yochelson stipulated that fear played a very prominent role in the criminal's chronic experience of anger. The link between fear and anger demonstrated that a unique relationship existed between one's emotion and one's behavior, and further established how the criminal's thinking patterns were different from those of noncriminals. As Yochelson explained it,

> Fear is the most common basis for anger in the criminal. Fear gives rise to anger in the noncriminal as well, but the criminal is more thin-skinned than the non-criminal is and thus can be reduced to nothing by even a slight criticism, which he interprets as a putdown. His response is anger. (p. 269)

Pride

The criminal pattern of pride is a key dimension to one's persona or process of thinking, acting, and existing. " 'Criminal pride' corresponds to an extremely and inflexibly high evaluation of oneself. It is the idea that one is better than others are, even when this is clearly not the case. Criminal pride is manifested in all aspects of the criminal's life" (Yochelson, 1976, p. 274). For the male offender, pride manifests itself in stereotypical masculine or "macho" contexts. He takes what he wants, when he wants, and from whomever he chooses. He is a man. He never backs down to threat, never lets anyone take advantage of him (either perceived or in reality), and always is in control.

In order to lead an extravagant lifestyle, the criminal not only lives well beyond his or her means but also believes he or she is entitled to such wealth and abundance. To maintain this lavishness, an extravagance that is essential to keeping the criminal's ego intact, the offender sometimes utilizes illegal methods. The criminal takes pride in his or her offenses, the way in which these criminal acts are perpetrated, and the ease with which they are conducted.

Another source of pride is the criminal's own self-image. Yochelson (1976) and Samenow (1984) reported that offenders generally regard themselves as good people. This sense of basic goodness can be attributed to a superficial appreciation of the arts, donations to charitable causes, helping others in distress, and identifying other offenders as "bad," warranting punishment. In this context, criminals do know right from wrong; however, the transgressions that they commit are not believed to be wrong in their minds. Thus, even the most violent assailant can harbor affirming feelings of self-worth and can adopt a positive self-image (Yochelson; Samenow).

There is some confusion surrounding the theory of criminal thinking patterns. In particular, critics question where criminal thinking patterns come from, especially because, according to the theory's proponents, they account for cognitive errors producing illicit conduct. Regrettably, researchers have not been able to adequately respond to this criticism. Indeed, the work of Yochelson (1976) and Samenow (1984) did not include elaborate criminogenic explanations. These are accounts that fully address the origin of criminal behavior. Thus, the basis for criminal thought processes, behavioral patterns, and thinking errors largely remains a mystery.

Although certainly controversial, the theory of thinking patterns and errors as a basis for explaining criminal personality has spawned more recent research (e.g., Andrews & Bonta, 1998). For example, in his book, *The Criminal Lifestyle,* Glenn Walters (1998) relied heavily on the insights of Yochelson (1976) to elaborate on the more impulsive character-istics of the criminal. In addition, Sharp (2000), employing a cognitive treatment approach, indicated that offenders need to be held responsible for their actions and that they need to stop making excuses. In his book, *Changing Criminal Thinking: A Treatment Program,* Sharp (2000) pointedly made his case for the utility of criminal thinking patterns.

> Criminals do not think like law-abiding prosocial people. . . . Criminal behavior is the result of erroneous thinking. Criminals' thinking leads to their feelings, their feelings lead to their behavior, and their behavior reaffirms their thinking. To use the words of Alcoholics Anonymous, the criminal is afflicted with "stinking thinking," which includes rationalizing, justifying, excuse-making, blaming, accusing, and being a victim. (p. 2)

California Psychological Inventory

To some extent, the idea that there is a criminal personality has been validated by the **California Psychological Inventory (CPI).** This psychometric instrument lends greater support to the conviction that criminals think differently than do noncriminals. Both the original and revised versions of this assessment tool indicate that the functions of the CPI are:

> . . . (1) to predict interpersonally consequential behavior in defined contexts and (2) to identify individuals describable in important and differentiating ways by knowledgeable observers. In particular, the inventory is directed to the assessment of facets of personality that all people, everywhere, recognize and denominate in their everyday lives. (Gough & Bradley, 1992, p. 299)

The CPI is a 480-item test divided into 20 scales. Some of the 20 profile scales include dom-inance (*Do*) = confident, assertive (high scores) versus unassuming, not forceful (low scores); capacity for status (*Cs*) = ambitious, independent, vying for success (high scores) versus self-uncertainty, avoiding competition (lower scores); and self-acceptance (*Sa*) = has good opinion of self, sees self as talented and attractive (high scores) versus self-effacing, self-blaming (low scores; Gough, 1987).

Laufer, Skoog, and Day (1982) reviewed those studies conducted between 1959 and 1974 that measured the CPI's ability to account for the criminal and noncriminal per-sonality structures. Given these studies, they addressed whether the CPI could evaluate the following:

> . . . (a) personality differences between delinquents and non-delinquents; (b) personality typologies, classifications, and taxonomic distinctions; and (c) personality variables that are predictive of future asocial or criminal behaviors. In addition, studies are listed that describe the (d) historical development of the CPI and its application to criminality, as well as (e) the CPI's ability to measure and quantify aspects of criminal behavior. (p. 562)

On the basis of their assessment of the published research, the investigators concluded that the CPI did possess significant explanatory capabilities regarding personality. Moreover, they concluded that there was statistical support for the existence of a homogenous crimi-nal personality.

More recent assessment tools employed to establish the presence of a criminal per-sonality include the MMPI, the MMPI-2, and the Inwald Personality Inventory (IPI; for a review of the varying ability of these instruments to account for criminal behavior, see Arrigo & Claussen, 2003). These instruments further validate the theoretical conviction that a criminal personality can in fact be identified (see also Gottfredson & Hirschi, 1990, as discussed in chapter 4). As such, these tools and their use are consistent with the work of Yochelson (1976) and Samenow (1984) on the criminal's cognitive processes, thinking errors, and behavioral patterns. This research notwithstanding, there are many critiques regarding the idea that a criminal personality in fact exists (e.g., Maruna, 2000), rendering such a notion a matter of ongoing debate and research.

DISCUSSION QUESTIONS

1. What are the four developmental approaches to personality? How are they similar and dissimilar? Think of an example of criminal behavior and explain how psychoanalytic, behavioral, humanistic, or sociocultural and biosocial approaches would account for this conduct.

2. What is human motivation and how is it related to criminal behavior?

3. What is antisocial personality disorder? What is its relationship to psychopathy?

4. How are antisocial personality disorder and future dangerousness connected?

5. How does impulsiveness as a personality characteristic relate to crime? What are some of the cognitive patterns that account for impulsive conduct?

6. According to psychoanalytic theory, what are the id, ego, and superego? Can you think of examples of delinquent or criminal behavior where these systems might be involved?

7. Name two defense mechanisms and explain how they are linked to deviant or criminal conduct. What is repression?

8. According to Sigmund Freud, what are the psychosexual stages of personality development?

9. What does it mean to have an underdeveloped superego? How is this related to delinquency?

10. How is Lacanian psychoanalysis relevant to an understanding of criminal behavior?

11. What are criminal thinking errors? Name two myths of criminal behavior as identified by Yochelson (1976) and Samenow (1984)? Describe two thinking patterns attributable to the criminal. What are the limits of criminal thinking pattern theory?

REFERENCES

Aichhorn, A. (1935). *Wayword youth*. New York: Viking.

Alloy, L. B., Jacobson, N. S., & Acocella, J. (1999). *Abnormal psychology: Current perspectives* (8th ed.). Boston, MA: McGraw-Hill College.

American Psychiatric Association. (2000). *Diagnostic and statistical manual of mental disorders* (4th ed., text revision). Washington DC: American Psychiatric Association.

Andrews, D. A., & Bonta, J. (1998). *The psychology of criminal conduct* (2nd ed.). Cincinnati, OH: Anderson.

Arlow, J. (1995). Psychoanalysis. In R. J. Corsini & D. Wedding (Eds.), *Current psychotherapies* (5th ed.). Itasca, IL: Peacock.

Aronson, E., Wilson, T. D., & Akert, R. A. (2002). *Social psychology* (4th ed.). Upper Saddle River, NJ: Prentice Hall.

Arrigo, B. A. (1996). The behavior of law and psychiatry: Rethinking knowledge construction and the guilty but mentally ill verdict. *Criminal Justice and Behavior, 23*(4), 572–592.

Arrigo, B. A. (1997). Insanity defense reform and the sign of abolition: Revising Montana's experience. *International Journal for the Semiotics of Law, X*(29), 191–211.

Arrigo, B. A. (2002). *Punishing the mentally ill: A critical analysis of law and psychiatry*. Albany, NY: State University of New York Press.

Arrigo, B. A., & Claussen, N. (2003). Police corruption and psychological testing: A strategy for pre-employment screening. *International Journal of Offender Therapy and Comparative Criminology, 47*(3), 272–290.

Arrigo, B. A., & Shipley, S. M. (2001). The confusion over psychopathy (I): Historical considerations. *International Journal of Offender Therapy and Comparative Criminology, 45*(3), 325–344.

Arrigo, B. A., & Williams, C. R. (2003). Victim voices, victim vices and restorative justice: Rethinking the use of impact evidence in capital sentencing. *Crime and Delinquency, 49*(4), 603–626.

Bandes, S. (1996). Empathy, narrative, and victim impact statements. *University of Chicago Law Review, 63*, 361–412.

Bowlby, J. (1953). *Childcare and the growth of love*. Baltimore: Penguin.

Corsini, R. J., & Wedding, D. (1995). *Current psychotherapies*. Belmont, CA: Wadsworth.

Caspi, A., Moffitt, T. E., Silva, P. A., Stouthamer-Loeber, M., Krueger, R. F., & Schmutte, P. S. (1994). Are some people crime-prone? *Criminology, 32*(2), 163–195.

Coles, M. G. H., Gale, A., & Kline, P. (1971). Personality and habituation of the orienting reaction: Tonic and response measures of electrodermal activity. *Psychosomatic Medicine, 30*, 12–22.

Davidson, R. J. (1991). Biological approaches to the study of personality. In V. J. Derlega, B. A. Winstead, & W. H. Jones (Eds.), *Personality: Contemporary theory and research* (pp. 88–112). Chicago: Nelson Hall.

Deci, E. L., & Ryan, R. M. (1985). *Intrinsic motivation and self-determination of human behavior*. New York: Plenum.

Derlega, V. J., Winstead, B. A., & Jones, W. H. (1991). *Personality: Contemporary theory and research*. Chicago: Nelson Hall.

Dweck, C. S. (1992). The study of goals in psychology. *Psychological Science, 3,* 165–167.

Elliot, A. J., & Sheldon, K. M. (1998). Avoidance personal goals and the personality-illness relationship. *Journal of Personality and Social Psychology, 75,* 1282–1299.

Freud, S. (1895). Studies on hysteria. In James Strachey (Ed.), *The complete psychological works of Sigmund Freud* (Standard ed., Vol. 2). London: Hogarth.

Freud, S. (1900). The interpretation of dreams. In James Strachey (Ed.), *The complete psychological works of Sigmund Freud* (Standard ed., Vol. 4). London: Hogarth.

Freud, S. (1914). On narcissism: An introduction. In James Strachey (Ed.), *The complete psychological works of Sigmund Freud* (Standard ed., Vol. 14). London: Hogarth.

Freud, S. (1920). Beyond the pleasure principle. In James Strachey (Ed.), *The complete psychological works of Sigmund Freud* (Standard ed., Vol. 18). London: Hogarth.

Freud, S. (1923). The ego and the id. In James Strachey (Ed.), *The complete psychological works of Sigmund Freud* (Standard ed., Vol. 19). London: Hogarth.

Freud, S. (1926). Inhibitions, symptoms, and anxiety. In James Strachey (Ed.), *The complete psychological works of Sigmund Freud* (Standard ed., Vol. 20). London: Hogarth.

Friedlander, K. (1949). Latent delinquency and ego development. In K. R. Eissler (Ed.), *Searchlights on delinquency* (pp. 205–215). New York: International University Press.

Glueck, S., & Glueck, E. (1950). *Unraveling juvenile delinquency*. New York: Commonwealth Fund.

Gorenstein, E. E., & Newman, J. P. (1980). Disinhibitory psychopathology. *Psychological Review, 87,* 301–315.

Gottfredson, M. R., & Hirschi, T. (1990). *A general theory of crime*. Stanford, CA: Stanford University Press.

Gough, H. (1987). *California Psychological Inventory: Administrators guide*. Palo Alto, CA: Consulting Psychologists Press.

Gough, H., & Bradley, P. (1992). Delinquent and criminal behavior as assessed by the Revised California Psychological Inventory. *Journal of Clinical Psychology, 48*(3), 298–308.

Graham, J. R. (2000). *MMPI-2: Assessing personality and psychopathology* (3rd ed.). New York: Oxford University Press.

Gray, J. A. (1977). Drug effects on fear and frustration. In L. L. Iversen, S. D. Iversen, & S. H. Snyder (Eds.), *Handbook of psychopharmacology: Drugs, neurotransmitters, and behavior* (Vol. 8). New York: Plenum.

Hare, R. D. (1993). *Without conscience: The disturbing world of the psychopaths among us*. New York: Guilford.

Hare, R. D. (1996). Psychopathy: A clincial construct whose time has come. *Criminal Justice and Behavior, 23*(1), 25–54.

Healy, W., & Bronner, A. (1931). *New light on delinquency and its treatment*. New Haven, CT: Yale University.

Henriques, J. B., & Davidson, R. J. (1989). Affective disorders. In G. Turpin (Ed.), *Handbook of clinical psychophysiology* (pp. 357–392). London: Wiley.

Hergenhahn, B. R. (1997). *An introduction to the history of psychology* (3rd ed.). Pacific Grove, CA: Brooks/Cole.

Hodes, R. L., Cook, E. W., & Lang, P. (1985). Individual differences in autonomic response: Conditioned association or conditioned fear? *Psychophysiology, 22,* 545–560.

Kagan, J., Reznick, J. S., & Snidman, N. (1988). Biological bases of childhood shyness. *Science, 240,* 167–171.

Kasser, T., & Ryan, R. M. (2001). Be careful what you wish for: Optimal functioning and the relative attainment of intrinsic and extrinsic goals. In P. Schmuck & K. M. Sheldon (Eds.), *Life goals and well-being*. Lengerich, Germany: Pabst Science Publishers.

Kenrick, D. T., & Funder, D. C. (1991). The person-situation debate: Do personality traits really exist? In V. J. Derlega, B. A. Winstead, & W. H. Jones (Eds.), *Personality: Contemporary theory and research* (pp. 150–174). Chicago: Nelson Hall.

Lacan, J. (1977). *Ecrits: A selection* (A. Sheridan, Trans.). New York: Norton.

Laufer, W., Skoog, D., & Day, J. (1982). Personality and criminality: A review of the California Psychological Inventory. *Journal of Clinical Psychology, 38*(3), 562–573.

Lerner, H. D. (1999). Psychodynamic theories. In V. B. Van Hasselt & M. Hersen (Eds.), *Handbook of psychological approaches with violent offenders: Contemporary strategies and issues.* New York: Kluwer Academic/Plenum.

Lilienfeld, S. O., Wood, J. M., & Garb, H. N. (2000). The scientific status of projective techniques. *Psychological Science in the Public Interest, 1,* 27–66.

Loeber, R., & Dishion, T. (1983). Early predictors of male delinquency: A review. *Psychological Bulletin, 94*(1), 68–99.

Martens, W. (2000). Antisocial or psychopathic disorders: Causes, course, and remission. A review article. *International Journal of Offender Therapy and Comparative Criminology, 44*(4), 406–430.

Maruna, S. (2000). Criminology, desistance and the psychology of the stranger. In D. Canter & L. J. Alison (Eds.), *The social psychology of crime* (pp. 287–320). Aldershot, UK: Dartmouth.

McAdams, D. P. (1991). Motives. In V. J. Derlega, B. A. Winstead, & W. H. Jones (Eds.), *Personality: Contemporary theory and research* (pp. 176–200). Chicago: Nelson Hall.

McCord, W. (1982). *The psychopath and milieu therapy: A longitudinal study.* New York: Academic Press.

Megargee, E. I. (1972). *The California Psychological Inventory handbook.* San Francisco: Jossey-Bass.

Megargee, E. I., & Bohn, M. J. (1979). *Classifying criminal offenders: A new system based on the MMPI.* Beverly Hills, CA: Sage.

Millon, T., Simonsen, E., Birket-Smith, M., & Davis, R. D. (Eds.). (1998). *Psychopathy: Antisocial, criminal, and violent behavior.* New York: Guilford.

Moffitt, T. E. (1993). Life-course-persistent and adolescent-limited antisocial behavior. *Psychological Review, 100,* 674–701.

Monahan, J. (1996). Violence prediction: The past twenty years and the next twenty years. *Criminal Justice and Behavior, 23,* 107–120.

Mosak, H. (1995). Adlerian psychotherapy. In R. J. Corsini & D. Wedding (Eds.), *Current psychotherapies* (5th ed.). Itasca, IL: Peacock.

Nash, R. (1994). Memory distortion and sexual trauma: The problem of false negatives and false positives. *International Journal of Clinical and Experimental Hypnosis, 42,* 346–362.

Palermo, G. B. (2002). A dynamic formulation of sex offender behavior and its therapeutic relevance. *Journal of Forensic Psychology Practice, 2*(2), 25–51.

Palermo, G. B., & Farkas, M. A. (2001). *The dilemma of the sexual offender.* Springfield, IL: Thomas.

Petrie, A. (1978). *Individuality in pain and suffering* (2nd ed.). Chicago: University of Chicago Press.

Plomin, R., DeFries, J. C., McClearn, G. E., & McGuffin, P. (2001). *Behavioral genetics* (4th ed.). New York: Worth.

Redl, F., & Wineman, D. (1951). *Children who hate.* New York: The Free Press.

Samenow, S. E. (1984). *Inside the criminal mind.* New York: Crown Business.

Schuessler, K. F., & Cressey, D. R. (1950). *Personality characteristics of criminals. American Journal of Sociology, 55,* 476–484.

Sharp, B. D. (2000). *Changing criminal thinking: A treatment program.* Lanham, MD: American Correctional Association.

Shipley, S. M., & Arrigo, B. A. (2001). The confusion over psychopathy (II): Implications for forensic (correctional) practice. *International Journal of Offender Therapy and Comparative Criminology, 45*(4), 407–420.

Shon, P. C. H. (2000). "Hey you c'me here!": Subjectivization, resistance, and the interpellative violence of self-generated police-citizen encounters. *International Journal for the Semiotics of Law, 13*(2), 159–179.

Silver, E. (2000). Race, neighborhood disadvantage, and violence among persons with mental disorders: The importance of contextual measures. *Law and Human Behavior, 24*(4), 449–456.

Sutherland, E. H. (1939). *Principles of criminology.* New York: Lippincott.

Toch, H. (1998). Psychopathy or antisocial personality disorder in forensic settings. In T. Millon, E. Simonsen, M. Birket-Smith, & R. D. Davis (Eds.), *Psychopathy: Antisocial, criminal, and violent behavior* (pp. 144–158). New York: Guilford.

Vaillant, G. E. (Ed.). (1992). *Ego mechanism of defense.* Washington DC: American Psychiatric Press.

Vold, G. B., Bernard, T. J., & Snipes, J. B. (1998). *Theoretically criminology.* New York: Oxford University Press.

Voruz, V. (2000). Psychosis and the law: Legal responsibility and the law of symbolization. *International Journal for the Semiotics of Law, 13*(2), 133–158.

Wade, C., & Tavris, C. (2003). *Psychology* (7th ed.). Upper Saddle River, NJ: Prentice Hall.

Waldo, G. P., & Dinitz, S. (1967). Personality attributes of the criminal: An analysis of research studies, 1950–1965. *Journal of Research in Crime and Delinquency, 4*(2), 185–202.

Walters, G. D. (1990). *The criminal lifestyle: Patterns of serious criminal conduct*. Newbury, CA: Sage.

Walters, G. D. (1998). *Changing lives of crime and drugs: Intervening with substance-abusing offenders*. New York: Wiley.

Walters, G. D. (2002). *Criminal belief systems: An integrated-interactive theory of lifestyles*. Westport, CT: Praeger.

Walters, P. L., & Cheek, J. M. (1991). Personality development. In V. J. Derlega, B. A. Winstead, & W. H. Jones (Eds.), *Personality: Contemporary theory and research* (pp. 114–148). Chicago: Nelson Hall.

Williams, C. R. (1998). The abrogation of subjectivity in the psychiatric courtroom: Toward a psychoanalytic semiotic analysis. *International Journal for the Semiotics of Law, XI*(32), 181–192.

Wilson, J. Q., & Hernstein, R. J. (1985). *Crime and human nature*. New York: Simon & Schuster.

Yochelson, S. (1976). *The criminal personality* (Vol. 1). New York: Aronson.

Zuckerman, M. (1989). Personality in the third dimension. *Personality and Individual Differences, 10,* 391–418.

chapter 3

Sociological Theories of Crime

OVERVIEW

Sociological theories of crime differ considerably from psychological and biological explanations. Sociological theories attempt to account for the social forces that cause or result in criminal behavior. In this respect, the sociological perspective acknowledges that factors such as strain, group conflict, subculture ideas, economics, and **language** are important facets to defining and interpreting delinquency and crime. This chapter explores several of the more fascinating sociological accounts of criminal behavior. In particular, subcultural, structural, **anomie,** strain, conflict, and critical approaches are summarily presented. Clearly, the ideas described in this chapter are not exhaustive; however, they do represent a major departure from previous explanations that associate crime in the physiology or personality of the offender. Indeed, from a sociological perspective, criminal behavior is deeply rooted in a host of factors external to the person. These forces significantly compel the person to act criminally or otherwise identify the individual as a transgressor.

KEY TERMS

Anarchist theory
Angry aggression
Anomie
Anomie theory
Chaos theory
Class
Conduct norms
Conflict theory
Criminal sentencing
Critical race theory
Emile Durkheim
False consciousness
Feminist theory
General strain theory
Group conflict theory
Integrative criminology
Language

Marxist theorists
Masculine power
Mechanical society
Negative affect
Organic society
Peacemaking criminology
Postmodern criminologists
Psychoanalytic semiotics
Radical criminology
Robert Merton
Social justice
Strain theory
Structural and process theories
Subcultural theories
Subculture of violence
Warmaking

SUBCULTURAL EXPLANATIONS OF CRIME

Introduction

Subcultural theories of crime focus on the "idea" of criminal behavior and law violation as occurring within a particular group context. In other words, subcultural theories start with the premise that the values, norms, and expectations pertaining to an understanding of delinquency and crime produce illicit conduct more so than do the actual social conditions in which these ideas are fostered. Although subcultural explanations do not rely heavily on environmental or ecological factors to account for crime, the interaction of these forces with the ideas pertaining to criminal behavior are considered. There are three prominent theories that further delineate that nature of crime from within a subcultural context. These theories are (a) Wolfgang and Ferracuti's perspective on the **subculture of violence,** (b) Curtis's adaptation of Wolfgang and Ferracuti's theory with an application to the African American population, and (c) Bernard's notion on the subculture of **angry aggression.** This portion of the chapter concludes by examining how subcultural explanations account for delinquent gang behavior.

Wolfgang and Ferracuti's Subculture of Violence

Wolfgang and Ferracuti's (1981) subcultural theory was formulated to explain homicide. More specifically, they were interested in "passion crimes that were neither planned intentional killings nor manifestations of extreme mental illness" (Vold, Bernard, & Snipes, 1998, p. 191). In their work, *The Subcultural of Violence* (1981), Wolfgang and Ferracuti hypothesized that passion homicides were symptomatic of certain ideas or values about both people and behavior. These values or norms were learned and were linked to societal conditions transmitted in group settings (e.g., Luckenbill & Doyle, 1989; Nelsen, Corzine, & Huff-Corzine, 1994).

Wolfgang and Ferracuti (1981) recognized that there was an absence of theoretical work accounting for the presence of violent criminal conduct. Thus, they attempted to explain the differences between violent members in the dominant culture and violent members in the subordinate culture. They reasoned that these differences were the result of conflicting interests, and that these circumstances only alienated the subculture from its dominant culture counterpart.

Wolfgang and Ferracuti (1981) reported several significant differences in cultural ideas between the two groups. Admittedly, these differences are reducible to competing value systems; however, they are important to a subcultural explanation of criminal behavior. For example, as Wolfgang and Ferracuti discovered, honor is a value differentially esteemed depending on the membership group to which one belongs. Violent subcultures placed greater importance on it than did violent dominant cultures. Clear differences were also detected in the value placed on human life. The worth assigned to it by the violent culture was greater than the value assigned to it by the violent subculture.

Examples of these conflicting group interests are observable even today. To illustrate, consider value differences based on geography or region. Some researchers assert that the Southern culture of violence is anchored in the honor of White gentlemen, dating back at least to the post-Colonial period of slavery (Gastil, 1971). In this context, violence is transmitted from generation to generation as part of an entrenched belief system in which ideas about race, region, and economic exploitation intersect, producing criminal behavior.

The value of human life takes on a decidedly unique interpretation in the gang subculture as well. Loyalty to the gang is esteemed above all else. Sometimes this may include killing another person in order to prove one's unshakable fidelity to the group (e.g., Miller, 1958). Under these conditions, the subculture's value system is conveyed to and embraced by members in the group, generating a commitment to delinquent conduct.

Wolfgang and Ferracuti (1981) identified other instances of conflicting group interests between cultural (dominant) and subcultural (subordinate) collectives. For example, individuals in the violent subculture responded to the killing of their members with brutality, resulting in homicidal acts toward nongroup members. In this situation, the subcultural idea at issue was survival, and a fight to the death was the only way to determine the victor.

Curtis's Subcultural Theory of Violence

A variation of Wolfgang and Ferracuti's theory of violent subculture was proposed by Curtis in his book, *Violence, Race, and Gender* (1975). He examined the "manliness" (p. 37) experienced by Black males in conjunction with the defensiveness exhibited by them in both trivial and more intense confrontations. Curtis found that these dilemmas were dealt with by either verbal or physical force. The use of physical force was utilized in the commission of homicide and other violent crimes, such as assault and rape. In the instance of rape, a man either relied on his verbal ability to coerce the woman into sexual encounters or he employed his physical prowess, forcing the woman to consent.

The theory proposed by Curtis (1975) investigated the link between violent behavior and general social conditions more so than did the study by Wolfgang and Ferracuti (1981). His position was that although historical ideas about violence, transmitted from one generation to the next, created a subculture, the social forces surrounding these historical conditions were important contributors as well. As Vold et al. (1998) summarily explained it,

> Curtis described culture as a key intervening variable between these current social conditions and the behaviors of each individual. Each individual independently experiences these social conditions, and to a certain extent his or her behavior is a direct response to the social conditions. (p. 193)

Given these circumstances, Curtis (1975) argued that the solution to violent subcultures was twofold. First, address the values of the subculture itself. Second, respond to the ecological conditions that inform the belief system harbored by members in the group. For Curtis, this two-pronged strategy was believed to be the best way to curtail criminal behavior among subordinate collectives over the long term.

Bernard's Subculture of Angry Aggression

Bernard (1990, 1993) postulated that a subculture of "angry aggression" developed as an embedded belief system for the group in certain circumstances. Similar to Wolfgang and Ferracuti (1981), Bernard (1990) was interested in the presence of violence (e.g., homicides) generated from seemingly harmless or incidental conflicts. Relying on biological and psychological research, Bernard (1990) explored how arousal (i.e., the body's fight-or-flight response) was activated when perceived threatening circumstances materialized. Based on the relevant scientific research on arousal, Bernard claimed that people respond aggressively if they are already highly aroused and if they regard a situation as threatening. The greater the perceived threat, the more likely that violence will occur, including extreme representations of it such as homicide.

Applying these observations to criminal behavior, Bernard (1990) asserted that poverty-stricken inner-city environments are breeding grounds for high arousal in the people who inhabit these locales. This is because discrimination, economic deprivation (i.e., low-skilled or underskilled employment), and poor or inadequate housing are structural conditions that manufacture threatening feelings, activate and elevate arousal, and result, at times, in violence. Bernard also explained that these environments are socially isolated from the rest of society. As a subculture, members from this group may perceive the behaviors of others outside the group as threatening, even when their conduct is quite harmless. By interacting with one another, socially isolated members of the subculture incorporate their aggressiveness and high arousal into a cultural belief system. This belief system informs the thinking processes of members in the group and is passed on from one generation of poor, inner-city subcultural group members to the next (Matsueda, Gartner, Piliavin, & Polakowski, 1992).

Subcultural Theory and Gangs

Two theories have attempted to explain gang delinquency from the perspective of subcultures. Both perspectives argue that, similar to the focus of **anomie theory,** criminal behavior can be explained through those social strains placed on an individual or a group. More detailed commentary on anomie theory is discussed elsewhere in this chapter. However, for purposes of this section of the chapter, subcultural theories exploring gang delinquency emphasize the behavior of lower-class individuals who live in urban settings.

Cohen (1955) articulated the first subcultural explanation for male gang delinquency. He concluded that juvenile criminal behavior frequently occurred in gang settings rather than in personal or individual settings. He ascertained that juvenile gang behavior did not have a purpose other than cruelty, and that this purpose was different from adult criminal conduct. Cohen maintained that the actions of gangs "were methods of gaining status among the delinquent's peers . . . gangs ha[d] a separate culture from the dominant culture, with a different set of values for measuring status" (Vold et al., 1998, p. 165).

Cohen (1955) explained that male youth who rebel against the values of the middle class form a new social structure for themselves. The members who subscribe to this new social structure form a group. This group becomes the gang. Within the gang culture, juveniles with similar social status characteristics can join it and work to create solutions for their low social and economic standing. Cohen acknowledged that juveniles from all social classes could experience this perceived sense of low status; however, the most affected group was the population of lower class youth.

Cohen's (1955) theory on the subculture of male gang delinquency relied on the insights of **Robert Merton** (1968) and his anomie theory. This theory is explained in subsequent sections of this chapter, and readers are encouraged to review Merton's perspective on criminal behavior and compare it to the theory proposed by Cohen. However, there are several important differences that can be summarily identified. The following table emphasizes the differences between Cohen's subcultural theory of gangs and Merton's anomie theory.

In reviewing the table, there are three important differences between the work of Cohen (1955) and that of Merton (1968). Cohen wanted to find an explanation for delinquent gang behavior that lacked purpose (other than cruelty). Merton wanted to explore the social strains that created functional delinquent behavior. Cohen wanted to explain the rebellious nature of gangs toward the middle class and to middle-class values. Merton wanted to explain adolescent rebellion in various forms (i.e., innovation and retreatism) and against various classes. Cohen linked the rebelliousness of the gang to group choices. Merton associated delinquent rebellion with individual choices.

Comparing Cohen's and Merton's Criminological Theories

Cohen's Subcultural Theory of Gangs	*Merton's Anomie Theory*
Nonutilitarian characteristics of crime	Utilitarian characteristics of crime
Rebellion against the middle class values	Rebellion seen in many different forms
Delinquency as a result of the choices made within the group	Delinquency as a result of individuals' choices

Cloward and Ohlin's Categories of Lower Class Juveniles

Categories of Youth	Seeking Middle-Class Membership?	Seeking Economic Improvement?
Type I	Yes	Yes
Type II	Yes	No
Type III	No	Yes
Type IV	No	No

The second subcultural theory of gang delinquency was proposed by Cloward and Ohlin (1960). The purpose of their research was to bridge the divide between Merton's (1968) anomie theory and Cohen's (1955) subcultural theory of gang delinquency. Moreover, they wanted to account for how delinquency was learned.

Similar to Merton (1968), Cloward and Ohlin (1960) concluded that delinquent behavior was an attempt to achieve status and money. Similar to Cohen (1955), Cloward and Ohlin explained that because both of these goals could occur, they could function independently from one another. This led them to identify four categories of juveniles within the lower classes. The following table depicts these categories or classifications.

Type I youth seek to change their class association to middle class and improve their economic standing. Type II youth also seek to change their class association to middle class; however, they do not intend to improve their economic standing. Type III youth do not seek to change their class association; however, they attempt to improve their economic standing. Type IV youth do not seek to change their class association, nor do they attempt to improve their economic standing.

Cohen (1955) hypothesized that most delinquent behaviors were committed by Type I and Type II youth. Cloward and Ohlin (1960) agreed with Cohen's position; however, they did not believe that these two categories made up the majority of youthful offenders who committed serious delinquent acts. Cloward and Ohlin argued that Type III youth were the most serious delinquents because they had the greatest amount of conflict with the middle class. Thus, the most violent juvenile crimes were committed when Type III adolescents formed a gang and expressed their anger toward society. Cloward and Ohlin also concluded that Type IV youth were engaged in the least amount of delinquent behavior. This is because they did not socialize with middle-class youth, did not join middle-class institutions, and did not participate in middle-class activities.

Implications of Subcultural Theories

Wolfgang (1958) suggested that there is a subculture of violence that accepts behaviors that the dominant culture would consider criminal and antisocial. Wolfgang further stated that within a violent subculture, a "quick resort to physical aggression is a socially approved and expected concomitant of certain stimuli. . . . [V]iolence has become a familiar but often deadly partner in life's struggles" (p. 329). Within this subgroup, violence becomes normalized, tolerated, and accepted. It is also transmitted from one generation to the next as part of the culture's belief system (i.e., ideas).

In a society that accepts such violent behaviors, these actions become second nature, instinctual, and a part of the cognitive processes for group members. In order to eliminate violent conduct, culturally sensitive social controls must be developed and implemented. When subcultures begin to dominate a society, the social controls of the greater public are weakened, and violence, especially homicide, is increased.

STRUCTURAL EXPLANATIONS OF CRIME

Introduction

Criminal behavior can be placed into one of two categories of criminological thought: **structural and process theories** or individual difference theories. This portion of the chapter focuses on the structural and process explanations for criminal behavior. There are many structural accounts of crime (e.g., differential association theory, **conflict theory, strain theory,** and developmental theory). Readers are encouraged to refer to these explanations discussed elsewhere in chapters 2 and 4 when considering how they represent structural and process explanations. However, in this section of the chapter, an overview of the structural approach to crime and its limits are presented.

Structural explanations of crime "attempt to identify variables in the situation itself that are associated with higher crime rates" (Vold et al., 1998, p. 324). In other words, structural theories support the claim that higher rates of crime are related to specific situations rather than to individual differences. Although structural arguments link the environment to rates of crime and criminal behavior, process arguments identify the reasons why individuals engage in criminal behavior when exposed to specific structural conditions. The premise of structural and process theories is based on three claims: (a) Crime is an elected response by individuals whose choices are controlled by the existing environment, (b) the quality of the environment in which crime occurs is a result of the structural characteristics of the social organization, and (c) criminals are "normal" because they respond to motives that direct their behavior and interact with their direct environment in the same manner as law-abiding citizens in a noncriminal environment.

There are eight structural conditions whose effects appear to produce elevated rates of crime and criminal behavior in society. First, increased rates of property crimes are correlated with economic modernization and development. As such, the rate of property crime will increase until society reaches its optimal level of economic development. At this point, property crime rates will become relatively fixed and remain relatively constant. Second, increased rates of violent behavior are coupled with economic inequality. Third, a cultural emphasis on economic success may result in utilitarian, nonutilitarian, and violent crime. This is because the ensuing rate of adherence to acceptable norms during times of economic prosperity decreases. Fourth, elevated crime rates are associated with poverty-stricken neighborhoods, few long-term neighborhood residents, and familial disorder. Fifth, extreme violence as a result of insignificant conflicts frequently occurs because of poverty, urban settings, racial prejudice, and social seclusion. Sixth, increased rates of criminal behavior are paralleled to media propaganda and the media's validation of illegal behaviors. Seventh, cultures that isolate law violators, as opposed to reincorporating them into society, tend to show greater rates of crime and deviant behavior. Eighth, totalitarian societies have higher rates of crime in comparison to democratic-run societies.

It is also important to consider the corresponding social processes through which these structural conditions occur. There are eight processes that increase an individual's likelihood to commit crime, notwithstanding the person's distinct characteristics. The following table describes these processes in relation to the structural conditions on which they are based. It also provides some examples of criminal behavior that may emerge given the interaction of structural conditions and social processes.

The processes that lead to crime, given economic modernization and development, are changes in daily activities and changes in criminal opportunities. Higher rates of violence, as a result of economic inequality, are based on perceptions of deficiency and frustrated reactions. Frustration is also one of the processes by which crime occurs in a society that emphasizes economic success. Additionally, the inclination to engage in behavior that is self-rewarding is a process that occurs in conjunction with a structure of material success. In some communities, high crime rates occur through the process of

Criminal Behavior Based on Social Structural/Process Explanations

Structural Situations	Process	Criminal Behavior
Economic modernization and development	Changes in daily activities and criminal opportunities	Property crimes (i.e., burglary)
Economic inequality	Perceived deficiency and frustration	Violence and violent behavior
Cultural views on economic success	Frustration; inclination to engage in self-rewarding behavior	Profitable crimes (i.e., drug dealing)
Poverty-stricken neighborhoods	Social disorganization and anonymity	Drug dealers taking over a "corner store"
Urban settings with poverty, racial prejudice, and social seclusion	Physiological arousal	Extreme violence (i.e., responding violently to an event perceived as threatening)
Media	Direct (rationalization) and indirect (observation) learning techniques	Modeling the behavior of a favorite media hero (i.e., resolving problems through violence because a TV character resolves conflicts in the same manner)
Isolation of law violators by the culture	Subcultures created through stigmas; denial of opportunities to criminals	Individuals have a criminal self-image and therefore engage in criminal behavior
Totalitarian society	Natural inclination to increase control of others	Deviant behavior as a resistance response to increased control

social disorganization. This is a result of neighborhood anonymity. Extreme violence associated with seemingly trivial conflicts blown out of proportion is fueled by situations in which an individual becomes highly physiologically aroused. These arousal states (i.e., fight-or-flight) are linked to perceived threats producing aggressive tendencies. These tendencies result in volatile and explosive reactions to a given situation. The processes by which the media reinforces criminal behavior include direct and indirect learning techniques. These techniques occur through rationalization (direct) and observation (indirect). Stigmatizing individuals who break the law denies them the opportunities availed to law-abiding citizens. It also helps establish subcultures into which these isolated individuals are not necessarily accepted. A tyrannical state in which one individual exerts the most power fosters an unhealthy environment. Individuals resort to their natural inclinations to increase control over others. Crime is a response to this excessive control.

Each of the previously delineated structural conditions and social processes result in specific types of criminal behavior. For example, poverty-stricken neighborhoods filled with social disorganization often have a drug dealer at the corner store. Despite the community's best efforts to resist this individual and the person's criminal behavior, the drug dealer is not removed from the corner store. Law-violating individuals who are isolated by society may engage in continued criminal behavior following the stigma or label that society assigns to them. The external image of being a criminal is then incorporated into the person's own self-image. This behavior maintains the stigma and the criminal conduct.

Limits of Structural Theories

There are a few broad-based criticisms of the structural and process approaches to crime. These limits extend to all cultural, racial, and ethnic groups. Vold et al. (1998) identified these shortcomings, indicating that they drew attention to the inherent disagreements across the structural explanations of crime. Commenting on these disagreements, the authors explained that:

> These theories tend to be more complex and descriptive, and it is sometimes hard to determine the location of independent variation. . . . [T]hese theories often have been interpreted and tested at the individual level [only]. . . . [S]ituations with high crime rates often have a large number of variables, all of which are correlated with each other and all of which are correlated with crime. . . . [I]t can be extremely difficult to determine which (if any) of these variables is causally related to high crime rates, and which have no causal impact on crime at all. (p. 325)

Based on the preceding observations, the criticisms of structural and process theories can now be identified. First, it is not possible to investigate structural and process theories with individual-level data. Structural and process theories should only be tested with aggregate-level data. Second, structural and process theories should not be compared to one another for reasons similar to the limits of relying on individual-level data. Inappropriate comparisons may result in multiple-factor causations of crime rates and criminal distributions.

Research on the Structural Explanation of Crime

In addition to the psychological, sociological, and social–psychological theories of criminal behavior discussed in this work throughout chapters 2, 3, and 4, respectively, Hagan and Palloni, in their 1986 work, developed a structural criminological approach to crime and delinquency. The purpose of structural theory is to "formulate more clearly how meaningful questions about crime and delinquency can be asked as well as answered" (Hagan & Palloni, 1986, p. 446). Based on this perspective, Hagan's work focused on three arenas of crime: (a) class and criminality, (b) **criminal sentencing,** and (c) the family and delinquency. According to Hagan (1989), the relationship between class and criminality is the basis for much of the literature on structural theories. As he explained, "a structural criminology urges that we incorporate relational class measures, reconsider what is meant by criminality, and move beyond the easy assumption that the relationship between class and criminality is linear or additive in form" (p. 6).

Hagan (1989) also believed that **class** was an important factor in sentencing. He claimed that "structural, that is relational, measures of class make more explicit than status measures the ways in which class might influence sentencing. . . . [I]t may be the fact of unemployment, more directly than low social status, that leads to punitive sentencing decisions" (p. 7). Last, Hagan described how power relations might play a significant role in the bond between the family and delinquency, eventually producing adult criminality. His principle focus in the family and delinquency research was on the decreased likelihood of females becoming engaged in delinquent and criminal behaviors. For example, as Hagan (p. 13) noted, "egalitarian families are more likely to reproduce themselves by treating daughters similarly to sons, with results that make daughters more like sons in attitudes toward risk-taking, work prospects, as well as delinquency."

Hagan (1985) also conducted a study to examine the interaction of race, gender, crime, and age through a structural approach. Hagan's first hypothesis stipulated that "differences between racial minority and majority group crime rates [would] be greater for women than men" (p. 130). His second hypothesis asserted that "differences between male and female crime rates [would] be greater within the racial majority than the minority group" (p. 130). The third hypothesis included race, gender, crime, as well as age. As he indicated, "the differences between racial minority and majority group crime rates [would]

The Chicago School of Criminology: From the Social Roots of Crime to Collective Efficacy

One sociological perspective that has received considerable research and practice-based attention is the Chicago School of Criminology. It has been useful in its explanation of juvenile delinquency (Shaw & McKay, 1972) and community involvement to prevent and informally control crime (Sampson, Raudenbush, & Earls, 1997). At the core of the Chicago School approach to criminal behavior is the conviction that the distribution of economic resources does not extend equally across all segments of society. Thus, persons who live in poor communities, ghettos, and other socially disorganized neighborhoods confront environments that compel some individuals to disproportionately engage in criminal behavior. This approach rejects biological predispositions and personality structures as the root causes of crime and delinquency.

The early work conducted by Chicago School researchers attempted to explain how the configuration of cities (divided into "zones" or "rings") would account for the presence of crime. Those zones in transition were littered with deteriorating homes, surrounded by abandoned or vacated factories. In addition, as industry and the business district expanded outward, residents in this zone were continuously displaced. This zone was the most susceptible to criminal activity. Its occupants were poor, often migrant and immigrant workers, who could not afford to reside elsewhere. The degree and intensity of social disorganization found within this zone produced and sustained a criminal tradition (Shaw & McKay, 1972).

The legacy of the Chicago School is found in the work of Sampson et al. (1997). Consistent with the pioneering work of early Chicago School theorists and researchers, Sampson and colleagues argue that as residents exercise informal social control in their neighborhoods, they can impact the presence of crime in their communities. They call this phenomenon "collective efficacy." Thus, as neighbors monitor the behavior of youth hanging out on street corners, or as residents support and work with police to prevent criminal activity, they can meaningfully affect the crime problem in their community. Engaging in such behavior sounds rather simple; however, it is not. The success of collective efficacy depends on "mutual trust and solidarity among neighbors" (Sampson et al., 1997, p. 919). This theme of collective efficacy is revisited in chapter 9, especially when discussing policing and community-based interventions.

increase faster for women than men with age, as [would] the differences between male and female crime rates for members of racial majority groups" (p. 131).

Hagan (1985) found that in the United States and Canada there were racial and gender differences in crime rates. In addition, the second hypothesis was supported in that "the total female race ratio [was] more than five times the total male ratio. This mean[t] that the ratio of Native to non-Native crime rates [was] much greater among women than men" (p. 136). Last, an analysis involving the structural perspective and age differences found that there was "an interaction of race, sex, and age on crime that result[ed] from the very low criminal involvement of older, non-Native women" (p. 138).

Overall, the research conducted by Hagan (1985) examined a structural theory of race, gender, and crime. The results and conclusions suggested some "promise [in] telling us much about the very different crime experiences of the two countries and their respective minority populations" (p. 144). As previously mentioned, when examining the structural explanations of crime and delinquency, it is very important to consider the cultural differences among different racial, ethnic, and cultural offender groups. Future research relying on structural approaches to criminal behavior need to bear this notion in mind.

ANOMIE THEORY

Introduction

Merriam-Webster's Collegiate Dictionary (10th ed.; Mish et al., 1996) defines the term anomie as "social instability resulting from a breakdown of standards and values" (p. 47). However, in the social sciences, the definition of anomie can be very ambiguous. For example, Orru (1987) states:

Anomie means ruthlessness and hybris in Euripides, anarchy and intemperance in Plato, sin and wickedness in the Old Testament, unrighteousness or unwritten law in Paul's letters, irregularity or formal transgression in Bishop Bramhall's treatises, a positive characteristic of modern morality in Jean Marie Guyau's books, and a human condition of insatiability in Durkheim. (p. 2)

According to Ronald Akers (1998), "theories emphasizing social structure propose that the proportions of crimes among groups, classes, communities, or societies differ because of variation in their social or cultural makeup" (p. 327). Anomie theory is a structural approach to examining behavior. The two main theorists who introduced the term *anomie* into the sociological lexicon of human behavior were **Emile Durkheim** (1858–1917) and Robert Merton (Durkheim, 1965; Merton, 1938). This section of the chapter generally reviews their respective approaches to anomie theory, provides a comparison of anomie theory to strain theory, and applies anomie theory to crime and criminal behavior.

Durkheim and Anomie

Durkheim (1965) used the term anomie to refer to "a weakening of the normative order in society" (Messner & Rosenfeld, 2001, p. 10). In addition, Orru (1987) contends that following the insights of the sociologist Talcott Parsons, Durkheim defined anomie as "the lack of equilibrium between means and ends of action, and by the unclean definition of the ends themselves" (p. 7). In his work, *The Division of Labor* (1965), Durkheim claimed that social change involves the development of society from a more primitive form to a more advanced form. Durkheim referred to more primitive societies as mechanical. In a **mechanical society** "each social group . . . is relatively isolated from all other social groups, and is basically self-sufficient" (Vold et al., 1998, p. 125). Durkheim referred to more advanced societies as organic. In an **organic society,** "the different segments . . . depend on each other in a highly organized division of labor" (Vold et al., p. 125).

Both forms of society depend on the law to preserve social solidarity; however, their dependence varies greatly. In a mechanical form, the function of the law is to maintain uniformity in order to safeguard against variation from the norm. Indeed, in such societies, the collective conscience, or the assemblage of similarities among group members, ensures that infractions will be kept to a minimum. In contrast, the law in an organic society attempts to control the relations among different individuals, and it sanctions (i.e., punishes) individuals who engage in unlawful behavior. In these cultures, rapid modernization (i.e., differentiation and industrialization) left unchecked, fosters a state of disharmony among people. Thus, Durkheim (1965) concluded that as a society moved toward an organic form, a state of anomie would take place. This state of normlessness (or weakened, ambiguous norms) would make the production of crime more likely.

Durkheim (1965) believed that criminals played a significant role in mechanical societies. In these cultures, criminals helped to maintain social solidarity by providing law-abiding citizens with a sense of individual and collective superiority. In general, crime was a normal and necessary activity, enabling the mechanical society to exist. In contrast, Durkheim maintained that social life within organic societies could produce a variety of maladies, including crime. He termed this state of inadequate regulation *anomie.* Durkheim indicated that the occurrence of criminal behavior would increase during large-scale phases of social change.

This tendency toward anomic crime is witnessed today. For example, as the former Soviet Union transitions from a communist regime to a more democratic government, rates of state crime are increasing there. As the practice of apartheid in South Africa is outlawed and the country comes to grips with its own version of democracy, social problems, including crime, are on the rise.

Similar to other realists of his time, Durkheim (1965) regarded "anomie as a corrupted and pathological condition of the ideal or normal social system" (Orru, 1987, p. 4). Moreover, similar to the writings of late Judaism, he also believed that anomie was a result of evil forces (Messner & Rosenfeld, 2001). The religious framework out of which Durkheim proposed his anomie theory distinguishes it from the one developed by Robert Merton (Messner & Rosenfeld).

In his theory of anomie, Durkheim recognized that social structure functions to provide opportunities to attain desired goals and functions to place limits on cultural necessities. These limits help ensure that some cultural necessities do not dominate others or inhibit the creation of still other necessities in the culture (Messner & Rosenfeld, 2001). In Durkheim's (1965) view, anomie was a theoretical construct. However, from an empirical point of view, it was flawed. As Orru (1987, p. 137) explained, Durkheim's notion of anomie was "illegitimately value-laden, disproven or unverifiable, historically grounded or historically limited, conceptually both equivocal and indistinct" (Orru, p. 137).

Orru (1987) also notes the limits of Durkheim's (1965) anomie theory. Specifically, it failed to separate facts from values. In addition, Durkheim placed a strong emphasis on the normative element of anomie, which in turn led to misjudgments about where it occurred and for whom it occurred. Indeed, Durkheim treated anomie as "a pathological phenomenon of modern societies instead of treating it as their distinguishing feature" (Orru, 1987, p. 135). Given these criticisms, we should not be surprised that modern-day anomie theories are much more empirically animated. Indeed, as we shall see shortly, Merton's theory (Messner & Rosenfeld, 2001) is not just descriptive but is anchored in considerably more research. As such, it offers a significant contrast to what Durkheim originally proposed.

Merton and Anomie

Similar to Durkheim's theory (1965), Merton claimed that the interaction of a society's culture and structure resulted in "a tendency for social norms to lose their regulatory force" (Messner & Rosenfeld, 2001, p. 11). However, Merton also proposed that these strains and pressures created high rates of crime and deviance, as seen in various facets of American culture. This is distinguished from Durkheim's position in which normlessness and crime were linked to rapid, unchecked modernization. Despite the contradictions noted between Durkheim and Merton, it is essential that the two viewpoints be seen as complimentary rather than conflicting (Agnew, 1997). This is because the similarities signal the evolution of the theory and its popular appeal to account for criminal behavior. In what follows, several of the more specific aspects of Merton's anomie theory are described.

Merton (1938) believed that nonconformity was a part of human nature, rather than a learned behavior. However, without social organization to respond to nonconformity, cultural chaos would materialize. Merton identified this cultural chaos as anomie. Anomie can also be examined in the context of criminal behavior. When doing so, Merton argued that there were three prominent factors that led individuals to pursue illegal means to obtained desired ends. These factors included (a) an insufficient ability to gain economic success legally, (b) the perceived efficiency of implementing illegal means rather than legal means, and (c) the lack of appropriate guidelines that provide a behavioral basis for success in a market economy (Deng & Cordilia, 1999). Deng and Cordilia further explained that:

> In a state of anomie, using legal means is less important than achieving the goal of economic success, and because aspirations for success have increased vastly, even those with access to legal means may be motivated to use illegal means when they are more efficient. (p. 217)

From this perspective, anomie theory is not only relevant to American society but also to all societies around the globe where economic fortune is valued. Indeed, the universal appeal of Merton's anomie theory stems from the fact that crime is found in all societies.

According to Merton (1938), when means and ends are unbalanced and there is an emphasis on an economically beneficial outcome, psychopathological personalities, antisocial conduct, and revolutionary activities may follow. Therefore, if antisocial behavior (i.e., crime) is to be understood through the perspective of anomie, the social sources of

Merton's Modes of Adaptation

Modes of Adaptation	Cultural Goals	Institutional Means
Conformity	Accepts goals	Accepts means
Innovation	Accepts goals	Rejects means
Ritualism	Rejects goals	Accepts means
Retreatism	Rejects goals	Rejects means
Rebellion	Rejects societal values; replaces with new values	Rejects societal means; replaces with new means

the behavior (i.e., emphasis on financial success) must be considered. Following Merton's theory, there are five ways in which an individual can choose to respond to anomie. The manner in which an individual responds depends on the person's "attitude toward the cultural goals and the institutionalized means" (Vold et al., 1998, p. 161). The following table summarily depicts the five anomie responses or modes of adaptation that an individual can have and the effects of these adaptation strategies on the means–ends relationship.

The modes of adaptation a person can elect to utilize are conformity, innovation, ritualism, retreatism, and rebellion. In a stable society, an individual will most likely choose conformity. In this response, the person accepts the cultural goals and the institutionalized means. In a more unstable and criminal society, individuals will respond through innovation. Individuals who utilize this mode of adaptation value the cultural goal of the wealth and expressions of it (e.g., home, car, and money), but are thwarted or frustrated in their ability to obtain them through institutional means. The path to economic success requires the use of illegitimate methods, and the innovator incorporates illicit strategies to secure such financial prosperity. The third mode of adaptation is ritualism. In this situation, the person does not value the goal of wealth or financial gain; however, the individual does regard hard work, loyalty, honesty, and other conventional social mores as valued, even cherished, means to experience a rewarding life. The fourth mode of adaptation is retreatism. Retreatists do not accept the cultural goals or the institutionalized means. Individuals who embrace this lifestyle are often psychotic, drug and alcohol addicted, or are in some other way societal outcasts. The fifth mode of adaptation is rebellion. This occurs when an individual rejects both the legitimately prescribed means and ends and substitutes them with new cultural forms and novel strategies by which to obtain them.

Despite its unquestionable appeal, Merton's (1938) anomie theory is not a comprehensive explanation of crime. Indeed, there are many limitations to this theory, including its focus on only one characteristic of social structure, namely, the inequality experienced by individuals in accessing legal means for monetary success (Messner & Rosenfeld, 2001). Interestingly, Merton noted that his approach to anomie theory was incomplete. As he insightfully explained,

> It has not included an exhaustive treatment of the various structural elements which predispose toward one rather than another of the alternative responses open to individuals; it has neglected, but not denied the relevance of, the factors determining the specific incidence of these responses; it has not enumerated the various concrete responses which as constituted by combinations of specific values of the analytical variables; it has omitted, or included only by implication, any consideration of the social functions performed by illicit responses; it has not tested the full explanatory power of the analytical scheme by examining a large number of group variations in the frequency of deviate and conformist behavior; it has not adequately dealt with rebellious conduct which seeks to refashion the social framework radically; it has not examined the relevance of cultural conflict for an analysis of culture-goal and institutional-means malintegration. (p. 682)

Strain Theory Versus Anomie Theory

During the 1970s, criminological theorists labeled the anomie perspective "strain theory" (Messner & Rosenfeld, 2001). Akers (1998, p. 197) compared the two orientations and concluded that anomie theory "makes no direct predictions about individual behavior . . . the strain may be experienced as a discrepancy between an individual's aspirations and expectations about access to appropriate means" (p. 197). However, strain theory "predicts that the greater the perceived discrepancy between aspirations and expectations, the higher the probability of deviant behavior" (p. 197).

Although the differences between strain theory and anomie theory are minimal, their affinities are quite appreciable. From Durkheim's (1965) theoretical frame of reference, anomie at a societal level results in strain at an individual level. This strain leads to anger and frustration, which in turn may lead to suicide or other violent acts. In contrast, Merton's theoretical perspective (Messner & Rosenfeld, 2001) maintains that strain at the individual level will lead to anomie at a societal level. The individual strain causes individuals to deviate from legal activities and norms (Agnew, 1997).

Anomie and Criminal Behavior

Anomie theory accounts for crime and criminal behavior through the importance of culture. As Messner and Rosenfeld (2001) explain, following Merton, "crime and deviance result . . . from the malintegration of elements within culture and from a similar lack of fit between culture and social structure" (p. 53). Thus, criminal behavior is a result not only of deviations from cultural conformity but also of deviations from structural conformity.

The cultural pressures to succeed economically generate desires within individuals that are at times difficult to achieve legally. Feelings of powerlessness, disappointment, and resentment may surface. In these instances, the pressure for financial reward may produce overwhelming sentiments of frustration. Individuals who harbor these feelings may rely on whatever resources or means they have at their disposal because they have no moral qualms about employing criminal strategies.

There are many instances where the pressure to achieve and benefit from monetary rewards can result in criminal behavior. Drug dealing and robbery are two examples. In these cases, the person's illicit conduct may be motivated by a desire to achieve some semblance of financial gain. The absence of legitimate outlets to secure such rewards may result in the pursuit of illegitimate outlets. Violent crimes that satisfy economic cravings are an even more significant result of an anomic environment. For example, muggings, carjackings, and home invasions are an efficient yet unlawful way to achieve financial success. Each of these wrongful acts tells us something about a culture in which financial wealth is valued, seemingly above all else. Indeed, as Messner and Rosenfeld (2001) state, "the distinctive cultural message accompanying the monetary success goal in the American Dream is the devaluation of all but the most technically efficient means" (p. 77). Clearly, this includes criminal methods, especially if they are strategic and efficient outlets.

STRAIN THEORY

Strain theory looks beyond the factors related to an individual. It considers subcultural influences and the various ways in which criminal behavior is actually learned through interactions with others. In this respect, strain theory seeks to integrate the cultural context in which crime occurs (as discussed earlier in this chapter) with the social mechanisms that teach one how to act criminally (see chapter 4 under Learning Theory for more). Thus, strain theory "point[s] to aspects of social culture and social learning that contribute to the creation of criminal [behavior] and attitudes" (White & Haines, 2000, p. 56).

The approach that strain theory takes toward crime and criminal behavior is that these are essentially social phenomena. "Strain theory proposes that criminality results from negative experiences, especially goal frustration associated with the discrepancy between an individual's aspirations, on the one hand, and achievements or expectations, on the other" (Messner & Rosenfeld, 2001, p. 45). The original (and principal) architect of strain theory was Robert Merton. Merton's ideas were previously discussed in relation to anomie theory, particularly as an extension of Durkheim's work in the area. Merton was especially interested in "the way in which the tensions between the legitimate and illegitimate means of acceding to the norms and values of a particular society resulted in deviant (rather than just criminal) [behavior]" (Walklate, 1998, p. 220).

Strain theories look to society as a whole, rather than to particular deviant individuals, for answers to criminological questions. According to Merton (1968), at the very foundation of social organization are strains, tensions, and contradictions. These tensions or strains are "generated by society itself; they do not reside within the individual (as in the case, e.g., of a person feeling strained or pressured by circumstance" (White & Haines, 2000, p. 56). Thus, unlike anomie theory where delinquency or crime arises because of conditions an individual confronts as disappointing or frustrating, strain theory locates the source of criminogenic conduct in society at large. As such, "[U]ndesirable forms of behavior, such as crime . . . may be inevitable features of the normal workings of the social system, just as more desirable forms of behavior [are a normal part of the social system]" (Messner & Rosenfeld, 2001, p. 11).

Merton (1968) argued that the United States fosters a social system embroiled with internal strain and contradiction. According to Steven F. Messner and Richard Rosenfeld, authors of *Crime and the American Dream* (2001), Merton is correct:

> . . . Merton observes that an exaggerated emphasis is placed on the goal of monetary success in American society, coupled with a weak emphasis placed on the importance of using the socially acceptable means for achieving this goal. This is a normal feature of American culture . . . it is an integral part of the American dream. (p. 11)

The fact that some can achieve this dream whereas others cannot is the result of an uneven playing field. This realization creates tremendous social unrest. "The result of these cultural and structural conditions is a pronounced strain towards anomie, that is, a tendency for social norms to lose their regulatory force" (Messner & Rosenfeld, 2001, p. 11). This social dynamic creates an atmosphere where crime can grow.

In the 1980s, Robert Agnew (1984, 1985, 1987) questioned the key elements of traditional strain theories. "He argued that there were broader, more general sources of strain which were not being considered" (Piquero & Sealock, 2000, p. 450). This led him to develop a **general strain theory** (Agnew, 1992), focusing primarily on negative relationships with others; that is, he concentrated on the relationship between how individuals expect to be treated and how they are actually treated. In this respect, Agnew's approach to strain theory differed considerably from conventional theories because he stressed "the individual social-psychological level rather than the strictly societal macro level" (Piquero & Sealock, 2000, p. 451).

Agnew (1992) reasoned that when an individual is treated in ways that he or she does not appreciate, a **negative affect** occurs. "Negative affect, most commonly characterized by anger or other unpleasant emotional states, can pressure adolescents into delinquency if other adaptations or coping strategies are not present or, if present, are not utilized" (Piquero & Sealock, 2000, p. 450). Williams (1999) offers a useful illustration of how this occurs in the realm of adolescent behavior:

> For instance, a juvenile may not be able to avoid a bad family situation, may drop out of school as a solution to poor grades, or even hide from peer rejection. All of these things may yield levels of frustration as high as those from blocked aspirations or immediate goals. (p. 38)

Agnew (1992) described three major categories of strain. The first category represents the core of what traditional strain theorists believe cause crime and deviance: the failure to achieve goals that one values and desires. Piquero and Selock (2000) elaborated on this specific category as follows:

> The failure to achieve positively valued goals is parceled into three categories: the disjunction between aspirations and expectations [such as the ghetto adolescent who aspires to be like the wealthy individuals he sees on television, yet expects to fall victim to gang warfare like many of his friends]; the disjunction between expectations and actual achievements [such as the teenage woman who expected to graduate high school rather than dropping out due to an unplanned pregnancy]; and the disjunction between just or fair outcomes and actual outcomes [e.g., at least 8 of every 10 automobiles searched by state troopers on the New Jersey Turnpike during the 1990s were driven by Blacks or Hispanics; see Kocieniewski & Hanley, 2000.] (p. 450)

These sources of strain certainly influence one's expectations and may influence one's behavior. For example, in chapter 9, a more in-depth analysis of racial profiling is presented. Consider how this experience may be linked to strain theory, giving way to criminal conduct.

The second category of strain is the elimination of the positively valued stimuli (Agnew, 1992). "This type of strain may lead to delinquency when an individual tries to prevent, recoup, substitute for, avenge, or manage the loss" (Piquero & Sealock, 2000, pp. 450–451). In chapter 7, James P. McGee and Caron R. DeBernardo (1999) describe "classroom avengers" as kids who are angered by authority figures or are rejected by others, who then seek revenge on their schoolmates in the form of deadly violence. Or, consider how many individuals cope with a loss (e.g., the death of a parent or child) by abusing alcohol and drugs.

The third category of strain identified by Agnew (1992) causing deviant behavior is the presentation of negative stimuli. "Delinquency may result when individuals try either to avoid or ameliorate the negative stimulus or to seek revenge against the source of the stimulus" (Piquero & Sealock, 2000, p. 451). To illustrate, imagine the strain a battered wife suffers in the wake of physical and emotional abuse administered by her husband. The presence of this negative stimulus (i.e., spousal battering) may lead the wife to harm or otherwise kill her tormentor. In chapter 5 of this work, domestic violence and the effects of spousal abuse are reviewed. Consider how strain theory may be a useful theoretical approach by which to account for this behavior. Overall, the highest rates of delinquency will occur when positively valued stimuli and the ability to avoid negative stimuli are blocked or otherwise thwarted (Williams, 1999).

Why might strained individuals turn to crime? Strained individuals might resort to deviance to regain some control over their troubling and frustrating situations. For instance, a young mother might turn to prostitution in order to feed her hungry children. The expectation that one must provide for one's children is strained by the limited opportunities to earn a decent, living wage in many segments of society. A juvenile might deal drugs in order to care for his sick mother. Indeed, the lack of socialized health care leaves many uninsured and unemployed individuals with nowhere else to turn. A person of color might lash out at a police officer in the hope of reclaiming the loss of dignity, following his or her experience of racial profiling. In this instance, even if it appears to be a superficial act, that individual may genuinely feel better, if only briefly. (Black rage as a criminal defense is detailed in chapter 8.)

The strain of coping with the pushes and pulls of life clash with what one feels he or she deserves. The resulting effect is an individual who turns to crime. This same logic applies to juveniles. As Agnew (1992) explains, "under certain conditions the experience of adversity may lead to beliefs favorable to delinquency, lead adolescents to join or form delinquent peer groups, and lead adolescents to blame others for their misfortune" (p. 160).

Crime is merely the mechanism by which those who are disadvantaged take something back in an attempt to level the playing field just a little bit more. Sometimes the results of strain are tragic (like the killings at Columbine High School), and sometimes the results are less transparent (like the investment banker who funnels money to a secret bank account in order to satisfy his or her sense of self-worth in a money-driven, success-oriented culture).

The Limits of Strain Theory

As with most theories regarding criminal behavior, the prominence and appeal of this perspective have evolved considerably. Along these lines, Piquero and Sealock (2000) comment that strain theory "achieved popularity during the mid-1960s, but excitement about this approach to explaining crime faded shortly thereafter" (p. 449). Strain theory is also subject to its own set of limitations. For example, some argue that empirical research on this perspective focuses almost exclusively on lower class crime (White & Haines, 2000). This tendency is a problem. What it means is that the theory neglects to account for criminal behavior committed by individuals of different socioeconomic standings or groupings. As White and Haines point out, "[d]espite understanding the need to gauge levels of crime not reported to police within communities, strain theorists largely accept the 'shape' of the official crime statistics, namely that the majority of offenses are perpetrated by the working class" (p. 72).

Kornhauser (1978) made a similar argument about the shortcomings of strain theory. Reviewing the research in the area, she argued that strain theory offered a limited explanation of delinquency because it "accepted that crime in working-class neighborhoods was that which needed explaining and eradicating" (White & Haines, 2000, p. 72). Moreover, she disagreed that frustration caused crime and that "the source of this frustration was . . . the 'gap' between what criminals and delinquents want (aspirations) and what they expect to get (expectations)" (Vold et al., 1998, p. 170). Kornhauser believed that the poor were not isolated in feeling the frustration of wanting more than they could ever get. Indeed, the rich often want more, too. Thus, "[s]train in this sense is evenly spread throughout society and is not greater among the poor" (Vold et al., 1998, p. 170). Interestingly, strain theorists are quick to point out that the wealthiest individuals in society have access to the best medical care, superior academic institutions, and the safest automobiles, and hold positions of political power and prestige. As such, the contention that there is equal frustration among rich and poor seems misguided at best, according to the theory's advocates.

Kornhauser (1978) also argued that strain theorists misrepresent the American culture, giving too much value to economic gain over hard work, perseverance, and honesty. Commenting on Kornhauser's position, Vold et al. (1998) offered the following explanation:

> On the one hand, [Kornhauser] interpreted the desire for economic success as a natural desire not requiring cultural supports. On the other hand, she argued that culture itself should be defined in terms of a design of a moral order that is passed as a valued heritage from generation to generation. Defined this way, economic success cannot be a component of any culture. Thus, in [Kornhauser's] view, American culture does not value monetary success. (p. 170)

Proponents of strain theory believe that there is a consensus of societal values. As they describe it, ultimately everyone wants to achieve the same goals and share the same lifestyle. "In this way, strain theory accepts the status quo. Rather than seeing the goals and aspirations of society as [molded] by those in positions of power, strain theory sees such aspirations as a genuine consensus of values" (White & Haines, 2000, p. 72).

Another criticism of strain theory relates to its acceptance of core, conventional beliefs. By endorsing such mainstream principles, the theory ignores the deep, structural inequalities inherent in all capitalist societies. This is a reference to the way in which money-driven, success-oriented cultures by their very nature render some people "marginal" and, as such, criminalize their behaviors (White & Haines, 2000, p. 73). For example, people who are homeless are routinely rounded up and arrested for vagrancy in cities, notwithstanding the fact that they have done nothing other than to live on the street (Barak, 1989). Indeed, as White and Haines explain:

> The system itself can be responsible for labeling some people and their activities criminal [medicinal marijuana users], while leaving alone other individuals whose activities are equally, or even more, harmful to society as a whole [illegal dumpers of toxic waste] . . . those who challenge the status quo are labeled as criminals. (p. 72)

In a society that measures social achievement by how much economic success an individual acquires, strain theory can be used to account for why crime is committed by people who are poor, minorities, or otherwise marginalized by the conforming culture. However, strain theory cannot explain all types of crime; in particular, white-collar crime, elite corporate crime, and crime committed by persons with mental illnesses. Why do the rich need to commit crimes in order to get richer, especially when they risk losing both their wealth and reputation? Do delusions cause psychiatrically disordered individuals to commit crimes? Or, are these behaviors linked to the strain individuals experience living in a society that is unfamiliar with or, worse, ignorant of the personal and emotional difficulties the mentally ill confront daily? Questions such as these are not easily addressed and, moreover, strain theory does not appear to have answers to them. As such, the theory's limitations have led investigators to look elsewhere for explanations concerning the causes of criminal behavior.

CONFLICT THEORY

> *"Wherever men live together conflict and a struggle for power will be found."*
> —*(Quinney, 1970, p. 11).*

As early as the 1930s scholars began to examine the occurrence of crime as an effect of conflicting interests among members of a community. In 1933, Frank Speck studied the primitive tribe of Labrador Indians. Speck characterized the Labrador Indians as a culture where

> . . . strife is scarcely present, violence is strenuously avoided; competition even courteously disdained. In their place are met subjection of self, generosity in respect to property, service and opinion . . . And these are the qualities that to them represent honor and a welcome place in the thoughts of their associates. (p. 559)

In 1938, Thorsten Sellin compared Speck's description of the Labrador tribe to modern Western culture of the time in order to elaborate on what he called "**conduct norms**" (p. 28). As he stated:

> [The industrialization of Western society results in] a culture which instead of the well-knit social fabric, which Speck pictured, shows a multitude of social groups, competitive interests, poorly defined interpersonal relationships, social anonymity, a confusion of norms and a vast extension of impersonal control agencies designed to enforce rules which increasingly lack the moral force which rules receive only when they grow out of emotionally felt community needs. (pp. 59–60)

According to Sellin, conduct norms represent the social attitudes of a group or community toward the ways in which a member of the group might act in various circumstances. These ways are solidified into rules, "the violation of which arouses a group reaction" (Sellin, 1938, p. 28). There is a considerable lack of conflicting interests when, as in the Labrador Indian tribe, members are held to the universal standards shared by everyone in the community. Therefore, a single cultural standard is effective in thwarting the conflict of conduct expectations. However, modern societies consist of tremendous diversity in terms of culture and conduct expectations. This is the point at which conflict theory offers an explanation of crime and criminal behavior.

Conflict theory is concerned with societies that consist of competing groups with contrasting values and interests (Bernard, 1983). "However, the organized state is not said to represent the values and interests of the society at large. Rather, it is said to represent the values and interests of groups that have sufficient power to control the operation of the state" (Vold et al., 1998, p. 235). Consequently, those with less voice in a society are at risk for being treated as criminal when they behave according to their own interests, especially when these interests conflict with those in power (Arrigo & Bernard, 1997).

Conflict theory points out that "power is the basic characteristic of social organization" (Quinney, 1970, p. 11). "This means that in every social organization some positions are entrusted with a right to exercise control over other positions in order to ensure effective coercion; it means, in other words, that there is a differential distribution of power and authority" (Dahrendorf, 1959, p. 165). This differential distribution of authority creates an environment where the ability of those in power "to protect themselves and their interests" inevitably leads vulnerable groups to seek greater power "thus leading those not in [authority] toward criminal behavior" (Dantzker, 1998, p. 59).

The consensus model of society (much like the society of the Labrador Indians) contrasts with the conflict theory of society (Bernard, 1983; Quinney, 1970). According to Ralf Dahrendorf (1959), the consensus model assumes that (a) society is a relatively stable structure; (b) society is well integrated; (c) every element of society has a function that helps to stabilize the system; and (d) society is a functioning, cohesive structure based on a consensus of values. Alternatively, the conflict model assumes that (a) at every point society is subject to change, (b) society displays at every point conflict and disagreement, (c) every element of society contributes to change, and (d) society is based on the coercion of some of its members by others. Thus, according to the conflict model, "society is held together by force and constraint and is characterized by ubiquitous conflicts that result in continuous change" (Quinney, 1970, pp. 9–10).

Dantzker (1998, pp. 58–59) notes that the conflict model promotes three themes:

1. **The relativity of criminal definitions.** Every act defined as immoral or criminal is always subject to redefinition, depending on the preferences of the societal group with the most power.
2. **Control of institutions.** There are three basic means to preserve and foster society's interests: force, compromise, and the dominance of social institutions (e.g., law, church, schools, and government).
3. **Law as an instrument of power.** Law is an extremely powerful weapon of social conflict. In other words, whoever has control over the laws retains power over all other groups.

Conflict theories attempt to identify and draw attention to society's power relationships in order to expose the role in which conflicts among groups actively promote criminal behavior (Bernard, 1983). As Dantzker (1998) explains, "Although conflict is viewed as an essential social process upon which society depends, group interests and their influence on legislation that arise from these conflicts are linked to criminal behavior" (p. 58). Vold et al. (1998) describe the process of legislative politics and its influence on criminal behavior. They refer to this process as "**group conflict theory**" (p. 236):

> Conflicts between opposing groups' interests exist in the community before there is any legislative action. As one group lines up against another, both may seek the assistance of the organized state to help them defend their rights and protect their interests . . . Whichever group interest can marshal the greatest number of votes will determine whether or not there will be a new law to hamper and curb interests of the opposing group. (p. 237)

It is also worth noting that, on occasion, underrepresented groups are not even afforded the opportunity to gather votes or to mobilize their constituency in support of their group's concerns (Lynch, Michalowski, & Groves, 2000). Even though the sole responsibility of the U.S. judicial branch of government is to interpret law, there is a propensity of appellate court judges to actually make new laws favoring one group over another through their (seemingly unregulated) powers of discretion (e.g., Arrigo & Bernard, 1997; Bernard, 1981). For example, most critics agree that the conservative-dominated Supreme Court of the United States, favoring the Republican candidate George W. Bush over his opponent, Democrat Al Gore, effectively decided the 2000 presidential election.

Group conflict theory then proposes that "once a new law is passed, the group who opposed the law in the legislature [or legal ruling] understandably does not take kindly to efforts at law enforcement" (Vold et al., 1998, p. 237). Consequently, Vold et al. make the following observations:

1. Those who opposed the law are more likely to violate it, because the law supports interests and purposes that are in conflict with the interests and purposes of those who oppose it.
2. Those who supported the law are more likely to obey and follow it.
3. Those who supported the law are more likely to demand that police enforce it against violators. This is because the law defends the interests and purposes of those who made it.

Following the logic of group conflict theory, the power of law enforcement is clearly with the majority. "Those who produce legislative majorities win control of police power of the state and decide the policies that determine who is likely to be involved in the violation of laws" (Vold et al., 1998, p. 237).

Conflict theory is not limited to explaining crime characteristically committed by lower income and less powerful individuals. Indeed, conflict theory is also applicable to white-collar crime (see chapter 6 for more details on this form of criminal behavior; Friedrichs, 1996). White-collar criminals are often involved in devastating acts that affect (sometimes lethally) countless people: insider trading (cheating investors), toxic-waste dumping (polluting the environment, killing animals, poisoning public drinking water), or insurance fraud (as a consequence, insurance companies raise premiums to maintain their profit margins, making insurance too expensive for those who need it). The fact that these criminals are underrepresented in prisons is not because their crimes are few. On the contrary, their crimes are committed frequently (Frank & Lynch, 1992). The issue is that individuals who commit white-collar crime also regulate the power of police in society (Frank & Cook, 1995). Poorer groups with much less power experiencing greater conflict with society's laws are being prosecuted, convicted, and incarcerated for petty crimes and drug offenses (Reiman, 2001). "The inference is that policing such relatively minor offenses [as opposed to major offenses by white-collar criminals] permits . . . harassment of young African-Americans" (Short, 1997, pp. 132–133).

Conflict theory is not without its limitations. One criticism is its generalization that the group with less power and fewer votes necessarily will resort to criminal acts. In particular, according to group conflict theory:

> . . . lawmaking, lawbreaking, and law enforcement directly reflect deep-seated and fundamental conflicts between group interests and more general struggles among groups for control of police power of the state. To that extent, criminal behavior is the behavior of *minority power groups*, in that these groups do not have sufficient power to promote and defend their interests and purposes in the legislative process [italics in original]. (Vold et al., 1998, p. 237)

Group conflict theory fails to explain the numerous occasions where minority groups prevail in advancing their agenda legislatively or succeed in calling for reform in existing laws, without criminal conduct.

McGarrell and Castellano (1991) proposed a three-tier, integrative conflict model of the criminal law and the process by which it is formed. The model's first level involves the

Minority Power

Led by Dr. Martin Luther King Jr. in the 1960s, Blacks united nonviolently to protest oppressive legislation of the powerful White majority. Through their struggle to unify, the minority gained momentum, broad-based power, and public support in the face of entrenched racism across the United States. Initiatives such as this demonstrate that criminal behavior is not always linked to conflicting group interests where the less powerful respond violently. Interestingly, despite the progress made in race relations since the civil rights movement of the 1960s, minority groups continue to struggle. For example, racial profiling, elevated rates of incarceration for African Americans, affirmative action reform, and professional and educational opportunities for women and people of color have often been lost or side-stepped in the political shuffle (Reiman, 2001). In each of these issues, the conflict being waged is over power and the minority group's ability to enjoy the benefits of society historically bestowed only upon majority (i.e., powerful) groups.

"structural foundations" (pp. 184–185) of crime and conflict in societies. Societies are differentiated if they consist of members of various races, ethnicities, and religions. McGarrell and Castellano also believed societies were differentiated if there was political and economic inequality among its citizens. "Experience teaches us that we cannot expect to find consensus on all or most values and norms in such societies" (Quinney, 1970, p. 9). The often substantially differing beliefs held by various groups in a society lead to conflict. "[The greater the differentiation the] higher the level of conflict [which] in turn leads to greater use of criminalization as a method of dealing with conflicts" (Vold et al., 1998, p. 245).

The second tier of McGarrell and Castellano's (1991) integrated conflict theory deals with the enforcement of criminal laws. Crime garners media attention. This attention creates a sense of victimization for all citizens who see the coverage on television or read about it in the newspapers. "The increased media attention results in feelings of 'vicarious victimization'—people who are not actually victims of crime may still feel victimized because they hear about the victimization of other people" (Vold et al., 1998, p. 245). This vicarious victimization fuels the misplaced fear that crime is spreading and is out of control. These fears lead to a more punitive response from the criminal justice system, increased enforcement of laws, and increased official crime rates, which inevitably increases peoples' fear of crime (Walker, 2001).

The Case of John Hinckley, Jr.

One of the best illustrations of how media attention and fear of crime work in tandem to produce new legislation is the case of John Hinckley Jr., the individual who attempted to assassinate former President Ronald Reagan. There was considerable concern for Hinckley's mental state at the time he engaged in his wrongful behavior. His defense team argued that Hinckley was insane and that therefore he should not be held legally responsible for his conduct. John Hinckley Jr. was found not guilty by reason of insanity. The outcome in this case led to tremendous social unrest. In fact, the public clamored for the repeal of the insanity defense. Public lawmakers, mindful of this unrest and mindful of the constant media exposure the case received, responded. In the wake of the verdict, the Federal Insanity Defense Reform Act of 1983–1984 was established. The Act made it more difficult for a defendant to invoke the defense of insanity. What is troubling about this legislation is that according to most experts, the insanity defense is invoked during the plea stage in less than 1% of all criminal cases. In those cases where it is invoked, it is typically not a successful defense strategy. Moreover, the media attention surrounding the Hinckley verdict fueled legislative efforts to establish the guilty but mentally ill verdict. In this instance, a person is found criminally responsible for his or her behavior, notwithstanding the presence of a psychiatric disorder. In short, this gives states who adopt the policy a license to define people as both "bad" and "mad."

(For more on the Hinckley case, the insanity defense, and the guilty but mentally ill verdict, see Steadman et al., 1993.)

Feminist Theory and Criminal Behavior

Interestingly enough, one example of a type of conflict theory explaining delinquency and crime is **feminist theory.** This is especially the case with the early work of Freda Adler (1975) and Rita Simon (1975). They both argued that gender differences in crime rates were a function of socialization rather than of biology. Thus, as they observed, to the extent that male dominance (i.e., patriarchy) was largely responsible for feminine identities (women's ways of thinking, feeling, and behaving), female criminality would remain an artifact of masculine logic and reasoning. Adler and Simon suggested that as gender equality materialized, women would more prominently display their own criminal behavior, consistent with that of their male counterparts. Although many critics agree that signs of gender equality during the past 30 years have been clear and appreciable, the theorizing of Adler and Simon has not been borne out in the relevant literature, leaving researchers to still speculate on the nature of female criminality.

There are several conceptual approaches to the study of women and crime. Some of these include socialist feminism (Eisenstein, 1979; Klein, 1982), radical feminism (Firestone, 1970; Stanko, 1985), and critical feminism (Smart, 1995; Young, 1996). Although each embraces different assumptions and values, at the core

of feminist criminology is a concern for **(masculine) power** and the exploitive and marginalizing effects it has on all women (Daly & Chesney-Lind, 1988). Indeed, the effect of such power is that it excludes women from decision making in various facets of social life and perpetuates gender inequality (Messerschmidt, 1993).

More recent attempts to explain female crime and interpret female criminal behavior emphasize detailed case study analyses of individual women offenders. The story of Aileen Wuornos is one illustration. According to Shipley and Arrigo (2004), Wuornos engaged in multiple acts of predatory homicide not because she was a "victim" of social forces but because of her poor psychological attachments with her parents. As an adolescent, Aileen's delinquent behavior (e.g., truancy, underage drinking) intensified because she was unable to resolve her deep-seated emotional scarring (e.g., mother who rejected her; father who abandoned her; grandmother who ignored her; and grandfather who abused her). Wuornos matured into a very calculated and ruthless killer—a psychopath—unable to show care or concern for others, especially those whom she murdered. In this context, questions about power and whether she was deprived of it by men are significantly called into question.

The third level identifed by McGarrell and Castellano (1991) in their integrated conflict model involves the enactment of criminal laws. They reasoned that media attention, compounded by fear of victimization, forced lawmakers to establish new legislation and implement more stringent punishments for behaviors previously thought to be legal or acceptable. "As a result, official crime statistics, media attention, and fear of crime again increase and the cycle continues" (Vold et al., 1998, p. 246).

Historically, conflicts among differing groups in society on occasion have led to radical changes. These reforms have benefited those groups with little power. However, lobbyists, political action committees (PACs), and other wealthy special interest groups have been extremely influential in bringing their concerns to the forefront of the political arena. Then, too, the impact of the media should not be underestimated. Indeed, once television, print, and radio outlets get wind of an intriguing, controversial issue where conflict group interests are at play, public sentiment can influence, if not force, those with power to take notice and react. Conflict, then, is not always a negative condition. Similar to crime, social change is born out of conflict. As Dantzker (1998) implied, what we currently view as criminal will be accepted as legal tomorrow. In other words, it all depends on the prevailing social climate.

CRITICAL CRIMINOLOGICAL THEORIES

Introduction

There are two foundational questions critical theorists address when exploring crime and criminal behavior: (a) What is justice?; (b) For whom is justice served (Arrigo, 1999)? Admittedly, the answers depend on who is asking the questions. However, this is precisely the point critical criminologists make. Indeed, everyone defines justice differently, depending largely on one's culture, social standing, gender, language, sexuality, and race. What critical criminologists remind us is that those who create and enforce laws also manipulate them, undermining prospects for a more diverse and inclusive social order (e.g., Chambliss & Zatz, 1993; Friedrichs, 2000; Michalowski, 1985). Law functions to benefit the needs and interests of those who govern and to oppress and pacify those who are governed. How the force of law operates tells us a great deal about the origins of crime and the behavior a society defines as criminal. Indeed, it tells us something about the nature of justice and whether it is attainable for all citizens through the very institutions and agencies that make up the criminal justice system.

In this final portion of the chapter, a number of the more prominent critical criminological theories are presented. The chronicling of perspectives is not exhaustive. Instead, some approaches that continue to demonstrate popular appeal from within the criminological and sociological communities are canvassed (for a more thorough review, see Arrigo, 2000). In addition to describing how each perspective interprets crime and justice, some reference to selected applications studies in the chosen areas are provided. Both the general descriptions and the targeted application work that follow are significant. In short, they provide a different set of conceptual lenses by which to frame our understanding of criminal behavior. In this respect, then, critical criminological theory offers some new and provocative approaches by which to advance the interests of justice for everyone in society.

Radical Criminology—Marxist Theory

Marxist or radical theorists believe that we are all alienated from the product of our work (Lynch et al., 2000). In every act of labor something personal is lost. In a capitalist society, what is lost or compromised is the essence or the humanity of the laborer. This is because our work is reduced to an artificial equivalent. This equivalent is money. In other words, the relationship between what we produce and its intrinsic value is conveyed in the form of monetary exchange.

In the Marxist or radical tradition, the reduction of labor to an artificial equivalent is problematic. Indeed, once we pay someone for his or her labor, money shapes our relationship to that person and it becomes a stand-in for the person's identity. In other words, by assigning an artificial value to what one produces through the equivalent of money, we mask the inherent worth of one's labor, and, more significantly, we reduce the value of that person to an artificial form.

Identity, personal worth, self-esteem, and loyalty are important values that people possess; however, in a capitalist society, these values are defined through dollars and cents. In many instances within the United States, the relative worth of people is translated into how much they make, what they own, whether they can afford to buy a new car or take a trip, or how they intend to diversify their investment portfolio. This is a far cry from valuing the character or intellect of people.

Interestingly, capitalist (i.e., money-driven, success-oriented) societies have remained viable in the face of tremendous poverty. This is because when we define ourselves by money and the accumulation of wealth, we endorse, mostly unknowingly, the belief that some will have more financial gain, that others will have less, and that those with more fortune will possess it at the expense of others (Lynch & Stretesky, 1999). Marxist or radical criminologists refer to this activity as **false consciousness.** False consciousness is a social and psychological condition in which people accept existing economic relations in society (e.g., the rich getting richer and the poor getting poorer) because they are believed to be the result of natural and inevitable forces.

False consciousness occurs all the time. Whenever we attend a sporting event, buy groceries, or rent an apartment, we accept money as the ultimate arbiter for our economic transactions. In doing so, we fortify the power of consumerism and capitalism to shape our identities and the identities of those with whom we interact.

Marxist theorists call our attention to the inherent injustice created and sustained by the powerful (Arrigo & Bernard, 1997; Lynch & Stretesky, 1999). Not only do the economically powerful regulate the flow and amount of financial reward they receive at the expense of others less powerful, but also they control what is defined as criminal so that their position of relative economic superiority and prosperity can be maintained. As Lynch and Stretesky explain:

> When we look at the criminal justice system, what do we see? Radical [theorists] see a system of class control and oppression. One reason they see this picture is because they look at *who is controlled by this system and who is omitted from this form of control*. Without a doubt, the criminal justice system controls the lower classes [italics in original]. (p. 24)

Society is structured in order to criminalize and marginalize those who cannot play by the rules imposed on them by those who make the rules. Radical or Marxist theorists have explored this dynamic in relation to a host of behaviors defined as criminal or regulated by those who exercise institutional control. Examples include homelessness (Barak, 1991), racial and ethnic bias (Lynch & Patterson, 1996; Mann & Zatz, 1998), punishment and penal discipline (Platt & Takagi, 1974), rape and inequality (Schwendinger & Schwendinger, 1983), the legal order (Quinney, 1974), gender and crime (Daly, 1994), crack cocaine (Brownstein, 1996), and policing in society (Harring, 1983). In Marxist or **radical criminology,** the goal is to promote **social justice** by changing or eliminating the political and economic systems that promote inequalities. This active engagement with the structures of oppression is believed to be the only way to liberate people from society's margins; boundaries that sustain their felt victimization.

Peacemaking Criminology

Peacemaking theorists argue that in order to restore true justice to society, people have to make peace with crime. This is not easy, especially when we experience the physical, personal, and emotional devastation that follows in the wake of criminal wrongdoing (Pepinsky & Quinney, 1991). However, genuinely and openly working through our anger, pain, and harm is essential to transform a **warmaking** culture into a peacemaking culture (Pepinsky, 1999). Indeed, as Arrigo (1999) explains:

> Peacemaking criminology challenges us to think about the presence of violence and democracy in society and in our lives. It considers how people, in the midst of conflict, build trust, community, and peace rather than distrust, separatism, and war. One form of conflict is crime. (p. 51)

In order to make the sort of change envisioned by **peacemaking criminology,** one has to look past the delinquent or criminal behaviors of people and realize that these actions do not define who they are. This is because peacemaking theorists believe that when individuals resort to offender conduct, they, too, are in pain, are afraid, and are in need of compassion. This is why peacemaking criminologists call for open and frank dialog during the recovery process with offenders, victims, and the community of which both are a part (e.g., Sulllivan & Tifft, 2001). Indeed, through such exchanges, we can all begin to reclaim our sense of selves as we struggle to be heard, accepted, and valued amidst the disappointments and frustrations of everyday life.

The peacemaking agenda is difficult to implement in practice. There are social, political, economic, and cultural forces that prevent or impede the kind of social change envisioned by the theory's advocates. However, moving in the direction of peace is about experiencing personal control and communal justice for oneself and for others. As Hal Pepinsky (1999) explains, social justice can be approached in one of two ways:

> "Social control" refers to achieving a sense of greater trust and social safety among one's associates, as manifested in the feeling of being happier and more secure in the next moment

> than at present. The other approach is . . . "warmaking." Warmaking entails the belief that our social insecurity and danger can be traced to identifiable persons who act out of evil or psychopathic motives, individually or in groups. (p. 56)

We are bombarded daily with events at work, at home, in our communities, in our society, and around the globe that stir our warmaking mentality. A child is sexually molested and raped by a pedophile, and we are outraged. A group of terrorists bomb a building killing thousands and wounding many others, and our passions are inflamed. However, instead of harboring anger and frustration, peacemaking criminology suggests that we mediate these feelings by addressing a number of transformative, life-affirming questions:

> What do I do that contributes to an attitude of peace among those causing others tremendous, concerted pain and fear? What do I do to stop the process of human separation or exclusion of victims and offenders, friends and enemies, from "normal," participative social discourse? (Pepinsky, 1999, p. 53)

If justice truly belongs to everyone, then we must be willing to address and respond to the pain and suffering of criminals. This is not an easy task. However, by failing to do this, not only is the humanity of the other person diminished but also is our own. Proponents of peacemaking have explored these ideas in a number of areas relevant to criminal behavior. Some recent examples include stalking (Vitello, 2003), corrections (Braswell, Fuller, & Lozoff, 2001), restorative justice (Sullivan & Tifft, 2001), and global violence (Williams & Arrigo, 2004). What these studies share in common is the belief that a just society grants everyone the opportunity to change and to experience mercy, forgiveness, and compassion.

Postmodern Criminology

Postmodernists believe that language is a variable that informs and shapes reality, including human behavior. More significantly, however, postmodern theorists maintain that this shaping or structuring of language is not a neutral endeavor. The words that are used to convey thoughts, feelings, impulses, and attitudes are always steeped in hidden values and implicit assumptions about people, institutions, and society. In some situations, the role of language or discourse to shape human affairs and civic life is not a problem at all. For example, the language of basketball, cooking, and computers represent a unique way to communicate meaning within these systems of communication. However, there are specific instances where this nonneutral structuring of reality is very much a problem. One example is crime and criminal behavior.

Postmodern criminologists recognize that the "texts" of crime, justice, law, and deviance are saturated in values, communicated in words and expressions (e.g., Arrigo, Milovanovic, & Schehr, 2005). However, these values typically represent the interests of those in positions of authority or power. For example, the field of mental health law describes persons with psychiatric disorders as experiencing a "disease" or "defect," and in "need of treatment" because they are "incompetent," "dangerous," and "ill." At first glance, these descriptions seem harmless enough. However, when looking closely at how these words and phrases are used to make decisions about persons with psychiatric disorders, we discover what unconscious messages are being communicated about this group of people or individuals within it.

Arrigo (1993, 1996, 2002a) has examined various aspects of this particular issue. Whether in the context of involuntary hospitalization, forced drug therapy over objection, competency restoration for purposes of execution, restricting the right to community-based care, or advocacy efforts in the psychiatric courtroom, one unmistakable truth emerges: Persons identified as "mentally ill" and "in need of treatment" are punished not so much for what they do or for who they are; rather, they are punished because they are different. This difference is conveyed in the system-supporting words and phrases used to articulate what mental illness signifies. However, persons experiencing psychiatric disorders are also "citizens," "differently abled," "psychiatric survivors," and "mental health system users." Yet, these are not the expressions we typically think of to describe such individuals. Indeed, they are not even in the lexicon of civil and criminal mental health law. Why? Because the hidden values and implicit assumptions communicated about psychiatric disorders are that persons with mental illness are not in control of themselves, need help, and must be corrected (Arrigo, 1996, 2002a).

Postmodern criminologists admit that persons with psychiatric disorders rely on speech patterns, thought processes, and behavioral interactions that are nonconventional, unfamiliar, and even uncomfortable to witness. However, these sentiments tell us more about the observer than they do about the person being observed. Again, for postmodernists, the issue is about how difference is valued. In the case of psychiatric citizens, difference is pathologized by the medical establishment and criminalized by the legal establishment (i.e., they are defined as ill, defective, diseased, and dangerous). In response to these interpretations, the spoken and lived reality of psychiatric patients is cleansed through institutional methods that contain, corral, or otherwise correct them. In this respect, language territorializes, indeed vanquishes, alternative realities; difference is reduced to sameness, and identities are homogenized (Arrigo, 2002b).

Postmodernists believe that there are no universal truths; that is, there is no single or best way to interpret phenomena. "Instead, there are multiple points of view that express our unique history, culture and identity" (Arrigo, 1999, p. 109). Retrieving these multiple and divergent perspectives validates difference. It is also the path to justice, dignity, and inclusiveness. This is why it is important to be careful in how we choose our words, speak about others and describe situations. However, this does not mean that justice is unattainable. Instead, it is provisional, positional, and relational (Arrigo, 1995). Indeed, as Wonders (1999) explained,

> Because postmodern . . . thinkers do not believe in objective truth or reality, instead viewing truth as a social construction that is always being (re-)created, it might seem impossible to develop a . . . postmodern conception of "justice." Is not justice different for everyone from this perspective? Does not any effort to define justice create a rigid boundary that necessarily benefits some people over others? But because postmodern . . . scholars recognize the limitations of *universal* definitions of justice (definitions that would be true for everyone all the time) does not mean that they believe we can afford to ignore our responsibility to make the best decisions we can, for the moment. In fact, once we understand that we shape the world and can change it, we have perhaps a greater responsibility to make choices that construct the world in ways that we can live with and feel good about [italics in original]. (p. 122)

Postmodern criminologists have addressed a number of issues and controversies in the realm of criminal behavior. Selected examples include gender and punishment (Howe, 1994), mental illness and dangerousness (Williams & Arrigo, 2002), race and crime (Russell, 1998), and policing in society (Manning, 1988). What these works share in common is a belief that words powerfully structure reality in ways that are not only value-laden but are system supporting, resulting in criminal justice polices that victimize, alienate, and oppress people.

Additional Critical Criminological Theories

There are additional strains of critical criminological theory that warrant some attention, as their insights have been relevant to an understanding of criminal behavior (for a brief overview, see Arrigo, 2002b). In particular, these include developments in new criminology (Taylor, Walton, & Young, 1973; Young, 1999), left realism (Matthews & Young, 1992; Young & Matthews, 1992), **anarchist theory** (Fox, 2000; Williams & Arrigo, 2001), **psychoanalytic semiotics** (Arrigo & Schehr, 1998; Milovanovic, 1992), **chaos theory** (Milovanovic, 1997; Pepinsky, 1991), **critical race theory** (Milovanovic & Russell, 2001), and **integrative criminology** (Barak, 1998). In these conceptual and applied areas of inquiry, investigators question how the criminological, psychological, and legal communities explain the causes of criminal behavior and, in doing so, undermine prospects for justice in society. Indeed, each one of these perspectives dramatically rethinks and reframes many of the enduring debates concerning offender conduct. Future efforts at exploring the origins of criminal behavior would do well to incorporate these critical lines of analysis into the overall research enterprise.

DISCUSSION QUESTIONS

1. What are some subcultural ideas that result in criminal conduct? How do adolescent gangs generate and sustain cultural belief systems that the dominant culture finds questionable if not delinquent?
2. How does the subculture of angry aggression work? Do you believe some individuals' arousal states are heightened when threatened, causing them to act aggressively and even violently over trivial conflicts? Explain your response using current examples.
3. Think of an example of criminal behavior. Identify three structural explanations for this crime. Identity the three corresponding process explanations that help account for this crime.
4. What is anomie? How did Emile Durkheim (1965) understand it? How did Robert Merton (1938, 1968) understand it?
5. What means–ends relationship does the innovator adopt, according to Robert Merton. What means–end relationship does the retreatist adopt, according to Robert Merton? Provide examples for each.
6. What are conduct norms and how do they relate to conflict theory?

7. What is the relationship among power, conflict theory, and criminal behavior? Use an example from American or European society for exemplification purposes.
8. What is the relationship among the media, conflict theory, and criminal behavior? Use an example from American or European society for exemplification purposes.
9. What makes critical criminological theories different from other sociological accounts of criminal behavior?
10. According to Marxist or radical criminology, what role does the economy play in crime? What is false consciousness? Can you think of an example of criminal behavior, best explained through Marxist or radical criminological theory?
11. What is peacemaking criminology? How does warmaking function in this theory of crime? From the peacemaking perspective, how is social justice achieved?
12. What is postmodern theory? According to postmodern criminology, what role does language play in the narratives of crime, law, delinquency, and justice? How does postmodern criminology promote social justice?

REFERENCES

Adler, F. (1975). *Sisters in crime: The rise of the new female criminal*. New York: McGraw-Hill.

Agnew, R. (1984). Goal achievement and delinquency. *Sociology and Social Research, 68*, 435–451.

Agnew, R. (1985). A revised strain theory of delinquency. *Social Forces, 64*, 151–167.

Agnew, R. (1987). On testing structural strain theories. *Journal of Research in Crime and Delinquency, 24*, 281–286.

Agnew, R. (1992). Foundations for a general strain theory of crime and delinquency. *Criminology, 30*, 47–87.

Agnew, R. (1997). The nature and determinants of strain: Another look at Durkheim and Merton. In N. Passas & R. Agnew (Eds.), *The future of anomie theory* (pp. 27–51). Boston: Northeastern University Press.

Akers, R. L. (1998). Social learning and social structure: *A general theory of crime and* deviance. Boston: Northeastern University Press.

Arrigo, B. A. (1993). *Madness, language and the law*. New York: Harrow & Heston.

Arrigo, B. A. (1995). The peripheral core of law and criminology: On postmodern social theory and conceptual integration. *Justice Quarterly, 12*(3), 447–472.

Arrigo, B. A. (1996). *The contours of psychiatric justice: A postmodern critique of mental illness, criminal insanity and the law*. New York/London: Garland.

Arrigo, B. A. (Ed.). (1999). *Social justice/criminal justice: The maturation of critical theory in law, crime, and deviance*. Belmont, CA: Wadsworth Publishing.

Arrigo, B. A. (2000). Social justice and critical criminology: On integrating knowledge. *Contemporary Justice Review, 3*(1), 7–37.

Arrigo, B. A. (2002a). *Punishing the mentally ill: A critical analysis of law and psychiatry*. Albany, NY: State University of New York Press.

Arrigo, B. A. (2002b). The critical perspective in psychological jurisprudence: Theoretical advances and epistemological assumptions. *International Journal of Law and Psychiatry, 15,* 151–172.

Arrigo, B. A., & Bernard, T. J. (1997). Postmodern criminology in relation to radical and conflict criminology. *Critical Criminology: An International Journal, 6*(2), 39–60.

Arrigo, B. A., Milovanovic, D., & Schehr, R. C. (2005). *The French connection in criminology: Rediscovering crime, law, and social change*. Albany, NY: SUNY Press.

Arrigo, B. A., & Schehr, R. C. (1998). Restoring justice for juveniles: A critical analysis of victim offender mediation. *Justice Quarterly, 15*(4), 629–666.

Barak, G. (1989). The crimes of the homeless or the crimes of homelessness? On the dialectics of criminalization, decriminalization, and victimization. *Contemporary Crises, 13,* 275–288.

Barak, G. (1991). *Gimme shelter: A social history of homelessness in contemporary America*. New York: Praeger.

Barak, G. (1998). *Integrating criminologies*. Boston, MA: Allyn & Bacon.

Bernard, T. J. (1981). The distinctions between conflict and radical criminology. *Journal of Criminal Law and Criminology, 72*(1), 362–379.

Bernard, T. J. (1983). *The consensus-conflict debate: Form and content in social theories*. New York: Columbia University Press.

Bernard, T. J. (1990). Angry aggression among the truly disadvantaged. *Criminology, 28*(1), 73–96.

Bernard, T. J. (1993). Angry aggression among the truly disadvantaged. *Criminology, 28*(1), 73–96.

Braswell, M., Fuller, J., & Lozoff, B. (2001). *Corrections, peacemaking, and restorative justice*. Cincinnati, OH: Anderson Publishing.

Brownstein, H. (1996). *The rise and fall of a violent crime wave: Crack cocaine and the social construction of a crime problem*. Guilderland, NY: Harrow and Heston.

Chambliss, W., & Zatz, M. (1993). *Making law*. Bloomington, IN: Indiana University Press.

Cloward, R. A., & Ohlin, L. E. (1960). *Delinquency and opportunity: A theory of delinquent gangs*. New York: The Free Press.

Cohen, A. K. (1955). *Delinquent boys: The culture of the gang*. New York: The Free Press.

Curtis, L. A. (1975). *Violence, race, and culture*. Lexington, MA: Heath.

Dahrendorf, R. (1959). *Class and class conflict in industrial society*. Stanford, CA: Stanford University Press.

Daly, K. (1994). *Gender, crime and punishment*. Princeton, NJ: Princeton University Press.

Daly, K., & Chesney-Lind, M. (1988). Feminism and criminology. *Justice Quarterly, 5,* 495–535.

Dantzker, M. L. (1998). *Criminology and criminal justice: Comparing, contrasting, and intertwining disciplines*. Woburn, MA: Butterworth-Heinemann.

Deng, X., & Cordilia, A. (1999). To get rich is glorious: Rising expectations, declining control, and escalating crime in contemporary China. *International Journal of Offender Therapy and Comparative Criminology, 43*(2), 211–229.

Durkheim, E. (1965). *The division of labor* (G. Simpson, Trans.). New York: The Free Press.

Eisenstein, Z. (Ed.). (1979). *Capitalist patriarchy and the case for socialist feminism*. New York: Monthly Review Press.

Firestone, S. (1970). *The dialectics of sex: The case for feminist revolution*. New York: Bantam.

Fox, D. (2000). A critical psychology's approach to law's legitimacy. *Legal Studies Forum, 25,* 519–538.

Frank, N., & Lynch, M. J. (1992). *Corporate crime, corporate violence: A primer*. Albany, NY: Harrow and Heston.

Frank, R. H., & Cook, P. J. (1995). *The winner-take-all society: Why the few at the top get so much more than the rest of us*. New York: Penguin.

Friedrichs, D. O. (1996). *Trusted criminals: White collar crime in contemporary America*. Belmont, CA: ITP/Wadsworth.

Friedrichs, D. O. (2000). *Law in our lives*. Upper Saddle River, NJ: Prentice Hall.

Gastil, R. D. (1971). Homicide and a regional subculture of violence. *American Sociological Review, 36,* 412–427.

Hagan, J. (1985). Toward a structural theory of crime, race, and gender: The Canadian case. *Crime and Delinquency, 31*(1), 129–146.

Hagan, J. (1989). *Structural criminology*. New Brunswick, NJ: Rutgers University Press.

Hagan, J., & Palloni, A. (1986). Toward a structural criminology: Method and theory in criminological research. *Annual Review of Sociology, 12,* 431–449.

Harring, S. (1983). *Policing in a class society: The experience of American cities 1865–1915.* New Brunswick, NJ: Rutgers University Press.

Howe, A. (1994). *Punish and critique: Towards a feminist analysis of penality.* London: Routledge.

Jurik, N. C. (1999). Socialist feminism, criminology, and social justice. In B. A. Arrigo (Ed.), *Social justice/criminal justice: The maturation of critical theory in law, crime, and deviance* (pp. 31–50). Belmont, CA: Wadsworth.

Klein, D. (1982). The dark side of marriage: Battered wives and the domination of women. In N. Rafter & E. Stanko (Eds.), *Judge, lawyer, victim, thief: Women, gender roles, and criminal justice* (pp. 83–107). Boston, MA: Northeastern University Press.

Kocieniewski, D., & Hanley, R. (2000, November 28). Racial profiling was the routine, New Jersey finds. *The New York Times,* p. 1.

Kornhauser, R. R. (1978). *Social sources of delinquency.* Chicago: University of Chicago Press.

Lynch, M. J., Michalowski, R., & Groves, W. B. (2000). *The new primer in radical criminology: Critical perspectives on crime, power, and identity.* Monsey, NY: Criminal Justice Press.

Lynch, M. J., & Patterson, E. P. (1996). *Justice with prejudice.* Albany, NY: Harrow and Heston.

Lynch, M. J., & Stretesky, P. (1999). Marxism and social justice: Thinking about social justice, eclipsing criminal justice. In B. A. Arrigo (Ed.), *Social justice/criminal justice: The maturation of critical theory in law, crime, and deviance* (pp. 14–29). Belmont, CA: Wadsworth.

Luckenbill, D., & Doyle, D. P. (1989). Structural position and violence: Developing a cultural explanation. *Criminology, 27,* 419–436.

Mann, C., & Zatz, M. (1998). *Images of crime, images of color.* Los Angeles, CA: Roxbury.

Manning, P. K. (1988). *Symbolic communication: Signifying calls and the police response.* Cambridge, MA: MIT Press.

Matsueda, R. L., Gartner, R., Piliavin, I., & Polakowski, M. (1992). The prestige of criminal and conventional occupations. *American Sociological Review, 57,* 752–770.

Matthews, R., & Young, J. (Eds.). (1992). *Issues in realist criminology.* London: Sage.

McGarrell, E., & Castellano, T. (1991). An integrative conflict model of the criminal law formation process. *Journal of Research in Crime and Delinquency, 28*(2), 174–196.

McGee, J. P., & DeBernardo, C. R. (1999). The classroom avenger: Behavioral profile of school based shootings. *Forensic Examiner, 8,* 16–18.

Merton, R. K. (1938). Social structure and anomie. *American Sociological Review, 3*(5), 672–682.

Merton, R. K. (1968). *Social theory and social structure.* New York: The Free Press.

Messerschmidt, J. (1993). *Capitalism, patriarch, and crime: Critique and reconceptualization of theory.* Totowa, NJ: Rowan & Littlefield.

Messner, S. F., & Rosenfeld, R. (2001). *Crime and the American dream* (3rd ed.). Belmont, CA: Wadsworth/Thomas Learning.

Michalowski, R. (1985). *Law, order, and power.* New York: Random House.

Miller, W. B. (1958). Lower class culture as a generating milieu of gang delinquency. *Journal of Social Issues, 14*(3), 5–19.

Milovanovic, D. (1992). *Postmodern law and disorder: On psychoanalytic semiotics, chaos theory, and juridic exegese.* Liverpool, UK: Deborah Charles.

Milovanovic, D. (Ed.). (1997). *Chaos, criminology and social justice: The new orderly (dis)order.* New York: Praeger.

Milovanovic, D., & Russell, K. (2001). *Petite apartheid in the U.S. criminal justice system: The dark figure of racism.* Durham, NC: Carolina Academic Press.

Mish, F. C., et al. (Eds.). (1996). *Merriam-Webster's Collegiate Dictionary* (10th ed.). Springfield, MA: Merriam-Webster.

Nelsen, C., Corzine, J., & Huff-Corzine, L. (1994). The violent West re-examined. *Criminology, 32*(1), 149–161.

Orru, M. (1987). *Anomie: History and meanings.* Boston: Allen & Unwin.

Pepinsky, H. (1991). *The geometry of violence.* Bloomington, IN: Indiana University Press.

Pepinsky, H. (1999). Peacemaking primer. In B. A. Arrigo (Ed.), *Social justice/criminal justice: The maturation of critical theory in law, crime, and deviance* (pp. 52–70). Belmont, CA: Wadsworth.

Pepinsky, H., & Quinney, R. (Eds.). (1991). *Criminology as peacemaking.* Bloomington, IN: Indiana University Press.

Piquero, N. L., & Sealock, M. D. (2000). Generalizing general strain theory: An examination of an offending population. *Justice Quarterly, 17,* 449–484.

Platt, T., & Takagi, P. (1974). *Punishment and penal discipline*. San Francisco, CA: Crime and Social Justice Associates.

Quinney, R. (1970). *Social reality of crime*. Boston, MA: Little, Brown.

Quinney, R. (1974). *Critique of legal order*. Boston, MA: Little, Brown.

Reiman, J. H. (2001). *The rich get richer and the poor get prison: Ideology, class, and criminal justice* (5th ed.). Boston: Allyn & Bacon.

Rosenfeld, R., & Messner, S. F. (1997). Markets, morality, and an institutional-anomie theory of crime. In N. Passas & R. Agnew (Eds.), *The future of anomie theory* (pp. 207–224). Boston: Northeastern University Press.

Russell, K. K. *The color of crime*. New York: New York University Press.

Sampson, R. J., Raudenbush, S. W., & Earls, F. (1997, August 15). Neighborhoods and violent crime: A multilevel study of collective efficacy. *Science, 277,* 918–924.

Schwendinger, J., & Schwendinger, H. (1983). *Rape and inequality*. Beverly Hills, CA: Sage.

Sellin, J. T. (1938). *Culture, conflict and crime*. New York: Social Science Research Council.

Shaw, C. R., & McKay, H. D. (1972). *Juvenile delinquency and urban areas*. Chicago: University of Chicago Press.

Shipley, S. L., & Arrigo, B. A. (2004). *The female homicide offender: Serial murder and the case of Aileen Wuornos*. Upper Saddle River, NJ: Prentice Hall.

Short, J. F., Jr. (1997). *Poverty, ethnicity, and violent crime*. Boulder, CO: Westview Press.

Simon, R. (1975). *The contemporary woman and crime*. Washington DC: U.S. Government Printing Office.

Smart, C. (1995). *Law, crime, and sexuality: Essays in feminism*. Newbury Park, CA: Sage.

Speck, F. G. (1933). Ethical attributes of the Labrador Indians. *American Anthropologist, 35,* 559–594.

Stanko, E. (1985). *Intimate intrusions: Women's experience of male violence*. London: Routledge.

Steadman, H. J., McGreevy, M. A., Morrissey, J. P., Callahan, L. A., Robbins, P. C., Cirincione, C. (1993). *Before and after Hinckley: Evaluating insanity defense reform*. New York: Guilford.

Sullivan, D., & Tifft, L. (2001). *Restorative justice: Healing the foundations of our everyday lives*. Monsey, NY: Willow Tree Press.

Tatum, B. L. (2000). Toward a neocolonial model of adolescent crime and violence. *Journal of Contemporary Criminal Justice, 16*(2), 157–170.

Taylor, I., Walton, P., & Young, J. (1973). *The new criminology: For a social theory of deviance*. New York: Harper & Row.

Vitello, C. (2003). Peacemaking criminology and stalking. *Journal of Forensic Psychology Practice, 3*(4), 1–41.

Vold, G. B., Bernard, T. J., & Snipes, J. B. (1998). *Theoretical criminology* (4th ed.). New York: Oxford University Press.

Walker, S. (2001). *Sense and nonsense about crime and drugs: A policy guide* (5th ed.). Belmont, CA: ITP/Wadsworth.

Walklate, S. (1998). *Understanding criminology: Current theoretical debates*. Buckingham, Great Britain: Open University Press.

White, R., & Haines, F. (2000). *Crime and criminology* (2nd ed.). South Melbourne, Australia: Oxford University Press.

Williams, C. R., & Arrigo, B. A. (2001). Anarchaos and order: On the emergence of social justice. *Theoretical Criminology: An International Journal, 5*(2), 223–552.

Williams, C. R., & Arrigo, B. A. (2002). *Law, psychology, and justice: Chaos theory and the new (dis)order*. Albany, NY: State University of New York Press.

Williams, C. R., & Arrigo, B. A. (2004). The geometry of peace: Reflections on violence and social change. In C. R. Williams & B. Arrigo (Eds.), *Theory, justice and social change: Theoretical integrations and critical applications,* (pp. 43–64). New York: Kluwer Academic/Plenum Publishing.

Williams, F. P. (1999). *Imagining criminology: An alternative paradigm*. New York: Garland Publishing, Inc.

Wolfgang, M. E. (1958). *Patterns of criminal homicide*. Philadelphia, PA: University of Pennsylvania Press.

Wolfgang, M. E., & Ferracuti, F. (1981). *The subculture of violence*. Beverly Hills, CA: Sage.

Wonders, N. A. (1999). Postmodern feminist criminology and social justice. In B. A. Arrigo (Ed.), *Social justice/criminal justice: The maturation of critical theory in law, crime, and deviance* (pp. 111–128). Belmont, CA: Wadsworth.

Young, A. (1996). *Images of crime*. London: Sage.

Young, J. (1999). *Exclusive society: Social exclusion, crime, and difference in late modernity*. London: Sage.

Young, J., & Matthews, R. (1992). *Rethinking criminology: The realist debate*. London: Sage.

chapter 4

Social–Psychological Theories

OVERVIEW

Biological, psychological, and sociological explanations rely on the theoretical and methodological tools of their respective disciplines to account for the presence of delinquency and crime in society. However, social–psychological theories are more eclectic and borrow heavily from various conceptions of human behavior to account for criminal conduct. This chapter examines three of the more prominent social–psychological theories that have received considerable research attention over the years. In particular, **social control theory, labeling theory,** and **social learning theory** are examined. What each of these perspectives uniquely discloses is that crime is an interactive process involving such factors as **social bonds,** ideas, meanings, definitions, cognitions, and associations. These important elements recast our understanding of the nature of criminal behavior. According to social–psychological accounts, crime is not so much a function of biological determinants, psychological predispositions, or sociological forces; rather, it is the result of ongoing, human social interaction. In this regard, both the condition of people and the environment of which they are a part are implicated in the process of making deviance, delinquency, and crime realities.

KEY TERMS

Attachment	Media violence
Behavior potential	Megan's Law
Belief	Modeling
Commitment	Racial profiling
Cue	Reciprocal determinism
Differential association	Reinforcement
Differential association theory	Reinforcement value
Differential reinforcement	Secondary deviance
Drive	Self-control
Expectancy	Sex stereotyping
General theory of crime	Social bonds
Generalized expectancies	Social control theory
Imitation	Social learning theory
Involvement	Specific expectancies
Labeling theory	Status degradation ceremony

CONTROL THEORY

Introduction

Many areas of psychological research address the growing problem of delinquency and crime. Chapter 2 reviews a number of these popular approaches. However, many of the psychological theories clash with or are incompatible with the perceptions of society as a whole. For example, Gottfredson and Hirschi (1990) offer the following scenario:

> If one asks an ordinary citizen, a probation officer, or a prison counselor which American institution is most responsible for crime and delinquency, he or she will typically answer "the family." If, on the other hand, one asks a delinquency theorist or researcher which American institution is most responsible, he or she will usually reply "the school." This perception follows from the major theories of delinquency and from the dominant research traditions of the field. (p. 159)

What this passage reveals is an inherent disconnect between society and the research community on the causes of delinquent or criminal conduct. In other words, many psychological investigators believe the educational system is most responsible for delinquent behavior; however, the general public's viewpoint is that the family is the cause of delinquency and crime.

One way to bridge the divide between societal and psychological accounts of criminal behavior is to look at social–psychological explanations. There are two major social–psychological perspectives that address crime: social control theory and **differential association theory** (Erickson, Crosnoe, & Dornbusch, 2000). Differential association is a social learning approach that is examined in the second portion of this chapter. However, in this section of the chapter, social control theory is reviewed.

Early control theories included the work of Reiss (1951), Toby (1957), Nye (1958), and, to a lesser extent, Matza (1964). Matza's work in *Delinquency and Drift* represented something of a departure from traditional control theories. Early control theorists insisted that delinquency was the product of constraint and differentiation (Vold, Bernard, & Snipes, 1998). Matza argued that wayward youth experience freedom and similarity. When social controls are weak, delinquents drift from one source of activity to the next, including responsiveness to criminal and noncriminal forces. Thus, for Matza, understanding delinquency meant addressing those factors that loosened social control; that is, made drift likely.

The modern-day understanding of control theory is perhaps best personified in the work of Travis Hirschi, especially in his text, *Causes of Delinquency* (1969). Hirschi's theory was initially used to explain juvenile delinquency, but its appeal and applicability has broadened considerably over the years. Indeed, researchers have relied on it to account for such behaviors as alcohol use, illegal drug use, and tobacco use (Aseltine, 1995). Social control theory was also originally conceived as a testable explanation for the criminal behavior exhibited by males (Erickson et al., 2000).

Most of the research generated by social control theory has been conducted on adolescents who complete a self-report survey. However, some studies examining control theory have also assessed adults (Alarid, Burton, & Cullen, 2000). A more recent reformulation of Hirschi's (1969) ideas is found in Gottfredson and Hirschi's text, *A General Theory of Crime* (1990). Briefly stated, their **general theory of crime** hypothesizes that an individual's engagement in criminal and antisocial behavior is caused by the same factors in every age group throughout the life course. Therefore, Gottfredson and Hirschi assert that the features of criminality are stable over time. This portion of the chapter explores the basic ideas of control theory and its social–psychological application to delinquency.

Social Control Theory: An Overview

The main assumption of social control theory is that the motivations for delinquent behavior are constant across all individuals. Hirschi (1969) believed that deviant acts were not learned behaviors; rather, they were an expression of natural tendencies. The basis for his assumption stemmed from the fact that deviant behaviors provide a rapid means of gratification for the unfulfilled needs and desires that all people possess (Erickson et al., 2000). In this regard, control theory does not question why people commit crime; instead, it wonders why more (or most) people do not commit crime.

Hirschi (1969) also hypothesized that different levels of deviance were triggered by the strength of one's bond to conventional societal practices. In other words, the stronger the bond, the less likely one would be to act delinquently or to engage in criminal behavior. This is because strong social bonds do not reinforce deviant behavior. If they did, the result would be the loss of personal relationships, broken commitments, and failed or blocked accomplishments (Erickson et al., 2000). Conversely, the weaker the social bond, the greater the likelihood that an individual would behave delinquently or commit criminal acts. This is especially the case if the deviance results in personal gain.

Some efforts to advance our understanding of control theory suggest that the bonds are strengthened and weakened by association. In simpler terms, most of a child's associations occur through one's parents or parental surrogates. As such, nonconforming or unconventional parents may weaken a child's social bond, resulting in adolescent displays of unacceptable, inappropriate, and deviant behavior (Elliot, 1985). Moreover, weakened social bonds caused by negative parental perceptions and attitudes may increase the probability of childhood delinquency (Wadsworth, 2000).

According to Hirschi (1969), there are four elements of the social bond that reinforce law-abiding behavior. From his perspective, it is not possible to have an individual with strong bonds who then acts delinquently. These elements include **attachment, commitment, involvement,** and **belief.** The following table summarily presents these elements and describes what each signifies. Attachment relates to an individual's investment in people, especially family, peers, and other close intimates. When an individual has strong attachments, he or she does not want to disrupt personal relationships that disappoint others. Hence, an attached individual is less likely to commit delinquent acts. Commitment refers to one's investment in conventional society. When a person is "dug in" or has a clear and rational stake in maintaining one's commitments, then delinquent conduct is not likely. When a person is goal oriented and focused on attaining positive ends, then the individual is less likely to engage in activities that will jeopardize the achievement of those goals. Involvement refers to the amount of time an individual spends engaging in conventional activities, for example, school. When an individual is frequently involved in positive, healthy, normative activity, there is less time for that individual to commit delinquent acts. Beliefs refer to one's adoption of society's rules. The extent to which an individual abides by social norms, conventions, and shared values is the extent to which that person will not act delinquently or criminally. Overall, an individual with strong social attachments, strong commitments, increased social involvement, and strong, prosocial beliefs is less likely to engage in deviant behaviors.

Fundamental Elements of Hirschi's Social Bond

Element	Description
Attachment	Facilitates internalization of conventional values and norms; emotional connection to others
Commitment	Logical, rational stake in conformity and the risks one faces when acting deviantly; pro-social goals
Involvement	Ongoing participation in conventional activities inhibits the likelihood for delinquent or criminal conduct
Belief	The extent to which one believes in and follows the rules of society; the lower the belief, the greater the likelihood of delinquent or criminal behavior

Control theory proposes that social bonds will have a significant impact on deviance, despite negative or positive peer associations. Opponents of control theory criticize it for its failure to significantly address the effect of peer relationships on adolescent deviance. Previous research has shown that an individual's association with delinquent peers is one of the most telling predictors of delinquent behavior (Erickson et al., 2000). For example, Agnew (1993) found that individuals are motivated to commit wrongful acts when delinquent peers provide a model for deviant action and when peers provide **reinforcement** for those behaviors. Indeed, as Gottfredson and Hirschi (1990) indicated:

> Adolescents do tend to commit delinquent acts in the company of others. This fact is traditionally taken as consistent with a group-support hypothesis and inconsistent with a control perspective. The delinquent commits delinquent acts because he is in a gang; breaking up the gang would therefore reduce the likelihood of delinquent acts. (p. 158)

Thus, although Hirschi's (1969) social control theory did not address the correlation between adolescent peer relationships and delinquent behavior in depth, his subsequent work with Gottfredson (Gottfredson & Hirschi, 1990) did take into account this correlation.

LaGrange and White (1985) conducted a study that simulated Hirschi's (1969) control theory. They demonstrated that it was accurate when the "mechanisms that should prevent it [i.e., deviance] . . . were not operating effectively" (p. 20). Their research focused on several factors that could induce delinquency. These factors included socioeconomic status, parental authority, school influence, and delinquent associates.

LaGrange and White (1985, p. 36) also commented on the role of self-report data. Self-report data imply that there is a developmental paradigm to delinquency. This developmental paradigm suggests that with most forms of adolescent misconduct, deviant behavior will increase until age 15 or 16 and will gradually decrease thereafter. As the researchers concluded, because adolescence is a period in which outside influences significantly affect the youth's personality development, reinforcement of antisocial behavior by external forces is simply not appropriate.

For example, consider the potentially harmful effects of placing a juvenile delinquent in a detention facility, jail, or prison with other offenders. In this instance, the question is whether and to what extent the incarcerated individuals will reinforce the delinquent's misbehavior in the facility. To the extent that they do, the juvenile will continue to practice antisocial behaviors throughout adolescence, while in correctional settings, and into adulthood.

Another pertinent issue in control theory is the ability to express self-control. **Self-control** is a determining factor in adolescent peer group relationships and in the quality of those relationships (Akers, 1991; Gottfredson & Hirschi, 1990). Gottfredson and Hirschi hypothesized that adolescents who had close social bonds within their peer group were less likely to be deviant than were those adolescents who had weak social bonds or no ties in their peer group. In their research, Gottfredson and Hirschi found that individuals who had less self-control were more likely to engage in deviant behavior. Commenting on their work, Vazsonyi, Pickering, Junger, and Hessing (2001) indicate that "high self-control . . . is a stable individual tendency that lets the actor avoid immediate or momentary acts and behaviors whose costs and consequences exceed the long-term benefits" (p. 92).

A study conducted by Arneklev, Grasmick, Tittle, and Bursik (1993) examined the relationship between self-control and noncriminal, irresponsible acts. Arneklev et al. found that a lack of self-control did not significantly predict an individual's engagement in noncriminal, irresponsible behaviors. However, these investigators did note that a significant relationship existed when extraneous variables (i.e., age, sex, and race) were held constant. In a similar study, Wood, Pfefferbaum, and Arneklev (1993) examined the relationship between adolescent risk taking and self-control. They concluded that levels of self-control were related to different types of risk-taking behaviors. Both studies suggest that self-control is an important factor in the prediction of delinquency (see also Polawski, 1994).

Social Control Theory and Adolescent Misconduct

According to Dukes and Stein (2001), "from the perspective of social control theory deviant behavior is the result of an absence of social (external) or personal (internal) controls" (p. 337). Given that control theory asserts that juvenile delinquents lack such controls, the absence of these internal and external inhibitors represent risk factors for deviant behavior. Again, this is because the theory posits that the main source of delinquent behavior is the weak link between an individual and the conventional norms of society (Bernberg & Thorlindsson, 1999).

Following control theory, adolescent violence is the result of a separation between the juvenile and his or her social bonds (i.e., attachment, commitment, involvement, and belief). These bonds are rooted in family systems, schools, and conventional beliefs. Additionally, delinquency and adolescent violence are influenced in the same manner as is non-violent behavior. In other words, positively enforced social controls work to minimize adolescent crime and violence, whereas nonenforced social controls and poorly enforced social bonds support delinquent behaviors (Akers, 1991; Polawski, 1994).

Bernberg and Thorlindsson (1999) conducted a study in which they hypothesized that violence, like other forms of delinquency, was influenced by social control variables. Their research explained how social bond processes and adolescent violence were correlated. In particular, the investigators found that social control variables affect not only conventional institutions but also all types of violent offending and illegal activities. Some illegal activities included in this category of adolescent offending were cigarette smoking and alcohol consumption. As agents of social control weaken or break down (e.g., family members, coaches, and teachers), adolescents become more vulnerable to suggestive learning from delinquent peers. Adolescents who become more vulnerable under these conditions are also more susceptible to suicidal thoughts and to membership in peer groups who engage in life-threatening rituals (Bernberg & Thorlindsson).

In another study, conducted by Houtzager and Baerveldt (1999), the researchers examined the relationship between adolescent petty crime and adolescent social bonds. The study found that more offenses were committed when school friends played a less significant role in the life of the adolescent. The study also noted that juvenile girls who had more intimate and emotional friendships with peers than did their male counterparts also had a decreased tendency to engage in delinquent behaviors. This research further confirmed Hirschi's (1969) control theory, highlighting the importance of social bonds.

A study conducted by Foshee, Bauman, and Linder (1999) examined the relationship between the tenets of social control theory and those of adolescent dating violence. The researchers found that the social bond and control variables were associated with the causes of dating violence. More specifically, the commitment variable was related to the commission of violence by females, and the belief variable was related to the commission of violence by males. In addition, the study indicated that exposure to family violence related more to control theory variables for males than it did for females. Males who were less attached to their family (specifically their mothers) were less committed to conventional activities and had fewer beliefs that were consistent with the traditional rules of the community. This study also explored the idea that social bond variables represent consequences of adolescent dating violence and not causes of adolescent dating violence. In short, the researchers argued that violent adolescent behavior might result in parental violence when the youth matured. Under these conditions, this makes control theory variables a consequence rather than a cause of adolescent violence.

Social Control Theory Beyond Adolescent Delinquency

A frequent question raised by social control theorists is whether the theory is generalizable to criminal behavior beyond the realm of juveniles. Most research testing the explanatory capabilities of social control theory focuses on adolescent delinquency, particularly less serious offenses. However, a study conducted by Alarid et al. (2000) examined the relationships between adult social bonds and criminality. In this investigation, the social bond was measured by marital attachment, attachment to parents, attachment to friends, involvement, and belief. When examining an adult population, it is important to measure one's attachment to one's significant other because cohabitation or marriage is an important aspect of informal social control. Indeed, a person's intimate partner can often protect or inhibit the individual from pursuing deviant or criminal activities.

Measuring attachment by an adult's bond to his or her parents is also significant because one's emotional investments in one's parents determines the effect of the parent–child relationship with respect to gender. Measuring attachment by assessing the quality, type, and intensity of one's friendships is a staple of conventional social control theory analysis of delinquent youth. This same logic applies to adults. Involvement, or the amount of idle time an individual possesses, is as consistent a measure of the social bond for adolescents as it is for adults. The beliefs of adults are measured through their moral regard for the law or, more specifically, their belief in the function and legitimacy of police work.

Overall, the study conducted by Alarid et al. (2000) found that the aforementioned measures provided support for the notion that social control theory is applicable to adults. The researchers indicated that parental bonds have a continuing effect on offenders into adulthood. In addition, the hypothesis that involvement in conventional activities is negatively associated with criminal behavior was supported by the research findings.

Limits of Social Control Theory

The limitations of social control theory are evident in three important areas. First, most research is based on self-report surveys. These data are inherently suspect because of the nature, quality, and accuracy of the reporting by youth. Second, most of the research addresses one type of criminal activity, namely, less serious forms of juvenile delinquency. Thus, the theory's ability to broadly explain adolescent misconduct is questionable. Third, the explanatory capabilities of control theory in relation to adult criminality have not been significantly tested. Thus, there is some question about the theory's generalizability. However, as Vold et al. (1998, p. 217) conclude, "the combination of a testable theory with a research technique [i.e., self-report surveys] that produces supportive results is very attractive [to researchers]." The future of social control theory, as a viable explanation for criminal and deviant behavior, depends on the efforts of investigators to test and evaluate the various aspects of the social bond.

LABELING THEORY

Labeling theory maintains that people are often led to believe the socially constructed definitions that are applied to them; therefore, they live up to or otherwise embrace the stigmatizing characterizations assigned to them. Our self-images are influenced by how we think, act, and react to the environment. Thus, people are likely to perform deeds consistent with how they define themselves and the meaning that they make in the face of these definitions (Cooley, 1902).

Where do these stigmatizing or marginalizing labels originate? According to the theory's proponents, they are mostly traceable to the very social organizations entrusted with eliminating or otherwise neutralizing the presence of such destructive characterizations. "Often mistrustful of institutions, such as schools, mental hospitals, police, courts, and correctional agencies, labeling advocates find it logical that these institutions produce the stigma that is so harmful to the very people they are trying to help, treat, or correct" (Siegel, 1992, p. 238).

Consider the example of how individuals are funneled through the criminal justice system. People are arrested, detained, tried, and sentenced in order to solidify and affix the label of "criminal" on them, notwithstanding any protests to the contrary on behalf of offenders and their self-image. Labeling theory suggests that societal institutions such as the legal or mental health system categorize and define persons as "guilty offenders" or "mentally ill" such that these labels become part and parcel of one's identity and, as such, a debilitating, lifelong burden. In this way, " . . . a criminal trial can be interpreted as a **'status degradation ceremony'** in which the public identity of the person is lowered on the social scale" (Vold et al., 1998, p. 222). This assessment is consistent with Garfinkel's (1965) position that every society has such ceremonies and that these ceremonies are instituted as a means of social control.

When an offender's sense of self is stripped away, it occurs in the form of a public trial or hearing that can have devastating and humiliating consequences. At the very least, the tarnished (social) image keeps the person at a considerable disadvantage, especially compared to those not so defined as criminal. This identity stripping is perhaps best illustrated by the relabeling process that takes place when an offender is released from prison and is identified as an "ex-con." Having served time behind bars and experienced the revocation of voting rights, the person now has his or her criminal records, fingerprints, and DNA samples on file for the length of the individual's life. Under these conditions, the label of ex-con serves only to ensure a greater sense of safety among society at large, as its members can readily identify those people who are different from others who follow the established social norms.

In some instances, individuals may refuse to accept or embrace the label assigned to them, even if their behaviors are consistent with the identity given to them by others and by social institutions. These are situations in which society conveniently classifies them by their actions. Thus, if the individual steals from another, then the person is a "thief." If the person has nonconsensual sex with another, then the individual is a "rapist." If the person takes the life of another, then the individual is a "murderer."

However, many offenders destabilize these labels by denying responsibility for their behaviors. In fact, individuals may incorporate techniques that undo the sting of the label, attempting to erode any accountability for their behavior (Sykes & Matza, 1957). These techniques of neutralization are employed so that the person can maintain a noncriminal self-image, enabling the individual to define his or her situation as harmless and his or her status as a nonoffender. In reality, though, society constructs and maintains labels for criminals, according to the theory. Therefore, no matter how hard offenders consciously, or unconsciously, attempt to define or to redefine their identities on their own terms, society will be reluctant to embrace or permit such changes.

Techniques of Neutralization

In *Delinquency and Drift* (1964), David Matza described several strategies youth employ to rationalize their deviant or illicit behavior. The most common of these and what they mean are listed in the following table. See if you have used any before.

Technique	Meaning
1. Denial of responsibility	"I'm not to blame; I was just a victim."
2. Denial of the victim	"Anybody would have done what I did if in my situation; I did what I had to do."
3. Denial of injury	"Nobody got hurt and if anyone had been injured their insurance would cover it."
4. Condemnation of the condemner	"I bet that my parents have done much worse than what I was punished for."
5. Appeal to higher loyalties	"A lot of people were counting on me; it wouldn't have been right to let them down."

For example, a clean and sober heroin abuser is assigned a label consistent with the person's past behavior. Indeed, the individual simply acquires a new, albeit just as marginalizing, self-definition. Typically, the person is identified as a "reformed heroin addict" or as a "heroin addict in remission." These characterizations retain their degrading status, stigmatizing the individual from the perspective of society and, more profoundly, from one's own perspective.

When a person begins to incorporate criminal behaviors into one's self-image, the individual experiences **secondary deviance** (Lemert, 1967). Once this occurs, the person allows the designation of criminal to become a driving force in his or her interaction with others. "At this point, Lemert argues, criminal behavior is no longer generated by the various biological, psychological, and social factors in the person's life, but is generated directly by the person's criminal self-image" (Vold et al., 1998, p. 222). Under these conditions, criminality is the result of a fearful society—a culture blinded to the fact that the very labels it constructs out of apprehension, misunderstanding, and ignorance set the stage for criminality and deviance to persist (e.g., Becker, 1963; Scheff, 2000).

Another consequence of labeling is that the stigmatized criminal may primarily associate with other people who have been similarly identified for help and support (Lemert, 1967). "At the conclusion of the labeling process, stigmatized people find themselves isolated from conventional society and locked into deviant careers and thereafter may identify themselves as members of an outcast group" (Siegel, 1992, p. 238). Outcasts form associations either because they are grouped or institutionalized together (e.g., a reform school, a jail, or a psychiatric facility) or because other people refuse to interact with them (Goffman, 1959, 1961). Moreover, "membership in an exclusively criminal group can increase the

Labeling Sex and Adolescent Rape

Consider the example of an 18-year-old boy who has sexual relations with his 16-year-old girlfriend. The girl's parents find out and bring charges of statutory rape against the boy (most states classify statutory rape as sex with a minor even if the act was consensual). Even if the boy is acquitted of such charges, he must live with the stigma that accompanies the accusations of rape. "As the negative feedback of law enforcement agencies, parents, friends, teachers, and other figures amplifies the force of the original label, stigmatized offenders may begin to reevaluate their own identities" (Siegel, 1992, p. 240). Labeling theory suggests that if the boy internalizes this image that was thrust on him by the rape charges, he may come to believe that he truly embodies the behavior underlying the label. Simply put, he may then be forced into a criminal role because of public stereotypes about criminals and about nonconsensual intercourse.

Prison

Vold et al. (1998, p. 223) provide another illustration of the labeling process and its relationship to criminal behavior: "On release from prison a person may be unable to obtain legitimate employment due to the criminal conviction and may then return to crime to survive" (the reintegration of criminals back into society is examined in chapter 11). This example amplifies one unintended consequence of the operation of the criminal justice system. In short, the impact of prosecuting and convicting an individual may lead the ex-offender to adopt a criminal lifestyle in order to make good in a society that defines the person as a deviant. Scheff (1975, p. 9) makes a similar argument in relation to the mentally ill: "[L]abeled deviants may be rewarded for playing the stereotyped deviant role [and] labeled deviants are punished when they attempt to return to conventional roles."

likelihood that individuals will resort to a criminal self-image rather than attempt to retain a noncriminal self-image" (Vold et al., 1998, p. 223). According to labeling theorists, these circumstances raise serious questions about whether social stigmas and marginalizing self-definitions generate more deviant, delinquent, and criminal conduct than they can possibly eliminate (Tittle, 1975).

Criticisms of Labeling Theory

There are numerous shortcomings to labeling theory. For example, Akers (1967) questioned if the power of a social label was not overestimated. As he explained:

> One sometimes gets the impression from reading this literature that people go about minding their own business, and then— "wham"—bad society comes along and slaps them with a stigmatized label. Forced into the role of deviant the individual has little choice but to be deviant. (Akers, 1967, p. 463)

This is a valid criticism. Indeed, people typically acquire public labels because they ignore societal rule in the first place. In response, however, labeling theorists assert persons in positions or relative authority and power establish the rules. As such, these established standards for behavior function to oppress and stigmatize certain groups of individuals (Goffman, 1959). Deviating from these rules means that the norm violator will be identified and labeled accordingly.

Another criticism of labeling theory is that it generally describes the deviant as refusing to accept his or her status, and then describes the person as accepting the label only when it is impossible to resist or do otherwise. Admittedly, this process does operate for some individuals; however, it does not operate for all individuals. As Vold et al. (1998) observe, in some cases "it would appear that the deviant identity is actively sought and that the person may form a deviant identity without ever having been officially or unofficially labeled" (p. 223). Thus, although all expressions of criminal behavior may have some relationship to the particular labels assigned to those who engage in deviant conduct, it is unclear whether, and to what extent, the label influences one's self-image or affects one's conduct. Indeed, the questions are: At what point, if at all, did the "criminal" stigma attach to the offender?; and how did the assigned definition get translated into a representation of the person's self-image, resulting in delinquent or criminal actions? (See Gove, 1975, for an explanation of this notion, especially in relation to mental illness.)

Recent studies conducted on juvenile delinquency, parental labels, and adolescent self-definitions have explored these questions at some length. For example, Matsueda (1992) found that the juvenile perceptions in which they are delinquent are significantly influenced by the interpretation others have of them as norm violators or as deviants. Moreover, these perceptions are strongly affected by the labels parents assign to their children. Complicating these definitions are instances in which youth embrace the delinquent role, irrespective of parental labels that they are rule violators (Heimer & Matsueda, 1994). Under these conditions, juveniles recognize that others perceive them as delinquents and so they incorporate this role into their self-image, giving rise to criminal conduct.

A third criticism of labeling theory is that fear of the legal system is typically sufficient to dissuade most law-abiding people from pursuing criminal behavior in the first place. "The average citizen is deterred from committing most crimes because he or she fears the conviction itself rather than the punishment associated with it" (Vold et al., 1998, p. 224). In other words, the threat of sanction (e.g., loss of income or prison time) rather than the actual administration of it, or the effect such punishment would have on one's self-image, works to prevent, deter, and control crime. Fear of criminal sanction is not synonymous with labeling, and the relationship between the two is difficult to assess.

Social Implications of Labeling Theory

Labeling theory attempts to demonstrate how society assigns or bestows power to certain institutions and individuals in order to keep entire groups of people on a social margin. In particular, the theory questions the efficacy of the entire justice system. Labeling theorists liken the system's behavior to a "social degradation ceremony." This is because social institutions (e.g., police, court, and correctional agencies) believe they can change or at least influence the conduct of individuals by affixing a stigmatizing identity on them. Then, too, society maintains that everyone should, generally speaking, embrace normative values, that is, culturally, ethnically, racially, and sexually similar outlooks on human interaction and civic life. Labeling theorists argue that these are social constructions designed to encourage us to rethink how we behave differently from the rest of conventional society. Moreover, in the face of our differences, these social constructions prompt personal change, making our behavior more consistent with rule followers rather than with rule violators.

One example of how this approach to normative or rule-bound values influences behavior comes from sexually violent predator statutes. Indeed, one popular policy gaining legislative and public approval across the country is **Megan's Law.** This law requires sex offenders to notify the community of their neighborhood presence. "Twenty-eight states run Internet sites listing such criminals. In the mid-1990s, judges in Texas, Louisiana, Florida, and Oregon [went so far as to order] individual sex offenders to post signs outside their homes" (Booth Thomas, 2001, p. 82; for more on sex offender registration, see chapter 11).

In Texas, District Court Judge J. Manuel Banales required that sex offenders place bumper stickers on their cars, "and even placards for traveling in someone else's car" (Booth Thomas, 2001, p. 82), alerting the public that the driver was convicted for sex-related crimes. This status-degradation ritual is consistent with a 1999 Texas law, signed by then Governor George W. Bush, "permitting judges to impose public punishment for some crimes" (Booth Thomas, p. 82). In Texas, convicted drunk drivers are often made to hold signs at busy intersections alerting pedestrians and motorists of their deviant behaviors.

The actions mandated by Judge Banales are extreme forms of labeling that can have profoundly detrimental effects on the offender, as well as on the community. "Landlords evict them and bosses fire them. One man attempted suicide after Banales' ruling [and] the families [of the sexual offender] worry about vigilantes" (Booth Thomas, 2001, p. 82). In most states, perpetrators of sex-related crimes are forced to register with their lo-

cal police. Local law enforcement officials then make public the person's name, address, and offense. For the rest of the individual's life, whenever he or she relocates, a public record of this movement must be provided. In other words, society has legislated labeling as an appropriate response to sex offenders.

Criminals are not the only group forced to bear socially constructed labels. In fact, we all are categorized or stigmatized in one form or another. Consider the following examples: African American youth congregate on an urban street corner and are perceived as "gangbangers"; homeless people live on heating grates and are defined as "drunken, lazy bums"; individuals of Arab or Middle Eastern descent travel and are defined as potential "terrorists"; professional athletes are labeled "greedy"; lawyers are defined as "snakes"; women are characterized as "weak and submissive"; and men, as "chauvinistic"; liberals are classified as "bleeding hearts"; and conservatives, as "mean-spirited." There are even laws that label parents "delinquent" as a consequence of the misdeeds of their children (see chapter 7 for more). It seems as if the labeling process is unavoidable. The question is whether, and to what extent, it fosters personal or collective harm.

One group unfairly burdened by the labeling process is the African American community. This is especially the case with **racial profiling.** Racial profiling occurs when someone is stopped by a police officer because of that person's skin color and a "fleeting suspicion that the person is engaging in criminal behavior" (Meeks, 2000, p. 5). For years, entire police departments have sanctioned this conduct based on the wrongful belief that data generated from past arrest practices represented a reliable indicator of which people were likely to engage in future criminal conduct. In other words, without carefully and thoroughly assessing the basis on which these practices and procedures occurred (e.g., a department's predisposition to act one way toward one group of citizens and another way toward another group of citizens), faulty police decisions become institutionalized. In the case of African Americans and racial profiling, some jurisdictions' arrest and crime statistics are used to justify disproportionately stopping, detaining, and arresting Blacks defined as "potential lawbreakers." This example illustrates the labeling theorist's contention that "the law is differentially constructed and applied" (Siegel, 1992, p. 238; for more on racial profiling, see chapter 9).

Another group of individuals who suffer greatly from the imposition of labels are the mentally ill

(Arrigo, 2002). Scheff (1975) poses the following illustration:

> Suppose that in your next conversation with a stranger, instead of looking at his eyes or mouth, you scrutinize his ear. Although the deviation from ordinary behavior is slight (involving only a shifting of the direction of gaze a few degrees, from the eyes to the ear), its effects are explosive. The conversation is disrupted almost instantaneously . . . the conversation is irretrievably damaged. Shock, anger, and vertigo are experienced not only by the "victim," but, oddly enough, by the experimenter himself. It is virtually impossible for either party to sustain the conversation, or even think coherently, as long as the experiment continues. (pp. 5–6)

The illustration points out the all-pervasive presence of public conformity we take for granted. According to Scheff (1975), there are numerous understandings humans possess when interacting—from gestures, language used, vocal fluctuations in speech, body comportment, and whether one should look into another's eye during conversation or look into the person's ear. "These understandings constitute part of our society's assumptive world, the world that is thought of as normal, decent, and possible" (p. 6).

The pressure of conformity is particularly problematic for persons who experience mental illness. Scheff (2000) and other social theorists (Williams & Arrigo, 2002) contend that labeling people who embody different views of and reactions to the world as mentally ill is a personally debilitating and socially damaging enterprise. Typically, the expression "mental illness" conjures up images of sick, mad, and dangerously perverted individuals who should be kept under close supervision for their own safety and for the security of society (Foucault, 1965). The interpretations associated with the term mental illness give rise to legal and psychiatric practices including involuntary civil commitment and forced drug therapy over the person's objection to it (for more on these topics, see chapters 8 and 11).

Commenting on the corrosive effect of the mental illness label, Scheff (1975) offers the following observations:

> Concepts of mental illness in general are not neutral, value-free, scientifically precise terms but are, for the most part, the leading edge of an ideology embedded in the historical and cultural present of the white middle class of Western societies. The concept of illness and its associated vocabulary— symptoms, therapies, patients, and physicians— reify and legitimate the prevailing public order at the expense of other possible worlds. (pp. 6–7)

In other words, the labels and images we use to describe individuals with mental illness are not chosen randomly, nor are they chosen because they best illustrate the behaviors associated with psychiatric disorder. Instead, they are selected as a way to conveniently validate some forms of behavior and interaction arbitrarily deemed socially appropriate and to denigrate others perceived to be inappropriate, deviant, or otherwise unacceptable.

Even women in our society carry a deviant label (Schur, 1983). As social psychologist Judith Long Laws (1979) explained, "Males as a group constitute the dominant class and females are the deviant class . . . In our society, male is normal (not merely different) and female is deviant, or Other . . . [B]eing female carries a stigma in and of itself" (p. 4). Women are seen as fragile, needing the security of a man for protection—both physically and financially. However, when a woman rejects this label, she is met with resistance and sometimes further discrimination by her male counterparts.

For example, consider the Supreme Court decision in *Price Waterhouse v. Hopkins* (1988). Ann Hopkins was turned down for partnership at Price Waterhouse despite credentials far exceeding those of her closest competitor for the promotion. She was denied partnership primarily because she was not as feminine as the men in her office expected her to be. As a woman, Hopkins was censured for being aggressive even though this personality characteristic was one of the job qualifications (Chamallas, 1990). The Court ruled in favor of Hopkins, relying on the illegal practice of **sex stereotyping** for support and justification. Sex stereotyping occurs when a person is negatively evaluated "based on that person's membership in a group" (Wrightsman, 2001, p. 10). Whether or not we are conscious of it, labels affect us all.

SOCIAL LEARNING THEORY

Introduction

The original school of thought regarding learning theory was that people gain knowledge as the product of a consistent pattern of scheduled reinforcements (Wade & Tavris, 2003). According to Phares (1991), this general model of learning had many shortcomings. First, learning theory failed to acknowledge the role of cognitive variables. "We think, we plan, we believe, and we imagine. Reinforcement does not just occur; it is interpreted, evaluated, and weighed" (p. 342). Second, early studies on human behavior and learning were dominated by Pavlov (1927) and his insights on classical conditioning, and by Skinner (1969) and his work on operant conditioning and radical behaviorism. These theories were based on experiments using animals, not humans. "This is probably why reinforcement came to be emphasized at the expense of cognitions" (Phares, 1991, p. 342). Third, these theories did not account for the fact that human learning takes place in very complex, social environments. "The lonely pigeon in the operant box or the human subject sitting before a complex reaction-time apparatus is not a good research model for human social behavior" (Phares, 1991, p. 342). Finally, early reinforcement theories depicted humans as passive learners, subjected to environmental influence. "In fact, however, we affect our environment just as we are affected by it, and we often choose the environments in which we behave" (Phares, 1991, p. 342).

The final portion of this chapter examines social learning theory. Social learning theory is an attempt to understand the social (and psychological) determinants of learning, giving rise to human conduct. In particular, this section of the chapter explores the relationship between the theory and its ability to account for criminal behavior. Specific and selective application studies along these lines are also discussed.

Social Learning Theory: The Origins

The earliest of social learning theories was developed by John Dollard and Neil Miller (1950). They were concerned with the impact the learning process had on personality development (Barone, Maddux, & Snyder, 1997). Their learning theory was based on a stimulus–response sequence. For Dollard and Miller, this sequence was a useful basis for explaining such personality functioning as intrapersonal processes, the nature and development of personality, the unconscious, and the origins of neurosis (Drapela, 1995).

Dollard and Miller (1950) identified the components of their learning theory in easily understood terms:

> The learner must be driven to make the response and rewarded for having responded in the presence of a cue. This may be expressed in a homely way by saying that in order to learn one must want something, notice something, do something, and get something. Stated more exactly, these factors are drive, cue, response, and reinforcement. (p. 2)

A **drive** can be any strong stimulus that results in a response. A drive can be external (e.g., an electric shock) or it can be internal (e.g., a craving for food). Internal drives are considered primary or innate stimuli, and include such things as hunger, pain, or sexual urges. Primary drives give way to acquiring and learning secondary drives. These are expansions of innate drives in the sociocultural framework of one's environment (Barone et al., 1997). "[Secondary drives] serve as a façade behind which the functions of the underlying innate drives are hidden" (Dollard & Miller, 1950, p. 32).

Similar to a drive, a **cue** is a motivator that determines when an individual will react to a stimulus, where the individual will respond, and how the individual will respond. However, a cue is more precise than a drive. A stimulus's driving power is modified in distinct ways by different cues:

> For instance, hunger pangs motivate a person to eat something; the marquee of a restaurant or the sign of a fast-food store may help the person decide how to respond to the stimulus: by having a full meal or getting a quick snack. It follows that drives and cues have a close functional relationship. (Drapela, 1995, p. 75)

According to Dollard and Miller (1950), a response is triggered by the incentive force of a drive and by the directional effect of a cue. For learning to take place, a response must be elicited and that response must be reinforced. Reinforcement is any occurrence "that strengthens the tendency for a response to be repeated" (Dollard & Miller, 1950, p. 39).

This is also known as drive reduction. For example, in the case of a reformed drug addict, success largely depends on the learner's (the addict's) ability to make appropriate responses (i.e., refuse drugs when offered) that will provide opportunities for reinforcement (self-gratification or the positive reaction from supporters).

According to Drapela (1995), the Dollard and Miller view on the social learning process occurs as follows:

> A previously neutral cue, when sufficiently often paired with a primary drive, acquires the capacity to elicit responses and thus becomes a secondary drive. For instance, the type of food offered to a hungry person will affect the person's taste. Instead of being hungry in general terms, an Italian is probably hungry for pasta, a Hungarian for goulash, and an American for steak or a hamburger. Secondary drives can be viewed as providing maintenance of human life in the context of a given society or culture. (p. 76)

According to Burgess and Akers (1968), criminal behavior is learned both by the positive and the negative reinforcements provided by one's environment (nonsocial situations) as well as by the positive and negative reinforcements provided by members of one's social group (social interactions). This theory recognized that the environment itself could influence and reinforce criminality independent of social interactions (Vold et al., 1998). Akers (1985) later amended this theory to include **modeling** as a factor in criminal conduct. Modeling contends that people learn deviance by observing the behaviors of others and by evaluating the consequences those behaviors have for other people (Meltzoff & Gopnik, 1993). Modeling theory is consistent with the work of Bandura (1977) discussed elsewhere in this section of the chapter.

Building on the insights of Dollard and Miller (1950), Julian Rotter (1954) offered another version of social learning theory. According to Rotter, in any given situation people have the ability to choose a variety of behaviors in order to achieve their goals. In Rotter's view, this human capacity is called **behavior potential.** Behavior potential is the range of actions a person may express in a certain situation in order to attain a particular outcome. Every behavior has the possibility of occurring in all situations; however, those behaviors with the highest potential for achieving one's objective are the actions most likely to follow. To illustrate, jogging with a friend for purposes of physical fitness has high potential, but jogging with a toddler for the same purpose has limited potential. Or, consider the example offered by Phares (1991), "Telling jokes may be high in potential at a party but very weak at a funeral" (p. 346).

Related to the concept of behavioral potential is **expectancy.** Rotter refers to expectancy as the probability that certain reinforcements will occur if a specific behavior is selected. "By the use of this concept, [Rotter] is stating that behavior potential is determined not just by how badly we want a certain goal but also by the extent to which we believe that a specific behavior will do the job" (Phares, 1991, p. 347). There are two types of expectancies: specific and generalized. **Specific expectancies** are applicable to a particular situation. **Generalized expectancies** are applicable to multiple situations. Expectancy is

Expectancy and Adolescent Gang Involvement

The notion of expectancy is relevant for purposes of explaining criminal behavior. Indeed, using Rotter's (1954) concepts of specific and generalized expectancies we can assess an adolescent boy's likely membership in a juvenile gang. If the youth sets unrealistic goals (e.g., to be as financially successful as are the corporate executives portrayed on television), he may be consistently let down by the environmental variables that keep him at home caring for younger siblings rather than attending school. In such a case, the juvenile may consistently set his expectancies to achieve wealth at a very low level, underestimating his potential to legitimately succeed despite the youth's current family situation. If the adolescent is asked by a gang member to join such a group, he may elect to do so given the promise of economic potential (specific expectancy) and his overall belief that he has no other means to achieve his goal of wealth (generalized expectancy).

subjective in nature. People may either be overconfident and set unrealistic expectancies for success with goals or may consistently underestimate the potential for success.

A final construct in Rotter's (1954) social learning theory is **reinforcement value.** Reinforcement value is the degree of preference one has for a particular outcome when all outcomes are equal. "[J]ust as people differ among themselves regarding their expectancies, they also differ in the value they place on various reinforcements. "I prefer steak over seafood; you do not. You order salad; I order soup. And so it goes" (Phares, 1991, p. 348). According to Rotter, the value of reinforcement is subjective and determined primarily by the expectancy that the reinforcement will lead to other reinforcements of value. "[Reinforcement] achieves value only through the individual's expectancy that it will, in turn, lead to something else. The idea that goals have no intrinsic value obviously will provoke a lively debate in some quarters" (Phares, p. 349).

Another approach to social learning theory was developed by Albert Bandura (1977). In his text, *Principles of Behavior Modification* (1969), Bandura emphasized the importance of explicit, figurative, and self-governing processes in psychological performance. In short, he asserted not only that behavior was reinforced through principles of reward and punishment, but also that learning occurred based on expectations generated through observing what happened to others. As he explained, "acknowledgment that human thought, affect, and behavior can be markedly influenced by observation, as well as by direct experience, foster[s] development of observational paradigms for studying the power of socially mediated experience" (Bandura, 1977, p. vii). In other words, learning for humans is very much a social process mediated by what we observe happening to other people and by our expectations that these same consequences will follow for others exposed to the same environmental conditions (Bandura, 1969, p. 118; see also Bandura, 1986).

Bandura (1977) also stressed the importance of the human function to interpret symbols in the learning process. "The extraordinary capacity of humans to use symbols enables them to represent events, to analyze their conscious experience, to communicate with others at any distance in time and space, to plan, to create, to imagine, and to engage in foresightful action" (Bandura, 1977, p. vii). In contrast to other behavioral theories popular during the time, Bandura asserted that human learning was more complex than the mere automated response to positive and negative consequences such as a bell, a treat, or an electric shock.

Another distinguishing feature of Bandura's social learning theory was the pivotal role it granted to self-regulatory processes, including higher mental functioning capabilities characteristic of humans. "People are not simply reactors to external influences. They select, organize, and transform the stimuli that impinge upon them. Through self-regulated inducements and consequences they can exercise some influence over their own behavior" (Bandura, 1977, p. vii). People learn by doing. People develop preferences often by experimenting with judgments and actions (Bandura, 1986). "Recognition of people's self-directing capacities provide[s] the impetus for self-regulatory paradigms of research in which individuals themselves serve as the principal agents of their own change" (Bandura, 1977, p. vii). For Bandura, this did not imply that the environment assumed minimal importance in the learning process; rather, human self-direction acknowledged that learning entailed mental processes that were, to some extent, self-generated and, therefore, were subject to self-regulation and change (Bandura, 1986).

Bandura believed that people behave in certain ways because of continuous reciprocal interaction among cognitive, behavioral, and environmental influences. He called this concept **reciprocal determinism.** As he defined it:

> Personal and environmental factors do not function as independent determinants, rather they determine each other. Nor can "persons" be considered causes independent of their behavior. It is largely through their actions that people produce the environmental conditions that affect their behavior in a reciprocal fashion. The experiences generated by behavior also partly determine what a person becomes and can do which, in turn, affects subsequent behavior. (p. 9)

Within the process of reciprocal determinism, people have the opportunity to exercise free will and to choose their future within limits. "This conception of human functioning then neither casts people into the role of powerless objects controlled by environmental forces nor free agents who can become whatever they choose. Both people and their environment are reciprocal determinants of each other" (Bandura, 1977, p. vii).

Using Bandura's concept of reciprocal determinism, learning is a matter of choice and preference within the limits or confines of one's environment. According to Bandura (1977), people learn by what they see. We behave in ways consistent with what we are exposed to and thus familiar with as a byproduct of our environment. Socially and legally, we are defined by the behaviors we commit as well as by where we live, work, and socialize. Consequently, our environment shapes our behaviors as much as our behaviors inform our environment. For example, a child growing up in a crime-ridden neighborhood has a greater chance of learning that dealing drugs is acceptable behavior than has a child growing up in a community that is more economically and socially stable. If the child grows up and *chooses* to be a drug dealer, then he or she reciprocally influences the neighborhood by promoting crime, behavior acquired from growing up in such an unstable neighborhood.

Bandura did not believe in a unique process by which one could account for deviant or criminal conduct. "Maladjusted behavior is learned in the same manner as adjusted behavior" (Phares, 1991, p. 371). For example, numerous studies indicate that male children run a greater risk of becoming abusive if they are raised in homes where their fathers continually batter their mothers (for more on domestic violence, see chapter 5). According to Bandura's social learning theory, the child has the opportunity to choose not to batter his future partners; however, his environment creates the knowledge (i.e., the expectancy) within the child that violence in the home is normal.

Bandura's (1973) insights on social learning were applied to aggression (see also, Bandura, 1983). He acknowledged that many theories relied on frustration as the root of aggression (e.g., instinct theory, drive theory as discussed in the psychoanalytic portion of chapter 2). However, Bandura did not believe frustration was the simple origin of aggression for human beings:

> In social learning theory, rather than frustration generating an aggressive drive, aversive treatment produces a general state of emotional arousal that can facilitate a variety of behaviors, depending on the types of responses the person has learned for coping with stress and their relative effectiveness. (Bandura, 1973, p. 53)

Thus, aggression represents just one way in which some people learn to deal with stress and, as such, they come to prefer it as a response to frustrating circumstances. However, this is not the case for all individuals. "When distressed, some people seek help and support; others increase achievement strivings; others show withdrawal and resignation; some aggress; others experience heightened somatic activity; still others anesthetize themselves against a miserable existence with drugs or alcohol" (Bandura, 1973, pp. 53–54). For the most part, however, people choose to overcome adversity by intensifying more constructive efforts. From a social learning perspective, what matters are the learned, anticipated consequences (reinforcements) a person expects to receive for making a particular choice in light of the stressors the individual confronts. (For a more in-depth examination of social learning, modeling, and aggression, see Bandura, Ross, & Ross, 1961, and their famous Bobo doll experiment.)

Social Learning Theory and Criminal Behavior

The most coherent application of social learning theory was developed by Edwin Sutherland (1947) over a period of years in revised versions of his text, *Criminology*. His theory has remained largely unchanged since the publication of the book's fourth edition (see also, Sutherland, Cressey, & Luckenbill, 1992). Because of the theory's importance for explaining

Edwin Sutherland's Principles of Differential Association

1. Criminal behavior is learned.
2. Criminal behavior is learned in interaction with other persons in a process of communication.
3. The principal part of the learning of criminal behavior occurs within intimate personal groups . . .
4. When criminal behavior is learned, the learning includes: (a) techniques of committing the crime . . . ; [and] (b) the specific direction of the motives, drives, rationalizations, and attitudes . . .
5. The specific directions of the motives and drives are learned from definitions of the legal codes as favorable or unfavorable . . .
6. A person becomes delinquent because of an excess of definitions favorable to violation of law over definitions unfavorable to violation of law. This is the principal of differential association . . .
7. Differential associations may vary in frequency, duration, priority, and intensity. This means that associations with criminal behavior and also associations with anticriminal behavior vary in those respects . . .
8. The process of learning criminal behavior by association with criminal and anti-criminal patterns involves all of the mechanisms that are involved in any other learning . . .
9. While criminal behavior is an expression of general needs and values, it is not explained by those general needs and values, since noncriminal behavior is an expression of the same needs and values. . . . The attempts by many scholars to explain criminal behavior by general drives and values, such as the happiness principle, striving for social status, the money motive, or frustration, have been, and must continue to be, futile, since they explain lawful behavior as completely as they explain criminal behavior . . .

criminal behavior and because of the straightforward way in which Sutherland summarized it, the essential components of the theory are presented in his own words.

What is significant about Sutherland's (1947) theory of differential association is the recognition that learning entails both a cognitive dimension and an interpersonal dimension. Indeed, the content of what is learned included motives, attitudes, and, more particularly, definitions about breaking the law. These represent ideas rather than behavior. The process of what is learned entails the intimate relationships one forms with others and the influence such group associations have on the person who then assigns meaning to the behavior based on these associations.

Given Sutherland's (1947) theory, defining what is criminal and what is lawful does not exist as an independent fact. Instead, it is subject to the meaning the conduct has for specific groups (e.g., family members, friends, and coworkers) and to the relative influence the group exerts on particular individuals intimately connected to those collectives.

Ronald Akers has elaborated on and expanded the social learning model developed by Edwin Sutherland (1947). According to Akers (1994), the most important aspect of social learning is **differential association.** "[Differential association] refers to the patterns of interaction with others who are the source of definitions that are either favorable or unfavorable to violating the law" (Vold et al., 1998, p. 196). For Akers, the use of the word "definitions" refers to the personal or intimate meanings people attach or assign to certain behaviors. This logic is consistent with other sociological efforts to understand the meaning-making process for individuals (Blumer, 1969), including the interpretation of criminal conduct (Katz, 1988).

According to Akers (1994), there are both specific and general definitions involved in this meaning-making process. General definitions entail an overall moral code, belief system, or ethical canon. Specific definitions involve the application of selected meanings to a particular behavior. The meanings that we assign to prostitution, underage drinking, gambling, adolescent consensual intercourse, jaywalking, truancy, rape, armed robbery, and murder, entail the use of specific definitions applied to these behaviors.

Akers (1994) calls the real or anticipated effects of a particular behavior **differential reinforcement.** The behavior of people is based on the achievement of rewards or benefits (e.g., the praise of a parent, salary adjustments, and greater social prestige) and on the avoidance of penalties or other forms of punishment (e.g., a traffic ticket, an employer reprimand, and parental disapproval). As these examples demonstrate, the rewards and penalties can be both social and nonsocial in nature. Regardless of their form, differential reinforcement helps people assign meaning to their behaviors and to the actions of others.

Another important feature to the social learning approach described by Akers (1994) is **imitation.** To imitate is to participate in the observed behaviors of other people. "Whether or not a behavior will be imitated depends on the characteristics of the person being observed, the behavior the person engages in, and the observed consequences of that behavior" (Vold et al., 1998, p. 197). For example, adolescents may imitate or replicate behaviors of other teens considered "cool" by juvenile standards. These kids may smoke, deal drugs, or join gangs because these behaviors appear highly rewarding and without consequence.

Recently, Skinner and Fream (1997) used the concepts of social learning theory to explain the relatively new phenomenon of computer crime. The investigators argued that differential association, differential reinforcement and punishment, definitions, and sources of imitation were significantly correlated with computer deviance. "As with other types of deviance, one of the major predictors of computer crime is associating with friends who engage in the activity" (Skinner & Fream, p. 512). The researchers went on to state that:

> Because peer groups are undoubtedly the major social context in which college students interact, they will undoubtedly have a great impact on learning computer crime . . . it is in the peer group where the individual is exposed to the various norms and values relating to legal and illegal computer activities. Thus . . . the more college students associate with peers who are engaging in illegal computer activity, the greater the frequency of the behavior. (p. 500)

In a somewhat related study, Hollinger (1992) found a strong negative relationship between perceived certainty of apprehension and software piracy. The significance of this research is linked to the definitions computer "hackers" establish with respect to breaking the law, and how these definitions influence others intimately associated with them. As Skinner and Fream (1997) observed, "Consequently, young computer criminals may realize from reading articles and from experiences they or their friends have had that they are very unlikely to get caught and, if they do, very little will be done to punish them" (p. 500; for more on other computer-related crime examples, see chapter 6).

Social Learning Theory, Violence, and the Media

The process by which learning occurs raises several questions about the impact of television, movies, videos, and other forms of entertainment on the behavior of people. In particular, "the role of perceptions in learning and observational learning have added fuel to an ongoing emotional debate: Does **media violence** make people behave more aggressively?" (Wade & Tavris, 2003, p. 260). Researchers following Bandura's (1983) lead have repeatedly demonstrated that when people watch aggression this increases their own aggressive tendencies (e.g., Bushman & Anderson, 2001; Surette, 1992).

The most common argument among experts is that children imitate the violence they witness on television or in movies (Felson, 1996; see also, Centerwall, 1989). Other researchers indicate that these findings obtain, even after controlling for the effects of race, gender, and class (Anderson & Bushman, 2001). Relatedly, investigators have demonstrated that when children decrease their exposure to watching television or playing video games, the effect is that they are less likely to act aggressively (Robinson et al., 2001).

However, not all research supports the claim that people learn violence by observing it through the media. For example, a study conducted by Felson (1996) found that exposure to television violence had a small effect on violent behaviors for some viewers. Yet, for those individuals with a propensity toward violent or criminal conduct in the first place, media exposure taught these viewers new skills in carrying out violence that they had not previously considered (see also, Bushman, 1995). As Felson explained:

> For example, young people may mimic karate and judo moves, or they may learn effective tactics for committing violent crime . . . such a modeling process could lead to more severe forms of aggression. [According to learning theories] it could increase the frequency of violence if people who are motivated to harm someone choose a violent method they have observed on television. (p. 117)

Perhaps what is most troubling about the relationships among social learning theory, media exposure to aggressiveness, and actual violence is that there is anecdotal evidence to support the claim that media violence is learned:

> In one widely reported case in Boston, six young men set fire to a woman after forcing her to douse herself with fuel. The scene had been depicted on television two nights before. In another instance, four teenagers raped a nine-year-old girl with a beer bottle, enacting a scene similar to one made-for-TV movie, *Born Innocent*. (Felson, 1996, p. 118)

Modeling can be used to explain copycat offenses following other highly publicized occurrences such as airplane hijackings or bombings. For example, the tragic events at Columbine High School initiated a rash of similar death threats and actual school shootings in the years following the intense media coverage of this particular incident. Troubling situations like this stand in stark contrast to the contention of critics who assert that the relationship between media violence and real violence is not strong enough to cause alarm or fear (Freedman, 1988).

Perhaps the best that can be said about the connection between media violence and actual aggression or criminal behavior is that there is an association, but that its influence is not sufficiently strong enough that it is universally experienced (Surette, 1992). This is because there are other mediating variables (e.g., predispositions to violence, mental illness, perceptions, or other personality traits) representing "crucial factors that intervene between what we see, what we learn, and how we respond" (Wade & Tavris, 2003, p. 261). However, this perspective is offered cautiously. Indeed, "when violence is justified or left unpunished on television, the viewer's guilt or concern about consequences is reduced" (Felson, 1996, p. 118). In the context of media violence, then, the value of social learning theory may very well be in how we educate young people about the potential downside of repeated exposure to aggressive, violent, and criminal acts displayed on television, in movies, or through other media outlets. Indeed, in the final analysis what really matters are the collective effects of ongoing, persistent viewing and the harm caused by such sustained exposure. As Wade and Tavris conclude:

> If 10 million people watch a violent TV program and only 1 percent of them become more violent afterwards, that's 100,000 people! And although the effects of one program may be short-lived, the *cumulative* effects over a period of years may be long-lasting [and devastating]. (p. 261)

DISCUSSION QUESTIONS

1. Unlike other theories exploring criminal conduct, social control theory is not interested in explaining why people commit crime. Instead, it is interested in accounting for the fact that more people choose not to commit more crime. Explain this perspective.

2. What are the elements of the social bond? Use an example from criminal behavior to account for how these elements function.

3. What are the three limitations of social control theory? What is your position on whether social control theory is a useful explanation for adolescent delinquency?

4. How does labeling theory work? Can you think of a good illustration from deviance to support your answer?

5. What is secondary deviance? How does secondary deviance influence one's self-image, resulting in criminal conduct?

6. What are some of the social implications of labeling theory? Can you think of a recent illustration where the label we assign to others produces harmful, even criminal, effects?

7. What is the relevance of Albert Bandura's (1973, 1977) research on learning theory, especially in relation to our understanding of criminal behavior today?

8. What is differential association? What is differential reinforcement? How do these concepts account for delinquency and crime?

9. What is the relationship between media violence and crime? Explain your answer using examples from television, film, or other media outlets.

REFERENCES

Agnew, R. (1993). Why do they do it? An examination of the intervening mechanisms between social control variables and delinquency. *Journal of Research in Crime and Delinquency, 30*(3), 245–266.

Akers, R. L. (1967). Problems in the sociology of deviance: Social definitions and behavior. *Social Forces, 46,* 455–465.

Akers, R. L. (1985). *Deviant behavior: A social learning approach* (3rd ed.). Belmont, CA: Wadsworth.

Akers, R. L. (1991). Self-control as a general theory of crime. *Journal of Quantitative Criminology, 7*(2).

Akers R. L. (1994). *Criminological theories.* Los Angeles: Roxbury.

Alarid, L. F., Burton, V. S., Jr., & Cullen, F. T. (2000). Gender and crime among felony offenders: Assessing the generality of social control and differential association theories. *The Journal of Research in Crime and Delinquency, 37*(2), 171–199.

Anderson, A. K., & Bushman, B. J. (2001). Effect of violent video games on aggressive behavior, aggressive cognition, aggressive affect, physiological arousal, and prosocial behavior: A meta-analytic review of the scientific literature. *Psychological Science, 12,* 353–359.

Arneklev, B. J., Grasmick, H. G., Tittle, C. R., & Bursik, R. J., Jr. (1993). Low self-control and imprudent behavior. *Journal of Quantitative Criminology, 9*(3), 225–247.

Arrigo, B. A. (2002). *Punishing the mentally ill: A critical analysis of law and psychiatry.* Albany, NY: State University of New York Press.

Aseltine, R. (1995). A reconsideration of parental and peer influences on adolescent deviance. *Journal of Health Society and Behavior, 3*(6), 103–121.

Bandura, A. (1969). *Principles of behavior modification.* Austin, TX: Holt, Rinehart, & Winston.

Bandura, A. (1973). *Aggression: A social learning analysis.* Upper Saddle River, NJ: Prentice Hall.

Bandura, A. (1977). *Social learning theory.* Upper Saddle River, NJ: Prentice Hall.

Bandura, A. (1983). Psychological mechanisms of aggression. In R. G. Geen & E. Donerstein (Eds.), *Aggression: Theoretical and empirical reviews* (pp. 1–40). New York: Academic Press.

Bandura, A. (1986). *Social foundations of thought and action: A social-cognitive theory.* Upper Saddle River, NJ: Prentice Hall.

Bandura, A., Ross, D., & Ross, S. (1961). Transmission of aggression through imitation of aggressive models. *Journal of Abnormal and Social Psychology, 63,* 575–582.

Barone, D. F., Maddux, J. E., & Snyder, C. R. (1997). *Social cognitive psychology: History and current domains.* New York: Plenum.

Bartusch, D. R. J., Lynam, D. R., Moffitt, T. E., & Silva, P. A. (1997). Is age important? Testing a general versus a developmental theory of antisocial behavior. *Criminology, 35*(1), 13–48.

Becker, H. S. (1963). *Outsiders: Studies in the sociology of deviance.* New York/Glencoe, IL: The Free Press.

Bernberg, J. G., & Thorlindsson, T. (1999). Adolescent violence, social control, and the subculture of delinquency. *Youth and Society, 30*(4), 445–460.

Blumer, H. (1969). *Symbolic interactionism.* Upper Saddle River, NJ: Prentice Hall.

Booth Thomas, C. B. (2001). A new scarlet letter. *Time, 157,* 82.

Burgess, R. L., & Akers, R. L. (1968). A differential association: Reinforcement theory of criminal behavior. *Social Problems, 14,* 128–147.

Bushman, B. J. (1995). Moderating role of trait aggressiveness in the effect of violent media on aggression. *Journal of Personality and Social Psychology, 69,* 950–960.

Bushman, B. J., & Anderson, C. A. (2001). Media violence and the American public: Scientific facts versus media misinformation. *American Psychologist, 56,* 477–489.

Centerwall, B. S. (1989). Exposure to television as a cause of violence. In G. Comstock (Ed.), *Public communication and behavior* (pp. 1–58). Orlando, FL: Academic Press.

Chamallas, M. (1990). Listening to Dr. Fiske: The easy case of Price Waterhouse v. Hopkins. *Vermont Law Review, 15,* 89–124.

Comstock, G. A., & Paik, H. (1994). The effects of television violence on antisocial behavior: A meta-analysis. *Communication Research, 21,* 516–545.

Cooley, C. H. (1902). *Human nature and the social order.* New York: Scribner's.

Dollard, J., & Miller, N. E. (1950). *Personality and psychotherapy: An analysis in terms of learning, thinking, and culture.* New York: McGraw-Hill.

Drapela, V. J. (1995). *A review of personality theories* (2nd ed.). Springfield, IL: Thomas.

Dukes, R. L., & Stein, J. A. (2001). Effects of assets and deficits on the social control of at-risk behavior among youth: A structural equations approach. *Youth and Society, 32*(3), 337–359.

Elliot, D. S. (1985). *Explaining delinquency.* Thousand Oaks, CA: Sage.

Erickson, K. G., Crosnoe, R., & Dornbusch, S. M. (2000). A social process model of adolescent deviance: Combining social control and differential association perspectives. *Journal of Youth and Adolescence, 29*(4), 395–425.

Felson, R. B. (1996). Mass media effects on violent behavior. *Annual Review of Sociology, 22,* 103–128.

Foshee, V. A., Baumann, K. E., & Linder, G. F. (1999). Family violence and the perpetration of adolescent dating violence: Examining social learning and social control processes. *Journal of Marriage and Family, 61*(2), 331–342.

Foucault, M. (1965). *Madness and civilization.* New York: Vintage Books.

Freedman, J. L. (1988). Television violence and aggression: What the evidence shows. In S. Oskamp (Ed.), *Television as a social issue (Applied Social Psychology Annual, Vol. 8).* Newbury Park, CA: Sage.

Garfinkel, H. (1965). Conditions of successful degradation ceremonies. *American Journal of Sociology, 61*(5), 420–424.

Goffman, E. (1959). *The presentation of the self in everyday life.* New York: Doubleday.

Goffman, E. (1961). *Asylums.* New York: Doubleday.

Gottfredson, M. R., & Hirschi, T. (1990). *A general theory of crime.* Stanford, CA: Stanford University Press.

Gove, W. R. (Ed.). (1975). *The labeling of deviance: Evaluating a perspective.* Beverly Hills, CA: Sage.

Heimer, K., & Matsueda, R. L. (1994). Role-taking, role commitment, and delinquency: A theory of differential social control. *American Sociological Review, 59,* 365–390.

Hirschi, T. (1969). *Causes of delinquency.* Berkeley, CA: University of California Press.

Hollinger, R. C. (1992). Crime by computer: Correlates of software piracy and unauthorized account access. *Security Journal, 4*(1), 2–12.

Houtzager, B., & Baerveldt, C. (1999). Just like normal: A social network study of the relation between petty crime and the intimacy of adolescent friendships. *Social Behavior and Personality, 27*(2), 177–195.

Katz, J. (1988). *Seductions of crime: Moral and sensual attractions in doing evil.* New York: Basic Books.

LaGrange, R. L., & White, H. R. (1985). Age differences in delinquency: A test of theory. *Criminology, 23*(1), 19–42.

Laws, J. L. (1979). *The second X: Sex role and social role.* New York: Elsevier.

Lemert, E. M. (1967). *Human deviance, social problems, and social control.* Upper Saddle River, NJ: Prentice Hall.

Matsueda, R. L. (1992). Reflected appraisals, parental labeling, and delinquency: Specifying a symbolic interactionist theory. *American Journal of Sociology, 97,* 1577–1611.

Matza, D. (1964). *Delinquency and drift.* New York: Wiley.

Meeks, K. (2000). *Driving while Black: What to do if you are a victim of racial profiling.* New York: Broadway Books.

Meltzoff, A. N., Gopnik, A. (1993). The role of imitation in understanding persons and developing a theory of mind. In S. Baron-Cohen, H. Tager-Flusberg, & D. Cohen (Eds.), *Understanding other minds.* New York: Oxford University Press.

Miller, N. E., & Dollard, J. (1941). *Social learning and imitation.* New Haven, CT: Yale University Press.

Nye, F. I. (1958). *Family relationships and delinquent behavior.* New York: Wiley.

Pavlov, I. P. (1927). *Conditioned reflexes.* London: Oxford Press.

Phares, E. J. (1991). *Introduction to personality* (3rd ed.). New York: HarperCollins.

Polawski, M. (1994). Linking self- and social-control with deviance: Illuminating the structure underlying a general theory of crime and its relation to deviant activity. *Journal of Quantitative Criminology, 10*(1), 41–78.

Price Waterhouse v. Hopkins, 490 U.S. 228 (1988).

Reiss, A. J. (1951). Delinquency as the failure of personal and social controls. *American Sociological Review, 16,* 196–207.

Roane, K. (2001, April 16). Risky trip through 'White Man's Pass' in New Jersey: A losing war on racial profiling. *U.S. News and World Report, 130,* 24–26.

Robinson, T. W., Wilde, M. L., Navracruz, L. C., et al. (2001). Effects of reducing children's television and video game use on aggressive behavior: A randomized controlled trial. *Archives of Pediatric and Adolescent Medicine, 282,* 1561–1567.

Rotter, J. B. (1954). *Social learning and clinical psychology.* Upper Saddle River, NJ: Prentice Hall.

Scheff, T. J. (Ed). (1975). *Labeling madness.* Upper Saddle River, NJ: Prentice Hall.

Scheff, T. J. (2000). *Being mentally ill* (3rd ed.). New York: Aldine de Gruyter.

Schur, E. M. (1983). *Labeling women deviant: Gender, stigma, and social control.* Philadelphia, PA: Temple University Press.

Siegel, L. J. (1992). *Criminology* (4th ed.). St. Paul, MN: West Publishing Company.

Skinner, B. F. (1969). *Contingencies of reinforcement: A theoretical analysis.* New York: Appleton–Century–Crofts.

Skinner, W. F., & Fream, A. M. (1997). A social learning theory analysis of computer crime among college students. *Journal of Research in Crime and Delinquency, 34*(4), 495–518.

Surette, R. (1992). *Media, crime, and criminal justice: Images and realities.* Belmont, CA: Wadsworth.

Sutherland, E. H. (1947). *Criminology* (4th ed.). Philadelphia: Lippincott.

Sutherland, E. H., Cressey, D. R., & Luckenbill, D. F. (1992). *Principles of criminology* (11th ed.). Dix Hills, NY: General Hall.

Sykes, G. M., & Matza, D. (1957). Techniques of neutralization: A theory of delinquency. *American Sociological Review, 22,* 667–670.

Tittle, C. R. (1975). Labelling and crime: An empirical evaluation. In W. B. Gove (Ed.), *The labelling of deviance: Evaluating a perspective* (pp. 181–203). New York: Wiley.

Toby, J. (1957). Social disorganization and stake in conformity: Complementary factors in the predatory behavior of hoodlums. *Journal of Criminal Law, Criminology, and Police Science, 48,* 12–17.

Vazsonyi, A. T., Pickering, L. E., Junger, M., & Hessing, D. (2001). An empirical test of a general theory of crime: A four-nation comparative study of self-control and the prediction of deviance. *Journal of Research in Crime and Delinquency, 38*(2), 91–131.

Vold, G. B., Bernard, T. J., & Snipes, J. B. (1998). *Theoretical Criminology* (4th ed.). New York: Oxford University Press.

Wade, C., & Tavris, C. (2003). *Psychology* (7th ed.). Upper Saddle River, NJ: Prentice Hall.

Wadsworth, T. (2000). Labor markets, delinquency, and social control theory: An empirical assessment of the mediating process. *Social Forces, 78*(3), 1041–1066.

Williams, C. R., & Arrigo, B. A. (2002). *Law, psychology, and justice: Chaos theory and the new (dis)order.* Albany, NY: State University of New York Press.

Wood, P. B., Pfefferbaum, B., & Arneklev, B. (1993). Risk-taking and self-control: Psychology correlates of delinquency. *Journal of Crime and Justice, 16*(1), 111–130.

Wrightsman, L. (2001). *Forensic psychology.* Belmont, CA: Wadsworth.

part II

Types of Offenders and Types of Criminal Behavior

Violent Crime and Criminals

OVERVIEW

There are many forms of criminal behavior and there are many types of offenders. The previous four chapters introduced us to the theoretical foundations of both; however, little attention was given to exploring specific expressions of crime or specific profiles of offenders. This chapter and those contained in the second section of this textbook address both of these matters. Chapter 5 is uniquely concerned with violent crimes and criminals. This is a world fraught with curiosity and consternation in part because the offenses are quite vile and the offenders are quite despicable. Where useful and appropriate, this chapter provides statistical information relevant to the prevalence or incidence of particular crimes, classifies offenders through typologies developed in the literature, and comments on the experience of harm for the victims. The areas of violent crime addressed in this chapter run the gamut from murder and sexual homicide, to domestic violence and **hate crimes**, to offenses perpetrated by the police and those committed within prisons. The domain of violent crimes and criminals is dark, seedy, and, in many ways, uncertain. However, this chapter reveals some of the more compelling and fascinating dimensions to this troubled and troubling underworld of criminal behavior.

KEY TERMS

Anger rapist
Anthropophagy
Armed robbery
Bioterrorism
Child abuse
Cult
Cyberterrorism
Cycle of violence
Domestic terrorism
Elder abuse
Erotophonophilia
Family annihilator
Flagellationism
Foreign terrorism
Gang
Gang bangers
Hate crimes
Hedonistic killer
Jockers

Lust murder
Mass murder
Mission-oriented killer
Necrosadism
Paraphilias
Pedophilia
Picquerism
Police brutality
Posttraumatic stress disorder
Power- or control-oriented killer
Power rapist
Prison violence
Psychopathic Deviate scale
Punks
Queens
Rape
Religious cults
Roofies
Sadistic rapist

Serial murder   Thought-reform programs
Sexual sadism   Trauma-control model
Skinheads   Transnational terrorism
Spousal abuse   Visionary killer
Terrorism

MURDER

Introduction

Murder assumes many forms and is understood in many ways. This portion of the chapter reviews the major types of this offense. These include serial, mass, spree, and general murder. Where useful and appropriate, important subclassifications are also identified. In addition, this section provides some basic information on what we know about each type of criminal offender. This information includes relevant demographics, profiles, and typologies.

Serial Murder and Serial Murderers

Serial murder is considered one of the most disturbing and puzzling phenomena in the world today. The definition of a serial murderer has been the topic of debate for many researchers (e.g., Fox & Levin, 1994; Hickey, 2002; Holmes & DeBurger, 1988; Holmes & Holmes, 1998). However, the definition that best describes the phenomenon, along with being general enough so as to not exclude certain populations (e.g., women), is the one offered by Holmes and Holmes. As they state, "serial murder is the killing of three or more people over a period of more than 30 days, with a significant cooling-off period between the killings" (p. 18). There are several elements that are part and parcel of the serial murderer's behavior. These include the following: (a) the crime is repetitive; (b) the murders are typically one-on-one; (c) the relationship between the killer and the victim is, generally speaking, unknown; and (d) the serial murderer is motivated by some driving force to commit the crime (Holmes & Holmes).

The prevalence of serial murderers and the number of their victims is not known precisely (Hickey, 1997; Holmes & Holmes, 1998). However, researchers approximate that there are 35 serial killers in America who take the lives of over 200 people each year. Interestingly, though, some investigators feel that this figure may be too low of an estimate (Fox & Levin, 1994; Holmes & Holmes).

Ronald Holmes and James DeBurger (1988) developed a four-factor classification for this unique type of criminal, based on countless years of researching serial murderers. The four classifications are as follows: (a) the **visionary killer,** (b) the **mission-oriented killer,** (c) the **hedonistic killer,** and (d) the **power- or control-oriented killer** (see also, White-Hamon, 2000). Visionary killers commit murder because of some inner voice that orders them to kill. The visionary killer is said to be psychotic and constantly out of touch with reality. Mission-oriented killers want to rid the world of certain people whose presence they feel is quite negative for society. One common example is the prostitute. As opposed to the visionary killer, the mission-oriented killer is in touch with reality and is aware of his or her actions. Hedonistic killers murder for a variety of reasons, with the major reason being the exhilarating thrill of it (see also, Katz, 1988). Sexual gratification is occasionally obtained in these types of serial crimes (Holmes & DeBurger, 1988). Power- or control-oriented killers completely dominate their victims. The rape, and various sexual and physical assaults against the person harmed are not motivated by sex; rather, they are motivated by the lust for power and control (Graney & Arrigo, 2002).

Researchers have also examined the profile of the serial murderer (Hickey, 2002). For example, the demographic characteristics of these killers suggest that they are predominantly White males, between the ages of 25 and 30, from various socioeconomic groups, and from different occupational sectors (Holmes & Holmes, 1998). Among the disparate jobs held by serial murderers, we find hotel porters, gas station attendants,

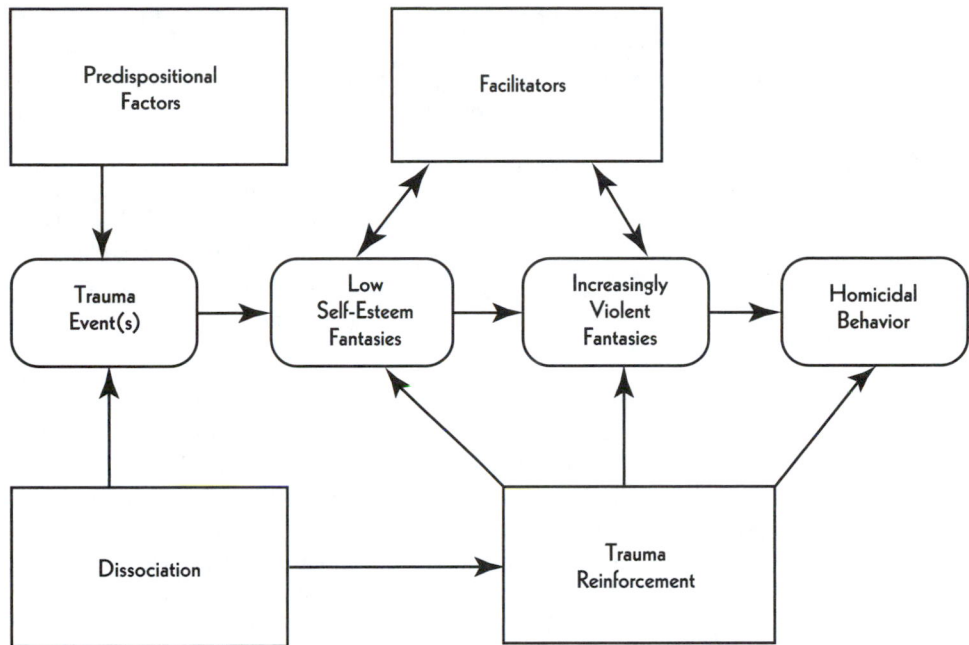

Figure 5–1 Eric Hickey's Trauma–Control Model

bartenders, house painters, car upholsterers, electronic technicians, and computer operators (Graney & Arrigo, 2002). The education level of serial murderers is generally low, with a majority having only a high school diploma or less. Some offenders attend college or vocational school for a few years; however, very few obtain a college degree. Geographic location of the offense also varies and, as previously mentioned, the killer is usually unknown to the victim. In other words, no prior relationship exists between the offender and the victim (Holmes & Holmes, 1994).

　　Several factors contribute to the overall etiology of a serial murderer. As a result, considerable confusion exists when determining what variables are common among a majority of serial killers and identifying those factors that are more causal in nature. As it stands, "It is unlikely that any one factor is directly responsible for homicidal behavior . . . In addition, no one factor has been useful thus far in predicting who may be prone to serial murder" (Hickey, 1997, p. 86; see also, Holmes & Holmes, 1988).

　　One of the more prominent models used to explain those factors contributing to and responsible for serial killing comes from the work of Eric Hickey (Arrigo & Purcell, 2001). Hickey (1997) refers to his approach as a **"trauma-control model."** As Figure 5–1 indicates, certain traumatic events occur during the critical developmental period of an adolescent's life. These events act as an impetus for serial crime. Examples include the divorce or death of parents, an overall unstable home life, and childhood sexual and physical abuse. The model also identifies several other important factors used to explain the origin and motivation of serial murder. For example, the role of violent fantasies, common among a large number of serial murderers, interacts with one's felt sense of low self-esteem. The latter occurs in the aftermath of the person's early childhood trauma. Both predispositional factors (biological and neurological problems) and the presence of dissociation (the offender reports no memory of certain parts, if not all, of the crime) work jointly or separately to form the traumatic, unresolved events at the core of the serial killer's behavior. In addition, facilitators (e.g., alcohol, drugs, and pornography) interactively contribute to or are enhanced by the individual's low self-esteem and increasingly violent fantasies. Finally, the role of trauma reinforcement is noted. Hickey (p. 87) contends that "childhood trauma for serial murderers may serve as a triggering mechanism or reinforcer, resulting in an individual's inability to cope with the stress of certain events, whether they are physical, psychological, or a combination of traumatizations." Trauma reinforcers include such things as experiencing emotional distance or indifference from a would-be lover or encountering hostile and incessant ridicule while at work or in the company of others. Assessing the trauma-control model and the role of reinforcers, Arrigo and Purcell offer the following comments:

> When the individual experiences . . . rejection, the person may internalize the feeling, may become immobilized, and may be unable to cope with it in a constructive manner. In these instances, the individual retreats psychologically into [a] fantasy world, often embracing cynical and negative sentiments, until [the person] finds comfort and relief in the (sadistic and sexual) images . . . conjure[d]. (p. 18)

Mass Murder and Mass Murderers

There are several important differences between serial murder and **mass murder** (Holmes & Holmes, 1994; White-Hamon, 2000, pp. 65–70). First, the amount of time that transpires between acts of multiple murder and serial murder is dissimilar. Unlike the serial killer, there is no cooling-off period for the mass murderer (Busch & Cavanaugh, 1986). Second, serial murderers tend to individualize their victims, killing them one-on-one and then cooling off before they pursue another victim. However, mass murderers kill multiple people over the course of a few minutes or hours, and in the same general area (Holmes & Holmes, 1998). Third, although serial killers make considerable efforts to avoid detection by police, multiple or mass murderers are almost always arrested, shot by the police, or succumb to suicide (Hickey, 2002).

Some researchers estimate that mass murderers will claim the lives of 150 to 200 people per year (Kelleher, 1997). However, these figures may vary because determining a universal definition of mass murder has been a problem for investigators. Holmes and Holmes (1998, p. 11) offer a more commonly used description, characterizing mass murder as "the killing of three or more people at one time and in one place." Elaborating on the concept of "one place," the researchers state that an offender may enter an establishment, kill a number of victims, and then travel to another nearby establishment and engage in the same behavior. The subsequent killings may still be classified as part of the same mass murder, notwithstanding spatial and temporal differences (White-Hamon, 2000).

Given the confusion over defining multiple or mass murder, it is no surprise that the demographics of this offender are also the subject of considerable debate. In spite of a few incidents of adolescent mass murder (e.g., the Columbine High School shootings), most researchers agree that the age of the multiple murderer is over 25, falling somewhere between 25 and 40 years of age (Kelleher, 1997; Palermo, 1999). Although there is general consensus that the majority of mass murderers are male, there is some disagreement on whether the males are predominately White (see Hickey, 2002), or whether the racial demographics are proportionate to the general population as a whole (see Palermo, 1999).

The most valid classification system used to explain the mass murderer was developed by Holmes and Holmes (1992). Drawing on the insights of other investigators, they tested five typologies or models of mass murder and had a 93% agreement rate among the four individuals who participated in classifying 47 individual offenders. Admittedly, research on multiple murder is scarce or addresses only a few isolated cases. However, for purposes of exploring this form of criminal behavior, these five typologies will be used as a basis to account for the phenomenon of mass murder.

The first type of mass murderer is the **family annihilator.** The annihilator or family slayer kills multiple family members (Busch & Cavanaugh, 1986). This type of murder takes place in the home, in contrast to other types of mass murder that take place in public settings (Palermo, 1999). Typically, these offenders believe that killing the family is a way of relieving personal suffering. After completing this act, mass murderers tend to kill themselves (White-Hamon, 2000).

The pseudocommando, or barricaded sniper, is a mass murderer who kills in order to lash out against society, or one who seeks revenge against specific individuals. Unlike the crimes of the family annihilator, this type of mass murder almost always takes place in a public setting. Regrettably, these killings have become all too prevalent among adolescents today (Palermo, 1999). An example of this type of mass murder would be the Columbine High School shootings that occurred in Littleton, Colorado.

Another type of mass murderer is the set-and-run killer. These individuals are similar to other types of mass murderers in that they choose to kill in a public place. However, set-and-run killers are different from other mass murderers because they seek to remain anonymous to or otherwise undetected by authorities (White-Hamon, 2000). An example of this type of mass murderer would be the bombing of the federal building in Oklahoma City, Oklahoma.

Disciple killers are distinguished from other mass murderers because their motivations are externalized; that is, they are told to kill by a leader whom they follow (Holmes & Holmes, 1994). Disciple murderers often harbor no ill will toward society or those they kill. Instead, they simply follow the instructions of their leaders. Similar to the set-and-run killer, the disciple murderer manages to avoid initial detection by authorities; however, they are eventually apprehended. A prominent example of this type of multiple killing was staged by Charles Manson and his **cult** followers.

The disgruntled worker seeks revenge against his place of employment, primarily because the person was laid off or fired. This killer often enters his former place of employment and begins to open fire on those he feels have wronged him. Common examples of this type of shooting include the highly publicized and controversial post office shootings that occurred during the early 1990s. More recently, a man killed 13 people in a computer company in Boston. However, this disgruntled worker had not been fired or laid off, nor had he received a pay cut prior to the shootings.

Workplace Violence, Criminal Behavior, and Threat Assessment

When we think about disgruntled workers, images of violence committed by postal service workers or manufacturing employees typically emerge (Braverman, 1998; Schell & Lanteigne, 2000). This was certainly the case with Bruce Clark, a veteran of the U.S. Postal Service for 22 years who shot and killed his supervisor in a mail-processing facility in Southern California; and with James Davis who murdered three and wounded four others at a manufacturing plant in North Carolina. Although these kinds of fatalities in the workplace are rare (Turner & Gelles, 2003; Vandenbos & Bulato, 1996), threat to employees must be taken seriously. According to the Workplace Violence Research Institute and a study it conducted in 1995, "[e]very workday, an estimated 16,400 threats are made, 723 workers are attacked and 43,800 are harassed" (Kaufer & Mattman, 2001, p. 2). What these figures suggest is that workplace violence is not just about the berserk and criminal behavior of employees who utilize semiautomatic weapons or other firearms to kill people; rather, workplace violence refers to any act that creates a hostile work environment, adversely impacting employees physically or verbally (Carll, 1999; Vandenbos & Bulato, 1996). These behaviors include coercion, assaults, intimidation, harassment, and threats (Kaufer & Mattman).

The best solution to workplace violence is prevention (Braverman, 1998). Several strategies linked to prevention include effective preemployment screening, broad-based employee assistance programs, annual employee review policies, and detailed procedures for termination. However, the most important component of prevention is early detection or threat assessment, focusing on high-risk behaviors (Schell & Lanteigne, 2000; Turner & Gelles, 2003). Although very difficult to accurately predict (Braverman, 1998), several indicators of likely workplace violence include drug and alcohol consumption, frequent tardiness and absenteeism, repeated substandard or poor job performance, consistent inability to engage in pro-social behavior, ongoing complaints from coworkers, erratic behavior on the job, and dramatic shifts in mood and interpersonal conduct (including acts of aggression). It is also important to assess the interplay of environmental factors (e.g., organizational and social factors such as constant shift work, level and intensity of job stress, supervisor–supervisee rapport), and individual employee dynamics in relation to potential job-related violence (Greenberg & Barling, 1999).

Spree Murder and Spree Murderers

To date, there is a dearth of research on spree killing (Holmes & Holmes, 1994; White-Hamon, 2000). Spree murder is defined as "a series of murders connected to one event committed over a time period of hours to days without a break or cooling off period and may be a subset of either mass or serial murder" (Busch & Cavanaugh, 1986, p. 6). The important element to note in this definition is that there is no cooling-off period, even though the killer may travel from place to place.

As the previous definition implies, there is some confusion about how best to classify spree murder. In short, researchers are uncertain if it is better to categorize it as a form of multiple murder or serial murder (White-Hamon, 2000). What distinguishes spree murders from either of these two forms of homicide is that the spree killer commits these crimes in a frenzy-like fashion, murdering in several sequences or stages (Gresswell & Hollin, 1994). Moreover, the spree killer does not attempt to avoid detection, thereby making the likelihood of repeated criminality remote. In fact, most spree murderers find themselves in a standoff with police where they are killed or where they elect to take their own lives.

Research on the spree killer is scarce; consequently, overall demographics, profiles, typologies, and causal factors are, at this time, mostly unavailable (Dietz, 1986). However, spree killers tend to be male and their racial identity is proportionate to the general population (White-Hamon, 2000). Spree killers are often mentally unstable and experience some kind of psychotic episode or "break" with reality, culminating in their efforts to seek revenge on unsuspecting others. Although spree killers choose their victims, their crimes are not as methodically planned or elaborately conducted as the activity of the serial or mass murderer (Holmes & Holmes, 1994). An example of a more recently publicized spree killer is Andrew Cunanan, the man who murdered Gianni Versace, the fashion designer, and four other individuals in 1999.

General and Passion Murder and Murderers

The United States has the highest murder rate of all industrialized, economically developed countries. As defined in the Federal Bureau of Investigation's (FBI) Uniform Crime Reporting Program, murder and non-negligent manslaughter represent "the willful (non-negligent) killing of one human being by another" (p. 33). The FBI estimated that there were 18,209 persons murdered in 1997. Surprisingly, this number represented a decrease of 7% as compared to murders in 1996 (FBI, 1997). More recent crime statistics reflect a similar trend (FBI, 2000).

Murder is regarded as a heinous and horrific offense, illustrated by the fact that there is no statute of limitations for this crime. In addition, it is the only offense where the offender can receive a death sentence. The crime itself is general, and those who commit this act do not fall under any universal profile. However, the following brief observations address important dimensions to understanding general or passion murder and those who engage in such criminal behavior. These dimensions include the demographics of the offender and a explanation as to why a person would take the life of another human being.

According to the FBI (1997), the demographics of the general homicide or passion murderer include the following aggregate figures on gender, age, and race. Ninety percent are male, 87% are 18 and older, and, of those for whom race is known, 53% are African Americans whereas 45% are Caucasian. The crime statistics further indicate that murderers tend to kill within their own race. For example, in 1997, 94% of African American murder victims were slain by African American men. Similarly, 85% of Caucasian victims were killed by Caucasian men, during the same reporting period. The FBI also notes that the most popular weapon for general murder was a firearm, used in 7 out of 10 instances (FBI).

One researcher who has conducted research on the causal factors of homicide is Scott Decker (1996). In his research, Decker describes the characteristics of those who commit the act of murder. He argues that murder serves to justify underlying offender beliefs or values, such as revenge, dispute resolution, jealousy, drug deals gone bad, and debunking threats to a person's authority or ego on the streets (i.e., murder as a means to maintain a callous image). Various criminological theories or approaches to criminal behavior address the motives for this offender's conduct (see, generally, chapters 1–4 for more details). For example, some investigators suggest that murder functions as one's response to tremendous interpersonal conflict in which violence acts to alleviate this inner turmoil. Two factors linked to such turmoil are poverty and income inequality.

Poverty is generally referred to as a form of economic deprivation wherein persons have extreme difficulty acquiring and maintaining the basic essentials to live a healthy life (Messner & Rosenfeld, 2001). When one confronts difficult circumstances where the principal goal is mere survival, intense anxiety can emerge and push a person to the brink of lethal violence. Williams and Flewelling (1988) explain this phenomenon as follows:

> It is reasonable to assume that when people live under conditions of extreme scarcity, the struggle for survival is intensified. A host of agitating psychological manifestations, ranging from a deep sense of powerlessness and brutalization to anger, annuity, and alienation, often accompanies such conditions. Such manifestations can provoke physical aggression in conflict situations. (p. 423)

The personal deprivation that accompanies the absence of economic resources has also been attributed to the breakdown of social controls (e.g., good, stable parenting) that might otherwise inhibit violent or aggressive impulses (Fiala & LaFree, 1988; Palermo, 1999). A majority of the evidence from which such an association is plausible comes from the disproportionate amount of people who serve time for murder, who are unemployed, or who come from significantly lower income populations (U.S. Department of Justice, Bureau of Justice Statistics, 1993). Whether or not poverty provides a direct and clear link to explaining homicide remains undetermined; however, when examining the amount of people in jail or prison with low socioeconomic status (SES), there is a formidable relationship that warrants ongoing concern and future research attention (Holmes & Holmes, 1994).

Nonlethal Violence: The Case of Armed Robbery

There are many forms of nonlethal violence as the subsequent sections of this chapter disclose. However, one example of criminal behavior that can be linked to murder is **armed robbery** (Wright & Decker, 1997). Other common expressions used to describe this behavior include muggings, stickups, or holdups. Some research suggests that there are specific types or categories of armed robbers (Correctional Service of Canada, 2003; Gabor, 1987). This insert provides some basic statistical information on and classifications of this form of criminal conduct.

There is some debate as to whether armed robbers are generally hostile and violent. Those who support this view believe that they are drawn to the subculture of violence in which this behavior develops. Those who argue that armed robbers are not violent indicate that the behavior is more closely correlated with the subculture of theft. According to the Correctional Service of Canada (2003), robbery felons are more likely to use weapons as compared with all other offenders. More specifically, based on data collected from a 1995 survey in Canada, 25% of robberies involve the use of a firearm, 25% entail the use of offensive weapons (i.e., knife or club), and about 50% involve the use of physical force or threat (Correctional Service of Canada). In addition, approximately 25% of robbery victims experience some physical injury. Most armed robbers are male, younger than 30 years of age, possess only a secondary-school education, use drugs and alcohol, meet the diagnostic criteria for antisocial personality disorder, and are sporadically employed (Gabor, 1987; Wright & Decker, 1997).

In a 1987 study conducted by a Montreal task force, researchers developed four typologies for the armed robber. The typologies were derived from a sample of robbery offenders in the Canadian Correctional System

(continued)

(Correctional Service of Canada, 2003). The "Chronic Armed Robber" engages in this criminality for approximately 7 to 8 years, averaging 20 to 25 armed robberies along with other related offenses (e.g., burglary). The planning of the robbery offense is often underdeveloped, sometimes occurring just a few minutes or hours before the actual crime is committed. Chronic offenders typically carry loaded firearms. The "Professional Armed Robber" engages in this criminal activity for 11 to 12 years, averaging 20 to 25 armed robberies along with many other offenses (e.g., safecracking). The planning of the robbery is often quite detailed, occurring many weeks and months prior to the actual crime. The "Intensive Armed Robber" experiences a short career spanning several weeks or months, averaging 5 to 10 offenses. These offenders commit very few related crimes. The planning of the armed robbery is modest at best, occurring just a few hours or days before the criminal event. The "Occasional Armed Robber" has a career that lasts anywhere from several months to a couple of years. These offenders average 1 to 6 crimes of this sort with many other related offenses occurring (e.g., auto theft). The planning of the armed robbery is typically very poor, as the offender is insufficiently armed and fails to conceal his or her identity.

SEXUAL HOMICIDE

Introduction

To date, the literature on sexual homicide and serial murder provides mostly descriptive or anecdotal accounts for these phenomena (Simon, 1996). However, what we know suggests that underscoring these crimes are a series of **paraphilias** (i.e., sexually deviant behaviors) that give rise to violent conduct (Ressler, Burgess, & Douglas, 1988). There are three typologies that help account for the current state of the literature on sexual homicide understood as a form of serial murder. These include the motivational model of Burgess, Hartman, Ressler, Douglas, and McCormack (1986), the trauma–control model of Hickey (1997), and the integrated model of Arrigo and Purcell (2001). The typology developed by Hickey was described in the previous section of this chapter where serial murder was discussed. Several relevant aspects of the Burgess et al. model are included in it, especially a number of the motivational factors linked to the behavior of the sexual killer. As such, these two typologies will not be recounted to any considerable degree within this section. Instead, this portion of the chapter examines what we know about sexual homicide, mindful of the three approaches that help explain it. This includes background information on sexual homicide (especially **lust murder**), the role and function of parphilias in the act of sexual murder, and the operation of the integrated model as developed by Arrigo and Purcell.

Background Information of Sexual Homicide

According to the Uniform Crime Reports (UCR), in general, sexual homicide is indexed under the unknown motive category because federal and state law enforcement agents are largely unaware of the underlying sexual dynamics for such criminal conduct (Hickey, 2002). Sexual homicide, particularly lust murder, does not have a specific classification within the UCR; therefore, statistics reflecting these types of offenses are often intangible, misleading, or otherwise unobtainable (Hazelwood & Douglas, 1980; Ressler et al., 1988).

The few investigations that specifically address sexual homicide suggest the existence of two types of offenders: the rapist or displaced anger murderer (e.g., Groth, Burgess, & Holmstrom, 1977; Prentky, Burgess, & Carter, 1986; Rada, 1978); and the sadistic, or lust murderer (e.g., Becker & Abel, 1978; Bromberg & Coyle, 1974; Groth et al.; Guttmacher & Weihofen, 1952; Podolsky, 1966; Rada; Scully & Marolla, 1985). Displaced anger murderers kill their victims after raping them primarily as a means of escaping detection. Consequently, these offenders do not become sexually satisfied from the rape (Ressler et al.,

1988). A growing, though admittedly limited, body of literature continues to explore the dynamic of the **anger rapist** and the serial nature of this sexual offense (Graney & Arrigo, 2002; Hazelwood, 1995; Hazelwood & Burgess, 1987; Hazelwood, Reboussin, & Warren, 1989; Hazelwood & Warren, 1990). Some additional comments on the sex crime of rape can be found following the material on sexual homicide.

What we know about sadistic, sexual homicide is that it is even more circumscribed than its displaced anger murder counterpart. Sexually aberrant or deviant behaviors, otherwise known as paraphilias, are mostly associated with crimes that are sexual in nature (Hickey, 1997). There are literally hundreds of paraphilias. Some are more familiar in name and more frequent in practice (e.g., cannibalism), and some people even find them exciting and attractive (e.g., Jeffery Dahmer). To most people, however, paraphilias are regarded as intrinsically bizarre. Deviant sexual behaviors exist on a continuum and vary in severity, with some indexed as criminal in nature (e.g., pedophilia), whereas others are classified as seemingly harmless (e.g., voyeurism). On the most extreme end of the paraphilic continuum is "erotophonophilia," commonly referred to as lust murder.

Erotophonophilia is the acting out of deviant sexual behavior by brutally and sadistically killing the victim to achieve ultimate sexual satisfaction (e.g., Hazelwood & Douglas, 1980; Holmes, 1991; Liebert, 1985; Simon, 1996). Lust murderers are likely to repeat their offenses, thereby making them serial in disposition. Mutilation of the body parts, especially the genitalia, is a standard feature of this paraphilia (Hickey, 1997; Money, 1990).

Currently, sadistic sexual homicide has been viewed as a perplexing phenomenon, defying efforts at explanatory and predictive models based on theory-driven conceptualizations for the behavior (Prentky et al., 1989; Simon, 1996). However, what investigators know thus far is that fantasy is a key component to understanding and interpreting lust murder (MacCulloch et al., 1983; Money, 1990). This notwithstanding, a cogent theoretical formulation regarding its role as a driving force or motive for explaining this form of sexual crime has eluded researchers.

Explaining Paraphilia

Paraphilia literally means abnormal love. "Para" is a Greek term for beyond, or outside the usual, and "philia" is a Greek term for love (Money, 1990, p. 27). Common exclusively in males, paraphilias, from a clinical perspective, are a group of persistent sexual behavioral patterns in which unusual objects, fetishes, rituals, or situations are required for full sexual satisfaction (American Psychiatric Association [APA], 1994; Money & Werlas, 1982). The average number of paraphilias is 4.8 per identified person (Holmes, 1991). Multiple paraphilias are often found in one person; however, one paraphilia typically becomes dominant until it is replaced by another (Abel et al., 1988; Hickey, 1997).

There are a number of essential components to most paraphilic behaviors, including fantasy, compulsive masturbation, and facilitators (e.g., alcohol, drugs, and pornography). Research on the role of fantasy demonstrates that it principally serves to influence, induce, or motivate violent and deviant sexual conduct (e.g., George & Marlat, 1989; Greelinger & Bryne, 1987; Hickey, 1997; Malamuth & McIlwraith, 1988; McGuire, Carlisle, & Young, 1965; Prentky et al., 1989). Studies on compulsive masturbation and paraphilias indicate that the former, as a reinforcer, is integral to sustaining the fantasy system. Indeed, the orgasm ultimately becomes a conditioned response to paraphilic imagery. Thus, the fantasies are bolstered by "powerful sex drives that, in turn, facilitate some unusual behaviors" (Hickey, p. 15). Inquiries addressing the connection between facilitators and paraphilic activity suggest that alcohol, drugs, and pornography are positively correlated with sexual and serial homicide (e.g., Hazelwood & Warren, 1990; Ressler, Burgess, Hartman, Douglas, & McCormack, 1986; Simon, 1996). However, a causal connection between facilitators and the etiology of paraphilic behavior remains inconclusive.

As previously described, paraphilias exist on a continuum and have the potential to become more violent over time. Diagnosed levels of paraphilic seriousness include mild, moderate, or severe (Abel & Osborne, 1992). What distinguishes "normal" paraphilics from their "abnormal" counterparts is that the former can function sexually without the sadistic stimuli and fantasy. The behavior is only considered abnormally paraphilic when the individual needs and depends on the aberrant fantasy for sexual arousal and gratification. In the absence of the paraphilic stimuli and fantasy, the dysfunctional individual loses his ability to behave in an appropriate sexual manner. In extreme cases, the paraphilic individual depends on the paraphilia so much that this reliance causes significant distress or impairment in interpersonal, social, and occupational contexts, as well as in other important areas of everyday life (Matthews, 1996).

In order to understand how paraphilias work, it is important to conceptualize the behaviors as functioning within a systemic process. Paraphilic activities are rooted in early childhood development (Hickey, 1997). Research indicates that many individuals who engage in such behavior experience traumatic events in their early adolescence, usually in the form of sexual and physical abuse (Burgess et al., 1986). For example, studies conducted on child molesters (Simon, 1996), rapists (Graney & Arrigo, 2002; Hazelwood, 1995), and lust murderers (Ressler, Burgess, & Douglas, 1988) report that offenders who utilized paraphilia and fantasy in their conduct were precipitated by childhood trauma, triggering their sadistic and deviant behavior or serial killing. The effects of such adolescent traumatization can be devastating, even producing, in some cases, revenge fantasies (Eth & Pynoos, 1985).

As previously mentioned, erotophonophilia, or lust murder, is at the extreme end of the paraphilic continuum. Interestingly, this severest of sexual deviations is comprised of several other paraphilias. Paraphilias typically associated with lust murder include **flagellationism, anthropophagy, picquerism,** and **necrosadism** (Holmes, 1991, p. 68). Flagellationism is an intense desire to beat, whip, or club someone. Anthropophagy involves an intense desire to eat the flesh or body parts of another. Picquerism is the intense desire to stab, wound, or cut the flesh of another person. Often, these stab wounds are inflicted near the genitals or breasts (DeRiver, 1956). Necrosadism involves sexual contact with a dead body.

Clearly, the previously mentioned paraphilias have a common element: All are sadistic in nature. According to Money (1990, p. 27), **sexual sadism** is an "obsessive and compelling repetition of sexual thoughts, dreams, or fantasies that may be translated into acts where the mental or physical suffering of a victim is intensely sexually arousing." Thus, the various combinations and interactive effects of the paraphilias that constitute lust murder make for a very troubling, disturbing, and volatile phenomenon.

In addition to the sadistic dimension of erotophonophilia is the role that lust or eroticism plays in forming and sustaining the paraphilic behavior. "The notion of lust suggests one who possesses a particular urge, not only to kill, but [also] to ravage [and devour] the victim" (Hickey, 1997, p. 69). The lust murderer is motivated and consumed by the need for ultimate sexual satisfaction. One example of this is torture. The offender tortures the victim, either pre- or postmortem, for the sole purpose of achieving climax. The orgasm, and the sexually sadistic nature by which it is reached, then symbolizes complete domination by the assailant over the victim, whether the offender's prey is alive or dead (DeRiver, 1956; Hazelwood & Douglas, 1980).

Lust murderers have a proclivity to engage in serial killing (Hickey, 2002). The FBI defines and classifies erotophonophilia as murder that involves more than three victims, where the offender has a cooling-off period between murders, indicating the premeditation of each sexual offense (Simon, 1996). Both the nature and content of the assailant's fantasy system act as catalysts for each subsequent killing. Thus, the lust murderer cannot escape his own sexually aggressive fantasies involving inappropriate sexual behavior (e.g., touching or fondling a victim). As the fantasies become increasingly violent, so too, do the offenses. The escalation in overt erotic aggression is linked to the fantasy system of the offender who associates sex with violence (Hickey, 1997). Indeed, routine themes identified within these fantasies include power, domination, molestation, revenge, and the degradation and humiliation of others (Simon, 1996).

Sexual Homicide: An Integrated Model

None of the previously developed models on sexual homicide and serial murder (e.g., the motivational model, Burgess et al., 1986; the trauma-control model, Hickey, 1997) examine lust murder with any appreciable degree of specificity. However, the efforts of these researchers have been assimilated. In particular, Arrigo and Purcell (2001) developed an integrated theoretical model of paraphilia and its extreme variant, namely, erotophonophilia. As they argued, the motivational model of Burgess et al. (1986) and the trauma-control model of Hickey possess key components suggestive of a viable and useful synthesis. Clearly, both models discuss some aspects of the paraphilic process as a system of behaviors. Figure 5–2 summarily depicts the integrated model proposed by Arrigo and Purcell.

As Figure 5–2 reveals, the integrative model is presented in a way that not only explains the development of paraphilic behaviors but also illustrates how the behaviors work as a process sustained by several elements comprising the paraphilic system itself. Thus, the model conceptually describes both the etiology of this phenomenon and its essential disposition. The troubled formative development of the offender (i.e., profound psychological difficulties in adolescent development) gives way to low self-esteem and childhood fantasies. As the adolescent matures,

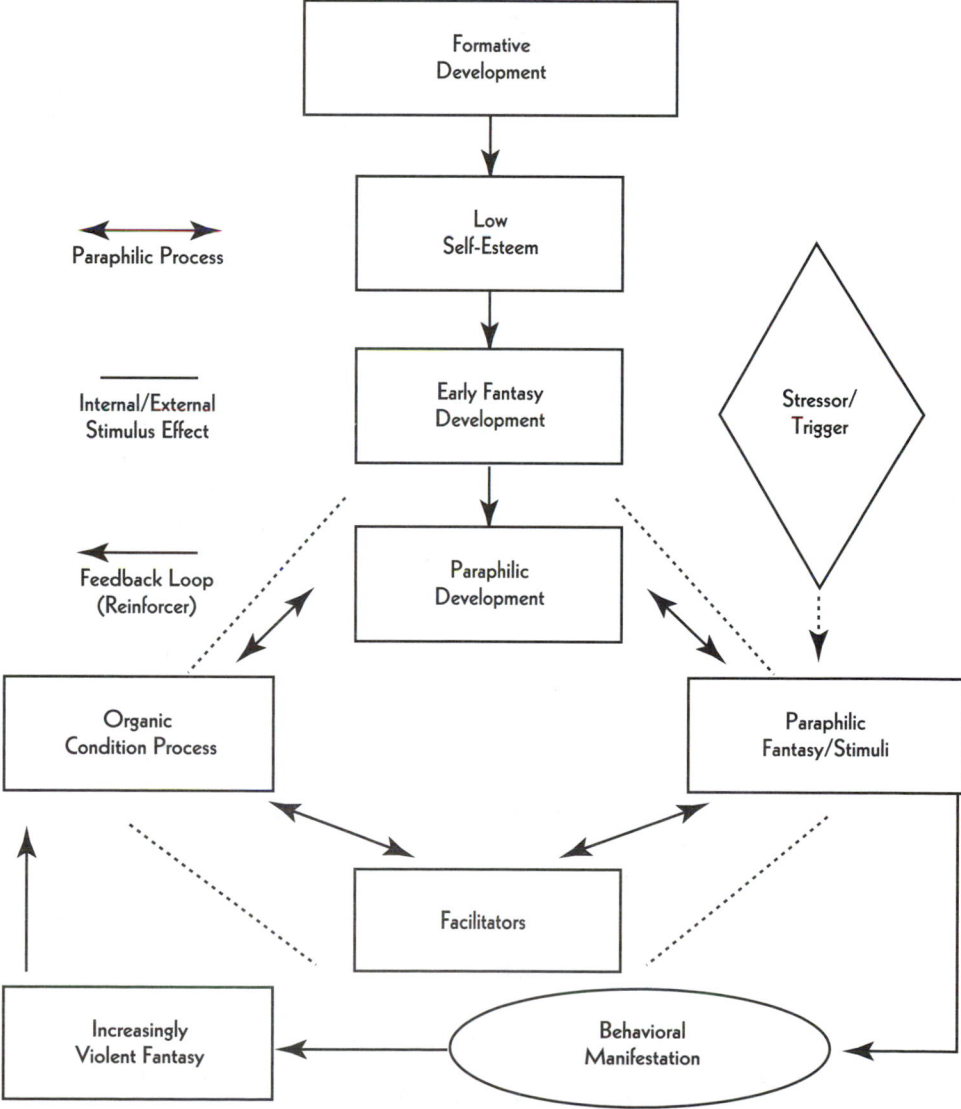

Figure 5–2 Arrigo and Purcell's Integrated Model on Lust Murder and Paraphilia

these factors contribute to sexually deviant and sadistic (i.e., paraphilic) thoughts and images. At this point, the paraphilic process is activated by continued sexually aberrant fantasies, facilitators (e.g., drug, alcohol, and pornography), and the desire for orgasmic fulfillment. Sustaining the paraphilic fantasies are stressors (i.e., triggering life experiences) that validate the person's troubled formative development and low self-esteem. As the individual struggles to achieve sexual gratification through sadistically charged sexual orgasms, the fantasies become increasingly violent. When these intensely aberrant and erotically aggressive fantasies offer no sexual relief for the person, the individual engages in violent and lethal behavior to achieve orgasm. As Figure 5–1 also suggests, there is a feedback loop operating in the process. The feedback loop illustrates how paraphilias manifest themselves, reinforce existing fantasies, and progress and cycle back into the overall sexually violent continuum for the lust murderer.

SEX CRIMES

Introduction

Rape is a deeply troubling phenomenon that impacts the lives of many women. There are various forms of rape and there are many models (especially motivational typologies) used to explain the behavior of this criminal. This portion of the chapter canvasses the crime of rape and the profile of the rapist. In particular, background material on what we know about this form of sexual assault is presented. In addition, a description of acquaintance and stranger rape is provided. Where useful, both demographic characteristics and personality features for different types of rapists are delineated.

Background Information on Rape

The Uniform Crime Report (UCR) defines rape in a manner that distinguishes forcible rape from statutory sexual assault and rape by fraud. According to the UCR, forcible rape is "the carnal knowledge of a female, forcibly and against her will" (FBI, 2000, p. 2). Sexual assault and attempts to commit rape either by threat or by force also are included in this definition (Graney & Arrigo, 2002). Statutory rape is the carnal knowledge of a female with or without her consent. The deciding factor in statutory rape is the age of the victim. Every state has a legal cutoff point for this offense. Thus, if a girl falls below this age (i.e., the point at which she would otherwise be deemed an adult), she is said to not possess the maturity to consent to sexual relations. Under these conditions, any male who engages in sexual intercourse with a female minor commits the offense of statutory rape. The age limits are arbitrarily set and vary from state to state (e.g., in the state of California, the cutoff is 18; in Ohio it is 13). The following comments on rape models and offender profiles address specific aspects of forcible, rather than statutory, rape.

The crime of rape is a significant problem in the United States, notwithstanding official statistics reporting that the incidences of this offense have been on the decline for the past several years (Bartol, 2002; FBI, 2000). For example, rape figures reported to law enforcement agencies in 1996 estimate that 150,000 of these crimes occurred in the United States (FBI, 1997). This means that a woman in the United States suffers this form of sexual abuse once every 2 minutes (U.S. Department of Justice, Bureau of Justice Statistics, 1997b). These statistics are 4 times higher than those in Germany, 13 times higher than those in England, and 20 times higher than those in Japan (Graney & Arrigo, 2002; Hazelwood & Burgess, 1995). However, compiling such statistics has been problematic for police personnel.

One of the major problems law enforcement agencies have in gathering statistics on rape is that a majority of these offenses go unreported. The U.S. Department of Justice, Bureau of Justice Statistics (1997a) estimates that 31% of all rapes are reported to the authorities, a significantly lower percentage than the total offenses that do occur (see also Ringle,

1997). Contributing to this underreporting is the emotional distress women confront when recounting their victimization and the legal (especially courtroom) ordeals they endure in the face of their sexual trauma.

Acquaintance Rape

There are a variety of categories for forcible rape (Graney & Arrigo, 2002). However, the most common term associated with acquaintance rape is "date rape." Hickman and Muehlenhard (1997, p. 528) define acquaintance rape as an act in which the female victim is assaulted by "someone known to her, ranging from a man she has just met to a close friend or boyfriend." This definition includes spousal rape.

Researchers report that 78% of all rape victims know their attacker (U.S. Department of Justice, Bureau of Justice Statistics, 1998), and that approximately 1 in 7 women are raped by their husbands (Russell, 1982). There is a high prevalence of date rape on college campuses with 1 in 4 college women either having been raped or having suffered an attempted rape (Schwartz & DeKeseredy, 1997). For example, in a survey of college women, 38% reported sexual victimization that met the legal definition of rape or attempted rate, yet only 1 in 25, or 4%, reported the incident to the police (U.S. Department of Justice, Bureau of Justice Statistics, 1997a). In another survey, 35% of college males reported that they would commit a violent rape if they were assured they could get away with it (Graney & Arrigo, 2002). Another survey of college male students revealed that 1 in 12 of them committed acts that met the legal definition of rape; however, 84% of these men definitely felt they had not committed such a crime based on their reported actions (Schwartz & Dekeseredy).

Seventy-five percent of male students and 55% of female students involved in acquaintance rape use drugs or alcohol (U.S. Department of Justice, Bureau of Justice Statistics, 1998). The most common drug associated with date rape is rohypnol (flunitrazepam), referred to by its street name as "**roofies.**" The common scenario is for the offender to slip the drug into a woman's drink and observe her as she becomes extremely sedated to the point of passing out. The effects of the narcotic begin within 30 minutes, peak after 2 hours, and last for 8 hours or more. Typically, the assailant volunteers to escort the apparently inebriated woman home, waits for the victim to pass out, and proceeds to take advantage of her sexually (U.S. Department of Justice, Bureau of Justice Statistics, 1997b). The victim rarely remembers anything after the drug hits its 2-hour peak. As such, she cannot say for sure whether or not the rape occurred (Graney & Arrigo, 2002). This condition further complicates and contributes to the gross underestimates for the actual incidents of rape.

In a survey of victims who did not report being raped, other explanations were identified. These included the following: the belief that nothing could be done (43%), the sense that it was a private matter (27%), the fear of police response or reprisal (12%), or the notion that it was not significant enough to warrant attention (12%; U.S. Department of Justice, Bureau of Justice Statistics, 1998). Rohypnol continues to be a highly accessible drug among college students, making the potential for sexual assault and other forms of acquaintance rape all the more prevalent.

Stranger Rape

According to the U.S. Department of Justice, Bureau of Justice Statistics (1994), approximately 29% of all rapes are committed by an offender the victim does not know (see also Hickman & Muehlenhard, 1997; Riedel, 1993). Stranger rapists are more likely to involve the use of a weapon (Koss et al., 1988), and the most frequently used weapon is a knife (Allison & Wrightsman, 1993). The stranger rapist also is more likely to employ threats of brutality and bodily harm, along with the actual use of physical violence perpetrated against the victim during the rape (Graney & Arrigo, 2002). Approximately 75% of female rape victims require medical attention after their attack (U.S. Department of Justice, Bureau of Justice Statistics, 1994).

There are many rapist typologies that have been developed over the years, emphasizing such factors as the victim–offender relationship, motivational intent, and the social and psychological dynamics of the sexual assault (e.g., Cohen, Seghorn, & Calamas, 1969; Gebhard, Gagnon, Pomeroy, & Christenson, 1965; Guttmacher & Weihofen, 1952; Kopp, 1962). However, the rapist typology developed by Groth and Birnbaum (1979; see also Groth et al., 1977) remains a major reference point in the victimological research community. According to Groth and Birnbaum (1979), the stranger rapist is not motivated by sexual forces; instead, other, previously unaccounted for factors primarily drive this assailant's behavior.

Groth and Birnbaum (1979) identified three, primary motivational typologies for the stranger rapist: anger, power, and sadism. The anger rapist harbors a great deal of aggression and hostility toward women. During this sexual assault, the offender exhibits an excessive amount of physically violent and degrading behaviors, including sodomy, fellatio, and even urinating on the victim. Hostility and contempt for women is further displayed in violent and degrading verbal outbursts. The anger rapist has a need to consciously express his anger toward women and does so in a myriad of dehumanizing ways. Sex is the weapon the anger rapist uses to achieve his goals of physically and verbally harming or otherwise humiliating his victims. The triggering event for the anger rapist is often a heated argument between the offender and another significant female in the rapist's life (e.g., sister, wife, mother, coworker, or supervisor).

The **power rapist** is recognized as the most common form of stranger rape (Graney & Arrigo, 2002). The power rapist seeks to exert complete and total domination and control over his victims (Groth & Birnbaum, 1979). Once again, sexual gratification is not the primary motive in this sexual assault. What drives the power rapist is a need to establish an identity of power, control, and authority over the victim; that is, to completely dominate the victim and to thoroughly make the woman aware of the assailant's mastery over her. This sexual conquest is further fueled by the rapist's need to (over) compensate for his perceived personal inadequacies and insecurities. Victims are often kidnapped or held captive in one form or another. The sexual experience is often anticlimactic and disappointing for the power rapist because the event fails to live up to the assailant's expectations. Consequently, the offender is left with reinforced feelings of inadequacy and insecurity.

For the **sadistic rapist,** aggression is eroticized (Groth & Birnbaum, 1979). The sadistic rapist receives sexual pleasure by torturing and tormenting his victim. Typically, the woman is bound and physical abuse is directed toward multiple areas of her body. The sadistic rapist may stalk and kidnap his victim and, on occasion, the injured party is murdered at the end of the sadistic ritual. This type of criminal behavior is consistent with the previous section exploring sexual homicide and lust murder. Sadistic rape offenses make up only 5% of all rape crimes (Graney & Arrigo, 2002).

Forty-seven percent of the physical injuries sustained by the victim during the sexual assault are not rape related (U.S. Department of Justice, Bureau of Justice Statistics, 1994). In other words, close to half of the injuries a woman sustains during a sexual assault are linked to ulterior motives. These motives are consistent with Groth and Birnbaum's (1979) observations on anger, power, and sadism.

Given the different motivational forces underpinning rape and the various manifestations this form of sexual assault assumes, it is difficult to establish one specific profile for the rapist (Graney & Arrigo, 2002). However, according to Scully and Marolla (1984), the general demographic features indicate that this sexual assailant is a White male with low wage-earning capacity. Only 20% of convicted rapists have the equivalent of a high school education or better, and 85% come from blue-collar, working-class backgrounds (Scully & Marolla, 1985). Moreover, Scully and Marolla (1984) also reported the prior conviction crimes and figures for the rapists in their study. They found that 12% were for rape, 39% were for robbery and burglary, 29% were for abduction, 25% were for sodomy, and 11% were for first- or second-degree murder. These figures reflect the multiple types of criminal behavior that individual rapists commit rather than totals for all prior convictions. The data are also consistent with the motivational influences Groth and Birnbaum (1979) presented in their rape typology.

PEDOPHILIA

Introduction

The sexual assault of a child is arguably one of the more repulsive crimes found in our society today. Moreover, adding to the frustration of law enforcement officials and the public at large, is the high incidence of child molestation that goes unreported. The crime itself is recognized as one of the most underreported offenses, and offenders are most likely to escape detection and prosecution by the criminal justice system (U.S. Department of Justice, Bureau of Justice Statistics, 1997a). The literature reflects that there is some debate in defining and classifying what constitutes a child molester and a pedophile. However, according to the *Diagnostic and Statistical Manual of Mental Disorders* (4th ed. [*DSM–IV*], APA, 1994, p. 528), **pedophilia** is defined as "recurrent, intense sexually arousing fantasies, sexual urges, or behaviors involving sexual activity with a prepubescent child or children (generally age 13 years or younger)."

For purposes of simplicity, in this portion of the chapter the terms *child molester* and *pedophile* are used interchangeably. Specific attention will be given to what we know about the incidence of child molestation in the United Sates. In addition, commentary on the profile of the pedophile will be addressed. Specifically, this section of the chapter concludes by reviewing the latest model for classifying child molesters, and discusses the overall utility the typology offers for both criminal justice and mental health professionals. Other paraphilias (i.e., deviant sexual acts) such as voyeurism, exhibitionism, and autoeroticism are not discussed here. Although certainly relevant to many sexual homicides (including pedophilia), they principally are expressions of deviance (Hickey, 2002) rather than acts of criminality (cf. Davis, 2002).

The Crime of Pedophilia

Despite the high incidence of underreported cases of child molestation, the U.S. Department of Health and Human Services (1996) compiled some startling statistics illustrating the prevalence of child sexual assault in the United States. These figures included the following: 1.6 million investigations of alleged **child abuse** and neglect were reported in 1996; 34% of the investigations resulted in substantiated or indicated child maltreatment; and 58% were not substantiated. Of the nearly 1 million (968,748) substantiated or indicated victims of abuse, 12% (119,397) were victims of sexual abuse (a decline of roughly 3% from 1990). Ten percent of the sexually abused victims were under the age of 4; 36% were 12 or older; girls made up 77% of the victims; boys accounted for 23%, and 65% of all victims were Caucasian.

The Profile of the Child Molester

With the incidence of child molestation alarmingly high, many investigators have attempted to identify what type of person commits such harmful acts against children (e.g., Finkelhor, 1979; Finkelhor & Araji, 1986). Unfortunately, there appears to be no one composite profile for the pedophile. However, the best classification model put forth thus far in the relevant research on child molestation is the Massachusetts Treatment Center: Child Molester Version 3 (MTC:CM3) taxonomic model. This typology was developed by Knight, Carter, and Prentky (1989).

As Figure 5–3 indicates, the model is divided into Axis I: Degree of Fixation, Axis II: Amount of Contact, and the decisional process within each axis resulting in the classification of the of the offender. Fixation (Decision 1, Axis I) refers to the strength or level of the offender's pedophilic interest; that is, the extent to which the person's sexual attraction to children occupies the pedophile's daily thoughts. Social Competence (Decision 2, Axis I) refers to the offender's ability to function in society (e.g., overall responsibility; ability to maintain steady employment; involvement in constructive, community organizations; and

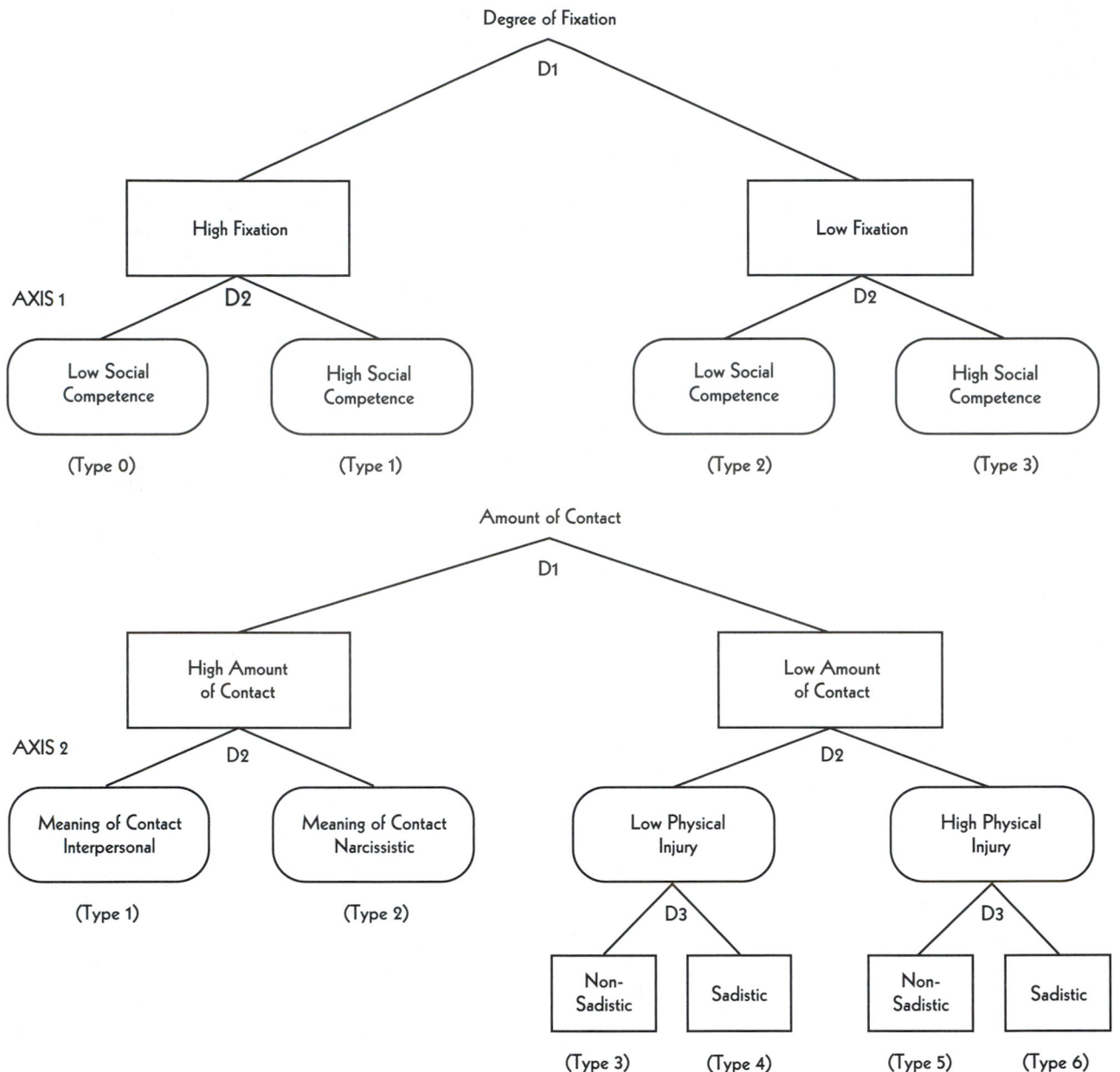

Figure 5–3 Knight et al. (1989) Model for Classifying Child Molesters

maintaining functional relationships both socially and sexually). Amount of Contact (Decision 1, Axis II) is the frequency and duration of close proximity an offender attempts to have with children. An example of a pedophile that seeks a high amount of contact would be a school teacher or a coach.

The high contact offender is subdivided into the Type 1-interpersonal and Type 2 narcissistic offender, differentiated by the meaning of the contact. The interpersonal offender (Type 1) seeks a relationship with the child to satisfy both social and sexual needs, and believes the friendship with the child is mutually appreciated. The narcissistic offender (Type 2) seeks the company of children solely to increase sexual opportunities. In this instance, the children are viewed merely as a means to an end, and little concern is given to the child's overall well-being. These offenders tend to be strangers to their victims. Offenders determined to be low-contact seekers are divided further into subdivisions based on the amount of physical injury they inflict on their victims (low physical injury = Type 3 and Type 4;

high physical injury = Type 5 and Type 6). The sexual assault itself is the only contact this offender traditionally has with the victim. Both levels of physical abuse are further divided into whether or not the injuries inflicted on the child are sadistic in nature. The Type 3 exploitative, non-sadistic offender typically uses no more physical force or violence than is necessary to commit the crime. Any physical abuse inflicted on the victim is not sadistic in nature. The Type 4 muted sadistic offender performs a number of painful sadistic rituals; however, these acts do not result in sustained physical damage or bodily harm to the child. The final two types of low-contact offenders are Type 5 and Type 6. Type 5 pedophiles are non-sadistic and aggressive; type 6 assailants are sadistic. However, both inflict high levels of physical injury on the child.

Admittedly, more research is needed to further test the current MTC:CM3 model; however, as a conceptual schema, the typology offers criminal justice and mental health practitioners a useful classification mechanism by which to interpret the criminal behavior of pedophiles. Recent studies and interviews also have revealed other personality characteristics of the child molester. These sex offenders typically deny responsibility for their actions. For example, pedophiles either claim they did not commit the offense at all or blame it on external forces over which they had no or little control (Palermo & Farkas, 2001). A majority of child molesters also demonstrate a lack of empathy for their victims. However, it is important to note that these individuals are capable of showing remorse, caring, or empathy in other settings or contexts. As such, they lack empathy toward their victims, thereby distorting the harm they inflict on the children they abuse (Marshall, 1999).

VIOLENCE IN THE CRIMINAL JUSTICE SYSTEM

Introduction

The United States has observed how the violence of **police brutality** has evolved from a sporadic anomaly to an event that is all too familiar. The very notion that those who are sworn to protect and serve the public abuse their power and inflict unnecessary and unlawful harm—sometimes resulting in death—on these same citizens is, at the very least, a cause for deep concern. The same alarming conditions present themselves in the prison and jail systems across the United States. Indeed, the criminal behavior of convicts and the corrupt conduct of guards who work the units housing offenders raise serious questions about the nature of correctional violence.

This portion of the chapter reviews both police brutality and **prison violence.** Police brutality is examined generally in the context of a law enforcement agent's use of excessive and deadly force, resulting, at times, in the brutal and unnecessary killings of citizens. Several theories are offered to help account for this behavior. In addition, an examination of the impetus for and the etiology of the brutal beatings and murders citizens endure at the hands of law enforcement personnel are also provided.

Relatedly, the phenomenon of prison violence is reviewed. The relevant research suggests that there are two types of relationships between convicts and guards: (a) hatred and malevolence, which is acted out violently; and (b) a business-like or professional association designed to maintain order, control, and stability. The former relationship is addressed in this section of the chapter. Specifically, the criminal interaction between prisoners and the deviant and the corrupt interaction between convicts and correctional officers are explored.

Police Brutality

As a function of a police officer's duty to uphold the law and to protect and serve the public, the agent is granted a tremendous amount of authority and power through one's precinct or department and by the criminal justice system itself (Kappeler, Sluder, & Alpert, 2001).

Accompanying this role in which officers protect citizens and safeguard communities is the discretion to make law enforcement decisions (Brooks, 2001). Undoubtedly, the decisions officers make can be significant. Indeed, they include such choices as whether to pull someone over while driving, whether to detain or arrest a suspect, when to use force, and when to use a firearm. As Arrigo (2000, p. 9) notes, "The decision to use force in the apprehension of a citizen, whether it becomes excessive or deadly, ultimately lies in the hands of the police officer at the moment of conflict." The implications for this choice making are profound. The police are entrusted with a great deal of authority and power mediated by their training, experience, and by their interpretation of discretion, including how best to use it (Ericson, 1982).

To be clear, discretion can be justified for several reasons. At the same time, it presents serious legal and social problems. Brooks (2001) succinctly summarizes these matters:

> Police discretion can be justified on many grounds including: the existence of vague laws, limited resources, community alienation, the need to individualize the law, and the fact that many violations are minor in nature . . . {However,] [t]he exercise of police discretion poses some difficulties, such as: unequal treatment of citizens, interference with due process, a reduction in deterrent effects, and the hidden or unreviewable nature of many discretionary decisions. (p. 119)

Given the tension implied in the use of police discretion, we should not be surprised when officers engage in questionable choices that challenge or erode the advisability of using discretion in the first place (Fyfe, 2001).

One way to understand discretion (especially in the context of police brutality and the use of deadly force) is to assess the personality of officers (Arrigo & Claussen, 2003; Bartol, 2001, pp. 68–70). Research on police personality provides some clues as to the characterological structure of officers, especially those who find themselves in difficult, intense, or otherwise problematic circumstances where discretion is used (e.g., Alpert, 1993; Alpert & Dunham, 1997). For example, a study performed by Cortina, Doherty, Schmitt, Kaufman, and Smith (1992) identified a number of police characteristics that arguably function to explain the cause of their violent interactions with the public. Their study involved profiles from the Minnesota Multiphasic Personality Inventory—Second Edition (MMPI-2), an objective personality test useful for measuring psychopathology (Graham, 2000). In their research, they discovered that police officers' scores on the **Psychopathic Deviate scale** were elevated. These scores are consistent with "individuals who have difficulty incorporating values and standards of society; are impulsive and often strive for immediate gratification without thinking [about] the consequences of their actions; are impatient and have limited frustration tolerance; show poor judgment and take risks; tend to be hostile . . . [and] may act in aggressive ways" (Graham, 2000, pp. 71–72). These specific personality characteristics do not easily lend themselves to interactions based on dispute resolution and conflict mediation techniques. When the variables of power and authority are factored into these intense police–citizen encounters, it is no surprise that the results may sometimes include violence (Blumberg, 2001).

Investigators speculate that the aforementioned personality features are the result of an officer becoming jaded, burned out, and estranged from society (Graves, 1996; Kappeler et al., 2001). For example, Graves suggests that these officers feel disappointed and let down by society in general. They see the worst aspects of people everyday and eventually lose faith in the system and the values they originally believed were sacrosanct (Skolnick, 1994). This cynicism is a precursor to the severe emotional problems and forms of misconduct that produce police brutality and acts of corruption (Arrigo & Claussen, 2003).

Other researchers maintain that there are violent people in the world, and that some of them seek employment as police officers (Toch, 1992). Toch does not support the theory that the values and beliefs of officers are diminished while on the force, that they become jaded, and that they then succumb to violence as a form of relief or other self-expression. Instead, he contends that police personnel have a certain penchant toward volatile conflict and violent interactions prior to entering the force. Indeed, he claims that existing personality tests cannot detect or screen out these job candidates, and that on-the-spot analysis is the only true measurement. Consistent with this line of thinking, Alpert (1993, p. 100) states that, ". . . no [psychological] test has been found that discriminates consistently and clearly between individuals who will and who will not make good police officers." In these circumstances, prospects for developing a proactive solution for the prevention of police brutality and violence do not appear forthcoming.

A third perspective addressing the problem of discretion in policing argues that departments and precincts need to hire more women for law enforcement work (Fitzsimmons, 1998). When examining the mediation skills required to successfully resolve disputes, and when considering whether male or female officers are more inclined statistically to resolve these conflicts nonviolently and peacefully, it is only logical that more women should be employed (Martin, 2001). Fitzsimmons's position is that society must work to establish and maintain peace. Precisely because women excel at conflict mediation, departments could benefit from having more women mediate potentially violent situations. Whereas, in theory this perspective represents a viable option, more empirical research would certainly enhance its credibility. The same observation applies to the other approaches previously described that attempt to explain police violence in relation to an officer's discretion, power, and authority.

A Typology of Violence for Police Officers

In his classic work, *Violent Men: An Inquiry Into the Psychology of Violence* (1992), Hans Toch develops a typology for the violence-prone person based, in part, on problem police officers, as well as on convict and parolee samples. The typology is briefly summarized below. It emphasizes violence "used to bolster and enhance the person's ego in the eyes of himself and others" (Toch, 1992, p. 133). This violence entails "self-preserving strategies." The typology also stresses behaviors "used by persons who see themselves (and their own needs) as being the only fact of social relevance" (p. 133). These behaviors represent "approaches that dehumanize others."

Self-Preserving Strategies	*Meaning*
1. Rep-defending	Defending the publicly authorized role assigned to the individual (e.g., police officer), including the use of aggression
2. Norm-enforcing	Employing the use of violence to promote and maintain what are taken to be universal rules of conduct
3. Self-image compensating (Self-image defending)	Utilizing aggression against others believed to be defaming or ridiculing the person's self-image
4. Self-image compensating (Self-image promoting)	Utilizing aggression against others to demonstrate self-worth, consistent with the value of toughness
5. Self-defending	Perceiving others as potentially dangerous or physically hostile, necessitating their control
6. Pressure-removing	Exploding (verbally or physically) because of an inability to cope with the demands or pressures of a given situation

Approaches That Dehumanize Others	*Meaning*
7. Bullying	Obtaining pleasure by victimizing others through the use of violence and terror
8. Exploitation	Manipulating others (including violently) so that they facilitate one's own pleasure and convenience
9. Self-indulging	Believing that others exist to satisfy one's own needs where violence is employed to ensure compliance
10. Catharting	Releasing built-up internal pressure violently

Prison Violence: Guard Versus Convict

Another form of violence within the criminal justice system is found within the area of corrections. Guards within prison facilities have been known to beat or physically assault convicts without proper cause (Ross & Richards, 2002). In a study conducted by McCorkle, Miethe, and Drass (1995), they estimated the rate of assaults on prisoners perpetrated by guards was less than 1%. This figure is indeed troubling, especially when we note that there are over 2 million persons incarcerated in prisons and jails today (U.S. Department of Justice, Bureau of Justice Statistics, 1999). Consequently, 20,000 individuals are subjected to correctional violence at the hands of prison guards annually.

Research addressing guard-on-convict violence offers some interesting findings. For example, in his study on correctional facilities, Carroll (1998) identified the incidents of guards ganging up against inmates and then beating them severely without cause or justification. In some of these brutal instances, the guards outnumbered the prisoners 4 to 1. Carroll also noted that some of these correctional officers possessed the equivalent of a third-grade education and had been previously arrested for violent offenses. The explosive temper exhibited by some guards was not directed completely toward the inmate population. Indeed, Carroll observed that one guard even paid a prisoner $150 to assault another officer.

Prison Violence: Convict Versus Convict

The one violent act committed by prisoners and feared the most is forcible rape. This type of crime is prominent in the convict subculture, especially in maximum-security facilities (Arrigo, 2000). Donaldson (1990) identified three groups of inmates who are a part of this subculture of rapists (or rape victims) within prisons. The first group constitutes the majority. These individuals are called "jockers." **Jockers** forcefully penetrate other prisoners, and this behavior serves to further their masculinity and sense of control. An important distinguishing characteristic for these convicts is that they consider themselves heterosexual. Indeed, although they engage in homosexual relations within the confines of prison, their sexual practices are exclusively heterosexual both before incarceration and after release from a correctional facility.

Another group of prisoners involved in the rape experience are the "queens." **Queens** engage in homosexual relations before and after incarceration. Unlike the jocks, they are predominantly rape victims. As such, they are isolated by the prison system or facility in an attempt to protect them from abuse and to curb homosexual activity. In spite of their protected status, these convicts endure brutal physical harm from guards and other prisoners (Long, 1993).

A third category identified by Donaldson (1990) is the "punks." **Punks** are heterosexual inmates who are gang raped by other convicts. This "turning-out" process represents a dramatic and horrific experience in which the person is completely dominated and, on occasion, sexually enslaved by other prisoners. Punks are usually nonviolent offenders with smaller physiques, making it more difficult for them to defend against unwanted bodily invasions. In these circumstances, they become easy prey for prison rapists. Over time, the psychological trauma endured by punks takes its toll on them. Indeed, some individuals are so severely damaged and emotionally scarred that they experience rape trauma syndrome. However, in other instances, when punks are released from prison they engage in homosexual relations, notwithstanding their exclusively heterosexual behavior prior to incarceration (Long, 1993).

Why does convict-on-convict violence occur in correctional facilities? According to Arrigo (2000, p. 248), "Measures of poor conditions, such as inadequate prison management and lack of prison programs due to over crowding, are associated with high levels of prison violence." To substantiate this perspective, a considerable amount of research reports that there is a negative relationship between prison conditions and the prevalence of violence in these facilities (May, 2000; U.S. Department of Justice, Bureau of Justice Statistics,

1999). With this in mind, it is logical to assume that as prison conditions improve, the likelihood for violence will decline. Moreover, the opposite is true. When prison conditions do not improve or are poor, there are higher rates of violence in these facilities (May; 2000; McCorkle et al., 1995).

In the McCorkle et al. (1995) study, poor prison conditions in male state correctional facilities increased the incidence of violence. However, when prisons provided convicts with access to programs (e.g., educational and vocational assistance), these prisons had a much lower rate of violence. These findings are consistent with the research conducted by Marquart et al. (1994). Along with his colleagues, Marquart demonstrated that the more overcrowded a prison was, the less likely prisoners were to participate in educational and vocational programs, initiatives that were clearly linked to the incidence and prevalence of prison violence. Other implications of the McCorkle et al. study showed that outside unemployment rates and employer turnover rates were positively correlated with within-prison violence.

DOMESTIC VIOLENCE

Introduction

The issue of domestic or family violence has most recently become more visible and more disturbing (Browne & Herbert, 1997). Changes in state and federal legislation have increased the penalties for those who resort to domestic violence as a disruptive method by which to cope with family problems or life issues. Generally speaking, domestic violence can be broken into three main categories: child abuse, **spousal abuse**, and **elder abuse**. This portion of the chapter examines each of these forms of criminal behavior. Where helpful, specific information on the offender and the victim are also provided.

Child Abuse

Child abuse has become one of the more prominent issues in society during the past several decades (Browne & Finkelhor, 1986). Interestingly, societal attitudes toward child abuse have changed substantially over the years. For example, what was once considered discipline, such as spanking a child with a paddle, is now considered abuse in some jurisdictions. Child abuse normally falls into one of four categories: physical abuse, emotional abuse, sexual abuse, and general neglect.

Physical abuse of a child involves bodily injury to anyone who is 17 years old or younger by a parent or caretaker. The extent to which physical harm meets the criteria for abuse varies across jurisdictions. Emotional abuse is any type of mental or psychological damage inflicted on a minor by one's parents or caretakers. Emotional abuse usually coexists with physical and sexual abuse. It is rare for emotional abuse to occur in the absence of another type of abuse directed toward children. Moreover, it is particularly prevalent among those youth that witness spousal abuse. Sexual abuse entails the fondling, molestation, or penetration of a minor by a parent, caretaker, or other individual above the age of consent. Sexual contact between two similar aged minors is not considered sexual abuse, nor is it investigated in many jurisdictions. However, when investigations do proceed, officials determine whether the minor was a victim of sexual abuse who learned his or her inappropriate sexual behaviors from another person (Waterhouse, 1993). General neglect is the broadest category of child abuse. Neglect can range from being unable to care for a child's basic needs to abandoning a youth. Generally speaking, neglect means that a child's basic needs (i.e., food, clothing, and shelter) are not being met, adversely affecting the adolescent's growth and development. Indicators of neglect include parental absence, a parent's debilitating medical illness, a mental illness that renders the parent unable to care for his or her child, or a parental substance abuse problem.

Child abuse statutes and mandatory reporting laws exist in federal and state jurisdictions, including all 50 states and the District of Columbia. Although the definition of child abuse varies across jurisdictions, most follow the guidelines derived from the federal Child Abuse Prevention and Treatment Act (CAPTA), originally passed in 1974 and last revised in 1996. All of the states require that members of certain occupations, such as educators, medical professionals, child care workers, police officers, and social service employees, report child abuse to local human service agencies (Smith, 1999).

Child abuse victims come from an array of backgrounds. All socioeconomic classes, races, and ethnic backgrounds are represented. The victims are relatively split between boys and girls, consistent with their representation in the general population. Characterologically, the victims are withdrawn, isolated, depressed, anxious, and act out abusive behaviors toward their siblings. They may be distracted in school and show a drop in grades during acute abuse episodes. Friends and family members in a child's life need to be aware of the changes a juvenile experiences in order to address and confront suspected abuse.

Perpetrators of child abuse, specifically physical abuse, emotional abuse, and general neglect, come from a variety of backgrounds as well. Some come from abusive and dysfunctional backgrounds, whereas others come from backgrounds in which no family violence occurred (Snow, 1997). Some researchers suggest that child abusers are more assertive and controlling with their children than are nonabusing parents. However, other investigators contend that abusing parents are inconsistent in their parenting techniques and tend to use more punitive types of discipline than nonabusing parents. These perspectives notwithstanding, other factors influence whether a parent becomes a child abuser. These factors include marital, work-related, and financial stressors; health problems; inadequate coping skills; and substance abuse problems.

The cycle of child abuse can be self-perpetuating (National Center on Child Abuse and Neglect, 1994). Abused children are more likely to act out inappropriately, resulting in additional parental stress, thereby increasing the likelihood of repeated physical child abuse. Research into sexual abuse perpetrators focuses on adult males; however, females are also known to sexually abuse children. Sexual abuse perpetrators range from those individuals who demonstrate extreme pathology and are dangerous, to those individuals who seem to function well in society but are involved in inappropriate relationships. These perpetrators have been described as socially immature and isolative, lacking boundaries, and having poor impulse control. They also are affected by external factors, including marital, family, financial, and health problems (Walker, Bonner, & Kaufman, 1998). As society changes its attitude toward child abuse and child abusers, the laws and penalties for those who commit this crime will continue to evolve as well. At the present time, legislation protects the rights of children more than it ensures the rights of parents. However, this trend is not guaranteed to continue (for more on child molestation see the previous section on pedophilia).

Spousal Abuse

The issue of spousal abuse has become another prominent phenomenon during the past several decades. Spousal abuse is defined as the emotional abuse, financial abuse, or physical battering of one's partner. This abuse occurs in marital or intimate relationships in the context of both heterosexual and homosexual relationships. Most of the current research literature focuses on the "traditional" male–female relationship. Although women can be the perpetrators, violence in marital and intimate relationships is typically characterized with women as victims. Previous research has shown that women are six times more likely to be abused in intimate relationships than are men (Hampton, Vandergriff-Avery, & Kim, 1999). Women of all races are equally susceptible to being abused by their partners. Spousal abuse can affect women of all socioeconomic backgrounds (Levinson, 1988). Women who are currently separated have a greater risk of being abused than those women who are currently married or divorced.

The violence that occurs in an intimate relationship typically follows a three-phase cycle. The first phase is the tension-building phase. In this phase, there is a slow buildup of stress and tension in the relationship. The perpetrator starts to criticize, blame, and berate the victim. The second phase is the battering incident. During this phase, the perpetrator will display physical, sexual, or emotional violence toward the victim. This is the phase of the cycle in which the victim is most likely to be killed. The third phase of the cycle is the honeymoon phase. This is the period when the perpetrator is remorseful and sympathetic, following his harmful and abusive actions. The offender promises to never act violently or aggressively toward the victim again. Because the perpetrator fears that the victim will end the relationship or will otherwise attempt to leave, the assailant showers the harmed party with gifts and affection to prevent or forestall the departure. Based on these actions, many victims want to believe that the behavior of the perpetrator will change. The victim remains in the relationship and the **cycle of violence** continues (Barnett, Miller-Perrin, & Perrin, 1997).

Given that spousal abuse is often unexpected and unprovoked, victims typically develop low self-esteem, a sense of loss and inadequacy, depression, and learned helplessness (Mills, 1996). Needless to say, the perpetrators are more aggressive than are nonabusers. However, they also suffer from low self-esteem and low levels of assertiveness. Abusers substitute aggression or passive–aggressive behavior for assertiveness. They exhibit a greater need for control in their life and are frequently unrealistically jealous of the other relationships in their partners' life. For many perpetrators, their abuse involves their children as well. When directly confronted, most perpetrators try to excuse or justify their actions, denying any personal responsibility for their violent behavior. These offenders would rather attribute their explosive tendencies to external forces beyond their control than to accept accountability for their conduct. Indeed, the abuser will often assign blame to the victim's behavior and personality as a contributing if not deciding factor for the assailant's actions. When perpetrators do admit to their abuse, they minimize the harm they caused or neutralize the amount of violence they inflicted, alleging that it was justified given the situation (Russell, 1995).

Some investigators maintain that it is likely that perpetrators are exposed to family violence at some prior point in their own lives (Browne & Herbert, 1997); however, this perspective is not supported by the current research. Feminists blame the patriarchal nature of our society for the current attitudes regarding spousal abuse (Mills, 1996). For example, police officers have been accused of responding to domestic violence calls and leaving the situation without arresting the perpetrator, or telling the couple they need to work out their problems on their own (Stanko, 1989). Police departments have started to educate their officers on spousal abuse laws and how to mediate domestic dispute situations (Buzawa & Buzawa, 2001). With increased education and training, the police can begin to protect the victims of spousal abuse.

Elder Abuse

A more recent issue regarding domestic violence is elder abuse. Elder abuse refers to physical abuse, emotional abuse, sexual abuse, general neglect, medical neglect, abandonment, isolation, fraud, and financial exploitation of a person age 65 or older by a caretaker (Barnett et al., 1997). The issues of physical abuse, emotional abuse, sexual abuse, and general neglect are similar to those issues described in the child abuse section. Medical neglect refers to a caretaker who refuses to have the medical problems of the victim addressed, potentially resulting in the victim's death. Abandonment refers to the practice of caretakers deserting an elderly person for whom they have been providing care. Abandonment occurs at hospitals, nursing facilities, police stations, and other public places. Isolation refers to keeping elderly victims from their family and friends in order to make them more vulnerable to other forms of abuse. At times, the perpetrator will not allow anyone to visit with the elderly person alone for fear that the victim will disclose the abuse. Fraud and financial exploitation are similar.

They involve the perpetrator gaining financial control of the elderly victim's resources for the perpetrator's economic gain. This could involve the assailant acquiring the victim's trust in order to persuade the elderly person to sign over his or her power of attorney. Having procured this degree of financial control, the offender raids the victim's accounts. This may include forgery wherein the perpetrator wrongfully and illegally signs financial documents for the elderly victim without the person's consent (Glendenning, 1997).

Unlike child abuse laws, there are currently no federal standards regarding elder abuse. Although the Older American Act provides a broad definition for this offense, it does not provide much direction for how best to interpret maltreatment of persons 65 years of age or older. The Act also authorizes funding for the National Center on Elder Abuse. This organization promotes awareness, training, and state and federal coordination of activities concerning the problem of elder abuse. Regrettably, the Older American Act does not provide funding for Adult Protective Services (APS) organizations nor does it financially support the development of shelters for victims of elder abuse (American Bar Association Committee on Legal Problems of the Elderly Research, 1999). APS organizations are found in all 50 states, including the District of Columbia. To date, no standardized laws regarding elder abuse have been developed; however, several APS organizations use the local Child Protective Services model as a method to report incidents of abuse and to conduct investigations.

Many victims of elder abuse are disabled or have some sort of hearing or visual impairment. They are frequently lonely, fearful, isolated, and occasionally mentally ill. There is a high prevalence of victims with cognitive impairment, such as dementia, Parkinson's disease, or Alzheimer's disease. The victims are equally likely to come from any social group or socioeconomic status. Females are more likely to be victims of elder abuse than are males, due to their longer life expectancies. Victims of elder abuse present with some of the following symptoms: recurring injuries, failure to receive daily medications or medical treatment for injuries, malnutrition, dehydration, depression, physical isolation, and social isolation.

Most perpetrators of elder abuse are related to and live with their victims. They frequently complain that they are experiencing extreme stress and feel isolated in their role of caretaker for their elderly family member. In many cases, the caretaker has quit work in order to assist the senior citizen. Some of the stressors contributing to elder abuse include marital or family disruptions in the perpetrator's life, the severity of the victim's disability, a history of violence in the perpetrator's family of origin, and the unavailability of outside services provided to the victim (Barnett et al., 1997). Other variables increasing the risk of elder abuse are a history of substance abuse by the assailant and poor communication between the perpetrator and the victim. Many offenders develop symptoms of depression and lack the requisite coping strategies to manage the stressors inherent in caring for the elderly. The abuse is more often a result of malfeasance from fatigue than intended harm.

The law defining elder abuse varies across jurisdictions. In some locales, the abuse must be inflicted by a relative in order to meet the relevant criteria or to otherwise qualify. In other jurisdictions, a primary caregiver, such as a nurse or a nursing home attendant, can be subjected to elder abuse laws. In some states, laws pertaining to long-term care facilities extend to victims of elder abuse. Other jurisdictions do not have specific laws to address this form of criminal behavior. As such, they rely on existing assault-and-battery statutes to prosecute crimes against the elderly.

As the issue of protecting the needs and interests of senior citizens in our society grows, more legislation will be passed to protect their rights. To some extent, these laws will become standardized. Indeed, given the shared goal of protecting specific segments of the population, it is likely that several important aspects of the laws on child, spousal, and elder abuse eventually will resemble one another. If this does occur, researchers will need to investigate how this uniformity will help further our regard for these unique forms of criminal behavior, the offenders responsible for their commission, and the victims who suffer as a consequence.

CULT VIOLENCE AND HATE CRIMES

Introduction

In this final section, four disturbing and controversial expressions of group-oriented criminal conduct are examined. These include domestic and international terrorism, gang-related offenses, **religious cults,** and minority-targeted crime. As with previous portions of this chapter, specific commentary is offered on each of these criminal acts. Where appropriate, observations on these offenders and their respective profiles are also considered. Admittedly, understanding cult violence and hate crimes is considerably more vast than what could ever be reasonably accomplished through the presentation of limited topics. This notwithstanding, the information provided deepens our regard for these crimes and for the offenders who commit them.

Terrorism: Domestic and Foreign

The political climate of the world today is as precarious as ever. International terrorists, angry at the injustices they perceive are incurred at the hands of the United States and its Western allies, are a major threat to the well-being of our homeland and to tourists abroad. It is also becoming apparent that **domestic terrorism,** that is, **terrorism** within a nation's borders, is a growing concern for the United States and for countries around the world. Regrettably, the recent attacks on the Twin Towers in New York City on September 11, 2001, confirm this.

The definition of terrorist activity is broad and, according to the U.S. Department of State, Office of Counterterrorism (1999), it includes the following dimensions:

> The hijacking or sabotage of any conveyance (including an aircraft, vessel, or vehicle), the seizing or detaining, and threatening to kill, injure, or continue to detain, another individual in order to compel a third person (including a governmental organization) to do or abstain from doing any act as an explicit or implicit condition for the release of the individual seized. (as cited in Pavlin, 2000, p. 1)

The definition of terrorism itself is rather expansive. The official position articulated by the U.S. Department of State, Office of Counterterrorism (1999) suggests the following:

> [Terrorism is] a violent attack upon an internationally protected person or upon the liberty of such person; an assassination; the use of, or a threat, attempt, or conspiracy to use any biological agent, chemical agent, or nuclear weapon or device or explosive or firearm with the intent to endanger, directly or indirectly, the safety of one or more individuals or to cause substantial damage to property . . . The objective of a terrorist is to instill terror in a population to further a political, religious, or ideological objective." (as cited in Pavlin, 2001, p. 1)

There are two classifications of terrorism: domestic and foreign (White, 2002). Domestic terrorism concerns acts of force or coercion that occur within the borders of the nation against whom the terrorist group or person is targeting. For example, a catastrophic act of domestic terrorism occurred on April 19, 1995, when, angered by the U.S. Federal Government, militia extremists Timothy McVeigh and Terry Nichols planted a truck bomb, leveling the Alfred P. Murrow Federal Building. As a result, "168 individuals were killed, more than 700 were injured and treated by physicians, and more than 16,000 in the [Oklahoma City metropolitan area] at the time experienced the effects of the blast and of the exposure to the disaster scene" (Tucker, Pfefferbaum, Nixon, & Dickson, 2000, p. 1).

Foreign terrorism, also called **transnational terrorism,** takes place outside of the country in conflict with the group's political, religious, or ideological belief. It also targets citizens of that nation abroad. As Enders and Sandler (2000) explain:

> Events that start in one country and end in another (e.g., the skyjacking of an international flight, a cross-border raid) are transnational. An event planned in one country that attacks the citizens or property of a second country but on the soil of a third country is also an act of transnational terrorism. (p. 2)

Tragic examples of transnational terrorism include the August 7, 1998, "simultaneous bombings of the United States embassies in Nairobi, Kenya (247 killed, 5,500 injured) and Dar es Salaam, Tanzania (11 killed, 57 injured), and the March 20, 1995, Sarin (a deadly chemical agent) attack on the Tokyo subway (12 killed, 5,500 injured)" (Enders & Sandler, 2000, p. 1). Occasions such as these demonstrate that extreme political or religious views can become intense and deadly. Indeed, a person may take his or her own life to further the terrorist cause (e.g., suicide bombing or airplane crash), thereby creating greater harm to one's adversary. Indeed, as recently as October 2000, a pair of suicide bombers crippled the destroyer, the USS Cole, in a Yemeni port, killing 17 sailors. This bombing has been linked to wealthy terrorist mastermind Osama bin Laden, who "finances and motivates a 'network of networks,' co-opting homegrown terrorist groups, from Egyptian Islamic Jihad to the Abu Sayyaf group in the Philippines to the Islamic Movement of Uzbekistan" (Strobel, Kaplan, Newman, Whitelaw, & Grose, 2001, p. 2). The more recent and tragic events of 9/11 in New York represent more visible and immediate signs of the devastation brought about by transnational terrorism.

Acts of violent terrorism create broad rippling effects long after the attack. For example, Tucker et al. (2000) found that many victims of the Oklahoma City bombing developed **posttraumatic stress disorder** (PTSD) symptoms. "PTSD symptoms, which encompass features of re-experiencing and avoiding reminders of the trauma as well as physiological hyper-arousal, have been noted to occur in varying degrees in survivors" (Tucker et al., p. 2). In addition to symptoms of PTSD, survivors may develop major depression, generalized anxiety, substance abuse, and other psychiatric disorders (White, 2002). Not only are surviving victims of a terrorist attack at risk for developing psychological symptoms, but also are those who assist in the rescue efforts, namely, police officers and firefighters. As Tucker et al. (p. 7) note, "The disaster scene in Oklahoma City was particularly grisly, replete with severely injured children and adults and mutilated bodies. Junior or untrained rescue workers would have had little or no preparation for such experiences."

As technology advances into the 21st century, so do new ways to commit acts of terror. Concerns have surfaced recently in military and civilian communities about the potential for biological pathogens (i.e., nerve gas) used for terrorism, better known as **bioterrorism** (Kortepeter et al., 2000). Not leaving anything to chance, "The [U.S.] federal government [has] allocated funding to improve laboratory infra-structures, set up a national pharmaceutical stockpile and electronic data networks, and [to] establish surveillance systems for bioterrorism defense" (Kortepeter et al., p. 1).

The threat of **cyberterrorism** (destructive acts via computer technology) is on the rise as well (White, 2002). Information warfare experts say "cyberterrorism and cyberwarfare are inevitable . . . hacking hobbyists have shown how easy it is to propagate viruses throughout Internet-connected mail systems. They have also shown they can hack armies of unwitting computers and make those computers do their bidding" (Radcliff, 2001, p. 2). Terrorists could shut down a city's power grid or emergency systems or potentially tap into government top-secret files, exposing vulnerabilities in a nation's security force (White, 2002). Circumstances such as these help explain why the United States established its Office of Homeland Security.

Gang-Related Crime

For many inner-city youth who live among adverse social conditions, joining a **gang** provides the advantages that mainstream society promises, but fails to deliver. Gang affiliation offers the promise of social identity, protection, respect, and economic advancement (Doucette-Gates, 1999). Often, gangs arise from troubled or disorganized neighborhoods where crime, violence, broken families, and poverty are the way of life.

Lower class juveniles are often raised in an environment that values immediate gratification, physical aggression, toughness, and loyalty. "Although they have been trained to endorse middle-class values, [lower class juveniles] are ill-equipped to translate these aspirations into effective actions" (Wrightsman, Nietzel, & Fortune, 1998, p. 106). Lower class juveniles often lack the parental support (particularly from fathers), social skills, and education necessary for successful middle-class achievement. In response to these conditions, juveniles form or join gangs. The formation of gangs by lower class juveniles is an attempt to achieve the ends valued in their culture through behaviors that appear best suited to obtain those ends (Sanchez-Jankowski, 1991). As Quamina (1999, p. 42) notes, "These men [and women] gather together for what a family sees itself as maintaining a sense of purpose, camaraderie, psychological and emotional support, entertainment, and economic well-being." Gangs can exist in response to racial identity and pride (as many prison gangs do), or they may arise as a profit-seeking entity within a particular neighborhood (McCorkle & Miethe, 2002).

Drug dealing is a major staple in the life of a street gang. In 1997, street gangs were estimated to be involved in 33% of the crack cocaine sales, 32% of the marijuana sales, 16% of the powdered cocaine sales, 12% of the methamphetamine sales, and 9% of the heroin sales nationwide. Between 43% and 78% of street gang members are involved in drug trafficking. Drugs are sold for profit, recreation, sex, as an escape from reality, social interactions, income, and currency within the street and prison subculture (Valdez, 2000).

Crime in the gang culture, whether drug trafficking, fighting, robbery, shooting, or hustling, amounts to one thing: survival. Participation of gang members in violent and destructive behaviors is indicative of the particular values and life struggles that many urban youth face on a daily basis (Sanchez-Jankowski, 1991). "Hundreds of gang-related murders occur in Los Angeles each year; many are done for the sole purpose of demonstrating loyalty to the gang's values" (Wrightsman et al., p. 107). In a world where hope for respect and status through economic advancement is limited, youths often turn to gang life as a means of solidarity, protection, loyalty, and social status (McCorkle & Miethe, 2002).

Gang bangers are an extremely violent group of individuals. Typically, a cadre of youths organize around a particular neighborhood and defend their community against threat of outside invasion. "[Gang bangers] almost see themselves as players in a militaristic or quasi-militaristic type organization with the principle aim to protect their identified territory or turf" (Quamina, 1999, p. 43). These individuals are short-term focused. Education means very little unless it satisfies their immediate needs (Sanchez-Jankowski, 1991). The benefits of education for future endeavors or for general stability are not considered. "[Gang bangers] unfortunately have a short life focus, because jail, death, drugs, or long-term disability resulting from injury is the prognosis" (Quamina, p. 44).

Defining the exact characteristics that constitute a "gang" has been difficult, therefore, enacting legislation to prevent them from cropping up and flourishing has been plagued by setbacks (McCorkle & Miethe, 2002). "While most experts acknowledge that gangs are present in every jurisdiction in America, almost every state has different laws pertaining to gangs, and some have different definitions of what actually constitutes a gang" (Domash, 2000, p. 1). Today, gang involvement by youths is on the rise, with no national solution in sight. "As each state struggles with its own ability to deal with the emerging and growing problem of gang violence, there has been no uniform, nationwide policy to assist communities that are either just beginning to face the problem or have become overwhelmed by it" (Domash, p. 1).

Religious Cults

In November 1978, 914 cult members, including 276 children and teenagers either committed suicide or were murdered following orders of the leader of the Peoples Temple, Jim Jones. This tragedy happened deep in the jungle of Jonestown, Guyana. In Waco, Texas, in the spring of 1993, after a 51-day standoff with the FBI, the compound housing the cult Branch Davidians went up in a fiery blaze. The fire killed 75 members, including 21 children. Officials believe it was set by the cult leader, David Koresh (Hamm, 1997). To an alarming degree, the disastrous endings to Jonestown and Waco illustrate "the control that a cult leader can exert over followers, and how difficult it is for relatives and families to help members" (Langone, 1993, p. xvi).

According to Michael Langone (1993), former member of the American Psychological Association Task Force on Deceptive and Indirect Techniques of Persuasion and Control, a cult is defined as a group or movement that (a) exhibits excessive devotion to some person, idea, or thing; (b) uses a thought-reform program to persuade, control, and socialize members; (c) systematically induces states of psychological dependency in members; and (d) exploits members to advance their leadership goals and causes psychological harm to members, their families, and the community. **Thought-reform programs** are methods of social learning (learning through social interactions in which the behavior of the group is reinforcing) used by cult leaders to produce the behavioral and attitude changes in the members of the group (Hamm, 1997).

Religious cults are founded on a religious philosophy. The first wave of cults recruited 18- to 25-year-olds and were often based on Eastern philosophies and religions (Langone, 1993). "Many [cult groups] incorporate as religious entities because of the many tax and other advantages, but close inspection often reveals that the religious properties are sparse compared to other aspects of these groups" (p. xviii). However, many groups that Americans once thought of as "religious cults" (e.g., the early Quakers, Seventh-Day Adventists, and Mormons) have received increased recognition as legitimate churches today (Szubin, Jensen, & Gregg, 2000).

Many cult groups characteristically coerce their members to cut off ties with their family and friends who do not share the same devotion to the group's philosophy or belief system. As the Peoples Temple and Branch Davidians tragedies demonstrated, often a cult leader will attempt to move the group to an isolated retreat or compound (Hamm, 1997). Allegations of "brainwashing" performed by members of religious cults is well documented by researchers. In these instances, members are physically coerced by "depriving them of food or [by] preventing them from freely leaving [while] subjecting them to lengthy prayer services during which [group leaders] emphasize and repeat certain themes or messages" (Szubin et al., 2000, p. 3). Cult leaders are also seen by some as charismatic "con artists"

Who Joins Cults and Why?

There is a misconception that depressed and vulnerable people join cults as a way of fulfilling a need that is missing from their lives. Though this may be the case for some, it is not the case for most people who participate in cult religions. As Langone (1993) explains,

> Most cultists were relatively normal persons experiencing an unusual level of stress when they encountered a cult. Those who had enduring psychological problems were not necessarily attracted to the cult because of their problems, although their problems may have made them more vulnerable to the cult's 'sales pitch' and control tactics. (p. 6)

People who join cults often are victims of poor judgment and naiveté. Consider the following analogy:

> A depressed young woman enters a dating bar seeking companionship. A charming, smooth-talking man persuades her to go for a ride in his convertible. If he takes her to a lonely place and rapes her . . . does one conclude that the young woman unconsciously wanted to be raped? Obviously no. (Langone, 1993, p. 6)

This analogy raises the point that people do not actively search out a cult to join when they are feeling depressed. However, cultists will seek out those they see as vulnerable for recruitment. "People are not always motivated to seek that which they get. People join cults, not because they make a rational, informed choice. They join because they are duped" (p. 6).

Cults, or "new religious movements" as many scholars of religion refer to them, no longer recruit merely the young. These groups now recruit the elderly, single mothers, and young couples (Langone, 1993). "For individuals who feel unfulfilled by existing outlets in their lives, spiritually adrift, or merely lonely, joining a [new religious movement] may provide a successful solution, at least temporarily" (Szubin et al., 2000, p. 3). We are reminded that, ". . . none of us is beyond being manipulated by an intense, dedicated, and persistent persuader who meets us at a time when we are vulnerable, needy, and lonely" (Langone, 1993, p. xviii). These groups can be very powerful and, certainly in the cases of Jonestown and Waco, deadly.

who establish these groups in order to "intentionally bilk followers out of money or to unilaterally promote their own interests" (p. 3).

Some religious cults pose a threat to the community, such as the Branch Davidians who were known to be stockpiling a massive arsenal (Hamm, 1997). Other cults pose a threat to themselves, such as the mass suicide by the Peoples Temple or, more recently, the suicides of the Heaven's Gate members in San Diego where "members killed themselves in order to 'beam up' to God's flying saucer" (Szubin et al., 2000, p. 3). Most new religions pose no harm to anyone; however, "each cult is a reflection of the personal interests, persuasion, and choices of the leader" (Langone, 1993, p. xviii). Under these conditions, it is an important challenge for federal and state law enforcement to determine how dangerous, if at all, a particular group is and what action, if any, needs to be taken to prevent harm, the loss of life, or physical destruction.

Minority-Targeted Crime

A minority-targeted crime, or hate crime, is defined as an act of intimidation, harassment, physical force, or threat of physical force, against a person, property, family, or supporter motivated in whole or in part by prejudice due to a person's race, color, religion, ethnicity, gender, disability, sexual orientation, or national origin (Jenness & Grattet, 2001). Hate crimes are bias-motivated acts that target members of a group based solely on their membership to that group (Grigera, 1999).

According to the FBI's (1998) Hate Crimes Statistics Act (HCSA) report, a total of 7,755 bias-motivated criminal incidents were reported by 10,730 law enforcement agencies in 46 states and the District of Columbia. That same year, the total number of reported victims was 9,722. However, according to Elena Grigera (1999), a hate crime produces much greater harm and creates many more victims than other criminal acts. "A violent offense motivated by bigotry can cause a broad ripple of frustration among members of a targeted group; and a violent hate crime can quickly spread feelings of terror through an entire community" (Grigera, 1999, p. 2). In other words, a minority-targeted offense unleashes tremendous fear, pain, and alarm not only on the individual victim but also across an entire community (Jenness & Grattet, 2001).

The largest target of bias-motivated crime in the United States is the African American community. Of the reported 9,722 hate crimes, 5,514 were racially biased crimes. Anti-Black incidents accounted for 366 (or 66%) of all racially biased incidents in 1998 (FBI, 1998). The most recently noted offense was the tragic dragging death of James Byrd, Jr., in Jasper, Texas, at the hands of White supremacist James William King. Such acts of hate can be seen as the mode of identification for some groups. ". . . [As] social beings we convey our identity through the image we present to others. **Skinheads** (i.e., a White supremacist group), for example, have defined their rallying point to be their indiscriminate use of violence toward minority groups" (Arena & Arrigo, 2000, pp. 228–229).

Crimes that target individuals based on religion accounted for 18% of all reported hate crimes (FBI, 1998). The Jewish community was the target in 1,235 out of 1,720 incidents. In Los Angeles in August 1999, White supremacist Buford O. Furrow Jr. attacked the North Valley Jewish Community Center preschool and day camp, leaving three children, a teenager, and one adult wounded by gunfire.

According to the HCSA (FBI, 1998), crimes committed on persons due to their sexual orientation totaled 1,488, compared to 1,016 two years earlier. Crimes toward male homosexuals accounted for 68% of all sexual-orientation-based offenses. One such case occurred in October 1998. Matthew Shepard was a 21-year-old homosexual college student who was savagely and fatally beaten and tied to a wooden fence in near-freezing temperatures. "Apart from their psychological impact, such bias-motivated crimes continue the oppression of marginalized groups, leaving victims and members of the victims' communities feeling isolated, vulnerable and unprotected by the law . . . [These acts] threaten the very fabric of the American sense of safety and basic understanding of differences" (Grigera, 1999, p. 2).

In 1998, law enforcement agencies reported that 66% of the known offenders involved in hate crimes were White, whereas 17% were Black. The majority of reported minority-targeted incidents occurred as follows: 31% in or on residential properties; 20% on highways, roads, alleys, and streets; and 9% at schools and colleges (FBI, 1998). One rare school-based assault occurred on January 19, 1998, while Christopher Kindinger and Brad Waite were walking on the campus of Miami University in Ohio. Two White men yelled racial and homophobic epithets toward them and attacked the men. Kindinger, an African American, was beaten with an ax handle (Winbush, 1999).

Why do people commit acts of hate against others? According to scholars, the perpetrator of a hate crime acts out of frustration and the desire to have power and domination over a particular group. These perpetrators often view their victims as deserving of punishment (Levin & McDevitt, 1993). Michael P. Arena and Bruce A. Arrigo (2000) offer four underlying social–psychological themes concerning the bias-motivated crime of White supremacists. As they explain:

> The first of these is power, which manifests itself in authority and domination. The second theme influencing white supremacist behavior is their sense of identity. This concept encompasses an individual's feelings of self-concept, self-worth, self-esteem, and self-definition. The third theme is gender, sexuality, and masculinity. The fourth theme is the definition of the situation. (pp. 215–216)

The White supremacist has a fragile self-concept that he or she must protect by maintaining power over others (Hamm, 1993). Often, perpetrators of hate crimes are young males who commit these offenses for excitement as part of social activities or acts of revenge based on perceived unfair benefits to the groups to which the victims belong (Levin & McDevitt, 1993). They commit acts deemed masculine, dominating, and righteous by their own warped definition of justice.

The debate in the national agenda is whether the government should enact a hate crime policy whereby perpetrators of such offenses would receive stiff penalties. Opponents of this policy argue that it would be difficult to conclude that a crime was minority targeted because if criminals knew they faced harsher sentences if convicted, they would be reluctant to confess to the true intentions of their actions. Given this scenario, attempts to objectively assess, prosecute, and sentence hate criminals may represent a waste of government time and resources (Hamm, 1993). However, proponents for the legislation assert that compared to other offenses in general, hate crimes are much more involved. Indeed, as advocates point out, hate crimes are more likely to involve excessive violence, multiple offenders, assailants who are strangers, serial attacks, greater psychological trauma to victims, a heightened risk of social disorder, and a greater expenditure of resources to resolve (Levin & Fein, 1998, p. 2). Therefore, proponents assert that these callous acts warrant more severe punishments.

DISCUSSION QUESTIONS

1. What is serial murder? How is it different from mass or multiple murder? Use current examples to justify your response.

2. What are the five typologies of mass murder? Give an example for each.

3. Is spree murder a type of serial or mass murder? Explain your response with relevant examples.

4. What is sexual homicide and how does lust murder relate to it? What are paraphilias and how do they help account for lust murder?

5. Discuss some of the more interesting aspects of the integrated mode of sexual homicide as developed by Arrigo and Purcell (2001).

6. Explain the differences between acquaintance and stranger rape. What are the three motivational typologies for the stranger rapist as identified by Groth and Birnbaum (1979)? Identify and explain some of the offender profile characteristics for each.

7. What is pedophilia and what do we know about the profile of this offender?

8. What is the relationship among police authority or power, discretion, and the police personality? How would you explain the presence of police brutality? Does a police personality really exist? Justify your response.

9. Rape in prisons perpetrated by convicts is a serious concern. What are the three subculture groups involved in prison rapes? Explain each of them.

10. What are some of the similarities and differences among child abuse, spousal abuse, and elder abuse?

11. What is transnational terrorism, bioterrorism, and cyberterrorism?

12. Why do juveniles join gangs? What is gang banging?

13. What are religious cults? How are they formed? Why do people join them? Are their activities criminal? Explain your answers.

14. What are minority-targeted crimes? Can you think of any examples of current-day minority-targeted crimes?

15. What role does religion play in hate crimes? Explain your answer. Should hate crimes be prosecuted, and should convicted individuals receive harsher penalties? Justify your response.

REFERENCES

Abel, G. G., Becker, J. V., Cunningham-Rather, J., Mittleman, M., & Rouleau, J. L. (1988). Multiple paraphilic diagnoses among sex offenders. *Bulletin of the American Academy of Psychiatry and the Law, 16,* 153–168.

Abel, G. G., & Osborne, C. (1989). The paraphilias: The extent and nature of sexually deviant criminal behavior. *Psychiatric Clinics of North America, 15,* 675–687.

Allison, J. A., & Wrightsman, L. S. (1993). *Rape: The misunderstood crime.* New York: Sage.

Alpert, G. P. (1993). The role of psychological testing in law enforcement. In R. G. Dunham & G. P. Alpert (Eds.), *Critical issues in policing: Contemporary readings* (2nd ed., pp. 96–105). Prospect Heights, IL: Waveland Press.

Alpert, G. P., & Dunham, R. G. (1997). *Policing urban America* (3rd ed.). Prospect Heights, IL: Waveland Press.

American Bar Association Committee on Legal Problems of the Elderly Research (Conducted on Westlaw, compliments of West Group). (1999). *Elder Abuse Laws.* Available at http://www.elderabusecenter.org.

American Psychiatric Association. (1994). *Diagnostic and statistical manual of mental disorders* (4th ed.). Washington DC: Author.

Arena, M. P., & Arrigo, B. A. (2000). White supremacist behavior: Toward an integrated social psychological model. *Deviant Behavior: An Interdisciplinary Journal, 21,* 213–244.

Arrigo, B. A. (2000). *Introduction to forensic psychology: Issues and controversies in crime and justice.* San Diego: Academic Press.

Arrigo, B. A., & Claussen, N. (2003). Police corruption and psychological testing: A strategy for pre-employment screening. *International Journal of Offender Therapy and Comparative Criminology, 47*(3), 272–290.

Arrigo, B. A., & Purcell, C. (2001). Explaining paraphilias and lust murder: Toward an integrated model. *International Journal of Offender Therapy and Comparative Criminology, 45,* 6–31.

Barnett, O. W., Miller-Perrin, C. L., & Perrin, R. D. (1997). *Family violence across the lifespan.* Thousand Oaks, CA: Sage.

Bartol, C. R. (2001). Police psychology: A profession with a promising future. In R. G. Dunham & G. P. Alpert (Eds.), *Critical issues in policing: Contemporary readings* (4th ed., pp. 66–81). Prospect Heights, IL: Waveland Press.

Bartol, C. R. (2002). *Criminal behavior: A psychosocial approach* (6th ed.). Upper Saddle River, NJ: Prentice Hall.

Becker, J. V., & Abel, G. G. (1978). Men and the victimization of women. In R. J. Chapman & M. R. Gates (Eds.), *Victimization of women* (pp. 33–51). Beverly Hills, CA: Sage.

Blumberg, M. (2001). Controlling police use of deadly force: Assessing two decades of progress. In R. G. Dunham & G. P. Alpert (Eds.), *Critical issues in policing: Contemporary readings* (4th ed.; pp. 559–582). Prospect Heights, IL: Waveland Press.

Braverman, M. (1998). *Preventing workplace violence: A guide for employers and practitioners.* Thousand Oaks, CA: Sage.

Bromberg, W., & Coyle, E. (1974, April). Rape!: A compulsion to destroy. *Medical Insight, 19,* 21–22.

Brooks, L. W. (2001). Police discretionary behavior. In R. G. Dunham & G. P. Alpert (Eds.), *Critical issues in policing: Contemporary readings* (4th ed.; pp. 117–131). Prospect Heights, IL: Waveland Press.

Browne, A., & Finkelhor, D. (1986). Impact of child sexual abuse: A review of the research. *Psychological Bulletin, 99,* 66–77.

Browne, K., & Herbert, M. (1997). *Preventing family violence.* New York: Wiley.

Burgess, A. W., Hartman, C. R., Ressler, R. K., Douglas, J. E., & McCormack, A. (1986). Sexual homicide: A motivational model. *Journal of Interpersonal Violence, 13,* 251–272.

Busch, K. A., & Cavanaugh, J. L. (1986). The study of multiple murder. *Journal of Interpersonal Violence, 1,* 5–23.

Buzawa, E. S., & Buzawa, C. G. (2001). Traditional and innovative responses to domestic violence. In R. G. Dunham & G. P. Alpert (Eds.), *Critical issues in policing: Contemporary readings* (4th ed.; pp. 216–237). Prospect Heights, IL: Waveland Press.

Carll, E. K. (1999). *Violence in our lives: Impact on workplace, home and community.* Philadelphia, PA: Allyn & Bacon.

Carroll, L. (1998). *Lawful order: A case study of correctional crisis and reform.* New York: Garland.

Cohen, M. L., Seghorn, T. K., & Calamas, W. (1969). Sociometric study of the sex offender. *Journal of Abnormal Psychology, 74,* 249–255.

Correctional Service of Canada. (2003). A profile of robbery offenders in Canada. Montreal, CA: Research Division, Correctional Service of Canada.

Cortina, J. M., Doherty, M. L., Schmitt, N., Kaufman, G., & Smith, R. G. (1992). The "Big Five" personality factors in IPI and MMPI: Predictors of police performance. *Personnel Psychology, 45,* 119–140.

Davis, J. (2002). Voyeurism: A criminal precursor and diagnostic indicator to a much larger sexual predatory problem in our community. In R. Holmes & S. Holmes (Eds.), *Current perspectives on sex crimes* (pp. 73–84). Thousand Oaks, CA: Sage.

Decker, S. H. (1996). Deviant homicide: A new look at the intersection of motives and victim offender relationships. *Journal of Research on Crime and Delinquency, 33,* 427–449.

DeRiver, J. P. (1956). *The sexual criminal.* Springfield, IL: Thomas.

Dietz, P. E. (1986). Mass, serial, and sensational homicides. *Bulletin of New York Academy of Medicine, 64,* 477–491.

Domash, S. F. (2000). Youth gangs in America: A national problem evading easy solutions. *Police, 24,* 22–30 (ProQuest citation, pp. 1–6).

Donaldson, S. (1990). Prison, jails, reformatories. In W. R. Dynes (Ed.), *Encyclopedia of homosexuality.* New York: Garland.

Doucette-Gates, A. (1999). Hope: Sustaining a vision of the future. In C. Branch (Ed.), *Adolescent gangs: Old issues, new approaches.* Philadelphia, PA: Taylor & Francis.

Enders, W., & Sandler, T. (2000). Is transnational terrorism becoming more threatening?: A time-series investigation. *The Journal of Conflict Resolution, 44,* 307–332.

Ericson, R. (1982). *Reproducing order: A study of police patrol work.* Toronto: University of Toronto Press.

Eth, S., & Pynoos, R. S. (1985). Developmental perspectives on psychic trauma in childhood. In C. R. Figley (Ed.), *Trauma and its wake: The study and treatment of post-traumatic stress disorder* (pp. 36–52). New York: Brunner/Mazel.

Federal Bureau of Investigation. (1997). *Uniform crime reports—1996.* Washington DC: United States Government Printing Office.

Federal Bureau of Investigation. (1998). *Hate crimes statistics act.* Washington DC: United States Government Printing Office.

Federal Bureau of Investigation. (2000). *Uniform crime reports—1999.* Washington DC: United States Government Printing Office.

Fiala, R., & LaFree, G. (1988). Cross-national determinants of childhood homicide. *American Sociological Review, 53,* 432–445.

Finkelhor, D. (1979). *Sexually victimized children.* New York: The Free Press.

Finkelhor, D., & Araji, S. (1986). Explanations of pedophilia: A four factor model. *Journal of Sex Research, 22,* 145–161.

Fitzsimmons, T. (1998). Engendering a new police identity? *Peace Review,* June 1998.

Fox, J., & Levin, J. (1996). *Overkill: Mass murder and serial killing exposed.* New York: Dell.

Fyfe, J. J. (2001). The split-second syndrome and other determinants of police violence. In R. G. Dunham & G. P. Alpert (Eds.), *Critical issues in policing: Contemporary readings* (4th ed.; pp. 583–598). Prospect Heights, IL: Waveland Press.

Gabor, T. (1987). *Armed robbery.* Springfield, IL: Thomas.

George, W. H., & Marlat, A. G. (1989). Introduction. In D. R. Laws (Ed.), *Relapse prevention with sex offenders* (pp. 1–13). New York: Guilford.

Glendenning, F. (1997). What is elder abuse and neglect? In P. Decalmer & F. Glendenning (Eds.), *The mistreatment of elderly people.* Thousand Oaks, CA: Sage.

Graham, J. R. (2000). *MMPI-2: Assessing personality and psychopathology.* New York: Oxford Press.

Graney, D. J., & Arrigo, B. A. (2002). *The power serial rapist: A criminology-victimology typology of female victim selection.* Springfield, IL: Thomas.

Graves, W. (1996). Police cynicism: Causes and cures. *FBI Law Enforcement Bulletin, 65,* 16–20.

Greelinger, V., & Bryne, D. (1987). Coercive sexual fantasies of college men as predictors of self-reported likelihood to rape and overt sexual aggression. *Journal of Sex Research, 23,* 1–11.

Greenberg, L., & Barling, J. (1999). Predicting employee aggression against coworkers, subordinates and supervisors: The roles of person behaviors and perceived workplace factors. *Journal of Organizational Behavior, 20,* 897–913.

Gresswell, G. M., & Hollin, C. R. (1994). Multiple murder: A review. *The British Journal of Criminology, 34*(1), 1–14.

Grigera, E. (1999). Hate crimes: State and federal responses to bias-motivated violence. *Corrections Today, 61,* 68–74 (ProQuest citation, pp. 1–7).

Groth, A. N. (1979). *Men who rape: The psychology of the offender.* New York: Plenum.

Groth, A. N., & Birnbaum, H. J. (1979). *Men who rape: The psychology of the offender.* New York: Plenum.

Groth, A. N., Burgess, A. W., & Holmstrom, L. L. (1977). Rape, power, anger, and sexuality. *American Journal of Psychiatry, 134,* 1239–1243.

Guttmacher, M. S., & Weihofen, H. (1952). *Psychiatry and the law.* New York: Norton.

Hamm, M. S. (1993). *American skinheads: The criminology and control of hate crime.* Westport, CT: Praeger.

Hamm, M. S. (1997). *Apocalypse in Oklahoma: Waco and Ruby Ridge revenged.* Boston, MA: Northeastern University Press.

Hampton, R. L., Vandergriff-Avery, M., & Kim, J. (1999). Understanding the origins and incidence of spousal violence in North America. In T. P. Gullotta & S. J. McElhaney (Eds.), *Violence in homes and communities: Prevention, intervention, and treatment.* Thousand Oaks, CA: Sage.

Hazelwood, R. R. (1995). Analyzing the rape and profiling the offender. In R. R. Hazelwood & A. W. Burgess (Eds.), *Practical aspects of rape investigation: An interdisciplinary perspective* (2nd ed.). New York: CRC Press.

Hazelwood, R. R., & Burgess, A. W. (1987, September). An introduction to the serial rapist: Research by the FBI. *FBI Law Enforcement Bulletin, 23,* 16–24.

Hazelwood, R. R., & Burgess, A. W. (1995). *Practical aspects of rape investigation: An interdisciplinary approach* (2nd ed.). New York: CRC Press.

Hazelwood, R. R., & Douglas, J. E. (1980, April). The lust murderer. *FBI Law Enforcement Bulletin, 16,* 18–22.

Hazelwood, R. R., Reboussin, R., & Warren, J. (1989). Serial rape: Correlates of increased aggression and the relationship of offender to victim resistance. *Journal of Interpersonal Violence, 4,* 65–78.

Hazelwood, R. R., & Warren, J. (1990, February). Rape: The criminal behavior of the serial rapist. *FBI Law Enforcement Bulletin, 26,* 18–25.

Hazelwood, R. R., & Warren, J. (1990, February). The serial rapist: His characteristics and victims. *FBI Law Enforcement Bulletin, 25,* 10–17.

Hickey, E. W. (1997). *Serial murderers and their victims* (2nd ed.). Belmont, CA: Wadsworth.

Hickey, E. W. (2002). *Serial murderers and their victims* (3rd ed.). Belmont, CA: Wadsworth.

Hickman, S. E., & Muehlenhard, C. L. (1997). College women's fears and precautionary behaviors relating to acquaintance rape and stranger rape. *Psychology of Women Quarterly, 21,* 527–547.

Holmes, R. (1991). *Sex crimes.* Newbury Park, CA: Sage.

Holmes, R., & DeBurger, J. (1988). *Serial murder.* Beverly Hills, CA: Sage.

Holmes, R. M., & Holmes, S. (1994). *Murder in America.* Thousand Oaks, CA: Sage.

Holmes, R., & Holmes, S. (1998). *Serial murder* (2nd ed.). Beverly Hills, CA: Sage.

Jenness, V., & Grattet, R. (2001). *Making hate a crime: From social movement to law enforcement.* New York: Russell Sage Foundation.

Kappeler, V. E., Sluder, R. D., & Alpert, G. P. (2001). Breeding deviant conformity: The ideology and culture of police. In R. G. Dunham & G. P. Alpert, *Critical issues in policing: Contemporary readings* (4th ed., pp. 290–316). Prospect Heights, IL: Waveland Press.

Katz, J. (1988). *Seductions of crime: Moral and sensual attractions of doing evil.* New York: Basic Books.

Kaufer, S., & Mattman, J. W. (2001). *Workplace violence: An employer's guide.* Palm Springs, CA: Workplace Violence Research Institute.

Kelleher, M. D. (1997). *Flash point: The American mass murderer.* Westport, CT: Praeger.

Knight, R. A. (1989). An assessment of the concurrent validity of a child molester typology. *Journal of Interpersonal Violence, 4,* 131–150.

Knight, R. A., Carter, D. L., & Prentky, R. A. (1989). A system for the classification of child molesters: Reliability and application. *Journal of Interpersonal Violence, 4,* 3–23.

Kopp, S. B. (1962). The character structure of sex offenders. *American Journal of Psychotherapy, 16,* 64–70.

Kortepeter, M. G., Pavlin, J. A., Gaydos, J. C., Rowe, J. R., et al. (2000). Surveillance at U.S. military installations for bioterrorist and emerging infectious disease threats. *Military Medicine, 165,* 571–575.

Koss, M. P., Dinero, T. E., Seibel, C. A., & Cox, S. L. (1988). Stranger and acquaintance rape: Are there differences in the victim's experience? *Psychology of Women Quarterly, 12,* 1–24.

Langone, M. D. (1993). *Recovery from cults: Help for victims of psychological and spiritual abuse.* New York: Norton.

Levin, B., & Fein, B. (1998). Symposium: Q: Does America need a federal hate-crime law? *Insight on the News, 14,* 24–27.

Levin, J., & Fox, J. (1985). *Mass murder: America's growing menace.* New York: Plenum.

Levin, J., & McDevitt, J. (1993). *Hate crimes: The rising tide of bigotry and bloodshed.* New York: Plenum.

Levinson, D. (1988). Family violence in cross-cultural perspective. In V. Van Hasselt, R. L. Morrison, A. S. Bellack, & M. Herson (Eds.), *Handbook of family violence* (pp. 435–456). New York: Plenum.

Liebert, J. A. (1985). Contributions of psychiatric consultation in the investigation of serial murder. *International Journal of Offender Therapy and Comparative Criminology, 29,* 187–200.

Long, G. T. (1993). Homosexual relationships in a unique setting: The male prison. In L. Diamant (Ed.), *Homosexual issues in the workplace.* Washington DC: Taylor & Francis.

MacCulloch, M. J., Snowden, P. R., Wood, P. J. W., & Mills, H. E. (1983). Sadistic fantasy, sadistic behavior, and offending. *British Journal of Psychiatry, 143,* 20–29.

Malamuth, N. M., & McIlwraith, R. D. (1988). Fantasies and exposure to sexually explicit magazines. *Communications Research, 15,* 753–771.

Marquart, J. W., Cuvelier, S. J., Burton, V. S., Adams, K., Gerber, J., Longmire, D., et al. (1994). A limited capacity to treat: Examining the effects of prison population control strategies on prison educational programs. *Crime and Delinquency, 40,* 516–531.

Marshall, W. M. (1999). Diagnosing and treating sex offenders. In A. K. Hess & I. B. Weiner (Eds.), *Handbook of forensic psychology.* New York: Wiley.

Martin, S. E. (2001). Women officers on the move: An update on women in policing. In R. G. Dunham & G. P. Alpert (Eds.), *Critical issues in policing: Contemporary readings* (4th ed., pp. 401–419). Prospect Heights, IL: Waveland Press.

Matthews, J. (1996). *The eyeball killer.* New York: Zebra Publishers.

May, J. P. (Ed.). (2000). *Building violence: How America's rush to incarcerate creates more violence.* Thousand Oaks, CA: Sage.

McCorkle, R. C., Miethe, T. D., (2002). *Panic: The social construction of the street gang problem.* Upper Saddle River, NJ: Prentice Hall.

McCorkle, R. C., & Miethe, T. D. & Drass, K. A. (1995). The roots of prison violence: A test of the deprivation, management, and "not-so-total" institution models. *Crime and Delinquency, 41,* 317–331.

McDonald, L. (1976). *The sociology of law and order.* Boulder, CO: Westview.

McGuire, R., Carlisle, J., & Young, B. (1965). Sexual deviations as conditioned behavior. *Behavior Research and Therapy, 2,* 185–190.

Messner, S. F., & Rosenfeld, R. (2001). *Crime and the American dream* (3rd ed.). Belmont, CA: Wadsworth/Thomas Learning.

Mills, L. (1996). Empowering battered women transnationally: The case for postmodern interventions. *Social Work, 41,* 261–267.

Money, J. (1990). Forensic sexology: Paraphilic serial rape (biastophilia) and lust murder (erotophonophilia). *American Journal of Psychotherapy, 64,* 26–36.

Money, J., & Werlas, J. (1982). Paraphilic sexuality and child abuse: The parents. *Journal of Sex and Marital Therapy, 8,* 57–64.

National Center on Child Abuse and Neglect. (1994). *Child maltreatment—1992: Report from the States to the National Center on Child Abuse and Neglect.* Washington DC: Department of Health and Human Services.

Palermo, G. B. (1999). Mass murder, suicide, and moral development: Can we separate the adults from the juveniles? *International Journal of Offender Therapy and Comparative Criminology, 43,* 8–20.

Palermo, G. B., & Farkas, A. (2001). *The dilemma of the sexual offender.* Springfield, IL: Thomas.

Pavlin, J. A. (2000). Bioterrorism and the importance of the public health laboratory. *Military Medicine, 165,* 25–29.

Podolsky, E. (1966). Sexual violence. *Medical Digest, 34,* 60–63.

Prentky, R. A., Burgess, A. W., & Carter, D. L. (1986). Victim responses by rapists type: An empirical and clinical analysis. *Journal of Interpersonal Violence, 1,* 73–98.

Prentky, R. A., Burgess, A. W., Rokous, F. R., Lee, A., Hartman, C., & Ressler, R. (1989). The presumptive role of fantasy in serial homicide. *American Journal of Psychiatry, 146*(7), 887–891.

Quamina, A. (1999). Adolescent gangs: A practitioner's perspective. In C. Branch (Ed.), *Adolescent gangs: Old issues, new approaches* (pp. 39–56). Philadelphia, PA: Taylor & Francis.

Rada, R. T. (1978). Psychological factors in rapist behavior. In R. T. Rada (Ed.), *Clinical aspects of the rapist* (pp. 109–123). New York: Grune & Stratton.

Radcliff, D. (2001). Info war games. *Computerworld, 35,* 44–46.

Ressler, R. K., Burgess, A. W., & Douglas, J. E. (1988). *Sexual homicide: Patterns and motives.* New York: The Free Press.

Ressler, R. K., Burgess, A. W., Hartman, C. R., Douglas, J. E., & McCormack, A. (1986). Murderers who rape and mutilate. *Journal of Interpersonal Violence, 1,* 273–287.

Riedel, M. (1993). *Stranger violence: A theoretical inquiry.* New York: Garland.

Ringle, C. (1997, November). *Criminal victimization 1996: Changes 1995–1996 with trends 1993–1996.* Washington DC: Government Printing Office.

Ross, J. I., & Richards, S. C. (2002). *Convict criminology.* Belmont, CA: Wadsworth.

Russell, D. E. H. (1982). *Rape in marriage.* Bloomington, IN: Indiana University Press.

Russell, M. N. (1995). *Confronting abusive beliefs: Group treatment for abusive men.* Thousand Oaks, CA: Sage.

Sanchez-Jankowski, M. (1991). *Islands in the street: Gangs in American urban society.* Berkeley: University of California Press.

Schell, B. H., & Lanteigne, N. M. (2000). *Stalking, harassment, and murder in the workplace: Guidelines for protection and prevention.* NY: Quorum Books.

Schwartz, M. D., & DeKeseredy, W. (Eds.). (1997). *Sexual assault on the college campus: The role of male peer support.* Thousand Oaks, CA: Sage.

Scully, D., & Marolla, J. (1984). Convicted rapists' vocabulary of motive: Excuses and justifications. *Social Problems, 31,* 530–544.

Scully, D., & Marolla, J. (1985). Riding the bull at Gilley's: Convicted rapists describe the rewards of rape. *Social Problems, 32,* 251–263.

Simon, R. I. (1996). Bad men do what good men dream: A forensic psychiatrist illuminates the darker side of human behavior. In R. I. Simon (Ed.), *Serial sexual killers: Your life for their orgasm* (pp. 279–312). Washington DC: American Psychiatric Press.

Skolnick, J. H. (1994). *Justice without trial: Law enforcement in a democratic society.* Beverly Hills: Sage.

Smith, S. K. (1999). *Mandatory reporting of child abuse and neglect.* Retrieved October 6, 2004, from http://www.smith-lawfirm.com/mandatory_reporting.htm

Snow, C. R. (1997). *Family violence: Tough solutions to stop the violence.* New York: Plenum.

Stanko, E. A. (1989). Missing the mark?: Police battering. In J. Hanmer, J. Radford, & E. Stanko (Eds.), *Women, policing, and male violence* (pp. 46–49). London: Routledge & Kegan Paul.

Strobel, W. P., Kaplan, D. E., Newman, R. J., Whitelaw, K., & Grose, T. (2001). A war in the shadows: The global fight against a terrorist leader and his network. *U.S. News and World Reports, 130,* 22–25.

Szubin, A., Jensen, C. J., III, & Gregg, R. (2000). Interacting with "cults": A policing model. *FBI Law Enforcement Bulletin, 69,* 16–24.

Toch, H. (1992). *Violent men: An inquiry into the psychology of violence.* Washington DC: American Psychological Association.

Tucker, P., Pfefferbaum, B., Nixon, S. J., & Dickson, W. (2000). Predictors of post-traumatic stress syndrome in Oklahoma City: Exposure, social support, peri-traumatic responses. *The Journal of Behavioral Health Services & Research, 27,* 406–416.

Turner, J. T., & Gelles, M. G. (2003). *Threat assessment: A risk management approach.* Binghamton, NY: Haworth.

U.S. Department of Health and Human Services. (1996). *Child maltreatment: 1996.* Washington DC: U.S. Government Printing Office.

U.S. Department of Justice, Bureau of Justice Statistics. (1993). *Survey of state prison inmates, 1991.* Washington DC: U.S. Government Printing Office.

U.S. Department of Justice, Bureau of Justice Statistics. (1994). *Violence against women.* Washington DC: U.S. Government Printing Office.

U.S. Department of Justice, Bureau of Justice Statistics. (1997a). *National crime victimization survey.* Washington DC: U.S. Government Printing Office.

U.S. Department of Justice, Bureau of Justice Statistics. (1997b). *Drug enforcement administration.* Washington DC: U.S. Government Printing Office.

U.S. Department of Justice, Bureau of Justice Statistics (1998). *Criminal victimization in the United States, 1995.* Washington DC: U.S. Government Printing Office.

U.S. Department of Justice. (1999). *Prisoners of 1998.* Washington DC: U.S. Government Printing Office.

U.S. Department of State, Office of Counterterrorism. (1999, October 8). *Background information on foreign terrorist organizations.* Washington DC: U.S. Government Printing Office.

Valdez, A. (2000). Street gangs profit in a bullish market. *Police, 24,* 52–55 (ProQuest citation, pp. 1–3).

Vandenbos, G. R., & Bulato, E. O. (Eds.). (1996). *Violence on the job: Identifying risks and developing solutions.* Washington DC: American Psychological Association.

Walker, C. E., Bonner, B. L., & Kaufman, K. L. (1998). *The physically and sexually abused child: Evaluation and treatment.* Elmsford, NY: Pergamon.

Waterhouse, L. (Ed.). (1993). *Child abuse and child abusers: Protection and prevention.* Great Britain: Athenaeum Press.

White, J. (2002). *Terrorism: An introduction* (3rd ed.). Belmont, CA: Wadsworth.

White-Hamon, L. S. (2000). *Mass murder and attempted mass murder: An examination of the perpetrator with an empirical analysis of typologies.* Doctoral dissertation, Institute of Psychology, Law, and Public Policy, California School of Professional Psychology—Fresno Campus.

Williams, K. R., & Flewelling, R. L. (1988). The social production of criminal homicide: A comparative study of desegregated rates in American cities. *American Sociological Review, 54,* 421–431.

Winbush, R. A. (1999). Campus hate crimes: Fruit on the American tree of violence. *Black Collegian, 30,* 145–149.

Wright, R., & Decker, S. H. (1997). *Armed robbers in action: Stickups and streetlife culture.* Boston, MA: Northeastern University Press.

Wrightsman, L. S., Nietzel, M. T., & Fortune, W. H. (1998). *Psychology and the legal system.* Pacific Grove, CA: Brooks/Cole.

Nonviolent Crimes and Criminals

OVERVIEW

Chapter 5 examined the complicated and often frightening world of violent crime and criminals. Equally complex, although in several important respects less frightening, is the domain of nonviolent crime and criminals. It is difficult to say with precision which behaviors amount to nonviolent criminal conduct. After all, every act of wrongdoing possesses an element of harm; however, not all transgressions produce devastating physical pain or debilitating emotional suffering. This chapter principally focuses on those actions that are self-violative, more passive in nature, or otherwise fail to produce personal harm. In particular, this chapter examines substance-related crime, organized crime, white-collar crime, **fraud**, Internet crime, **stalking**, **sexual harassment**, property crime, and **prostitution.** Each of these behaviors deepens our appreciation for the nature of nonviolent criminals and illicit conduct. As this chapter demonstrates, the individuals who engage in these actions, although in many ways less sinister or dangerous than their violent criminal counterparts, are most assuredly complex, troubled, and provocative. Accordingly, where appropriate, this chapter provides useful information on what we know about the profiles of these offenders and the nature of their criminal behavior.

KEY TERMS

Alcohol intoxication

Anti-Kickback statute

Arson

Burglary

Controller

Criminalization

Decriminalization

Diminished capacity

Drug abuse

Dumpster diving

Epiphenomenal approach

Erotomanic stalker

Ethics in Patient Referral Act

False Claims Act

Fencing

Fraud

Gambling

Health care fraud

Hostile work environment

Identity theft and fraud

Integrated model

Intellectual property crimes

Internet fraud

Involuntary intoxication

Kleptomania

Loan sharking

Larceny-theft

Lifestyle theory

Love obsessional stalkers

Mass arsonist

Mens rea

Money laundering

Motor vehicle theft
Numbers running
Physical sexual harassment
Prostitution
Quid pro quo
Racketeering
Reloading
Runners
Scamming
Securities fraud
Serial arsonist
Sex work
Sexual abuse
Sexual harassment

Shoplifting
Shoulder surfing
Simple obsessional stalker
Skimming
Spammers
Spree arsonist
Stalking
Telemarketing fraud
Telemarketing schemes
Unidirectional approach
Verbal sexual harassment
Victimization
Visual sexual harassment
Voluntary intoxication

SUBSTANCE-RELATED CRIMES AND CRIMINALS

Introduction

Criminal behavior is often highly correlated with the use and abuse of chemical substances. Substance-related crime generally follows when a person attempts to gain access to narcotics or endeavors to resolve a drug-related dispute. Substance-related criminality is also a behavioral reaction to the mind-altering influence of some drugs. Behavioral changes linked to chemical use include loss of control, impaired judgment, induced grandiosity, and the stimulation of uncontrollable conduct (Miller, 2000). This section explores these issues in relation to the use of both drugs and alcohol. In addition, commentary on drug dealing, women, substance use and crime, legal aspects of drugs and alcohol, and treatment options are all explored.

Drug-Related Crimes and Criminals

The definition of substance abuse varies; however, a useful description of it is found in the American Psychiatric Association's (APA) *Diagnostic and Statistical Manual of Mental Disorders* (4th ed., revised, 2000). According to the *DSM–IV–TR,* it is defined as "a maladaptive pattern of substance use manifested by recurrent and significant adverse consequences related to the repeated use of substances" (APA, 2000, p. 198). There are three commonly identified risk factors that significantly affect the nexus between **drug abuse** and crime. These risk factors are the pharmacological effects of alcohol and drugs, the economic impulses caused by the acquisition of drugs, and a systemic connection generated by drug consumption.

The pharmacological effects of drugs and alcohol illustrate that violence is associated with their use, especially because they affect brain functions including perception. Economic impulses occur when an individual becomes criminally inclined in order to obtain illicit drugs. A person may act on criminal impulses, both violent and nonviolent, if the offender believes that crime is the only way to obtain the substances, thereby maintaining their dependence and avoiding withdrawal (Deitch, Koutsenok, & Ruzi, 2000). Substance dependence is "a pattern of repeated self-administration that can result in tolerance, withdrawal, and compulsive drug-taking behavior" (APA, 2000, p. 192). A systematic connection arises when an individual is involved in selling drugs. Criminal behavior frequently occurs when a drug dealer seeks justice with clients who have unpaid debts (Deitch et al., 2000). Although a majority of drug users and abusers report their primary illegal activity to be the distribution or sale of narcotics, a representative portion of offenders report engaging in other nondrug crimes such as **burglary** or robbery (Farabee, Joshi, & Anglin, 2001).

There are three explanations for the drug–crime relationship. (A more detailed explanation is found in chapter 7 in the section addressing juvenile drug use.) These include (a) a noncausal, epiphenomenal explanation; (b) a unidirectional explanation; and (c) a bidirectional explanation (Walters, 1998). Each of these approaches is briefly described.

The **epiphenomenal approach** suggests that neither crime nor drugs are a result of the other. In other words, drugs are not the cause of crime and crime is not the cause of drug use. The **unidirectional approach** contends that crime causes substance abuse and substance abuse causes crime. Thus, there is an additive effect between criminal activity and substance abuse. The bidirectional approach suggests that drugs and crime are causes and effects of one another. In this instance, drugs and crime function interactively.

Each of these approaches also has a unique orientation to the treatment of substance-abusing offenders. The epiphenomenal approach suggests that appropriate intervention methods include psychoanalytic and behavioral therapy techniques. The unidirectional approach maintains that the use of 12-step programs, such as Alcoholics Anonymous and Narcotics Anonymous, are necessary to curb the conduct of chemically addicted criminals. The bidirectional approach argues that establishing therapeutic communities is the most appropriate and effective intervention when treating substance-abusing offenders.

Walters (1998) proposed an **integrated model** regarding drug–crime interactions. This model used **lifestyle theory** as a basis and emphasized three interrelated components. These three elements were (a) incentive and opportunity; (b) attributions, expectancies, and the person–situation interaction; and (c) the initiation and maintenance of lifestyles.

According to lifestyle theory, incentive for an individual is often established through fear. Therefore, a lifestyle of drugs and crime may be the result of fear. Fear in this instance includes such things as rejection or ostracism from the substance-using group, or the denial of privileges or resources that the drug- and crime-using collective possesses. Under these conditions, fear manifests itself when exposure to the drug culture (i.e., opportunity to use illicit substances or engage in criminal conduct) is great.

The second component of the integrated model deals with the nature of one's associations with others. In short, a person is drawn to a life of crime and drug use, given "the interactions that form between dispositional and situational influences" (Walters, 1998, p. 17). These dispositional and situational factors involve the personality of the individual, the person's expectations regarding drug use, and the quality and type of associations and communications that occur through one's involvement in the drug-crime culture.

The third component of the integrated model entails the initiation and maintenance of a delinquent or criminal lifestyle. Walters (1998) described three factors or variables in which an individual's lifestyle may become vulnerable. These situations include (a) predisposing variables, (b) precipitating variables, and (c) maintenance variables. Predisposing variables often put an individual at risk for involvement in a drug–crime lifestyle because the individual is already inclined to adopt this way of living. Examples of predisposing variables include a family history of drug use and crime, or a preexisting tendency to behave impulsively and to act aggressively. Precipitating variables introduce an individual to a life of substance abuse and criminal activity. Examples of precipitating factors include the involvement in a crime–drug lifestyle by a close friend or intimate, or the firsthand experience of economic rewards or social benefits (e.g., prestige) that can accompany a drug–crime lifestyle. Maintenance factors encourage sustained involvement in the substance-using and criminal behavior lifestyle. Examples of maintenance factors include the ready source of income and recreational drug stimulants that encourage ongoing involvement in the substance-using and criminal offender lifestyle. Following the integrated approach, interventions for the drug-abusing offender include generating or producing confidence in the ability to change, developing decision-making skills, and participating in resocialization efforts through strong social support (Maruna, 2001)

Behavioral characteristics of a criminal lifestyle include irresponsibility, self-indulgence, interpersonal intrusiveness, and social rule breaking. The behavioral characteristics that define a drug lifestyle are irresponsibility or pseudoresponsiblity, stress-coping imbalance, interpersonal triviality, and social rule breaking or bending (Walters, 1998). It is interesting to note that when comparing the two lifestyles, there is considerable overlap in behavioral characteristics.

Alcohol-Related Crimes and Criminals

Often, personality traits are linked to the likelihood of committing criminal acts while under the influence of alcohol. One trait that appears to have a high correlation between alcohol and criminal behavior is sensation seeking. Sensation seeking refers to the search for gratification or pleasure for the senses (e.g., taste, smell, and sight). Sensation seeking often leads to risk-taking behaviors that can result in criminal activity. Other traits include impulsivity, low self-esteem, low self-efficacy, and aggression (Parent & Newman, 1999). The risk of criminal conduct is influenced on the basis of not only personality traits but also behavioral changes. Indeed, behavioral alterations occurring from the consumption of alcohol can increase the chance of criminality. Examples of behavioral changes include increased aggression or violence, following the consumption of large quantities of alcohol.

Alcohol intoxication is "the presence of clinically significant maladaptive behavioral or psychological changes (e.g., inappropriate sexual or aggressive behavior, mood lability, impaired judgment, and impaired social or occupational functioning) that develop during, or shortly after, the ingestion of alcohol" (APA, 2000, p. 214). Alcohol intoxication appears to produce higher risk-taking behaviors in men than in women. However, both sexes appear to sustain multiple physical injuries while under the influence of alcohol. Behaviors that produce these injuries can be criminal in nature. Examples of nonviolent criminal behaviors that can be a result of alcohol intoxication are a willingness to drive under the influence, damaging property, **gambling,** and high-risk sexual behavior (Parent & Newman, 1999). Researchers contend that individuals who engage in these behaviors—specifically driving under the influence—are more likely to be categorized as a subtype of offender possessing high sensation-seeking needs, drinking problems, negative affect, and hostility (Parent & Newman, 1999).

Drug Dealing

Recently, drug arrest rates have been higher than the arrest rates for any other category of crime. This increase has been attributed to the "war on drugs" that began in the mid-1980s (Mosher, 2001). Drug offenses have resulted in relatively harsh penalties within the United States. As Mosher reports, "The mean sentence length for convicted drug traffickers in 1994 was 82.5 months, compared with 111 months for convicted murderers, 94.6 months for convicted robbers, and 68.4 months for convicted rapists" (p. 84).

Some communities are more susceptible to drug-related offenses than are others. There are several neighborhood characteristics related to the prevalence of illegal drug use and trafficking activities. These characteristics include (a) the central location of the community, (b) evidence of physical deterioration, and (c) the presence of social disorganization. However, according to Mosher (2001), the most important factors predicting drug use and trafficking operations are not the neighborhoods. Instead, the (low) income of community members and the low-status jobs of residents are highly correlated with drug-related offenses. As Mosher found, the illegal drug industry is a prominent source of money for individuals in disorganized and deteriorating communities, given the decreasing number of blue-collar jobs in these areas and the increase of deindustrialization in society.

What do we know about the profile of today's drug dealer? The typical profile is a young male who sells illegal substances as an alternative to a low-paying job or unemployment. Investigators report that minority individuals, specifically African Americans, have higher drug possession and trafficking arrest rates than do their nonminority counterparts, and that the arrest rates of Blacks are disproportionately higher than their representation in the general population. This overrepresentation is attributed to the ease with which arrests are made in disorganized areas of a city where many minority drug dealers conduct their business. In addition, arrest practices are more difficult in middle- and upper-class neighborhoods where White dealers often conduct their affairs. A related feature to the apprehension of minority drug dealers and traffickers is the patrol and enforcement activities of local law enforcement in socially decaying communities. Police officers believe that these deteriorating neighborhoods are more crime infested than are other nondeteriorating locales; hence, they patrol them with more frequency and intensity than they do other portions of a city or other geographical areas (Mosher, 2001).

Drug- and Crime-Involved Women

The context of social relationships must be taken into consideration when considering crime-involved female drug users. Generally speaking, women identified as drug-related offenders come from families where drug dependence and criminal histories are commonplace (Dowden & Blanchette, 2002; Pottieger & Tressell, 2000). Relatedly, women drug users often find themselves implicated in other crimes, given their association or contact with the criminal element.

For example, in a study conducted by Pottieger and Tressell (2000), the researchers found that female cocaine users were frequently charged as co-defendants in the other crimes alleged in their indictments. Moreover, relationships with individuals outside of the crime and drug circle were minimal or nonexistent. However, Pottieger and Tressell also reported that the number of positive non-drug- and non-crime-related social relationships increased as a function of their participation in rehabilitation initiatives. In addition, women in treatment programs were more likely to have increased levels of financial assistance, child care help, and family and social support. Fewer women involved in counseling and related treatment services reportedly were identified as co-defendants than women not enrolled in similar rehabilitation programs. Overall, the study concluded that criminally involved cocaine-using women who enter treatment become highly dependent on the social and family support received while in drug treatment. This increased level of support leads to more positive rehabilitative outcomes. This study suggests that women who are not enrolled in treatment initiatives to address their illicit substance use are more likely to maintain a lifestyle of drugs and crime than are those who are enrolled.

Several ethnographic studies have reached similar conclusions but also point out the devastating **victimization** women confront when involved in the drug scene. For example, Dunlap, Johnson, and Maher (1997) described the abuse (i.e., beatings) that female street dealers experience when they fail to provide the full amount of cash for the drugs they sell. In addition, Maher and Daly (1996) reported that women assume a range of roles in the drug culture and economy including independent drug dealers and equal partners (typically with a boyfriend or husband), to "mules" (small-time participants used to smuggle drugs into the country), "steerers" (individuals who refer potential customers to dealers), and crack "hoes" (women who exchange sex for drugs; see also Maher & Curtis, 1992). Investigations such as these confirm the fact that although women are involved in the drug subculture their roles are somewhat different from those of men (Pollock, 2001, p. 53).

Legal Aspects of Substance-Related Crime

There is substantial debate about whether drug and alcohol addictions are a disabling illness or an act of deliberate misconduct. When examining substance-related crime from a legal perspective, **mens rea** is the central legal consideration. *Mens rea* is defined as a "guilty mind," which is essential for the classification of guilt (Wrightsman, 2001). *Mens rea* can be established by determining an individual's level of mental capacity. **Diminished capacity** can result from the intoxicating effects of chemical substances that disinhibit an individual's intent to commit a crime. However, diminished capacity is not an appropriate defense in the case of **voluntary intoxication.** Voluntary intoxication occurs when an individual knowingly engages in substance use. However, in the case of **involuntary intoxication,** a person can rely on a defense of diminished capacity. Involuntary intoxication occurs when an individual becomes intoxicated as a result of the external actions of others. Other mental states in which diminished capacity can be claimed are pathological intoxication and psychosis with the primary condition as alcoholism (Miller, 2000). According to the *DSM–IV–TR* (APA, 2000), chemical substances are involved as etiological factors for numerous substance-induced disorders and states of psychosis. Some substance-induced disorders include, but are not limited to, substance-induced delirium, substance-induced psychotic disorder, and substance-induced mood disorders.

Treatment Opportunities

In some states, statutes exist that are designed to provide treatment programs for drug or alcohol addicts, provided certain criteria are met. One such program exists in Illinois, enacted through the Alcoholism and Other Drug Abuse and Dependency Act (2001). Several crimes exclude one from eligibility consideration in this program. These exclusionary offenses include violent crime, numerous drug offenses, pending felony charges, previous enrollment in a designated treatment program, conviction of residential burglary, more than one felony offense conviction, charge of driving under the influence of any substance, reckless homicide while under the influence of chemical substances, and individuals currently enrolled in probation or parole programs (Hardy, Patel, & Paull, 2000).

Some specific crimes are strongly correlated with alcohol and drug use. Alcohol, drug use, and addiction are often associated with physical child abuse, sexual child abuse, and neglect. Substance abuse has been considered a treatable cause of child abuse. Parents who commit acts of child abuse while under the influence of drugs or alcohol are offered an alternative to incarceration. This alternative is addiction treatment and monitoring. However, if a parent does not comply with the court's treatment orders, one's parental rights may be terminated. Termination of parental rights can be either voluntary or involuntary (Miller, 2000).

Annually, only a small percentage of drug users receive needed treatment and rehabilitation services. In fact, "of the 13 million to 16 million Americans who need drug and alcohol treatment each year, only 3 million receive it" (Vastag, 2000, p. 3114). Moreover, in 1998, 60 percent of federal prisoners were incarcerated for drug-related offenses (Vastag, 2000). In addition, the majority of female inmates were convicted of drug-related offenses. Of the 2 million individuals in U.S. jails or prisons today, approximately 500,000 are there for drug-related crimes (Ross & Richards, 2002). Most of these individuals are drug users and abusers, and most of them have committed nonviolent crimes. Presently, Arizona, California, and New York appear to be taking steps to transfer drug users into treatment programs rather than into penal institutions (Vastag, 2000).

ORGANIZED CRIME

Introduction

Defining the term *organized crime* has been a daunting task for scholars and law enforcement officials for years (e.g., Abadinsky, 1999). As far as public opinion is concerned, it is merely a technical term describing "Mafioso" criminal activity. Images of New York shootouts and John Gotti's rise to (and fall from) the top of the Gambino crime family are suddenly conjured up in the minds of many individuals. Alternatively, visions of the Home Box Office cable series, *The Sopranos,* reflect media representations of the criminal enterprise. Although these portrayals constitute aspects of organized crime, the term itself encompasses *all* sophisticated networks engaged in a variety of criminal activities, both violent and nonviolent alike (Liddick, 1999; Ryan, 1995). This portion of the chapter examines the latter dimension of organized criminal activity. The most common nonviolent criminal behaviors associated with the criminal enterprise are **money laundering,** gambling or **numbers running,** and **racketeering** (Ryan). Other illegal activities associated with these criminal activities include **loan sharking,** "**scamming,**" "**skimming,**" bookmaking, and **fencing.** Collectively, these dimensions of organized crime illustrate the actions of those involved in this form of criminal behavior.

Money Laundering

Similar to the difficulty of reaching consensus on what organized crime is, the meaning of money laundering has evolved, defying efforts at a universal definition. Researchers maintain that the term originated in the 1920s as a result of organized crime figures, such as Al Capone, using the money earned from bootlegging and gambling to purchase legitimate businesses, such as laundries. The term itself did not appear in print until 1973, during the Watergate scandal (Richards, 1999). The first time it appeared in legal print was in 1984, in the case of *United States v. Powell.*

According to Richards (1999), definitions for money laundering are wide-ranging and include the "process by which one conceals the existence, illegal source, or illegal application of income and then disguises that income to make it appear legitimate" [as well as] "the process of taking the proceeds of criminal activity and making these proceeds appear legal" (Richards, pp. 43–44). Possibly the best definition for the term was developed by the U.S. Customs Service. As this agency explained,

> Money laundering is the process whereby proceeds, reasonably believed to have been derived from criminal activity, are transported, transferred, transformed, converted, or intermingled with legitimate funds, for the purpose of concealing or disguising the true nature, source, disposition, movement or ownership of those proceeds. The goal of the money-laundering process is to make funds derived from, or associated with, illicit activity appear legitimate. (as cited in Richards, 1999, p. 44)

The Financial Crimes Enforcement Network (FinCEN) estimates that of the $750 billion that is laundered annually around the world, a total of $300 billion is laundered either within, or through, the United States (Richards, 1999). As the Financial Action Task Force reports, the major participants in this multibillion-dollar-a-year swindle are the illegal drug traffickers. Following these individuals are the illegal arms dealers and terrorists (FATF, 1996–1997, as cited in Richards).

There are three essential activities involved in the money-laundering process. These include placement, layering, and integration (Abadinsky, 1999). Placement refers to changing the bulk money derived from illicit activities into a less conspicuous form and then placing these proceeds into the legitimate financial system. Layering is the movement of these funds, often intermingled with legitimate businesses, through worldwide financial accounts in an attempt to conceal the illicit funds. After the funds have gone through placement and layering, the process of integration reintroduces the money into the legitimate financial economy where the individual can then spend or invest the laundered money.

Gambling, Loan Sharking, and Numbers Running

Organized crime syndicates have long since used gambling as a primary source of income. The proceeds received from gambling and gambling-related activities are second only to the proceeds received from the illegal sale and distribution of drugs (Ryan, 1995). For the purpose of this subsection of the chapter, gambling encompasses booking bets, loan sharking, and numbers running.

Bookmaking consists of taking bets and manufacturing point spreads and odds on sporting events. A person is able to place a bet with a "bookie," either by using the point spread or the odds in the newspaper. If the bettor wins (say on a $25 dollar bet) he or she is paid $25 dollars, plus whatever the odds were on the sporting event. If the odds were 3:1

and the bettor wins, the person receives three times the actual bet ($75 dollars). However, if the bettor loses, he or she loses what was bet plus interest or a "kickback" to the bookie. This usually amounts to 10% of the total bet. Sometimes bettors overestimate their chances of winning and actually lose a considerable amount of money that they do not have. When this occurs, bookies are usually more than happy to provide a loan, especially because a considerable interest rate attaches to the loan.

The practice of lending money under the previously cited conditions is called loan sharking. It typically involves a bookie that lends a bettor or gambler a set amount of money, under the condition that the loan or debt will be repaid at a specific date and with a sizeable interest rate attached. If the person fails to meet these conditions, the loan shark sends "collectors" to obtain the only thing the person in debt has as collateral: his or her body. Obviously, entering into a business transaction with a loan shark can be a precarious, and often painful, experience. Rich businessmen and women who are unsuccessful gamblers are a prime target for loan sharks (Ryan, 1995).

The final aspect of organized crime (gambling) is that of numbers running. Running numbers is another popular activity of organized crime syndicates. The numbers racket in organized crime circles is similar to the legislated "daily number" of most state lotteries. In 1970, Kaplan and Maher researched racketeering and developed an analysis of this crime, the process by which it unfolds, and the members who participate in it. Their assessment is still regarded as an effective approach to understanding this dimension of the criminal enterprise (Abadinsky, 1999; Liddick, 1999; Ryan, 1995).

Numbers running is preferred over the state lottery because it is cheaper and the pay-off odds are 600:1 as opposed to the 500:1 available in most state lotteries (Kaplan & Maher, 1970; Ryan). The person manipulating this project is the "**controller**," who organizes the particular numbers racket event. The controller employs "**runners**" who take bets from people in a given area and who run them back to the banker. When it is time to pay out, the runners do the distributing and collecting for the banker who holds all the money (Ryan). The three numbers used for this illegitimate lottery were once taken from stock market quotes. However, crime syndicates now rely on three digits taken from the results of races at a specified horse track or from the total amount of money bet that day (Liddick). This aspect of organized crime predominantly caters to, and is facilitated by, poor, urban constituents (Liddick; Ryan).

Racketeering

As a technical matter, the material thus far presented on organized crime falls under the broad category of racketeering. As defined by the Racketeer Influenced and Corrupt Organization Act of 1970 (RICO), racketeering activity includes, but is not limited to, murder, kidnapping, gambling, **arson,** robbery, bribery, extortion, embezzlement, and dealing in narcotics. In addition, following the implementation of this important piece of legislation, a person does not have to commit this crime in order to be charged with racketeering. Instead, the individual needs only to belong to or be a co-conspirator with the organization that is committing these unlawful acts (Viano, 1999).

One of the more notable forms of racketeering is labor racketeering. This is the illegal infiltration into labor unions by organized crime syndicates for personal profit (Ryan, 1995). Mob infiltrators take kickbacks from the employers of the union to ensure that everything operates smoothly. In this situation, the people who suffer the most are members of the union themselves. The significant political influence held by organized crime syndicates makes it difficult to curtail or address this form of criminal behavior (Abadinsky, 1999). Indeed, few union leaders are able to withstand the brutal threats and acts of coercion on the part of these organized crime affiliates.

There are also some minor, nonviolent aspects of organized crime that warrant some consideration. Skimming is a very popular offense among associates within and outside of organized crime circles. Skimming occurs when money is taken "off the top" of any cash transaction. This money is hidden and becomes a source of unreported, tax-free income. Businesses involved in skimming can range from locally owned grocery stores to nationally recognized food chains to casinos owned by organized crime figures. Frequently, crime syndicates partner with legitimate establishments and use their professional relationship to commit bankruptcy fraud. When the legitimate business owner acquires solid credit, large orders are placed for merchandise, but payments on the goods are not submitted. The merchandise is fenced out the back door without the knowledge of the bank or lending institution. Large amounts of loans also are assigned through the business, yet repayments are never made to the lender for the merchandise. The organized crime syndicate escapes with the merchandise and the money, and bankruptcy is filed on the part of the legitimate business.

Is There a Personality Profile for Organized Crime Members?

Research shows that there are no demographics or personality profiles specific to individuals who engage in organized crime. In the field today, there are three theories or models accounting for why a person enters this lifestyle or criminal career that extend beyond mere social and economic class (Abadinsky, 1999). The first theory is the Alien-Conspiracy/Bureaucracy paradigm. This model has received tremendous criticism in the field and is not commonly held as an explanation for organized crime per se. Nonetheless, the basis for this theory centers on the idea of La Cosa Nostra, or "this thing of ours." It is the term applied to Italian organized crime syndicates, believed to control the criminal enterprise nationwide. This specific element is what establishes the conspiratorial nature of the theory. The structure of these families is set up in a bureaucratic way. There are bosses, under-bosses, soldiers, counseling agents or "consigliore" who advise the crime boss, and other people who work in crews beneath the soldiers. The development of this theory perpetuates the myth painted by Hollywood motion pictures, cable television series, and paperback crime fiction novels.

The Alien-Conspiracy/Bureaucracy paradigm is flawed in several important respects. First, we know that organized crime activity is not composed primarily of Italian Americans. The demographics of organized crime offenders are as diverse as the types of crimes themselves. Second, researchers agree that the criminal enterprise in America is not set up by one formal bureaucratic superstructure; rather, it is arranged by many smaller and informal organizations, some of which are not well organized at all (Liddick, 1999). Third, the scholarly foundation for this theory grew out of the work done by Donald R. Cressey in the late 1960s and early 1970s, along with the Organized Crime Hearings set up by then President Lyndon B. Johnson in the 1960s. More recently, testimony has been provided confirming the existence of certain crime families operating in New York City, composed of a majority of Italian Americans. However, to assume the presence of these families represents the controlling aspect of a nationwide conspiracy is, at the very least, absurd. Fourth, the Alien-Conspiracy/Bureaucracy paradigm evolved from unsubstantiated stereotypical ideas perpetuated by the media and the motion picture industry.

The Enterprise paradigm is a theoretical approach that appears to have a fair amount of face validity when applied to certain nonviolent organized crime behaviors. Fundamentally, this approach to crime syndicates argues that organized criminal behaviors are an extension of legitimately based markets into illegal domains (Liddick, 1999). When applied to certain crimes, this model provides a solid explanation for activities such as numbers running and loan sharking (Abadinsky, 1999).

A number of states have a legitimate lottery in which citizens can pay a fee for a ticket and guess the winning numbers. Organized crime number circuits operate in a very similar fashion; however, they function within illegitimate domains. When a person needs money for whatever reason and is not approved by a bank, the individual can borrow the money through an illegitimate source such as a loan shark. There are a variety of intermingled behaviors that can be explained by this theory, such as legitimate businesses purchasing legal goods illegally to sell legally in a store, or illegally purchasing illegal goods to sell illegally in a back-door operation (Liddick, 1999).

The third explanation for why a person would pursue a career in the criminal enterprise is linked to a number of prominent sociological theories as discussed in chapters 3 and 4 of this textbook. In short, theories that explain criminal behavior on the basis of economic deprivation, strain, and inequalities can be applied to many aspects of nonviolent organized crime. Indeed, in these instances, the main reason why a person would engage in conduct linked to the criminal enterprise is to achieve personal success and monetary gain.

WHITE-COLLAR CRIME

Introduction

White-collar crime costs this country billions of dollars per year in stolen revenue (Friedrichs, 1996; Simpson, 2002). Researchers estimate that the figure may reach anywhere from $200 to $400 billion annually (Benson, 1998; Simpson, 2002). In addition to the money lost directly from the actions of these elite offenders are the criminal justice costs involved in the apprehension and prosecution of such felons. Indeed, attempts by law enforcement officials to track and arrest white-collar offenders, and efforts by the legal system to investigate and prosecute them are extremely time-consuming and financially draining (Benson, 1998). It is not uncommon for an investigative unit to take months to sort through hundreds of documents, accounting journals, bank statements, contracts, and other records pertinent to a particular case (Friedrichs, 1996). Complicating this situation are law enforcement agencies that lack a formal, white-collar crime investigative unit. Moreover, not every inquiry into alleged embezzlement, fraud, and other white-collar crime warrants the use of federal agencies such as the Internal Revenue Service (IRS) or the Federal Bureau of Investigation (FBI). Overreliance on these entities can lead to incomplete and inadequate investigations and prosecutions, factors that only contribute to the economic and criminal justice problems linked to white-collar crime (Benson).

This portion of the chapter reviews three specific types of white-collar crime. These forms of criminal behavior include embezzlement, insider trading, and security fraud. However, before addressing these matters, some commentary on the difficulty that exists within the literature regarding the appropriate definition for white-collar crime is warranted.

Defining White-Collar Crime

The history of the term *white collar crime* and its definition date back over half a century (Friedrichs, 1996). Edwin Sutherland first introduced the term in 1939, in his presidential address to the American Sociological Society. In his book, *White-Collar Crime* (1949), Sutherland defined this form of behavior as "a crime committed by a person of respectability and high social status in the course of his occupation" (p. 31; see also Sutherland, 1983). Although criticized for a number of reasons (especially including the overly generalized nature of the definition), Sutherland's work paved the way for other criminologists to establish a more inclusive and composite meaning for white-collar crime.

For example, Donald Gibbons (1977) asserted that white-collar crime was a violation of business rules and occupational practices, but only insofar as those offenses were committed to benefit legitimate enterprises or organizations. However, by focusing on the actions of larger administrations, businesses, and corporations, the definition supplied by Gibbons failed to account for crimes such as fraud and embezzlement. Marshall Clinnard and Richard Quinney (1980) also attempted to define white-collar crime by linking it to what they described as occupational crime (see also, Clinnard & Yeager, 1983). For Clinnard and Quinney, occupational crime focused on nonviolent infractions of legal codes within an otherwise legitimate occupation or enterprise. Examples of this offense include elements of fraud and deception. In an effort to establish a more inclusive and less convoluted definition for the phenomenon of white-collar crime, the U.S. Congressional Subcommittee on Crime (USC) introduced its own interpretation for this form of criminal behavior. As the Committee noted, white-collar crime is "an illegal act or series of illegal acts committed by nonphysical means and by concealment or guile, to obtain money or property, or to obtain personal or business advantage" (USC, 1979, p. 27). Interestingly, this definition represents the most functional interpretation supplied to date for many criminal justice scholars and law enforcement officials (Simpson, 2002).

Embezzlement

Embezzlement comes from an old English common law established in 1799, revising the definition of larceny (Friedrichs, 1996). The offense of larceny did not account for the theft of goods that one had been entrusted with by another. Thus, the crime of embezzlement was born. Today, the Uniform Crime Reports differentiate among the crimes of theft, larceny, and embezzlement. Although, as we shall see, it is difficult to keep accurate records on the offense of embezzlement because incidences of it are grossly underreported (Benson, 1998).

Embezzlers are a unique type of criminal. They are often highly educated and, in many instances, are known to the person from whom they are stealing. Some researchers estimate that roughly 85% of known embezzlements by a company are not conveyed to the criminal justice system (Ermann & Lundman, 2002; Simpson, 2002). Instead, these businesses address the problem internally, using a payback arrangement or dismissal from the corporation or company (Benson, 1998). Embezzlement is estimated to account for roughly 30% of all business bankruptcies (Friedrichs, 1996; Simpson, 2002).

Consistent with other discussions on the profile of offenders entertained throughout this book, the personality and behavioral portrait of the embezzler varies. However, there are common characteristics, events, and circumstances attributable to this offender type, and these factors represent a catalyst for the embezzler's behavior. In the work setting, the embezzler is the model employee: outgoing, aggressive, industrious, hard working, and seemingly honest. This persona establishes the requisite conditions and opportunity for the individual to act criminally. Prior to the commission of an offense, the embezzler creates an elaborate plan to ensure success without any detection. However, if the person is suspected or detected, the embezzler typically leverages unflattering or less than complimentary information regarding certain officials within the company, and uses the information for extortion purposes. As this description suggests, the embezzler is manipulative, scheming, and deceptive (Ermann & Lundman, 2002).

Why would someone embezzle? There is a range of precipitating factors that could trigger this criminal behavior. For example, immediate and genuine economic hardship may incline a person to obtain money illegally rather than seek legitimate financial assistance. Alternatively, some embezzlers manufacture their monetary needs, believing that they are entitled to or otherwise deserve the additional income (Simpson, 2002).

Other triggers may appear more noble or admirable. For example, some people embezzle in order to care for a chronically ill loved one whose alcoholism, drug abuse, or gambling addiction has produced sizeable health care and treatment needs. Clearly, the justification process utilized by this offender type is important when interpreting their behavior and assessing whether the offense represents a one-time occurrence or a repeated act of criminal wrongdoing (Friedrichs, 1996). Embezzlers are prone to justifying their actions (Benson, 1998). Indeed, they convince themselves that they are just "borrowing" money. Explanations such as this are delusional. They enable the embezzler to rationalize the criminal conduct and establish, at least in the mind of the offender, the perception that the behavior was not deviant or illicit. Instead of feeling guilt, the embezzler often conveys a sense of entitlement and superiority.

Securities and Exchange Commission Violations: Insider Trading

Securities and Exchange Commission (SEC) violations are varied in description and often vague in definition. One example of a SEC violation is called insider trading. This concept is somewhat convoluted and it is often misrepresented to society at large. One misperception is that all insider trading is illegal. This is not accurate. In addition, many people believe that all profits generated by insiders must be illegal. Again, this is not true. Indeed, persons not identified as insiders still could be guilty of this SEC violation.

Part of the problem with these misperceptions is one of definition. In short, the question is who is and who is not an insider, and what is it that constitutes insider trading. According to Seyhun (2000, pp. xxvi–xxvii), insiders are "officers, directors, and owners of more than 10% of any equity class of securities . . . [that] must have decision-making authority that affects the entire organization." Securities laws impose restrictions on this group of insiders. Insider trading occurs when information or material that is not made public is used for personal profit. As Seyhun (2000) explains it,

> A central feature of the insider-trading regulations involves disclosure. The securities laws require all insiders to report all their stock transactions in their own firms to the Securities and Exchange Commission (SEC) and the stock exchange where the transaction took place in a timely fashion. Failure to report their transactions in a timely fashion is a violation of the securities laws, which currently involves fines of up to $2.5 million as well as ten years in prison. Insiders must report all transactions within 10 days of the calendar month following the month in which the trade took place (p. xxviii).

Currently, there is no clear definition of what comprises insider information. Even with the implementation of the Insider Trading Sanctions Act of 1984 and the Insider Trading and Securities Fraud Enforcement Act of 1988, a great deal of ambiguity remains. Moreover, at the implicit request of the SEC, the ambiguity is endorsed particularly when defining and prosecuting these offenses.

Securities and Exchange Commission Violations: Securities Fraud

Illegal stock trading, or the illegal trading in convertible securities and equity derivatives, is another SEC violation falling within the realm of insider trading. One of the biggest examples of this form of nonviolent criminal conduct witnessed in the United States involved the actions of Dennis Levine and Ivan Boesky. They were convicted in highly publicized, very controversial, and extremely profitable insider-trading business scams and takeovers in the 1980s. These men bought and sold information not made public, made a sizeable profit as a result, and did not report the transaction to the SEC because they knew the activity was illegal.

Securities and commodities fraud is among the more notable SEC violations. "**Securities fraud** involves fraudulent activities including the sale, transfer, or purchase of securities or of money interests in the business activities of others" (Bintliff, 1993, p. 376). This type of crime covers a broad range of illicit activity. Some examples of these activities are the following:

> . . . securities of no value are sold, or are misrepresented to be worth more than their value; purchasers are not informed of all facts regarding securities, and there is a failure to file proper disclosures with federal and state regulatory agencies; broker-dealers and investment advisers act for their own benefit instead of for the benefit of their corporate clients; false information is supplied to the security holder and the investing corporation in financial statements published or filed with securities, regulatory agencies, or by payments to financial writers or publications; [and] manipulation of the price of securities by purchases and sales occurs in stock exchange or over-the-counter markets. (Bintliff, 1993, pp. 376–377)

Finally, there are the "boiler-room" operations. These operations are used to promote the sales of fraudulent securities and to acquire charitable donations from unwitting victims who believe their money is going toward a legitimate cause or beneficial purpose. Boiler-room operations are performed primarily through telemarketing sales procedures. In some instances, the name of a legitimate organization is used as a cover for the solicitation of charitable donations, especially when the business entity sees very few of the returns itself (Bintliff, 1993).

FRAUD

Introduction

Fraud is a nonviolent crime that has become increasingly prevalent in today's society. According to the *Merriam-Webster's Collegiate Dictionary* (10th ed., 1996, p. 463), fraud is "an act of deceiving or misrepresenting." Following this definition, people engage in fraudulent behavior every day, although not all fraudulent behavior is illegal. Nevertheless, there are many types of illegal fraud in which individuals engage. The most prevalent categories are **Internet fraud, telemarketing fraud,** and **identity theft and fraud.** These topics are reviewed in this portion of the chapter.

Internet Fraud

One factor contributing to the growth of fraudulent crime is the widespread availability of computers and the Internet. Fraud schemes can be found throughout the Internet on message boards, Web sites, e-mails, and chat rooms (U.S. Department of Justice, 2000b). There are five general types of Internet fraud: auction and retail schemes, business opportunity schemes, identity theft and fraud, investment schemes, and credit card schemes (U.S. Department of Justice, 2000b).

In an attempt to successfully deal with Internet fraud, the Computer Fraud and Abuse Act was established in 1996 (Samoriski, 1999). Under this Act, the number of successful cases against e-mail solicitors, also known as "**spammers,**" is on the rise. The Communications Privacy Act has also been established to prevent spamming activity (Samoriski, 1999). According to the U.S. Department of Justice (2000b), offenders of Internet fraud can incur legal consequences such as imprisonment and serious fines. Both civil and criminal lawsuits have emerged from Internet fraud. For example, spammers have been prosecuted under civil, federal, and state law (Samoriski, 1999). Some prominent cases in computer fraud are *People by Vacco v. Lipsitz,* 663 N.Y.S.2d 468 (1997); *In Re. Apple Computer Security Litigation,* No. C-84-20148(A)-JW (N.D. CAL 2000); and *Shugard Storage Centers v. Safeguard Self-Storage, Inc.,* 119 F. supp, 2d 1121 (W.D. WASH. 2000). Many other cases regarding Internet fraud have arisen throughout the country. These cases encompass all of the different classifications of Internet fraud.

Telemarketing Fraud

Telemarketing fraud occurs when false and misleading statements, representations, and promises are made, offering goods and services, requesting investments, or asking for donations for charitable causes (U.S. Department of Justice, 1998). There are three factors that differentiate fraudulent telemarketing practices from legitimate entrepreneurship. The first of these factors or elements relates to the goals of the illegitimate enterprise.

Individuals who engage in telemarketing fraud have three primary goals: (a) to make the scheme appear to be a good service or charitable cause worth the payment that consumers are asked to send; (b) to obtain immediate payment before the victim can inspect the item of value they expect to receive; and (c) to devise a perception of validity about the venture by attempting to resemble valid telemarketing operations, valid businesses, or valid government agencies (U.S. Department of Justice, 1998).

A second factor differentiating fraudulent **telemarketing schemes** from legitimate telemarketing businesses is "**reloading.**" Reloading means that the fraudulent operation re-approaches its "victims" after their first contact with a telemarketer has been successful. When the subject is re-approached, the fraudulent telemarketer then initiates solicitation for additional payments.

There is a third factor distinguishing fraudulent telemarketing activity from valid telemarketing operations. This element relates to the geographical location of the illegitimate business and the unsuspecting consumer. Generally speaking, fraudulent tele-marketers are opposed to contacting prospective buyers who live in the same state as the headquarters of the criminal operation (U.S. Department of Justice, 1998). This is because the tracking, detection, and apprehension by law enforcement officials is considerably more likely when the illegitimate business and the victim are located in the same state or jurisdiction.

Telemarketing schemes or plans vary considerably. Among the more distinctive criminal enterprises are charity schemes, credit card schemes, credit repair and loan schemes, investment and business opportunity schemes, lottery schemes, magazine promotion schemes, and prize promotion schemes (U.S. Department of Justice, 1998). Each of these illegitimate business ventures is designed to bilk money from unsuspecting or otherwise innocent, ordinary citizens.

Identity Theft and Identity Fraud

Identity theft and identity fraud are loosely defined as crimes in which a person wrongfully acquires and uses another individual's personal information in a manner that involves fraud or deception. Identity theft and fraud are generally used for purposes of economic gain (U.S. Department of Justice, 2000a). Personal information that is typically used by an offender includes Social Security numbers, bank account numbers or credit card numbers, telephone calling card numbers, and other data that identify a particular individual.

Most people do not realize how effortlessly an identity theft and fraud offender can obtain personal data without having to commit other crimes such as breaking and entering. Offenders of identity theft and fraud can obtain private information in a few significant ways. These methods include **"shoulder surfing"** and **"dumpster diving"** (U.S. Department of Justice, 2000a). Shoulder surfing occurs when the perpetrator observes an individual using an ATM card or a calling card. The perpetrator can determine pin numbers and calling card numbers through this simple shoulder surfing method. Dumpster diving occurs when an offender sorts through trash cans looking for data, such as credit card receipts, checks, names, addresses, and phone numbers, all of which assist the offender in assuming a new identity.

The U.S. Department of Justice (1998) created a law that prohibits identity theft. The Identity Theft and Assumption Deterrence Act of 1998 established identity theft as a criminal offense. As the Act stipulates, it prohibits the following:

> . . . knowingly transfer[ring] or us[ing], without lawful authority, a means of identification of another person with the intent to commit, or to aid or abet, any unlawful activity that constitutes a violation of Federal law, or that constitutes a felony under any applicable State or local law. (18 USC 1028(a)(7))

An offense under this act may result in a prison term of 15 years, monetary penalties, and the revocation of personal property used or designed to be used to commit an identity theft or fraud offense (U.S. Department of Justice, 2000a).

Other Types of Fraud

According to Kalb (1999), the U.S. Department of Justice has declared **health care fraud** to be one of its two foremost priorities, with the number one priority being violent crime. Health care fraud is a prevalent issue in today's society given the substantial rise in health care costs, perceived flaws in the quality of health care and health care delivery, and legislative initiatives established to reduce the prevalence of fraud.

Legislation designed to prevent health care fraud targets three types of behavior: the submission of false claims, the payment or receipt of bribes, and self-referrals. The **False Claims Act,** the federal **Anti-Kickback statute,** and the **Ethics in Patient Referral**

Act established guidelines to avoid health care fraud (Kalb, 1999). The False Claims Act of 1998 prohibits the knowledgeable submission of invalid claims, statements, or certifications to the government. This act also prohibits conspiracies with others to submit false claims. The Anti-Kickback statute of 1998 prohibits the receipt and dispersal of bribes and kickbacks intended to influence the exchange of heath-care-related services. Last, the Ethics in Patient Referral Act of 1998 established that patients may not be referred to health care providers who are associated with (either by familial or financial relationship) the referring physician or psychologist.

If physicians or psychologists violate these laws, the consequences can be devastating to their professional careers and to their livelihoods. In particular, infractions may result in the loss of licensure, exclusion from the participation in health care programs, imprisonment, fines, and other monetary damages. Health care laws are enforced by numerous regulatory agencies or related authoritative bodies. Federal criminal actions are mostly controlled by the U.S. Department of Justice, whereas civil actions are regulated by the U.S. Attorney's Office. State actions are monitored and prosecuted by the individual states, and administrative actions are pursued by the Office of the Inspector General.

Most of the fraudulent behavior referred to in this chapter focuses on individuals committing a deceitful act. However, fraud is not always a one-person crime. Securities fraud occurs when publicly traded firms commit acts of disclosure. As discussed in the subsequent section under Offenders and Victims, disclosure occurs when a firm provides, "misleading public reporting as a result of the information production process" (Latham & Jacobs, 2000, p. 170).

Offenders and Victims

Any person of any age can be a victim of fraud. Those factors most likely to make a person a victim of fraudulent conduct are vulnerability and carelessness. However, some research suggests that elderly individuals are more vulnerable to crime than are other members of a community, particularly when crimes of consumer fraud and financial abuse are involved (Anetzberger, 2001). The following two inserts summarize the characteristics of victims and offenders for the various fraudulent schemes and practices discussed previously in the chapter.

Fraudulent Crimes: A Summary of Victim Characteristics

The U.S. Department of Justice (2000b) developed a profile of victims succumbing to Internet fraud. These individuals frequently make a positive judgment of a virtual site relying only on initial appearance. For example, one might judge a scheme based on the aesthetic or artistic quality of the Web page, assuming its legitimacy on the basis of creativeness alone. Other victims are careless in disclosing valuable personal data online (i.e., Social Security number or credit card numbers), or communicating online with an individual who conceals his or her true identity. Finally, many Internet fraud victims agree to pay advance-fee demands before researching the legitimacy of the proposed scheme.

Identity theft and fraud victims generally disclose personal information to others, despite warnings about trusting people. Therefore, preventing identity theft and fraud can be as simple as checking financial information on a regular basis, looking specifically for unexpected financial transactions, asking periodically for a copy of credit reports, and maintaining precise records of banking and financial accounts.

Unlike other acts of fraud and fraudulent behavior, illicit telemarketing operations do not choose their victims at random. Telemarketers pursue and purchase "leads" (i.e., the names of potential buyers or consumers) from lead brokers. Leads are typically listings of names, addresses, and phone numbers of individuals victimized by fraudulent behavior in previous telemarketing schemes. Lead brokers are companies that disclose this information about individuals scammed by telemarketing operations in the past (U.S. Department of Justice, 1998). With telemarketing schemes, more so than in other fraudulent activities, the perpetrators have more control of the victims.

Fraudulent Crimes: A Summary of Perpetrator Characteristics

Perpetrators of nonviolent crime are motivated by factors that are different from those who engage in violent criminal behavior. More specifically, fraudulent offenders are often influenced and stimulated by dissimilar interests than are offenders of assault, rape, and murder. Given the previous commentary on fraud and fraudulent conduct, adult offenders who engage in these behaviors are frequently motivated by monetary gain. Additionally, research suggests that adolescents who engage in fraudulent activities are generally susceptible to a diagnosis of conduct disorder (Rodney, Tachia, & Rodney, 1999. For a more detailed discussion on adolescent crime or conduct disorder, please refer to chapters 7 and 8, respectively.)

There are other contrasts between nonviolent and violent offenders. For example, prison sentences for subsequent fraudulent criminal activity generally run 11 months, whereas subsequent robbery crimes run anywhere from 24 to 36 months. After serving their prison sentences, approximately 13% of individuals convicted for either fraud or drug offenses return within 3 years of their release (Sabol, Adams, Parthasarathy, & Yuan, 2000). The recidivism rate for fraud is significantly lower as compared to other violent (and nonviolent) crimes and criminals. For example, 36% of robbery offenders return to prison within 3 years, and 50% of public-order offenders return to prison within 3 years (Sabol et al.).

Notwithstanding this important information about victims and offenders of fraudulent conduct, these forms of criminal behavior continue to be difficult offenses to extinguish. For example, according to Latham and Jacobs (2000), disclosure manipulation is a motivation for individuals to engage in misleading behavior. In their study investigating disclosure fraud, the investigators found that misleading firms are more closely monitored, have higher quality investment professionals, and have more stock owned by management individuals. These findings illustrate that monitoring a company's behavior will not reduce the amount of fraudulent behavior within the company. However, monitoring a company will increase the reliability of their disclosure of fraudulent behavior. Although monitoring may not prevent a company from releasing deceptive information to the public, it will assist in revealing fraud.

INTERNET CRIME

Introduction

Internet crime is quickly becoming a serious threat to all segments of society. The creation and spread of malicious computer viruses, identity theft, patent infringement, child exploitation, fraud, and technological terrorism threaten the sanctity of the information superhighway. As Godwin (1995) observes:

> Extortion is one of the many imaginative, daring, and increasingly publicized crimes that have gone high tech in recent years. In addition to the predictable tax, insurance, and credit card scams, software infringements and eavesdropping, the computer is now the site of crimes that range all the way up to homicide. (p. 62)

Although computer crimes can assume many forms and can be used for numerous devious and delinquent purposes, this section of the chapter focuses on nonviolent Internet crime. In particular, child pornography, online solicitation of children, and cyberstalking are examined. Additional Internet behaviors such as the dissemination of hate-filled messages to certain groups of people, or Web sites that instruct juveniles on how to build a pipe bomb are protected under the free speech clause of the First Amendment. In other words, these actions are not deemed criminal, although, they certainly are expressions of deviance. Accordingly, these topics are not explored in this portion of the chapter.

The Internet is an enormous arena that allows people from all over the world to exchange ideas, to dialog, and to entertain. However, in this vast universe of digitized information, extremely offensive (and criminal) material is being exchanged. "[Material] which seems to cause the greatest consternation (in rough descending order of concern) is sex involving children; sex between humans and animals; nonconsensual sex; homoerotic activity; and depictions of consensual sexual activity between adult males and females" (Grabosky & Smith, 1998, pp. 119–120). According to Grabosky and Smith, the regulation of the transmission of sexually explicit and offensive material is a contentious issue:

> First, there are, within and between nations, substantial differences of opinion as to what is offensive and what is not. Second, there are in some places equally strong differences of opinion relating to the balance between the rights of the individual and those of the state (the First Amendment to the Constitution of the United States protects material that many U.S. citizens, not to mention those from less tolerant cultures, would find totally abhorrent). (p. 119)

With these thoughts in mind, this section addresses nonviolent Internet crime whose context is sexual in nature.

Electronically Generated Child Pornography

According to Denning (1999, p. 128), child pornography is defined as "any visual depiction, including any photograph, film, video, picture, or computer-generated image or picture of sexually explicit conduct of a minor (any person under the age of eighteen years)." The United States Code § 2252A (2001) provides for the arrest or fines anyone who "knowingly mails or transports, or ships in interstate or foreign commerce by any means, *including by computer,* any child pornography" [italics added, p. 23]. Clearly, the possession and distribution of child pornography is one area where one's First Amendment free speech rights have little weight, including the fast-paced information superhighway of the Internet (Denning, 1999).

However, as technology advances, society faces a new dilemma: Is it illegal to produce or possess *electronically generated* child pornography? Interestingly, the marvels of "modern technology have brought us virtual child porn: images that look exactly like children engaging in sexual conduct but are created by computers, without using real children" (Taylor, 2001, p. 51). The Child Pornography Prevention Act (CPPA) of 1996 bans any computer transmission of erotic images that are altered to resemble depictions of minors. "Congress found not only that pedophiles use such images to whet their own appetites and lure children into sexual activities" (Taylor, 2001, p. 51), but also computer-generated child pornography can desensitize the viewer to the pathology of **sexual abuse** or exploitation of children (CPPA, 1996).

Cyberstalking

In addition to the Internet practice of computer-generated child pornography is the general practice of cyberstalking. "In 1990, after five women were murdered by stalkers, California became the first state in the United States to enact a law to deal with this specific problem" (Casey, 2000, p. 187). In 1998, California specifically addressed cyberstalking in its antistalking legislation.

Cyberstalking involves the use of the Internet as a medium for harassment and is legally defined as:

> . . . any person who willfully, maliciously, and repeatedly follows or harasses another person and who makes a credible threat, including that performed through the use of an electronic device, or a threat implied by a pattern of conduct or combination of verbal, written or electronically communicated statements and conduct made with the intent to place that person in reasonable fear of death or grave bodily injury. "Electronic communication device" includes, but is not limited to, telephones, cellular phones, computers, video recorders, fax machines, or pagers. (California Penal Code 646.9, p. 47)

Sexual Stalking of Children on the Internet

Related to electronically manufactured images of child pornography are the cyberspace interactions that can develop between unsuspecting juveniles and adult pedophiles. As chapter 5 disclosed, a pedophile is one who is sexually attracted to a minor. "Individuals with pedophilia who act on their urges with children may limit their activity to undressing the child and looking, exposing themselves, masturbating in the presence of a child, or gentle touching and fondling of the child" (DSM–IV, APA, 1994, p. 527). Unfortunately, in some instances, pedophiles persist in their behaviors using "various degrees of force to do so" (DSM–IV, APA, 1994, p. 527). What distinguishes acts of pedophilia from computer-generated and socially inappropriate interaction between children and adults is the role of the Internet. In brief, computer contact can facilitate an eventual physical encounter between the child and the pedophile. On these occasions, the Internet becomes a sophisticated medium by which to stalk children and adolescents.

To avert potential computer-generated stalking of children for erotically explicit purposes, parents should discuss these dangers with their children and monitor their journeys through cyberspace. Janal (1998) cited instances of juveniles being given and accepting airline tickets to rendezvous with individuals whose initial contact occurred on the Internet. Not only are these children considered missing, several may have been sexually abused or murdered at the hands of a violent cyberspace predator.

Equally compelling is the study provided by the National Center for Missing and Exploited Children. According to this organization, one in five children who use the Internet report being exposed to unwelcome sexual solicitations, and one in four come across unwanted pornography (Finkelhor, Mitchell, & Wolak, 2000). Notwithstanding the lack of a comprehensive database, the incidence of reported sexual stalking of children appears to be rising sharply. For example, "in 1995 the FBI investigated 113 cases involving online enticement of children. By [the year 2000], the number soared to 1500" (McDonald, 2001, p. 57).

Children engage in numerous daily conversations with others in online chat rooms. The anonymity these forums provide make it possible for sexual stalkers of children to read about and partake in conversations with them. In addition, the anonymity allows cybersex offenders to pretend and act as if they are children, too. Unsupervised children utilizing the Internet may interact naively, providing details on where they live and what they look like. Unfortunately, not everyone who participates in these online conversations has the best of intentions. Young people need to be made aware of this. Indeed, as Janal (1998, pp. 20–21) observed, "The Internet is not a model community. Instead, it mirrors the real world. . . . Miscreants can ply their trade online with ease since they can hide their identities and spread their maliciousness with little fear of being caught."

In the subsequent section of this chapter, the characteristics of "real-world" stalking (as opposed to "cyberworld" stalking) are discussed in greater detail. However, it is important to point out that the latter is as real and can be as frightening and dangerous as traditional forms of stalking. Casey (2000, p. 188) noted that "many offenders combine their online activities with more traditional forms of stalking and harassment such as telephoning the victim and going to the victim's home." Janal (1998, p. 11) provides a useful illustration of this phenomenon:

> A New Jersey woman was the victim of a cyberstalker who harassed her online and then stole $2,500 from her checking account. He also called her on the phone, recited her Social Security number, knew the names of her family members, and described her neighborhood.

In the previous example, the stalker knew that the more information he gathered and revealed to the victim, the more likely it was that the victim would become afraid and, consequently, the greater his power would be over her. Stalkers gather personal phone numbers, addresses, daily routines, preferences, and related material in order to eventually access and manipulate the victim's emotions and increase the impact of their harassment. The behavior of cyberstalkers, then, amounts to the acquisition of information electronically obtained without the consent of the person from whom the personal data are retrieved.

As a general practice, cyberstalkers browse through online profiles and spend time in chat rooms in search of potential victims. Cyberstalkers look for "vulnerable, under-confident individuals who [are] easy to intimidate" (Casey, 2000, p. 189). The Internet affords them anonymity and privacy, granting these offenders the ability to spy on a person's online activities while concealing their own identity. Women who use the Internet as one might use a singles' bar are at a greater risk for being cyberstalked (Casey, 2000). Moreover, as speaker, author, and marketing consultant, Daniel Janal (1998) asserts, "Reaching out and touching someone can lead to nasty situations on the Internet" (p. 8). As he warns, "While many pen pals pursue healthy, happy relationships online, [people] should use great caution when talking to [others] online and agreeing to meet them in person. People are not necessarily who they say they are, and their motives might not be innocent" (p. 11).

To date, there is no consensus regarding the typical profile for or description of a cyberstalker. "It is difficult to make accurate generalizations about cyberstalkers because a wide variety of circumstances can lead to [this behavior]" (Casey, 2000, p. 197). An online stalker may be a pedophile, a scorned and retaliatory-minded lover, or perhaps a person who feels wronged by a victim. "The list goes on, and any attempt to generalize or categorize necessarily excludes some of the complexities and nuances of the problem" (Casey, 2000, p. 197).

Other Computer Crimes

According to D. E. Denning, author of *Information Warfare and Security* (1999), there are countless crimes being committed via computer. These include, but are not limited to, **intellectual property crimes** (illegal acquisition and distribution of copyright materials); fraud (telemarketing scams where victims divulge their credit card number); and identity theft (access gained to another person's name, Social Security number, driver's license, etc., in which the information is used to do harm). Computer crimes involving hardware include computer fraud and abuse that involves "accessing computers without authorization, exceeding authorization, and performing malicious acts against computing resources," such as "downloading sensitive information, initiating bogus transactions, tampering with records, disrupting operations, and destroying files and equipment" (Denning, p. 56).

In summary, cyberspace is no more protected than is reality. Many of the same dangers found in everyday life exist along the information superhighway. Pedophiles may solicit children. Stalkers may harass innocent victims. Personal information may be stolen. Although these criminal behaviors are essentially nonviolent, the personal harm experienced is profound. Thus, those precautions taken in the real world to curb abuses or to forestall victimization are just as vital and necessary when traversing the virtual world of the Internet.

STALKING

Introduction

Among the topics discussed in the previous section on Internet crime was cyberstalking. This section explores the phenomenon of stalking, without the aid of computers. Where useful, commentary on the various types of stalkers is also delineated. However, to initiate this material, some observations on the definition of stalking, the development of laws to prevent this criminal behavior, and characteristics of the offense are provided.

Background Information on Stalking

According to Meloy (1998, p. 2), "Stalking is a crime involving acts of pursuit of an individual over time that are threatening and potentially dangerous." Moreover, the *Merriam–Webster's Dictionary* (10th ed., 1996) refers to this concept as "the stealth pursuit of game." There is some debate about whether stalking is a violent or nonviolent offense, especially because more than half of them arise from domestic disputes involving temporary restraining orders (Mullen et al., 2000). However, most researchers concede that stalkers are potentially predatorily violent (Davis, 2001)

The first stalking law was established in California in 1990, and since that time a variety of legal definitions have appeared across the states. For the most part, they all possess three common elements: "(1) a pattern (course of conduct) of behavioral intrusion upon another person that is unwanted; (2) an implicit or explicit threat that is evidenced in the pattern of behavioral intrusion; and (3) as a result of these behavioral intrusions, the person who is threatened experiences reasonable fear" (Meloy, 1998, p. 2). Marked differences in the definition are related to the fact that some states require criminal intent to cause fear, whereas other states regard the intent element of the crime as sufficient for placing the victim in reasonable fear. Meloy and Gothard (1995, p. 258) summarize stalking as "the willful, malicious, and repeated following and harassing of another person that threatens his or her safety." Stalking laws currently exist in all 50 states and at the federal level.

Clinical definitions of stalking also vary; however, they seem less convoluted and more easily explained than their legal counterparts. Meloy and Gothard (1995) coined the clinical term "obsessional following," which is defined as "an abnormal or long term pattern of threat or harassment directed toward a specific individual" (p. 259). They further defined the pattern of threat or harassment as "more than one overt act of unwanted pursuit of the victim that was perceived by the victim as being harassing" (p. 259). Meloy (1998) later noted that the reason why the legal and clinical definitions vary is because of their respective purposes. The legal meaning seeks to define concepts to facilitate prosecution, and the clinical definition seeks to identify the behavioral aspects for further scientific research and treatment understanding.

Though the phenomenon of stalking is rather old, treating this behavior as a crime is rather new. As such, the collection of data has been extremely scarce, if not nonexistent, at least until recently (Davis, 2001). Researchers estimate that about 8% of the women and 2% of the men in America have been stalked. However, these percentages are an underestimation because only about half of these cases are ever reported. Of those known incidences of stalking, about 12% make it to criminal prosecution. The majority of obsessional followers are male and the majority of victims are female (Tjadan, 1997). About 25% to 30% of these crimes involve violence; however, the homicide rate is less than 2% (Meloy, 1998). These statistics help confirm the perspective that stalking is, for the most part, a nonviolent crime.

Stalking Typologies

The most useful typology on stalking was developed by Zona, Sharma, and Lane (1993). They placed these offenders into three categories (1) simple obsessional, (2) love obsessional, and (3) erotomanic. Each of these stalker types is briefly examined.

The **simple obsessional stalker** can emerge following either an intimate or a nonintimate relationship. Moreover, in this instance, the victim and the stalker typically have had some prior relationship or have had some prior knowledge of one another. Simple obsessional stalkers generally materialize in the aftermath of relationships that failed or were otherwise terminated, and this offender's behavior represents the most frequent type of stalking. Some examples of relationships in which simple obsessional stalking occur are husband and wife or boyfriend and girlfriend. A common variable in these cases is a breakup that ensues as a result of domestic violence. Following the breakup, one former partner (usually the male) attempts to sustain the relationship, resulting in the continued harassment and intimidation of the other former partner.

Motives for the obsessional stalker's actions are typically of two sorts. The offender either wants to reestablish the intimate relationship with the victim, or wants to punish the victim for ending the romantic association. Obsessional stalking also occurs when two people briefly date and then breakup. In these instances, one partner may be left harboring extremely unrealistic, though emotionally profound, feelings of attachment for the other person. For example, the scorned or jilted partner may perceive the relationship to have been more stable and healthy than it apparently was, resulting in a significant assault on the person's self-image and self-esteem when the breakup occurs. These factors precipitate stalking behaviors. As such, the obsessional following represents an effort to achieve one of the two goals previously mentioned.

Simple obsessional stalking also occurs in nonintimate relationships. These are predominantly found in workplace environments. A common example involves an employee terminated from a job where the person believes the decision was unfair or unjust. In this instance, the individual proceeds to stalk the supervisor, promoting a sense of terror or at least fear in response to the wrongful termination as a form of punishment. This occurrence is a common precursor to workplace violence.

A related instance of simple obsessional stalking in a nonintimate context takes place when a co-worker attempts to forge a romantic relationship with another co-worker and is unsuccessful. Men are more likely to engage in this form of stalking than are women. Typically, the rejection by the office employee is not handled well. The rebuffed worker insists on establishing more than office rapport or collegiality with the co-worker. This behavior escalates to the point that stalking commences. Other examples in which nonintimate relationships can evolve into threatening stalking relationships include business partners, physician and patient, psychologist and client, and student and teacher relationships (Zona, Palarea, & Lane, 1998).

Love obsessional stalking is the second category identified by Zona et al. (1993). Our familiarity with these offenders is linked to the stalking experienced by celebrities such as Madonna, David Letterman, or Jodi Foster. In these cases, no prior relationship exists between the victim and the perpetrator. The high-profile victims are usually known to the stalker through various media outlets, including television, radio, and film (Zona et al., 1998). A significant number of these offenders suffer from mental illness such as bipolar disorder or schizophrenia. Generally, **love obsessional stalkers** have not had any successful, intimate relationships in their lives. Moreover, they are often severely maladjusted socially, and they develop a delusional thought pattern. This thought pattern allows the person to believe that if the famous object of their obsession (i.e., the celebrity) were to meet the stalker, they would fall in love and have a long-lasting, intimate relationship.

Love obsessional stalkers initiate some sort of correspondence (usually letters) expressing their attraction to, admiration for, and desire to meet with the well-known media figure. When the letters receive no response, over time this acts as a frustrating and anger-provoking agent. The tone of these letters begins to change from that of esteem and affection to persecution and disdain. Eventually, the person relies on threats of physical harm to convey his (or her) sentiments; this is a message filled with resentment and outrage for being rebuked, dismissed, or worse, ignored.

The third classification developed by Zola et al. (1993) is the **erotomanic stalker.** Erotomanic and love obsessional stalkers are different. The primary difference is that the delusional thought pattern of the former offender escalates to the point where the person truly believes that he or she is loved by the victim. Another unique feature of the erotomanic stalker is that this perpetrator is usually female and the victims are typically men of considerable socioeconomic status, or are well-known celebrities. These female stalkers are described as very aggressive and difficult to handle, given the severity of their delusion; however, they rarely act in a physically violent way toward their victims.

Research on stalking also includes some interesting profile information, including the factors that motivate or cause this criminal behavior to materialize in the first place (Davis, 2001; Meloy, 1996; Mullen et al., 2000). Research shows that a majority of these offenders can be clinically diagnosed with personality disorders found in the Cluster B group. This group includes antisocial, borderline, histrionic, and narcissistic personality disorders. In the study done by Zona et al. (1993), as many as 63% of the perpetrators had some form of mental illness. Stalkers with antisocial personality disorder (ASPD) are usually more violent toward their victims, having been domestically abusive in prior relationships (Meloy, 1998). They tend to prey on women perceived to be highly vulnerable and weak. When the relationship is terminated (usually because the victim can no longer endure the physically abusive nature of the contact), the perpetrator threatens the victim, relying on harassing phone calls or letters and by engaging in stalking behavior. Given their violent nature, these obsessional followers are dangerous, and the victim is advised to have law enforcement intervene as soon as possible (Meloy, 1998).

The stalker with borderline personality disorder (BPD) creates an unrealistic sense of importance or level of commitment and intensity in his or her relationships with victims. This obsessional follower begins stalking after experiencing severe hurt and rejection, following the termination of a short relationship. The pathological mentality in this case appears to be "If I can't have her, nobody can!" (Meloy, 1998, p. 74).

Stalkers with histrionic personality disorder also consider their relationships to be more intimate than they are in reality. These obsessional followers are described as extremely dramatic in their emotional expressions and inappropriately sexually seductive (Meloy, 1998). Histrionic stalkers create elaborately designed scenes, adopt a variety of seductive roles, and go to considerable theatrical lengths to pursue their victims.

The final personality disorder most commonly associated with stalking is narcissistic personality disorder (NPD). "These individuals demonstrate a grandiose sense of self-importance and are preoccupied with fantasies of power, brilliance, beauty, and ideal love . . . They require excessive amounts of admiration and are interpersonally exploitive" (Meloy, 1998, p.74). These obsessional followers are deeply wounded and rely on their stalking fantasies and behaviors to fill the psychological emptiness in their lives.

There are other theories related to stalking and obsessional followers. For example, predispositional theories focus on disturbances in early attachment relationships (i.e., bonding with parents), adversely impacting the person's psychological development. Other predispositional theories examine how a recent loss in adulthood can serve as a triggering mechanism for stalking conduct.

In a study done by Kienlen, Birmingham, Solberg, O'Regan, and Meloy (1997), the investigators found that 63% of the stalkers in the sample suffered a change or loss of a primary caregiver in childhood. In addition, they noted that at least 42% experienced some sort of disruption in caregiver relationships during the early childhood years of age 6 or younger. Parents who were separated or divorced were listed as the major reasons for these disruptions during childhood. Consequently, after the attachments were severed, the subjects had little to no subsequent contact with their caregiver. Kienlen et al. also hypothesized that the parents of these individuals may have suffered from some sort of mental illness. A number of the subjects in this study reported emotional trauma in the form of physical or sexual abuse by their primary caregivers, leading to further attachment disruption. Some examples of loss in adulthood acting as triggering factors included (a) a terminated marriage or the end of another significant intimate relationship; (b) the loss of a job; (c) a messy divorce proceeding (i.e., custody battle); and (d) the loss of a parent through death, usually occurring within 7 months of the stalking behavior. Investigators contend that the factors pertaining to predispositional theories are related to the likelihood that a person will become a stalker. However, the manner in which these factors operate on their own or in combination to establish such an obsessional follower have not been ascertained or significantly tested in the relevant research.

SEXUAL HARASSMENT

Introduction

Sexual harassment is a crime that has been generalized to the workplace; however, it can occur in many different situations or contexts. In addition, sexual harassment is typically believed to affect women, but can be (and is) directed toward men as well. According to Richman, Rospenda, Nawyn, and Flaherty (1999), sexual harassment "encompasses unwanted sexual advances, requests for sexual favors, and other verbal or physical conduct of a sexual nature" (p. 358). Noting this definition, Berman, McKenna, Arnold, Taylor, and MacQuarrie (2000) reported that the American Association of University Women (AAUW) published the results of a study revealing that of girls ages 9 to 15, 81% experienced some form of sexual harassment.

This section examines the phenomenon of sexual harassment as a form of nonviolvent criminal conduct. In particular, both **quid pro quo** and workplace sexual harassment are reviewed. In addition, commentary on the three modalities of sexual harassment is provided, as are the mental health and physical health consequences that victims suffer. The section concludes by exploring the problems with identifying sexual harassment in the educational arena. However, before these matters are addressed, some background information on the development of sexual harassment in the law are warranted.

Sexual Harassment: Developments in the Law

Developments in sexual harassment law emerged in 1964 with the passage of Title VII of the 1964 Civil Rights Act. Although sexual harassment legislation began in 1964, the Supreme Court did not address the issue until the case of *Meritor Savings Bank v. Vinson* (1986). This case established that "the language of Title VII [was] not limited to 'economic' or 'tangible' discrimination" (Wiener & Hurt, 1999, p. 64). The court ruled for the first time on a **hostile work environment** theory. The Supreme Court again addressed the issue of sexual harassment in *Harris v. Forklift Systems, Inc.* (1993). Justice Sandra Day O'Connor defined a hostile work environment as one that "a reasonable person would find hostile or abusive" (p. 21).

With regard to the health consequences of a hostile work environment, Justice O' Connor stated, "so long as the environment would reasonably be perceived, and is perceived, as hostile or abusive, there is no need for it to also be psychologically injurious" (*Harris v. Forklift Systems, Inc.*, 1993, p. 22). Both the reasonableness standard identified and the perception standard referenced here established a two-prong test to determine a hostile work environment. However, the sexual harassment standard has been challenged. This two-prong test is comprised of objective and subjective measures; therefore, the law "does not treat hostile work environment sexual harassment as codified and prohibited conduct. Instead, it treats sexual harassment as the outcome of a legal test that takes into consideration the totality of the circumstances in the workplace" (Wiener & Hurt, 1999, p. 568).

Sexual Harassment: Types, Models, and Modalities

There are two identifiable types of sexual harassment. These include *quid pro quo* and hostile work environment. According to Wiener and Hurt (1999), *quid pro quo* involves an act, ". . . in which a supervisor demands sexual favors in exchange for tangible job benefits" (p. 560). Hostile work environment sexual harassment represents a situation ". . . in which an employee is the victim of severe and/or pervasive sexual conduct which she or he did not welcome" (Wiener & Hurt, 1999 p. 560).

Two broad-based models of sexual misconduct are frequently addressed. The first model is the sex-role spillover theory as proposed by Gutek (1985). Gutek asserted that men have a tendency to invoke sex-based stereotypes when interacting with female workers, resulting in sexual misconduct. The second model was introduced by Pryor, LaVite, and Stoller (1993). They argued that sexual harassment is a result of the presence of an encouraging individual and situational factors that increase the likelihood of misconduct. Persons who support sexual misconduct (including harassment) may be supervisors who promote the dissemination of erotically explicit photographs, magazines, or related paraphernalia to be displayed at work and shared among coworkers. In this instance, the workplace atmosphere breeds the necessary conditions for sexual harassment to occur.

There are three modalities related sexual harassment: verbal, physical, and visual (Berman, McKenna, Arnold, Taylor, & MacQuarrie, 2000). **Verbal sexual harassment** includes, but is not limited to, demeaning statements, insults, demands, harassing phone calls, and whistling. **Physical sexual harassment** includes grabbing, touching, and threatening acts. Sexual harassment can be considered a violent crime if it is physical in nature. Persons with antisocial tendencies are inclined to engage in violent crimes. Predictors that are useful in identifying prospective sexual harassment offenders are antisocial behavioral patterns and high levels of aggression experienced during childhood (Sprague & Walker, 2000). In childhood, these offenders may have been diagnosed with psychiatric conditions such as conduct disorder or oppositional defiant disorder. Early warning signs of violent tendencies can be inferred from juvenile arrest data and educational history. In adulthood, sexual harassment offenders may have been diagnosed with antisocial personality disorder (Sprague & Walker, 2000). **Visual sexual harassment** includes leering or ogling, sexual gestures, and pornographic material.

Sexual Harassment: Mental Health and Physical Health Concerns

In today's culture, sexual harassment is a significant social problem. Not only are mental health interests at stake but also are public health needs. These concerns have spawned two noteworthy areas of research identified in the field: organizational behavior studies and epidemiological studies. Organizational behavior studies focus on interpersonal interactions that lead to sexual harassment. Epidemiological studies concentrate more on task-related aspects of stressors caused by a work environment, conducive to sexually harassing behavior (Richman, Rospenda, Nawyn, & Flaherty, 1999).

Sexual harassment occurs when three conditions are met within an environment. These conditions are the presence of a motivated offender, the availability of a suitable target, and the absence of individuals who could prevent the crime from occurring. In a study conducted by DeCoster, Estes, and Mueller (1999), the investigators found that a lack of guardianship was a strong predictor for sexual harassment. In addition, women who were routinely involved in male-dominated settings were more likely to be victims of sexual harassment than were women who were not in male-dominated settings. Third, the researchers discovered that the attractiveness of the targeted victim was a significant predictor; that is, women who held powerful positions were more attractive targets to would-be assailants. The latter finding suggests that one motivational factor in some acts of sexual harassment is the presence of a power threat.

Recently, a number of mental health concerns have been raised in relation to sexual harassment. Typically the victim suffers from anger, depression, anxiety, and substance use or abuse as a form of self-medication (Richman et al., 1999). Over time, these poor coping mechanisms lead to more serious psychopathologies, such as alcoholism. The study conducted by Richman et al. also concluded that both males and females are subject to sexual harassment; however, males were more likely to experience harassment in low-status jobs, whereas females were more likely to experience harassment in high-status jobs. In addition, Berman et al. (2000) noted that females tend to experience higher levels of psychological distress than do their male counterparts. Therefore, although males may experience sexual harassment, they are less likely to endure psychological trauma as a result of the harassment.

Sexual Harassment and the Educational System

Aside from the consequences of workplace sexual harassment, there are educational and emotional effects that victims of school-based sexual harassment suffer. These consequences include a reluctance to attend school, increased self-consciousness, embarrassment, lower self-confidence, identity confusion, self-blame, helplessness, and self-doubt (Stone, 2000). Clearly, the emotional costs of school-based sexual harassment can be devastating to an adolescent.

For example, in a study conducted by Berman et al. (2000), it was apparent that girls who participated in the research shared a sense of fear and intimidation, given their similar experiences with sexual harassment. This fear and intimidation, brought on by the harassment, resulted in a decline of self-confidence. The study also found that girls and young women felt that despite the trauma inflicted on them, the harassing offenders did not experience any negative consequences. The participants also believed that sexual harassment was an acceptable form of male domination in society.

Clearly, sexual harassment is identifiable in the education system. The purpose of Title IX in the Education Amendments of 1972 was to "protect students in schools that receive[d] federal funds from discriminatory practices" (Wiener & Hurt, 1999, p. 562). Under this amendment, a public school is not liable for discriminatory damages caused to any student by a teacher. For example, a school is not liable for the actions of a teacher who sexually harasses a student. However, a school is liable for sexual harassment if school officials are notified of the harassment and do not act on the notification (Stone, 2000). A second implication of Title IX is that schools are not financially liable for the behaviors of the school's teachers. Again, this is only true if the school is unaware of the teacher's misconduct. In *Davis v. Monroe County Board of Education* (1999), the U.S. Supreme Court addressed sexual harassment in the education system. This case established that a public school can be held liable for damage incurred when failing to stop student-on-student sexual harassment.

Sexual Harassment in Schools: Identifying and Responding to the Problem

A scenario illustrating the serious nature of and challenges to identifying sexual harassment in educational settings was given by Stone (2000). The vignette is as follows:

> Until sixth grade, Sarah was a conscientious student consistently given high marks by teachers in her work ethic. Sarah's elementary academic life was not without struggle, but her motivation allowed her to maintain above-average grades with an occasional C. However, the sixth grade brought a marked change in grades and attitude for Sarah. At first her teachers and parents attributed the change to middle-school adjustment, but when Sarah began to make health excuses to miss school, her parents called the school counselor for help . . . Sarah's counselor began to learn the truth of her first 5 months of sixth grade. Sarah was a victim of sexual harassment. Sarah was unusually well developed for a 12-year-old and found herself the target of jokes and sexual comments about her physical development. Changing classes was the worst time for Sarah as boys leered, jeered, brushed up against her, and sometimes a hand would grope her . . . [On one occasion] Sarah found herself trapped against her locker by a group of boys who made lewd remarks to her and wouldn't let her pass. Their leader, who frequently harassed Sarah, was a boy she recognized as having slid his hand up her blouse while she was trying to negotiate a crowded hallway . . . Perplexed by the unwelcome attention and how to respond to it, Sarah hinted that she may in some way be responsible for bringing the harassment on herself, and she wished she could just learn to ignore the attention or develop a sense of humor about it all. (p. 23)

In this case, the school counselor would need to assist Sarah by organizing a safe educational environment for her, free of any sexual harassment possibilities. If the counselor failed to offer more security to Sarah—or any student in a similar situation—the school officials would assume responsibility, including settlement for monetary damages if sued. This position is consistent with the holding in the case of *Davis v. Monroe County Board of Education* (1999).

Some Concluding Thoughts on Sexual Harassment

Research suggests that young girls and women are socialized to expect violence (including sexual harassment) in their lives (Berman et al., 2000). The assumptions on which this type of finding is based vary. However, two important factors appear constant. First, females believe that violence becomes normalized for girls as a result of their socialization; that is, violence for them occurs in many facets, including psychological, emotional, physical, and sexual. Second, women believe that all girls, regardless of ethnicity, socioeconomic status, culture, and geography, are at risk for becoming victims of sexual harassment. Given these presuppositions, the only way to eliminate the social problem of sexual harassment is for both men and women to leave their gender identity at the door before entering a social situation. However, as Wiener and Hurt (1999) observe, this position is not only unrealistic but also constitutionally not required. This perspective suggests that meaningfully addressing the problem of sexual harassment is not only difficult but also possibly unrealizable.

PROPERTY CRIMES

Introduction

According to the U.S. Department of Justice (1997), the property crime index includes the offenses of burglary, **larceny-theft, motor vehicle theft,** and arson. When a property crime is committed, there is no force, or threat of force, against the victim. However, some property crimes may escalate to more violent forms of behavior. This section reviews two of the more common forms of property crime: theft and arson. Where helpful and appropriate, profiles on these offender types are provided.

Theft

The object of a theft crime is to take money or property. The U.S. Department of Justice (1997) estimated that over $15 billion represented the value of property stolen in 1997, and the average loss per offense was approximately $1,300. Larceny-theft accounted for the highest percent of all property crimes that year, comprising 67% or two thirds of all property-related offenses. Larceny-theft is defined as the following:

> . . . unlawful taking, carrying, leading, or riding away of property from the possession or constructive possession of another. It includes crimes such as **shoplifting,** pocket-picketing, purse-snatching, thefts from motor vehicles, thefts of motor vehicle parts and accessories, bicycle theft in which no use of force, violence, or fraud occurs. (U.S. Department of Justice, 1997, p. 52)

Burglary is defined as the "unlawful entry of a structure to commit a felony or theft" (U.S. Department of Justice, 1997, p. 54). This offense accounted for 21% of all property crimes, and motor vehicle theft accounted for 12%. Law enforcement has a lower clearance rate for property crimes than for violent crimes. Clearance rates for property crime range from 16% to 19% as compared to 48% for violent offenses. According to the FBI (2000), the estimated property crime total in 1999 decreased 1% to 12.1 million offenses, representing the lowest since 1987. The highest arrest counts were for larceny-theft and drug-abuse violations. Larceny-theft was the offense resulting in the most arrests of females and of persons under the age of 18 (U.S. Department of Justice, 1997).

When considering the motivation for property offenses, Patterson, Lennings, and Davey (2000) examined methadone clients and found that 52% of them reported some criminal offending, with drug-related and property crimes accounting for the majority of their criminal activity. Other studies substantiate the conclusion that drug use leads to criminal behavior, specifically property crimes, given the need to acquire money to support

Burglary and Shoplifting

Burglary and shoplifting are two other property crimes linked to theft that continue to receive their share of research attention. According to the U.S. Department of Justice, Bureau of Justice Statistics (2003), burglary rates over the last 30 years have steadily declined. Burglary entails the illegal entry of not just one's household but any structure (e.g., shed or garage) in which the burglar is not authorized to enter. Even if someone unlawfully breaks into and enters a hotel room, the crime of burglary has occurred against the person (or family) occupying that residence at that time. A number of investigators have examined the motivational states of burglars (e.g., Cromwell, Marks, Olson, & Avary, 1991), demonstrating how their thrill-seeking behavior is also fueled by a desire for money and drugs or is otherwise linked to the subculture of theft.

Shoplifting takes place when the person intends to permanently deprive a store of the value of its merchandise. Typically, shoplifters conceal the items they steal, placing them in a coat, a purse, or a pocket. Most shoplifters are amateurs, although some individuals make a criminal career out of this activity. Shoplifting impacts retail stores around the world with annual merchandise losses projected at $33 billion. This estimate includes customer, employee, and vendor theft. Often linked to **kleptomania,** or the compulsion to steal (Goldman, 1997), shoplifters engage in this behavior for a variety of reasons, including excitement, pursuit of material possessions, economic need, and peer pressure (Katz, 1988). Some shoplifters are compulsive in their behavior, opportunistically taking advantage of a situation because of their drug addiction, alcoholism, or homelessness (Cupchik, 1997).

addictive habits (De Li, Priu, & MacKenzie, 2000). The research by De Li et al. found that drug use led to property crimes more often than did violent offenses.

A person's lifestyle is also an important factor in explaining various property crimes. For example, associating with persons who routinely engage in deviance increases the likelihood that more opportunities will present themselves, leading to offender behavior. More specifically, two factors that lead to property crime offenses include exposure and vulnerability to criminal activities, and an absence of capable guardians. This perspective is consistent with a recent finding from the Office of Juvenile Justice and Delinquency Prevention (OJJDP). The OJJDP noted that juveniles are disproportionately involved in arrests for property crimes such as arson, larceny-theft, motor vehicle theft, and burglary (Snyder & Sickmund, 1999). Exposure and vulnerablity to delinquency, along with the lack of adequate parenting, were noted as causal factors generating this criminality.

Additional research has examined the relationship between economic factors and property crime. According to Witt, Clark, and Fielding (1999), the change in unemployment has a positive impact on criminal conduct, specifically on property crimes. The study found that high crime is associated with increases in male unemployment, and a reduction in property crime is related to an increase in the size of the police force.

Arson

Arson is also considered a property crime and is defined as the "willful and malicious burning of property" (Douglas, Burgess, Burgess, & Ressler, 1992, p. 165). There are three essential components necessary to designate an act as arson: the burning of property or the actual destruction of a target, the presence of intent, and the condition of malice.

Researchers report that the motivation for arson varies widely (Davis, 1999). Some arsonists are purposeful and seek monetary gain, whereas others set fires for erotic gratification (Holmes & Holmes, 1996). There is a relative lack of agreement regarding the statistics on arson. This is because of the unreliable methods used to collect the data. However, arson is a very serious personal and financial problem that costs society millions of dollars, and can take the lives of many innocent people.

According to Douglas et al. (1992), three types of arson are serial arson, spree arson, and mass arson. The **serial arsonist** engages in three or more separate fire-setting incidents with an emotional cooling-off period in between each fire. This type of arson is considered the most serious, given the unpredictability of the fire setting and choice of victims. The **spree arsonist** also sets three or more fires at separate locations; however, the difference between a serial and a spree arsonist is that a spree arsonist does not have an emotional cooling-off period between each incident. The **mass arsonist** sets three or more fires at the same location within a limited amount of time.

John Douglas, formerly of the FBI, identified five categories to explain the motivations of arsonists (Douglas et al., 1992). They include fire setting for the purpose of vandalism, excitement, revenge, crime concealment, and profit. The individual who commits arson for the purpose of vandalism is typically young and immature. The individual often targets schools or residential areas, setting fires on weekdays or weekends when school is out. These individuals typically live at home and are from a lower class neighborhood. Generally, arsonists motivated by the need to vandalize do not return to the crime scene.

The fire setter motivated by excitement uses the act of arson to gain attention. The behavior is usually committed alone and sexual gratification may play a secondary role in one's actions. For example, pornography or other evidence related to sexual gratification may be found at the crime scene. Most often, this individual is from a middle-class family and lives with his (or her) parents.

The arsonist motivated by revenge generally targets a business or a facility believed to be responsible for the unjust or unfair treatment the offender experienced in his (or her) life. Although a person who chooses to take revenge through the act of fire setting may come from a lower class background, the offender usually has a higher level of education than the previously discussed arsonists. For the fire setter motivated by revenge, typically the crime is a one-time occurrence, and it may take place months or even years after the perceived injustice occurred. The offense is frequently committed in conjunction with alcohol use, when the individual's inhibitions are lowered. Women who commit arson are generally motivated by revenge. For example, a woman motivated by revenge may burn the clothing or other possessions of a former lover.

Individuals who commit arson in an effort to conceal a crime have a simple motivation for the event. In short, they hope to destroy any evidence that may be related to a previous crime of homicide, burglary, or theft. If the primary crime committed is homicide, it is likely that the arson is a one-time event.

Arson for profit is committed by an individual who has a sole motive, namely, material or economic gain. This person is generally hired by another individual attempting to collect insurance money for a failing business. The hired arsonist may be between 25 and 40 years of age and have an extensive arrest record for robbery, burglary, public drunkenness, and arson (Holmes & Holmes, 1996).

The Arsonist Profile

Does a composite profile for the arsonist exist? According to Holmes and Holmes (1996), the answer is yes. Interestingly, a typology can be created through the identification of characteristics that are common to different types of fire setters.

Arsonists are usually White males between 16 and 28 years of age. Although they generally function within a wide range intellectually, their academic adjustment is poor. They are reared in an inconsistent, harsh environment. Arsonists come from all economic classes, and they experience severe problems in developing friendships, interpersonal relationships, and intimacy. Generally speaking, arsonists possess criminal histories linked to delinquency, including offenses such as burglary, theft, running away, and other property crimes. The personality profile of an arsonist can best be described as an individual who feels inadequate, inferior, reclusive, and lacks ambition. In addition, fire setters tend to have repressed rage toward society and authority figures. Following the setting of a fire, the emotional state of an arsonist is characterized by exaltation and relief of tension. Many arsonists stay at or near the fire as a spectator, or assist firefighters in first aid or in rescuing victims. Similar to other nonviolent crimes, alcohol and other drugs play an important role in reducing the inhibitions of arsonists, making it easier for them to commit their crimes.

PROSTITUTION

Introduction

By definition, a prostitute is a person who exchanges sex or sexual favors for money, drugs, or other desirable commodities (Dalla, 2000). Prostitution is often referred to as the oldest profession in history and a crime of last resort (Patterson et al., 2000). The National Task Force on Prostitution suggests that about 1% of American women have worked as prostitutes. There are approximately 90,000 arrests annually for violations of prostitution laws, and $120 million is spent yearly to enforce statutes against the sex trade industry (Delacoste & Alexander, 1987). Some scholars argue that the resources used to arrest and prosecute women involved in **sex work** could be utilized more efficiently to address the social, psychological, and economic problems that accompany or are associated with this profession. In addition, there is a lack of research on the male customer or "john" who participates in the act of prostitution. This final section explores the nonviolent criminal behavior of prostitution. In particular, the material entertained here examines the reasons why women pursue prostitution, assesses the impact of sex work on their lives, and comments on the limitations of research on women whose profession is sex work.

Women in the Sex Trade Industry

Women often attribute their involvement in sex work to a desperate need to establish some form of existence or to otherwise survive. Indeed, for far too many streetwalkers, they earn an income to support the essentials of living and their drug habits. As Pettiway (1997, p. xxi) explains it, "sex is part of the economic reality of their lives. Acquiring money is directly tied to their bodies; pleasure is perhaps more directly tied to the money and drugs they receive." These are women who may earn their incomes from prostitution combined with welfare benefits, or they may trade sex for drugs, shelter, or safety from their pimps (Weiner, 1996).

Several studies have examined the reason why women become engaged in prostitution. Researchers have found that the social dynamics of the sex trade industry involve a multiplicity of factors, including discrimination based on sex, race, and social class (Sanchez, 1999). Given the life circumstances of many women involved in sex work, prostitution helps provide needed resources for females of minority races and low socioeconomic class, including their children (Reanda, 1991; Weiner, 1996).

Previous studies have documented lifelong patterns of abuse for women who prostitute themselves. A qualitative examination of the lives of streetwalking prostitutes revealed career patterns of abuse, exploitation, and degradation at the hands of men, including fathers, brothers, intimate partners, clients, and pimps (Nandon, Koverola, & Schludermann, 1998). These researchers acknowledged that background factors such as childhood victimization could lead one to enter prostitution; however, numerous contextual factors accumulate and influence continued involvement in the sex trade industry (Sanchez, 1997).

Some theorists suggest a causal link between childhood sexual abuse and prostitution. For example, West, Williams, and Siegel (2000) investigated the consequences of abuse and found that Black women with documented histories of childhood sexual abuse were three times more likely to be victims of partner violence during adulthood and while involved in prostitution. Other studies estimate the percentage of female prostitutes with a sexual abuse history to vary between 10% and 70% (Bagley & Young, 1987).

Dalla (2000) found that abandonment, either literal or psychological, was a defining characteristic of women involved in prostitution. Over 50% of the women in this sample reported losing a parent through death desertion, being reared in an environment with parental alcoholism, and experiencing mental instability or drug abuse. Dalla found that 66% of the women had used drugs prior to entering the sex trade industry. Severe

> *The Case of Aline*
> *Aline, a professed Buddhist and lesbian who works as a topless dancer and prostitute, analogizes sex work to the actions of counselors, nurses, and psychologists who often function as good listeners for others in a "touch-deprived" society. Aline makes the argument that we are all sexual creatures and that religion, media, and culture dictate our actions, including the prohibition of sexual intimacy. Therefore, Aline believes that her chosen profession represents an important and useful avenue by which people can participate in a "simple, uncomplicated, get-laid genital exchange" (Delacoste & Alexander, 1987, p. 43).*

domestic violence also contributed to these women's experiences of emotional abandonment. As children, 10% of them were moved to foster homes as a result of domestic violence, and 30% reported sexual abuse within their foster homes. Other research suggests that women become involved in prostitution as a consequence of runaway behavior.

Many theories have been offered explaining why women engage in sex work; however, the evidence that has emerged thus far is either inconsistent or contradictory. For example, according to Bullough and Bullough (1996, p. 171), "when all is said and done, no single factor stands out as causal in a woman becoming a prostitute." In essence, a profile of a woman who eventually turns to a life of prostitution does not exist.

In his book, *Sex Crimes* (1991), Ronald Holmes suggests that prostitution would appear abnormal based on statistical, religious, and cultural standards in this country. However, in relation to the subjective standard, which is described as how persons judge their own behavior, sex workers are successful in legitimizing their behavior. For example, consider the story of the following woman in the sex industry as reported by Delacoste and Alexander (1987).

The Impact of Prostitution on Women's Lives

According to Weinberg, Shaver, and Williams (1999), the emotional damage that results from sex work occurs not from the act of sex, but from negative social attitudes, loss of control over the work situation, and harassment from clients and the police. Most sex workers featured in research studies make a strong argument for prostitution to no longer be viewed as a crime. Indeed, being a prostitute makes a woman vulnerable to termination of parental rights, loss of social services, rape, violence, arrest, and loss of social support systems such as family or church, given the socially degrading label attached to sex work. These stigmatizing factors make it difficult for women to reach out for services, such as job training or educational advancement, skills that would enable them to develop a lifestyle deemed noncriminal by society.

In one research study the personal perceptions of approximately 30 different sex workers were requested (Delacoste & Alesander, 1987). This project attempted to develop a broader appreciation for the political issues involved in the **criminalization** of prostitution and the social consequences incurred by sex trade workers as a result. Several of the study's participants advocated for the **decriminalization** of prostitution. They argued that the criminalization of the sex industry increased opportunities for violence against women. For example, the Black Coalition Fighting Black Serial Murders was founded in response to police inaction and media inattention to the deaths of over 17 Black prostitutes in South Central Los Angeles. The police waited until 10 women were dead before notifying the public of the dangers of a serial murderer in their community. The delayed response by media, elected officials, and police gave the impression that the killing of prostitutes was not sufficient to garner public attention, given the belief that the murders merely impacted "street women."

There are several different organizations that represent the interests of women involved in the sex industry. Some organizations, such as the National Task Force on Prostitution, work from the perspective that women have the right to determine how they use their bodies, whether the issue is prostitution or reproductive rights. Other organizations, such as the U.S. Prostitutes' Collective, maintain that sex work is a class issue, and that poverty forces women to work in the sex industry (Pheterson, 1989). Other organizations such as Whisper (Women Hurt in Systems of Prostitution Engaged in Revolt) believe that all prostitutes are victims, and the profession is an institution created by a patriarchal structure used to control and abuse women. Clearly, organizations such as these differ in philosophical approach on issues such as the legalization or decriminalization of prostitution. However, they share a common purpose, namely, creating a social and legal climate that promotes safety and empowerment for women who work in the sex industry.

In spite of the evidence suggesting that most women become involved in prostitution because of economic oppression, it is clear that many women experience independence and power as a result of their careers in the sex trade industry. For example, Judy, a mother of two, supported her family through employment as a sex worker. Judy indicated that she was able to achieve a sense of self-reliance through the financial independence she felt as a street worker. Judy relished her ability to use sexual attractiveness to achieve (sexual) power over her male clients. Similar to other women in the study conducted by Delacoste and Alexander (1987), Judy found this power to be a satisfying component of her work (see also Sanchez, 1999).

The sense of liberating power through sex work is also contained in the narrative of Donna, a 19-year-old prostitute. She described her experience in a "straight job" as a secretary as one in which she was invisible to her coworkers, was treated with disregard, and felt patronizing contempt from others in the office (Delacoste & Alexander, 1987). Not only did Donna report feeling more disrespect while employed as a secretary than she did when working as a prostitute, but also she made less money and had less time to herself when working in a conventional corporate environment. Implied in these statements by Donna is the belief that prostitution translates into sexual power, financial independence, and personal autonomy.

The Limits of Research on Prostitution

Prostitution is blamed for the spread of heterosexual AIDS, often promoted in the public discourse as the etiology of sexually transmitted infections, including the HIV disease. According to Kanouse, Berry, Duan, and Lever (1999), female prostitutes are known to play an important role in the epidemiology of certain sexually transmitted infections, given their sexually active work and their (or their client's) use of intravenous drugs. However, much of the empirical research in this area is underdeveloped and is not based on scientifically rigorous investigations. Indeed, most studies on prostitutes rely on convenience samples (e.g., Sanchez, 1997), such as prostitutes who are in jail, sexually transmitted disease (STD) clinics, outreach recruitment street initiatives, or methadone maintenance programs.

Clearly, research on prostitution varies, depending on the sample chosen by the investigator. Under these conditions, the realities of sex work can be portrayed from the perspective of street prostitutes, high-class call girls, exotic dancers, porn actresses, massage parlor workers, nude models, and escorts, all of whom may be defined as "sex workers." Each group's perspective may be different; however, these respective points of view offer valuable insight into the racial, religious, political, psychological, social, and cultural implications of sex work. Admittedly, the illegality of sex work makes research in the area difficult (Sanchez, 1999). For example, rosters of sex workers are not available, and screening of persons in the general population is unlikely to draw a representative sample, because prostitutes are mostly unwilling to admit to being involved in the sex trade industry (Kanouse et al., 1999).

DISCUSSION QUESTIONS

1. What are the three explanations for the drug–crime relationship? How would you define substance abuse? What is the APA's interpretation of substance abuse?
2. What is the relationship between alcohol and crime? Identify some examples of criminal behavior brought on by alcohol abuse.
3. What are some of the factors that must be considered when examining female drug users who commit crime?
4. What is money laundering and how does it relate to organized crime? What are gambling, loan sharking, and numbers running, and how do these forms of criminal behavior relate to the criminal enterprise?
5. What does the acronym RICO stand for? How does RICO relate to organized crime?
6. Explain the Alien-Conspiracy/Bureaucracy approach and the Enterprise approach to the criminal enterprise. Use relevant examples.
7. What is white-collar crime? Explain how embezzlement, insider trading, and securities fraud operate. Use relevant, criminal behavior examples to support your explanation.
8. Take one type of fraudulent conduct and explain how it represents a form of noviolent criminal behavior.
9. Are computer-generated images of children depicted in sexually explicit poses examples of criminal behavior? Justify your response. What are some of the victimization concerns related to Internet stalking of children? How are these concerns similar or dissimilar to cyberstalking?
10. What are the three types of stalkers? Explain them with reference to relevant examples. Does a generic profile for obsessional followers exist? Justify your response.
11. What is sexual harassment? What is the difference between *quid pro quo* and workplace sexual harassment?
12. What are some of the mental health concerns related to sexual harassment? What is the relationship between sexual harassment and the educational system?
13. What are the three types of arsonists? Does a profile for the fire setter exist? Please explain your response.
14. What is prostitution? Why do women enter the sex trade industry? What are some of the victimization effects of prostitution for women?
15. Are there justifications for pursuing a career as a sex worker? Explain your response. Is prostitution criminal or deviant behavior?

REFERENCES

Abadinsky, H. (1999). *Organized crime* (6th ed.). Belmont, CA: Wadsworth.

Alcoholism and other Drug Abuse and Dependency Act. Public Act 90-0135 (Illinois 2001).

American Psychiatric Association. (1994). *Diagnostic and statistical manual of mental disorders* (4th ed.). Washington DC: American Psychiatric Association.

American Psychiatric Association. (2000). *Diagnostic and statistical manual of mental disorders* (4th ed., Text Revised). Washington DC: Author.

Anetzberger, G. J. (2001). Crime and older people: Truth or consequences. *The Gerontologist, 41*(1), 137–139.

Anti-Kickback Statute, 42 U.S.C. 1320 (1998).

Bagley, C., & Young, L. (1987). Juvenile prostitution and child sexual abuse: A controlled study. *Canadian Journal of Community Health, 6*, 5–26.

Benson, M. L. (1998). *Combating corporate crime: Local prosecutors at work*. Boston, MA: Northeastern University Press.

Berman, H., McKenna, K., Arnold, C. T., Taylor, G., & MacQuarrie, B. (2000). Sexual harassment: Everyday violence in the lives of girls and women. *Advances in Nursing Science, 22*(4), 32–46.

Bintliff, R. L. (1993). *The complete manual of white collar crime: Detection and prevention*. Upper Saddle River, NJ: Prentice Hall.

Bullough, B., & Bullough, V. (1996). Female prostitution: Current research and changing interpretations. *Annual Review of Sex Research, 7*, 158–180.

Casey, E. (2000). *Digital evidence and computer crime: Forensic science, computers and the Internet*. San Diego: Academic Press.

Child Pornography Prevention Act, Pub. L. No. 104-208, Title I, § 121(a), 110 Stat. 3009, 3009-26 to 3009-31 (1996).

Clinnard, M. B., & Quinney, R. (1980). *Criminal behavior systems: A typology*. New York: Holt, Rinehart & Winston.

Clinnard, M. B., & Yeager, P. C. (1983). *Corporate crime*. New York: The Free Press.

Cromwell, T., Marks, A., Olson, J., & Avary, D. (1991). Group effects on decision making by burglars. *Psychological Reports, 69,* 579–588.

Cupchik, W. (1997). *Why honest people shoplift and commit other acts of theft: Assessment and treatment of atypical theft offenders*. Toronto: University of Toronto Press.

Cyberstalking, California Penal Code § 646.9 (1998).

Dalla, R. (2000). Exposing the "pretty woman" myth: A qualitative examination of the lives of female streetwalking prostitutes. *Journal of Sex Research, 37,* 344–353.

Davis, J. A. (1999). Criminal behavior assessment of arsonists, pyromaniacs, and multiple firesetters. *Journal of Contemporary Criminal Justice, 15,* 291–301.

Davis, J. A. (Ed.). (2001). *Stalking crimes and victim protection: Prevention, intervention, threat assessment, and case management*. Boca Raton, FL: CRC Press.

Davis v. Monroe County Board of Education, 120 F.3d 1390. (1999, Supreme Court, May 24).

DeCoster, S., Estes, S. B., & Mueller, C. W. (1999). Routine activities and sexual harassment in the workplace. *Work and Occupations, 26*(1), 21–49.

Deitch, D., Koutsenok, I., & Ruzi, A. (2000). The relationship between crime and drugs: What we have learned in recent decades. *Journal of Psychoactive Drugs, 32*(4), 391.

Delacoste, F., & Alexander, P. (1987). *Sex work: Writings by women in the sex industry*. Pittsburgh, PA: Cleis Press.

De Li, S., Priu, H., & MacKenzie, D. (2000). Drug involvement, lifestyles, and criminal activities, among probationers. *Journal of Drug Issues, 30,* 593–619.

Denning, D. E. (1999). *Information warfare and security*. Reading, MA: Addison-Wesley.

Douglas, J., Burgess, A.W., Burgess, A.G., & Ressler, R. (1992). *Crime classification manual*. Lexington, MA: Lexington.

Dowden, C., & Blanchette, K. (2002). An evaluation of the effectiveness of substance abuse programming for female offenders. *International Journal of Offender Therapy and Comparative Criminology, 46,* 220–230.

Dunlap, E., Johnson, B., & Maher, L. (1997). Female crack sellers in New York City: Who they are and what they do. *Women and Criminal Justice, 8,* 25–55.

Ermann, M. D., & Lundman, R. J. (Eds.). (2002). *Corporate and governmental deviance: Problems of organizational behavior in contemporary society*. New York: Oxford University Press.

Ethics in Patient Referral Act, 42 U.S.C. 1395 (1998).

False Claims Act, 31 U.S.C. 3729 (1998).

Farabee, D., Joshi, V., & Anglin, M.D. (2001). Addiction careers and criminal specialization. *Crime and Delinquency, 47*(2), 196–220.

Federal Bureau of Investigation. (2000). *Uniform Crime Reports—1999*. Washington DC: U.S. Government Printing Office.

Finkelhor, D. J., Mitchell, K., & Wolak, J. (2000, October 2). Online victimization: A report on the nation's youth. Alexandria, VA: National Center for Missing and Exploited Children. Retrieved October 6, 2004 from http://www.missingkids.com.

Friedrichs, D. O. (1996). *Trusted criminals: White collar crime in contemporary society*. Belmont, CA: ITP/Wadsworth.

Gibbons, D. C. (1977). *Society, crime, and criminal careers* (3rd ed.). Upper Saddle River, NJ: Prentice Hall.

Godwin, M. (1995). Cops on the I-way. *Time, 145,* 62–64.

Goldman, M. J. (1997). *Kleptomania: The compulsion to steal—What can be done?* New York: New Horizon Press.

Grabosky, P. N., & Smith, R. G. (1998). *Crime in the digital age: Controlling telecommunications and cyberspace illegalities*. New Brunswick, NJ: Transaction Publishers.

Gutek, B. A. (1985). *Sex in the workplace: Impact of sexual behavior and harassment on women, men and organizations*. San Francisco: Jossey-Bass.

Hardy, D. W., Patel, M., & Paull, D. (2000). Basic law for addiction psychiatry. *Psychiatric Annals, 30*(9), 574–585.

Harris v. Forklift Systems, Inc., 114 S. Ct. 367 (1993).

Holmes, R. (1991). *Sex crimes*. Newbury Park, CA: Sage.

Holmes, R., & Holmes, S. (1996). *Profiling violent crimes: An investigative tool*. Thousand Oaks, CA: Sage.

Identity Theft and Assumption Deterrence Act, 18 U.S.C. 1028(a)(7) (1998).

Janal, D. S. (1998). *Risky business: Protect your business from being stalked, conned, or blackmailed on the web*. New York: Wiley.

Kalb, P. E. (1999). Health care fraud and abuse. *The Journal of the American Medical Association, 282*(12), 1163–1168.

Kanouse, D., Berry, S., Duan, N., & Lever, J. (1999). Drawing a probability sample of female street prostitutes in Los Angeles county. *Journal of Sex Research, 36,* 45–51.

Kaplan, L. J., & Maher, J. (1970). The economics of the numbers game. In L. J. Kaplan & D. Kessler (Eds.), *An economic analysis of crime* (pp. 113–141). Springfield, IL: Thomas.

Katz, J. (1988). *Seductions of crime*. New York: Basic Books.

Kienlen, K. K., Birmingham, D. L., Solberg, K. B., O'Regan, J. T., & Meloy, J.R. (1997). A comparative study of psychotic and non-psychotic stalking. *Journal of the American Academy of Psychiatry and Law, 25*(3), 317–334.

Latham, C. K., & Jacobs, F. A. (2000). Monitoring and incentive factors influencing misleading disclosures. *Journal of Managerial Issues, 12*(2), 169–187.

Liddick, D. (1999). *The mob's daily number*. New York: University Press of America.

Maher, L., & Curtis, R. (1992). Women on the edge of crime: Crack cocaine and the changing contexts of street-level sex work in New York City. *Crime, Law, and Social Change, 18,* 221–258.

Maher, L., & Daly K. (1996). Women in the street level drug economy: Continuity or change? *Criminology, 34,* 465–498.

Maruna, S. (2001). *Making good: How ex-convicts reform and rebuild their lives*. Washington DC: APA Press.

McDonald, M. (2001, February 5). New kids' video games spotlights web predators. *U.S. News and World Report,* p. 57.

Meloy, J. R. (1996). Stalking (obsessional following): A review of some preliminary studies. *Aggression and Violent Behavior, 1,* 147–162.

Meloy, J. R. (Ed.). (1998). *The psychology of stalking: Clinical and forensic perspectives*. San Diego: Academic Press.

Meloy, J. R., & Gothard, S. (1995). A demographic and clinical comparison of obsessional followers and offenders with mental disorders. *American Journal of Psychiatry, 152,* 258–263.

Meritor Savings Bank v. Vinson, 477 U.S. 57 (1986).

Merriam–Webster's collegiate Dictionary (10th ed.). (1996). Springfield, MA: Merriam–Webster.

Miller, N. S. (2000). Addictions and the law. *Psychiatric Annals, 30*(9), 609–624.

Mosher, C. (2001). Predicting drug arrest rates: Conflict and social disorganization perspectives. *Crime and Delinquency, 47*(1), 84–104.

Mullen, P. E., Pathe, M., & Purcell, R. (2000). *Stalkers and their victims*. Cambridge, MA: Cambridge University Press.

Nandon, S., Koverola, C., & Schluderman, E. (1998). Antecedents to prostitution: Childhood victimization. *Journal of Interpersonal Violence, 13,* 206–221.

Parent, E. C., & Newman, D. L. (1999). The role of sensation-seeking in alcohol use and risk-taking behavior among college women. *Journal of Alcohol and Drug Education, 44*(2), 12–29.

Patterson, S., Lennings, C., & Davey, J. (2000). Methadone clients, crime, and substance use. *International Journal of Offender Therapy and Comparative Criminology, 44,* 667–680.

Pettiway, L. (1997). *Workin' it: Women living through drugs and crime*. Philadelphia: Temple University Press.

Pheterson, G. (Ed.). (1989). *A vindication of the rights of whores*. Seattle: Seal Press.

Pollock, J. M. (2001). *Criminal women*. Cincinnati, OH: Anderson.

Pottieger, A. E., & Tressell, P. A. (2000). Social relationships of crime-involved women cocaine users. *Journal of Psychoactive Drugs, 32*(4), 445–461.

Pryor, J. B., LaVite, C. M., & Stroller, L. M. (1993). A social-psychological analysis of sexual harassment: The person/situation interaction. *Journal of Vocational Behavior, 42,* 62–83.

Racketeer Influenced and Corrupt Organization Act of 1970, 18 U.S.C. 96 (1961–1968).

Reanda, L. (1991). Prostitution as a human rights question: Problems and prospects of United Nations action. *Human Rights Quarterly, 13,* 202–228.

Richards, J. (1999). *Transnational criminal organizations, cybercrime, and money laundering: A handbook for law enforcement officers, auditors, and financial investigators*. Boca Raton: CRC Press.

Richman, J. A., Rospenda, K. M., Nawyn, S. J., & Flaherty, J. A. (1999). Sexual harassment and generalized workplace abuse among university employees: Prevalence and mental health correlates. *American Journal of Public Health, 89*(3), 358–363.

Rodney, H. E., Tachia, H. R., & Rodney, L. W. (1999). The home environment and delinquency: A study of African American adolescents. *Families in Society, 80*(6), 551–559.

Ross, J. I., & Richards, S. (2002). *Convict criminology*. Belmont, CA: Wadsworth.

Ryan, P. (1995). *Organized crime: A reference handbook.* Santa Barbara, CA: ABC-CLIO Inc.

Sabol, W. J., Adams, W. P., Parthasarathy, B., & Yuan, Y. (2000). *Federal justice statistics program: Offenders returning to federal prison 1986–97.* Retrieved October 6, 2004, from http://www.ojp.usdoj.gov/bjs/pub/ascii/orfp97.txt.

Samoriski, J. H. (1999). Unsolicited commercial e-mail, the Internet and the First Amendment: Another free speech showdown in cyberspace? *Journal of Broadcasting and Electronic Media, 43*(4), 670–689.

Sanchez, L. E. (1997). Boundaries of legitimacy: Sex, violence, citizenship and community in a local sexual economy. *Law and Social Inquiry, 22,* 543–554.

Sanchez, L. E. (1999). Sex, law, and the paradox of agency and resistance in the everyday practices of women in the "Evergreen" sex trade. In S. Henry & D. Milovanovic (Eds.), *Constitutive criminology at work: Applications to crime and justice* (pp. 39–66). Albany, NY: State University of New York Press.

Seyhun, H. N. (2000). *Investment intelligence from insider trading.* Cambridge, MA: MIT Press.

Simpson, S. (2002). *Corporate crime, law and social control.* Cambridge, MA: Cambridge University Press.

Snyder, H. N., & Sickmund, M. (1999). *Juvenile offenders and victims: 1999 National Report.* Washington, DC: Office of Juvenile Justice and Delinquency Prevention.

Sprague, J., & Walker, H. (2000). Early identification and intervention for youth with antisocial and violent behavior. *Exceptional Children, 66*(3), 367–379.

Stone, C. B. (2000). Advocacy for sexual harassment victims: Legal support and ethical aspects. *Professional School Counseling, 4*(1), 23–31.

Sutherland, E. H. (1949). *White-collar crime.* New York: Holt, Rinehart & Winston.

Sutherland, E. H. (1983). *White-collar crime: The uncut version.* New Haven, CT: Yale University Press.

Taylor, S., Jr. (2001, March 19). Is it sexual exploitation if victims are "virtual"? *Newsweek,* p. 51.

Tjadan, P. (1997). *The crime of stalking: How big is the problem?* Washington DC: U.S. Department of Justice, Office of Justice Programs, National Institute of Justice.

United States Code (Title 18) § 2252. Certain activities relating to material involving the sexual exploitation of minors (2001).

United States v. Powell 469 U.S. 57 (1984).

U.S. Congressional Subcommittee on Crime (1979).

U.S. Department of Justice. (1998). *What's the U.S. Department of Justice doing about telemarketing fraud?* Retrieved October 28, 2004, from www.usdoj.gov/criminal/fraud/telemarketing/doj.htm

U.S. Department of Justice. (2000a). *Identity theft and fraud.* Retrieved on October 6, 2004, from http://www.usdoj.gov/criminal/fraud/idtheft.html

U.S. Department of Justice. (2000b). *Internet fraud.* Retrieved on October 6, 2004, from http://www.internetfraud.usdoj.gov

U.S. Department of Justice, Bureau of Justice Statistics. (2003). *Crime and victim statistics.* Retrieved October 6, 2004, from http://www.ojp.usdoj.gov/bjs/cvict.htm

U.S. Department of Justice, Federal Bureau of Investigation. (1997). *Uniform crime reports for the United States: Crime in the United States, 1997.* Washington DC: U.S. Government Printing Office.

Vastag, B. (2000). Federal plan asks for increased drug treatment. *The Journal of the American Medical Association, 284*(24), 3114.

Viano, E. C. (1999). The criminal justice system facing the challenges of organized crime. In E. C. Viano (Ed.), *Global organized crime and international security* (pp. 38–61). Aldershot, UK: Ashgate.

Walters, G. D. (1998). *Changing lives of crime and drugs: Intervening with substance-abusing offenders.* Chichester, England: Wiley.

Weinberg, M., Shaver, F., & Williams, C. (1999). Gendered sex work in the San Francisco tenderloin. *Archives of Sexual Behavior, 28,* 503–521.

Weiner, A. (1996). Understanding the social needs of streetwalking prostitutes. *Social Work, 41,* 97–105.

West, C., Williams, L., & Siegel, J. (2000). A prospective examination of serious consequences of abuse. *Child Maltreatment, 5,* 49–57.

Wiener, R. L., & Hurt, L. E. (1999). An interdisciplinary approach to understanding social sexual conduct at work. *Psychology, Public Policy, and Law, 5*(3), 556–595.

Witt, R., Clarke, A., & Fielding, N. (1999). Crime and economic activity: A panel data approach. *The British Journal of Criminology, 39,* 391–400.

Wrightsman, L. S. (2001). *Forensic psychology.* Belmont, CA: Wadsworth/Thomas.

Zona, M., Palarea, R., & Lane, J. (1998). Psychiatric diagnosis and the offender—Victim typology of stalking. In J. R. Meloy (Ed.), *The psychology of stalking: Clinical and forensic perspectives* (pp. 70–84). San Diego: Academic Press.

Zona, M., Sharma, K., & Lane, J. (1993). A comparative study of erotomanic and obsessional subjects in a forensic sample. *Journal of Forensic Sciences, 38*(4), 94–903.

Juvenile Delinquency

OVERVIEW

Violent and nonviolent criminal behavior is not the exclusive domain of adults. Indeed, **juveniles** are also susceptible to criminal wrongdoing. In fact, several investigators argue that the wayward actions of individuals in childhood and adolescents, if sustained and untreated, will produce persistent patterns of criminal conduct in adulthood. Thus, how children are cared for, nurtured, understood, disciplined, or otherwise dealt with by parents, families, peers, educators, and other agents of socialization, will have a profoundly stabilizing or destabilizing influence on their maturation.

Chapter 7 examines the phenomenon of juvenile delinquency, featuring a spectrum of issues related to this type of illicit conduct. In particular, parental responsibility, status crimes, substance-related crimes, **school violence**, kids killing kids, **juvenile sex offenders,** and the waiver process are all explored. Each of these matters is significant, especially in relation to understanding childhood and adolescents. Indeed, by focusing on those topics comprising or contributing to juvenile delinquency, we learn something more about this form of criminal behavior, the offenders responsible for their commission, and a society that endeavors to comprehend both.

KEY TERMS

Addiction	Marital violence
Antisocial tendencies	MTC:CM3
Bullying	Murder
Classroom avenger	Parental responsibility laws
Conduct disorder	Runaway
Criminal lifestyle	School violence
Curfew violation	Serious violent crime
Drug lifestyle	Sexual abuse cycle
Firearm	Status offenders
Incorrigibility	Substance abuse
Juveniles	Truancy
Juvenile homicide	Underage drinking
Juvenile sex offenders	Vandalism

PARENTAL RESPONSIBILITY

Introduction

There are many reasons why juveniles commit crimes. Some of the major contributing factors include peer pressure, gang involvement, social status, financial difficulty, drug and alcohol abuse, and psychiatric illness (especially **conduct disorder** and oppositional defiant disorder). Several of these factors are examined throughout this chapter and elsewhere in the first section of the book where various theories of crime and delinquency are explored. Another dimension of juvenile delinquency involves the adolescent's home life. Clearly, there are many things parents can do to help keep their children stay crime free; however, there are also many things parents do that create the social and psychological ingredients that breed and sustain troubled adolescent conduct. This section examines several parental forces that impact the likelihood of juvenile crime. In brief, these include parents as poor role models, physical abuse directed toward children, exposure to **marital violence,** divorce and single-parenting, and **parental responsibility laws.** Admittedly, the presence of these factors alone does not guarantee that a child will become a wayward youth; however, these conditions are quite distressing and they can have a devastating affect on the life of a juvenile, including the onset of deviant and delinquent behavior.

Parents as Role Models

Parents are role models for their maturing children. Young people learn to think and act for themselves by watching and mimicking the various ways in which their parents interact with one another, socialize with people outside of the home, and react to different environments. When children observe and subsequently imitate their parents, they learn how adults are rewarded or punished in specific situations, and these experiences influence their own sense of morality (Atkinson, Atkinson, Smith, & Bem, 1990). Moreover, during early childhood development, a young boy or girl looks for and expects to receive help from parents when experiencing unfamiliar, uncomfortable, or otherwise awkward feelings and emotions. One example of this is aggressive impulses. The child looks to the parents for guidance, especially when it comes to managing these urges in a positive and creative way (Davies, 1997; Sutton, 1988). However, "if both parents have problems with their own aggression then they will be ill equipped to 'stand the strain' of the child's repeated and 'hopeful' attempts to gain help with [the adolescent's] aggressive impulses" (Davies, 1997, p. 112). In the absence of parental direction, there is no model of proper moral judgment for the child to emulate. Indeed, "The child will be inhibited in his [or her] attempts to acquire positive and fruitful outlets for [the] aggression. . . . " (p. 112). As such, children run the risk of acting on their own aggressive or violent inclinations when they should have learned how to appropriately control or contain them from their caregivers (Sutton, 1988).

Often, when parents attempt to guide and shape the behaviors of their children, they do not feel in control themselves. For example, a temperamental child who exhibits impulsive, unresponsive, or overactive behavior receives less positive and constructive parenting than children who are more responsive and compliant (Stern & Smith, 1999). When parents give in to a difficult son or daughter, the child may become more belligerent and uncontrollable (Sutton, 1988; Stern & Smith, 1999). In short, the child learns that parents reward negative behaviors. Without question, parenting skills and characteristics can be blatant, subtle, or somewhere in between. Regardless of their form, they have a significant impact on the child's development of moral judgment and interpersonal behavior. This is why positive, healthy parenting is so important.

Physical Abuse Against Children

When parents target their aggression, anger, and violence toward a child, psychological and behavioral problems often follow. According to Kaplan et al. (1999), physically abused adolescents, compared with nonabused adolescents, exhibit internalizing (anxiety and depression) and externalizing (aggression and alcohol or drug use) conduct problems. Many youth become depressed and confused because they think they are the cause of their parents' hostility. In an earlier study, Kaplan et al. (1998) found not only that physical abuse during adolescence was associated with a greater risk for developing adolescent psychiatric and disruptive disorders, but also that drug abuse and cigarette use were correlated with it. In these instances, the children attempted to cope with the parental abuse by escaping reality through the consumption of controlled substances. In fact, the investigators found that physically abused adolescents were 19 times as likely to abuse drugs as nonabused children were, and that abused adolescents were 9 times as likely to be diagnosed with conduct disorder than were their nonabused counterparts (Kaplan et al., 1998). According to the *DSM–IV–TR,* conduct disorder is described as a repetitive and persistent pattern of behavior in which the basic rights of others or major age-appropriate societal norms are violated (APA, 2000).

Clearly, parental interactions with their children significantly affect whether their sons and daughters will make appropriate and acceptable judgments in life. Furthermore, how parents treat each other has a tremendous effect on the behaviors of their children. Indeed, as Rossman, Hughes, and Rosenberg (2000) noted, "children's behavioral problems [are] mostly a function of violence in the child's immediate family, with violence against the child exerting the most powerful impact but witnessing violence adding to that impact" (p. 17). Thus, the adverse ways in which parents respond to one another and to their offspring significantly contribute to the development of the juvenile delinquent.

Children's Exposure to Marital Violence

Numerous investigators have linked exposure to marital violence (spousal abuse) to a range of dysfunctional behaviors and adjustment problems for children (Holden, 1998). For example, according to Barnett, Miller-Perrin, and Perrin (1997), children's problems associated with exposure to marital violence include attention deficit disorder, aggression, alcohol or drug abuse, anger, conduct disorder, oppositional problems, anxiety, depression, low self-esteem, self-blame, suicidality, and posttraumatic stress disorder (symptoms such as hypervigilance, flashbacks, and nightmares). Children may develop cognitive distortions related to relationships, such as beliefs in violence within relationships; deficits in social skills; low empathy (compassion); and poor problem-solving skills. Children who are exposed to marital conflict exhibit poor behavior in school, as well as poor academic performance, poor classroom attendance, and **truancy.** Moreover, these children often transfer the violence they witness to their future spouse and children (Barnett et al., 1997). Indeed, "[The male child who is exposed to marital violence] may then in his own future life repeat his parent's relationship by finding 'willing' partners who will fall into this [type of relationship]. He may also come to the point where he treats people as if they are 'willing,' whether they are or not" (Davies, 1997, p. 113).

In situations where marital violence occurs, it is usually precipitated by the father who acts against the mother. A developing child who witnesses such behavior acquires a skewed sense of reality. As Davies (1997) observed:

> While the child may be frightened and disturbed by father's violence he [or she] may wonder why mother continues to suffer the violence. Rather than acquiring an uncomplicated perception of a powerful male perpetrator and a helpless female victim, the child may thus feel and think that his [or her] mother in some ways enjoys the suffering and that his [or her] father enjoys inflicting the pain. (p. 113)

Children reared in the presence of frequent violence are less likely to perceive aggression as inappropriate and are therefore more likely to be comfortable with their own aggressive and delinquent behavior (Kaplan et al., 1999). This comfort with aggression is often associated with criminal behavior.

Divorce and Single-Parenting

Approximately 95% of adults in the United States get married and have children. However, the divorce rate is at 50% in the United States, and it remains among the highest in the world (Stevenson & Black, 1996). Children of divorced families may be at a greater risk for becoming juvenile delinquents; though, this is not as clear-cut as it appears. Indeed, as the available evidence suggests,

> The majority of offspring of divorce will not show behavior problems; however, as compared to the general population, a greater proportion of both male and female offspring of divorce will have some overt, inappropriate behaviors (i.e., use of controlled substances, academic problems). (Stevenson & Black, 1996, p. 101)

Divorce may create residual effects in children such as stress; therefore, the use of drugs might be an escape or coping strategy for the juvenile (Stevenson & Black, 1996). Nonetheless, over the years, research into the effects of divorce as a cause of juvenile delinquency has shifted away from regarding divorce as a major variable (Stevenson & Black, 1996). For example, as Fox (1998) argues:

> While the negative socializing forces of drugs, guns, gangs, and the media have become more threatening, the positive socializing forces of family, school, religion, and neighborhood have grown relatively weak and ineffective. Increasingly, children are being raised in homes disrupted by divorce and economic stress; too many children emerge undersocialized and unsupervised. (p. 117)

Thus, divorce, in conjunction with other social variables, might better explain juvenile delinquency than the effect of marital separation itself.

In addition to the potential delinquency problems posed by divorce is the social and psychological impact of being raised in a single-headed household. The percentage of African American children born into families headed by single mothers has increased from 22% in 1960 to 68% in 1996, and European American children born into single-mother households has grown from 2% in 1960 to 22% in 1996 (Rubenstein, 1998). Many researchers believe that these high illegitimacy rates reflect an increasing lack of morality and that "single parent families, and the culture that condones them, are the root cause of most violent crimes" (Rubenstein, 1998, p. 19).

Parental Responsibility Laws

Parental responsibility laws are statutes or codes that make parents legally responsible for the intentional damage and injuries inflicted by their children (Simpson, 1999). These laws hold parents accountable for the antisocial behavior of their sons and daughters, and require parents to pay fines, attend court, frequent parenting classes, do community service, and attend school with their children (Samborn, 1996; Turpin, 2000). Under these legal ordinances, parents often must participate in their child's probation and counseling, pay restitution to the state for the youth's care while in custody, and spend time in jail for the actions of their son or daughter (Samborn). These laws have been passed in order to compel or otherwise force parents into making better choices in how they raise and discipline their children, eliminating or reducing the likelihood that these adolescents will stay out of trouble.

Some mothers and fathers believe they are not physically capable of keeping their troubled offspring from acting delinquently. Indeed, some parents abdicate parental control and authority early in the juvenile's life and, as such, become fearful of and intimidated by the aggressiveness of their children. In these instances, parents may be unable to manage the behaviors of their children. Holding a mother or father liable for the delinquency of their child sends a message to the parents that the courts will always second-guess parental judgments. Unfortunately, not only do laws such as these label the parents criminal,

Are Single-Parent Families Responsible for Juvenile Crime?

Is it fair to say that single-parent households are indicative of an immoral society and that they should therefore be blamed for the growing crime rate? To some extent, the answer to this question depends on the research you accept.

For example, because some unmarried mothers often lack the skills to support a family or to manage a household effectively, their children are more prone to commit crime due to a lack of supervision, lack of moral development, or financial need. Children from single-parent families are two to three times more likely than children from two-parent families to have emotional and behavioral disturbances (Maginnis, 1997). Robert L. Maginnis, policy analyst for the Family Research Council (a conservative research organization concerned with preserving the traditional family), reports that when looking at the data on children from single-parent families compared with children from two-parent families,

> [Adolescents from single-parent families] use drugs more heavily and commit more crimes throughout their lives; are more likely to be gang members; make up 70% of juvenile delinquents in state reform institutions; account for 75% of adolescent murderers and are 70% more likely to be expelled from school. (p. 64)

However, there are other investigators who argue that the quality of family relationships is more significant than the absence of a parent in causing juvenile delinquency (Wright & Wright, 1998). Indeed, blaming juvenile crime on single-parent homes is much too inadequate. "Thirty-six years and hundreds of studies later . . . the literature reveals conflicting findings and opinions regarding the relationship between family structure and [juvenile] delinquency" (pp. 68–69). Other factors that might present better predictors of delinquency include (a) marital discord (unhappily married mothers supervise their children less diligently and more of them have negative opinions of their children than happily married women); (b) economic deprivation (studies show that delinquency is related to the mother's income level at the time of the child's birth and to the father's irregular employment); (c) socialization (single parents may be less able to properly monitor, support, and guide their children to conform to societal expectations); and (d) one's neighborhood (many single-parent families live in social isolation and in economically deprived neighborhoods, leading to decreased opportunity for economic mobility and a greater likelihood that children will drop out of school or become pregnant as teenagers; Wright & Wright, 1998). Thus, as Wright and Wright conclude, "Most [single-parent] families do not produce delinquent children" (p. 74).

but also they potentially stigmatize the parents as failures. In situations like these, improving parental skills cannot be expected without their genuine participation in specific remedial training classes, often mandated by the court.

Clearly, the underlying assumption of parental responsibility laws is that mothers and fathers fail to adequately supervise or control their children, and that this failure directly contributes to the delinquency of their offspring. Opponents of these laws maintain that society should not label parents criminal for the actions of their teenagers (Schrof & Thomas, 1999). According to this perspective, teenagers, and even most children, know right from wrong. Thus, the choices juveniles make may be a reflection of numerous variables outside the context of parental neglect and irresponsibility. As Fox (1998) explains it:

> For the sake of short-term economic savings, we have closed down the neighborhood movie houses, community recreation centers, and local swimming pools. To control taxes, we have neglected zoos, playgrounds, ball fields, and lakes. School districts everywhere have abandoned after-school activities and intramural sports. (p. 117)

When children have no meaningful or ongoing outlets for positive and healthy recreation or socialization, they often turn to whatever sources of interaction are available to them. This includes adopting mischievous, deviant, and delinquent patterns of behavior. Under these conditions, rather than blaming parents as principally responsible for the wayward conduct of their children, perhaps we should consider how social, economic, and political forces are created for adolescents that breed and sustain criminal behavior.

STATUS CRIMES

Introduction

Notwithstanding the role of parents in curtailing or contributing to juvenile delinquency, some adolescents do engage in antisocial and criminal behavior. In 1946, Massachusetts passed the Stubborn Child Law, which created the first status offense defined as an act that is illegal for minors only (Drowns & Hess, 2000). Status offenses are based solely on a person's chronological age and, in most state jurisdictions, a person must be younger than 18 for a status offense to take place, with the exception of **underage drinking** violations that occur if the person is younger than 21. There are several behaviors considered violations of the law if committed by a juvenile. Representative examples include habitual truancy, curfew infractions, running away, **incorrigibility,** ungovernable conduct, uncontrollable by parents, and using tobacco and alcohol.

This portion of the chapter reviews what we know about status offenses. In particular, the section examines the historical context in which juvenile crime emerged and was understood, reviews the literature on status offenses, and offers several psychological theories that explain this form of criminal conduct. More than just chronicling what acts are socially defined as status offenses, the purpose of this section is to develop a broader basis by which to appreciate why and how this form of adolescent delinquency occurs.

Historical Perspective

In 1899, when the first juvenile court was established in Chicago, Illinois, the state was supposed to act as a wise and loving parent for neglected and dependent children (Bernard, 1992). However, prior to the 1960s, most states treated **status offenders** and juvenile delinquents the same. This changed in the late 1960s when the President's Commission on Law Enforcement and the Administration of Justice surveyed juvenile detention and correctional facilities. The survey showed that 93% of juvenile court jurisdictions across the country had no place for the detention of juveniles other than county jails or local lockups (Feld, 1999). These facilities were holding adolescents who were simply dependent, neglected, or involved in noncriminal conduct. During this time period, there was very little distinction between child neglect and criminal behavior committed by juveniles (Howell, 1998).

In 1961, California was the first state to separate status offenses from the category of delinquency. In 1962, New York followed and created a new classification for criminal conduct known Person in Need of Supervision (PINS). Other states adopted New York's perspective and used other labels such as CINS (Children in Need of Supervision), MINS (Minors in Need of Supervision) and JINS (Juveniles in Need of Supervision) in an effort to reduce the stigma of being labeled a delinquent.

A major contribution to the juvenile justice reform movement occurred in the 1970s with the White House Conference on Youth. This conference led to a series of decisions aimed at preventing delinquency and rehabilitating offenders outside of the traditional criminal justice system. Referring status offenders outside of the juvenile justice system was intended to conserve limited court resources, commodities that should be reserved for serious juvenile recidivists. In addition, the Juvenile Justice and Delinquency Prevention Act of 1974 (JJDP) embodied the juvenile justice reform movement. The purpose of the JJDP Act was on prevention, requiring the development of alternative interventions and practices external to the formal juvenile justice system (Howell, 1998). The Act had two goals: the deinstitutionalization of status offenders and the separation of juveniles from adult facilities. It also provided funds to states that removed status offenders from jails and prisons, and it helped to create reforms such as community-based interventions for these troubled youth (Bernard, 1992; Feld, 1999).

Court data show a substantial decline in the use of detention for status offenders, according to the OJJDP (Snyder & Sickmund, 1999). For example, in 1975 status offenses were twice as likely as delinquency cases to involve secure detention between the time of referral to court and the disposition of the case. However, by 1992, the likelihood that a status offense would involve detention dropped to less than half of that for delinquency cases.

Status Offenses

In 1996, status offenses accounted for approximately 14% of the court's formal delinquency caseload. The OJJDP stated that among adolescents detained in secure juvenile facilities in 1997, 49% were held for running away, 22% for incorrigibility, 9% for truancy, 8% for underage drinking, and 6% for **curfew violation** (Snyder & Sickmund, 1999). The following is a description of the more common status offenses.

Running away from home is a status offense that is typically found among teenage girls (Chesney-Lind & Shelden, 1992). Girls who run away are often likely to engage in prostitution and other criminal acts in an effort to survive (Drowns & Hess, 2000). According to the OJJDP, 60% of juveniles brought to court for running away in 1996 were female (Snyder & Sickmund, 2000). However, self-report studies show that boys and girls are equally likely to run away from home.

Vandalism is a destructive status offense performed to garner attention, seek revenge, or release hostility. In 1996, 141,600 juveniles were arrested for vandalism (Drowns & Hess, 2000). This kind of destructive behavior is frequently an overt sign that a child is experiencing difficulty communicating and is in need of professional assistance.

Curfew violations are another common status offense and are enacted so police officers can maintain control over youth during times when they are most likely to get into trouble. As a result, approximately 125,000 youths are arrested each year for curfew violations (Siegel & Senna, 2000). These laws have created large numbers of new status offenders. Violations of curfew often result in a warning, fine, or detention at the police station until the youth's parents take the child home. Currently, curfew laws are being challenged on constitutional grounds, with some communities claiming that these laws discriminate against those who are not yet legal adults (Drowns & Hess, 2000; Feld, 1999).

For juveniles under 15 years of age, the most likely status offense is truancy. For juveniles over the age of 16, the most likely status offense is a liquor violation. Girls are more likely than are boys to be arrested for status offenses, with these crimes accounting for 23% of juvenile female arrests compared to only 10% for all juvenile male status offense arrests (Regoli & Hewitt, 2000). In addition, females were involved in 4 out of 10 status offense cases formally processed in 1996, according to the OJJDP (Snyder & Sickmund, 1999). These figures suggest that the juvenile justice system may be inadvertently reinforcing a more passive and domestic role for adolescent girls, given the frequency with which they are arrested and processed for minor infractions (Regoli & Hewitt, 2000).

States vary in how they process status offenders (Feld, 1999). For example, a **runaway** may be filed through juvenile court in one state and a child welfare agency in yet another state. Some state jurisdictions do not consider status offenses a violation of law. Instead, these behaviors are viewed as indicators that the child is in need of supervision. Given this framework, these particular states handle status offenders through the provision of social services. In this model, the social, economic, and psychological needs of wayward youth are addressed rather than attending to the delinquent act through the formal juvenile justice system.

Psychological Theories

Several theories have been offered to explain the occurrence of status offenses. For example, psychologist Erik H. Erikson (1902–1994) suggested that adolescents go through an identity crisis, or a period in which they experience inner turmoil and uncertainty about their role in life (Erikson, 1963). The confusion during this period, if unsuccessfully resolved, may cause a child to become more emotionally distraught or impulsive than usual and, subsequently, to feel incapable of channeling his or her behavior in appropriate directions. As a result, the youth may run away, miss curfew, or engage in underage drinking.

Why Do Juveniles Commit Status Offenses?: Some Insights From Social Psychology

Why do juveniles commit status offenses? One explanation comes from social psychology. For example, control theory suggests that skipping school, using drugs, having sex, fighting, and engaging in other forms of delinquency are attractive to most teenagers. The only reason why more adolescents do not become involved in these behaviors is because of their attachment to certain social and familial institutions and norms. These youngsters are able to resist the urge to engage in such delinquent acts because they possess a meaningful bond with these control factors (see chapter 4 for more details on this perspective).

Travis Hirschi (1969) created his own version of control theory in an effort to explain the causes of delinquency. His theory accounts for some of the reasons why juveniles commit crime in general, and it may offer some insight into why adolescents commit status offenses in particular. According to Hirschi, all individuals have the potential to be delinquent or to commit crimes. The social order establishes various norms and cultural beliefs, and each person creates a bond with society, ascribing (more or less) to these basic tenets. If an adolescent has a weak bond with society, given the type of attachments, commitments, and involvements the person possesses,

or if the person subscribes to alternative beliefs, then the youth is likely to violate the law.

Consider the instance of an adolescent who has a lot of free time on his or her hands. This individual is prone to more illegal behavior than is a youth whose time is filled with activities (e.g., work, school and sports). If this same adolescent comes from a family shattered by divorce and if there is little attachment to the child's parents, the juvenile has an even stronger likelihood for delinquency. Hirschi argued that the interrelationship of these (and other) social–psychological variables contribute to a youth's involvement in conventional or unconventional behavior (see also, Gottfredson & Hirschi, 1990).

Another consideration is whether status offenders are more likely to escalate to serious crimes than those adolescents whose criminal pasts do not include status offending. A longitudinal study conducted by Sheldon, Horvath, and Sharon (1989) found that whether status offenders go on to commit more serious crimes depends on the gender and the specific type of status offense committed. However, there is little current research revealing whether status offenders escalate to more serious criminal behavior.

Other status offenses (e.g., truancy) may be linked a child's learning disability or psychological deficits, preventing the youth from receiving optimal educational benefits (Bartollas, 2000; Dryfoos, 1990). However, the prevailing view is that status offenders and juvenile delinquents share similar social and developmental problems. These problems contribute to their involvement within the criminal justice system (Siegel & Senna, 2000).

SUBSTANCE-RELATED JUVENILE CRIME

Introduction

Another factor accounting for juvenile delinquency is the use of drugs and alcohol. In chapter 6, some commentary on substance use was offered as a way of understanding nonviolent crime. Reference to this material will be helpful, and readers are encouraged to refer to it for guidance. However, in this section, the focus is on the illicit use of drugs and alcohol and their impact on juvenile delinquency. In particular, general background information on **substance abuse** related to juveniles is presented. In addition, the risk factors for adult criminality, given adolescent substance abuse, are examined. Finally, the behavioral lifestyle characteristics of the drug-consuming juvenile offender are delineated.

Background Information on Substance-Related Juvenile Crime

According to the American Psychiatric Association (2000), substance abuse is a maladaptive pattern of drug and alcohol consumption in which a person repeatedly experiences profoundly adverse effects from the ongoing use of these substances. In the context of adolescents, substance abuse represents a poor coping mechanism for the many stressors of life. In addition, it appears to have a high correlation with increasing crime rates among both the juvenile and the adult offender populations. For example, when looking at all juveniles, incarcerated youth are seven times more likely to participate in drug use. Moreover, substance abuse is linked to an increased risk of criminal behavior, whereas substance abuse treatment is associated with a reduction in criminal conduct (Tsytsarev, Manger, & Lodrini, 2000).

An important question to consider regarding the drug use and crime connection is whether the consumption of illicit substances precedes criminal activity, or whether criminal conduct precedes drug use. Research has shown that approximately 50% of juvenile offenders engage in criminal behavior prior to their drug use, that 25% of juvenile offenders engage in substance use prior to their criminal behavior, and that 25% of juveniles simultaneously engage in the drug use and criminal behavior (Deitch, Koutsenok, & Ruzi, 2000). Findings such as these do not clearly tell us whether delinquency is precipitated by substance use or vice versa. Nonetheless, it is clear that drugs and crime are closely related in many juvenile offenses (Bartol, 2002; Bartollas, 2000).

One way to appreciate the adverse relationship between drugs and crime is to consider the effects specific substances have on offender behavior. The interaction between crime and substance use begins in one of two ways. Either individuals support their drug behavior through criminal acts or individuals engage in substance use because of their criminal involvement (Deitch et al., 2000). Drug use multiplies the crime rate and helps to maintain criminal behavior. Statistics report that over half of all crimes committed are drug related (Siegel & Senna, 2000). Upon arrest, juveniles are tested for drugs. Among those tested, between 60% and 70% test positive for drugs. The most common drugs found in juvenile offenders are marijuana, cocaine, and methamphetamine (Deitch et al., 2000).

Substance use reportedly increases the possibility that one will engage in criminal conduct. Opiate and multidrug abusers commit unlawful acts more routinely than do their nonabusing counterparts (Patterson, Lennings, & Davey, 2000). Researchers indicate that substance abuse is either the result of a genetic predisposition or is the result of an individual's inability to resist the temptation to engage in negative behavior (Walters, 1998). Heroin addicts are six times more likely to engage in criminal acts while intoxicated than when they remain drug free (Patterson et al., 2000). With respect to opiate use, continual use of heroin is perceived as a significant risk factor for engaging in illicit behavior. Lower rates of opiate-related crime correlate with methadone treatment and employment opportunities (Patterson et al., 2000). Overall, the drug consumption **criminal lifestyle** pattern becomes a cycle for many offenders. In addition, the increase in economic standing, given the capital generated from committing a crime, leads to greater heroin use because more funds are available to purchase drugs (Walters, 1998). This same cycle operates for drug-using juvenile offenders.

Risk Factors

There are specific psychological testing measures or instruments used to determine different levels of criminality. Examples of these scales include the Lifestyle Criminality Screening Form–Revised, the Drug Lifestyle Screening Interview, the Estimated Self-Efficacy in Avoiding Drugs, the Estimated Self-Efficacy in Avoiding Crime, the Lifestyle Stress Test, the Psychological Inventory of Criminal Thinking Styles, and the Psychological Inventory of Drug-Based Thinking Styles (Walters, 1998). These instruments are useful when evaluating or interpreting the type and level of delinquency committed by an adolescent. For example, the types of criminality perpetrated by male versus female juvenile substance abusers are considerably different. Males are apt to engage in violent crimes such as burglary and robbery while intoxicated. In comparison, females are more likely to engage in acts of prostitution, drug sales, and shoplifting (Patterson et al., 2000).

Notwithstanding the effect of gender, youth who become involved in both delinquent behavior and substance use at a young age are more likely to adopt criminal behavioral patterns throughout their lives than are other adolescents not inclined to act criminally (Deitch et al., 2000). Some investigators speculate that because of the combinatory effect of these delinquent actions, risk factors for drug abuse and crime occur conjointly (Bartollas, 2000). Prevalent risk factors for substance use include depression, conduct disorder, delinquency, and poor cognitive ability or the inability to appropriately interpret an environmental situation. Poor cognitive ability leads to aggression, which may lead to further drug use and criminal activity (Bartol, 2002).

Significant risk factors for criminality detected in youth include impulsivity, low frustration tolerance, thrill-seeking, the pursuit of dangerous activities, manipulation, and dissatisfaction with tasks. Factors that are prevalent in combined substance use and criminal behavior include violence due to the consumption of alcohol and other illicit substances, economic impulsivity from drug **addiction,** and sustained involvement with criminal activity because of drugs (Deitch et al., 2000). As these factors indicate, there is a strong connection between criminal behavior and substance use. Indeed, there appears to be an increased likelihood for criminal behavior when perpetrated by substance users (rather than nonsubstance users), and substance-abusing criminals appear to have higher recidivism rates than do non-substance-abusing offenders.

Juvenile Characteristics

Many criminal and drug behaviors are grounded in an individual's lifestyle. Lifestyles are established through incentives and opportunities to engage in a specific behavioral pattern. In other words, an individual's motivation and learning "blueprint" forms the groundwork for one's lifestyle (Walters, 1998). Both the criminal and the **drug lifestyle** have common characteristics in their behavioral patterns. Four behavioral characteristics define a delinquent lifestyle. These include irresponsibility, self-indulgence, interpersonal intrusiveness, and social rule breaking. Irresponsibility is the lack of accountability for and an unwillingness to meet obligations to family, friends, and oneself. Self-indulgence is an attempt to achieve instant gratification. Interpersonal intrusiveness is a violation of others' privacy, dignity, or personal space. Social rule breaking is a violation of society's conventional rules.

Four behavioral characteristics define a juvenile drug lifestyle. These include irresponsibility and pseudoresponsibility, stress-coping imbalance, interpersonal triviality, and social rule breaking and bending. Pseudoresponsibility is the failure to meet personal or family obligations while maintaining individual appearances. Examples include employment, paying bills, and staying out of prison. Stress-coping imbalance means that an individual's approach to accommodating tension contributes to long-term stress, even though short-term discomfort may be reduced. Interpersonal triviality occurs when a person downplays the importance of close, interpersonal relationships with family, friends, or other loved ones. These relationships are understood to be a necessity for human existence. Social rule breaking and bending occurs when an individual engages in dishonest acts with the intention of avoiding conventional rules because they are perceived as unjust or otherwise unfair. Clearly, the criminal and substance abuse lifestyles have similar characteristics.

Lifestyle theorists believe that substance use and crime exist on a continuum of increasing criminality or drug involvement rather than as a dichotomy of criminality and noncriminality or drug use and nonuse (Walters, 1998). For example, according to this perspective, juveniles are not categorized as either delinquent or nondelinquent. Rather, they operate somewhere along a spectrum that defines their illicit conduct. An individual may be at the most criminal end of the spectrum or at the most noncriminal end of the continuum. What determines where an individual is positioned on this spectrum are the behavioral styles (i.e., crime and drug patterns) that he or she employs.

SCHOOL VIOLENCE

Introduction

Substance abuse may be linked to increasing delinquent conduct; however, there are expressions of juvenile crime that appear to be beyond clear quantifiable explanation. One example is the disturbing phenomenon of school violence. Recent displays of adolescent shootings raise serious questions about this form of delinquent and criminal behavior committed by teenagers. This section provides general background and statistical information on school violence, explores some of the reasons why this criminal conduct occurs for boys and girls, and comments on the phenomenon of **bullying.**

General Background and Statistical Information on School Violence

School violence, or violence that takes place in educational settings or at school-related functions, has become a significant concern for lawmakers, educators, and parents, especially in the wake of the tragic massacre at Columbine High School, in Littleton, Colorado. In this particular instance, 12 students and 1 teacher were shot and killed, whereas 23 others were wounded by 2 male classmates. In addition to being armed with an arsenal of guns, the 2 teenage murderers prepared 95 explosive devices that failed to go off because of a simple electronic failure (Aronson, 2000). Interestingly, the 2 youths prepared for the slaughter of their fellow students months in advance. As Aronson notes, commenting on the premeditated nature of this gruesome event:

> [Of these explosives], one set, placed a few miles from the school, was intended to explode first and distract police by keeping them busy away from school; a second set was supposed to go off in the cafeteria killing a great many students there and causing hundreds more to evacuate the building, in terror, where Eric Harris and Dylan Klebold [the assailants] would be waiting to gun them down; a third set was planted in their cars in the school parking lot, these timed to explode after police and paramedics had arrived on the scene, creating more chaos and increasing the number of casualties. (p. 2)

Littleton, Colorado, stands as a grim reminder that school violence is not exclusive to inner cities. If such senseless violence can happen at Columbine, it can happen anywhere.

> [Unfortunately], it does seem to be happening anywhere and everywhere—small towns and little cities that conjure up Norman Rockwell paintings: Littleton, Colorado; Conyers, Georgia; Notus, Idaho; Springfield, Oregon; Fayetteville, Tennessee; Edinboro, Pennsylvania; Jonesboro, Arkansas; West Paducah, Kentucky; Pearl, Mississippi; [and] Fort Gibson, Oklahoma. (Aronson, 2000, p. 3)

According to the National Center of Education Statistics and the U.S. Department of Justice, reports released in 1999 indicated that for the year 1996 to 1997, 10% of all public schools reported at least one **serious violent crime.** Serious violent crimes included **murder,** rape, or other types of sexual battery, suicide, physical attack and fight with a weapon, or robbery. For the year 1996 to 1997, of the high schools that reported a violent crime, 8% of the offenses were rape and sexual battery, 8% robbery, 13% physical attack and fight with a weapon, and 55% physical attack without a weapon (U.S. Department of Education, Office of Educational Research and Improvement, 1999). For the same year, another 47% of public schools reported a less serious violent or nonviolent crime. These offenses included physical attack or fight without a weapon, theft and larceny, and vandalism.

Deadly school violence has received a great deal of attention. News reports over the 10-day span between February 5 and February 15, 2001, alerted the nation of three separate Columbine-like plots involving teenagers bent on massacring their classmates in Hoyt, Kansas; Fort Collins, Colorado; and Elmira, New York. "Increasingly, it appears that school buildings and even playgrounds have become zones of death" (Heide, 1999, p. 18). Though it appears that school violence is on the rise, the annual number of school shootings has actually decreased since 1990 (Aronson, 2000). "There are approximately some 108,000 public schools [in the United States], but fewer than 1% of adolescent homicides occur in or around schools" (Aronson, 2000, p. 4). Thus, as Lawrence (1998) noted, "There is no strong evidence that serious crime in schools is an extensive problem or that the problem has increased significantly; serious physical injuries or financial loss are rare in schools . . ." (p. 29).

Why Does School Violence Occur?

What causes someone to commit violence on school grounds? First, it is important to remember that for many youth, school is a central feature of their lives. The fact that violence occurs at school or at educational functions is indicative of where children are spending most of their time. In addition, the educational environment is an important factor accounting for school violence as well. Indeed, "The incidence of violence is increasing as the size of school classes increase. Crowding, anonymity, and a greater sense of alienation are variables that some researchers believe are related to aggression" (Fried & Fried, 1996, p. 24). So what social lessons are being taught at schools outside of the classrooms?

> Unfortunately, many [students] learn that the world is a difficult, unfriendly place. Many learn that the law of the jungle prevails, that might makes right, and that they can't look to adults to help solve their personal problems. Many learn that they are unattractive and unpopular, that others do not want them around. (Aronson, 2000, p. 90)

Regrettably, far too many adolescents are psychologically and socially unprepared to handle such devastating realizations.

During the school year, a child faces a perplexing maturation process that is awkward and sometimes cruel. For example, the gunmen at Columbine were considered by many to be outcasts, igniting resentment and hatred toward their more "popular" classmates. "One of the most important things we need to know is the enormous power a social situation can exert on an individual's behavior" (Aronson, 2000, p. 21). When social rejection is combined with an aggressive predisposition, given genetic or prenatal factors, an at-risk and violent environment is formed (Fried & Fried, 1996). Moreover, the family atmosphere can play a profound role in how children perceive situations and, therefore, how they choose to react to certain stimuli. Indeed, issues of neglect or abuse at home influence the development of appropriate versus aggressive behavior. "Schools become the arena where these influences collide, creating a climate of terror for too many young people" (p. 28).

James P. McGee and Caron R. DeBernardo (1999) described the potentially dangerous student as the "**classroom avenger.**" These students perpetrate violence at school when they experience "discipline by parents or authorities and/or rejection by peers or girlfriends . . . [In these instances,] the motive is vengeance and the action is a premeditated shooting spree with parents, fellow students and/or faculty [or] school administrators as target victims" (McGee & DeBernardo, 1999, p. 16). As these children mature, they develop slower than expected and have problems with social attachments and bonding (Lawrence, 1998). The profile of the classroom avenger is an adolescent who, as a child, was unaffectionate, aloof, and overly fearful of strangers. During childhood, they exhibit "indications of **antisocial tendencies** such as excessive lying and deceit, bed wetting, fire setting, and animal abuse may be present . . . [A]s adolescents, they do not show evidence of blatant mental disorders; [however, classroom avengers] are friendless, immature, and socially inadequate loners" (McGee & DeBernardo, 1999, p. 17). Even though they do not appear outwardly psychotic, there are psychological indicators of emotional and social deficits present in the classroom avenger.

Often violent students are depressed and angry; they anticipate rejection from their peers and they blame others for their personal failings (Bartollas, 2000). "They think of themselves as victims of the unfairness and malevolent intent of others. They are insightless youngsters who are easily frustrated and lack adequate coping skills for dealing with intense emotional states such as anger, anxiety, or embarrassment" (McGee & DeBernardo, 1999, pp. 17–18). On March 5, 2001, another teenage male was fed up with being picked on by his classmates and open fire at Santana High School in Santee, California. He was seen smiling as he killed 2 people and wounded 13 others (McDonald, 2001).

For the most part, male students commit violence at school. However, according to Sibylle Artz (1998), Associate Professor at the School of Child & Youth Care at the University of Victoria, Canada, females are very much in the forefront of the rise in violence in schools, both as victims and as perpetrators. "In many respects, the violent school girl looks much like the violent school boy: [She] misuses drugs and alcohol; engages in rule-breaking, deviance, and delinquency; [and] endorses aggression. She enjoys similar pastimes and she is affiliated with the same [delinquent or marginal] social groups" (Artz, 1998, p. 54). Although it is a popular misconception, bullying (i.e., inflicting physical, verbal, or emotional harm on another, as well as sexual harassment) is not limited to boys. "As perpetrators, girls are more likely to engage in verbal and emotional bullying, rather than physical or sexual harassment, but they are not exempt from such behavior" (Fried & Fried, 1996, p. 21). However, there are key differences between the sexes when it comes to school violence. The violent schoolgirl places little value on her connection with her mother and has a "greater fear of abuse, and actual experience of physical and sexual abuse, than [violent and nonviolent boys and nonviolent girls]" (Artz, 1998, p. 55).

Bullying and School Violence

Although investigators note that school violence is not significantly increasing, "minor victimizations and verbal threats do occur regularly" (Lawrence, 1998, p. 29). These actions are the product of juvenile bullies: adolescents who prey on other youth believed to be weak or vulnerable. Bullies acquire destructive power at the expense of children who perceive themselves as defenseless (Fried & Fried, 1996). However, bullies often pose as much of a threat to teachers as they do to their helpless classmates. For example, according to the U.S. Department of Justice (1999), from 1993 to 1997 teachers were the victims of approximately 1,771,000 nonfatal crimes at school. This number included 657,000 violent crimes (rape or sexual assault, robbery, aggravated assault, and simple assault). Fried and Fried described several harrowing examples of this victimization.

> [A] seventh grader in New York was arrested for setting fire to his teacher's hair; [t]wo middle school students in Ohio were charged with plotting to kill their English teacher with a 12-inch fish-filleting knife while fifteen students placed bets on the plot; [and a] substitute teacher in St. Louis died of a heart attack after being attacked by a fourth-grade student who didn't like the assignment the teacher handed out. (p. 160)

In a study conducted by Petersen, Pietrzak, and Speaker (1998), teachers, building supervisors, and district administrators were asked about their feelings of school safety and whether they experienced threats or acts of violence while attending these institutions. A majority of the respondents reported encountering some form of violence at least one or more times from 1996 to 1998. "In the past two years, 64% of [school personnel] had been verbally threatened or intimidated, 28% had been physically threatened or intimidated, and 11% had been sexually threatened one or more times" (Petersen et al., 1998, p. 348). Violence directed toward educators appears to be growing (Lawrence, 1998). Indeed, as the results from the previous study suggest "If these actions remain constant, school personnel have a greater than 50% chance of being verbally attacked, a 25% chance of being physically intimidated, and a 10% chance of being sexually harassed in the next two years" (Petersen et al., 1998, p. 348).

Some Concluding Thoughts of School Violence

Not that long ago, if a student had a disagreement with another classmate, the dispute might be settled with a punch to the nose. The worst case of school violence was a black eye. Today, however, with the availability of guns, students (and teachers) are faced with a greater threat than ever before. "Every school day 160,000 students skip classes because they fear physical harm and forty are killed or hurt by firearms" (Fried & Fried, 1996, p. 20). How do we account for this?

Interestingly, violence in movies, video games, and music lyrics may contribute to a student's acceptance of guns, aggression, and outright disregard for authority (Lawrence, 1998). "The fragile state of many families, the easy accessibility of handguns, and the glossy, idealized images of violence without consequences that pervade the culture have changed the [passage from childhood to adulthood] dramatically" (Fried & Fried, 1996, p. 26). It is becoming increasingly apparent that metal detectors, increased police surveillance, strict enforcement policies, and other zero-tolerance initiatives at schools cannot resolve, let alone respond to, the complicated and troubling youth interactions that surface daily in classrooms and school yards across the country. However, the solution may be linked to how we value adolescence, understand identity development, and foster a climate of respect, difference, and tolerance. These are weighty issues that researchers, policy analysts, and educators need to consider if society is to meaningfully address this devastating form of criminal behavior.

KIDS KILLING KIDS

Introduction

School violence is not the only expression of serious delinquent conduct receiving widespread attention in the media and elsewhere today. When children take the lives of other youth, the effects are as incomprehensible as they are terrifying. This section examines the phenomenon of **juvenile homicide.** In particular, statistical information on this offense is provided. In addition, the demographics of adolescent murderers and the risk factors associated with this form of delinquent conduct are presented. Collectively, these observations help us understand this phenomenon, the offenders who commit them, and the harm caused by this form of criminal behavior.

Juvenile Homicide: Some Statistical Information

As the previous section documented, adolescent violence is a troubling occurrence. Recently, high-profile cases have generated much of this concern, especially among the general public, for the safety of children. For example, in 1998, a 15-year-old male shot and killed his parents at home, then drove to school and killed 2 students, wounding 23 other students. In 1999, a school shooting in Littleton, Colorado involved 18- and 17-year-old classmates, who opened fire on faculty and students, targeting athletes and minorities. Twelve students and 1 teacher were killed, and 23 other students were injured in the shooting spree. These and other similar incidents have garnered the attention of parents, teachers, policymakers and researchers (Ewing, 1995). The question that everyone wants answered is: Why are these shootings and killings taking place in classrooms and schoolyards across the country?

Notwithstanding the controversy and publicity surrounding school violence, the Office of Juvenile Justice and Delinquency Prevention (OJJDP) reported that students are safer at school than they are away from school (Sickmund, Snyder, & Poe-Yamagata, 1997). Moreover, according to the FBI and the National Incident-Based Reporting System, from 1991 to 1996, one in five of all violent crimes with juvenile victims occurred outside of school between 3 p.m. and 7 p.m. on school days (Snyder & Sickmund, 1999). Although these statistics confirm the belief that schools are not the dangerous havens some pundits and politicians make them out to be, the question remains: How do we account for violent juvenile crime, especially homicide?

The National Center on School Safety (2000) listed murder as the second leading cause of death for persons between the ages of 15 and 24, the third leading cause of death for youth ages 5 to 15, and the fourth leading cause of death for children ages 1 to 4. Given the presence of juvenile homicide in society, the United States has a higher child mortality rate than do other industrialized countries. For example, between 1980 and 1997, nearly 38,000 juveniles were murdered in the United States.

A disturbing factor related to the homicide of children and adolescents is that juveniles perpetrate 26% of these crimes (Sickmund et al., 1997). According to the OJJDP's 1999 national report entitled, *Juvenile Offenders and Victims,* 1 in 4 juvenile murders involved an adolescent offender (Snyder & Sickmund, 1999). The victim and the offender were the same race in 91% of these crimes. These rates are alarming; however, studies reveal that among adolescent murders involving a juvenile offender, a decrease has occurred since 1997. Indeed, in 1980 approximately 400 juveniles were killed by adolescent offenders, and by 1994 this figure rose to 900 slain youth. However, by 1997 the number of youth murdered by adolescents dropped to 500 juveniles (Snyder & Sickmund).

According to the FBI (1997), youth involvement in homicide increases directly with age. For example, juvenile arrests in 1996 show that 16% were 15 years of age, 30% were 16 years of age, and 42% were 17 years of age. Youths 12 and under accounted for less than 1% of all homicide arrests. The OJJDP data indicate that of the juveniles killed by other youth, 13% of the victims were less than 6 years of age (Snyder & Sickmund, 1999). In 47% of youth homicides, the juvenile offender was the parent of the victim, and in 18% of these cases the juvenile offender was another family member. Of juveniles murdered by other adolescents, approximately 76% were slain by acquaintances and 19% were murdered by strangers.

The weapon of choice among children and adolescents ages 5 to 14 is a **firearm** (Ewing, 1995; Sickmund et al., 1997). Of the older juveniles killed by other adolescents, 77% were murdered with a firearm. According to the Center for Disease Control and Prevention, homicides involving a firearm accounted for about 10% of all murders among children ages 0 to 4. In contrast, 66% of homicides among children ages 5 to 14 involved a firearm. In other industrialized countries, firearms were involved in less than 25% of all killings in either age group. For example, Finland has the second highest rate of firearm-related homicides in children, and the rate in the United States is still more than twice the rate of Finland (Snyder & Sickmund, 1999). The accessibility to firearms is believed to account for part of the dramatic differences in homicide rates between the United States and other industrialized nations (FBI, 1997). Research suggests that the dramatic increase in juvenile homicides occurring since the mid-1980s is directly linked to gun-related homicides; therefore, restricting access of guns to juveniles should be an important consideration for Congress in the prevention of violent crime committed by youth (Snyder & Sickmund).

Demographics

Juveniles who commit murder are predominately male (Sickmund et al., 1997). Between 1980 and 1997, 93% of known juvenile homicide offenders were male (Snyder & Sickmund, 1999). Of the juvenile male offenders, 56% were Black, and between 1985 and 1994, the rate for Black youth committing homicide tripled from 44.3 to 139.6 per 100,000. The per year rates for adolescent girls committing homicide has risen consistently since 1984 (Snyder, Sickmund, & Poe-Yamagata, 2000). However, when compared to males, these rates are extremely low. For example, 6% of juveniles arrested in 1996 were girls. Girls tend to engage in more indirect, verbal, and relational aggression such as excluding peers from groups, and are less frequently engaged in the most serious forms of violence such as homicide and sexual violence. Moreover, males and females appear to have different motivations for their crimes as demonstrated by their different choices in victims. Fifty-four percent of the victims of male juvenile offenders are acquaintances, and 39% of the victims of females are family members (Snyder & Sickmund, 1999).

Juvenile homicide appears to be concentrated in major urban cities (Ewing, 1995; Snyder et al., 2000). The Federal Bureau of Investigation Supplementary Homicide Reports for 1997 indicated that one in four juvenile homicides occurred in five counties in the following cities: Los Angeles, Chicago, New York, Philadelphia, and Detroit. These findings demonstrate that juvenile homicide is concentrated in a small portion of the United States (Snyder & Sickmund, 1999).

Risk Factors

Risk factors for violence and aggression among youth have been identified in an effort to prevent and treat juveniles at risk for committing homicide (Snyder et al., 2000). Attention to these factors is of the utmost importance if the safety and prosperity of our nation's youth are to be ensured. The one factor consistently shown to be the best, single predictor of future violence is prior violent behavior (Farrington, 1991). Moreover, some researchers argue that a history of nonviolent behavior may not predict the severity of subsequent violence (Cornell, Benedek, & Benedek, 1987). Other key risk factors for violence and aggression in youth include poor school performance, a history of maltreatment or abuse, familial discord and maladjustment, substance abuse and access to drugs, mental or behavioral disorders, risk-taking behavior and impulsivity, negative attitudes, negative peer relations such as gang involvement or rejection by peers, limited parent–child interpersonal interactions, personal loss; neighborhood crime, and lack of social support (Heide, 1999).

Are There Patterns of Juvenile Violence?

In addition to specific personal or environmental risk factors for adolescent violence, investigators have identified four patterns that provide a theoretical basis for the origin of juvenile homicide (Elliott, Huizinga, & Ageton, 1985). When adolescents display one of these four patterns, they are at risk for juvenile delinquency and, in the extreme, youth homicide.

The first pattern involves situational violence. This is a type of violence driven by contextual factors such as aggression by another person, negative peer relations, or being part of a criminogenic environment. A criminogenic environment is highly disorganized, given the perceived high rates of crime, drug availability, poor housing, and gangs.

Relationship violence is the second pattern. This is common for adolescents and adults, and occurs within the context of existing associations. Relationship violence may take place as a result of interpersonal disputes or revenge that involves family members or friends.

Predatory violence is another pattern of adolescent violence. Predatory violence is perpetrated because of a youth's strong desire to take over the victim. Approximately 7% of male juveniles and 5% of female juveniles account for predatory violence.

Psychopathological violence is the final type of violence. It is caused by mental or emotional disturbance and is less predictable than are the other types of violence. For each of these categories, both an assessment of risk factors and an assessment of protective factors are important. Protective factors reduce the likelihood of future violence by curbing violence directly, or by lessening the negative impact of an existing risk factor

(Borum, 2000). An example of a protective factor may be the absence of substance-abusing behavior in the presence of other known risk factors.

The case example of a 17-year-old adolescent, convicted of murdering his best friend and sentenced to life in prison, highlights a number of factors that may contribute to a juvenile's decision to kill. In many respects, the youth may have seemed like the "boy next door." However, on closer inspection a number of situational factors such as societal influences, resource availability, and personality characteristics that provide greater insight into the motivation for the crime are revealed. He was a "latchkey child" and had little contact with his parents. He was obsessed with the military and he spent a lot of time watching war movies and idolizing military heroes. He learned to accept killing as an acceptable solution to problems, often practiced shooting, and fantasized about killing. When the adolescent killer found out that his friend had become involved with his girlfriend, the youth became enraged and was unable to deal with his feelings of betrayal. He felt that his friend had broken a rule of honor within their relationship and deserved to die. The adolescent had access to firearms and was mentally prepared to use one. In a follow-up interview conducted by Dr. Kathleen Heide, the youth stated he had been reading Stanton Samenow's book, *Inside the Criminal Mind* (1984), and was able to attribute his motivations for killing his friend to the need for power, excitement, control, and acceptance. The adolescent murderer said he felt he had no control and he wanted "everybody to know you can't do this to me" (Heide, 1999).

JUVENILE SEX OFFENDERS

Introduction

In the past, juveniles were excused from taking responsibility for their deviant sexual behaviors. The rationale was that these actions were part of the maturation process, and that these aggressive and exploitative behaviors were "adolescent adjustment reactions" or "exploratory" stages that would pass with age (Ryan & Lane, 1991, p. xi). Today, however, we know that sex offenses are extremely important to address, regardless of the age of the perpetrator (Flitton & Brager, 2002). Unfortunately, in the past 10 or 15 years we have only just begun to look at the incidence, prevalence, and causal factors surrounding this troubling form of antisocial conduct (Bartollas, 2000; National Center on Child Abuse and Neglect Reporting System, 2000). This section reviews a number of definitional matters pertaining to juvenile sex crimes, comments on both offender and victim characteristics, and explores some theories that account for this disturbing form of adolescent behavior.

Juvenile Sex Crimes and Definitional Matters

Sexually abusive behavior is defined as "any sexual interaction with person(s) of any age that is perpetrated (a) against the victim's will; (b) without consent; or (c) in an aggressive, exploitative, manipulative, or threatening manner. It may be characterized by one or more of a wide array of behaviors or multiple paraphilias (more than one type of sexual deviancy) . . . seen in a single individual" (Ryan & Lane, 1991, p. 3). When dealing with adolescent sex offenders, it is difficult to discern what can (and should) be identified and treated as a sex crime because the customary markers used for adults, such as age and behavior, do not function (or necessarily apply) as substantial requirements (Flitton & Brager, 2002). However, the identifier most commonly employed when distinguishing juvenile offenders from nonoffenders is the presence or absence of exploitation in the interaction (Allan, Middleton, & Browne, 1997; Hanson, 2000). Clearly, the violent rape and molestation of a 6-year-old at the hands of a 15-year-old is treated as a sex offense. However, when the chronological ages of the juveniles are closer together and the sexual interaction is less aggressive or intrusive, then other factors or variables regarding the situation must be evaluated, prior to treating the incident as a sex offense. The factors considered when assessing whether an adolescent sexual relationship is exploitative are equality, consent, and coercion (Ryan & Lane, 1991). Each of these variables is briefly explained.

If the two children involved in the sexual interaction are physically, developmentally, cognitively, and emotionally equal to each other, then exploitative behaviors are less likely to be present. According to the National Task Force on Juvenile Sexual Offending, in order for consent to be present, an agreement must be struck by the participants (Ryan & Lane, 1991). This agreement must include *all* of the following criteria: "(1) understanding what is proposed based on age, maturity, developmental level, functioning, and experience; (2) knowledge of societal standards for what is being proposed; (3) awareness of potential consequences and alternatives; (4) assumption that agreements or disagreements will be respected equally; (5) voluntary decision; [and] (6) mental competence" (p. 5). Coercion occurs when the victim feels pressured or forced to engage in the sexual interaction. One way to gauge coercion is to assess the power imbalance that may exist between the two children.

A related feature to the exploitative character of adolescent sexual behavior is whether any secondary gains are employed in the interaction. Secondary gains include such things as the use of monetary or nonmonetary services in exchange for sex. In these instances, the transaction is mediated by something other than a genuine adolescent sexual relationship in which a youth is enticed to participate in sex. All of these variables must be considered when determining whether the interaction between the two juveniles entails exploitation.

Offender Characteristics and Victim Characteristics

It is difficult to develop a universal profile on juvenile sex offenders for the same reasons the adult sex offender typology is difficult (Graves, Openshaw, Ascione, & Ericksen, 1996; U.S. Department of Justice, 1995). Adolescent sex offenders are a heterogeneous group and the process of determining whether or not the interaction itself can be classified criminally is daunting (Knight, Rosenberg, & Scheinder, 1985; National Center on Child Abuse and Neglect Reporting System, 2000). Thus, it should come as no surprise that a global portrait for the juvenile sex offender does not exist (Flitton & Brager, 2002). However, researchers have been able to identify incidence and prevalence rates, as well as common characteristics, including the demographics for this population.

The prevalence of juvenile sex offenders in the United States today is alarming. Indeed, according to the National Center on Child Abuse and Neglect (NCCAN, 1987), it was estimated that in 1986 there had been 2.25 million cases of alleged child abuse reported, and 1.5 million of these cases were confirmed that same year. The incidence rate of sexual child abuse was 2.5 per 1,000. By 1993, there were reports of nearly 3 million alleged cases of child abuse (U.S. Department of Justice, 1995). More recent research suggests that the incidence rate of child sexual abuse has not fluctuated significantly, remaining at approximately 2 per 1,000 cases (National Center on Child Abuse and Neglect Reporting System, 2000). Investigators report that juveniles are responsible for approximately 30% of child sexual abuse cases (Finkelhor, 1996). Problems with compiling data on the incidence and prevalence of adolescent sex offenders are perhaps best illustrated with research done on first-time offenders (U.S. Department of Justice, 1995). Although a majority of juveniles were held for their initial sex crime, the average number of victims reported was seven. These findings demonstrate the high incidence of the offense, as well as the chronic under-reporting common with such an offense type (National Center on Child Abuse and Neglect Report System).

As previously indicated, a universal profile of the juvenile sex offender does not exist. However, there are some general characteristics shared by a majority of these offenders (Fehrenbach, Smith, Monastersky, & Deisher, 1986; Graves et al., 1996). At the time of arrest, an estimated 70% of juvenile offenders are currently living in a two-parent household, although half reported that at some time in their life there had been some form of parental loss, by divorce, separation, or death. A significant number of these offenders are enrolled in school and achieve average grades. Socioeconomic status (SES) varies among these individuals; although a majority come from middle and lower SES families (Flitton & Brager, 2002). Overwhelmingly, these offenders are male (between 91% and 93%) and predominantly White (Graves et al., 1996). A prior sexual offense is reported among a significant number of the juveniles, along with a majority of them diagnosed with a psychiatric disorder at one point in their lives (Flitton & Brager, 2002).

The victims of juvenile sex offenders tend to be young children (Bartollas, 2000; U.S. Department of Justice, 1995). Research indicates that 62% are under 12 years old and 44% are under the age of 6 (Finkelhor, 1996). The majority of victims (69% to 84%) are female (National Center on Child Abuse and Neglect Reporting System, 2000). Figures such as these clearly suggest that juvenile sex offender behavior entails the victimization of adolescent girls more than any other cohort, and treatment and prevention strategies should be tailored to address this particular form of adolescent sexual misconduct (U.S. Department of Justice, 1995).

Theories of Juvenile Sexual Offending

A number of theories accounting for the onset of sexual offending committed by juveniles have been proposed. However, the sex offender research community generally acknowledges that there is a process or a series of stages that this offender passes through, commencing with the initial thought of the sex crime and concluding with the feelings and behaviors the individual experiences after the offense has been committed. This process is identified as the **sexual abuse cycle** (Lane, 1991). Understanding this cycle is beneficial not only in relation to the offense but also in treating the youthful sex offender with the goal of preventing future criminality (Flitton & Brager, 2002). "The sexual abuse cycle represents the antecedents, components, patterns, and progression of sexually abusive behavior" (Lane, 1991, p. 77). This concept, originally named the "rape cycle," was developed by the Closed Adolescent Treatment Center (CATC) of the Colorado Division of Youth Services in 1977 to 1978 (Lane & Zamora, 1984) and subsequently revised into its present form. The sexual abuse cycle describes the cognitive, affective, and behavioral processes that occur within the juvenile offender before, during, and after the offense (Perry & Orchard, 1992). Thus, it is not an empirically validated causal model.

The sexual abuse cycle begins when the juvenile responds to a triggering event. His views of the world, his beliefs, and his overall life experiences have given him a negative outlook toward the future. This stage is called *negative anticipation.* The individual begins to feel hopeless and attempts to avoid the issue altogether. When this avoidance is unsuccessful, the youth becomes resentful and angry and endeavors to exert power over others in nonsexual ways. As this power is displayed and celebrated, the child fantasizes about other controlling and gratifying behaviors, such as sex. This exertion of control and power is eventually expressed outwardly in a sexual manner. The offender then attempts to deal with the offense and the feelings that go along with the fear of being apprehended for the misconduct. This is called *fugitive thinking.* Finally, through the use of thinking errors, the individual assimilates the behavior. The cycle is then set to repeat itself. It is important to note that every time a trigger occurs, a sexual offense is not necessarily committed. The juvenile only goes as far through the cycle as is needed to feel relief and improved self-esteem.

In chapter 5 the typologies and classifications of adult sex offenders are reviewed. Although researchers continue to debate the viability of creating a specific model for the juvenile offender, adult typologies, such as the Massachusetts Treatment Center: Child Molester, Version 3 **(MTC:CM3)** instrument (Knight, 1989; Knight, Carter, & Prentky, 1989), is a useful tool by which to understand the juvenile sex offender (Knight & Prentky, 1993). Thus, readers are encouraged to review the material presented in chapter 5 on adult sex offenders to further assess how best to respond to the problems posed by juvenile sex offenders and this form of criminal behavior (Perry & Orchard, 1992).

BINDING OVER OR WAIVER PROCESS

Introduction

In addition to assessing the delinquent and criminal behaviors committed by youth, it is important to understand the judicial decision that must be made about how they will be tried and treated under the law. In many jurisdictions, youth are tried as adults, especially if their offenses are grave enough to warrant this determination. This is called the *binding over* or *waiver process.* In this final section, the phenomenon of waiving juveniles to the adult criminal court system is examined. In particular, commentary on the types of adolescent waivers that exist are described, the implications of transfer to the adult system are discussed, and the possible effects of the waiver process on the adolescent's behavior and development are considered.

Types of Adolescent Waivers

The objective of juvenile justice is to pursue the best interests of the child (Singer, 1999). A separate justice system was created for juveniles because of the developmental differences between adults and adolescents. Juveniles are thought to be capable of rehabilitation and are vulnerable to negative influences within the adult criminal justice system (Coalition for Juvenile Justice, 1995). Adolescent offenders are involved in one of three types of proceedings: juvenile proceedings with no possibility of adult punishment, juvenile proceedings with some possibility of adult punishment, and criminal proceedings with adult punishment (Grisso & Schwartz, 2003). The latter two processes require that the adolescent offender be evaluated for competence to be tried as an adult (Barnum, 2000; McKee, 1998).

According to the law, a juvenile is anyone under the age of 18; however, individuals between the ages of 16 and 18, and as low as 12 in some states, are often prosecuted as adults (Grisso & Schwartz, 2003). When an adolescent is transferred from juvenile court to the criminal court system the process is called a *waiver* or a *transfer*. Core principles behind waivers include removing violent youthful offenders from the juvenile justice system and eliminating confidentiality for serious adolescent offenders (Garcetti & O'Leary, 1994). Prior to waiving the jurisdiction of juvenile offenders to criminal court, the Virginia waiver statute mandates that the juvenile court must find the offender competent for adjudication (Bonnie & Grisso, 2000).

There are two types of waivers that assist in determining whether a youth should be tried as an adult. These are legislative waivers and judicial waivers. In some states, legislative waivers are also known as *direct file waivers*. Legislative waivers, or direct filing, exclude certain offenses from the jurisdiction of the juvenile courts, requiring adult criminal courts to handle adolescents charged with specific offenses (Singer, 1999).

Legislative waivers are designed to elicit a stronger response to serious juvenile crime than the response elicited by the process of judicial waivers (Feld, 1999). When considering a plea for a legislative waiver, several evaluations must be made. These evaluations include (a) the level of criminal sophistication demonstrated by the youth, (b) the possibility of rehabilitation before the juvenile court jurisdiction ends, (c) previous delinquent history, (d) the success or failure of previous rehabilitation attempts, and (e) the severity of the offense committed and the circumstances in which the crime occurred. Some of the crimes that subject juveniles between the ages of 16 and 18 to prosecution in adult criminal courts are murder, rape with force or threat of bodily harm, robbery while armed with a deadly or dangerous weapon, kidnapping with bodily harm, assault with a firearm or destructive device, escape from any juvenile hall or group home by use of force or violence, and carjacking while armed with a deadly or dangerous weapon (Scott, 2002).

Judicial waivers, however, give discretionary power to the judges who can waive juveniles into the adult system on their authorization. Judicial waivers are a frequently pursued alternative for dealing with serious juvenile offenders (Grisso & Schwartz, 2003). The purpose of judicial waivers is to impose harsher punishments than those administered by the juvenile court system (Fritsch, Caeti, & Hemmens, 1996). Judicial waivers are influenced by several factors. These factors include (a) the offender's age, (b) the present offense committed by the adolescent, (c) the youth's past record, (d) the weapon or weapons used during the crime, (e) the severity of the harm inflicted on or caused to the victims of the offense, (f) the gender of the juvenile, and (g) the race of the offender. Judicial waivers are often subject to a judge's personal prejudices and they may illustrate racial biases (Scott, 2002). Juvenile transfer hearings often occur if a judicial waiver is not mandated. In a judicial transfer hearing, the state must prove that the adolescent was not responsive to treatment in the juvenile justice system. In a transfer hearing, the youth must be deemed competent (Barnum, 2000). In other words, the juvenile must be able to understand the wrongfulness of his behavior, be aware of available alternatives to imprisonment, and be able to communicate effectively with counsel (Steinberg & Schwartz, 2000).

The Implications of Transfer to the Adult System

Through the implementation of waivers, the juvenile offender's due process rights guaranteed by the Sixth and Fourteenth Amendments may be violated. There are two principal cases that have influenced the due process rights for juveniles. These cases are *Kent v. United*

States (1966) and *In Re Gault* (1967). The United States Supreme Court in the *Kent* case concluded that juvenile waiver procedures required a full hearing, that adolescents possessed the right to counsel at waiver hearings, that counsel had the right to access all records used in the waiver hearing, and that the judge was compelled to issue a statement explaining the reasons for the waiver. The decision in *Kent* indicated that the criteria for being waived to criminal court included sophistication and maturity expressed in the home, impact of the environment, emotional outlook, and lifestyle (Cauffman & Steinberg, 2000). The Court in the case of *Gault* found that children who commit serious crimes should be treated the same as adults in criminal court. Moreover, the Court in the *Gault* decision ruled that juveniles have certain due process rights in court hearings. In other words, youth are required to have adequate, timely, written notice of the charges against them; the right to counsel; the right to confront and cross-examine witnesses; and the privilege against self-incrimination.

Once waived to criminal court, adult sanctions, such as the death penalty, can be administered to an adolescent. The United States is only one of three countries that currently executes juveniles for the crimes they commit if waived to the adult system. The other two countries that endorse this practice are Iran and Iraq. Since 1979, 14 juvenile-convicted executions have occurred, 9 of which were in the United States. Opponents of waivers believe that imposing the death penalty on juvenile-committed crimes ignores or dismisses the possible reasons for the offense. Some of these reasons may be higher impulsivity and vulnerability among the juvenile population rather than the adult population, and a false sense of power and immortality in the perceptions of youth (Coalition for Juvenile Justice, 1995). However, advocates of the waiver process maintain that the primary goal of society must be to punish adolescent offenders and not rehabilitate them. Therefore, as these critics contend, sanctions such as life imprisonment or the death penalty should parallel the heinousness of the crime and not the age of the offender (Garcetti & O'Leary, 1994).

There may be dangerous implications in sending juvenile offenders to the adult criminal court system (Feld, 1999). Once transferred, adolescent offenders are often regarded as outcasts and negatively stereotyped. The stigma associated with being an accused adult criminal is far greater than the stigma of being accused and tried in the juvenile court system. Society's response to criminally convicted juveniles is mostly unflattering (Scott, 2002). Indeed, often youth convicted of adult crimes are considered adults who lack the potential for rehabilitation rather than juveniles who possess the possibility of reform (Bishop, Frazier, Lanza-Kaduce, & Winner, 1996).

The use of waiver legislation can be examined through a comparison of arrest data. In 1971, less than 1% of juveniles were taken to criminal court; that is, less than 1% of individuals under the age of 18 were waived to adult criminal court and prosecuted as adults. However, in 1996, 6% of juveniles arrested were taken to adult criminal court. Another statistic that measures the use of waivers is the rate at which adolescents are sent to criminal court in small versus large cities. In the latter instance (cities with over 250,000 inhabitants), the average rate of sending juveniles to criminal court is 1%. In the former instances (cities with fewer than 10,000 inhabitants), the average rate of sending juveniles to criminal court is 9% (Singer, 1999). Both of these statistics are useful in determining the level of implementation on juvenile waivers.

Possible Effects of the Waiver Process on the Adolescent's Behavior and Development

When adult sanctions are imposed on most juvenile offenders, the likelihood of becoming a career offender increases (Feld, 1999). An adult sentence may have direct and indirect negative effects on long-term factors such as education, employment, and social adaptability. Most adolescent offenders will outgrow their desire to engage in criminal activity; therefore, adult penalties will not generate positive outcomes. One method suggested as a more effective strategy than the waiver process for dealing with wayward youth is to teach them lessons in accountability that successfully prepare them to develop appropriate adult roles

How Are Individual States Implementing and Responding to Juvenile Waiver

Increasingly, states are now taking the initiative to handle juveniles who commit serious crimes (Scott, 2002). Most of these actions are adopted from New York's 1978 Juvenile Offender Law, which makes the adult criminal court the tribunal of initial jurisdiction for eligible youth (Singer, 1999). For example, in Oregon, children who are 12 years old and over cannot claim an "incapacity due to immaturity" defense and, therefore, they are tried in criminal court. In Kansas, children age 10 and over can be sent to the adult system, depending on the seriousness and severity of the crime. Connecticut has implemented an automatic transfer to criminal court of any juvenile, 14 years of age or older, who engages in a class A or B felony (Loken & Rosettenstein, 1999). In California, the Welfare and Institutions Code Section 707 states that if a juvenile is over the age of 16 and commits a serious crime, he or she could be prosecuted in adult criminal court (Scott, 2002). In Florida, prosecutors are allowed to file criminal charges against juveniles of any age without a prior judicial waiver hearing. This procedure in Florida is known as direct filing (Loken & Rosettenstein, 1999).

One of the most significant reforms in waiver legislation took place in Florida. In 1978, Florida began implementing a direct file system of waivers in which prosecutors were given authority to file criminal charges against juvenile offenders without prior judicial waiver hearings. Florida has continuously increased this power for prosecutors; however, it has led to a decline in transfers. In Georgia, similar legislation has been implemented to expand the power of prosecutors, allowing them to try juveniles in adult court more effortlessly. Youth arrested in Georgia and in other states for offenses requiring a transfer to criminal court often receive juvenile sanctions despite the legislative waivers transferring them to criminal court. This reverse-waiver procedure prevents juveniles from being incarcerated in adult correctional facilities (Loken & Rosettenstein, 1999).

Many states have adopted reverse-waiver legislation. Typically, these statutes stipulate that (a) juveniles may be arraigned in criminal court, but they are given the right to transfer back to the juvenile court; and (b) there are "mandatory" waiver requirements for certain offenses (Loken & Rosettenstein, 1999). The implementation of reverse waivers reduces the number of juvenile offenders sentenced and classified as adults. Moreover, providing the right to transfer back to juvenile court gives the juvenile offender an opportunity to escape the possibility of being detained with adult career offenders in the prison system.

(Scott, 2000). However, investigators note that juveniles who frequently commit serious crimes at a young age are likely to become career offenders (Moffit, 1993). Thus, severe sanctions sought through the waiver process may be justified for these chronic delinquents (Scott, 2000). Overall, the transfer process is becoming a more routine practice in the prosecution and sentencing of juvenile offenders (Feld, 1999).

Advocates of waiver reform argue that children who commit serious crimes should receive the same treatment as that of their adult criminal counterparts (Scott, 2002). As they argue, this does not occur, especially when acknowledging that punishment has replaced rehabilitation as the preferred method of intervention for adolescent misconduct (Bernard, 1992). Indeed, the adult system focuses on punishment *and* retribution, whereas the juvenile system focuses on rehabilitation alone. In this context, individual differences among adolescent offenders are not taken into account when these widely adopted legislative and judicial waiver practices are implemented. This model of courtroom justice raises significant questions about the nature of retribution and rehabilitation for adults and juveniles. Readers are encouraged to read the section addressing this debate in chapter 11 in relation to correctional intervention.

DISCUSSION QUESTIONS

1. What role do parents play in preventing or curbing the possibility of juvenile delinquency? How does physical abuse against children and exposure to marital violence increase the likelihood for adolescent misconduct?

2. Are divorced and single-parent families responsible for the presence of adolescent

misconduct in society? Explain your response. Should parents be accountable for the delinquency of their children under the law? Justify your response.

3. What are status crimes? How can we account for this form of criminal behavior, according to social psychological theory?

4. What are the three explanations for the drug–crime relationship? What are some of the risk factors for substance-abusing adolescent offenders?

5. What are the similarities between the drug and criminal lifestyles? Explain how these likenesses operate in the everyday lives of adolescents.

6. Is school violence a problem in society today? On what do you base your position? What is the classroom avenger? How are boys and girls who engage in school violence different and similar?

7. What role do bullies play in perpetuating school violence? How are teachers and other educational personnel affected by the behavior of bullies in classrooms and elsewhere on school grounds?

8. What are some of the demographics for juvenile murderers? What are some of the risk factors for violence among youth? From your perspective, is juvenile homicide a significant problem? Justify your response.

9. What is the definition of a juvenile sex offender? What are the demographic and related characteristics of offenders? How does the sexual abuse cycle function and what are its major components?

10. What are the two types of adolescent waivers and how do they function? What are the implications of juvenile transfer to the adult system? Does transfer make adolescents more likely to become adult criminals? Explain your response. Is the waiver process just another form of punishing youth? Justify your answer.

REFERENCES

Allan, J., Middleton, D., & Browne, K. (1997). Different clients, different needs? Practical issues in community-based treatment for sex offenders. *Criminal Behavior and Mental Health, 7,* 69–84.

American Psychiatric Association. (2000). *Diagnostic and statistical manual of mental disorders* (4th ed., Text revision). Washington DC: American Psychiatric Association.

Aronson, E. (2000). *Nobody left to hate: Teaching compassion after Columbine.* New York: Worth.

Artz, S. (1998). *Sex, power, and the violent school girl.* New York: Trifolium Books.

Atkinson, R. L., Atkinson, R. C., Smith, E., & Bem, D. (1990). *Introduction to psychology.* Orlando, FL: Harcourt Brace Jovanovich.

Barnett, O. W., Miller-Perrin, C. L., & Perrin, R. D. (1997). *Family violence across the lifespan.* Thousand Oaks, CA: Sage.

Barnum, R. (2000). Clinical and forensic evaluation of competence to stand trial in juvenile defendants. In T. Grisso & R. G. Schwartz (Eds.), *Youth on trial: A developmental perspective on juvenile justice* (pp. 193–223). Chicago: University of Chicago Press.

Bartol, C. R. (2002). *Criminal behavior: A psychosocial perspective.* Upper Saddle River, NJ: Prentice Hall.

Bartollas, C. (2000). *Juvenile delinquency* (5th ed.). Boston: Allyn & Bacon.

Bernard, T. J. (1992). *The cycle of juvenile justice.* New York: Oxford University Press.

Bishop, D. M., Frazier, C. E., Lanza-Kaduce, L., & Winner, L. (1996). The transfer of juveniles to criminal court: Does it make a difference? *Crime and Delinquency, 42*(2), 171.

Bonnie, R. J., & Grisso, T. (2000). Adjudicative competence and youthful offenders. In T. Grisso & R. G. Schwartz (Eds.), *Youth on trial: A developmental perspective on juvenile justice* (pp. 73–103). Chicago: University of Chicago Press.

Borum, R. (2000). Assessing violence risk among youth. *Journal of Clinical Psychology, 56,* 1263–1288.

Cauffman, E., & Steinberg, L. (2000). Researching adolescents' judgment and culpability. In T. Grisso & R. G. Schwartz (Eds.), *Youth on trial: A developmental perspective on juvenile justice* (pp. 325–343). Chicago: University of Chicago Press.

Chesney-Lind, M., & Shelden, R. G. (1992). *Girls, delinquency, and juvenile justice.* Pacific Grove, CA: Brooks/Cole.

Coalition for Juvenile Justice. (1995). Fewer juveniles should be tried as adults. In D. Bender & B. Leone (Eds.), *Juvenile crime: Opposing viewpoints* (pp. 180–186). San Diego: Greenhaven Press, Inc.

Cornell, D., Benedek, E., & Benedek, D. (1987). Juvenile homicide: Prior adjustment and a proposed typology. *American Journal of Orthopsychiatry, 57,* 383–393.

Davies, R. (1997). Violent child and his family. In V. Varma (Ed.), *Violence in children and adolescents* (pp. 111–122). London: Jessica Kingsley.

Deitch, D., Koutsenok, I., & Ruzi, A. (2000). The relationship between crime and drugs: What we have learned in recent decades. *Journal of Psychoactive Drugs, 32*(4), 391–407.

Drowns, R., & Hess, K. (2000). *Juvenile Justice* (3rd ed.). Stamford, CT: Wadsworth.

Dryfoos, J. G. (1990). *Adolescent at risk: Prevalence and prevention*. New York: Oxford University Press.

Elliott, D. S., Huizinga, D., & Ageton, S. S. (1985). *Explaining delinquency and drug use*. Beverly Hills, CA: Sage.

Elliott, D. S., Huizinga, D., & Morse, B. (1986). Self-reported violent offending. *Journal of Interpersonal Violence, 1,* 472–514.

Erikson, E. H. (1950/1963). *Childhood and society* (2nd ed.). New York: Norton.

Ewing, C. P. (1995). *Kids who kill*. New York: Avon.

Farrington, D. (1991). Childhood aggression and adult violence: Early precursors and later life outcomes. In D. Pepler & K. Rubin (Eds.), *The development and treatment of childhood aggression* (pp. 5–29). Hillsdale, NJ: Erlbaum.

Federal Bureau of Investigation. (1997). *Uniform Crime Reports—1996*. Washington DC: U.S. Department of Justice.

Fehrenbach, P. A., Smith, W., Monastersky, C., & Deisher, R. W. (1986). Adolescent sexual offenders: Offender and offense characteristics. *American Journal of Orthopsychiatry, 56,* 225–233.

Feld, B. C. (1999). *Bad kids: Race and the transformation of the juvenile court*. New York: Oxford.

Finkelhor, D. (1996, August). Keynote address. Presented at the International Conference on Child Abuse and Neglect, Dublin, Ireland.

Flitton, A. R., & Brager, R. C. (2002). Juvenile sex offenders: Assessment and treatment. In N. G. Ribner (Ed.), *The handbook of juvenile forensic psychology* (pp. 343–362). San Francisco, CA: Jossey-Bass.

Fox, J. A. (1998). Both prevention programs and punishment are needed to control juvenile crime. In P. A. Winters (Ed.), *Crime: Current controversies* (pp. 115–120). San Diego: Greenhaven Press.

Fried, S., & Fried, P. (1996). *Bullies and victims: Helping your child survive the schoolyard battlefield*. New York: M. Evans and Company.

Fritsch, E. J., Caeti, T. J., & Hemmens, C. (1996). Spare the needle but not the punishment: The incarceration of waived youth in Texas prisons. *Crime and Delinquency, 42*(4), 593–609.

Garcetti, G., & O'Leary, B. S. (1994). More juveniles should be tried as adults. In D. Bender & B. Leone (Eds.), *Juvenile crime: Opposing viewpoints* (pp. 175–179). San Diego: Greenhaven Press.

Gottfredson, M. R., & Hirschi, T. (1990). *A general theory of crime*. Stanford, CA: Stanford University Press.

Graves, R. B., Openshaw, D. K., Ascione, F. R., & Ericksen, S. L. (1996). Demographic and parental characteristics of youthful sexual offenders. *International Journal of Offender Therapy and Comparative Criminology, 40,* 249–254.

Grisso, T., & Schwartz, R. G. (2003). *Youth on trial: A developmental perspective on juvenile justice*. Chicago: University of Chicago Press.

Hanson, R. K. (2000). Will they do it again? Predicting sex-offense recidivism. *Current Directions in Psychological Science, 9,* 106–109.

Heide, K. M. (1999). *Young killers: The challenge of juvenile homicide*. Thousand Oaks, CA: Sage.

Hirschi, T. (1969). *Causes of delinquency*. Berkeley, CA: University of California Press.

Hirschi, T., & Gottfredson, M. R. (1983). Age and the explanation of crime. *American Journal of Sociology, 89,* 552–584.

Holden, G. W. (1998). Introduction: Development of research into another consequence of family violence. In G. W. Holden, R. Geffner, & E. N. Jouriles (Eds.), *Children exposed to marital violence: Theory, research and applied issues* (pp. 1–18). Washington, DC: American Psychological Association.

Howell, J. (1998). National council on crime and delinquency's survey of juvenile detention and correctional facilities. *Crime and Delinquency, 44,* 102–109.

In re Gault, 387 U.S. 187, S. Ct. 1428 (1967).

Johnson, J. (1992). *Criminal victimization in the United States*. Washington DC: Bureau of Justice Statistics.

Kaplan, S. J., Labruna, V., Pelcovitz, D., Salzinger, S., Mandel, F., & Weiner, M. (1999). Physically abused adolescents: Behavior problems, functional impairment, and comparison of informants' reports. *Pediatrics, 104,* 43–49.

Kaplan, S. J., Pelcovitz, D., Salzinger, S., Weiner, M., Mandel, F. S., Lesser, M. L., et al. (1998). Adolescent physical abuse: Risk for adolescent psychiatric disorders. *American Journal of Psychiatry, 155,* 954–959.

Kent v. United States, 383 U.S. 451 (1966).

Knight, R. A. (1989). An assessment of the concurrent validity of a child molester typology. *Journal of Interpersonal Violence, 4,* 131–150.

Knight, R. A., Carter, D. L., & Prentky, R. A. (1989). A system for the classification of child molesters: Reliability and application. *Journal of Interpersonal Violence, 4,* 3–23.

Knight, R. A., & Prentky, R. A. (1993). Exploring characteristics for classifying juvenile sex offenders. In H. E. Barbaree, W. L. Marshall, & S. M. Hudson (Eds.), *The juvenile sex offender.* New York: Guilford.

Knight, R. A., Rosenberg, R., & Schneider, B. A. (1985). Classification of sexual offenders: Perspectives, methods, and validation. In A. W. Burgess (Ed.), *Rape and sexual assault* (pp. 222–293). New York: Garland.

Lane, S. (1991). The sexual abuse cycle. In G. Ryan & S. Lane (Eds.), *Juvenile sexual offending: Causes, consequences, and corrections* (pp. 103–141). San Francisco: New Lexington Press.

Lane, S., & Zamora, P. (1984). A method for treating the violent sex offender. In R. Mathias, P. Demuro, & R. Allinson (Eds.), *Violent juvenile offenders.* San Francisco: National Council on Crime and Delinquency.

Lawrence, R. (1998). *School crime and juvenile justice.* New York: Oxford.

Loken, G. A., & Rosettenstein, D. (1999). The juvenile justice counter-reformation: Children and adolescents as adult criminals. *Quinnipac Law Review, 18,* 351–392.

Maginnis, R. L. (1997). Single-parent families cause juvenile crime. In A. E. Sadler (Ed.), *Juvenile crime: Opposing viewpoints* (pp. 62–66). San Diego: Greenhaven Press.

McDonald, J. (2001, March 6). Teen smiled and reloaded witnesses say; anger over bullying may be the motive. *San Diego Union-Tribune,* p. 1.

McGee, J. P., & DeBernardo, C. R. (1999). The classroom avenger: Behavioral profile of school based shootings. *Forensic Examiner, 8,* 16–18.

McKee, G. (1998). Competency to stand trial in preadjudicatory juveniles and adults. *Journal of the American Academy of Psychiatry and the Law, 26,* 88–99.

Moffit, T. E. (1993). Adolescence-limited and life-course persistent antisocial behavior: A developmental taxonomy. *Psychological Review, 100,* 674–701.

National Center on Child Abuse and Neglect. (1987). *Child abuse and neglect national statistics.* Washington DC: U.S. Department of Health and Human Services.

National Center on Child Abuse and Neglect Reporting System. (2000, April). *Child abuse and neglect national statistics.* Washington DC: U.S. Department of Health and Human Services.

National Center on School Safety. (2002). *School associated violent deaths.* Westlake Village, CA: National Center on School Safety.

Patterson, S., Lennings, C. J., & Davey, J. (2000). Methadone clients, crime, and substance abuse. *International Journal of Offender Therapy and Comparative Criminology, 44*(6), 667–680.

Perry, G. P., & Orchard, J. (1992). *Assessment and treatment of adolescent sex offenders.* Sarasota, FL: Professional Resource Press, Professional Resource Exchange.

Petersen, G. J., Pietrzak, D., & Speaker, K. M. (1998). The enemy within: A national study on school violence and prevention. *Urban Education, 33,* 331–359.

Regoli, R., & Hewitt, J. (2000). *Delinquency in society* (4th ed.). Boston: McGraw-Hill.

Rossman, B. B., Hughes, H. M., & Rosenberg, M. S. (2000). *Children and interpersonal violence: Impact of exposure.* Philadelphia, PA: Taylor & Francis.

Rubenstein, E. (1998). Social factors cause crime. In P. A. Winters (Ed.), *Crime: Current controversies* (pp. 17–21). San Diego: Greenhaven Press.

Ryan, G., & Lane, S. (Eds.). (1991). *Juvenile sexual offending: Causes, consequences, and corrections.* San Francisco: New Lexington Press.

Samborn, H. V. (1996). Kids' crimes can send parents to jail. *American Bar Association Journal, 82,* 28–37.

Samenow, S. E. (1984). *Inside the criminal mind.* New York: Crown Business.

Schrof, J. M., & Thomas, G. (1999). Who's guilty? *U.S. News & World Report, 126,* 60–62.

Scott, C. L. (2002). Juvenile waivers to adult court. In D. Schetky & E. Benedek (Eds.), *Principles and practice of child and adolescent forensic psychiatry.* Washington DC: American Psychiatric Association.

Scott, E. S. (2000). Criminal responsibility in adolescence: Lessons from developmental psychology. In T. Grisso & R. G. Schwartz (Eds.), *Youth on trial: A developmental perspective on juvenile justice* (pp. 291–324). Chicago: University of Chicago Press.

Sheldon, R., Horvath, J., Tracy, J., & Sharon, T. (1989). Do status offenders get worse? Some clarifications in the question of escalation. *Crime and Delinquency, 35,* 202–216.

Sickmund, M., Snyder, H. N., & Poe-Yamagata, E. (1997). *Juvenile offenders and victims: 1997 update on violence.* Washington DC: Office of Juvenile Justice and Delinquency Prevention.

Siegel, L., & Senna, J. (2000). *Juvenile delinquency: Theory, practice, and law.* Belmont, CA: Wadsworth.

Singer, S. I. (1999). The significance of place in bringing juveniles into criminal court. *Quinnipiac Law Review, 18,* 643–668.

Simpson, M. D. (1999). Laws that make parents pay. *NEA Today, 17,* 25.

Snyder, H. N., & Sickmund, M. (1999). *Juvenile offenders and victims: 1999 national report.* Washington DC: Office of Juvenile Justice and Delinquency Prevention.

Snyder, H. N., Sickmund, M., & Poe-Yamagata, E. (2000). *Juvenile transfer to criminal court in the 1990s: Lessons learned from four studies.* Washington DC: Office of Juvenile Justice and Delinquency Prevention.

Steinberg, L., & Schwartz, R. G. (2000). Developmental psychology goes to court. In T. Grisso & R. G. Schwartz (Eds.), *Youth on trial: A developmental perspective on juvenile justice* (pp. 9–31). Chicago: University of Chicago Press.

Stern, S. B., & Smith, C. A. (1999). Reciprocal relationships between antisocial behavior and parenting: Implications for delinquency intervention. *Families in Society, 80,* 169–181.

Stevenson, M. R., & Black, K. N. (1996). *How divorce affects offspring: Research approach.* Boulder, CO: Westview Press.

Sutton, J. R. (1988). *Stubborn children: Controlling delinquency in the United States, 1640–1981.* Berkeley, CA: University of California Press.

Tsytsarev, S., Manger, J., & Lodrini, D. (2000). The use of reinforcement and punishment on incarcerated and probated substance-abusing juvenile offenders. *International Journal of Offender Therapy and Comparative Criminology, 44,* 22–32.

Turpin, J. (2000). Juvenile justice legislation 1999: Change in focus. *Corrections Today, 62,* 159.

U.S. Department of Education, Office of Educational Research and Improvement. (1999). *Indicators of school crime and safety* (NCES 1999-057, NCJ-178906). Washington DC: U.S. Government Printing Office.

U.S. Department of Justice. (1995). *Victims of childhood sexual abuse: Later criminal consequences.* Washington DC: Office of Justice Programs, Bureau of Justice Statistics.

Walters, G. D. (1998). *Changing lives of crime and drugs: Intervening with substance-abusing offenders.* Chichester, England: Wiley.

Wright, K. N., & Wright, K. E. (1997). Single-parent families may not cause crime. In A. E. Sadler (Ed.), *Juvenile crime: Opposing viewpoints* (pp. 67–74). San Diego: Greenhaven Press.

Mental Illness

In addition to examining criminal behavior from the perspective of juvenile conduct and adolescent development, some researchers question whether there is a link between offender behavior and the presence of **mental illness**. This chapter examines this relationship in some detail. In particular, considerable attention is given to what we know about psychiatric disorders, especially their onset, maintenance, and treatment, and how specific manifestations of mental illness correlate with antisocial or criminal conduct. Along these lines, chapter 8 provides statistical information on the prevalence of psychiatric illness among various types of offenders, discusses the connection between specific mental disorders and expressions of criminality and reviews the literature on how the legal and psychiatric systems understand the competency of persons with mental illness in various contexts. The chapter concludes by examining several unique situations in which mental illness can be used as a defense in a criminal court. In short, **battered woman syndrome, posttraumatic stress disorder,** and the **Black rage defense** are explored. As this chapter reveals, not all offenders who engage in violent criminal acts are mentally ill, and not all psychiatrically disordered individuals are prone to behave violently. However, there is a connection between crime and mental illness, and this association deepens our regard for the nature of criminal behavior.

Antisocial personality disorder	Delusions
Axis I disorders	Depressive symptoms
Battered child syndrome	Dissociative state
Battered woman syndrome	Dual diagnosis
Bipolar disorder I or II	Flat affect
Black rage defense	Hypomania
Borderline personality disorder	Hypomanic episodes
Civil commitment	Insanity defense
Competency restoration	Learned helplessness
Competency to be executed	Manic episode
Competency to stand trial	Mental illness
Conduct disorder	Mixed mania
Co-occurring disorders	Multiaxial system
Cycle of violence	Paranoia

Paranoid schizophrenia
Parens patriae
Parental abuse syndrome
Personality disorders
Police power
Posttraumatic stress disorder
Psychopathy

Psychopathy Checklist Revised (PCL-R)
Psychosis
Pure mania
Right to refuse treatment
Schizophrenia
Substance abuse
Twinkie Defense

PREVALENCE OF MENTAL ILLNESS IN CRIMINAL POPULATIONS

Introduction

The prevalence of psychiatric disorder among criminal populations is an important marker for ascertaining what the relationship is between mental illness and crime. This section examines this matter in several important respects. In particular, background statistical information on mentally disordered offenders and non-mentally-disordered offenders is provided, and the link between violence and certain types of psychiatric illnesses (including **co-occurring disorders** such as **substance abuse**) is presented.

Background Statistical Information on Mentally Ill Offenders

In a special report concerning the mental health of incarcerated felons filed by the U.S. Department of Justice, 16% of state convicts, 7% of federal convicts, and 16% of those in local jails indicated either a preexisting mental condition or a previous overnight stay in a psychiatric hospital (Ditton, 1999). Interestingly, estimated rates of mental illness among incarcerated populations vary depending on the methods used to conduct the study, the definition of mental illness, and the institution developing the report. However, investigations undertaken in New York, Philadelphia, and Chicago county jails during the 1980s and 1990s looked at the diagnoses of **schizophrenia,** bipolar disorder, and major depression and found that they were similar to the statistics published by the U.S. Department of Justice. In short, the rates of mental illness for these incarcerated offenders were between 8% and 16% (e.g., Lamb & Weinberger, 1998; Steadman et al., 1998). Some differences were noted in relation to race in that White convicts were more likely than Blacks or Hispanics to report a mental illness. Moreover, variations in gender were also found, with 24% of females reporting the presence of some psychiatric disorder as compared with 16% for males (Ditton, 1999).

The U.S. Department of Justice also found that mentally ill prisoners were more likely than other prisoners to be incarcerated for a violent offense (Ditton, 1999). This conclusion is consistent with other studies addressing this relationship (e.g., Wallace et al., 1998). For example, about 53% of psychiatrically disordered convicts were in prison for a violent offense, as compared to 46% of offenders who were not. Approximately 13% of the mentally ill convicts in state prisons committed murder, 12% committed sexual assault, 13% committed robbery, and 11% committed assault. Overall, nearly 1 in 5 violent offenders incarcerated or on probation was identified as mentally ill (Steadman et al., 1998). However, psychiatrically disordered offenders are less likely than other non-mentally-ill prisoners to be incarcerated for a drug-related offense, with 13% of the former group subject to confinement for a substance-related crime as compared with 22% for all other convicts. In addition, the U.S. Department of Justice conducted personal interviews with prisoners and found that 6 out of 10 mentally ill offenders were under the influence of alcohol or drugs at the time their crime was committed (Ditton, 1999). This particular finding is very important, especially given the more recent research reporting that substance abuse is a risk factor for persons with mental illness to engage in violent behavior (Monahan, 1996; Steadman et al., 1998).

The Link Between Violence and Psychiatric Illness: What Do We Know?

Previous research acknowledges a relationship between violent criminal acts and certain mental disorders. For example, some investigators report that persons with schizophrenia, in comparison with the general population, are 4 to 7 times more likely to commit violent acts (Hodgins, 1992). In addition, research conducted by Eronen, Tiihonen, and Hakola (1996) found that people with schizophrenia and alcoholism, as compared with nonalcoholic schizophrenic subjects, were twice as likely to engage in violence. More recently, Rasanen and colleagues (1998) reported that individuals suffering from schizophrenia and alcoholism were 7 times more likely to commit a violent crime than were their nonalcoholic schizophrenic counterparts. Clearly, the risk of violence for a person experiencing psychiatric illness is exacerbated when alcoholism is also indicated.

Typically, the term **dual diagnosis** is applied to individuals who meet the criteria for a diagnosis of a severe mental illness and an alcohol- or drug-related disorder (Scott et al., 1998). Several studies support the finding that a comorbid diagnosis of substance abuse is associated with the risk of aggression and violent behavior (Hodgins, Lapalme, & Toupin, 1999; Rasanen et al., 1998; Scott et al., 1998; Soyka, 2000; Wallace et al., 1998; Steadman et al., 1998). Based on this research, prevention of criminal behavior among persons experiencing co-occurring disorders (i.e., psychiatric illness and substance abuse) requires a diagnosis of both conditions with the appropriate clinical interventions and treatments administered to address these related psychiatric phenomena.

Admittedly, there are problems with the research on threat assessment for the mentally ill, given several methodological constraints and limits. For example, selection bias, the absence of control groups, a misdiagnosis, and the lack of a diagnosis by a treating clinician make it difficult to reach definitive conclusions about the relationship between psychiatric disorder and violent behavior. However, this association is an extremely important matter, especially given the power that such determinations possess to influence mental health law and policy (e.g., Williams & Arrigo, 2002). Indeed, how our society attempts to control the behavior of disordered people is regulated by public and professional perception. Thus, as Monahan (1992) notes, belief in the violence potential of the psychiatrically ill "not only drive[s] formal law and policy toward [them] as a class, but [it] also determine[s] our informal responses and modes of interacting with individuals who are perceived to be mentally ill" (p. 511). In essence, how we understand and interpret the relationship between mental illness and violence is crucial to whether these citizens are stigmatized, mistreated, or otherwise wrongly punished (Arrigo, 2002; Holstein, 1993).

Some research questions the nature of the association between crime and mental illness. For example, a study conducted by Wallace et al. (1998) investigated serious criminal offending and psychiatric disorders and discovered that although a relationship exists, the extent of the association remains in doubt. In particular, persons diagnosed with major mental health disabilities such as schizophrenia or affective disorders were found to exhibit a modest increase in offending most often accompanied by substance abuse. Thus, as Wallace et al. (1998) concluded: "The risk of a serious crime being committed by someone with a major mental illness is small and does not justify subjecting them, as a group, to either increased institutional containment or greater coercion" (p. 477).

The most comprehensive study to date investigating the relationship between psychiatric disorder and crime looked at patients discharged from acute inpatient mental hospitals and their rates of subsequent violence (Steadman et al., 1998). The study found that those subjects who did not abuse alcohol or drugs were not inclined to commit violent acts any more frequently than were a random selection of their non-mentally-ill neighbors in the same urban communities. Violent acts were defined as threats with weapons, physical assaults, and pushing or hitting that caused injuries. The investigators also reported that 18% of those people who exhibited no signs of substance abuse but had been diagnosed with schizophrenia or bipolar disorder engaged in a violent act. However, the proportion of people who committed a violent act diagnosed with a co-occurring major psychiatric condition and a substance abuse disorder was 31%. On the basis of these findings, the authors concluded that an important distinction could (and should) be made when assessing the risk of violence for persons with mental disorders. In short, one of the key distinctions for predicting future violence is whether persons with psychiatric illness abuse alcohol or drugs.

What can we conclude about crime and mental illness? Overall, the research suggests that a significant proportion of persons convicted of serious crime have had contact with psychiatric services. However, persons experiencing substance abuse issues and **personality disorders** appear to account for the bulk of this association. For example, 43% of persons with personality disorders and substance abuse commit a violent act (Ditton, 1999). Moreover, even though the chance of any person with an affective disorder or with schizophrenia engaging in a violent crime is greater than that in the general population, the risk is still quite small (Wallace et al., 1998). Given these findings, attempts to draw attention to the criminality of the mentally ill as a persuasive argument for enforced drug compliance, greater coercion, and general containment do not appear justified (Arrigo, 2002; Williams & Arrigo, 2002).

The links among substance abuse, mental illness, and the likelihood of criminal conduct warrant further empirical and policy consideration. Indeed, the presence of these co-occurring disorders is useful in predicting future violence. As such, increased clinical awareness and improved (and targeted) intervention is critical to meeting the complex needs of some persons with psychiatric disorders. This approach would not only improve the health of the person suffering from a debilitating mental illness but also contribute to public safety (Wallace et al., 1998). In addition, other predictors of violence not associated with psychiatric illness require attention from legislators, researchers, and the general public. Indeed, as Marzuk (1996) noted, if society wants to address the problems posed by aggression and violence, then it must carefully evaluate those factors responsible for it. Indeed, as he perceptively states:

> . . . social and moral rules about behavior, the likelihood of apprehension, the severity of punishment, the accessibility of firearms, the immediate availability of alcohol and other drugs, the characteristics of the physical setting, the personality of the people involved, the presence of racial and religious discrimination, economic inequality, poverty, and crowding all influence the likelihood of violence. (p. 484)

MENTAL DISORDERS: AXIS I

Introduction

One way to appreciate the relationship between crime and mental disorder is to explore what we know about various expressions of psychiatric illness. This section focuses on Axis I clinical disorders. The subsequent portion of the chapter focuses on Axis II or personality disorders. In particular, observations on bipolar disorder, schizophrenia, and **conduct disorder** are presented in this section. These comments include some discussion on their respective subtypes and the symptoms and warning signs for each of them. However, before reviewing these matters, some cursory remarks on what **Axis I disorders** represent are provided.

Axis I Disorders: Background Information

As identified in the *DSM-IV-TR*, Axis I disorders are psychiatric conditions that may be a focus of clinical attention (APA, 2000). Axis I excludes personality disorders and mental retardation. These are listed as Axis II conditions. The *DSM–IV–TR* uses a **multiaxial system,** and each axis refers to a different domain of information that can assist the mental health professional in planning treatment and predict outcome. There are five axes included in the *DSM–IV–TR,* but for purposes of our discussion, attention is directed only to Axis I. Clinical disorders that may be included under Axis I are (a) disorders usually first diagnosed in infancy, childhood, or adolescence, excluding mental retardation, delirium, dementia, and amnestic or other cognitive disorders; (b) mental disorders due to a general medical condition; (c) substance-related disorders; (d) schizophrenia and other psychotic disorders; (e) mood disorders; (f) anxiety disorders; (g) somatoform disorders; (h) factitious disorders; (i) dissociative disorders; (j) sexual and gender identity disorders; (k) eating disorders, sleep disorders, impulse–control disorders not elsewhere classified; (l) adjustment disorders; and (m) other conditions that may be a focus of clinical attention (*DSM–IV–TR;* APA, 2000).

Not all of the previously listed psychiatric conditions are linked to criminal behavior. However, bipolar disorder, schizophrenia, and conduct disorder are positively correlated with antisocial behavior, including offender conduct. Indeed, according to evidence provided by the Epidemiological Catchment Area Survey in 1990, a modest association exists between a current diagnosis of major psychoses (i.e., bipolar disorder and schizophrenia) and violence in the community (Melton, Petrila, Poythress, & Slobogin, 1997). Given this association, additional information on these three psychiatric conditions is presented.

Bipolar Disorder

The prevalence of bipolar I disorder ranges from 1 million to 3.5 million people, and bipolar II disorder is found in another 2 million people. Bipolar I disorder is found in men and women equally, but bipolar II is more common in women (Evans, 2000). Women are more likely to experience their first episode as a major depressive episode, and men are more likely to experience their first episode as a **manic episode** (APA, 2000). The age of onset appears to range from 15 to 19, and the mean age of individuals with bipolar disorder is 21. Onset of bipolar disorder prior to the age of 12 appears to be uncommon (Evans, 2000).

Bipolar disorder is a life-threatening disease, given the high rate of suicide affecting 10% to 15% of all patients. Clinicians suspect that 15% to 20% of untreated people with bipolar disorder will eventually kill themselves (Evans, 2000). Suicidal behavior is more common in the depressive phase, and some research has found that individuals with an early age of onset may be at greater risk for self-injurious behavior (Sands & Harrow, 2000).

Bipolar disorder often goes unrecognized and is misdiagnosed and not adequately treated. In particular, clinicians experience difficulty in differentiating bipolar disorder from schizophrenia and schizoaffective disorder, because each of these psychiatric conditions includes the mimicking of symptoms such as **delusions, flat affect,** incoherence, and hallucinations (Brady, 2000).

There are three main subtypes of bipolar disorder recognized by the *DSM–IV–TR* (APA, 2000). Bipolar I disorder is the most common subtype and involves both full manic and full depressive symptoms. A manic episode is characterized by a distinct period of abnormally and persistently elevated, expansive, or irritable mood, lasting at least 1 week, or any duration if the episode requires hospitalization (APA, 2000). Bipolar II disorder involves full **depressive symptoms** in conjunction with **hypomanic episodes,** characterized as a less severe form of mania. Bipolar disorder not otherwise specified (NOS) includes disorders with bipolar features, but with those that do not meet the formal criteria for **bipolar disorder I or II.** For example, a person exhibiting manic symptoms and depressive symptoms rapidly over a period of days, not exhibiting these symptoms for the specified duration of a manic, hypomanic, or depressive episode, would be diagnosed as bipolar disorder NOS (APA, 2000).

In an effort to accurately diagnose bipolar I from bipolar II, manic episodes must be distinguished from hypomanic episodes. A *manic episode* is a mood disturbance that is sufficiently severe to cause marked impairment in occupational, social, or relationship functioning and may require hospitalization. In addition, a manic episode may have psychotic features necessitating a diagnosis of bipolar I disorder (APA, 2000).

There are three distinct manic states: **pure mania, hypomania,** and **mixed mania.** These states are important to differentiate in terms of diagnosis and treatment considerations. Pure mania, which is common in persons with bipolar I, is a classic acute mania characterized by euphoria and grandiosity. Hypomania is less severe than pure mania and is characterized by a distinct period of a persistently elevated, expansive, or irritable mood lasting at least 4 days, which is clearly different from the usual nondepressed mood. A hypomanic episode is defined by the absence of psychotic symptoms and is not sufficiently severe to cause marked impairment in social or occupational functioning. Mixed mania includes symptoms of depression and mania. The person may present with manic symptoms, but the content of their thoughts is clearly depressive in nature. Approximately 40% of all persons with bipolar disorder have mixed mania (Tondo, Baldessarini, Hennen, & Floris, 1998).

Research indicates that misdiagnosis of persons with bipolar disorder occurs approximately 40% of the time (Ghaemi, 2000). An accurate diagnosis relies on clinical judgment to differentiate an emotional state that is abnormal, inappropriate, or excessive from normal happiness. For example, the emotional component of bipolar disorder may be characterized by an elated, expansive, or irritable mood. There are behavioral and cognitive features that must be examined in combination with the emotional component for accurate diagnosis. The behavioral features help to ensure additional certainty when diagnosing the syndromes of mania or hypomania (Sands & Harrow, 2000). Diagnostic criteria specify that the manic or hypomanic episode must include three of the following symptoms (or four of the following if the mood is only irritable): (a) grandiosity; (b) decreased need for sleep; (c) excessive talkativeness; (d) flight of ideas or racing thoughts; (e) distractibility; (f) increased goal-directedness either socially, sexually, or occupationally; or (g) excessive involvement in pleasurable activities that potentially have negative consequences (APA, 2000).

Schizophrenia

Schizophrenia is another Axis I disorder. Its association with antisocial and criminal behavior is very problematic. The following two case illustrations provocatively demonstrate this.

Schizophrenia and Crime: What's the Connection?

In 1996, John du Pont, heir to the du Pont chemical fortune, went on a tour of his estate to survey the damage the winter storms had done to his property. According to Patrick Goodale, du Pont's private security expert, du Pont drove his car to the driveway of David Schultz, an Olympic gold-medal wrestler who lived on du Pont's property and trained at the state-of-the-art training facility built by du Pont. As Schultz was sitting in his Toyota Tercel, du Pont suddenly pulled out a .44-magnum revolver and shot Schultz three times, killing him almost instantly.

Colin Ferguson lived and worked in New York. In 1993, this 35-year-old Black Jamaican immigrant killed 6 train passengers and wounded 19 others on a Long Island commuter line. When law enforcement personnel arrested Ferguson and checked him for identification, several items were found. Among them were "rambling notes intimating that the act was spurred by a rage against Caucasians, Asians, 'Uncle Tom Blacks,' and many other 'racist' people and organizations" (Bardwell & Arrigo, 2002a, p. 148). Prior to the criminal trial, it was determined that Ferguson had a history of delusional and paranoid thoughts. In fact, a pretrial hearing was conducted to assess whether he was competent to stand trial. Various psychiatric experts testified, raising considerable questions about whether the Long Island Railway shooter was schizophrenic.

Although the facts of these two cases are different, they are troubling for similar reasons. Mr. du Pont had been previously diagnosed with schizophrenia, paranoid type. He was known to have displayed periods of bizarre behavior over several years, and many people had expressed their fear of him. He was prone to hallucinations, rages, and paranoid behavior. He was also rumored to have had serious drug and alcohol problems that exacerbated his psychiatric condition (Wrightsman, Nietzel, & Fortune, 1998).

Mr. Ferguson had a history of **paranoia** and delusions, dating back to 1982. His previous work history, academic experiences, and interpersonal relationships were based on protests of racism, governmental conspiracies against people of color, and unfair treatment of minorities (Bardwell & Arrigo, 2002a). Ferguson even went so far as to represent himself in his criminal case, believing that his attorneys, the law enforcement community, the judicial system, the Mayor of New York, and former President William J. Clinton were all prejudiced against Black people. Both of these cases raise deeply troubling questions about the relationship between schizophrenia and crime.

Schizophrenia is a disorder that lasts for at least 6 months and includes at least 1 month with two or more of the following symptoms: delusions, hallucinations, disorganized speech, and grossly disorganized or catatonic behavior. The term *psychotic* is often used in association with schizophrenia and refers to delusions, prominent hallucinations, disorganized speech, and disorganized or catatonic behavior. The characteristic symptoms of schizophrenia are either positive or negative, indicating an excess or distortion of normal functions. The positive symptoms may include distortions in thought content known as delusions, perceptions, or hallucinations, and language and thought processes such as disorganized speech and grossly disorganized or catatonic behavior. The content of the delusions may include themes that are persecutory, somatic, religious, or grandiose. The persecutory delusions are most common and include beliefs that the person is being followed, tricked, ridiculed, or spied on. Auditory hallucinations are the most common and include hearing familiar or unfamiliar voices; however, hallucinations of any of the five senses are possible. Negative symptoms include restrictions in the range and intensity of emotional expression known as flat affect, the fluency and productivity of speech and thought, and the initiation of goal-directed behavior. All the symptoms are associated with a marked social or occupational dysfunction (APA, 2000).

The prevalence of schizophrenia is reported to be approximately 0.5% to 1.5%, and the incidence is estimated to be 0.5 to 5 persons per 10,000 with no differences related to culture or race. The onset of schizophrenia may occur between the late teens and mid-30s. Schizophrenia is expressed differently in men and women, with the onset in men occurring between 18 and 25 years of age; and that in women, between 25 and 30 years of age. Women with schizophrenia manifest symptoms such as paranoid delusions and hallucinations. Men express symptoms such as social withdrawal, absence of emotional expression, and lack of goal-directed behavior (APA, 2000).

There is a strong genetic component to the etiology of schizophrenia (Marder, 1996). In first-degree relatives, the risk of schizophrenia is about 8%. Studies also indicate an increased risk in adopted offspring whose biological mothers are schizophrenic, notwithstanding being raised in families without schizophrenia. Other factors associated with an increased risk of schizophrenia include winter birth, exposure to viral infections during the second trimester, and birth complications (Marder, 1996).

The individual diagnosed with schizophrenia, paranoid type, may have delusions that are typically grandiose or persecutory. The persecutory themes may predispose the individual to suicidal behavior. The delusions are typically organized around a coherent theme, such as religion, somatic issues, or jealousy. Hallucinations are also typically related to the content of the delusional theme. Other features include anger, anxiety, aloofness, and argumentativeness. The combination of grandiose and persecutory delusions combined with anger may predispose the individual to violence. The onset of paranoid-type, schizophrenia may occur later in life, and the distinguishing characteristics are more stable over time. The person with **paranoid schizophrenia** may have a greater capacity than a person with other types of schizophrenia for independent living and have more success in occupational functioning (APA, 2000).

Conduct Disorder

Thus far in this section, the focus has been on mental illness as linked to adults. However, children and adolescents can also be diagnosed with psychiatric conditions. One of the more common diagnoses is conduct disorder (a related disorder for youth is oppositional defiant disorder). The *DSM–IV-TR* offers useful information on the diagnostic criteria for this psychiatric condition. As the *Manual* explains:

> The essential feature of Conduct Disorder is a repetitive and persistent pattern of behavior in the basic rights of others or major age-appropriate societal norms or rules are violated (Criterion A). These behaviors fall into four main groupings: aggressive conduct that causes

or threatens physical harm to other people or animals (Criteria A1-A7), non-aggressive conduct that causes property loss or damage (Criteria A8-A9), deceitfulness or theft (Criteria A10-A12), and serious violations of rules (Criteria A13-A15). Three (or more) characteristic behaviors must have been present during the past 12 months, with at least one behavior present in the last 6 months. The disturbance in behavior causes clinically significant impairment in social, academic, or occupational functioning (Criterion B). (APA, 2000, pp. 93–94)

Associated personality features for children diagnosed with the Axis I diagnosis of conduct disorder are lack of empathy and complete disregard for the welfare and feelings of other people. Adolescents with this disorder may display violent–aggressive behaviors across a variety of situations (Loeber, Burke, Lahey, Winters, & Zera, 2000). These acts may include rape, assault, and much less frequently, homicide. Other crimes committed among conduct-disordered children are muggings, breaking and entering, robbery, vandalism, and petty and grand theft. These individuals are usually very deceitful and cunning and display a very manipulative "charm" similar to those diagnosed with **antisocial personality disorder** (Loeber & Stouthamer-Loeber, 1998). Feigning remorse or guilt is also characteristic of the individual with this psychiatric condition (Haroun, 2002).

According to the *DSM–IV–TR,* conduct disorder is often associated with an early onset of sexual behavior, drinking, smoking, using illegal substances, and reckless and risk taking acts. Illegal drug use may increase the risk that conduct disorder will persist" (APA, 2000, p. 96). The onset of conduct disorder falls traditionally within the period from mid-childhood to midadolescence or as early as the preschool years (Loeber et al., 2000). Early symptoms for this psychiatric condition include cruelty to animals, fire starting, problems in school (e.g., poor grades, discipline problems, and truancy), vandalism, lying, cheating, and stealing. The disorder is more common in males than in females (Haroun, 2002). Moreover, children who have either a biological or adoptive parent with antisocial personality disorder or a sibling with conduct disorder are at higher risk for being diagnosed with this disorder (Loeber et al., 1998). Conduct disorder is also more prevalent among children of biological parents with alcohol dependence, mood disorders, schizophrenia, or biological parents who have a history themselves of attention-deficit/hyperactivity disorder or conduct disorder (APA, 2000). Finally, conduct disorder (and oppositional defiant disorder) is recognized as a precursor to antisocial personality disorder (for a relevant and topical criminal justice example, see Shipley & Arrigo, 2004).

MENTAL DISORDERS: AXIS II

Introduction

Axis II psychiatric conditions include all personality disorders. The *DSM–IV–TR* defines a personality disorder as "an enduring pattern of inner experience and behavior that deviates markedly from the expectations of the individual's culture, is pervasive and inflexible, has an onset in adolescence or early adulthood, is stable over time, and leads to distress or impairment" (APA, 2000, p. 685). Similar to the previous section, those disorders most commonly associated with criminal behavior are examined in this portion of the chapter. These Axis II conditions include **psychopathy,** antisocial personality disorder, **borderline personality disorder,** and conduct disorder.

Psychopathy

The personality disorder most frequently associated with crime is psychopathy. According to Arrigo and Shipley (2001, p. 325), "Psychopathy is an elusive and perplexing psychological construct. Problems posed by this mental disorder are linked to changing historical interpretations, impacting the current clinical community's general understanding of it, especially in relation to antisocial personality disorder (ASPD)." After extensive, but not exhaustive, review, many practitioners and researchers now maintain that psychopathy should be treated as a separate entity when examining dysfunctions in personality and their relationship to crime (e.g., Cleckley, 1982; Gacono, 2000; Hare, 1991, 1996). In part, this position is linked to a number of factors. As Arrigo and Shipley (2001, p. 325) explain it:

> . . . a great deal of confusion currently exists regarding the relationship between Antisocial Personality Disorder (ASPD), as identified by the Diagnostic and Statistical Manual of Mental Disorders (DSM-IV), and the modern construct of psychopathy as explained by Cleckley (1941), and further refined and empirically validated by Hare (1991). While contemporary research supporting the diagnosis of psychopathy is at its strongest, mental health professionals remain perplexed when diagnosing, treating or making recommendations to the court system about these individuals . . . (also see Gacono, 2000, pp. xvi–xvii)

Indeed, as a practical and historical matter, the construct of psychopathy in the clinical diagnostic literature has been used interchangeably with terms such as sociopathy and ASPD. These concepts are not synonymous. Moreover, the *DSM* Axis II Steering Committee has reviewed the compatibility and fit of these constructs for decades. Over the years, psychopathy has been assigned many labels (Arrigo & Shipley, 2001). Some of these include *manie sans delire* or "mania without frenzy" (Pinel, 1801/1962), moral alienation of the mind (Rush, 1812), moral insanity (Prichard, 1837/1973), psychopathic inferiority (Koch, 1891), moral imbecility (Maudsley, 1897/1977), and moral depravity (Krafft-Ebing, 1915). It was not until the work of Cleckley (1941) that the modern construct of psychopathy was established.

Hare's (1991, 2003) **Psychopathy Checklist Revised (PCL-R)** describes a number of the characteristics that constitute the psychopath. These include glibness, superficial charm, grandiose sense of self-worth, pathological lying, conning and manipulative, lack of remorse, lack of empathy, shallow affect, impulsivity, and failure to accept responsibility for one's own actions. As discussed in the next subsection, these personality traits are similar to some of the diagnostic criteria for ASPD (Gacono, 1998). In fact, the *DSM–IV–TR* even states that sometimes ASPD is referred to as psychopathy or sociopathy (APA, 2000). Obviously, this nomenclature can make things difficult and confusing for students, researchers, and practitioners, especially when attempting to differentiate between these phenomena and their respective association to criminal behavior (Millon, Simonsen, Birket-Smith, & Davis, 1998; Shipley & Arrigo, 2001).

These dilemmas notwithstanding, psychopathy and ASPD are mostly separate entities (Gacono, 2000). In fact, some investigators suggest that the former term is, at best, a more extreme manifestation of the latter construct (Arrigo & Shipley, 2001). Thus, it is very important that the characteristics of psychopaths and persons suffering from antisocial personality disorder be carefully assessed (Gacono & Hutton, 1994). Typically, crimes committed by psychopaths include serial murder, mass or spree murder, and serial rape (Millon et al., 1998). To best illustrate the connection between psychopathy and ASPD, some review of antisocial personality disorder is warranted.

There are several critics of the PCL-R and its ability to validly assess for psychopathy. Many observers note that the first edition was not normed for women, making its application in these instances thoroughly suspect if not altogether unfounded. This is particularly problematic when psychologically evaluating a female prisoner confined for such crimes as murder or multiple homicides (e.g., Shipley & Arrigo, 2004). Others point out that small sample sizes inadequately accounted for substance abusers, sex offenders, special populations, and forensic psychiatric patients, especially in terms of descriptive and validation data (Toch, 1998). Admittedly, many of these concerns are now addressed in the revised PCL-R (Hare, 2003). However, only through future and repeated use of the instrument will criminologists and psychologists be able to determine if it more accurately assesses for psychopathy than its predecessor.

Antisocial Personality Disorder

The *DSM–IV–TR* offers useful diagnostic information on the nature of ASPD. As the *Manual* explains:

> The essential feature of Antisocial Personality Disorder is a pervasive pattern of disregard for, and violation of, the rights of others that begins in childhood or early adolescence and continues into adulthood. This pattern has also been referred to as psychopathy, sociopathy, or dyssocial personality disorder. Because deceit and manipulation are central features of Antisocial Personality Disorder, it may be especially helpful to integrate information acquired from systematic clinical assessment with information collected from collateral sources. (APA, 2000, pp. 701–702)

There are two important diagnostic criteria for this personality disorder. The individual must be at least 18 years of age and have had a history of conduct disorder symptoms before age 15 (APA, 2000).

The *DSM–IV–TR* also provides useful personality or character information on persons experiencing ASPD. As the *Manual* reports:

> Individuals with ASPD fail to conform to social norms with respect to lawful behaviors . . . They are frequently deceitful and manipulative in order to gain personal profit or pleasure . . . They may repeatedly lie, use an alias, con others or malinger . . . (they) tend to be irritable, aggressive and may repeatedly get into physical fights or commit acts of physical assault (including spouse beating or child beating) . . . Individuals with Antisocial Personality Disorder show little remorse for the consequences of their acts. (APA, 2000)

Typical crimes committed by those with ASPD are theft and robbery. Violent crimes include assault, rape, and homicide.

Is the Beltway Sniper a Psychopath or Someone Suffering from ASPD?

In the autumn of 2002, Washington DC and several surrounding suburban communities in Virginia and Maryland lived in fear of the Beltway Sniper. Linked to the murders of 10 citizens in which several others were seriously injured, John Allen Muhammad, 41, preyed on his unsuspecting victims, killing them from a distance with a Bushmaster AR-15 rifle, the civilian version of the M-16 military assault rifle. The Beltway Sniper eluded local law enforcement officials for 3 weeks until his apprehension. What kind of person commits such vicious and cold-blooded acts? One explanation may be related to our understanding of psychopathy and antisocial personality disorder.

Recalling the diagnostic criteria and characterological information on these two types of personality disorders may be helpful. Psychopaths lack remorse and empathy, possess a shallow affect, and maintain a grandiose sense of self-worth. They are also prone to commit serious crimes such as serial and mass murder. Persons suffering from ASPD do not follow the law, are manipulative and deceitful, and show little remorse for their actions. Among other criminal transgressions, ASPD felons engage in homicidal conduct.

The behavior of the Beltway Sniper appears to be consistent with these diagnostic and personality criteria. The callous killing of so many innocent citizens suggests an utter disregard for human life. The high visibility of these crimes and their repetitive nature indicate the assailant's need to fill a deep, emotional void of low self-esteem falsely expressed as inflated self-appraisal. The ability to avoid detection and apprehension is consistent with a highly methodical, well-organized, and extremely controlling individual. These traits are often found in persons who are successful at manipulating others and their environment. The multiple homicides are the product of a serial killer. The Beltway Sniper was found guily of murder and weapons charges. He was sentenced to death. It will be interesting to see whether over time experts characterize him as a psychopath, as a person who suffered from ASPD, or whether he is otherwise labeled mentally ill.

Borderline Personality Disorder

Borderline personality disorder (BPD) is another Axis II psychiatric condition. The *DSM–IV–TR* provides useful information on this disorder. As the *Manual* stipulates, the primary diagnostic features of BPD are:

> . . . a pervasive pattern of instability of interpersonal relationships, self-image, and affects, and marked impulsivity that begins by early adulthood and is present in a variety of contexts. Individuals with Borderline Personality Disorder make frantic efforts to avoid real or imagined abandonment (Criterion 1) . . . Individuals with Borderline Personality Disorder have a pattern of unstable and intense relationships (Criterion 2) . . . There may be an identity disturbance characterized by markedly [and] persistently unstable self-image or sense of self (Criterion 3). There are sudden and dramatic shifts in self-image, characterized by shifting goal values and vocational aspirations . . . Individuals with this disorder display impulsivity in at least two areas that are potentially self-damaging (Criterion 4) . . . Individuals with Borderline Personality Disorder display recurrent suicidal behavior, gestures, or threats or self-mutilating behavior (Criterion 5). (APA, 2000, pp. 706–707)

Behaviors typically found among those diagnosed as BPD include unsafe sex, reckless driving, gambling, and substance abuse. Self-destructive, undermining conduct is also common among this population (Millon & Davis, 2000). For example, dropping out of school just prior to graduation and withdrawing from a relationship when it is clear the relationship has good potential to last are acts of personal sabotage (APA, 2000). BPD individuals are clearly emotionally unstable and present a danger to themselves and others. Indeed, 8% to 10% of BPD-diagnosed persons successfully commit suicide (APA).

BPD is diagnosed more frequently in females than in males. It is estimated that 2% of the population as a whole is diagnosed with BPD (APA, 2000). There are also some indicators for acquiring this disorder. In particular, high at-risk populations include adolescent to early-adult females with identity and substance abuse problems, complicated by affective difficulties and poor interpersonal relationships (Millon & Davis, 2000; APA). Moreover, this disorder is common among those with childhood histories of prior sexual abuse, loss of a parent, and separation from loved ones. Compared with the rest of the general population, biological relatives of those with the disorder are 5 times as likely to be diagnosed with this condition (APA).

Borderline Personality Disorder and the Crime of Stalking

In the movie, *Fatal Attraction,* Glenn Close plays a love-starved corporate executive obsessed with a successful attorney, portrayed by Michael Douglas. The only problem is that Douglas is happily married. The two have an affair when Douglas's family is out of town for the weekend. Although the sex is steamy and satisfying, Douglas realizes that his wife and child (whom he professes to love) will be returning from their trip, and that his weekend sexual encounter regrettably must end.

Douglas attempts to break off the relationship and finds that this is more difficult than it appears. Close begins to follow him and spontaneously visits him at work. At first, she indicates that her interests are platonic and that she wants to develop a friendship. However, Douglas is resistant to any relationship. Close then appears at his house sharing coffee and conversation with his unsuspecting wife who is told that Close is a work colleague. When Douglas becomes annoyed and frustrated, Close becomes angry and hostile. The relationship between Douglas and Close intensifies. What was once a passion-filled romantic weekend becomes a devastatingly frightening and trauma-inducing mistake. Close attempts suicide, stalks Douglas in New York and Connecticut, and kills the family pet. Presumably, all of this is because she loves Douglas. Eventually, she attempts to murder Douglas and his family. If she can't have him, no one will.

How can someone's behavior be so extreme? BPD individuals are known for their intense and severe interactions with others. The conduct of Glenn Close in the film *Fatal Attraction* exemplifies this tendency. For the borderline, people are loved or hated, wonderful or horrible, good or bad. Stalking is a common offense among persons diagnosed with BPD.

COMPETENCY AND CRIMINAL BEHAVIOR

Introduction

Assessing the relationship between criminal behavior and mental illness extends beyond diagnostic classifications and statistical information on the prevalence of psychiatric disorder among offenders. The association also entails an evaluation of those specific legal conditions in which a person diagnosed as mentally ill is nonetheless competent to make decisions on his or her own behalf. This section examines two specific criminal law controversies surrounding this matter: **competency to stand trial** and **competency to be executed.** In addition, commentary on forced drug treatment over patient objection for purposes of **competency restoration** and capital punishment is also provided. The section concludes by reviewing the practice of civilly committing involuntarily an individual identified as mentally ill and dangerous to oneself or to others.

Competency to Stand Trial

In most cases, *competency to stand trial* refers to a person's "ability to understand the nature and purpose of the court proceedings, and it is applicable at every stage of the criminal justice process, from interrogations and pretrial hearings to trials and sentencing hearings" (Wrightsman, 2001, p. 224). The definition of competency used by the courts comes from a decision by the Supreme Court in *Dusky v. United States* (1960). The *Dusky* standard for competence to stand trial focuses on the accused's (a) present ability to sufficiently consult with one's attorney with a reasonable degree of understanding and (b) rational, as well as factual, comprehension of the proceedings against the defendant (Bardwell & Arrigo, 2002b). Given this two-prong approach as articulated by the *Dusky* Court, competency to stand trial entails "not only the presence of mental illness, but also the individual's ability to function as a defendant in light of the effects of his/her mental illness" (Arrigo, 2000, p. 122). Indeed, for an accused to effectively assist in his or her criminal case, it is essential that the person have at least a modicum of understanding regarding the legal proceedings surrounding the criminal matter at hand.

Competency to stand trial is quite different from the legal defense of insanity (Bardwell & Arrigo, 2002b). Competency refers to the *current* ability of the defendant to comprehend what is going on, whereas insanity refers to the ability of the individual to understand and appreciate the wrongfulness of his or her act, at the time the alleged criminal offense occurred. "For example, an individual may have been legally insane at the time he/she committed a crime, but perfectly competent to stand trial and be sentenced" (Arrigo, 2000, p. 122). In addition, a person may have been sane at the time of the crime, but months later when the case goes to trial the defendant may be unable to meet the *Dusky* standard of competence required to stand trial (Bardwell & Arrigo, 2002b).

Courts require that persons on trial must be competent for numerous reasons (Bonnie, 1992; Bonnie et al.,1997). Wrightsman et al. (1998, p. 281) succinctly summarize this criminal law rationale.

> First, legal proceedings are more likely to arrive at accurate results with the participation of competent defendants. Second, punishment of convicted defendants is morally acceptable only if they understand the reasons they are being punished. Finally, the perceived fairness of our adversary system of justice requires participation by defendants who have the capacity to defend themselves against the charges of the state.

Given these justifications, investigators contend that if an incompetent mentally ill defendant cannot participate fully and knowledgeably in his or her defense, then justice is not only deferred but also denied in these specific criminal courtroom instances (Bardwell & Arrigo, 2002b).

The "Unabomber" and Competency to Stand Trial

During a span of 18 years, the Federal Bureau of Investigation worked in vain to apprehend Theodore Kaczynski (a.k.a., the Unabomber). However, in 1996 the case finally broke when Kaczynski's brother, David, compared the infamous "Manifesto" (a document originally titled "Industrial Society and Its Future" authored by Mr. Kaczynski and published in the New York Times) with letters and journal entries written by the elder Theodore. Kaczynski was "arrested and charged with 16 bomb attacks that killed 3 people and injured 23 others" (Bardwell & Arrigo, 2002a, p. 338). As the pretrial evidence was reviewed, Kaczynski's attorneys believed that they could successfully mount a mental defect defense during the penalty phase because the evidence pointing to the Unabomber's guilt was overwhelming.

As the case unfolded, tension grew between the Unabomber and his attorneys, especially because Mr. Kaczynski adamantly refused to be identified as psychiatrically ill. To avoid such a designation or defense, the Unabomber made a motion to secure new attorneys. This request was denied. Thereafter, he unsuccessfully attempted suicide, exercised his right to waive counsel, and sought to represent himself. Again, these efforts were designed to avoid the mental status defense planned and developed by his legal team.

Eventually, given the Unabomber's bizarre behavior and his courtroom requests, experts questioned whether Theodore Kaczynski was even competent to stand trial. Following the court-ordered evaluation of Mr. Kaczynski, Dr. Sally Johnson tendered a provisional diagnosis of schizophrenia, paranoid type. However, on the ultimate legal issue of whether the Unabomber was competent to stand trial, the psychiatrist indicated that Kaczynski was competent, and that, moreover, he was capable of representing himself. Indeed, as she explained, Mr. Kaczynski's suicide attempt was a rational preference for life over death and not evidence in support of incompetency.

Based on this testimony, Judge Garland Burrell ruled that Theodore Kaczynski was competent to stand trial. However, he did not grant the Unabomber's request to waive counsel and represent himself, indicating that these motions were nothing more than deliberate attempts to delay the trial proceedings (Arrigo & Bardwell, 2000). Soon thereafter, Mr. Kaczynski pled guilty in a federal court to the criminal charges filed against him in association with the bombings. Although the Unabomber effectively avoided any designation of mental illness or any defense based on such a theory, he was sentenced to prison without the possibility of parole.

One way to appreciate the meaning of competency is to distinguish it from rationality (Bonnie, 1992). As Barrett, Taylor, Pullo, and Dunlap (1998, p. 245) note, "Competent people can make irrational decisions. Therefore, one way to define rationality is that it is only a characteristic of a person's decision." An irrational decision is one in which a person clearly chooses an action that the party knows will elicit negative consequences (Bardwell & Arrigo, 2002a, 2002b; Culver, 1991). The idea that a competent person can make an irrational decision often comes into play when discussing the **right to refuse treatment** (Winick, 1997). Barrett et al. (1998) explain this connection:

> The three components of valid consent or refusal of treatment are a) the person must have adequate information about the treatment including harms and benefits, and the probability of harm occurring as a result of treatment (e.g., death, permanent disability); b) there must be no coercion; and c) the person must be fully competent to understand and appreciate information about the treatment. Forced treatment is only an issue when the person's decision-making capabilities (competence) are in question. (p. 245)

Consequently, when a person is competently making an informed but bad decision, it is well within the person's right to exercise that choice, no matter how ill-advised the decision may be (Smith & Meyer, 1987; Winick, 1997).

Competency to Be Executed

Another area of criminal law where the issue of competency is raised is in cases of execution. Under the American system of jurisprudence, the death penalty cannot be administered unless the offender is mentally competent. The case that best illustrates this position is *Ford v. Wainwright* (1986).

Competency to Be Executed and the Alvin Ford Case

Alvin Ford was a prisoner whose mental condition deteriorated to the point where his competency was questionable while awaiting his death sentence. In response to this development, the U.S. Supreme Court intervened and halted Ford's execution (Ford v. Wainwright, 1986). The Court felt that it would be in violation of Ford's Eighth Amendment right against cruel and unusual punishment if the death penalty were administered while he was incompetent (Arrigo & Tasca, 1999). The Court decided that a person could not be executed absent the ability to understand (a) the death penalty and (b) the reasons for execution in one's particular case (Ford v. Wainwright).

Although in the *Ford v. Wainwright,* (1986) decision the U.S. Supreme Court addressed the unconstitutionality of executing a mentally incompetent death row convict, the Court did not address whether the state could force a death row prisoner to take medications in order to restore the offender to competency for purposes of execution (Winick, 1997). This matter was addressed in *Perry v. Louisiana* (1990), in which the Court explored whether a convict had a right to refuse drug treatment that would ultimately make the person mentally fit to face capital punishment. The Court concluded that a prisoner could not be forced to take medication if the state's sole justification was competency restoration for purposes of execution. In other words, medicate to execute was not constitutionally permissible. At the same time, the U.S. Supreme Court rendered another opinion on the matter of competency restoration for death row prisoners clarifying its previous decision in *Ford v. Wainwright*.

In *Washington v. Harper* (1990), the Court concluded that a convicted death row prisoner had a right to refuse drug treatment for competency restoration purposes that resulted in execution. However, a mentally incompetent person on death row could not successfully exercise his or her right to refuse treatment if the medication was in the convict's best medical interest or if the absence of such intervention endangered the lives of prison personnel or other convicts. Based on the Court's ruling in *Washington,* is it possible to easily reconcile the issue of competency, treatment refusal, and capital punishment? Most experts believe the answer is no.

One way to explore this relationship is to question whether mentally incompetent death row prisoners genuinely pose a threat to prison personnel or other convicts if left unmedicated. As Winick (1997, p. 299) asserts, "In the context of treating incompetent death row inmates to restore [competency], these security considerations are rarely implicated. Death row inmates are isolated and subjected to intensive [custody] measures that, other than under the most unusual circumstances, significantly diminish any risk to other inmates or prison staff." In addition, employing drug therapy for purposes of restoring the competency of a prisoner awaiting execution as found in the *Perry* case had very little to do with the safety issues considered in the *Harper* decision (Arrigo & Tasca, 1999). In other words, forced and intrusive drug treatment, in the absence of any risk posed to prison staff or other convicts, violates a person's constitutional right to refuse that treatment, even if the person is a prisoner (Winick, 1997). Consequently, the state's interest in coercing incompetent convicts to take medication over their objection for purposes of competency restoration is simply not tenable, especially when the essential purpose of treatment is to facilitate the individual's execution (Arrigo & Williams, 1999).

Finally, there is an ethical dilemma surrounding the determination of competence for a prisoner facing the death penalty. "Often, psychologists conducting [competency] evaluations find themselves in a difficult position, given that their expert opinion can lead directly to an individual's execution" (Arrigo, 2000, p. 237). If a convict is found incompetent for purposes of capital punishment, the prisoner is sent to a treatment facility for competency restoration. However, in these instances, the correctional psychologist or psychiatrist and mental health team are charged with returning the convict to a fit mental state for the sole purpose of being put to death. "As might be expected, the psychologist often has ambiguous feelings about providing treatment under such circumstances" (Arrigo, p. 237).

Involuntary Civil Commitment

Discussions of forced treatment and refusal in the relevant literature are not simply reducible to drug therapy for purposes of competency restoration and execution. Indeed, there are many other areas where coerced intervention is considered, impacting our understanding of offenders and their criminal behavior. However, perhaps one of the most contentious domains where debate about forced treatment surfaces is with the practice of involuntary **civil commitment.**

Defendants found incompetent to stand trial were once confined to locked psychiatric facilities for extremely lengthy periods of time while the state attempted to restore these disordered individuals to competency (Arrigo, 1993). In fact, "at times, this period exceeded the sentence the individual would have faced if tried and convicted" (Arrigo, 2000, p. 123). However, a limit was established on the amount of time an incompetent defendant could be confined against his or her will in the U.S. Supreme Court decision of *Jackson v. Indiana* (1972). The Court ruled that the duration of psychiatric confinement would be reasonable if a substantial likelihood existed, indicating that the individual would be found competent to stand trial in the near future. "The Jackson decision was the first Supreme Court case to place legal limits, though imprecise and not well defined, on the commitment of [incompetent to stand trial] individuals" (Arrigo, 2000, p. 123).

Civil commitment is the process by which an individual is detained in a psychiatric facility because the person is mentally ill, is dangerous to self or to others, and engages in behaviors suggestive of the nature and quality of one's psychiatric disorder (e.g., Arrigo, 1993; Resiner & Slobogin, 1997). "Consistent with basic due process, [the U.S. Supreme Court] has held that an individual who is not mentally ill cannot be involuntarily committed for civil purposes" (Arrigo, 2000, p. 164). Typically, justification for involuntary hospitalization is drawn from one of two sources: the **police power** authority or *parens patriae* justification (Myers, 1983/1984). States (and psychiatric facilities as agents of the state) are authorized to use police power commitments when a person poses a threat of danger to others. States (and mental health hospitals as agents of the state) are authorized to employ ***parens patriae*** commitment when a person poses a treat of danger to oneself. In this latter instance, the state operates much like a parent making important life decisions (i.e., hospitalization) for a person presumably incapable of making decisions on his or her own behalf. Different state jurisdictions rely on various interpretations for what constitutes "mental illness," "danger," and their relationship, making the process of determining whether an individual's behaviors rise to the level of civil commitment very complicated (Williams & Arrigo, 2002).

An attempt at clarifying what constitutes mental illness for purposes of involuntary psychiatric hospitalization was articulated in the case of *Foucha v. Louisiana* (1992). In this decision, the Court ruled that although an individual must be shown to be mentally ill and dangerous, dangerousness and antisocial personality disorder alone are not sufficient. Indeed, according to the *DSM–IV–TR* antisocial personality disorder is described as a "pervasive pattern of disregard for, and violation of, the rights of others that begins in childhood or early adolescence and continues into adulthood" (APA, 2000, p. 645). Thus, as Arrigo (2000, p. 166) concludes, "the implication is that personality disorders, at least antisocial personality disorder, do not constitute mental illness for purposes of involuntary confinement."

Although the *Foucha v. Louisiana* (1992) Court endeavored to further define the conditions under which civil commitment would be warranted in particular instances, there continues to be some considerable speculation surrounding how best to use this mental health law practice (Resiner & Slobogin, 1997). Indeed, persons diagnosed as mentally ill can be tried in a criminal court of law and can be found guilty, not guilty, not guilty by reason of insanity, and in some jurisdictions, guilty but mentally ill (Steadman et al., 1993). In addition, a defendant in a criminal case can be declared incompetent to stand trial and can be sent to a psychiatric facility until competency restoration occurs, enabling the individual to participate appropriately in the trial and to assist, if called on, in his or her own defense. Finally, a person identified as mentally ill and dangerous to self or to others can be civilly committed involuntarily for short-term and extended psychiatric treatment. Each of these possible outcomes is important to understanding how mental illness and crime are related and how criminal behavior and psychiatric disorder can, and in some cases do, function in tandem.

MENTAL DISORDERS AS UNIQUE DEFENSES

Introduction

The conclusion of the previous section on competency and criminal behavior suggests that there are certain situations in which mental illness can mitigate responsibility for one's otherwise illicit and wrongful actions. One highly publicized and controversial area where this occurs is with the defense of insanity (Arrigo, 1996). Researchers exploring the relationship between psychology and the legal system have examined this phenomenon in considerable detail (e.g., Melton et al., 1997), and readers are encouraged to review this material for more direction on how the defense of insanity functions under the law. However, there are other, emerging psychiatric conditions whose affects raise considerable doubt about the criminal responsibility of people. This final portion of the chapter explores these mental disorders in relation to a defendant's criminal culpability. In particular, three such conditions are reviewed. These include battered woman syndrome, posttraumatic stress disorder, and the Black rage defense.

The Battered Woman Syndrome as a Defense

Women who are constant recipients of physical abuse, verbal abuse, emotional abuse, threats, and intimidation by their husbands or significant others are susceptible to a psychiatric condition called battered woman syndrome or spousal abuse (Toffel, 1996). Moreover, according to a report filed by the APA (1995), nearly 1,000 women murder their current or former abusers each year. Interestingly, however, "Although battered woman syndrome is becoming increasingly popular in the mental health arena, it has yet to receive substantial support in the courtroom" (Arrigo, 2000, p. 202). Still, experts in the field of psychology are often called on to testify concerning the mental state of the battered spouse. As such, even though "the claimed presence of this syndrome is not a legal defense in and of itself, it can be used as justification for arguing, as a defense, either self-defense or insanity" (Wrightsman, 2001, p. 244).

In chapter 5 several comments on the causes, prevalence, and effects of spousal or partner abuse were presented. In other words, understanding the behavior of batterers was mostly emphasized. Here, however, the focus is on the victim. One way to appreciate the victimization women confront in the instance of spousal abuse is to examine the syndrome itself.

What is meant by the term *syndrome*? "A syndrome is usually defined as a collection of symptoms, most of which appear in every case of a particular disease or bodily response" (Wrightsman et al., 1998, p. 415). Consequently, the term *battered woman syndrome* refers to the constellation of symptoms characteristic of women who have endured abuse at the hands of their spouse or partner. According to Lenore Walker (1979), battered woman syndrome is defined as the presumed reactions to a pattern of continual psychological and physical abuse inflicted on a woman by her companion.

Walker (1979, 1989) suggests that there is a common set of components experienced by adult females subjected to battered woman syndrome. These components include the following: (a) **learned helplessness** or exposure to painful situations over which the woman believes she has no control and no ready recourse to escape, (b) lowered self-esteem, (c) impaired functioning, (d) loss of the assumption of invulnerability and safety, (e) fear and terror in response to the abuser based on past experiences or encounters with him, (f) anger and rage, and (g) the belief in impending loss of life at the hands of her partner. Moreover, women afflicted with this devastating and crippling syndrome may also find themselves trapped in a cycle of abuse (Walker, 1989). As discussed in chapter 5, this **cycle of violence** involves three stages: (a) a tension-building phase leading to injury; (b) the battering incident itself in which physical, emotional, and verbal abuse are prominent; and (c) a contrition stage in which the battering spouse or partner apologizes and seeks forgiveness (Walker, 1979).

How successful is the defense of battered woman syndrome in acquitting women accused of murdering their spouses or partners? Based on expert testimony identifying the symptoms of this mental disorder, "battered woman's syndrome has been used successfully to acquit many women, or in other cases, to reduce their sentence" (Oltmanns & Emery, 2001, p. 622). However, expert testimony of this sort does not always benefit the defendant. For example, Dr. Lenore Walker testified in the case of *People v. Aris* (1989) on behalf of Ms. Aris. Walker indicated that the accused suffered from battered woman syndrome (Arrigo, 2000). However, Ms. Aris was found guilty of murder, because the jury did not believe the accused was acting in self-defense when she killed her husband while he slept.

Although at least five states have enacted statutes expressly acknowledging the battered woman syndrome as a legitimate defense (Toffel, 1996), several courts have concluded that expert testimony in support of this defense is inadmissible (Faigman, Kaye, Saks, & Sanders, 1997). Indeed, according to critics, not only is the scientific evidence in support of battered woman syndrome modest at best (Schopp, Sturgis, & Sullivan, 1994; Faigman et al.), but also endorsing such a defense may promote vigilantism (Dershowitz, 1994). Moreover, referring to the defense as the "abuse excuse," critics conclude that battered woman syndrome "is nothing more than a symptom of a general abdication of responsibility. . . . " (Dershowitz, 1994, p. 4). This line of attack seems particularly compelling, especially when one wonders how a person suffering from learned helplessness can sufficiently mobilize herself to kill another human being. These comments

Battered Child Syndrome as a Criminal Defense

Battered child syndrome is an offshoot of battered woman syndrome. Some children endure physical and emotional abuse from their parents. Consequently, these battered children develop the same "learned helplessness" witnessed in the cycle of violence that battered women experience. Similar to the physically or emotionally abused wife who believes that killing her tormentor is the only way to stop the terror she confronts daily, a child who kills his or her mother or father also may have been repeatedly victimized by a parent. Indeed, in this instance, murdering one's parents could be interpreted as an act of self-defense. Consider the following two, real-life vignettes.

On August 30, 1988, 17-year-old Andrew G. Janes shot and killed his abusive stepfather, Walter Jaloveckas. Janes skipped school and waited for Jaloveckas to arrive home from work where he shot him twice in the head (Washington v. Janes, 1992). At his original trial, Janes was not allowed to offer expert testimony that he suffered from battered child syndrome; thus, Janes was convicted of second-degree murder and sentenced to 10 years in prison (Alexander,

1995). However, in June 1993, the United States Supreme Court ruled that the battered child syndrome was admissible, and that it could be used as part of a self-defense argument. Thus, Janes was given another trial.

*Lyle and Erik Menendez used the battered child syndrome as part of their defense in relation to the deaths of their parents. More specifically, the Menendez brothers claimed to be suffering from "**parental abuse syndrome.**" In his book, The Abuse Excuse (1994), Alan M. Dershowitz argues that parental abuse syndrome "claims that years of emotional, physical, or sexual abuse inflicted upon a child at the hands of his or her parent can cause that person to lose control of his or her behavior, usually manifested in an act of revenge against the abusive parent" (p. 332). Though the Menendez brothers were ultimately found guilty, the pair did win a mistrial in their original trial, "largely on the basis of expert testimony about the affects of parental abuse on Lyle and Erik's mental state" (Dershowitz, p. 332). Both the case of Andrew G. Janes and the experience of the Menendez brothers raise important criminal behavior questions about child abuse syndrome and the devastating mental state in which such murderous actions can, and sometimes do, occur.*

notwithstanding, battered woman syndrome is a defense that draws attention to the mental state of the defendant at the time the crime occurred. As such, if successfully employed in a court of law, battered woman syndrome can mitigate one's criminal responsibility or otherwise impact one's criminal sentence. Indeed, as Arrigo (2000, p. 203) concludes, "There is no consistency in the sentencing of these women and verdicts depend largely on the jury of each particular case and the differences from crime to crime."

Posttraumatic Stress Disorder as a Defense

Posttraumatic stress disorder (PTSD) is a condition linked to one's direct experience of or extreme exposure to life-threatening traumatic events that produce symptoms of intense fear, helplessness, or terror (Schiraldi, 2000). The diagnostic criteria for this psychiatric condition include (a) a persistent reexperience of the traumatic event, (b) persistent avoidance of or non-responsiveness to the stimuli (e.g., thoughts, feelings, or other factors associated with the life-threatening situation) linked to the traumatic event, (c) persistent symptoms or increased arousal (e.g., inability to concentrate, outbursts of anger, and sleep difficulties); and (d) persistent duration for at least 1 month. The condition is acute if the disturbance lasts 1 month; it is chronic if the disturbance lasts 3 or more months (APA, 2000). Typical symptoms include flashbacks, recurrent nightmares, and painful memories or images of the traumatic event.

Posttraumatic stress disorder has been linked to a number of individuals or groups exposed to harrowing life situations. Among these groups are war veterans, Holocaust survivors, persons released from solitary confinement, and survivors of sexual abuse (Appelbaum et al., 1993; Herman, 1997). Recently, PTSD has been applied to the firefighters, police officers, and emergency medical service personnel who witnessed the physical devastation and human destruction of the 9/11 airplane suicide crashes in New York City.

Early research on PTSD indicated that it was not a chronic problem (e.g., Helzer, Robins, & McEvoy, 1987). However, more recent statistics paint a different picture. According to some studies, about 10% of women and about 5% of men will experience PTSD at one point or another in their lives (e.g., Kessler, Sonnega, Bromer, Hughes, & Nelson, 1995; Schiraldi, 2000). More alarming figures on Vietnam-era veterans suggest that 31% of these military personnel suffer from PTSD (Kulka et al., 1991).

PTSD has been successfully employed in several contexts, from correctional work (*Wertz v. Workmen's Compensation Appeal Board,* 1996) to support for the **insanity defense** (Monahan & Walker, 1994). In the latter instance, the use of PTSD usually results in a finding of diminished capacity (Bartol, 2002). Diminished capacity is not the same as the total absence of responsibility for one's behavior. Researchers note that persons suffering from battered woman syndrome accused of a capital crime have successfully employed PTSD to substantiate their claim of insanity (Appelbaum et al., 1993). In these instances, the defendant argues that her emotional condition deteriorated so extensively and dramatically because of the constant threat or administration of abuse that, in a **dissociative state,** she killed her batterer. This dissociative state is a condition in which a person is unaware of his or her actions (McCord, 1987; Schiraldi, 2000).

Black Rage as a Defense

On occasion, psychologists, mental health professionals, criminologists, and other trained specialists are asked to advocate for defendants in a criminal trial. However, credible experts are expected to remain objective, impartial, and fair, especially because courts rely on their testimony and expertise. Regrettably, this expectation is not always met. For example, "Sometimes, when the advocate role becomes paramount, the psychologist may create a diagnosis to fit the behavior . . . when no proof exists for the validity of the diagnostic construct" (Wrightsman, 2001, p. 27). Testimony related to Black rage illustrates the dilemma mental health experts confront when attempting to explain, justify, or otherwise account for criminal behavior in the absence of scientific evidence (Dershowitz, 1994; Wilson, 1997).

The Black Rage defense asserts that "black people who are constantly subjected to actions that are perceived by them to be unfair and oppressive become angry, despite an appearance of external calm" (Dershowitz, 1994, p. 323). Further, Black rage "can cause an individual to commit acts of violence by becoming the 'catalyst' for an individual who already suffers from severe mental problems" (Dershowitz, p. 323). One prominent case where the Black rage defense was tested was in the criminal trial of Colin Ferguson (Bardwell & Arrigo, 2002a). "Colin Ferguson was convicted of murder for shooting several passengers on the Long Island railroad despite his lawyers' claims that he was a victim of racism venting black rage" (Wilson, 1997, p. 24). Presently, Ferguson is appealing his case on constitutional grounds, alleging that he was a victim of courtroom prejudice against people of color.

Dershowitz (1994) contends that the phenomenon of Black rage is an abuse excuse. Indeed, as he argues, "it is an insult to millions of law-abiding black Americans. The vast majority of African Americans who never break the law have not used the mistreatment they have suffered as an excuse to mistreat others" (Dershowitz, 1994, p. 90). What is troubling about the defense of Black rage is that, if endorsed in courtrooms, it has the potential to label an entire group of people as vengeful, given the deep-seated rage they harbor operating beyond their control (Wilson, 1997). Acknowledging this sentiment serves only to "reaffirm racist fears among too many Americans that violent crime is a 'black problem'. If black rage produces violent crime, or even is a 'catalyst' for it, then racists will be quick to justify their fear of blacks as a group" (Dershowitz, 1994, p. 90). Relatedly, if the defense is upheld in a court of law, given expert testimony in support of it, then treatment of African Americans in the legal system will be adversely affected because of Black rage (Bardwell & Arrigo, 2002a). Indeed, if it is believed that "blacks as a group have more 'rage' than others, and are thus more inclined towards violence, some [people] will argue for longer sentences for black

Junk Food, Depression, and Criminal Behavior

Does the food that we eat, along with the presence of chronic depression, impact our behavior? Most researchers say the answer is yes. However, can behavior that rises to the level of killing someone be attributed to junk food and depression? The answer was yes in at least one controversial case.

On November 27, 1978, a man by the name of Dan White shot and killed San Francisco Mayor George Moscone and Supervisor Harvey Milk. "Examined by a psychiatrist immediately after the shootings, White showed no signs of **psychosis** *and seemed able to appreciate the wrongfulness of his act" (Wilson, 1997, p. 22). Moreover, evidence that the crime was premeditated was linked to the fact that White carried extra bullets with him to City Hall, climbed through a window so as not to be detected, and even reloaded his weapon between shootings. It sounds like an open and shut case for first degree murder, right? Wrong.*

"White was convicted only of involuntary manslaughter. He was sentenced to 7 years and 8 months in prison rather than life [for the killing of Moscone and Milk]" (Wilson, 1997, p. 22). White's case became known as the infamous **"Twinkie Defense."** *An expert witness testified that White suffered from periodic bouts of depression arising from the*

pressures of his job aggravated by the consumption of twinkies. As such, the defense argued that White's mental state was diminished due to the effects of junk food and depression. Following their deliberations, the jury found White to be "incapable of fully forming a malicious or premeditated intent to kill Moscone and Milk" (Wilson, 1997, p. 23). This case demonstrates that juries can be persuaded by scientific evidence, even if it is testimony on the effects of a snack food. Not surprisingly, then, the jury was inclined to conclude that Dan White was not wholly responsible for his criminal actions.

More recent research prepared by Wade White and Mark Wolraich (1995) provided an overview of the scientific evidence both supporting and refuting the connection between sugar and human behavior (evidence Dan White's jury was not privy to). The authors found that numerous clinical investigations with children have not demonstrated a significant effect of sugar on aggressive behavior, motor activity, or cognitive performance. So, the next time you get angry or do something you regret, remember you are not going to be able to successfully blame your actions on the sugar coated cereal you had for breakfast!

recidivists, earlier and harsher police intrusion against black suspects, and other forms of 'preventative' intervention in black neighborhoods" (Dershowitz, 1994, p. 90).

As a defense mitigating criminal responsibility, Black rage creates a public sentiment that questions the validity of legitimate defense strategies such as the insanity defense, battered woman syndrome, and PTSD (Wilson, 1997). "Insanity and other traditional defenses serve an important function in our system of law enforcement, by distinguishing between culpable [deserving of blame] and nonculpable [not deserving of blame] harm-doers" (Dershowitz, 1994, p. 91). Thus, the interests of justice cannot be served when these established and proven defenses are either disregarded or abused. To date, the Black rage defense has not done anything other than undermine the integrity of recognized criminal defense strategies where legitimate psychiatric disorders are involved. To the extent that psychiatric experts testify in support of the existence of such a condition, their actions are less than responsible, especially because they are inaccurately testifying about the relationship between mental illness and criminal behavior.

DISCUSSION QUESTIONS

1. Comment on the relationship between mental illness and crime. Are psychiatrically disordered individuals more likely to act violently than non-mentally-ill individuals? What relationship, if any, does substance abuse figure into your response?

2. What are the differences between Axis I and Axis II disorders? What is bipolar disorder? In what ways are bipolar disorder I and bipolar disorder II distinguishable?

3. What are some of the diagnostic criteria for schizophrenia? What is the relationship between schizophrenia and paranoia? Can you think of any recent cases of persons who acted violently and who were subsequently diagnosed with schizophrenia?

4. What is the definition of a personality disorder? How are psychopathy and antisocial personality disorder related? Can persons diagnosed as psychopathic or with ASPD traits act criminally? Explain your response.

5. What are some of the diagnostic criteria for conduct disorder? What types of delinquent behaviors are associated with adolescents diagnosed with conduct disorder?

6. Define competency to stand trial. How is it different from the defense of insanity?

7. Can mentally incompetent prisoners be restored to competency for purposes of execution? Can you think of any controversial cases where the issue of competency restoration for death row convicts was raised?

8. What is involuntary civil commitment? What is its relationship to competency to stand trial? How do police power commitments and *parens patriae* commitments differ?

9. What are the elements of battered woman syndrome? In what way is this syndrome linked to the defense of insanity? In what ways are battered woman syndrome and battered child syndrome similar?

10. What is posttraumatic stress disorder? How is it linked to the defense of insanity?

11. What is the Black rage defense? Is it a credible criminal defense strategy? Explain your response.

REFERENCES

Alexander, K. (1995, February 13). Jury deadlocks in murder trial of abused youth. *The Seattle Times,* p. A1.

American Psychiatric Association. (2000). *Diagnostic and statistical manual of mental disorders* (4th ed., text revision). Washington DC: Author.

American Psychological Association. (1995). *Violence in the family.* Washington DC: APA Press.

Appelbaum, P. S., Jick, R. Z., Grisso, T., Givelbar, D., Silver, E., & Steadman, H. J. (1993). Use of posttraumatic stress. *Psychiatry, 150,* 229–334.

Arrigo, B. A. (1993). *Madness, language, and the law.* Albany, NY: Harrow and Heston.

Arrigo, B. A. (1996). *The contours of psychiatric justice: A postmodern critique of mental illness, criminal insanity, and the law.* New York: Garland.

Arrigo, B. A. (2000). *Introduction to forensic psychology.* San Diego, CA: Academic Press.

Arrigo, B. A. (2002). *Punishing the mentally ill: A critical analysis of law and psychiatry.* Albany, NY: State University of New York Press.

Arrigo, B. A., & Bardwell, M. C. (2000). Law, psychology, and competence to stand trial: Problems with and implications for high profile cases. *Criminal Justice Policy Review, 11*(1), 16–43.

Arrigo, B. A., & Shipley, S. L. (2001). The confusion over psychopathy (1): Historical considerations. *International Journal of Offender Therapy and Comparative Criminology, 45*(1), 325–344.

Arrigo, B. A., & Tasca, J. J. (1999). Right to refuse treatment, competency to be executed, and therapeutic jurisprudence: Toward a systematic analysis. *Law and Psychology Review, 23,* 1–47.

Arrigo, B. A., & Williams, C. R. (1999). Law, ideology, and critical inquiry: Case of treatment refusal for incompetent prisoners awaiting execution. *New England Journal on Criminal and Civil Confinement, 25,* 367–412.

Bardwell, M. C., & Arrigo, B. A. (2002a). *Criminal competency on trial: The case of Colin Ferguson.* Durham, NC: Carolina Academic Press.

Bardwell, M. C., & Arrigo, B. A. (2002b). Competency to stand trial: A law, psychology, and policy assessment. *Journal of Psychiatry and Law, 30*(2), 147–269.

Barrett, K. E., Taylor, D. W., Pullo, R. E., & Dunlap, D. A. (1998). The right to refuse medication: Navigating the ambiguity. *Psychiatric Rehabilitation Journal, 21*(3), 241–249.

Bartol, C. R. (2002). *Criminal behaivor: A psychosocial approach* (6th ed.). Upper Saddle River, NJ: Prentice Hall.

Bonnie, R. (1992). The competence of criminal defendants: A theoretical reformulation. *Behavioral Science and the Law, 10*(3), 292–313.

Bonnie, R., Hoge, S., Monahan, J., Poythress, N., Eisenberg, M., & Feucht-Haviar, T. (1997). The MacArthur adjudicative competence study: A comparison of criteria for assessing the competence of criminal defendants. *Journal of the Academy of Psychiatry and Law, 24*(2), 149–159.

Brady, K. (2000). Difficulties in diagnosis and management of bipolar disorder: Three case presentations. *Journal of Clinical Psychiatry, 61,* 32–37.

Cleckley, H. (1941, 1982). *The mask of sanity* (1st & 7th eds.). St. Louis, MO: Mosby.

Culver, C. M. (1991). Health care ethics and mental health law. In S. A. Shah & B. D. Sales (Eds.), *Law and mental health* (pp. 25–47). Rockville, MD: Department of Health and Human Services, National Institute of Mental Health.

Dershowitz, A. M. (1994). *The abuse excuse: And other cop-outs, sob stories, and evasions of responsibility.* Boston: Little, Brown.

Ditton, P. M. (1999). *Mental health treatment of inmates and probationers (Special Report NCJ 174463).* Washington DC: U.S. Department of Justice, Office of Justice Programs, Bureau of Justice Statistics.

Dusky v. United States, 362 U.S. 402 (1960).

Eronen, M., Tiihonen, J., & Hakola, P. (1996). Schizophrenia and homicidal behavior. *Schizophrenia Bulletin, 22,* 83–89.

Evans, D. (2000). Bipolar disorder: Diagnostic challenges and treatment considerations. *Journal of Clinical Psychiatry, 61,* 26–31.

Faigman, D. L., Kaye, D. H., Saks, M. J., & Sanders, J. (1997). *Modern scientific evidence: The law and science of expert testimony.* St. Paul, MN: West.

Ford v. Wainwright, 477 U.S. 399 (1986).

Foucha v. Louisiana, 504 U.S. 71 (1992).

Gacono, C. B. (1998). The use of the Psychopathy Checklist-Revised (PCL-R) and Rorschach for treatment planning with antisocial personality disordered patients. *International Journal of Offender Therapy and Comparative Criminology, 42*(1), 49–64.

Gacono, C. B. (Ed.). (2000). *The clinical and forensic assessment of psychopathy: A practitioner's guide.* Mahwah, NJ: Lawrence Erlbaum Associates.

Gacono, C. B., & Hutton, H. E. (1994). Suggestions for the clinical and forensic use of the Hare Psychopathy Checklist-Revised (PCL-R). *International Journal of Law and Psychiatry, 17*(3), 303–317.

Ghaemi, S. (2000). New treatments for bipolar disorder: The role of atypical neuroleptic agents. *Journal of Clinical Psychiatry, 61,* 33–40.

Hare, R. D. (1991). *The Hare psychopathy checklist-revised.* Toronto: Multi-Health.

Hare, R. D. (1996). Psychopathy: A clinical construct whose time has come. *Criminal Justice and Behavior, 23,* 25–54.

Hare, R. D. (2003). *The Hare psychopathy checklist-revised* (2nd ed.). North Tonawanda, NY: Multi-Health.

Haroun, A. (2002). Conduct disorder or disordered conduct? In N. G. Ribner (Ed.), *Handbook of juvenile forensic psychology* (pp. 117–133). San Francisco: Jossey-Bass.

Helzer, J. E., Robins, L. N., & McEvoy, L. (1987). Post-traumatic stress disorder in the general population: Findings of the epidemiological catchment area survey. *New England Journal of Medicine, 317,* 1630–1634.

Herman, J. (1997). *Trauma and recovery*. New York: Basic Books.

Hodgins, S. (1992). Mental disorder, intellectual deficiency, and crime: Evidence from a birth cohort. *Archives of General Psychiatry, 49,* 476–483.

Hodgins, S., Lapalme, M., & Toupin, J. (1999). Criminal activities and substance use of patients with major affective disorders and schizophrenia: A 2-year follow-up. *Journal of Affective Disorders, 55,* 187–202.

Holstein, J. A. (1993). *Court-ordered insanity: Interpretive practice and involuntary commitment*. New York: Aldine de Gruyter.

Jackson v. Indiana, 406 U.S. 715 (1972).

Kessler, R. C., Sonnega, A., Bromer, E., Hughes, M., & Nelson, C. B. (1995). Post-traumatic stress disorder in the National Comorbidity Survey. *Archives of General Psychiatry, 52,* 1048–1060.

Koch, J. L. (1891). *Die psychopathischen Mindwerigkeiten*. Ravensburg, Germany.

Krafft-Ebing, R. von. (1915). *Textbook of insanity* (C. G. Chaddock, Trans.). Philadelphia, PA: F. A. Davis.

Kulka, R. A., Schlenger, W. E., Fairbank, J. A., Jordon, B. K., Hough, R. L., Marmar, C. R., et al. (1991). Assessment of post-traumatic stress disorder in the community: Prospects and pitfalls from recent studies of Vietnam veterans. *Psychological Assessment: A Journal of Consulting and Clinical Psychology, 4,* 547–560.

Lamb, H. R., & Weinberger, L. E. (1998). Persons with severe mental illness in jails and prisons: A review. *Psychiatric Services, 49*(4), 483–492.

Levrant, S., Cullen, F. T., Fulton, B., & Wozniak, J. F. (1999). Reconsidering restorative justice: The corruption of benevolence revisited? *Crime and Delinquency, 45*(1), 3–27.

Loeber, R., Burke, J. D., Lahey, B. B., Winters, A., & Zera, M. (2000). Oppositional defiant and conduct disorder: A review of the past 10 years, Part 1. *Journal of the American Academy of Child and Adolescent Psychiatry, 39,* 1468–1484.

Loeber, R., & Stouthamer-Loeber, M. (1998). Development of juvenile aggression and violence: Some common misconceptions and controversies. *American Psychologist, 53,* 242–259.

Marder, S. (1996). Management of schizophrenia. *Journal of Clinical Psychiatry, 57*(Suppl. 3), 9–13.

Marzuk, P. (1996). Violence, crime and mental illness: How strong a link? *Archives of General Psychiatry, 53,* 481–486.

Maudsley, H. (1897/1977). *Responsibility in mental disease*. New York: Publications of America.

McCord, D. (1987). Syndromes, profiles and other mental exotica: A new approach to the admissibility of nontraditional psychological evidence in criminal cases. *Oregon Law Review, 66,* 19–108.

Melton, G. B., Petrila, J., Poythress, N., & Slobogin, C. (1997). *Psychological evaluation for the courts* (2nd ed.). New York: Guilford.

Millon, T., & Davis, R. (2000). *Personality disorders in modern life*. New York: Wiley.

Millon, T., Simonsen, E., Birket-Smith, M., & Davis, R. (1998). *Psychopathy: Antisocial, criminal, and violent behavior*. New York: Guilford.

Monahan, J. (1992). Mental disorder and violent behavior: Perceptions and evidence. *American Psychologist, 47,* 511–521.

Monahan, J. (1996). *Mental illness and violent crime*. Washington DC: U.S. Department of Justice, Office of Justice Programs, National Institute of Justice.

Monahan, J., & Walker, L. (1994). *Social science and law: Cases and materials* (3rd ed.). Waterbury, NY: Foundation Press.

Myers, J. E. B. (1983/1984). Involuntary civil commitment of the mentally ill: A system in need of change. *Villanova Law Review, 29,* 367–433.

Oltmanns, T. F., & Emery, R. (2001). *Abnormal Psychology* (3rd ed.). Upper Saddle River, NJ: Prentice Hall.

People v. Aris, 215 Cal. App. 3d 1178.

Perry v. Louisiana, 494 U.S. 1015 (1990).

Pinel, P. (1801/1962). *A treatise on insanity* (D. Davis, Trans.). New York: Hafner.

Prichard, J. C. (1837/1973). *A treatise on disorders affecting the mind*. London: Sherwood, Gilbert, & Piper.

Rasanen, P., Tiihonen, J., Isohanni, M., Rantakallio, P., Lehtonen, J., & Moring, J. (1998). Schizophrenia, alcohol abuse, and violent behavior: A 26-year followup study of an unselected birth cohort. *Schizophrenia Bulletin, 24,* 437–441.

Resiner, R., & Slobogin, C. (1997). *Law and the mental health system: Civil and criminal Aspects* (2nd ed.). St. Paul, Minnesota: West Publishing.

Rush, B. (1812). *Medical inquiries and observations upon the diseases of the mind*. Philadelphia, PA: Kimber & Richardson.

Sands, J., & Harrow, M. (2000). Bipolar disorder: Psychopathology, biology, and diagnosis. In M. Hersen & A. Bellack (Eds.), *Psychopathology in adulthood* (2nd ed., pp. 326–347). Boston: Allyn & Bacon.

Schiraldi, G. R. (2000). *Post-Traumatic Stress Disorder Sourcebook*. New York: McGraw-Hill.

Schopp, R. F., Sturgis, B. J., & Sullivan, M. (1994). Battered woman syndrome, expert testimony, and the distinction between justification and excuse. *University of Illinois Law Review, 54*, 45–113.

Scott, H., Johnson, S., Menezes, P., Thornicroft, G., Marshall, J., Bindman, J., et al. (1998). Substance misuse and risk of aggression and offending among the severely mentally ill. *British Journal of Psychiatry, 172*, 345–350.

Shipley, S. L., & Arrigo, B. A. (2001). The confusion over psychopathy: Implications for forensic (correctional) practice. *International Journal of Offender Therapy and Comparative Criminology, 45*(4), 407–420.

Shipley, S. L., & Arrigo, B. A. (2004). *The female homicide offender: Serial murder and the case of Aileen Wuornos*. Upper Saddle River, NJ: Prentice Hall.

Smith, S. R., & Meyer, R. G. (1987). *Law, behavior, and mental health: Policy and practice*. New York: New York University Press.

Soyka, M. (2000). Substance misuse, psychiatric disorder and violent and disturbed behavior. *British Journal of Psychiatry, 176*, 345–350.

Steadman, H. J., McGreevy, M. A., Morrissey, J. P., Callahan, L. A., Robbins, P. C., & Cirincione, C. (1993). *Before and after Hinckley: Evaluating insanity defense reform*. New York: Guilford.

Steadman, H., Mulvey, E., Monahan, J., Robbins, P., Appelbaum, P., Grisso, T., et al. (1998). Violence by people discharged from acute psychiatric inpatient facilities and by others in the same neighborhoods. *Archives of General Psychiatry, 55*, 393–401.

Stevens, G. F. (1993). Applying the diagnosis antisocial personality to imprisoned systems. *Criminal Justice and Behavior, 23*(1), 25–54.

Toch, H. (1998). Psychopathy or antisocial personality disorder in forensic settings. In T. Millon, E. Simonsen, M. Birket-Smith, & R. D. Davis (Eds.), *Psychopathy: Antisocial, criminal, and violent behavior* (pp. 144–158). New York: Guilford.

Toffel, H. (1996). Crazy women, unharmed men, and evil children: Confronting the myths about battered people who kill their abusers, and the argument for extending battering syndrome self-defenses to all victims of domestic violence. *Southern California Law Review, 70*, 337–380.

Tondo, L., Baldessarini, R., Hennen, J., & Floris, G. (1998). Lithium treatment and risk of suicidal behavior in bipolar disorder patients. *The Journal of Clinical Psychiatry, 59*, 405–420.

Walker, L. (1979). *The battered woman*. New York: Harper & Row.

Walker, L. (1989). Psychology and violence against women. *American Psychologist, 44*, 695–702.

Wallace, C., Mullen, P., Burgess, P., Palmer, S., Ruschena, D., & Browne, C. (1998). Serious criminal offending and mental disorder. *British Journal of Psychiatry, 172*, 477–484.

Washington v. Harper, 494 U.S. 210 (1990).

Washington v. Janes, 64 Wn. App. Ct. 134 (1992).

Wertz v. Workmen's Compensation Appeal Board, 683 A.2d 1287 (Penn. 1996).

White, W. J., & Wolraich, M. (1995). Effect of sugar on behavior and mental performance. *The American Journal of Clinical Nutrition, 62*, 242–247.

Williams, C. R., & Arrigo, B. A. (2002). *Law, psychology, and justice: Chaos theory and the new (dis)order*. Albany, NY: State University of New York Press.

Wilson, J. Q. (1997). *Moral judgment: Does the abuse excuse threaten our legal system?* New York: Basic Books.

Winick, B. J. (1997). *Right to refuse mental health treatment*. Washington DC: American Psychological Association.

Wrightsman, L. S. (2001). *Forensic psychology*. Belmont, CA: Wadsworth/Thomas Learning.

Wrightsman, L., Nietzel, M. T., & Fortune, W. H. (1998). *Psychology and the legal system* (4th ed.). Pacific Grove, CA: Brooks/Cole.

part III

Justice System Approaches to Criminals and Criminal Behavior

Policing

OVERVIEW

How does society respond to violent and nonviolent forms of criminal behavior? One mechanism is law enforcement. The system of policing represents the frontline approach to the problems posed by delinquency and crime. At times, police intervention is spontaneous, immediate, and reactive. On other occasions, law enforcement work is planned, calculated, and proactive. Both strategies are designed to reduce the likelihood of antisocial behavior and offender conduct. This chapter examines various mechanisms used by the police in the tracking, detection, and apprehension of criminals, as well as in the prevention or reduction of delinquency and crime.

In particular, this chapter examines community-based policing methods, reports on the effect of **neighborhood watches** and **D.A.R.E. (drug abuse resistance education)** programs, and explores useful strategies in law enforcement training and related instruction. In addition, this chapter reviews the use of criminal and **racial profiling** and other techniques or devices employed in routine police investigation and apprehension work. The chapter concludes by exploring the role of officers in schools and the impact this strategy has on curbing violence in educational settings.

As the criminal justice gatekeepers of society, law enforcement personnel endeavor to promote public welfare and prevent civic unrest. These are not easy tasks. When antisocial, delinquent, and criminal behavior emerges, the police are called on to address these problems and protect us from harm. Clearly, the decisions they make and the strategies they employ represent important approaches to understanding offenders and their criminal behavior.

KEY TERMS

Beanbag guns
Community-oriented policing (COP)
Contextual discrimination
Crime scene analysis
Criminal profiling
D.A.R.E. (drug abuse resistance education)
Front porch phenomena
Knock and talk
Less-than-lethal weapons
Memorandum of Understanding (MOU)
Modus operandi

Neighborhood Watches
Nets
Police education
Police training
Porcupine spikes
Racial profiling
Road spikes
Robots
Signature
Stinger spikes
Stop sticks
Tire deflation devices

COMMUNITY POLICING

Introduction

Community policing programs are being implemented in cities all over America (Wycoff, 1995). When they first emerged around the country in 1994, it was estimated that 46% of all law enforcement units or precincts in America had adopted this form of policing in some aspect within their respective departments (Roche, Adams, & Arcury, 2001). In addition to their regular duties, officers all over the country are now expected to establish more direct and intimate relationships with people in the communities they serve. Part of this task includes facilitating the resolution of problems that citizens confront and mediating interpersonal disputes that might otherwise result in violence (Dietz, 1997).

Intervention programs of this sort were established to deter crime and raise the quality of life within lower income neighborhoods. As such, police personnel are charged with identifying the most salient problems within their particular patrol area, and working closely and cooperatively with residents in those communities to resolve them. These police strategies help create a more stable and healthy neighborhood where people believe their input is valued, makes a difference, and ensures public safety. When problems exist beyond the scope of police expertise, local law enforcement is responsible for identifying and relying on appropriate public or private agencies that can best address these concerns (Sadd & Grinc, 1996).

This section briefly examines the structure and practice of **community-oriented policing (COP)** programs. In addition, the underlying philosophical, programmatic, and activity levels of policing are reviewed. To situate this commentary, material on the efficacy of such programs is presented at the end of the section, featuring particular initiatives around the country that have implemented community-oriented policing.

The Structure and Practice of Community-Oriented Policing

To date, there exists no universally accepted definition for what constitutes community-oriented policing. However, veteran researchers maintain that it involves a solution-focused, problem-solving, decision-making process in which the police address the needs and issues that community residents confront daily (e.g., Hickman & Reaves, 2001; Mastrofski, Worden, & Snipes, 1996; Sadd & Grinc, 1996; Skogan & Hartnett, 1997). Moreover, investigators contend that COP is not a specific set of tactical plans, but a broad concept or idea to which law enforcement personnel can actively adhere (Skogan & Hartnett, 1997).

In addition, community-oriented policing entails prevention work and proactive intervention. Proactive law enforcement anticipates and resolves problems before they occur in a neighborhood and seeks to curtail the use of incident response or reactive policing to address neighborhood issues (Radelet & Carter, 1994). In this context, the community plays an important, active, and vital role (Rosenbaum, 1998). Indeed, the positive relationship established between law enforcement agents and local residents is crucial to maximizing prospects for successful community-oriented policing (Wycoff, 1995).

Given the structure and practice of community-oriented policing, it is clear that it represents an ongoing process of institutional change (Peak, 2003). The change envisioned by this strategy of law enforcement recasts the way in which officers engage in patrol work, emphasizing the resolution of neighbor problems or resident disputes. Moreover, COP signifies an ever-increasing multicultural awareness (Shusta, Levine, Harris, & Wong, 2002) in which departments and precincts rethink how they understand public safety in a diverse society, and how they recruit, educate, train, evaluate, and reward officers for their police work (Hickman & Reaves, 2001).

The Philosophical, Programmatic, and Activity Levels of Community-Oriented Policing

There are three main levels at which to examine community policing: the philosophical level, the programmatic level, and the activity or strategic level (Langworthy & Travis, 2003; Roche, Adams, & Arcury, 2001). At the philosophical level, there are three main principles that distinguish COP from the traditional, enforcement style of policing. These principles are briefly examined in the following paragraphs.

First, there is a sense of shared responsibility among officers and community members for the overall safety and well-being the neighborhood can (and should) experience. Achieving this goal requires constant communication between police and citizens, in which local residents assume a more active role in preventing crime, keeping the community safe, and improving the quality of life for everyone in the neighborhood (Wycoff, 1995). In order to assure this sense of collective responsibility, officers are assigned permanent "beats," enabling them to become better acquainted with the people who inhabit a given jurisdiction or locale. These assignments typically entail foot patrol in which officers stop and talk to members of the community, become familiar with residents while on patrol, or otherwise invest themselves in the needs of the neighborhood (Hickman & Reaves, 2001).

The second philosophical principle of COP relates to crime prevention. Conventional law enforcement tends to be very reactive in its crime-deterring methods. Consequently, it is not oriented to prevention at all (Rosenbaum, 1998). In this model of policing, the interaction among officers and citizens consists mainly of the police responding to calls for assistance and not of much more (Radelet & Carter, 1994). Conversely, community policing attempts to identify those conditions responsible for the occurrence of crime, working to solve or rectify these circumstances before a problem materializes. This is the core of what proactive crime prevention represents (Roche et al., 2001).

The third philosophical principle linked to COP entails a reassessment of officer discretion. Community-oriented policing encourages law enforcement agents to be more flexible, within limits, when addressing neighborhood needs, including their response to crimes occurring within their area of patrol (Ponsaers, 2001). This approach displaces reactive, mechanical decision making in which arrests for criminal wrongdoing are automatic. Indeed, the degree of discretion attributable to COP enables officers to build trust within the community and establish rapport with residents (Wycoff, 1995). As such, officers receive support in their efforts to locate creative ways to minimize arrest practices while nonetheless addressing the problem at hand in a fair, just, and constructive manner for all parties concerned (Roche et al., 2001).

At the programmatic level, there is also no universal format followed by all departments or precincts (Mastrofski et al., 1996). Each community-oriented policing program has its own unique set of characteristics depending on the city or jurisdiction examined (Hickman & Reaves, 2001). However, one common aspect of COP initiatives is the emphasis on community awareness (Ponsarers, 2001). While on shift, COP personnel are "off radio." In other words, they are not expected to respond to any calls because they are building trust and rapport within the community (Pino, 2001). Typically, these officers work out of small, neighborhood-based substations, patrolling small, contained, and accessible communities. However, over time some departments expand their COP efforts, adding additional officers to a larger region within their jurisdiction (Roche et al., 1996).

The activity or strategic level of community-oriented policing involves a wide array of behaviors on the part of law enforcement personnel. Patrol may consist of walking or bicycling. These activities facilitate the establishment of personal relationships with residents—a relationship that would otherwise be hindered by the use of traditional and impersonal patrols by squad cars. Another strategy employed through COP initiatives is called **knock and talk.** In this scenario, police make an effort to formally introduce themselves to the residents of the neighborhood. In addition, patrol officers may initiate community projects such as youth service efforts and Neighborhood Watch programs (Roche et al., 2001). These and related community-oriented policing activities are designed to enhance and compliment the presence of traditional law enforcement in residential neighborhoods and are not a substitute for these police practices (Wycoff, 1995).

The Efficacy of Community-Oriented Policing

Police departments and precincts around the country have been encouraged to implement specific curricula to train officers properly in the practice of community-oriented policing (Palmiotto & Donahue, 1995). Not surprisingly, there has been some resistance to this initiative, given the shift in established law enforcement work (Palmiotto, Birzer, & Unnithan, 2000; Russell & MacLachlan, 1999). As such, it is important to examine the overall efficacy of COP and to determine whether such an approach to policing in society is worthwhile, especially with regard to addressing the problems posed by criminal behavior.

The most comprehensive evaluation of community policing programs and their effect on residential neighborhoods was done by Skogan (1994). In his quasi-experimental design, Skogan conducted a pretest and posttest on 14 neighborhoods in 6 cities. In his analysis, he found that 9 of the neighborhoods experienced a statistically significant improvement in the residents' attitudes toward the police; 7 neighborhoods experienced reductions in *fear of crime;* 6 neighborhoods showed decline in perceived neighborhood disorder; and 3 of the neighborhoods experienced an actual reduction in victimization rates.

Another study focusing on the problem-solving activities of community-oriented police officers yielded similar, positive results. In their investigation of a commercial strip in Joliet, Illinois, Wilkinson, Rosenbaum, Bruni, and Yeh (1994) found that over the course of 4 years, Part I crimes decreased significantly. Indeed, there was a 68% decrease in reported incidents, along with significant declines in violent crimes, property crimes, and code violations (Wilkinson, Rosenbaum, Bruni, & Yeh, 1994).

More recently, research conducted in Greensboro and Asheville, North Carolina, provided additional evidence supporting the efficacy of community-oriented policing (Roche et al., 2001). The researchers found that 66% of the people in Asheville believed that law enforcement protection offered by COP represented a significant improvement over traditional policing. Moreover, 56% of the people in Asheville felt that COP officers were doing a very good job and were a positive asset to the community (Roche et al., 2001). In Greensboro, 48% of the residents believed that community-oriented policing was an improvement in protection, and 75% felt that the officers were doing a good job within the community (Roche et al, 2001).

Interestingly, the data reported on the reduction of fear of crime did not support the efficacy of community-oriented policing in the Roche et al. (2001) study. Indeed, in Greensboro, only 19% of the residents expressed less fear of crime with the implementation of the COP initiative. In addition, 26% reported experiencing more fear following the implementation of the COP program. Moreover, during the 2-year period assessed, there was only a 1.6% decrease in crime rates. Similar results were found in Asheville. A total of 15% of the people reported feeling less fearful of crime, whereas 20% indicated feeling more fearful following COP programming. These figures are difficult to interpret, especially because there was an 8% decrease in the incidence of crime in Asheville (Roche et al., 2001). Clearly, some research questions the efficacy of community-oriented policing in relation to reducing the fear of crime; however, other studies affirm the positive aspects of COP programming on this particular measure (Skogan, 1994).

Presently, detailed and systematic evaluation regarding the long-term effectiveness of community-oriented policing is wanting (McLauglin & Donahue, 1997; Zhao, Lovrich, & Thurman, 1999). Despite some positive indications, especially from the previously cited research, more investigations are sorely needed. If the aim of COP is to prevent crime and to promote improved police–citizen relationships, then its effect must be to offer a much different strategy to understand offender behavior. Although COP efforts are designed to address and anticipate problems posed by an increasingly diverse and multicultural society, we need to learn more about how community-oriented policing can attend to these very important matters through the institutional changes it endeavors to establish (Shusta et al., 2002).

Defiance Theory and Policing Domestic Violence

In addition to preventing and predicting crime through community policing efforts, it is also important that law enforcement personnel understand variations in criminal events. For example, criminal sanctions (i.e., punishments) can (and do) increase crime. Theories that emphasize the effects of labeling (Lemert, 1972), brutalization (Bowers, 1988), and thrill seeking (Katz, 1988) exemplify this. However, another illustration is defiance theory (Sherman, 1993).

Defiance theory represents the total increase in the degree, frequency, and intensity of future criminality, given societal sanctions perceived by the shameless offender to be unjust and unfair. In other words, defiance occurs as a reaction to the perceived unfair punishment that one receives. These sanctions are defined as unfair if the offender believes that he or she is treated disrespectfully, notwithstanding the relative fairness of the punishment, or if the sanction is considered arbitrary, discriminatory, and excessive.

In his explanation of policing domestic violence, Sherman (1993) theorized how some violators regarded the criminal sanctions they receive (e.g., arrest) as unfair, giving rise to future acts of violence against women. In addition to believing that the criminal sanction is unfair, Sherman (1993) hypothesized that the offender's subsequent defiance would occur because (a) the violator was poorly bonded to or alienated from the community or law enforcement agent imposing the punishment; (b) the offender defined the punishment as stigmatizing and degrading and failed to regard his behavior as a violation of the law; and (c) the violator denied, dismissed, or otherwise did not own the personal shame that followed, given the punishment assigned to him. Thus, to the extent that punishment (i.e., arrest) can be meted out in ways perceived by domestic violence offenders (and other violators) to be legitimate (i.e., fair and respectful of their humanity), control of this criminal behavior might be possible (Sherman, 1992).

NEIGHBORHOOD WATCHES

Introduction

As the previous section suggests, one activity linked to community-oriented policing is participation in Neighborhood Watch programs. In addition, the previous material suggests that people fear crime. Indeed, as Warr and Ellison (2000, p. 576) note, "Confronted with the risks posed by crime in everyday life, adults in our society understandably worry about their own safety. But many of those same adults worry as much or more about the well-being of others as they do about their own safety." Neighborhood Watch initiatives are a proactive response to crime and to offender behavior. This section defines the phenomenon, links it to community policing, and comments on its success in addressing offender conduct.

Neighborhood Watch and Criminal Behavior

As the following caption indicates, communities all across the country take crime seriously. Billboards, signs, and pamphlets are being distributed among citizens in residential neighborhoods invested in preventing antisocial behavior, delinquency, or criminal wrongdoing (Smith, Novak, & Hurley, 1997). This is because fear of crime is a crippling social problem that has many people worried about prospects for victimization. One popular strategy used by community members to alleviate much of this growing fear is to establish Neighborhood Watch or community Block Watch programs. According to Priscilla Stegenga (2000), crime prevention director for the National Sheriff's Association:

> Neighborhood Watch is a basic crime prevention program that stresses education and common sense. It teaches citizens how to help themselves through target hardening and other home security techniques. It also teaches citizens how to identify and report suspicious activity in their neighborhoods. By encouraging citizens to be aware of their surroundings and to look out for one another, it decreases the likelihood of their becoming victims. (p. 11)

Neighborhood Watch Meeting

Neighborhood Watch Meeting

Come learn how to better protect
your home,
your property, and
yourself.

WHEN: WEDNESDAY, June 20, 2005
WHERE: Northwest corner of rear complex (Please bring your own chair)
TIME: 6:30 PM (Meeting will last about 1 hour)
HOSTED BY: **YOUR PALM LAKES NEIGHBORS**

Community Service Officer Dan Noonan
555-0138 or 555-5321

The basic premise behind the Neighborhood Watch effort is citizen participation (Langworthy & Travis, 2003), by which residents protect their homes (and those of others) from burglary or vandalism. In addition, the philosophy behind Block Watch initiatives is that when people work cooperatively and closely with their neighbors and with local law enforcement officials, they can reduce the likelihood of criminal activity from occurring (Stegenga, 2000; Wycoff, 1995). Indeed, according to a study on community cohesion and violent predatory victimization by Matthew R. Lee (2000):

> Well-integrated communities actually lower the risk of violent victimization among individuals because such communities tend to exhibit active social control. That is, they tend to be characterized by high levels of informal guardianship because the residents of said communities are more likely to intervene in public deviant and criminal activities. (pp. 702–703)

Some researchers refer to citizen participation along these lines as *collective efficacy* (Sampson, Raudenbush, & Earls, 1997). As Lee (2000, p. 700) observes, participation of this sort "lend[s] substantial support to the notion that neighborhood context, specifically the degree of community cohesion, is an important determination of victimization risk." Given the practice of collective efficacy, the question is how Neighborhood Watch helps reduce crime, victimization, and fear in modern society. According to the National Neighborhood Watch Program (NNWP; 1981), Block Watch initiatives bring communities closer together through what is termed the **Front Porch phenomena.** As the NNWP (1981) explains it:

> The American way of life is changing rapidly. Americans don't know their neighbors as well as they once did. Churches, schools, and neighborhoods are no longer social institutions linking entire families into a single community. The front porch has disappeared, and the family has moved its social activities to the back yard—often behind a tall fence or hedge. As our towns become more crowded, we all seek more and more privacy. That privacy—that move from the front porch to the back patio—has had its price. Neighborhood Watch has helped to restore the front porch to America. It is bringing neighbors in contact with each other again for a common purpose—to make our homes and streets safe. It has created a spirit of cooperation between law enforcement and the people they serve. (p. iii)

Stegenga (2000) believes that Neighborhood Watches can adapt to today's ever-changing and fast-paced lifestyle. As she notes, "[Block Watch] gives citizens an opportunity to contribute to the well-being of their community. It can be something as simple as agreeing to collect a neighbor's mail and newspapers while they are on vacation. Or it can be a more extensive effort such as organizing ongoing citizen patrols" (p. 11). Activities such as these emphasize residential cooperation (Smith et al., 1997), while providing a safer community in which to live and raise one's family.

The Link Between Neighborhood Watch and Community Policing

One of the most important aspects of a successful Neighborhood Watch program is the cooperation that exists between the community residents and the local police. Indeed, as Skogan (1996, p. 31) asserts: "It is widely assumed that crime prevention is probably more dependent on the community than on the police." With the emphasis today on COP efforts, "the goal of many law enforcement agencies is to form a cooperative relationship with the community built on trust, problem solving, and the exchange of information. Neighborhood Watch meetings can be a useful forum to discuss neighborhood problems and practice problem-solving techniques" (Stegenga, 2000, p. 11). However, many inner-city neighborhoods have a longstanding distrust of the police; therefore, cooperation with law enforcement may not be the first option. "Without citizen trust and cooperation, police officers work in an information vacuum and lack the criminal information needed to perform their basic duties. Identifying the fundamental causes of crime depends largely on citizens who make observations and report illegal activity" (Baker, 2001, p. 72).

Communities that are fearful or distrustful of the police often find it difficult to collaborate with law enforcement and to establish successful Block Watch groups. As Montague (2001) comments on the creation of viable Neighborhood Watch initiatives, "First, police had to build bridges of trust to the communities. [But] police also had to convince citizens that effective policing, whether enforcement, protection or prevention, was a shared responsibility" (p. 51).

The way in which a department goes about building positive community–police relations can take many years to nurture (Bohm, Reynolds, & Holmes, 2000). This is especially the case when local residents disagree about how best to address crime and delinquency in their neighborhoods. For example, community members tend to place greater emphasis on traditional enforcement efforts than they do on prevention practices. Under these conditions, it may be difficult for citizens to understand how law enforcement involvement in "neighborhood trash clean-ups and graffiti removal efforts [helps] reduce crime. . . ." (Webb & Katz, 1997, p. 21). Thus, as Montague (2001) contends, building police–citizen trust has meant that the "police have had to reach out to . . . communities to convince them of the validity and human character of [their] mission" (p. 51).

The Success of Neighborhood Watch Programs

The value of Block Watch efforts is in their ability to reduce crime and foster civic awareness and police–citizen cooperation. In the absence of a positive relationship between communities and local law enforcement, Neighborhood Watch programs are considerably less likely to be successful (Bohm et al., 2000; Sadd & Grinc, 1996). As Stephens (1999) reported, crime reduction through Block Watch initiatives is highly dependent on ongoing and meaningful citizen participation. Commenting on a 1998 National Institute of Justice study that reviewed the major findings of a 2-year, congressionally mandated examination of over 500 crime-prevention programs, the researcher found that "the highly touted centerpiece of crime-prevention programs, Neighborhood Watch, failed to diminish burglary or other targeted crimes" (Stephens, 1999 p. 31). Moreover, inner-city community mobilization against crime was ineffective given that "inner-city residents feared getting involved because the criminals [might] retaliate" (p. 31). However, in other, more promising evaluations, Neighborhood Watch was found to be successful, "but only when initiated and sustained by citizen groups. Police-initiated efforts were not sustained by residents" (p. 31).

What are some techniques that facilitate the success of Neighborhood Watch initiatives? In many communities, technological advancements help residents stay abreast of local-interest news. For example, an automated telephone-dialing system provides daily messages to members of Neighborhood Watch programs (Judd & Shriver, 1999). "These messages include reports of news making activity, community meeting notifications, suggested personal safety precautions, crime prevention tips, information to help in locating suspects or identifying sexual predators, and patterns of property crimes within problem areas" (Judd & Shriver, 1999, p. 23). Another tool that is increasingly useful for Block Watch program members is the World Wide Web:

> The information highway makes it possible for customers to be apprised of news bulletins as soon as they are added to the Web page of the sheriff's office. Anyone accessing the Web page can conduct searches for inmates in custody, query local and statewide listings of fugitives and registered sexual predators/offenders, and view warrant records. (Judd & Shriver, 1999, p. 23)

Notwithstanding these useful devices, the success of Block Watch programs varies considerably (Bohm et al., 2000). "Some police departments have implemented Neighborhood Watch successfully; others have difficulty initiating and sustaining citizen and group participation. Unfortunately, this proves particularly true in troubled neighborhoods that need police assistance" (Baker, 2001, p. 72). In response to this problem, some investigators suggest that police leaders should provide appropriate cyberspace training for Neighborhood Watch participants. "For example, [learning to use] computerized mapping and crime statistics [to identify criminal patterns or trends] would help organizers facilitate and focus citizens on the problems of their communities" (Baker, 2001, p. 72). In addition, proponents of this approach contend that law enforcement officials should establish and update a cyberspace training Web site, and Neighborhood Watch leaders should have a laptop computer "because it serves as an excellent training opportunity for police crime prevention programs" (p. 72).

Neighborhood Watch has evolved since its inception in the 1960s. Its goal of reducing crime and the fear associated with it remains the same. However, its current interventions are more proactive and community oriented; indeed, Block Watch participants no longer represent just another pair of eyes and ears for police departments (Smith et al., 1997). "Neighborhood Watch groups are now incorporating activities that not only address crime prevention issues but that also restore pride and unity to a neighborhood. It is not uncommon to see Neighborhood Watch groups participating in [local] cleanups" (Stegenga, 2000, p. 11) or in other activities that impact community residents' quality of life. Interestingly, what Neighborhood Watch efforts remind us about is that the presence of criminal behavior can also be a powerful source for much needed change through collective solidarity. Indeed, "As Durkheim observed long ago, crime can unite and consolidate communities. But it also exposes the number and strength of social bonds that were already in place" (Warr & Ellison, 2000, p. 576). This is the promise of Neighborhood Watch programming, and its effects, if successfully implemented, can be significant for crime reduction.

DRUG ABUSE RESISTANCE EDUCATION PROGRAMS

Combating the drug problem, especially among society's youth, has been and continues to be a top priority in the United States and abroad. Most experts agree that there are two ways to address this problem. First, incarcerate the offender or refer the individual to a drug and alcohol treatment facility. This approach is reactive and punitive, emphasizing deterrence as the appropriate strategy. Second, educate young people about the potentially harmful effects of substances early in their lives, promoting awareness, discussion, and proactive intervention. To date, neither model has been completely effective in curbing illicit drug consumption. However, this section examines the highly controversial D.A.R.E. (Drug Abuse Resistance Education) initiative; a program based on the philosophy of educating adolescents about drugs and alcohol. In particular, information on the operation of D.A.R.E. is provided, and its effectiveness in reducing criminal and delinquent behavior is explored.

The Operation of D.A.R.E. Programs

In 1983, the Los Angeles Police Department, in cooperation with the Los Angeles Unified School District, initiated a pioneering, proactive project in response to the war on drugs, directed toward the youth of America. The D.A.R.E. program immediately became one of the most popular endeavors in schools all over the United States. Indeed, researchers reported that in 1993 over 6 million students (target ages including fifth- and sixth-graders) were exposed to the D.A.R.E. program (Rosenbaum & Hanson, 1998). The estimated cost of this nationwide educational project was roughly $750 million (Hansen & McNeal, 1997). The program was so popular that, in 1994, the Safe and Drug-Free Schools and Communities Act mandated that all law enforcement agencies provide D.A.R.E. programs as part of a national effort to curb drug usage in America (Hansen & McNeal). In 1996, the number of D.A.R.E. participants grew to over 25 million students in 44 countries (Rosenbaum & Hanson, 1998).

What is D.A.R.E.? These programs are intervention-oriented initiatives "designed to prevent violence and the use of tobacco, alcohol, marijuana, and inhalants (e.g., paints, glue, and markers) by America's youth" (Zagumny & Thompson, 1997, p. 33). Working in conjunction with the local law enforcement community and with Unified School Districts, the ultimate goals of D.A.R.E. are to reduce, if not altogether eliminate, substance use among children and establish drug-free schools, based on the philosophy that intervention and education at an early age are the best ways to achieve these ends (Rosenbaum & Hanson, 1998).

How does D.A.R.E. operate? A trained, uniformed police officer frequents elementary school classrooms once a week for a semester and educates children on the dangers of drug and alcohol use and tobacco products through a 17-session curriculum. There are two major reasons for using a police officer as the primary educator in D.A.R.E. programs. First, the initiative requires that an effective communicator impart the message that drug, alcohol, and tobacco consumption is hazardous. Arguably, a strong authority figure working in the community, such as a police officer, commands the attention and respect of children (Donnermeyer, 1998). Second, proponents maintain that it is important for young people to experience positive interactions with law enforcement personnel in a supportive setting (Donnermeyer, 1998).

D.A.R.E. Programs and Their Effectiveness

Thus far, the research on D.A.R.E. has offered mixed results on the program's ability to curb or eliminate criminal behavior. For example, during 1985 to 1994, drug abuse violations among youth in the United States rose from 73,446 to 121,951 (U.S. Department of Justice, 1995). In addition, one of the early longitudinal studies of D.A.R.E. participants was conducted by Wysong, Aniskiewicz, and Wright (1994). In particular, the researchers sought to measure the coping skills and attitudes of D.A.R.E. participants and control group subjects toward drugs. No significant differences were found between the two groups. The balance of this section reviews the research history on the success (and failure) of D.A.R.E. in relation to drug use and abuse.

Following the implementation of D.A.R.E. in 1983, Congress enacted the Drug-Free Schools and Communities Act in 1987. However, it was not until July 1, 1998, that local school districts were expected to provide evidence of the effectiveness of their programs in order to receive continued federal funding (Rosenbaum & Hanson, 1998). Moreover, Congress required that this evidence be the product of empirical research. Under the new and improved Safe and Drug-Free Schools and Communities Act (SDFSCA), educational units were compelled to expend serious time and energy evaluating the efficacy of the programs for which they had been receiving financial support.

Rosenbaum and Hanson (1998) conducted one such analysis on the efficacy of D.A.R.E. involving a 6-year, multilevel investigation. The researchers engaged in a randomized longitudinal field experiment that assessed both the short- and the long-term effects of the program. Randomization lends itself to fewer threats in experimental validity when evaluating programs. In the past, very few studies used a large sample size or implemented a longitudinal design. The variables assessed included the student's attitudes, beliefs, social skills, and drug use behaviors. The sample consisted of 1,798 adolescents in Grades 6 to 12 from schools in urban and suburban Illinois. These students were followed from the inception of the program for more than a 6-year period. The students were evaluated yearly with surveys. Teachers were also questioned on the extent to which their students were exposed to additional (post-D.A.R.E.) educational training. This is another confounding aspect that previous research failed to consider. Throughout the study, the investigators reported effectiveness with the program at various points. They also commented on its limitations. The results of their study are outlined as follows.

When students in the experimental group were evaluated 30 days after graduation from the D.A.R.E. program, the only substance abuse difference between the experimental and the control group was that those who had graduated from D.A.R.E. reported a significant decline in the use of cigarettes. No other significant differences among the groups concerning substance abuse were reported at the 30-day checkpoint (Rosenbaum & Hanson, 1998). Follow-up studies and evaluations done at 1-, 2-, and 3-year intervals produced no significant main effects for the D.A.R.E. program relating to substance abuse. After the 4-year period, the researchers measured different effects the D.A.R.E. program appeared to be showing. For example, they discovered that students in the project reported getting drunk for the first time and reported the onset of drinking at a later age than those in the control group. Unfortunately, after the 5-year checkpoint, D.A.R.E. students scored significantly higher than those in the control group on the Total Drug Use and Total Alcohol Use indices. The severity of alcohol abuse was also higher among students in the experimental D.A.R.E. group (Rosenbaum & Hanson).

When measuring mediating variables, such as attitudes, beliefs, and social skills, early findings produced the following: Students in the D.A.R.E. program were more likely, than those in the control group, to have negative attitudes toward drugs overall, and they exhibited a greater awareness for the social and media influences pertaining to cigarettes and beer. The students in the experimental group showed more signs of greater self-esteem and greater assertiveness in social situations in response to peer pressures, and they had more positive attitudes toward police officers than did those students in the control group (Rosenbaum & Hanson, 1998). However, after just 1 year, there was a severe decline in self-esteem, assertiveness, and positive attitudes held toward the police. After the 3-year interval, all attitude effects completely disappeared, except that D.A.R.E. students were still more confident in their ability to resist peer pressure. After the 4-year mark, all previously displayed effects concerning attitudes, beliefs, and social skills were completely gone (Rosenbaum & Hanson, 1998). When examining ancillary benefits such as school behavior and academic performance, student exposure to D.A.R.E. resulted in no significant effect on reported grades or number of times children skipped class, got into trouble with teachers, or engaged in delinquent or criminal activity. Overall, the study conducted by Rosenbaum and Hanson indicated that D.A.R.E. had no long-term effects in accomplishing its philosophy; any success attributed to it was entirely scarce or ephemeral at best.

POLICE TRAINING AND EDUCATION

Introduction

Understanding the principles behind **police training** and **police education** requires some familiarity with what both of these terms mean and how these related but separate instructional experiences are useful in the detection and apprehension of offenders. As Bennett and Hess (1996) note, police training is "vocational instruction that takes place on the job and deals with physical skills, [whereas] police education is . . . academic instruction that takes place in a college, university, or seminar-type setting and deals with knowledge and mental skills" (p. 351). This distinction is significant. Indeed, as Whetstone (1993) explains:

> There is a small but important difference between education and training. Education presents material in a broad context where it may be applicable to a variety of experiences. Training can be broad in scope but is primarily focused on a particular activity or skill. In what may be oversimplified terms, education shapes how we think; training shapes how we do. (p. 150)

Clearly, officer training and education are vital to law enforcement work. However, it is imperative that police instruction be appropriate to the tasks assigned. Overall, the instruction must be tailored to address (proactively and reactively) the problems posed by offender conduct. This section examines police training, police education, and the effects of both in relation to combating crime and criminal behavior.

Police Training

Training for police officer recruits teaches them the basic competencies needed to perform the duties of a police officer (McCampbell, 2001). Generally, local police departments require 640 hours of training, including 425 hours of classroom instruction and 215 hours of field instruction (U.S. Department of Justice, 1997). Most training is done within a classroom environment; however, it is essential to take the instruction beyond this formal setting. Field training programs provide recruits with an opportunity to apply the principles learned in a classroom context to a real-life situation (Birzer & Tannehill, 2001). Field training typically begins once the recruit completes the in-class segment of basic training (McCampbell, 2001).

Field training is composed of at least three phases, including an introductory stage, several intermediate training or encounter phases, and an evaluation or metamorphosis phase (Langworthy & Travis, 2001; Van Maanen, 1973). According to McCampbell (2001), "during the introductory phase, the recruit becomes familiar with agency policies and local laws; during the training and evaluation phases, the recruit is gradually introduced to the more complicated tasks patrol officers confront" (p. 107). The final phase of training determines whether the recruit is capable of working on his or her own, and whether the officer is adequately socialized into the police culture (Farkus & Manning, 1997). During this phase, the field-training officer evaluates the recruit and assesses whether the individual can successfully perform the duties associated with being a patrol officer.

Training programs beyond field instruction are also necessary for police officers. For example, Buzawa and Buzawa (2001) maintain that law enforcement personnel "have not been well trained to cope with domestic violence incidents. In many cases, police had profound ignorance of the proper methods of handling domestic violence cases" (p. 219). Research has shown that officers trained in domestic violence handle these incidents more appropriately than do officers not exposed to such field instruction. Indeed, law enforcement personnel trained in domestic violence and spousal abuse matters are better suited to diffuse the emotional intensity generated by these situations (Stanko, 1989). However, exposure to such instruction may be affected by other cultural and organizational factors located within police departments. As Buzawa and Buzawa suggest:

> Training may be overshadowed by: the contradictory pressures of the police organization's paramilitary structure, coupled with an inability to control officer conduct on the street; inability to provide rewards for appropriate behavior; and the retrograde informal "training" that new officers receive from cynical, hardened peers. (p. 226)

Overall, however, officers trained in supplemental areas (i.e., domestic violence and intervention with the mentally ill) are better equipped to face the challenges of policing, especially when they engender attitudes supportive of the need for this ancillary instruction (Patch & Arrigo, 1999). Not surprisingly, though, these pro-social attitudes cannot thrive unless the police subculture teaches and encourages them through the appropriate instructional training.

Additional Police Training Efforts Designed to Combat Crime

Another area in which officers are often not properly trained is in the use and proficiency of firearms. Typically, the police receive extensive training in shooting a gun or rifle; however, ethical responsibilities associated with them are often neglected. In order to train officers in the use of firearms and instill ethical responsibility, police departments have developed a training method named "Shoot–Don't Shoot" (Blumberg, 2001). This method presents officers with a set of vignettes and asks them to fire their weapon only when appropriate. This strategy differs significantly from previous methods in which recruits were taught to shoot at fixed objects from a stationary position. Other precincts and departments around the country have implemented related training efforts. Examples of these initiatives include martial arts training, ethics training, conflict resolution training, and hostage negotiation training (Blumberg, 2001). These instructional initiatives are designed to address the problems posed by crime and delinquency.

Another type of police training includes stress management and stress reduction. Most police academy training programs do not include exposure to these exercises, despite the fact that stress relief is essential to job satisfaction in law enforcement (Abdollahi, 2002; Arrigo & Garsky, 2001). Indeed, Arrigo and Garsky (2001) assert that "policy setting within precincts can and must include on-going staff development designed to address stress related to police work, family life, and alcohol use" (p. 677). In addition, coping strategies for anxiety need to be included in police training programs. Instructing officers on how best to deal with job-related stress can be accomplished through group process sessions in which officers openly and supportively discuss the pressures of work. However, law enforcement personnel are often very reluctant to participate in these sessions for fear of ridicule or other reprisals from fellow officers. Consequently, they are not adequately schooled in those preventive methods designed to help them cope with work-related anxiety and other symptoms of job stress (Arrigo & Garsky, 2001). This training is essential if officers are to be adequately prepared in their efforts to fight crime.

Police Education

In 1993, almost all local police departments had formal education requirements (U.S. Department of Justice, 2001). The typical, minimum education requirement for police officer recruits was the completion of high school. Furthermore in 1993, 12% of local police departments required some college course work (Reaves & Goldberg, 2000). In 1990, only 6% of departments required some college course work. In addition, approximately 1% of police departments required a 4-year college degree, and 7% required a 2-year college degree (U.S. Department of Justice, 1997).

An increased commitment to police education has resulted in a growing number of departments offering incentives for individuals who have earned college credits (Carlan & Byxbe, 2000). Currently, over half of all police officers have completed at least 1 year of college and nearly one fourth of all officers have obtained a 4-year degree (Carlan & Byxbe, 2000). Typically, the college program that police officers and potential recruits enter is linked to the academic discipline of criminal justice. Commenting on educational success through college preparation, Stevens (1999) notes that this goal is "highest among young officers, females, single persons, nonwhite, higher ranking officers, persons undecided about staying in law enforcement, and those receiving incentive pay to attend school" (p. 37).

Some investigators argue that higher education produces numerous benefits for police officers (Hoover, 1995). Included among these benefits are (a) development of a broader knowledge base that can positively affect decision making; (b) increased maturity of officers gained through experience; (c) a deepening sense of responsibility achieved through the completion of course requirements; and (d) a heightened awareness of the democratic processes and the history of the United States and its policing methods (Stevens, 1999).

In addition to these benefits, there are widespread ideals that support or reject officer education. According to Hawley (1998), there are four foci behind the push for this instruction. These foci include (a) the professionalization of policing, (b) the improvement of the performance of individual officers, (c) the development of improved critical thinking skills in officers, and (d) the improvement of officers' understanding of diverse populations. However, other researchers question the value of baccalaureate education for the police (Swanson, 1977). Hawley identifies five factors: (a) the ability of noneducated administrators to set policies within their departments, (b) the notion that police officers should represent their communities demographically, (c) the effect of education on both individual and police force professionalism, (d) the requirement of a college education for further professionalization of the police, (e) and the incentives needed for individual police officers to attain higher education.

Effects of Police Training and Education on Criminals and Criminal Behavior

Notwithstanding the pushes and pulls for college-level instruction among the police, "the available evidence suggests that educational attainment does matter in police behavior. . . " (Langworthy & Travis, 2003, p. 251). Indeed, as the research indicates, officers who attend college are better equipped to endure the intricacies of policing (Carlan & Byxbe, 2000). College-educated police officers have a broader understanding of human behavior, are more supportive of community relations between officers and the community, and bear a higher standard of neighborhood and civic service (Carlan & Byxbe, 2000; Hoover, 1995). Research suggests that police officers that frequent college are more accepting of alternatives to punishment (Farnworth, Longmire, & West, 1998). Indeed, officers who graduate from criminal justice programs often complete their degree with attitudes that are less harsh than those of their non-college-educated counterparts (Farnworth et al., 1998; Reaves & Goldberg, 2000).

Police officers exposed to higher education are also more likely to employ nonviolent strategies, such as conflict resolution, and more ethical reasoning in their discretionary decision making when apprehending criminals (Blumberg, 2001). These police practices represent a service rather than a force orientation toward the public (Carlan & Byxbe, 2000). Admittedly, education alone cannot adequately prepare law enforcement personnel for the rigors of police work, especially when antisocial behavior, delinquency, and offender conduct are involved. However, establishing a departmental climate in which education matters is an important first step in the process. This is not as easy as it sounds, especially because it entails altering the police subculture in many departments and precincts around the country (Hoover, 1995). Ultimately, though, as the higher education of officers becomes more acceptable, this will produce a more promising future for law enforcement agencies in their efforts to apprehend criminals (Blumberg, 2001).

CRIMINAL AND RACIAL PROFILING

Introduction

Although community-oriented policing, Neighborhood Watch efforts, D.A.R.E. programs, and police training and education are all designed to prevent crime, police officers must be prepared to track, detain, and apprehend offenders. This section focuses on two approaches that equip officers along these lines. In particular, **criminal profiling** and racial profiling are reviewed. As the section explains, although these techniques assist law enforcement personnel, they also raise some serious questions about the nature of police investigation work.

Criminal Profiling

What is criminal profiling? According to most investigators, it is "the process of inferring distinctive personality characteristics of individuals responsible for committing criminal acts" (Turvey, 1999, p. 1) based on offender and victim data. Typically, profiling takes place after law enforcement personnel examine a crime scene (Alison & Canter, 1999). Indeed, as Copson (1995) argues, profiling is an attempt to determine the attributes of an unknown perpetrator based on evaluating minute details of the crime scene, the victim, and any other obtainable evidence. In this context, then, criminal profiling "is an attempt to provide investigators with more information on the offender who is yet to be identified" (Egger, 1999, p. 243). Criminal profiling is often referred to as psychological profiling, investigative profiling, or **crime scene analysis.** (Bartol, 2001; Egger, 2002).

What is the purpose of profiling? "The purpose of profiling is to develop a behavioral composite, combining sociological and psychological assessments of the offender" (Egger, 1999, p. 243). According to Brent E. Turvey (1999), forensic scientist and crime scene analyst, "Criminal profiling is a multi-disciplinary forensic practice [that] requires, at the very least, applied knowledge in criminalistics, medico-legal death investigation, and psychology" (p. xxvii). This wide range of knowledge and experience is crucial to the specialist so that an impression of the offender can be formulated. As Egger (1999) explains it:

> Profiling is generally based on the premise that an accurate analysis and interpretation of the crime scene and other locations related to the crime can indicate the type of person who committed the crime. Because certain personality types exhibit similar behavioral patterns (in other words, behavior that becomes routine), knowledge and understanding of the patterns can lead investigators to potential suspects. (p. 243)

Often, crime scene analysts seek to understand a perpetrator's unique **modus operandi** (MO) in an attempt to predict the offender's behavior and form a personality portrait from such data. According to Douglas and Olshaker (1998), "MO is what an offender has to do to accomplish a crime. It is learned behavior and gets modified and perfected as the criminal gets better and better at what he [or she] does" (p. 90). For example, a serial rapist might begin to use duct tape to cover a victim's mouth after realizing that her screams for help could get the assailant caught.

Investigative profilers also attempt to ascertain the criminal's **signature.** The signature "is something the offender has to do to fulfill himself [or herself] emotionally. It is not needed to successfully accomplish a crime, but it is the reason he [or she] undertakes the particular crime in the first place" (Douglas & Olshaker, 1998, p. 90). An example of an offender's signature would be to leave a Bible at the scene of every crime the person commits. Leaving the Bible is unnecessary to the administration of the criminal act, and it does not facilitate departure from the crime scene; rather, it is "something special to that particular offender" (Douglas & Olshaker, 1998, p. 90). By uncovering a perpetrator's MO or signature, a profiler can link a crime scene to a particular personality and behavioral type (Egger, 2002). This linkage can help investigators narrow their search for suspects.

What do we know about who profilers are? As Egger (1999) reports, "The terms psychological profiling, offender profiling, criminal profiling, or criminal personality profiling have become almost household words when the public hears about serial killers or

What Does It Take to Be a Successful Profiler?

If you want to be a profiler and you want to be good at it, there are some basic skills you must acquire. In fact, according to Hazelwood, Ressler, Depue, and Douglas (1995), the most important features of successful profilers include the following: (a) an appreciation of the psychology of the criminal (how a criminal mind might function), (b) investigative experience (no amount of classroom education can replace the experience of investigating crimes), (c) the ability to think objectively and logically (a profiler must think logically without being influenced by personal feelings toward the crime, criminal, or victim), and (d) intuition (the act of knowing or sensing without the use of rational processes). "The media often depict[s] the profiler as able to evoke apparently mystical visions of the way in which the crime was committed" (Kocsis, Irwin, Hayes, & Nunn, 2000, p. 313). Police agencies have even invited psychics to use their intuitive faculties to assist in solving difficult cases (Kocsis et al., 2000).

unsolved murders in the mass media or in works of fiction." Unfortunately, most of the impressions people have when they hear the word "profiler" are incorrect. "All of these popular portrayals of profiling [e.g., Agent Starling from the film, *The Silence of the Lambs*] are inaccurate, and they are beginning to construct icons in our popular culture who promote the myth that profiling is a magical skill [beyond intuition], frequently encompassing precognitive psychic ability" (Egger, p. 243). David Canter, Director of the Center for Investigative Psychology at the University of Liverpool, and Laurence Alison further criticize the manipulation by the media regarding criminal profiling:

> There seems to be a reluctance for the media to relinquish fully the notion that psychologists can provide some special insight into the human mind. This is especially true when the actions being examined involve rape and murder. With a morbid fascination reminiscent of the attitudes to freak shows, there appears to be an inability to resist the desire to probe into the darker recesses of the more bizarre features of criminal behavior. "Experts" are commonly credited by the press with almost mythical powers of deduction if they appear to have contributed to police investigations and there appears to be a strong relationship between the presumed powers of the expert and the bizarre nature of the offense. (Alison & Canter, 1999, p. 3)

In other words, "Fiction blurs with reality for the general public who expect profiling to be the answer to solving murders, rapes, and other violent crimes" (Egger, 1999, p. 243). Sometimes, in a desperate effort to find a perpetrator of a heinous crime, one's objectivity gets lost in a mix of human emotion, fear, and outrage.

Forensic psychiatrist, Park Dietz, has worked on numerous high-profile cases from the Unabomber to Jeffrey Dahmer. In an interview for *Psychology Today* (Toufexis, 1999), Dietz explained the importance of neutrality in the role forensic psychiatrists play in criminal investigations:

> Our job should be like any other forensic scientists'. We should be truth seekers who are non-partisan, who do not have interest in the outcome, who call it as we see it no matter the consequences. But it seems a lot easier for chemists and anthropologists and pathologists to take that neutral role than it does for psychiatrists . . . the innocuous reason is that psychiatrists are usually very well imbued with the clinical role, where helping the sick person is the goal. And that's quite incompatible with the truth-seeking role." (p. 58)

This incompatibility can pose great obstacles for investigators and prosecutors alike (Egger, 2002).

Is profiling a profession? In part fueled by the media's portrayal of profilers in television crime dramas, many people believe that this investigative work is, by definition, a profession. However, this is not true. "It has been said that any profession is defined by its ability to regularize, to criticize, to restrain vagaries, to set a standard of workmanship and compel others to conform to it. This definition assumes uniform terms, definitions, ethics, standards, practices and methodology" (Turvey, 1999, xxvii). But, as Turvey explains, "Despite any belief to the contrary, such things do not exist in the community of individuals that are engaged in criminal profiling . . . profilers just do not seem to agree on anything" (p. xxvii).

Disagreement among profilers can be best understood by analyzing the process by which a psychological portrait is created. In short, the issues involved with the construction of an offender profile are rarely black and white (Egger, 2002). Indeed, as Alison and Canter (1999, p. 4) note, "Conditions under which any single offense has been committed often have features unique to that case. Moreover, information is often partial, potentially inaccurate and/or irrelevant, and errors early on in an enquiry can compound subsequent misguided interpretations." Moreover, a profile is never established under controlled laboratory conditions, free of outside influence (Egger, 1999). "Experts consult with an enquiry team who have their own opinions and agendas. Thus the opinions given regarding the characteristics of the offender may be profoundly shaped by the nature of the interaction between police and psychologist" (Alison & Canter, 1999, p. 4). Clearly, then, this process opens the door for the distortion of facts, leading to disagreement among experts (Turvey, 1999).

How Does Criminal Profiling Work?

Even though there is no single standardized way in which to engage in criminal profiling, the approach developed by the FBI Behavioral Science Unit is widely accepted. According to Ressler, Burgess, and Douglas (1988), the profiling process entails five interrelated steps (see also Davis, 1999).

Step 1: A comprehensive assessment of the nature of the criminal event and the offender types likely to have committed this particular crime.

Step 2: An exhaustive and systematic assessment of the particular crime scene in question.

Step 3: A detailed and systematic review of the victims' backgrounds and potential suspects.

Step 4: An assessment of the likely motivating factors giving rise to the criminal event.

Step 5: The creation of a descriptive profile for the offender as linked to overt personality features gleaned from the criminal act or scene and associated with the assailant's probable psychological character.

More recently, Jackson and Bekerian (1997) summarized the systematic FBI approach as follows:

Stage 1: data assimilation—involves the collection of all available information from as many sources as possible (e.g. police reports, autopsy reports, photographs of the crime scene); Stage 2: crime classification—attempts to classify the type of crime on the basis of the data collected; Stage 3: crime reconstruction—attempts to reconstruct the crime and to generate hypotheses about the behavior of victims, sequence of crime or modus operandi; Stage 4: profile generation—the generation of a profile including hypothesis about demographic and physical characteristics, behavioral habits and personality dynamics of the perpetrator. (p. 5)

The investigative process outlined here is useful in the police tracking and apprehension of particular offenders (Egger, 1999). Indeed, according to the FBI, "offenses most suitable for profiling involve those where the suspects' behavior at the crime scene reveal important details about themselves" (Jackson & Bekerian, 1997, p. 5). Thus, profiling can be most effective when examining offenses such as "arson and sexually motivated crimes where the criminal has demonstrated some form of psychopathy [such as] a crime scene revealing evidence of sadistic torture, ritualistic behavior, evisceration [disembowelment], posturing of the body, staging, or acting out of a fantasy" (Jackson & Bekerian, 1997, pp. 5–6). So, are you ready to be a profiler?

Racial profiling occurs when a person is stopped by a police officer or security guard due to his or her skin color and because there is "a fleeting suspicion that the person is engaging in criminal behavior" (Meeks, 2000, p. 5). According to Kenneth Meeks, author of *Driving While Black* (2000), this form of profiling "is generally targeted more towards young Black American men and women than any other racial group, although Asians, Hispanics, and even young Whites with long hair and a hip-hop flair about them get profiled more every day" (p. 5). Thus, as Meeks (p. 5) notes, "A police officer or security guard or anyone in a role of authority can detain and question people, and some believe that racial profiling is a justified form of law enforcement and detective work" (p. 5).

"White Man's Pass" and Racial Profiling

More than a decade ago, the New Jersey Turnpike came to be known as "White Man's Pass" to Black and Hispanic drivers. Many suspected they were being pulled over and searched by state police far more often than Whites. They were right. But it wasn't until White officers shot three minority travelers on the turnpike in 1998 that the perils of DWB—Driving While Black—forced the Garden State to try to clean up its act. New Jersey's Highway Patrol hired its first Black superintendent, and the U.S. Justice Department ordered a series of reforms to stop racial profiling (U.S. News and World Report, April 16, 2001).

One way to assess the practice of racial profiling is to question what it represents and accomplishes (Cooper, 2001). For example:

> Is racial profiling a subtle form of legal prejudice? Or is it a legitimate way to stop crime before it takes place? And what are the consequences of racial profiling for African Americans—or Asians, or Middle Eastern Muslims, or even Hispanic and Latinos—as a matter of local, state, or federal government practice? (Meeks, 2000, pp. 5–6).

The answers to these questions are not easy or simple. Indeed, police officers, law enforcement agencies, the media, social science researchers, and the general public are concerned with what racial profiling represents, especially when innocent or noncriminal citizens are injured or killed (Cooper, 2001).

New Jersey's acknowledgment of racial profiling by highway state troopers garnered national attention to this widespread and often overlooked problem. Regrettably, New Jersey is not alone. Indeed, since 1999, "10 states passed laws to discourage racial profiling. Another 13 are considering similar legislation. And one state, Oklahoma, allows cops to be charged criminally for the practice" (Roane, 2001, p. 24). Decisions such as these draw attention to the suspicion that police organizations around the country employ tactics and procedures harmful to racial minorities (Cooper, 2001).

To be clear, however, there is also opposition to the eradication of racial profiling. For example, as Roane (2001) reports:

> Johnny Hughes, spokesman for the National Troopers Coalition, said during testimony before the U.S. Senate [2000] that including race as one of the factors in identifying criminals was about "reason, not race." Hughes claimed that Blacks were more likely than whites to be carrying drugs along the interstate in New Jersey. (p. 24)

However, research into the accuracy of such statements remains unfounded (Cooper, 2001; Roane, 2001). In fact, the evidence seems to suggest that in at least some jurisdictions the standard operating procedure for law enforcement personnel in relation to people of color has been to shoot first and ask questions later. Indeed, as the Christopher Commission (1992) reported following alleged incidents of police brutality in the wake of the Los Angeles riots linked to the trial of officers accused of using excessive force in their arrest of Rodney King, this police practice appears customary.

Racial profiling does not end with traffic stops. As a result of criminal justice policy and differential enforcement of drug laws, the term *criminal* is increasingly associated in the public's mind with Black youth, (re)producing the identity of Black and the identity of criminal (Cooper, 2001). However, according to Tonry (1995), Whites are more likely to use all major drugs except for heroin, yet African Americans are disproportionately arrested and prosecuted for substance use. African Americans comprise 12% of the U.S. population and make up 13% of all monthly drug users. Yet, they represent 35% of those arrested for drug possession, 55% of those convicted of drug possession, and 74% of those sentenced to prison for drug possession (Donziger, 1996).

Walker, Spohn, and DeLone (2000) analyzed dozens of studies investigating the relationship between the defendant's race and the severity of the sentence. Although the researchers reported no significant racial differences in sentencing, the authors asserted that "discrimination ha[d] not declined or disappeared, but simply ha[d] become more subtle and difficult to detect . . . [D]iscrimination against racial minorities is not universal but is confined to certain types of cases, settings, and defendants" (p. 218). Indeed, as Walker et al., explained, when determining appropriate sentences for non-White individuals, racial profiling often comes into play in many jurisdictions, and it assumes the form of **contextual discrimination.** As the investigators reported:

> Judges in some jurisdictions continue to impose harsher sentences on racial minorities who murder or rape Whites, and more lenient sentences on racial minorities who victimize members of their own racial or ethnic group . . . [I] less serious cases, racial minorities [in some jurisdictions] get prison, whereas Whites get probation. (Walker et al., p. 218)

As recently as 2001, the Bush administration and Attorney General John Ashcroft called for "an eradication of racial profiling nationwide" (Roane, 2001, p. 24). Eliminating this practice will not be easy. In part, this is because of the opposition to it. More than this, however, is the problem with proving that racial profiling exists at all (Cooper, 2001). To prove its existence, proponents would have to systematically demonstrate the extent to which racism is institutionalized within law enforcement training academies and within the culture of police departments and precincts around the country. However, a more modest approach would entail tracking the behavior of the police when engaged in ongoing investigative work. Some efforts along these lines have already been implemented. As Meeks (2000) explains:

> This is why a national movement has been launched by politicians of color and civil-rights leaders to mandate that law-enforcement agencies keep statistics of whom they are stopping, questioning, detaining, and searching. Black leaders say it's the only way to be sure that people of color are not being stopped because of their skin. (p. 7)

Efforts such as these represent the best chance for society to eliminate the "White Man's Pass" phenomenon, reorienting the police to the appropriate apprehension and arrest of criminal wrongdoers.

APPREHENSION OF CRIMINALS

Introduction

Law enforcement officials often resort to using several methods of criminal apprehension during the pursuit of suspects. Several technological advances have contributed significantly in these investigative efforts. This section reviews some of the more recent strategies, techniques, and devices employed in the apprehension of offenders. These include the use of **robots, nets, tire deflation devices,** and **less-than-lethal weapons.**

Robots

Two of the more popular uses for robots in law enforcement are found among bomb squad units and within hostage situations. For example, robots are used to complete bomb disarmament tasks (Sorid, 2000). Investigators note that recent developments in robot building suggest that these mechanical devices eventually will be able to complete their work in half the time currently needed to disarm a bomb (Sorid, 2000). Moreover, breakthroughs in robot technology anticipate that these sophisticated machines will be able to adapt to new types of bombs developed by terrorists and other threat groups.

The use of robots in policing is also common in hostage negotiations (Moore, 1999). For example, tactical hostage negotiation teams are now using these mechanical devices in their rescue efforts. The use of robots in these cases minimizes the amount of danger experienced by law enforcement officers. Thus, the maximization of police safety is one of the most powerful arguments in favor of the use of robots in hostage or similar threat situations (Moore, 1999).

Although technological advances are facilitating the use of robots in law enforcement, there are several negative aspects to their use in policing. The first disincentive is that they are extremely costly. Robots used in law enforcement agencies generally cost in excess of $100,000 (Moore, 1999). In addition, the training needed to teach officers adequate skills to deploy robots is expensive. Relatedly, police who receive instruction in robot deployment also train with strategic weapons and tactics (SWAT) teams. SWAT preparation adds to the already high cost of training with robots (Moore, 1999).

The second disincentive for the use of robots in policing is that these mechanical devices are extremely limited in their mobility. For example, many robots cannot climb stairs or maneuver in small spaces such as airplane aisles or overhead compartments (Moore, 1999). The inability of these sophisticated machines to access these areas reduces the scope of their law enforcement effectiveness.

The third disincentive for the use of robots in policing is their battery life. Typically, a robot's battery will last 2 hours. In most instances, this is insufficient time to apprehend a suspect. Other robots are equipped with a 110-volt power supply; however, extension cords are necessary to give power to this supply. Thus, the need for ancillary equipment to facilitate the deployment of robots (i.e., extension cords) represents another limitation to their use (Moore, 1999).

A fourth disincentive with respect to robots in law enforcement is the fear they instill in suspects as well as in victims. Offenders often have a negative reaction to robots; consequently, it is necessary to notify the suspect of robot entry. In addition, experimental testing of robots has documented the fear they engender in young children. For example, Moore (1999) notes the following about an experiment with "Lonnie," a law enforcement robot:

> During a recent school bus hijacking scenario, Lonnie was utilized to talk with the "suspect," who had driven the bus into a large open area. The suspect agreed to release several of the children, but when it came time for them to leave the bus, they were too frightened to walk past the robot. Scenario proctors had to go onto the bus and carry the kids off. (p. 45)

Nets

One of the more recent developments in criminal apprehension is the use of nets, also known as portable vehicle-arresting barriers (PVAB; Willingham, 2000). A net is a nonlethal device that stops a moving vehicle, thereby confining the vehicle's occupants (News Roundup, 2000). Nets are extremely powerful. Indeed, some devices can halt a 7,500-pound car or truck traveling at speeds of up to 45 miles per hour. This type of PVAB is efficient for stopping vehicles within 200 feet. Moreover, at this range, neither the vehicle nor the passengers suffer damage or injury, respectively (News Roundup, 2000). Experiments conducted on the net conclude that it is effective for vehicles weighing a maximum of 14,000 pounds (Willingham, 2000). In addition, the system is also effective for lighter weight automobiles traveling at speeds of up to 60 miles per hour (News Roundup).

Tire Deflation Devices

Many law enforcement agencies now use tire deflation devices when in pursuit of offenders or criminal suspects. Mechanical tire deflating devices are practical and effective. Overall, there are two types of tire deflation devices—stationary devices and nonstationary, or flexible, devices (Stockton, 1999). The main advantage in using stationary mechanisms is their reduced cost. However, the main disadvantage in using stationary devices is the inability (i.e., inflexibility) to move the apparatus to other locations. When a law enforcement agency decides to use tire deflation devices, the department or precinct must also consider their relative strengths and limits for police officers. Although using these devices may reduce the stress experienced during pursuit, police personnel must take the time to undergo the appropriate training to operate these mechanisms safely.

There are four basic tire deflation devices used by police departments. These devices are **stop sticks, road spikes, stinger spikes,** and **porcupine spikes** (Stockton, 1999). Each of these mechanisms is briefly described in the following paragraphs.

Stop sticks were first designed in 1993. These devices are placed on a roadway to deter fleeing suspects. Stop sticks are either 3 or 4 feet long and can be joined together to create a longer device. Stop sticks are armed with Teflon-coated quills and sharp tips. In order to make the stop stick less visible, they can be inserted into a black sleeve and then placed on a roadway.

Road spikes are retractable tire deflation devices that, unlike stop sticks, are activated by an operator in the distance. The operator can trigger the road spikes at his or her own

Do Tire Deflation Devices Effectively Combat Crime?

Can tire deflection mechanisms reduce or contain criminal behavior? According to some experts, the answer is yes. Consider the following real-life vignette.

Officer Paul Gaspich was responding to a call on Pennsylvania State Route 422 when Robert Carney, a 31-year-old trucker hauling a 50,000 pound load of onions, swerved across the highway in an attempt to hit the officer's patrol vehicle. Carney apparently believed the officer was coming after him for an earlier hit and run incident . . . Gaspich turned around and initiated a pursuit that lasted almost two hours and covered five counties. Despite the best efforts of officers from several agencies, attempts to stop the truck were futile as the driver refused to yield and roared down the highway, scattering cars in a manner that a district attorney later said was "like a moving steam roller." Complicating the efforts to stop the huge vehicle was the fact that Carney's two children, ages 3 and 11, were in the cab of the truck. Although officers were successful in laying out spike strips that deflated several of the truck's tires, Carney, who was high on methamphetamine, continued driving even after the tires were shredded. Ultimately, he was unable to maintain sufficient traction to make it up a steep exit ramp and was forced to stop . . . A review of the pursuit showed the successful deflation of the truck's tires permitted the ultimate apprehension of the suspect. (Stockton, 1999, p. 199)

discretion. The spikes on the mechanism remain retracted until activated by the operator. This device is especially effective at checkpoints and other parallel situations. Stinger spikes are different from road spikes. Stinger spikes are thrown across the road. Upon activation, the apparatus expands considerably. When this mechanism is run over, the spikes remain in the tires.

Another tire deflation device frequently used by law enforcement agencies is the porcupine. The porcupine is an apparatus with 178 spikes, each at least 2 inches in length. The spikes cut into the tires on all three sides, causing them to deflate, not allowing the suspect to travel any further.

Less-Than-Lethal Weapons

Recently, law enforcement agencies have begun using alternative means of force to combat crime. These replacement methods include the use of less-than-lethal weapons (Bailey, 1996). Some examples of these weapons are pepper spray, rubber bullets, and beanbag guns. **Beanbag guns** and other less-than-lethal weapons are used not only in policing efforts but in military excursions as well. This subsection specifically comments on the deployment of beanbag guns in law enforcement work.

Beanbag guns were formally known as less-than-lethal .12-gauge shotguns. Beanbag guns are kinetic devices that rarely cause fatalities (Willingham, 2000). Typically, it takes more than a single round to sufficiently incapacitate or otherwise control a suspect or offender.

The impact of this less-than-lethal weapon can be extremely forceful and immobilizing. Indeed, "a square beanbag fired from a .12-gauge shotgun has about the same impact as a line-drive hit in baseball" (Willingham, 2000, p. 27). A beanbag hit can be particularly fatal if shot at the chest area of the suspect. Thus, experts recommend that these less-than-lethal weapons be aimed at other vulnerable areas of the body, for example, the abdomen and the lower back. The most unsafe condition for firing a beanbag gun is when the subject is less than 10 feet away from the shooter (Willingham, 2000).

Willingham (2000) reports that when shot from .12-gauge shotguns, beanbags are difficult to control. At a distance beyond 15 feet, beanbags begin to lose their accuracy. However, law enforcement officials like to keep a distance of at least 21 feet between themselves and their target. In crowded areas, the gap preferred by officers is increased to 30 feet. According to statistics on less-than-lethal weapons, the longest beanbag hit occurred at a distance of 67 feet (Willingham, 2000).

Today, numerous law enforcement departments are experimenting with the alternative-force method of employing beanbag guns (Bailey, 1996; Suhay, 1999). Moreover, research indicates that less-than-lethal weapons are particularly effective in five law enforcement situations. These situations include (a) the apprehension of rebellious suspects, (b) the response to criminals armed with a weapon other than a firearm, (c) the response to a hostage situation, (d) the transportation of prisoners, and (e) the response to riots and other disorderly group phenomenon (Bailey, 1996).

Some Concluding Remarks on Psychology and Criminal Apprehension

A police officer's goal is to "apprehend the suspect and make the arrest" (Alpert, 2001, p. 601). However, achieving this goal may endanger the cop as well as the public (Dunham, Alpert, Kenney, & Cromwell, 1998). Thus, as Alpert notes, "the trend has been to restrict [police firearm] use to defense or preservation of life situations" (p. 603). To reduce the use of firearms, technologists have devised mechanisms that effectively apprehend criminals in a nonlethal fashion. To be clear, when these devices are employed by the police, it is essential that officers receive the appropriate physical and cognitive training in their use. When assessing the training that officers are required to receive, significantly less time is spent on when and how to use the weapons skills they acquire (Alpert & Fridell, 1992). In other words, officers are trained in the skills needed to apprehend criminals. However, they are not adequately prepared to apply this training to real-life situations (Dunham et al., 1998).

Notwithstanding a lack of systematic and ongoing training in the area of apprehension devices, the use of these mechanisms can decrease stress levels for officers (Bailey, 1996). Criminal pursuit is a highly debilitating activity that police officers endure (Alpert, 2001). Moreover, apprehension devices assist law enforcement officers by depersonalizing criminal situations. For example, the use of robots in hostage negotiations "allows the subject to surrender to a 'thing,' rather than police. This allows the subject to 'save face'" (Moore, 1999, p. 44). When suspects are granted the opportunity to "save face" during apprehension or are taken into custody in a nonviolent manner, the outcome is less psychologically burdensome for all parties involved. In the final analysis, then, addressing criminal wrongdoing through law enforcement efforts requires that one understand the psychology of offender behavior as well as the psychology of police work.

COPS IN SCHOOLS

The tragic massacre at Columbine High School in Littleton, Colorado, has alerted educators across the nation of a potential danger that children face every day at school. This danger is school violence. At a recent symposium entitled "Creating a violence free school for the twenty-first century," the then Attorney General of North Dakota, Heidi Heitkamp (2000), made the following observations:

> We need to ask the question about what rights do students sitting in a classroom have to a safe environment, to a quality education, to an education uninterrupted by chair throwing, and to an education uninterrupted by drugs and alcohol in the schools. How many of you would go to work every day and sit next to someone who brought a gun to work or who is peddling drugs in your workplace? Kids are forced to be there . . . in order to get an education they have to be there, and they have to be treated appropriately. (p. 4)

In an effort to increase school safety both physically and psychologically, one popular tactic employed is to hire school resource officers (SRO) and have police officers patrol school campuses. In this section, the relationship between policing and school violence is examined. In particular, background information on law enforcement personnel in schools is provided, and commentary on the function, roles, and responsibilities of SROs in schools is presented.

Background on Police in Schools

Placing police officers in schools is not a new phenomenon. In fact, the idea was first introduced in Liverpool, England, in 1951 (Bond, 2001). In the United States, as early as 1958, the first SRO was assigned to a high school in Flint, Michigan with the same goal "as it had been in England: to build positive police-student relationships" (Bond, 2001, p. 53).

Today, however, police officers in schools across the country carry out a wide range of duties in order to ensure a safe environment where children can learn, free of the interruptions and distractions noted by Attorney General Heitkamp. For example, in Miami-Dade County, the public school police department consists of 170 sworn personnel who serve 312,000 students in the county (Vardalis & Kakar, 2000). These police officers "not only patrol school property, but conduct background investigations on teachers, staff, and bus drivers, record all crime and related reports, and arrest offenders" (Vardalis & Kakar, 2000, p. 39).

In 1994, Congress passed the Safe Schools Act. "This act, among other things, allowed school districts with high rates of crime, violence, and disciplinary problems to compete for federal grants" (Stefkovich & Miller, 1999, p. 4). Since Congress passed the Safe Schools Act of 1994, "police and quasi law enforcement officers [have become] increasingly involved in public schools for a variety of reasons from protection of students to education programs, such as peer mediation and crime prevention" (Stefkovich & Miller, 1999, p. 4). As Portner (1994) explains it:

> Twenty years ago, most school officials would never have dreamed of allocating their precious resources to hire armed police to protect campuses. If increased security was required for a football game or a school dance, a district typically hired security officers for the night . . . [In 1994], more than 50 school districts have spent millions of dollars to set up professionally trained school police forces that operate around the clock. In the late 1970s, there were fewer than 100 school police officers in the United States. [In 1994], there [were] more than 2,000 [school police officers]. (p. 13)

Recently, in the wake of several tragedies involving school violence across the nation, the number of school districts utilizing police officers has increased dramatically (Bond, 2001). "In Kentucky, for example, there were four districts with SROs during 1997–1999. By the start of the 2000 school year, that number had increased to 67 districts" (p. 53). These figures reflect an alarming trend designed to address growing concern for, and the possibility of, school violence.

The Function, Roles, and Responsibilities of Police in Schools

James Vardalis and Suman Kakar (2000) suggest that there are three models of providing specialized security services in schools: (a) The School Security Department Model, (b) The School Resource Officer Model, and (c) The School Police Department Model. "The School Security Model engages contractual or proprietary private security personnel. The School Resource Officer Model contracts with a law enforcement agency to provide assigned officers to schools . . . [T]he School Police Department Model creates a public police department for the school system" (Vardalis & Kakar, 2000 p. 40).

Law enforcement personnel who work in schools have different responsibilities compared to police officers who patrol city neighborhoods (Bond, 2001). Indeed, "because the academic environment is driven by institutional goals, school police have a different role than typical city police in their approach to law enforcement" (Vardalis & Kakar, 2000, p. 41). For example, school police approaches may include the following activities: "(1) Offenses are handled both administratively and criminally, (2) crime reporting is a positive safety tool, and (3) security requires student relations and cooperation" (Vardalis & Kakar, p. 41). Moreover, according to Trump (1997), owner and chief consultant of National School Safety and Security Services, SROs must enact a multifaceted approach when it comes to school safety. This approach requires that officers remember that the educational setting informs their decision making.

What is the best way for the police to respond to school violence? Vardalis and Kakar (2000) contend that school violence "can be addressed most effectively by a collaborative effort between the schools, law enforcement officials, social service agencies, and the community as a whole" (p. 42). Police officers in schools need to be aware that crime in schools often is indicative of a larger societal problem. Indeed, "It must be understood that crime in schools is an extension of crime in the community" (Vardalis & Kakar, 2000, p. 42). Therefore, police officers in schools must have adequate knowledge of the particular problems the students are facing at home and in their neighborhoods. In this way, school officers, in conjunction with education officials, can be on the alert for potential problems, intervening before an act of violence takes place. As Bond (2001) describes it:

> School resource officers are security experts, just as school nurses are health specialists, and they can devote 100 percent of their time and effort to this vital function . . . [T]heir backgrounds allow them to anticipate and plan to deal with illegal activities that an educator might miss, and as employees of the local police departments, they have many resources to help prevent problems before they occur. (p. 53)

Another area where SROs can assist school personnel in maintaining a safe environment is with crisis management. "School officials and law enforcement personnel should have a plan to deal with any crisis situation that might arise, including, but not limited to, hostage situations, bomb threats, and natural disasters such as hurricanes, earthquakes, tornados, and fire" (Vardalis & Kakar, 2000, p. 42). Typically, school police have the training and skills necessary to deal with these occurrences more effectively than do school personnel.

It is also worth noting that SROs can create conflicts with the established roles found within the school community. "Having police officers in schools is a new experience for most educators and officers; [thus], a complete understanding of each group's expectations must be clearly defined" (Bond, 2001, p. 53). Frequently, schools that intend to use SROs will draft what is referred to as a **Memorandum of Understanding (MOU).** "A Memorandum of Understanding is a document typically developed between the superintendent and the sheriff or police chief, and it describes in detail the areas of responsibilities and expectations of the school and the local police" (p. 53).

Authority and chain of command are important components of the MOU. "SROs typically work for local sheriffs or police chiefs and are directly supervised by the police department. Principals are responsible for safety, discipline, and order. Only when a state or federal law is broken does the SRO's authority supercede that of the principal" (Bond, 2001, pp. 53–54). SROs also have the authority to arrest individuals and to take the lead in the investigation of any criminal violations occurring within the school (Vardalis & Kakar, 2000). However, "In all other cases of conduct and school policy, the principal is in charge" (Bond, 2001, p. 54).

SROs are also responsible for student searches occurring on school grounds. As Stefkovich and Miller (1999) explain, police involvement in school searches may take place in a variety of ways—from patrolling schools, participating in crime prevention programs, teaching about drug abuse and prevention, and addressing truancy. Commenting on such activities occurring on campus, the authors note the following:

> First, police may give tips to school officials that a crime has been committed or is about to be committed on school property. In this situation the police have shared information with school administrators but have not told them what to do with the information. Second, police may give tips to school security guards. The information shared usually relates to criminal activity, warning the guards that a crime has been committed on school property. Third, police may become involved in school searches when they investigate a crime that started outside of school. Fourth, school officials may request police presence to witness a search or to act as consultants. Fifth, police are involved in school searches when they are called into school to help with a discipline problem and end up conducting an investigation and then a search. In the latter situation, police may be the fact finders, make the decision to

Should SROs Be Allowed to Carry Firearms?

One of the most controversial areas surrounding the use of police officers in schools is whether or not they should be allowed to carry a firearm. "Many principals and parents have strong feelings about having an armed individual in a school setting, but police departments feel that SROs must carry a sidearm to carry out their mission as law enforcement officers" (Bond, 2001, p. 55). However, psychologically speaking, students and their parents are concerned that a mistake in judgment by a school officer could lead to devastating and deadly results. "All parties should remember that SROs are highly trained and experienced professionals who know when deadly force is required" (p. 55). Ultimately, most schools allow police officers to carry firearms. "It is estimated that 95 percent of all school police officers across the United States are armed" (p. 55).

search, and direct and conduct the search with the outcome being possible criminal prosecution for the student. Police may also simply "stand by" while school officials conduct a search. In this latter capacity, police are present but involved neither in the fact-finding nor in the search. Sixth, police may be involved in school searches when they are hired by school districts. In such situations, police help deter crime by patrolling the halls and school grounds. Finally, they also do routine police work in a school setting. (p. 4)

In the case of searches and seizure taking place at school (i.e., searches of student lockers and automobiles on campus), the Supreme Court addressed this matter in the case of *New Jersey v. T. L. O.* (1985). In this instance, the Court ruled that school officials could not conduct *unreasonable* student searches. However, the Court's opinion did establish the reasonable suspicion standard, "which clarified the criteria under which school officials could conduct student searches" (Steftkovich & Miller, 1999, p. 3). The reasonable suspicion standard states that school officials must have reasonable belief that the search will provide evidence that the student committed a crime or violated a school regulation (Steftkovich & Miller, 1999). This is a useful standard because many school police officers routinely use drug-sniffing dogs to search for contraband on school property in order "to control the use and sale of drugs in public schools" (p. 14). The dogs' ability to sniff out drugs provides the school reasonable suspicion to search a student's locker or automobile.

DISCUSSION QUESTIONS

1. What is community-oriented policing (COP)? What are some of the philosophical, programmatic, and activity-level aspects of COP? What are some of the limits of community-oriented policing?
2. How do Neighborhood Watch efforts combat crime? What role does citizen participation play successfully in Block Watch efforts? How does fear or distrust of the police impact Neighborhood Watch programs?
3. What is D.A.R.E.? Are D.A.R.E. programs successful in responding to criminal or delinquent behavior? Explain your response.
4. What are some of the differences between police training and education? What are the arguments in support of higher education for law enforcement personnel? What are some of the arguments against higher education for law enforcement personnel?
5. What is criminal profiling? Is criminal profiling a profession? Justify your response. How does criminal or investigative profiling assist the police efforts with crime?
6. What is racial profiling? What are some of the arguments in favor of this police practice? What are some of the arguments opposed to this police practice? Has racial profiling become institutionalized in law enforcement? Explain.
7. What are some of the techniques officers employ in the apprehension of suspects or offenders? What are the limitations of using robots in law enforcement? Distinguish among the various types of tire deflation devices used by the police.

8. How is the discipline of psychology important to apprehending offenders and to understanding policing?

9. What are school resources officers (SROs)? How do they combat school violence? What are some of the roles and responsi-

bilities of SROs in relation to school personnel? Do you believe that the presence of armed officers at educational settings have an impact on juvenile crime? Explain your response.

REFERENCES

Abdollahi, M. K. (2002). Understanding police stress research. *Journal of Forensic Psychology Practice, 2*(2), 1–24.

Alison, L., & Canter, D. (1999). Profiling in policy and practice. In D. Canter & L. Alison (Eds.), *Profiling in policy and practice* (pp. 3–19). Brookfield, VT: Ashgate Publishing.

Alpert, G. P. (2001). Managing the benefits and risks of police pursuit driving. In R. G. Dunham & G. P. Alpert (Eds.), *Critical issues in policing: Contemporary readings* (4th ed., pp. 599–618). Prospect Heights, IL: Waveland Press.

Alpert, G. P., & Fridell, L. (1992). *Police vehicles and firearms: Instruments of deadly force.* Prospect Heights, IL: Waveland Press.

Arrigo, B. A., & Garsky, K. (2001). Police suicide: A glimpse behind the badge. In R. G. Dunham & G. P. Alpert (Eds.), *Critical issues in policing: Contemporary readings* (4th ed., pp. 664–680). Prospect Heights, IL: Waveland Press.

Bailey, W. C. (1996). Less-than-lethal weapons and police-citizen killings in U.S. urban areas. *Crime and Delinquency, 42*(4), 535–552.

Baker, T. E. (2001). A cyberspace approach. *Law & Order, 49,* 72–75.

Bartol, C. R. (2001). Police psychology: A profession with a promising future. In R. G. Dunham & G. P. Alpert (Eds.), *Critical issues in policing: Contemporary readings* (4th ed.). Prospect Heights IL: Waveland Press.

Bennett, W. W., & Hess, K. M. (Eds.). (1996). *Management and supervision in law enforcement* (2nd ed.). Minneapolis, MN: West Publishing Company.

Birzer, M., & Tannehill, R. (2001). A more effective training approach for contemporary policing. *Police Quarterly, 4*(2), 233–252.

Blumberg, M. (2001). Controlling police use of deadly force: Assessing two decades of progress. In R. G. Dunham & G. P. Alpert (Eds.), *Critical issues in policing: Contemporary readings* (4th ed., pp. 559–582). Prospect Heights, IL: Waveland Press.

Bohm, R., Reynolds, K., & Holmes, S. (2000). Perceptions of neighborhood problems and their solutions: Implications for community policing. *Policing: An International Journal of Police Strategies and Management, 23*(4), 439–465.

Bond, W. (2001). Principals & SROs: Defining roles, principal leadership. *High School Education, 1,* 52–55.

Bowers, W. J. (1988). The effect of executions is brutalization, not deterrence. In K. C. Haas & J. A. Inciardi (Eds.), *Challenging capital punishment.* Newbury Park, CA: Sage.

Buzawa, E. S., & Buzawa, C. G. (2001). Traditional and innovative police responses to domestic violence. In R. G. Dunham & G. P. Alpert (Eds.), *Critical issues in policing: Contemporary readings* (4th ed., pp. 216–237). Prospect Heights, IL: Waveland Press.

Carlan, P. E., & Byxbe, F. R. (2000). The promise of humanistic policing: Is higher education living up to societal expectation? *American Journal of Criminal Justice, 24*(2), 235–245.

Christopher Commission. (July, 1992). *Report of the independent commission on the Los Angeles Police Department.* City of Los Angeles.

Cooper, C. (2001). An Afrocentric perspective on policing. In R. G. Dunham & G. P. Alpert (Eds.), *Critical issues in policing: Contemporary readings* (pp. 376–400). Prospect Heights, IL: Waveland Press.

Copson, G. (1995). *Coals to Newcastle? Part 1: A study of offender profiling.* London: Police Research Group Special Interest Series, Home Office.

Davis, J. A. (1999). Criminal personality profiling and crime scene assessment. *Journal of Contemporary Criminal Justice, 15,* 273–290.

Dietz, A. (1997). Evaluating community policing: Quality police service and fear of crime. *Policing: An International Journal of Police Strategies and Management, 20*(1), 83–100.

Donnermeyer, J. F. (1998). Educator perceptions of the D.A.R.E. officer. *Journal of Alcohol and Drug Education, 44*(1), 1–7.

Donziger, S. (1996). *The real war on crime: The report of the National Criminal Justice Commission*. New York: Harper Perennial.

Douglas, J., & Olshaker, M. (1998). *Obsession*. New York: Scribner's.

Dunham, R. G., Alpert, G. P., Kenney, D., & Cromwell, P. (1998). High-speed pursuit: The offender's perspective. *Criminal Justice and Behavior, 25,* 30–45.

Egger, S. A. (1999). Psychological profiling: Past, present, and future. *Journal of Contemporary Criminal Justice, 15,* 242–261.

Egger, S. A. (2002). *The killers among us: An examination of serial murder and its investigation* (2nd ed.). Upper Saddle River, NJ: Prentice Hall.

Farkus, M., & Manning, P. (1997). The occupational culture of corrections and police officers. *Journal of Crime and Justice, 20*(2), 51–68.

Farnworth, M., Longmire, D. R., & West, V. (1998). College students' views on criminal justice. *Journal of Criminal Justice Education, 9,* 39–57.

Hansen, W. B., & McNeal, R. B. (1997). How D.A.R.E. works: An examination of program effects on mediating variables. *Health Education and Behavior, 24,* 165–176.

Hawley, T. J. (1998). The collegiate shield: Was the movement purely academic? *Police Quarterly, 1*(3), 35–59.

Hazelwood, R., Ressler, R., Depue, R., & Douglas, J. (1995). Criminal investigative analysis: An overview. In R. Hazelwood & A. Burgess (Eds.), *Practical aspects of rape investigation: A multidisciplinary approach* (2nd ed., pp. 115–126). Boca Raton, FL: CRC Press.

Heitkamp, H. (2000). Symposium: Creating a violence free school for the twenty-first century. *New England Law Review, 34,* 581–588.

Hickman, M., & Reaves, B. (2001). *Community policing in local police departments, 1997 and 1999*. Washington, DC: Bureau of Justice Statistics, Government Printing Office.

Hoover, L. (1995). Education. In W. B. Bailey (Ed.), *The encyclopedia of police science* (2nd ed., pp. 245–248). New York: Garland.

Jackson, J., & Bekerian, D. (1997). Does offender profiling have a role to play? In J. Jackson & D. Bekerian (Eds.), *Offender profiling: Theory, research and practice* (pp. 1–7). Chichester, England: Wiley.

Katz, J. (1988). *Seductions of crime*. New York: Basic Books.

Kocsis, R., Irwin, H., Hayes, A., & Nunn, R. (2000). Expertise in psychological profiling: A comparative assessment. *Journal of Interpersonal Violence, 15,* 311–331.

Langworthy, R. H., & Travis, L. F. (2003). *Policing in America: A balance of forces* (3rd ed.), Upper Saddle River, NJ: Prentice Hall.

Lee, M. R. (2000). Community cohesion and violent predatory victimization: A theoretical extension and cross-national test of opportunity theory. *Social Forces, 79,* 683–706.

Lemert, E. (1972). *Human deviance, social problems, and social control* (2nd ed.). Upper Saddle River, NJ: Prentice Hall.

Mastrofski, S., Worden, R., & Snipes, J. (1996). *Law enforcement in a time of community policing*. Washington DC: National Institute of Justice.

McCampbell, M. S. (2001). Field training for police officers: State of the art. In R. G. Dunham & G. P. Alpert (Eds.), *Critical issues in policing: Contemporary readings* (4th ed., pp. 107–116). Prospect Heights, IL: Waveland Press.

McLaughlin, C., & Donahue, M. (1997). Problem-oriented policing: Assessing the process. *Justice Professional, 10*(1), 47–59.

Meeks, K. (2000). *Driving while Black: What to do if you are a victim of racial profiling*. New York: Broadway Books.

Montague, A. (2001). Ottawa's police have something to sing about. *Law & Order, 49,* 51–54.

Moore, R. (1999). Consider 'RoboCops' for the 21st century. *Police, 23*(8), 42–45.

New Jersey v. T. L. O., 469 U.S. 325 (1985).

News Roundup. (2000, December 22). *Defense Daily International, 1*(37), 1.

Palmiotto, M., Birzer, M., & Unnithan, P. (2000). Training in community policing: A suggested curriculum. *Policing: An International Journal of Police Strategies and Management, 23*(1), 8–21.

Palmiotto, M., & Donahue, M. (1995). Evaluating community policing: Problems and prospects. *Police Studies, 18*(2), 33–53.

Patch, P., & Arrigo, B. A. (1999). Police officer attitudes and use of discretion in situations involving the mentally ill: The need to narrow the focus. *International Journal of Law and Psychiatry, 22*(1), 23–35.

Peak, K. J. (2003). *Policing America: Methods, issues, challenges* (4th ed.). Upper Saddle River, NJ: Prentice Hall.

Pino, N. (2001). Community policing and social capital. *Policing: An International Journal of Police Strategies and Management, 24*(2), 200–215.

Ponsarers, P. (2001). Reading about "community (oriented) policing" and police models. *Policing: An International Journal of Police Strategies and Management, 24*(4), 470–496.

Portner, J. (1994, June 22). Cops on campus. *Education Week*, 13.

Radelet, L., & Carter, D. (1994). *The police and the community* (5th ed.). New York: McMillan.

Reaves, B., & Goldberg, A. (2000). *Local police departments, 1997*. Washington DC: Bureau of Justice Statistics, U.S. Government Printing Office.

Ressler, R. K., Burgess, A. W., & Douglas, J. E. (1988). *Sexual homicide: Patterns and motives*. Lexington, MA: Lexington Books.

Roane, K. (2001). Risky trip through 'White Man's Pass' in New Jersey: A losing war on racial profiling. *U.S. News and World Report, 130*, 24–28.

Roche, W., Adams, R., & Arcury, T. (1996). *Community oriented policing: The North Carolina experience*. Chapel Hill, NC: Center for Urban and Regional Studies.

Roche, W., Adams, R., & Arcury, T. (2001). Community policing and planning. *Journal of the American Planning Association, 67*(1), 78–90.

Rosenbaum, D. (1998). The changing role of the police: Assessing the current transition to community policing. In Jean-Paul Brodeur (Ed.), *How to recognize good policing: Problems and issues*. Thousand Oaks, CA: Sage.

Rosenbaum, D. P., & Hanson, G. S. (1998). Assessing the effects of school-based drug education: A six-year multilevel analysis of project D.A.R.E. *The Journal of Research in Crime and Delinquency, 35*(4), 381–412.

Russell, G., & MacLachlan, S. (1999). Community policing: Decentralized decision making and employee satisfaction. *Journal of Crime and Justice, 22*(2), 31–54.

Sadd, S., & Grinc, R. (1996). *Implementation challenges in community policing*. Washington DC: National Institute of Justice.

Sampson, R. J., Raudenbush, S. W., & Earls, F. (1997). Neighborhoods and crime: A multilevel study of collective efficacy. *Science, 277*, 918–924.

Sherman, L. W. (1992). *Policing domestic violence: Experiments and dilemmas*. New York: Free Press.

Sherman, L. W. (1993). Defiance, deterrence, and irrelevance: A theory of criminal sanction effects. *Journal of Research in Crime and Delinquency, 30*, 445–473.

Shusta, R. M., Levine, D. R., Harris, P. R., & Wong, H. Z. (2002). *Multicultural law enforcement: Strategies for peacekeeping in a diverse society*. Upper Saddle River, NJ: Prentice Hall.

Skogan, W. (1994). The impact of community policing on neighborhood residents: A cross-site analysis. In D. P. Rosenbaum (Ed.), *The challenge of community policing: Testing the promises* (pp. 167–181). Thousand Oaks, CA: Sage.

Skogan, W. (1996). The community's role in community policing. *National Institute of Justice Journal* (August), 31–34.

Skogan, W., & Hartnett, S. (1997). *Community policing Chicago style*. New York: Oxford University Press.

Smith, B. (2000a). Police service dogs: The unheralded training tool. *Police, 24*(1), 36–39.

Smith, J. P. (2000b). Portland (Ore.) police bureau: Building bridges in the City of Roses. *Police, 24*(2), 42–43.

Smith, B., Novak, K., & Hurley, D. (1997). Neighborhood crime prevention: The influences of community-based organizations and neighborhood watch. *Journal of Crime and Justice, 20*(2), 69–86.

Sorid, D. (2000, June 22). Trying to give bomb squad robots brains to match their brawn. *New York Times*, p. G14.

Stanko, E. A. (1989). Missing the mark? Police battering. In J. Hanmer, J. Radford, & E. Stanko (Eds.), *Women, policing, and male violence* (pp. 46–49). London: Routledge & Keagan Paul.

Stefkovich, J. A., & Miller, J. A. (1999). Law enforcement officers in public schools: Student citizens in safe havens? *Brigham Young University Education and Law Journal, 25*, 1–35.

Stegenga, P. (2000). Classic crime prevention: Neighborhood watch. *Sheriff, 52*, 10–12.

Stephens, G. (1999). Preventing crime: The promising road ahead. *The Futurist, 33*, 29–34.

Stevens, D. J. (1999). College educated officers: Do they provide better police service? *Law and Order, 47*(12), 37–41.

Stockton, D. (1999). Getting the point. *Law and Order, 47*(10), 199–202.

Suhay, L. (1999, October 17). Nonlethal force. *New York Times*, p. 5–14.

Swanson, C. (1977). An uneasy look at college education and the police organization. *Journal of Criminal Justice, 5*(4), 311–320.

Tonry, M. (1995). *Malign neglect: Race, crime and punishment in America*. New York: Oxford Press.

Toufexis, A. (1999). Dancing with devils. Forensic psychiatrist Park Dietz tracks America's serial killers, bombers and mass murderers. *Psychology Today, 32,* 54–58.

Trump, K. S. (1997). Security policy, personnel, and operations. In A. P. Goldstein & J. C. Conoley (Eds.), *School violence intervention: A practical handbook* (pp. 265–289). New York: Guilford.

Turvey, B. (1999). *Criminal profiling: An introduction to behavioral evidence analysis*. San Diego, CA: Academic Press.

U.S. Department of Justice. (1995). Bureau of Justice Statistics. Washington DC: U.S. Government Printing Office.

U.S. Department of Justice. (1997). LEMAS reports—1993. In R. G. Dunham & G. P. Alpert (Eds.), *Critical issues in policing: Contemporary readings* (3rd ed., pp. 36–73). Prospect Heights, IL: Waveland Press.

U.S. Department of Justice. (2001). Highlights of the 1999 LEMAS Survey. In R. G. Dunham & G. P. Alpert (Eds.), *Critical issues in policing: Contemporary readings*. Prospect Heights, IL: Waveland Press.

Van Maanen, J. (1973). Observations on the making of policemen. *Human Organization, 32,* 407–418.

Vardalis, J. J., & Kakar, S. (2000). Crime and the high school environment. *Journal of Security Administration, 23,* 37–48.

Walker, S., Spohn, C., & DeLone, M. (2000). *The color of justice: Race, ethnicity and crime in America* (2nd ed.). Belmont, CA: Wadsworth.

Warr, M., & Ellison, C. G. (2000). Rethinking social reactions to crime: Personal and altruistic fear in family households. *The American Journal of Sociology, 106,* 551–578.

Webb, V., & Katz, C. (1997). Citizen ratings of the importance of community policing activities. *Policing: An International Journal of Police Strategies and Management, 20*(1), 7–23.

Whetstone, T. S. (1993). Training police officers: Misplaced priorities and missed opportunities. *Law and Order, 41*(9), 150–153.

Wilkinson, D., Rosenbaum, D., Bruni, M., & Yeh, S. (1994). *Community policing in Joliet: Year 2 process evaluation*. Chicago: University of Illinois at Chicago, Center for Research in Law and Justice.

Willingham, S. (2000). Peacekeeping duties bolster demand for kinder weapons. *National Defense, 84*(558), 26–27.

Wycoff, M. (1995). *Community policing strategies*. Washington DC: National Institute of Justice.

Wysong, E., Aniskiewicz, R., & Wright, D. (1994). Truth and D.A.R.E.: Tracking drug education to graduation and as symbolic politics. *Social Problems, 41,* 448–472.

Zagumny, M. J., & Thompson, M. K. (1997). Does D.A.R.E. work? An evaluation in rural Tennessee. *Journal of Alcohol and Drug Education, 42*(2), 32–41.

Zhao, J., Lovrich, N., & Thurman, Q. (1999). The status of community policing in American cities: Facilitators and impediments revisited. *Policing: An International Journal of Police Strategies and Management, 22*(1), 74–92.

The Legal System

OVERVIEW

In the aftermath of police work, some offenders are funneled through formal and informal court processes. When this occurs, the mechanics of the legal system are at work, endeavoring to respond to a host of problems linked to delinquency and crime. Chapter 10 examines the relationship between criminal behavior and law, mindful of some of more salient court administration stages to which an offender can be subjected.

In particular, this chapter reviews (a) the pretrial phase of a case; (b) the trial process, especially as it relates to the introduction and use of mental disorders; (c) the posttrial stage, including **sentencing guidelines** and related matters; and (d) the death penalty phase of a case, highlighting problems and practices connected to capital punishment. As the chapter discloses, the link between offenders and the courts raises a number of immediate, complex, and controversial issues for society, especially in its understanding of offender conduct. Ultimately, however, the role that the courts assume in this process tells us a great deal more about how the legal system interprets criminal behavior, attempts to respond to the problems posed by delinquency and crime, and seeks to promote the administration of justice.

KEY TERMS

Actus reas	Fines
Aggravating factors	Guilt phase
Appeal	Guilty but mentally ill
Bifurcated trial	*Habeas corpus*
Boot camps	Hanging
Capital trials	Home confinement
Community release	Imprisonment
Conviction appeal	Incapacitation
Determinate sentencing	Intensive probation supervision (IPS)
Deterrence	Intermediate sanctions
Diminished responsibility	Lethal injection
Diversion	Mandatory minimum sentencing
Electrocution	Mens rea
Electronic monitoring	Mental disease or defect
Execution	Mitigating factor

Murder	Rehabilitation
Not guilty by reason of insanity	Remand
Parole	Retribution
Parole boards	Reverse
Penalty phase	Sentence appeal
Plea bargain	Sentencing
Presentence investigation report	Sentencing guidelines
Probation	Three Strikes law

PRETRIAL MATTERS

Introduction

Persons apprehended and suspected of illicit conduct do not automatically go through the formal court process in order to have their criminal case addressed. Instead, there are a series of pretrial matters that can effectively reroute the person away from the traditional courtroom setting. This section examines several of the more important components involved in this informal decision making. These pretrial matters include the plea-bargaining process, **probation,** and **diversion** programs.

Plea Bargaining

The majority of criminal cases do not go to trial. Instead, they are disposed of through the plea-bargaining process. *Plea bargaining* is defined as "a defendant's agreement to plead guilty to a criminal charge with the reasonable expectation of receiving some consideration from the state" (LaFave, Israel, & King, 1999, p. 35). Researchers indicate that plea bargaining resolves approximately 90% of all criminal cases (e.g., Melton, Petrila, Poythress, & Slobogin, 1997). During this phase of a criminal case, the prosecutor selects the appropriate charge or charges, given the available information and facts, and negotiates a plea arrangement with the defendant through the accused's counsel.

There are three types of plea-bargaining options. At the state level, it is common for the defendant and prosecutor to agree that the accused will plead guilty to a crime that is less serious than is the charge supported by the evidence. There are perceived advantages for an accused opting to pursue this plea arrangement. For example, if a defendant has been charged with a sex offense, he or she may plead guilty to a charge of disorderly conduct. Agreeing to the crime of disorderly conduct avoids conviction of a sex offense and the imposition of a stigmatizing label that has severe consequences both legally and socially. A second type of plea-bargaining arrangement occurs when the defendant pleads guilty to the original charge in exchange for the prosecutor promising to recommend leniency or a specific disposition, such as probation. A third type of plea-bargaining arrangement takes place when a defendant is charged with multiple offenses, with the prosecutor agreeing to drop all of them in exchange for the accused pleading guilty to one, usually very serious, charge. This plea-bargaining scenario is recognized as "illusory" because most crimes involve multiple charges, and these charges are rarely brought against a defendant who does not plead guilty to some combination of them in the first place.

The U.S. Supreme Court upheld plea bargaining as a necessary and proper practice in *Bordenkircher v. Hayes* (1978). Plea-bargaining practices exist for a variety of reasons, especially the need to deal more efficiently with crowded court dockets. Other reasons for the use of plea bargaining include the high costs of jury trials, the desire on the part of prosecutors and judges to offer a sentence that would be more appropriate to the individual offender not otherwise permissible under rigid sentencing statutes, and validating the due process rights of the defendant, thereby strengthening the accused's bargaining position (LaFave et al., 1999).

Does Everyone Get Perry Mason for an Attorney?

Under the U.S. system of courtroom justice, every criminal defendant charged with a misdemeanor or felony is entitled to counsel, understood as adequate legal representation. However, many poor or indigent defendants find that counsel assigned to them amounts to assistance from the public defender's office. So, the question is whether public defenders are adequately equipped to represent their clients, especially those who profess their innocence.

In an article titled "Did you have a lawyer when you went to court? No, I had a public defender," Casper (1992) explains what happens from the defendant's perspective. At play is the tension between client representation and the need to settle cases as quickly as possible. Commenting on these matters from the defendant's perspective, Casper notes:

> Most of the men spent very little time with their public defender. In the court in which they eventually pled guilty, they typically reported spending . . . five to ten minutes with their [counsel]. These conversations took place in the bull-pen of the courthouse or in the hallway . . . The brief conversations usually did not involve much discussion of the details surrounding the alleged crime, mitigating circumstances or the defendant's motives or backgrounds. Instead, they focused on the deal, the offer the prosecution was likely to make or had made in return for a cop out. (pp. 239–240)

There are concerns and criticisms about the plea-bargaining process, typically voiced by the police, legal scholars, and the general public. Opponents generally argue that some offenders may receive sentences that are too lenient for their crimes and that an innocent person may be convicted. If an innocent person is charged with a serious offense, there may be a great temptation to plead guilty to a lesser charge rather than risk conviction at trial for a more severe penalty. This is especially the case for persons who possess limited financial resources to secure skilled legal representation (Reiman, 2001).

PROBATION AND DIVERSION PROGRAMS

Probation is defined as the supervised release of offenders (Abadinsky, 2003a). The legal system can be involved in probation decision making following an agreed-on **plea bargain.** Under these conditions, probation can be part of the negotiated arrangement in which the prosecutor's office recommends this sentence to a judge, stipulating that defense counsel supports this resolution (Meyer & Grant, 2003). Thus, similar to the plea-bargaining process, probation can represent a pretrial issue designed to respond to criminal behavior. Probation arose out of the rehabilitative model of punishment and was approved in all states in 1967 (LaFave et al., 1999). Probation is also referred to as **community release** and allows a defendant's sentence to be suspended as long as the defendant meets all the requirements set forth by probation. Conditions of probation may include attendance in treatment programs, work release, restrictions on travel, and drug testing.

Each state has its own statute, authorizing the use of probation for only certain offenses. The statute authorizing probation will often outline the length of the probation term, list mandatory conditions of probation, and provide a general standard for the judge to use when setting the conditions of probation. There is no state that allows probation for all offenses. For example, probation is not available for offenses that result in life **imprisonment** or the death penalty. Also, the majority of states deny probation for other serious offenses such as **murder,** kidnapping, crimes involving the use of a weapon, and sexual assault (Champion, 1988a).

Historically, imprisonment and probation have been the primary options for **sentencing** offenders (Abadinsky, 2003a). However, these options fail to address the problems of prison overcrowding, increased violence among convicts, the housing of violent criminals with nonviolent offenders, and the lack of resources available to probation departments (Champion, 1988b). In the latter instance, probation officers typically are assigned extremely large caseloads, and supervise a growing number of released ex-prisoners designated as violent and aggressive in the community.

The problems identified previously plague the criminal justice system, creating a profound need for alternative sentencing options and other diversion programs (del Carmen et al., 2001; Geerken & Hayes, 1993). **Intermediate sanctions** are one option that combine probation and incarceration (Durham, 1994). For example, the defendant may be required to spend a brief period in jail as a condition of his or her probation, or be sentenced to a specific jail term followed by a set period of probation. If a defendant violates any of the conditions of release, the judge has the right to impose any sentence that could have been imposed originally (Geerken & Hayes, 1993). Also, **boot camps** are used as intermediate sanctions for young, inexperienced, and nonviolent offenders. Judges may sentence a youthful offender to boot camp for approximately 3 to 4 months. Upon release, the youthful offender will be on probation for the remainder of his or her sentence (LaFave et al., 1999).

Another intermediate sanction is called **home confinement.** Home confinement requires that offenders remain at their residences for specific periods of the day (Durham, 1994). Probation officers enforce home confinement by calling the individual randomly, by making home visits, and by **electronic monitoring** (Arrigo, 2000). Electronic monitoring tracks the movement of the offender. Another intermediate sanction used in some form in every state is called **intensive probation supervision (IPS).** IPS programs are designed for offenders who may be at higher risk and need more intensive supervision. For example, individuals participating in IPS programs have more contact with probation officers, participate in community service, are under some form of house arrest, have evening curfews, and are frequently drug tested (LaFave et al., 1999).

Diversion programs are another form of alternative sentencing, typically used for first-time offenders, younger persons, minor law violators, and individuals who pose little societal risk (Abadinsky, 2003a). Diversion programs are often community-based initiatives offering alternatives to prosecuting persons formally charged with criminal offenses (Alexander, 1999). Diversion programs generally involve completion of a contract that can include treatment, counseling, restitution, community service, or other sanctions or requirements (Gebelein, 2000).

Intensive Probation Supervision, Risk Control, and Criminal Behavior

IPS is a form of community risk control in correctional programming and management (O'Leary & Clear, 1984). It is designed to ensure control in an environment (i.e., a neighborhood or community) over offenders who would otherwise be imprisoned. Typical programs entail such things as weekly face-to-face contact between the probationer and the supervising agent, strict and mandatory curfews, unscheduled and unannounced alcohol and drug testing, and weekly arrest record checks (Clear & Hardyman, 1990; Petersilia, 1998; Petersilia & Turner, 1990).

IPS correctional officers emphasize a team approach and share a joint case load of about 25 to 40 probationers (Petersilia, 1998). In this mode, one agent specializes in rehabilitative intervention and risk reduction, whereas the other agent specializes in surveillance and risk control. Although caseloads for IPS correctional officers are low compared to those of their non-IPS counterparts, making management less cumbersome, IPS is not without its drawbacks. Durham (1994) summarizes these limitations as follows:

> First . . . probation represents a lenient sanction that fails to adequately punish offenders. Second, the leniency of the sentence interferes with the creation of either specific or general deterrent effects. Third, the presence of offenders in the community creates risks of additional citizen victimization. Fourth . . ., research on intensive supervision does not demonstrate that **rehabilitation** is a likely product of the probationary process. Finally . . ., intensive supervision may widen the legal net. Relatively minor offenders who would otherwise have received traditional probation may find themselves in unnecessary high-surveillance, high-punishment programs. (pp. 184–185)

Legal scholars suggest several purposes for diversion programs. Among others, these purposes include (a) an attempt to reverse the serious sanctions on those adversely impacted by social, economic, and personal factors linked to criminal behavior; (b) reduction of recidivism; and (c) reduction of justice system costs (Palmer, 1995). An example of a diversion program is the drug treatment court, established in the late 1980s to provide speedy prosecution of substance using criminals and, in some cases, to offer treatment programs for drug offenders (Boldt, 1998).

Diversion programs designed for youth are intended to prevent the assigning of stigmatizing labels to adolescents for petty acts that may best be handled outside the criminal justice system (Feld, 1999). These programs are designed to help prevent overcrowding of detention facilities while allowing courts to focus on the more serious offenders. In theory, diversion programs are supposed to decrease crime and recidivism rates and offer a promising strategy for rehabilitation. However, according to Polk (1984), increases in neither punishment nor diversion programs show much promise for decreasing crime (see also, Sutton, 1988).

Diversion of the mentally disordered from the legal arena is also considered appropriate, given the criminal justice system's limited capacity to deal with the treatment, control, and safety issues presented by persons experiencing persistent and severe psychiatric illness. However, according to Steadman et al. (1999), despite the support of diversion programs that are community based for the mentally ill and for individuals suffering from substance abuse disorders, few studies have actually documented their success. Presently, the Substance Abuse and Mental Health Services Administration (SAMHSA) is in the process of examining the characteristics and outcomes of various types of jail diversion programs, in an effort to establish their impact on persons with psychiatric illness.

THE TRIAL PROCESS, CRIME, AND BEHAVIOR

Introduction

In chapter 8, material is presented on mental disorders as unique defenses. In particular, battered woman syndrome, posttraumatic stress disorder, and Black rage were all identified as strategies attorneys could employ when preparing their cases. However, chapter 8 does not examine the relationship between the trial process per se and the presence of psychiatric illness. This section addresses this matter. Accordingly, various criminal responsibility standards are explored, and the role of the mental health professional with respect to these standards is considered.

The Use of Mental Disorders in the Trial Process

*Socorro Caro of Santa Clara County, California, was accused of shooting and killing her three children in November 1999. Ms. Caro subsequently shot herself in the head, but survived. She pled not guilty to three counts of first-degree murder and later amended her plea to **not guilty by reason of insanity** (NGRI). If Ms. Caro is convicted, she faces the death penalty or life in prison. If she is found NGRI, she may face automatic commitment to a psychiatric facility for an indefinite period of time.*

The defendant, Ms. Caro, is not claiming that she is innocent of the crime of murdering her three children. Instead, her defense is that when the crime was committed, she could not tell right from wrong or that she could not control her

*behavior because of mental illness. In legal terms, the defense of NGRI is based on the premise that an individual should not be held criminally responsible for his or her behavior because **retribution** and **deterrence**, the principal grounds for punishment, do not apply to individuals who do not know what they are doing or who have no control over themselves.*

*Ms. Caro's case demonstrates how a mental disorder may be introduced and used as a defense in a criminal case. The material that follows in this portion of the chapter examines the various ways that a **mental disease or defect** can be introduced in a criminal trial. Not surprisingly, guidelines vary from state to state as to the specific legal requirements needed to successfully mount a mental disorder criminal defense.*

Criminal Responsibility Standards

There are three legal impairments based on mental disorders that are applicable to defendants involved in a criminal trial. These include criminal incompetence, criminal responsibility, and criminal dangerousness (Bardwell & Arrigo, 2002a). These legal concepts are important to understanding how psychiatric illnesses are introduced and used in a trial. For purposes of this section of the chapter, the focus is on the first two legal matters. Criminal dangerousness is already examined in chapter 8, especially in relation to the psychopathic offender, antisocial personality disorder, and schizophrenia.

Criminal incompetence may be raised in a number of circumstances. These circumstances include whether a defendant (a) is unable to consult with his or her lawyer or does not have a rational or factual understanding of the trial or **appeal** proceedings; (b) is unable to make a knowing, intelligent, and voluntary waiver of rights; (c) is unable to be restored to competency; (d) is unable to testify reliably or truthfully; and (e) is unable to make reasoned choices among those available for a plea agreement and to understand the nature and consequences of the plea (Bonnie, 1992). In addition, a person may be found criminally incompetent if he or she is unable to understand the sentence and the reason for the punishment (Parry, 1998). In all of the aforementioned instances, a defendant's mental health status may be brought up as an important variable, impacting the accused's ability to competently function during the criminal trial (Bardwell & Arrigo, 2002b).

For example, some defendants whose mental state is questionable exercise their right to request a waiver of counsel. This issue presented itself in the controversial and highly publicized cases of the Long Island Rail Road gunman, Colin Ferguson, and the Unabomber, Theodore J. Kaczynski (Arrigo & Bardwell, 2000). In these instances, the defendants were found competent to stand trial. Ferguson's request to waive counsel was granted. He represented himself and was found guilty of murdering 6 train passengers and critically wounding 19 others. Kaczynski's request to waive counsel was not granted. Desperately seeking to avoid being labeled psychiatrically ill, the Unabomber pled guilty to killing 3 people and seriously injuring 23 others.

Criminal responsibility is another legal matter that often brings mental health issues into the trial process. It is important to note that any act identified as illegal (e.g., robbery, theft, and sexual assault) *on its own* is insufficient for assigning criminal responsibility to a person who engages in this behavior. This is because, "[I]n our legal system, guilt is a quality of the individual, not of the act. . . ." (Levine & Wallach, 2002, p. 181). Among legal circles, the guilty act alone is termed **actus reas.** In addition, there must be a guilty mind, also known as **mens rea.** In other words, the issue fact finders (i.e., judges and juries) must weigh whether the defendant possessed the appropriate mental capabilities sufficient to form the requisite intent to commit the crime for which the individual was accused. Finally, there must be a proximate relationship between one's guilty act (*actus reas*) and one's guilty mind (*mens rea*), such that a finding of criminal responsibility can attach to the defendant.

The Model Penal Code and Criminal Responsibility

The way in which the Model Penal Code (MPC) interprets crime helps illustrate the link between *actus reas* and *mens rea* and their overall relationship. Indeed, the MPC places criminal offenses into four levels. These levels include negligence, recklessness, knowledge, and purposefulness. Attorneys rely on these levels to present evidence explaining the defendant's mental state during the commission of a crime.

Consider the example of a man who finds his wife in bed with another person and subsequently and instantaneously shoots the individual. The man may be found to have lacked "purposefulness" as it relates to the crime's intent. In other words, the offense occurred "in the heat of the moment." This is different from a planned killing. As such, the absence of purposefulness may result in a reduction in the charge of murder to manslaughter, based on the man's decreased mental awareness.

Can Defendants Be Both "Bad" and "Mad"?

Another defense strategy available in some states is the guilty but mentally ill (GBMI) option (Arrigo, 1996b). This approach acknowledges that persons with psychiatric disorders are mentally fit enough to be found guilty of a criminal act. In short, these defendants are understood to be both "bad" and "mad."

One case in point was Michael Carneal. Michael, age 15, pled **guilty but mentally ill** after being charged with the killing of three high school classmates. In this instance, the judge accepted the plea on the condition that the maximum penalty would be imposed. Carneal is now serving a sentence of life in prison without the possibility of **parole** for 25 years. Carneal was found to suffer from paranoia and from a personality disorder with characteristics similar to schizophrenia. The plea of GBMI will allow Carneal to receive mental health treatment in prison as long as he needs it or until his sentence has been completed. This option is used for defendants found legally sane, but mentally ill. Critics of this strategy contend that the GBMI verdict obscures the defense of NGRI, and promises, but does not provide, treatment for mentally disordered offenders (Parry, 1998).

This proximate relationship varies depending on the offense; however, the point is that the time frame or sequence within which one contemplates a criminal act and performs an illegal behavior determines whether and what type of crime has been committed.

Diminished responsibility due to mental impairment is another defense used by defendants who show evidence of a psychiatric disorder. Persons with conditions that cause psychoses, delusions, or impaired reality testing are likely to meet the criteria establishing diminished criminal responsibility due to mental defect. Defendants with cognitive, brain, organic, medical, or neurological disorders are also likely to meet the legal criteria to establish insufficient *mens rea* (Parry, 1998). An accused utilizing a diminished responsibility defense argues that he or she was unable to formulate the requisite intent to commit the crime (Levine & Wallach, 2002). This defense is often used in cases of homicide. For example, if a person is found to have diminished responsibility in a case of murder, the results may include a reduction in punishment or it may be considered a **mitigating factor** at the defendant's sentencing.

The defense of NGRI requires a defendant to show that he or she was mentally ill at the time the illicit act occurred (Arrigo, 1996b). This defense is available in most jurisdictions under the standard of M'Naghten or the American Law Institute (ALI; Arrigo, 2002). The M'Naghten standard states that as a result of mental disorder or defect the defendant did not know the nature and quality of the conduct, or that he or she did not know that the act was wrong. A second standard in addition to M'Naghten is the *irresistible impulse test*. This defense alleges that the accused was unable to control his or her conduct. The ALI standard states that if the defendant did know the conduct was wrong, then as a result of mental disease or defect, the defendant lacked "substantial capacity either to appreciate the criminality or wrongfulness of his [or her] conduct or to conform [the] conduct to the requirements of the law" (Parry, 1998, pp. 30–31). Research investigating the NGRI defense indicates that the majority of persons acquitted are diagnosed as psychotic (Steadman et al., 1993). Moreover, most successful insanity defenses are based on defendants found to be psychotic or mentally retarded (Melton et al., 1997). Despite public perception, NGRI verdicts in felony cases are successful less than 1% of the time (Cirincione & Jacobs, 1999).

The Role of Mental Health Professionals

Often, psychologists and psychiatrists are called on by the legal system to evaluate defendants accused of crimes where mental disorder is thought to play a significant role in the intent or execution of these offenses (Arrigo, 2000). These forensic experts are asked by various agents of the legal system (e.g., prosecutors, defense attorneys, and judges) to look for and identify symptoms indicative of clinical syndromes that could explain an individual's criminal behavior. The DSM-IV-TR (APA, 2000) is the standard diagnostic classification system in the mental health field today. It encompasses the most widely accepted definitions of psychiatric disorders. This manual is a diagnostic guide, reflecting a consensus of opinion at the time of publication. However, this guide is not a definitive, final, or unchangeable source (Winick, 1995). There are other syndromes and disorders not listed in the *DSM–IV–TR* that may be relevant to a legal decision (Parry, 1998). The legal definitions of mental disorders are usually broad and may include conditions that are not officially recognized as psychiatric illnesses. One example is epilepsy.

In general, the evidence necessary to show the existence of a mental disorder is based on widely agreed on definitions in the *DSM–IV–TR*. There are five areas, called axes, in the *DSM–IV–TR* that offer different information about the individual's mental health history (APA). The first two areas address psychiatric and personality disorders, and the last three address information on relevant medical factors, psychosocial stressors, and the level of past and current adaptive functioning.

It is worth noting that not all the mental disorders found in the *DSM–IV–TR* satisfy the legal definition of incompetence. For example, a psychologist may discover that a defendant has a mental disorder as identified in the *DSM–IV–TR*, but the question

A Review of Legal Standards Pertaining to Mental Illness and Criminal Responsibility

STANDARD	DESCRIPTION
M'Naghten (1843)—First prong of ALI test	Defendant did not know the nature and quality of criminal act or did not know the act was wrong.
"Irresistible Impulse"—Second prong of ALI test	Defendant lacked the substantial capacity to conform to the requirements of the law and was unable to control conduct.
Model Penal Code	As a result of mental disease or defect, person lacks substantial capacity either to appreciate the criminality of conduct or to conform conduct to the requirements of the law.
Guilty but Mentally III (1975)	Defendant is held responsible for the crime, but the presence of a mental disorder is recognized.
Insanity Defense Reform Act (1984)	Federal Standard states as a result of a severe mental disease or defect, defendant was unable to appreciate the wrongfulness of his acts. In federal suits, there is no "irresistible impulse" defense.

Who Raises Defense?

In nearly all states, the defendant is required to come forward with evidence showing that he or she is insane—only then does the defendant's sanity enter the case.

Burden of Persuasion

First, the defendant must show some evidence of insanity. Once the defendant has shown some evidence of insanity, the courts are split as to who bears the burden of convincing the fact-finder on the insanity issue.

- In half the states, the prosecution must prove beyond a reasonable doubt that the defendant is not insane.
- In the other half of the states, the defense is required to prove insanity.
- In the federal system, the defense must prove insanity.

Percentage

- When burden rests on prosecution, must prove "beyond a reasonable doubt" (90%-95% degree of certainty).
- When burden rests on defendant, must prove by a "preponderance of the evidence" (51% degree of certainty).
- In the federal system, the defendant must prove by "clear and convincing evidence" (75% degree of certainty).

remains as to whether this condition is severe enough to justify a legal finding of diminished responsibility or NGRI (Bardwell & Arrigo, 2002a). Indeed, anxiety disorders are typically not considered severe enough to meet legal standards unless the anxiety is found in extreme cases where the symptoms are associated with posttraumatic stress disorder or dissociative symptoms (Parry, 1998). Notwithstanding these observations, the decision concerning the defendant's criminal responsibility, given the testimony of the forensic mental health specialist, is reserved for the fact finder and not for the expert witness (Arrigo, 2000).

Psychologists and psychiatrists base their clinical diagnoses of criminal defendants on medical and neurological examinations, personal interviews, clinical testing, and an analysis of the accused's psychosocial history (Melton et al., 1997). These four methods allow the clinician to assess and diagnose mental disorder (if warranted) and provide the court with requested information regarding the defendant's mental state.

A psychological evaluation of this sort does not focus exclusively on the emotional well-being of a defendant. Other extraneous factors may exacerbate mental health symptoms. As such, they must be considered in the overall approach to an individual's psychological state. For example, physical conditions such as migraine headaches, epilepsy, and hypoglycemia may exacerbate mental health symptoms or complicate treatment plans. Therefore, a comprehensive psychological evaluation includes a medical and neurological exam. In addition, there are several specific objective tests available to psychologists and psychiatrists conducting psycholegal evaluations. For example, if a defendant's competency to stand trial is being questioned, there are measures to assess personality and cognitive functioning abilities. These instruments enable the forensic specialist to provide the court with enough information to answer the legal question under consideration (Bardwell & Arrigo, 2000a).

Regardless of the thoroughness contained within a mental health evaluation prepared for a criminal court, there is a less than perfect fit between what the law endeavors to determine and what clinical assessments and diagnoses can provide (Melton et al., 1997). For example, even if the forensic mental health expert determines that a criminal defendant suffers from schizophrenia, this may not be sufficient to establish the legal criteria needed to prove to the fact finder that the defendant suffers from a mental defect or disease. Therefore, clinicians that find a link between the commission of the crime and the defendant's mental status must also describe the symptoms and the severity of the individual's condition. This testimony is essential if the magnitude of the accused's psychological condition is to be appropriately communicated.

In addition to assessing and diagnosing mental disorders, psychologists investigate and report on mitigating factors that may have impacted the defendant's judgment, perception, or intent in relation to committing the criminal act (Arrigo, 2000). There are several mitigating factors that can help explain or justify the defendant's behavior (e.g., neurological impairments). Mitigating factors clarify how the disorder affected the individual's ability to form the mental state necessary to commit the offense. In addition, reporting this kind of information is relevant for effective treatment, reducing the likelihood of future criminal behavior by the accused in question.

POSTTRIAL MATTERS

Introduction

The processing of a defendant through the legal system does not end with the conclusion of the trial. There are several issues related to the posttrial phase of a case that raise important questions about the appropriate response to criminal behavior. This section examines a number of these matters. In particular, the sentencing of offenders is discussed, various state and federal sentencing guidelines are assessed, Three Strikes legislation is explored, and the appellate process is reviewed.

Sentencing

Sentencing is the phase in courtroom processing that occurs only after a person has been convicted of a crime. In essence, a judge or jury determines how the guilty offender should be punished. Historically, punishment has been the principal purpose of the sentencing process (e.g., Foucault, 1977); however, there are four important goals inherent in the criminal justice system's philosophical approach to crime and punishment (Cassel & Bernstein, 2001). These goals include rehabilitation, retribution, deterrence, and **incapacitation.** Most recently, some efforts based on the principles of restorative justice (RJ) have also been identified as a philosophical basis for punishment (Sullivan & Tifft, 2001). The value of RJ in relation to understanding and responding to criminal behavior is examined further in chapter 12.

Each of the four established goals listed previously plays an important part in the sentence imposed on convicted criminals. Not surprisingly, then, the sentencing of offenders is a complicated process. In part, this is because of the conflicting objectives embedded within these four goals. The following section describes these goals in more detail.

There are four entities, or sentencing authorities, that determine the type and length of incarceration (Abadinsky, 2003b). These authorities include legislatures, prosecutors, courts, and **parole boards,** and all of them assume different roles in the administration of a sentence (Meyer & Grant, 2003). The legislature establishes state laws by defining what acts are criminal and by determining the penalties for each offense. The prosecutor selects the charges to be brought against the defendant and then engages in the plea-bargaining process. Ideally, a successful plea arrangement is negotiated with the accused's attorney. Judges determine the majority of sentences, except in jurisdictions where juries are mandated to assume this responsibility. Judges evaluate the individual characteristics of the offender and the particulars of the offense. In some cases, judges must follow rigid guidelines, known as **determinate sentencing,** and are required to justify in writing any deviation from these standards. In other jurisdictions, judges have considerable discretion when deciding what kind of sentence to administer in a particular case. They receive recommendations on the imposition of sentence from three sources: the prosecutor, the defendant's attorney, and the probation officer. The probation officer prepares a report for the judge that includes information on the accused's personal history (e.g., employment, education, and family circumstances), prior convictions, and related material relevant to the disposition of the case. This document is called a **presentence investigation report.**

Persons convicted of the same offense do not necessarily receive the same sentence. Research reveals that four factors best predict the variation in sentencing outcomes. These four factors include (a) the type of crime; (b) the extent of the offender's past record; (c) what guidelines were placed on the defendant between the time of arrest and the time of

The Goals of Punishment: Can They Be Reconciled?

The goals of punishment represent vastly different ways to address offender conduct. Because of this, some researchers question whether it is even possible to reconcile them. One way to respond to this concern is to define what each goal represents. See if you think an argument can be made for their reconciliation.

Rehabilitation—designed to reform, treat, or otherwise cure the criminal through therapeutic interventions in a jail, prison, or community setting.

Retribution—designed to punish the offender with a sentence that would be proportionate to the crime committed. In this way, retribution makes the criminal "pay their debt to society" through incarceration.

Deterrence—designed to impose a sentence that would inhibit the offender from engaging in similar criminal behavior (specific deterrence), and to send a message to society that such actions will not be tolerated in the future (general deterrence).

Incapacitation—designed to isolate the offender, preventing the possibility that similar criminal actions will occur.

conviction (i.e., released on bail or held in jail); and, most importantly, (d) the race and class composition of the criminal and victim (Beck, 2000; U.S. Sentencing Project, 1998). Investigators also note that judges agree with the probation officer's report 84% of the time (Wrightsman, Nietzel, & Fortune, 1998). The types of sentences that can be imposed by a judge or jury are discussed in the subsequent subsection.

As a sentencing authority, the parole board is usually composed of probation officers and citizens from the community (Abadinsky, 2003a). Parole boards are responsible for determining the length of a prisoner's continued confinement once the individual becomes eligible for parole. The parole board considers a variety of factors in making this decision. Among other things, these include the seriousness of the offense committed, the behavior of the offender while incarcerated, and whether the convict became sufficiently rehabilitated such that he or she no longer posed a threat to the community.

There are several options to consider when sentencing a convicted defendant. The most severe option is the death penalty. **Execution** can be imposed on an individual convicted of a very narrow class of felonies (e.g., first-degree murder) in 38 states and the federal government (Arrigo, 2000). The goal of this sentence is deterrence, retribution, and incapacitation. Community release is another sanction applied to offenders who commit less severe crimes. Community release is based on the rehabilitation model of justice. Typically, it entails varying degrees of supervision by a probation officer. Community release is not available in most states for offenders who commit the crime of murder, kidnapping, sexual assault, or who perpetrate offenses involving the use of a dangerous weapon (LaFave et al., 1999).

Other options to consider when sentencing a convicted felon include intermediate sanctions (Cassel & Bernstein, 2001). Generally speaking, intermediate sanctions entail the use of a variety of punishments. For example, an individual may be incarcerated for a certain period of time, subsequently released, and then placed on closely supervised probation. Other intermediate sanctions include boot camp or home confinement (Durham, 1994). Boot camps are hierarchically arranged, military-style training facilities designed to instill the values of discipline, responsibility, and respect in the offender. Delinquent youth are often sent to boot camps; however, the research documenting their success in reducing adolescent recidivism has not been promising (Blair, 2000). Home confinement keeps offenders secure in their own living space through the use of electronic monitoring for specific periods during the day. It is also called house arrest or home detention. Some success has been demonstrated in the use of home confinement for low-risk offenders (e.g., Baumer & Mendelsohn, 1992; Lilly, Ball, Curry, & McMullen, 1993); however, the ability of house arrest to curb recidivism at a greater rate than other sentencing options has yet to be documented (Sherman et al., 1997). Other sentencing options include financial penalties or **fines.** When combined with incarceration they represent another intermediate sanction.

State and Federal Sentencing Guidelines

Given the variation in sentencing, especially when disparities can (and do) appear, a number of states and the federal government follow strict guidelines. One example is **mandatory minimum sentencing.** This is a form of determinate sentencing specifically designed to support the goal of deterrence and incapacitation by limiting the discretion of judges and parole boards (LaFave et al., 1999). Mandatory minimums are laws that require a minimum term of incarceration for an offender who commits a particular offense. One practice consistent with this sentencing philosophy is Three Strikes legislation. As the subsequent subsection explains, the **Three Strikes law** was originally developed with the intent of imposing mandatory and lengthy prison terms on repeat offenders (Reynolds & Kramer, 1999). Examples of crimes that fall under mandatory minimum guidelines include burglary, drug offenses, possession of a weapon, and robbery. Mandatory minimum sentences often exceed prison terms that would be imposed under normal sentencing conditions and generally impact low-level offenders convicted of repeat drug crimes (LaFave et al., 1999). This approach to sentencing has been highly criticized for several reasons including the high cost of implementation, the failure to demonstrate an observable impact on crime, and the creation of unfair sentencing practices (Stolzenberg & D'Alessio, 1997).

Given these limitations, Congress adopted a statute allowing judges to bypass mandatory minimum sentences for first-time and nonviolent offenders. This strategy is particularly noteworthy in the case of drug offenders. Indeed, the race and class disparities inherent in mandatory minimum sentences are evident in the different prison terms imposed for crack versus powder cocaine possession (LaFave et al., 1999). Longer and harsher sentences are administered for crack cocaine use than for powder cocaine use (National Drug Control Policy, 2001). As a result, stiffer sentences for economically disadvantaged minority offenders follow, given that poor people of color are more frequently convicted for the use of crack cocaine than are their White counterparts.

The U.S. government instituted federal sentencing guidelines with the passage of the Sentencing Reform Act of 1984. These standards were made effective on November 1, 1987, and were intended to make sentencing more predictable and less open to judicial discretion. The federal guidelines are composed of a sentencing table consisting of 43 offense levels and 6 criminal history categories. These categories focus on the actual offense rather than on the offender and are used to determine what type of sentence corresponds with the defendant's crime.

Adjustments to the sentence imposed are possible. However, in order to do this, several factors must be considered. Among those factors considered are the following: (a) the harm to the victim, (b) the defendant's role in the offense, (c) whether there was any obstruction of justice, (d) whether the defendant was convicted of multiple counts, and (e) whether the defendant accepted personal responsibility for the offense (LaFave et al., 1999). To illustrate, if an individual commits the crime of murder while engaged in a burglary and if the individual has a prior criminal conviction history related to violence, the defendant might receive a sentence at the high end of the available range, given the **aggravating factors** of multiple charges and a violent criminal history. However, a judge may also depart from the sentencing guidelines if there are mitigating factors to consider, including the defendant's diminished responsibility or the victim's instigation of the crime.

The federal sentencing guidelines were developed in order to promote a more humane and effective approach to punishment; however, these guidelines have been criticized (Abadinsky, 2003b). For example, recent research indicates that most determinate sentencing schemes do not inhibit the power of prosecutors to select charges. Moreover, judicial discretion has been limited when considering individual characteristics, producing unjust results. Finally, penalties have become harsher with the guidelines, despite the use of mitigating factors (Melton et al., 1997).

Some scholars argue that determinate sentencing will not achieve the goal of equal and fair treatment for offenders (Lacasse & Payne, 1999). This is especially the case as long as prosecutors possess the power to select charges and bargain with the defendant. In addition, judges have little discretion within the determinate sentencing guidelines and may only evaluate offense and offender characteristics considered relevant according to the sentencing guidelines.

Three Strikes Legislation

Three Strikes legislation is a form of mandatory minimum sentencing designed to incarcerate repeat offenders for long periods of time and, in some instances, for life (Clark, Austin, & Henry, 1997). In most cases, offenders with prior criminal records are sentenced to longer prison terms. However, California's famous Three Strikes law is more specific. Indeed, an offender with two prior convictions for serious or violent felonies must be sentenced to at least 25 years to life in prison on the third offense that qualifies as a felony (Stolzenberg & D'Alessio, 1997).

Is "Three Strikes and You're Out" a Good Policy Response to Criminal Behavior?

Brandon, a 51-year-old mechanic, was arrested for attempted forgery of a $300 check. Four years ago Brandon was arrested for attempted burglary, and 2 years before that Brandon was arrested for burglary. Brandon has a history of substance abuse and is mentally disabled. However, due to the Three Strikes law, Brandon was sentenced *to 25 years to life for the current offense of forgery. Randy, age 49, was arrested and convicted for stealing a spare tire. Because he had prior convictions in 1972 and in 1986 for burglary, Randy was sentenced to 27 years to life. Again, this sentence followed, given the Three Strikes law.*

In 1997, the legislative analyst's office of California published an update on the Three Strikes law (Reynolds & Kramer, 1999). The California Department of Corrections found that less than one fourth of second-strikers were admitted to prison for a serious or violent crime. The most common second-strike offenses included possession of a controlled substance, petty larceny with a prior theft, and second-degree burglary. Slightly more than half of the third-strikers were admitted to prison for a serious or violent offense. The most common third-strike crimes included robbery, first-degree burglary, possession of a controlled substance, second-degree burglary, and possession of a weapon (Legislative Analyst's Office, 2001).

Three Strikes legislation originated in California after a repeat offender kidnapped and murdered 12-year-old Polly Klaas (Clark, Austin, & Henry, 1997). A growing number of states as well as the federal government have enacted similar statutes to deal with repeat offenders. Some states require a life sentence once a defendant is convicted of a third felony, regardless of the class of felony committed. Other states require that the prior felonies involve violence, narcotics, or the use of a firearm (LaFave et al., 1999).

In California, a prior strike is defined as a conviction for a violent or serious felony (Greenwood et al., 1996). A judge decides whether the evidence proves beyond a reasonable doubt that the prior conviction qualifies as a strike. If an individual is convicted of any felonies outside of California identified as violent or serious, these crimes are considered strike priors and count in the application of the Three Strikes law (Stolzenberg & D'Alessio, 1997). Certain violent offenses are also counted as strikes for juveniles aged 16 or 17 at the time of the offense.

There have been many challenges and developments with respect to Three Strikes laws (Shichor & Sechrest, 1996). For example, the Supreme Court ruled that judges have power to dismiss strike priors in the interest of justice. In addition, crimes committed out of state can be used as a strike in a third-strike case, and trial courts have the power to reduce offenses to misdemeanors in instances where strike priors have been alleged (Menaster & Ricciardulli, 1997).

In California, approximately 120 third-strikers are admitted to prison each month (Reynolds & Kramer, 1999). One of the greatest challenges confronting the state's Department of Corrections is how to respond to its serious housing gap, given that an increasing number of third-strike offenders are being admitted to state facilities (Greenwood et al., 1996). Researchers from California's Justice Policy Institute have been studying the impact of the Three Strikes law. To date, they find no evidence to support the contention that this legislation has a deterrent effect on the crime rate (Macallair & Miles, 1999; see also Stolzenberg & D'Alessio, 1997). As a result, some researchers and analysts have called for a repeal of the current version of the Three Strikes law, and have urged further investigation of its crime control capabilities and its financial impact on various states (Macallair & Miles, 1999).

The Appellate Process

After an individual has been found guilty within the legal system, there is an opportunity to appeal the conviction. The appeal process is designed to ensure that constitutional rights are protected and that persons convicted unjustly have an avenue to pursue a new

What Are Some Grounds for an Appeal?

There are many circumstances in which a person may request an appeal. Some involve errors in the application of law; others involve errors in the application of courtroom procedures; and still others involve new evidence. On occasion, questions concerning the trial's overall fairness to the defendant may also be raised. The following vignette represents an example of this last category.

Steve Jake, a 42-year-old man, was convicted of attempted murder. The victim in the case was the daughter of a well-known politician. Given the extensive media publicity and exposure surrounding this legal matter, Steve's defense attorney requested that the trial judge grant a change of venue. Venue refers to the particular jurisdiction where a case is presented before a judge and jury. Arguably, a change of venue would allow Steve to be tried in a specific location where potential jurors would not be unduly and adversely influenced by the highly visible and controversial coverage linked to this case.

The judge denied the defense attorney's request. Steve was tried and found guilty of attempted murder. He was sentenced to life in prison. Steve's attorney will file for an appeal based on the judge's seemingly "incorrect" decision to deny a change of venue in this case. The appeal does not entail new evidence and it does not challenge any facts pertaining to the criminal dispute. However, the defense attorney is pursuing the legitimacy of the appeal based on an issue objected to within the original trial.

trial. There is a time limit in which an individual can petition a higher court for an appeal. Generally, a person must file a notice of appeal within 60 days; however, this time frame may vary by jurisdiction. There are two common types of appeals that can be requested. A **conviction appeal** is an appeal that requests the higher court to overturn a guilty verdict. A **sentence appeal** is a request to appeal the sentence due to its severity.

The appellate process is used to promote consistency in trial procedures, uncover any courtroom errors, and correct mistakes that may have been made by sentencing authorities, such as judges or juries (Meyer & Grant, 2003). When a decision is appealed, the appellate court reads the transcript of the trial in question, reviews any motions filed by the attorney, and assesses the briefs prepared by the defense and prosecution, outlining the issues brought forward in the appeal. The judge may listen to oral arguments drafted by the prosecution and the defense and may ask questions about the case. New evidence is not allowed during the appeal. The only issues raised during this posttrial process are those objected to during the original criminal case.

The judge has four options in response to the appeal. The judge may affirm the trial court's decision. This means that the appellate court agrees with the ruling made by the lower court. The judge may **reverse** the decision. This means that the appellate court sets aside the guilty verdict or the sentence, depending on the type of appeal requested. The judge may reverse and **remand** the case. This means that the appellate court overturns the guilty verdict but has sent the case back to the trial court for a new trial. Finally, the judge may remand the case. This means that the case is neither reversed nor affirmed; however, the appellate court has found reason to send the case back to the trial court for further proceedings. In this instance, the defendant may receive a new trial or have the charges dismissed.

THE DEATH PENALTY

Introduction

Defendants found guilty of having committed serious acts of criminal behavior (e.g., first-degree murder) may receive a sentence of death. Execution is the most extreme form of punishment available in the United States and in several other countries around the world. In this final section, the phenomenon of capital punishment is examined. In particular, background statistical information on this sentence is provided, the methods of execution are reviewed, the issue of wrongful convictions is discussed, and the process of appealing one's conviction and death sentence is described.

Background Statistical Information on the Death Penalty

According to the Bureau of Justice Statistics, 98 prisoners were executed in 1999 (Snell, 2000). This figure represented the largest number of convicts put to death since 1951 (U.S. Department of Justice, 2000). Moreover, by the end of 1999, 3,527 prisoners were sentenced to death (Snell, 2000). Of these convicts, 553 persons were on death row awaiting execution in California, 460 were similarly situated in Texas, 365 were located in Florida, and 230 were stationed in Pennsylvania (Salinas, 2002). There were also 20 people under a federal death sentence (Snell, 2000). Despite the fact that more executions occurred in 1999 than in any year since 1951, the ambivalence surrounding capital punishment appears to be increasing (Akers, Bohm, & Lanier, 1998). This is especially the case, given recent calls for a moratorium on capital punishment and attempts by legislators to restrict the death penalty (e.g., Connors, Lundregan, Miller, & McEwen, 1996; Scheck, Neufeld, & Dwyer, 2000; Shapiro, 2000).

The frequency with which capital punishment is administered has varied considerably over the years (Akers et al., 1998). One explanation for this is the evolving legal basis for its legitimacy. For example, between 1968 and 1976 there were no executions. During this period, the constitutionality of the death penalty was tested in the courts. In particular, the U.S. Supreme Court rendered its decision in *Furman v. Georgia* (1972). In this instance, the Court ruled that the death penalty was cruel and unusual punishment in violation of the Eighth and Fourteenth Amendments. As such, capital punishment was declared unconstitutional. However, the Court in *Furman* did not stipulate that the death penalty was unconstitutional for all crimes in all circumstances.

Several important decisions followed *Furman*. These cases endeavored to decrease the arbitrariness of imposing the death penalty, making it constitutional to execute only specific felons under precise conditions. For example, mandatory executions for certain crimes were abolished, and no instance of capital punishment was to be administered without automatic review of the conviction by a state appellate court. In the wake of *Furman,* the states enacted their own death penalty statutes. These efforts were undertaken in an attempt to guide and narrow the ability of judges and juries to impose a death sentence. The intent here was "to ensure that like crimes would be punished equally" (Levine & Wallach, 2002, p. 211). The most significant post-*Furman* case was *Gregg v. Georgia* (1976). This decision reinstated the constitutionality of the death penalty, specifying the crimes for which capital punishment could be administered. It also established the **bifurcated trial** process. This two-stage process includes the **guilt phase** (i.e., the trial) and the **penalty phase** (i.e., the sentence).

As of 1999, there is little variation among the states regarding the crimes punishable by death (Snell, 2000). Of those 38 states that rely on capital punishment, criminal homicide is one offense that can result in execution if the accused is convicted. In the context of the death penalty, these cases are also known as **capital trials.**

There are considerable differences among the states regarding the necessary requirements to secure the death penalty in a murder case (Akers et al., 1998). For example, in Alabama and Arkansas, capital murder is a crime punishable by death with the presence of at least 1 of 10 aggravating circumstances. The penal code in some states lists offenses other than homicide that are punishable by execution. To illustrate this practice, consider the following: California, Louisiana, and Arkansas cite treason; Florida names capital drug trafficking; Georgia lists aircraft hijacking; Kentucky and Idaho specify kidnapping; and Montana cites capital sexual assault (Snell, 2000). Again, these crimes are identified by these states as warranting the death penalty following conviction.

The Federal Bureau of Investigation reports approximately 22,000 criminal homicides per year, and only a fraction of defendants are subjected to a possible death sentence (U.S. Department of Justice, 2000). Of the 39 jurisdictions that authorize the use of capital punishment (38 states and the federal government), each one has its own set of laws that determine which offenses can result in execution. For detailed information about state statutes, readers are encouraged to visit the Death Penalty Information Center Web site at www.deathpenaltyinfo.org.

As was previously indicated, there is a bifurcated or split process that occurs in capital cases. If a defendant is found guilty of a capital crime, the individual proceeds to the penalty phase of the trial. The penalty or sentencing stage entails a decision to be reached by a jury or judge regarding the individual circumstances of the case and whether they warrant the imposition of capital punishment. Commenting on this matter, the Court in *Lockett v. Ohio* (1978) concluded that the jury must be allowed to hear "any aspect of the defendant's character or record and any of the circumstances of the offense that the defendant proffers as a basis for a sentence less than death" (p. 587). In other words, there may be mitigating factors that require some consideration before a death sentence is issued. Examples of such mitigating factors include, among other things, the presence of mental retardation or related disability, the absence of a prior record, the relative age of the person, and any other circumstances that may have unduly influenced the defendant's criminal behavior.

In addition, for the death penalty to be imposed, the prosecution must introduce at least one aggravating factor. Aggravating factors are unequivocal facts that support the reasonableness of execution in a given case. These factors vary by state; however, they typically include the offender's prior criminal history, prediction of future dangerousness, and the heinousness of the offense. In an effort to more fairly and justly determine the appropriateness of the death penalty, the judge or jury must weigh all relevant mitigating and aggravating evidence concerning the person convicted of capital murder, prior to reaching a sentencing decision (Melton et al., 1997). Moreover, according to the U.S. Supreme Court ruling in *Presnell v. Georgia* (1978), a decision to execute will be declared invalid if the jury fails to specify aggravating circumstances during the penalty phase of the trial.

Methods of Execution

In 2001, there were five methods of execution available throughout the United States. These include **lethal injection, electrocution,** lethal gas, firing squad, and **hanging.** Some states have more than one option available and allow the prisoner to make a choice about the method of capital punishment to be used. The most common form of execution is lethal injection, which is authorized in 34 of the 38 states that have the death penalty (Snell, 2000). Death by lethal injection results from an anesthetic that is administered in order to put the condemned person to sleep; however, the amount that is given results in death by overdose. In addition, a drug is administered to paralyze the entire muscular system and to stop the person's breathing, resulting in respiratory and cardiac arrest. Interestingly, the ethics of the medical profession prevent physicians from participating in administering capital punishment; therefore, inexperienced technicians involved in the process can (and do) create medical problems during the execution, at times causing considerable pain to the convict and protracted delays in the administration of death.

Electrocution is another method of execution. It is available in 11 states (Snell, 2000). The first electric chair, built in New York in 1888, was developed in response to the need for a more humane form of capital punishment. Prior to this time, hanging was the most common form of execution. Death by the electric chair involves shaving the convict; strapping the person to the chair with belts across the chest, groin, leg, and arm areas; and blindfolding the prisoner. A metal cap is attached to the person's scalp and forehead and placed over a sponge moistened with saline solution. An additional electrode is dampened with conductive jelly and attached to the prisoner's shaved leg. This process allows the force of electricity, which ranges between 500 and 2,000 volts, to surge through the body. After each jolt, a physician determines if the person's heart is still beating. The electrical charges continue until the person is declared dead by the attending medical examiner.

Death By Electrocution: What Is It Like?

Have you ever wondered what death by execution looks and feels like? If you have, you are not alone. One description comes from William Brennan, U.S. Supreme Court Justice. As he indicated:

The prisoner's eyeballs sometimes pop out and rest on [his] cheeks. The prisoner often defecates, urinates, and vomits blood and drool. The body turns bright red as its temperature rises, and the prisoner's flesh swells and his skin stretches to the point of breaking. Sometimes the prisoner catches fire . . . witnesses hear a loud and sustained sound like bacon frying, and the sickly sweet smell of burning flesh permeates the chamber. (Death Penalty Information Center, 1997, p. 3)

Exposure to the gas chamber is available in four states as a form of execution; however, each state offers lethal injection as an alternative method to gas inhalation (Snell, 2000). In 1924, the use of cyanide gas was introduced in Nevada as a more humane approach to meting out death to prisoners. In addition, the gas chamber was constructed and became the appropriate venue for administering capital punishment when it was discovered that gas leaked out from the condemned person's cell. The operation of this apparatus involves the release of crystals of sodium cyanide. These crystals cause a chemical reaction that discharges hydrogen cyanide gas. The condemned person is instructed to breathe deeply to expedite the process; however, some convicts try to hold their breaths and resist inhaling. The side effects of doing this are gruesome. The eyes of the prisoner burst, extreme pain is experienced, the skin turns purple, and the convict succumbs to strangulation. Eventually, the individual dies of cerebral hypoxia, that is, the cutting off of oxygen to the brain.

The firing squad is also available in three states and it represents a rather infamous method of execution. The firing squad was employed in the 1977 death of Gary Gilmore (Snell, 2000). Gilmore, convicted of murder in Utah, refused to pursue appeals, accepted his sentence, and was subsequently killed by the state. His case was the first execution after reinstatement of the death penalty. As recently as 1996, John Albert Taylor chose to be executed by a firing squad as well.

The procedures used by a firing squad involve strapping a prisoner to a chair surrounded by sandbags designed to absorb the convicted felon's blood. A black hood is placed over the convict's head and five shooters armed with .30-caliber weapons aim at the white cloth target placed over the person's heart. One of the shooters is given blank rounds. None of the participants know who will be using blanks. This strategy is employed to psychologically protect the shooters from experiencing any adverse effects from the incident. Death occurs as a result of blood loss caused by a rupture of the heart or other large blood vessel. However, if the shooters miss the heart by accident or by intention, the prisoner will bleed to death slowly.

Hanging is still available as an option for execution in three states. This method of capital punishment was primarily used until the 1890s. Preparation for the hanging involves weighing the convict the day before the death event. A sandbag matching the prisoner's exact weight is used to rehearse the execution and to determine the length of the drop necessary to ensure a smooth process. Any mistakes can result in decapitation or slow, painful asphyxiation.

When a hanging occurs, the convict is placed on top of a chair or other stationery object. A noose is then placed around the condemned person's neck. Once the object is removed, the person is unable to breathe. Alternatively, the prisoner is positioned in such a way that a removable door is located beneath him or her. Once this door is dislodged, the condemned man or woman again is unable to breathe. In both cases, however, the force of carrying one's full body weight by the neck typically causes it to snap in the process.

Wrongful Convictions

The death penalty is currently one of the most intensely debated issues in our criminal justice system (Akers et al., 1998; Scheck et al., 2000). Regardless of any moral and political convictions or any factual information derived from social science research, the strongest argument against the death penalty is that innocent people have been executed (Cohen, 1999). In addition, since 1973, over 80 convicted men and women sentenced to death have had their convictions overturned and have been released due to the higher court's finding of innocence (Snell, 2000). Interestingly, the increase in the number of persons being proved innocent is not because of the appeals process. Instead, it is the result of new technology such as DNA testing (Connors et al., 1996; Dieter, 1997). Before DNA testing, the criminal justice system relied on confessions, forensic experts, eyewitnesses, police officers, prosecutors, and defense attorneys (Scheck et al., 2000). However, today with DNA testing, it is possible to uncover human errors and free persons wrongly convicted of crimes for which they had been accused. For example, in 1984, Kirk Bloodsworth was convicted and sentenced to death for the rape and murder of a young girl. The panties of the young girl were stained with semen, and subsequent DNA testing convincingly demonstrated that the semen stain was not from Bloodsworth. Wrongfully convicted, Kirk Bloodsworth was released in 1994 and given a pardon by the governor of Maryland (Bedau, 1997).

Between 1975 and 1993, an average of 2.5 people were released from death row every year. Between 1994 and 2000, this rate increased to 4.6 persons per year (Scheck et al., 2000). According to Radelet, Bedau, and Putnam (1992), there are several explanations for why people are wrongfully convicted. Sometimes, witnesses simply provide false information. The bases for this vary but generally include lying to ensure a conviction, accusing a person because of a grudge, or making an honest mistake. People are also wrongfully convicted for more troubling reasons. For example, prejudice because of race, mental disability, or class can produce discrimination, adversely impacting a defendant's criminal case. In addition, police officers can (and do) make mistakes. At times, they may feel pressured to arrest someone for a crime given the presence of organizational or political pressure. As a result, evidence may be withheld from defense counsel, and witnesses may be coerced into providing information that supports the prosecution's case (Dieter, 1997).

Appealing the Death Penalty

For persons convicted and sentenced to death, most states authorize an automatic review. In Idaho, Indiana, Kentucky, Oklahoma, and Tennessee, a review is required for the sentence only; in Indiana and Kentucky, the defendant can waive a review of the conviction. The highest appellate court in the state conducts the examination of the case. If the appellate court vacates the conviction or the sentence, the case can be sent back to the lower court for a retrial. Even in the instance of a retrial or a resentencing hearing, the possibility that the defendant may be sentenced to death a second time does exist.

Federal *habeas corpus* petitions (i.e., a request to release the person confined) have been used in death penalty cases, challenging the constitutionality of imprisonment because it unjustly violates one's personal liberties (e.g., freedom of movement). In some instances, these claims have been shown to possess merit, given the high number of cases in which the federal court has overturned the decision of the state court (Bedau, 1997). However, the appellate process has been severely restricted by the Anti-Terrorism and Effective Death Penalty Act (AEDPA). This act was signed into legislation on April 24, 1996, by former President William Jefferson Clinton (U.S. Sentencing Project, 1998). The AEDPA restricts the ability of death row prisoners to gain federal review of their cases. This legislative outcome followed in the wake of concerns raised by the judicial and legislative branches of government, reporting that too many state death penalty convictions were being invalidated by federal courts due to violations of federally protected rights (Bedau). Indeed, some lawmakers maintained that death row prisoners were abusing the federal *habeas corpus* writ, and that these petitions were becoming far too common in postconviction death penalty cases.

Designed to place severe restrictions on convicts wishing to utilize federal *habeas corpus* writs, the AEDPA requires that these petitions be filed within 6 months of a conviction. In addition, only claims of actual innocence can be granted an evidentiary hearing, and only "unreasonable," unconstitutional state court rulings can be overturned. With the enactment of AEDPA, the law forbids federal courts from overturning state convictions or sentences, unless the state proceeding resulted in a decision that was contrary to clearly established federal law as articulated by the U.S. Supreme Court (Bedau, 1997).

DISCUSSION QUESTIONS

1. What is the plea-bargaining process? What types of plea-bargaining strategies are employed in criminal cases? Do you believe that negotiating the defendant's guilt (or innocence) is an effective way to respond to criminal behavior?

2. What is probation? What are some intermediate sanctions? Do you believe that these interventions are effective mechanisms designed to address offender conduct?

3. Should persons with substance abuse disorders and mental health diagnoses be diverted from the formal justice system? Explain your response.

4. What is the difference between criminal competency and criminal responsibility? List some examples of diminished responsibility and explain how *actus reas* and *mens rea* operate here.

5. What is the difference between not guilty by reason of insanity and guilty but mentally ill? What is your position on the use of these strategies in response to criminal behavior?

6. What are the four established goals of punishment? Do you believe they can be reconciled? From your perspective, which goal is the most effective response to criminal behavior?

7. List the four authorities that determine the type and length of sentence. What are mandatory minimum sentences? What concerns, if any, exist with these types of determinate sentences? How does the Three Strikes law operate?

8. Following a conviction, what are the four options a judge considers when a case is reviewed for an appeal?

9. Describe the five methods of execution. Identify some recent cases where capital punishment was administered.

10. Do you believe that persons convicted of a crime may be wrongfully condemned? What are some of the reasons why prisoners are wrongfully convicted?

REFERENCES

Abadinsky, H. (2003a). *Probation and parole: Theory and practice* (8th ed.). Upper Saddle River, NJ: Prentice Hall.

Abadinsky, H. (2003b). *Law and justice: An introduction to the American legal system* (5th ed.). Upper Saddle River, NJ: Prentice Hall.

Akers, J. R., Bohm, R. M., & Lanier, C. S. (1998). *America's experiment with capital punishment.* Durham, NC: Carolina Academic Press.

Alexander, V. (1999). Ethics-based decision-making: A psychoeducational workshop for adult diversion programs. *Journal for Specialists in Group Work, 24,* 208–219.

American Psychiatric Association. (2000). *Diagnostic and statistical manual of mental disorders* (4th ed., text revision). Washington DC: Author.

Arrigo, B. A. (1996a). *The contours of psychiatric justice: A postmodern critique of mental illness, criminal insanity, and the law.* New York/London: Garland.

Arrigo, B. A. (1996b). Rethinking knowledge construction and the guilty but mentally ill verdict. *Criminal Justice and Behavior: An International Journal, 23*(4), 572–592.

Arrigo, B. A. (2000). *Introduction to forensic psychology: Issues and controversies in crime and justice.* San Diego, CA: Academic Press.

Arrigo, B. A. (2002). What is "forensic psychology." In D. Levinson (Ed.), *Encyclopedia of crime and punishment* (pp. 1295–1301). Thousand Oaks, CA: Sage.

Arrigo, B. A., & Bardwell, M. C. (2000). Law, psychology, and competency-to-stand-trial: Problems with and implications for high profile cases. *Criminal Justice Policy Review, 11*(1), 16–43.

Bardwell, M. C., & Arrigo, B. A. (2002a). Competency to stand trial: A law, psychology, and policy assessment. *Journal of Psychiatry and Law, 30*(2), 1–115.

Bardwell, M. C., & Arrigo, B. A. (2002b). *Criminal competency on trial: The case of Colin Ferguson.* Durham, NC: Carolina Academic Press.

Baumer, T. L., & Mendelsohn, R. I. (1992). Electronically monitored home confinement: Does it work? In J. M. Byrne, A. J. Lurigio, & J. Petersilia (Eds.), *Smart sentencing: The emergence of intermediate sanctions.* Newbury Park, CA: Sage.

Beck, A. J. (2000). *Prisoners in 1999.* Washington DC: U.S. Department of Justice, Office of Justice Programs.

Bedau, H. A. (1997). *The death penalty in America: Current controversies.* New York: Oxford University Press.

Blair, J. (2000, January 2). Boot camps: An idea whose time came and went. *New York Times Week in Review,* p. 3.

Boldt, R. C. (1998). Rehabilitative punishment and the drug treatment court movement. *Washington University Law Quarterly, 76,* 1205–1306.

Bonnie, R. (1992). The competence of criminal defendants: A theoretical formulation. *Behavioral Sciences and the Law, 10,* 291–316.

Bordenkircher v. Hayes, 434 U.S. 357 (1978).

California Legislative Analyst's Office. (2001, July 30). Retrieved October 12, 2004, from www.lao.ca.gov

Casper, J. D. (1992). Did you have a lawyer when you went to court? No, I had a public defender. In G. F. Cole (Ed.), *Criminal justice, law and politics* (6th ed., pp. 231–253). Pacific Grove, CA: Brooks/Cole.

Cassel, E., & Bernstein, D. A. (2001). *Criminal behavior.* Boston, MA: Allyn & Bacon.

Champion, D. (1988a). *Felony probation: Problems and prospects.* New York: Praeger.

Champion, D. (1988b). Felon plea bargaining and probation: A growing judicial and prosecutorial dilemma. *Journal of Criminal Justice, 16,* 291–301.

Cirincione, C., & Jacobs, C. (1999). Identifying insanity acquittals: Is it any easier? *Law and Human Behavior, 23,* 487–497.

Clark, J., Austin, J., & Henry, D. A. (1997). *Three strikes and you're out: A review of state legislation.* Washington DC: National Institute of Justice.

Clear, T. R., & Hardyman, P. L. (1990). The new intensive supervision movement. *Crime and Delinquency, 36,* 42–60.

Cohen, A. (1999, September 13). Innocent, after proven guilty. *Time,* 26–28.

Connors, E., Lundregan, T., Miller, N., & McEwen, T. (1996). *Convicted by juries, exonerated by science: Case studies in the use of DNA evidence to establish innocence after trial.* Washington DC: U.S. Department of Justice, Office of Justice Programs, National Institute of Justice.

Death Penalty Information Center. (1997). Retrieved October 12, 2004, from www.deathpenaltyinfo.org

del Carmen, R., Barnhill, M. B., Bonham, G., Hignite, L., & Jermstad, T. (2001). *Civil liabilities and other legal issues for probation/parole officers and supervisors.* Washington DC: National Institute of Corrections.

Dieter, R. (1997). *Innocence and the death penalty: The increasing danger of executing the innocent.* Washington DC: Death Penalty Information Center.

Durham, A. M. (1994). *Crisis and reform: Current issues in American punishment.* Boston, MA: Little, Brown.

Feld, B. C. (1999). *Bad kids: Race and the transformation of the juvenile court.* New York: Oxford University Press.

Foucault, M. (1977). *Discipline and punish: The birth of a prison.* New York: Pantheon.

Furman v. Georgia, 408 U.S. 238 (1972).

Gebelein, R. S. (2000). *The rebirth of rehabilitation: Promise and perils of drug courts.* Washington DC: Office of Justice Programs.

Geerken, M. R., & Hayes, H. D. (1993). Probation and parole: Public risk and the future of incarceration alternatives. *Criminology, 31,* 549–564.

Greenberg, M., & Ruback, R. (1982). *Social psychology of the criminal justice system.* Pacific Grove, CA: Brooks/Cole.

Greenwood, P. W., Rydell, C. P., Abrahamse, A. F., Caulkins, J. P., Chiesa, J., Model, K. E., et al. (1996). Estimated benefits and costs of California's new sentencing law. In D. Shichor & D. K. Sechrest (Eds.), *Three strikes and you're out* (pp. 53–89). Thousand Oaks, CA: Sage.

Gregg v. Georgia, 428 U.S. 153 (1976).

Lacasse, C., & Payne, A. A. (1999). Federal sentencing guidelines and mandatory minimum sentences: Do defendants bargain in the shadow of the judge? *Journal of Law and Economics, 42,* 245–268.

LaFave, W., Israel, J., & King, N. (1999). *Criminal procedure: Criminal practice series.* St. Paul, MN: West Group.

Legislative Analyst's Office. (2001). *California's three strikes law.* Sacramento, CA: Department of Corrections.

Levine, M., & Wallach, L. (2002). *Psychological problems, social issues, and law.* Boston, MA: Allyn & Bacon.

Lilly, J. R., Ball, R., Curry, G. D., & McMullen, J. (1993). Electronic monitoring of the drunk driver: A seven year study of the home confinement alternative. *Crime & Delinquency, 39,* 462–484.

Lockett v. Ohio, 438 U.S. 586 (1978).

Macallair, D., & Miles, M. (1999). *Striking out: The failure of California's "three strikes and you're out" law.* San Francisco, CA: The Justice Policy Institute.

Melton, G., Petrila, J., Poythress, N., & Slobogin, C. (1997). *Psychological evaluations for the courts* (2nd ed.). New York: Guilford.

Menaster, A., & Ricciardulli, A. (1997). *3 strikes manual.* Woodland Hills, CA: Courtroom Compendiums.

Meyer, J. F., & Grant, D. R. (2003). *The courts in our criminal justice system.* Upper Saddle River, NJ: Prentice Hall.

Mitchell, G., & Lifton, R. (2000). *Who owns death? Capital punishment, the American conscience, and the end of executions.* New York: Morrow.

National Drug Control Policy. (2001). *2001 annual report.* Washington DC: U.S. Office of National Drug Control Policy.

O'Leary, V., & Clear, T. R. (1984). *Directions for community corrections in the 1990s.* Washington DC: U.S. Department of Justice, National Institute of Corrections.

Palmer, T. (1995). Programmatic and non-programmatic aspects of successful intervention: New directions for research. *Crime and Delinquency, 41,* 100–131.

Parry, J. (1998). *National benchbook on psychiatric and psychological evidence and testimony.* Washington DC: American Bar Association.

Petersilia, J. (1998). A decade of experimenting with intermediate sanctions: What have we learned? *Federal Probation, 62,* 3–9.

Petersilia, J., & Turner, S. (1990). Comparing intensive and regular supervision for high-risk probationers: Early results from an experiment in California. *Crime and Delinquency, 36,* 87–111.

Polk, K. (1984). Juvenile diversion: A look at the record. *Crime and Delinquency, 30,* 648–659.

Presnell v. Georgia, 439 U.S. 14 (1978).

Radelet, M., Bedau, H., & Putnam, C. (1992). *In spite of innocence: Erroneous convictions in capital cases.* Boston: Northeastern University Press.

Reiman, J. (2001). *The rich get richer and the poor get prison: Ideology, class, and criminal justice* (6th ed.). Boston, MA: Allyn & Bacon.

Reynolds, M., & Kramer, J. (1999). Is the "three strikes and you're out" a useful sentencing policy? In J. Fuller & E. Hickey (Eds.), *Controversial issues in criminology* (pp. 240–258). Boston, MA: Allyn & Bacon.

Salinas, P. S. (2002). Death row inmates. In D. Levinson (Ed.), *Encyclopedia of crime and punishment* (pp. 478–482). Thousand Oaks, CA: Sage.

Scheck, B., Neufeld, B., & Dwyer, J. (2000). *Actual innocence: Five days to execution and other dispatches from the wrongly convicted.* New York: Doubleday.

Shapiro, B. (2000, March 26). Capital offense. *New York Times Magazine,* pp. 19–20.

Sherman, L. W., Gottfredson, D., MacKenzie, D., Eck, J., Reuter, P., & Bushway, S. (1997). *Preventing crime: What works, what doesn't, what's promising.* Washington DC: U.S. Department of Justice, Office of Justice Programs, National Institute of Justice.

Shichor, D., & Sechrest, D. K. (Eds.). (1996). *Three strikes and you're out.* Thousand Oaks, CA: Sage.

Snell, T. (2000, December). *Capital punishment 1999.* Bureau of Justice Statistics Bulletin. Washington DC: U.S. Department of Justice, Office of Justice Programs.

Steadman, H., Deane, M., Morrissey, J., Westcott, M., Salasin, S., & Shapiro, S. (1999). A SAMHSA research initiative assessing the effectiveness of jail diversion programs for mentally ill persons. *Psychiatric Services, 50,* 1620–1623.

Steadman, H., McGreevy, M. A., Morrissey, J. P., Callahan, L. A., Robbins, P., & Cirincione, C. (1993). *Before and after Hinckley: Evaluating insanity defense reform.* New York: Guilford.

Stolzenberg, L., & D'Alessio, S. J. (1997). "Three strikes and you're out": The impact of California's new mandatory sentencing law on serious crime rates. *Crime and Delinquency, 43,* 457–469.

Sullivan, D., & Tifft, L. (2001). *Restorative justice: Healing the foundations of our everyday lives.* Monsey, NY: Willow Tree Press.

Sutton, J. R. (1988). *Stubborn children: Controlling delinquency in the United States.* Berkeley, CA: University of California.

U.S. Department of Justice. (2000). *The federal death penalty system: A statistical survey (1998–2000).* Washington DC: U.S. Department of Justice.

U.S. Sentencing Project. (1998). *Variations in sentencing—A report.* Washington DC: U.S. Government Printing Office.

Winick, B. (1995). Ambiguities in the legal meaning and significance of mental illness. *Psychology, Public Policy and the Law, 2*(1), 534–611.

Wrightsman, L., Nietzel, M. T., & Fortune, W. H. (1998). *Psychology and the legal system* (4th ed.). Pacific Grove, CA: Brooks/Cole.

The Correctional System

OVERVIEW

Systematic responses to criminal behavior extend beyond law enforcement and courtroom justice. On occasion, persons convicted of illicit conduct are processed through the system of corrections. Chapter 10 addresses some of these matters, especially in relation to sentencing guidelines and the death penalty. However, the way in which offenders are treated in and respond to penal environments is especially noteworthy.

Chapter 11 examines how the correctional system addresses criminal behavior. In particular, an assessment of **retribution** versus **rehabilitation** is presented, focusing on how this philosophical tension impacts overall correctional practice. In addition, the phenomenon of **parole** is explored, highlighting its relationship to mentally ill offenders, **sex offender registration**, substance abuse and crime prevention, and **halfway houses.** Moreover, an analysis of the correctional milieu is described, emphasizing the federal and state systems, general prison conditions, forensic psychiatric wards, and the subculture of confinement. Finally, some commentary on reintegrating criminals back into society following release from prisons is discussed.

As this chapter reveals, the correctional response to criminal behavior raises some deeply troubling questions about offender conduct and society at large. In short, what is at stake is whether the prison environment is itself a generating milieu for violence and recidivism. If so, the system of corrections has a long way to go before it can effectively and humanely attend to the problems posed by criminal behavior.

KEY TERMS

Deprivation model	Prisoner mother program
Determinate sentencing	Proposition 36
Discretionary parole	Rehabilitation
Faith-based rehabilitation programs	Retribution
Federal Bureau of Prisons	Security Housing Units
Halfway houses	Sex offender registration
Importation models	Solitary confinement
Mandatory release	Supermax prisons
Megan's law	Technical parole violation
Parole	10–20–Life law
Parole board	The Young Offender Initiative
Parole grant hearing	Three Strikes law

RETRIBUTION VERSUS REHABILITATION

Introduction

The tension between retribution and rehabilitation underscores much of what passes for punishment and treatment within correctional settings. This section examines this philosophical and practical conflict. As such, some initial commentary on this tension is presented, the presence of retribution in various legislative acts or statutes is described, and the model of correctional rehabilitation is outlined.

Retribution Versus Rehabilitation: Exploring the Tension

In chapter 10, some observations on the goals of punishment are discussed. Not surprisingly, goals such as deterrence, incapacitation, retribution, and rehabilitation do not appear easily reconcilable. This is particularly the case when examining the tension between rehabilitation and retribution (for commentary outlining a "third way" with respect to this tension, see Maruna & LeBel, 2003; Travis, 2000; and Travis & Petersilia, 2001).

Proponents of rehabilitation believe that the correctional system has a duty to help offenders change their criminal or delinquent ways through various vocational, social, and psychological interventions. Advocates of this philosophical approach contend that sustained and meaningful treatment is the best response to offender conduct, especially if the goal is to change behavior and to curb recidivism. However, supporters of retribution maintain that harsh sentencing practices and capital punishment are the best answers to crime. Indeed, as these proponents assert, not only do retributive efforts deter future illicit behavior, but also they acknowledge that convicted killers or other serious offenders are beyond rehabilitation. Commenting on this distinction, Jacoby (1983) notes the following:

> For those whose concept of justice is concerned primarily with the criminal's rights and prospects for rehabilitation, any extended punishment is simply another crime. For those focused totally on the victim's rights, only executions or other severe penalties will suffice to restore a sense of moral balance. (p. 291)

For those citizens who support the victim's rights approach, they believe that individuals are chiefly accountable for their successes and failures. In part, this notion explains why there is so much popular support today for a retributive system of justice. Underpinning this correctional approach is the general public's perception that those who fail on their own merit deserve the punishment that awaits them. However, there are certainly those who disagree with this logic:

> Few proponents of [retributive justice] seem to be aware that it rests upon two fundamentally contradictory views of human nature: it is both deterministic (in holding that punishment can cause others to be deterred from crime) and indeterministic (in proclaiming that incarceration cannot cause the culprit to be rehabilitated. (Partridge, 2001, p. 43)

The tension that exists between retribution and rehabilitation, especially when evaluating the best or preferred correctional response to criminal behavior, is not easy to resolve. Subsequent sections of this chapter examine this conflict in several practical contexts. However, regardless of the approach emphasized in specific situations or with particular offenders, the fundamental question to be addressed is whether the strategy employed reduces the likelihood of future criminal conduct.

Retribution in Legislation

Those who favor retribution in sentencing want to see offenders punished for their wrongdoings; that is, proponents of retribution want criminals to receive their just desserts. "Whereas the goals of deterrence, incapacitation, and rehabilitation are based on what might happen or what the offender might do, [just] dessert focuses on the event that led to

Deciding to Punish or to Treat

On July 27, 2001, 14-year-old Florida boy Nathaniel Brazill was sentenced to 28 years in prison for the shooting death of his favorite teacher, Barry Grunow. Brazill received a verdict of second-degree murder. However, the prosecution sought a first-degree murder conviction that would have carried a mandatory sentence of life in prison without the possibility of parole. Brazill was 13 at the time of the shooting. Even though Brazill did not receive a life sentence, he will still be locked away until he is almost 40 years old.

The philosophy of retribution holds people accountable for their actions, even when circumstances make it difficult to do so. The philosophy of rehabilitation argues that convicted murderers such as Nathaniel Brazill are not beyond redemption. Based on the facts of the case presented here, how would you decide Brazill's fate? Would your decision have any impact on the possibility of future delinquent or criminal conduct?

conviction" (Siegel, 1998, p. 532). To make things right, criminals are required to pay society back for the harms they committed. According to Jacoby (1983), "The symbolic 'scales of justice' have a real meaning for most citizens, who believe that the legal system exists to maintain a moral and social equilibrium, and to restore that equilibrium when it has been violently disturbed" (p. 291). Consequently, a barrage of more punitive sentencing laws has flooded the legal landscape in the last 2 decades, reflecting society's correctional preference in the face of criminal and delinquent conduct.

Popular support for new legislation such as California's **Three Strikes law**, Megan's Sexually Violent Predator law, Florida's **10–20–Life law** (the law in which Nathaniel Brazill's crime falls under), and increased support for capital punishment all have frustrated proponents of rehabilitation. As Jacoby (1983) explains:

> In a society of laws, popular feeling cannot be allowed to dictate either a particular form of punishment or the application of that punishment to a specific individual. This principle is valid insofar as it applies to the ultimate penalty of death but also it applies to all lesser punishments. Popular support alone is not sufficient to confer legitimacy on a legal penalty, whether that penalty is extremely cruel or extremely mild. (p. 294)

However, popular opinion often triumphs over logic. For example, do the majority of Americans truly believe that a 13-year-old child is beyond redemption? The answer is probably not. Yet, when young Nathaniel Brazill received a 28-year sentence, the judge (and the prosecutor who actually sought a life sentence under first-degree murder) made a statement that retribution on behalf of the victim's family was more important than rehabilitating the offender. In response to the judge's sentence, Brazill's defense attorney, Robert Udell, was quoted as saying, "It tells you all you need to know about the United States of America in the year 2001, doesn't it? We've lost our soul" (Quotation retrieved February 10, 2002, from http://www.CNN.com).

Forms of Retribution: Three Strikes, 10–20–Life, and Megan's Law

Chapter 10 describes the Three Strikes law in relation to posttrial sentencing matters. But this legislation also represents a retributive mechanism by which to address criminal behavior. California's Three Strikes law was initiated by wedding photographer, Mike Reynolds, following the murder of his daughter, Kimberly Reynolds, killed by career offender, Joe Davis (Olson, 2000). When the heinous and vicious slaying of 12-year-old Polly Klass, occurred, "Reynolds' three strikes bill gained public backing. With both Reynolds' and the public's insistence, legislators refocused on 'lock' 'em up' legislation to combat violent crime" (Olson, 2000, p. 548; Reynolds & Kramer, 1999). In March 1994, California's Three Strikes and You're Out bill was enacted by the legislature (Cal. Penal Code 667, 1999). Popular support for this legislation clearly was evident when California voters approved the law by enacting Proposition 184 in November of that same year (Olson, 2000).

Under California's Three Strikes law, a mandatory sentence is imposed for repeat offenders (Cal. Penal code 667, 1999). The first violent or serious felony conviction is not subject to sentencing enhancements under this law because it is identified as the first strike. However, if a defendant is convicted of a second felony (hence, a second strike), the law mandates a double sentence for that conviction. If a defendant is then convicted of a third felony, he or she receives a mandatory tripled sentence, a 25-year-to-life sentence, or a discretionary sentence by the court, whichever is most severe (Menaster & Ricciardulli, 1997). The glaring defect in this legislation is that "California's 'Three Strikes' law results in disparate treatment of criminal defendants because it allows first strike defendants to plea bargain without requiring rehabilitation, but then severely punishes them if they commit a new offense" (Olson, 2000, p. 547). This type of inconsistent treatment for convicted defendants undoubtedly disturbs those in favor of criminal rehabilitation and fairness in the legal system (Macallair & Miles, 1999).

Additional criticisms have been leveled against the punitive philosophy embedded in the Three Strikes law. Indeed, as Olson (2000, p. 557) explains, "The law is poorly written, over broad, and fails to take into account the defendant's individualized circumstances." On this latter point, the offender's circumstances include his or her " . . . particular disposition, rehabilitative history, [and] the likelihood of future criminal acts" (Owens, 1995, p. 144). Furthermore, despite the public's misperception, California's Three Strikes law is not working to decrease incidences of violent crime (Macallair & Miles, 1999). Therefore, the retributive effect of the legislation seems to be its only sustaining value. (For further analysis of the Three Strikes law, see chapter 10.)

Another legislative enactment that prioritizes retribution over rehabilitation is the 10–20–Life law. This legislation is designed to punish anyone who uses a gun to commit a crime by enforcing harsh mandatory sentencing. Under this law, persons convicted of carrying a gun during the commission of a crime face 10 years in prison. Those who fire a gun during a crime receive an automatic 20 years in prison. Those who fire a gun harming or killing someone during the commission of a crime can receive 25 years to life without parole and without time deducted for good behavior (Fla. Stat. § 775.087, 2001).

Megan's law is another example of retributive philosophy in correctional practice. It began in New Jersey when Megan Kanka was abducted, sexually abused, and murdered by her neighbor, a convicted sex offender (Pratt, 2000). Public outcry for retribution led to legislation requiring sex offenders to register with local law enforcement upon release from jail (Tier & Coy, 1997). Many states followed New Jersey's lead, and some states additionally require law enforcement to notify the public when a released sex offender moves into their neighborhood. A federal version of Megan's law was enacted in 1996, receiving Congressional approval and former President William Jefferson Clinton's signature with little debate (Freeman-Longo & Blanchard, 1998).

For some states, there is a community notification provision, representing a particularly controversial issue for Megan's law. By notifying the community that a sex offender is in their midst, fearful and vengeful people can (and do) resort to vigilantism to satisfy their need for retribution. Critics of Megan's law (and many of those in support of the rehabilitation philosophy in corrections) argue that sex offenders are not afforded ample opportunities for adequate treatment and reform while incarcerated; consequently, releasing the offender from prison and subjecting the ex-convict to community mistreatment is worse than leaving the person in prison for the remainder of the individual's life.

To address this issue, California enacted a Sexually Violent Predator law, which keeps offenders locked away after their sentence is over (Cal. Wel. & Inst. Code § 6600, 2001). Those offenders still deemed a risk to the community can be civilly committed until a panel of psychiatrists renders them safe for community reintegration. However, as some critics caution, to sustain incarceration beyond an individual's given sentence merely represents another mode of retribution. (See chapter 8 for more on civil commitment.)

The Rehabilitation Model in Corrections

The rehabilitative model in corrections argues that criminals can change their errant behavior and become productive members of society, provided proper treatment, rather than punishment, is availed to them (e.g., Cullen & Gilbert, 1982). To be sure, harsh punitive sentencing, including the death penalty, is contrary to the tenets of the rehabilitative ideal (Akers, Bohm, & Lanier, 1998).

Supporters of rehabilitation and treatment believe that offenders are victims. ". . . [C]riminals themselves are the victims of social injustice, poverty, and racism; and their acts are a response to a society that has betrayed them" (Siegel, 1998, p. 462). Supporters of rehabilitation argue that this victimization causes emotional scarring or problems in individuals who might otherwise not commit criminal offenses (VanVoorhis, Braswell, & Lester, 1999). However, these concerns are of little consequence for those who maintain that individuals are morally blameworthy and socially accountable for their wrongful transgressions. "Retributive desires . . . flow from a need to restore 'something missing'—a sense of physical and emotional integrity that is shattered by violence" (Jacoby, 1983, p. 298). For retributivists, blaming society for the commission of crime against a loved one can never provide the "something missing." Instead, according to this approach to punishment, people must be held responsible for their actions.

Supporters of the rehabilitation philosophy maintain that in order to deal effectively with crime, public passion must be excluded from correctional policy. Attacking the root causes of crime is the only method of minimizing criminal behavior (VanVoorhis et al., 1999). "First, funds must be devoted to equalize access to conventional means of success. If individuals run afoul of the law, efforts should be made to treat and not punish them" (Siegel, 1998, p. 462). This makes sense because prison overcrowding mandates the release of convicts sooner than retributivists would like. Additionally, simply locking up offenders without treatment cannot keep prisoners from recidivating when they are released into the same environment that produced (or contributed to) the condition for law breaking in the first place (Sechrest, White, & Brown, 1979). Rehabilitation "means emphasizing counseling and psychological care in community-based treatment programs. Whenever possible, offenders should be placed on probation in halfway houses or in other rehabilitation-oriented programs" (Siegel, 1998, pp. 462–463).

However, critics of rehabilitation claim that it does not work (e.g., Logan & Gaes, 1993; Martinson, 1974; von Hirsch, 1976). Further, victim's rights are ignored when offenders receive treatment and privileges in prison. Indeed, from the victim's perspective:

> The punishment of criminals provides some measure of assurance . . . that the assault was an exception to the rule, a violation of an order that society is determined to uphold. Retribution alone cannot provide such assurance—nor should it become the single determinant of criminal punishments—but it is an indispensable element in the process of restoration. The absence of sufficient retribution becomes a twofold attack on the sense of moral order that most people require to sustain their existence. . . . (Jacoby, 1983, pp. 298–299)

To be sure, the debate surrounding whether the retribution-focused interests of the victim should outweigh the rehabilitative interests of the offender will be with us for some time to come. Moreover, the durability of the debate may last as long as criminal behavior occurs. The question, then, is whether the correctional policy that is in place helps reduce crime and delinquency. The balance of this chapter examines this matter in several important though controversial contexts.

PAROLE

Introduction

One area where correctional policy intersects with the retribution–rehabilitation tension described previously is in the parole or release of offenders. This section examines the phenomenon of parole in specific criminal behavior contexts. Three such contexts are considered and include (a) the release of mentally ill offenders, (b) sex offender registration, and (c) halfway houses. However, before these matters are addressed, some background information on parole is provided.

Background Information on Parole

Parole is the planned release and community management of incarcerated offenders before the actual termination of their prison sentences.

> It is usually considered to be a way of completing a prison sentence in the community and is not the same as a pardon; the paroled offender can be legally recalled to serve the remainder of his or her sentence in an institution if the parole authorities deem the offender's adjustment inadequate or if while on parole the offender commits a further crime. (Siegel, 1998, p. 579)

Historically, parole has mostly been regarded as a tool of reform. Though it is still commonly employed today, parole does have flaws. "In general, there [is] no supervision of offenders on parole, parole decisions are made based on idiosyncratic subjective criteria applied in the briefest and most perfunctory manner; and the popular media [blames] the parole system for each new crime wave" (Quinsey, Harris, Rice, & Cormier, 1998, pp. 7–8). Despite these criticisms, parole is a necessary component of the corrections system.

According to the U.S. Department of Justice (2001a), at the conclusion of 2000, there were 725,527 men and women on parole across the country. Further, 97% of all adults on parole were released to conditional supervision following a prison term for committing a felony. During the 1990s, those offenders entering parole increased by 2.4% each year (U.S. Department of Justice, 2001b). Over 50% of those offenders entering parole during 2000 received a **mandatory release** from prison because of a sentencing statute or good-time provisions, whereas 37% entered parole because of a **parole board** decision. (Some states do not use parole boards because they have **determinate sentencing** statutes where offenders are released at the conclusion of their maximum sentence minus any good time they may have earned while in prison. This is called *mandatory release.*)

The parole system was designed to treat offenders and not punish the crime (Abadinsky, 2003). Those individuals interested in correctional reform believed that by using the case study method deviants could be distinguished from one another (Quinsey et al., 1998). "This method involved recording the facts of each individual case. The observed differences would then lead to different treatments and disposition decisions [such as parole]" (Quinsey et al., 1998, p. 7). According to Quinsey et al., (1998), there is wide support for parole from wardens who gain control over convict behavior because prison authorities participate in parole decisions. Additionally, prosecutors favor parole. A paroled inmate could be reincarcerated without trial upon commitment of further offenses. Even though major participants in the criminal justice system support parole, in practice convicts are not really getting a break. "[I]t [is] doubtful that parole actually decrease[s] the amount of time inmates [spend] imprisoned because judges simply [raise] the maximum time to be served for the offense, effectively increasing the amount of time offenders [are] involved in the criminal justice system" (Quinsey et al., 1998, p. 8).

Parole is determined by a statutory requirement and typically mandates that the prisoner complete a portion of his or her sentence (Abadinsky, 2003). Parole boards determine whether an offender is suitable for release on parole. This is known as **discretionary parole:** Parole boards have discretionary authority to conditionally release prisoners based on statutory or administrative determination of eligibility (U.S. Department of Justice, 2001b). These boards consist of men and women who review cases and decide whether an offender has rehabilitated adequately to deal with the stressors of the outside world. Whether or not a convict attains parole is decided at a **parole grant hearing.** "There, the full board or a selected subcommittee reviews information, may meet with the offender, and then decides whether the parole applicant has a reasonable probability of succeeding outside of prison" (Siegel, 1998, p. 580). Additionally, the board provides the parolee the specific rules he or she is to obey once released.

> Parolees are subject to a strict standardized and/or a personalized set of rules that guide their behavior and set limits on their activities. If at any time these rules are violated the offender can be returned to the institution to serve the remainder of the sentence. [This is called a **technical parole violation.**] (Siegel, 1998, p. 579)

Moreover, parolees may be tried and sentenced for any subsequent crimes committed while on release. In order to assist a parolee on his or her transition from jail to the community, a trained set of parole officers help the offender search for work while monitoring the offender's activities. This ensures that there are no violations of the conditions of early release.

Parole is seen as an act of leniency on behalf of the criminal justice system (Abadinsky, 2003). Parole is a method of assimilating criminals back into society with restrictions. Although offenders are released, they are subject to immediate revocation of parole and rearrest if they violate any of the imposed limitations set by the parole board. According to Siegel (1998), there are two conflicting perspectives regarding parole:

> . . . [one view], The paroled offender is given a break and allowed to serve part of the sentence in the community; [the opposing view], the sentiment exists that parole is a privilege and not a right and that the parolee is in reality a dangerous criminal who must be carefully watched and supervised. The conflict between the treatment and enforcement aspects of parole has not been reconciled by the criminal justice system, and the parole process still contains elements of both orientations. (p. 579)

Recidivists and absconders (those who flee) pose an inherent risk that burdens the parole system. According to the U.S. Department of Justice (2001a), parole violators more than doubled from 17% in 1980 to 35% in 1999. The criminal justice system looks to remedy these risks while balancing the need for alternatives to lengthy sentencing that inevitably results in prison overcrowding.

Parole and the Reentry Court Experiment

Recently, some researchers have questioned whether programming based on either the philosophy of rehabilitation or that of retribution serves the interests of society and offenders, especially those ex-convicts returning to the community (Maruna & LeBel, 2003). Central to this debate are the staggering statistics regarding recidivism and incarceration. For example, whereas 459,000 U.S. parolees were released from community supervision in 2000, 42% returned to prison *U.S. Department of Justice,* 2001a). In addition, Hughes, Wilson, and Beck (2001) report that 27,177 ex-convicts violated their parole in 1980 resulting in reincarceration and that 197,606 ex-convicts violated their parole in 1999 resulting in a return to prison. Thus, it is no surprise that the phenomenon of ex-convict reentry is a significant issue confronting the field of corrections today (Austin, 2001; Travis, 2000).

One response to these disturbing statistics has been the emergence of the reentry court experiment (Maruna & LeBel, 2003). Operating in a number of state jurisdictions around the country, the operating assumption is that "offenders respond positively to the fact that a judge is taking an interest in their success" (Office of Justice Programs, 1999, p. 6). Whether based on the needs-based approach (assessing what should happen to an offender, given the person's violation) or the strength-based approach (assessing what the person can do to compensate for his or her criminal behavior; Maruna & LeBel, 2003), this initiative endeavors to transcend the conventional rhetoric of retribution versus rehabilitation (Bazemore, 1999).

Modeled after various problem-solving courts (mental health, domestic violence, and drug treatment), the reentry court experiment is based on six fundamental practices involving the judge, the community, the offender, treatment agencies, and various civic organizations (Travis & Petersilia, 2001). In brief, these include (a) assessment and strategic reentry planning, (b) regular status assessment meetings, (c) coordination of multiple support services, (d) accountability to the community, (e) graduated and parsimonious sanctions, and (f) rewards for success (Office of Justice Programs, 1999, pp. 7–9).

Mentally Ill Offenders and Parole

There are two criticisms of parole: (a) It is beyond the capacity of parole authorities to predict and assess future harm and risk to society, and (b) it is unjust to decide whether to release an individual from custody on what one expects that person will do in the future. Further, "the specter of recidivism is especially frustrating to the U.S. public: It is so difficult to apprehend and successfully prosecute criminal offenders that it seems foolish to grant them early release so they can prey upon more victims" (Siegel, 1998, p. 580). This concern is especially true for offenders with mental illness.

Of the 10 million adults incarcerated in local jails each year, approximately 700,000 have active symptoms of serious mental illness (Ditton, 1999). Criminal offenders with mental illness often recidivate largely because the individuals are released to the streets untreated for their psychiatric disorders and co-occurring substance abuse disorders (The Sentencing Project 2002). According to a report released by The Sentencing Project (2002), "People with mental illness are more likely to exhibit the kinds of behaviors that will bring them into conflict with the criminal justice system" (p. 7). Further, crimes committed by the mentally disordered can be classified as (a) illegal acts that are a byproduct of a psychiatric illness (e.g., disorderly conduct, criminal trespassing, disturbing the peace, and public intoxication; (b) economic crimes to obtain money for subsistence (e.g., petty theft, shoplifting, and prostitution); and (c) more serious offenses such as burglary, assault, and robbery (The Sentencing Project, 2002, p. 7). In order to preserve public safety, parole boards must assess and predict whether or not a mentally ill offender will commit a new offense, especially a serious violent crime.

Serious violent crimes committed by psychiatrically disordered individuals cannot be accounted for by a mere diagnosis of mental illness. Rather, serious violent crimes committed by these offenders are most often linked to active psychotic symptoms that can be managed through medication and treatment (Lurigio & Swartz, 2000). In reality, " . . . the contribution of mental illness to overall levels of violence in the United States is considered to be very small" (The Sentencing Project, 2002, p. 8). In addition, according to Torrey (1997), the seriously mentally ill only commit approximately 4% of all homicides. Vigilant parole boards and parole officers should be able to make certain that psychiatrically disordered parolees take their medications, thus safeguarding the public from this minimal risk. However, parole boards are reluctant to take chances with mentally ill offenders.

> The misunderstanding of the level of violence among mentally ill persons contributes to a climate of fear in which confrontational police tactics, intervention of the criminal justice system [a closer scrutiny of the possibility of parole], and prolonged periods of incarceration are seen as acceptable, even necessary, steps [to ensure public safety]. (The Sentencing Project, 2002, pp. 8–9)

Sex Offender Registration

Sex offender registration laws gained considerable popularity in the 1980s (Freeman-Longo & Blanchard, 1998). "Registration laws require convicted sex offenders, upon their release, or placement, to provide local law enforcement agencies in the community with their name, a description of their conviction crime, and their new address" (Pullen & English, 1996, p. 5). Most states have these laws and require offenders to frequently update their addresses and other pertinent information (Pratt, 2000; Pullen & English, 1996). Once a person is convicted of a sex crime, he or she is subject to registration for life (Edwards & Hensley, 2001).

Sex offender registration laws are designed to assist police and corrections departments in tracking the location of sex offenders released from prison (Freeman-Longo & Blanchard, 1998). Congress passed the Violent Crime Control and Law Enforcement Act of 1994 mandating that all states adopt a sex offender registry to avoid losing portions of their federal crime control grants (Freeman-Longo & Blanchard, 1998; Pullen & English, 1996). The theory behind these federally supported registration laws is that registries provide law enforcement officials with a head start when investigating a sex crime (Pullen & English, 1996). According to Freeman-Longo and Blanchard (1998):

> Generally, sex-offender registration laws make good sense for the limited purpose of finding a repeat offender after a crime has been committed. They require law enforcement agencies, corrections departments, and probation and parole agencies to track the locations of convicted sexual abusers. Often, a description of the abuser's criminal patterns and modus operandi are also kept on file. When a sexual abuse crime is reported and there is no obvious suspect, sexual offender registration can help investigative agencies obtain leads to track down the abuser. (p. 107)

However, such a database is not without its drawbacks. One drawback to sex offender registration is compliance by those who are required to register (Pratt, 2000; Tier & Coy, 1997). When a released sex offender refuses to register or if he or she moves and does not update his or her whereabouts, sex offender registries are of little help to corrections and law enforcement agencies. Community safety is one goal of offender registration; however, it remains to be seen how such a law can protect the community if police officers are unable to find many offenders. "One might argue that sexual offenders who do not register are the most dangerous, have not participated in [sex offender treatment] programs, and pose the greatest risks of re-offending" (Freeman-Longo & Blanchard, 1998).

A second drawback to sex offender registration is that some states require the listing of offenders as young as 10 years old "who, developmentally, are not yet clear about their own sexual identity . . . Imagine the impact of this [sex offender] label on the child's psychological and social development" (Freeman-Longo & Blanchard, 1998, p. 108). The excessive nature of this punishment might force a family to move from state to state in order to protect their child from the stigmatizing effects of sex offender registration. Even with adults, the punitive nature of these laws can tempt offenders to avoid registration in order to safeguard their identities (Pratt, 2000). The law cannot work to assist law enforcement if offenders keep their whereabouts a secret.

A third limitation to these registration laws is that they do not necessarily deter sex offenders from recidivating (Freeman-Longo & Blanchard, 1998). "[Registration laws] may provide some limited deterrence for compliant parolees, but they do not prevent hard core, untreated, noncompliant abusers from re-offending or address the large number of sex offenders who have not been identified" (Freeman-Longo & Blanchard, 1998, p. 108). However, according to Pullen and English (1996), the merits of lifetime sex offender registration cannot be ignored when registration includes the following five components:

1. criminal justice oversight and enforcement,
2. consequences for failure to register,
3. lifelong registration,
4. statewide accessibility of offender information, and
5. laws and oversight ensuring registration of sex offenders who move into the state. (pp. 5–6)

Arguably, with these five components in place, sex offender registration can be an effective instrument in law enforcement's struggle to ensure community safety.

Halfway Houses

Halfway houses are sometimes referred to as "community-based psychiatric home care facilities" (Rothwell & Doniger, 1996; Shu, Lung, Lu, Chase, & Pan, 2001). In order to address the psychosocial needs of mentally disordered individuals, especially for those released from prison, "community-based multi-disciplinary teams are being developed as a way of delivering coordinated comprehensive community services" (Shu et al., 2001, p. 52).

According to Rothwell and Doniger (1996), psychiatric halfway houses became popular in the United States in the 1950s as institutions for the severely and persistently

Proposition 36: California's Substance Abuse and Crime Prevention Act of 2000

One novel form of parole in California targets nonviolent drug offenders, endeavoring to keep them out of prison. This radical version of community supervision is Proposition 36. Prop 36 represents a paradigm shift from incarceration and punishment to treatment and cooperation (Jett, 2001). In 2000, over 60% of California's voters supported Prop 36—the Substance Abuse and Crime Prevention Act of 2000—mandating treatment rather than jail time for certain nonviolent drug offenses. **Proposition 36** "is the product of a gradual change in public sentiment; it provides a policy shift which reflects this change, creates opportunities for new directions, and will help 'scientifically' demonstrate the benefits of years of treatment and incarceration outcome research" (Jett, 2001, p. 322). According to Kathryn Jett, Director of California's Department of Alcohol and Drug Programs, Health and Human Services Agency, Prop 36 is an attempt to divert drug offenders from incarceration to treatment programs, to preserve jails and prison cells for serious and violent offenders, to address drug abuse as a public health problem, to enhance public safety, and to recognize the effectiveness of treatment over incarceration for nonviolent drug offenders. Further, the proposition assumes that nonviolent drug offenders who receive treatment are less likely to abuse drugs and commit future crimes while living healthier, more productive lives (Riley, Ebener, Chiesa, Turner, & Ringel, 2000). This policy shift makes sense. For example, consider the fact that 51% of nonmentally ill convicts in State prison were under the influence of alcohol or drugs at the time of their current offense (Ditton, 1999).

Given the significance of Proposition 36, the California Legislative Analyst's Office (CLAO; 2000) estimates that as many as 24,000 offenders per year will be diverted to drug treatment rather than to incarceration, and an additional 12,000 will be diverted from short-term jail sentences to probation and treatment. In addition to the relief these numbers could have for prisons and jails across California, the CLAO projects that from 2001 to 2006, Prop 36 could result in a savings of $1.5 billion to be spent elsewhere.

mentally ill began to lose favor among policymakers. Halfway houses were meant to protect patients from the debilitating effects of institutionalization, maintain patients in the community as long as possible, and assist patients in leading relatively normal and independent lives (Rothman, 1980).

Halfway houses aim to foster independence while allowing mentally ill individuals to remain in contact with family members (Shu et al., 2001). They provide services that are similar to outpatient treatment facilities and are a viable alternative to inpatient hospitalization (Pelletier, 1988). Paroled offenders are often linked to psychiatric home care facilities in order to assist them with the transition from incarceration to community living. "Psychiatric home care helps patients create, within their homes, a physical and psychological environment that facilitates healthy social functioning" (Shu et al., 2001, p. 53). For released mentally ill offenders, halfway houses can provide stability and accessibility to treatment that are crucial to thwarting future contact with the criminal justice system. (For more information on community reintegration for offenders and what prisons and jails are doing to keep released psychiatrically disordered convicts from recidivating, see the section Assimilating Criminals Back into Society.)

PRISONS

Introduction

Another way to comprehend how the retributive–rehabilitative tension operates in relation to correctional practice and criminal behavior is to examine the function and operation of prisons. Accordingly, this section reviews several noteworthy facets of confinement and correctional life. In particular, the federal and state systems are discussed, prison conditions are examined, problems with state psychiatric units are reviewed, and the subculture of prisons and convict violence is described.

The Federal Prison System

The federal **Bureau of Prisons** (BOP) consists of 100 prisons throughout the United States. According to the federal BOP (U.S. Department of Labor, 2001b), the total offender population as of October 2001 was 156,238. Of these prisoners, 12,668 were held in privately operated detention centers and juvenile facilities, whereas the remainder were confined through arrangements with state and local governments (U.S. Department of Justice, 2001b).

The number of prisons maintained by the federal BOP has grown tremendously since its inception in 1930. Indeed, according to a report prepared by the U.S. Department of Justice (2001b):

> At the end of 1930, the agency operated 14 institutions for just over 13,000 inmates. In 1940, the Bureau had grown to 24 institutions with 24,360 inmates. Except for a few fluctuations, the number of inmates did not change significantly between 1940 and 1980; however, the number of institutions almost doubled (from 24 to 44) as the Bureau gradually moved from operating large institutions confining inmates of many security levels to operating smaller, more cost effective facilities that each confined inmates with similar needs. (p. 3)

The federal BOP operates institutions at four security levels—minimum, low, medium, and high—to "meet the various security needs of its diverse inmate population and [it] has one maximum-security prison for the less than 1 percent of the inmates who require that level of security" (U.S. Department of Justice, 2001b, p. 3). The security level of a facility depends on perimeter controls (fences, patrol officers, and guard towers), staffing patterns (the internal personnel monitoring of convict movement and accountability), and whether the penitentiary keeps convicts in conventional barred cells or open dormitories. Those prisoners who pose less of a safety threat to other offenders and correctional staff are typically housed in less secure institutions (U.S. Department of Justice, 2001a).

According to the federal BOP, as of October 2001, 54.9% of federal prisoners were held in low- to minimum-level security facilities, whereas 38.3% of convicts were housed in medium- to high-level security prisons (6.8% of prisoners had not been assigned a security level). Males comprised 145,285 of all federal inmates (or 93%), whereas women accounted for 10,953 (or 7%). Whites and Hispanics combined to make up 56.1% of the entire federal convict population. Blacks and other African Americans made up 40.8%. To understand why these percentages were (and are) so high for the African American community, readers are encouraged to review chapter 3, especially Strain Theory and Conflict Theory, as well as chapter 9, Racial Profiling.

In 2001, the most frequent length of imprisonment for a federally held convict was between 5 to 10 years (28.5%), and only 2.7% of federal prisoners were released in less than a year. There were 4,719 offenders serving life sentences and 19 prisoners on death row. Federal prisons hold individuals who commit federal crimes, such as kidnapping across state lines, treason, and transnational drug trafficking. As of 2001, 55% of federal prisoners were serving time for drug-related offenses, whereas only 2% were incarcerated for homicide, aggravated assault, and kidnapping combined (U.S. Department of Justice, 2001a).

The State Prison System

In recent years, states have been challenged to build new correctional facilities in order to accommodate the nationwide increase in convicted offenders (Blumstein & Beck, 1999). For instance, since the 1980s, there has been a sense of urgency in California to construct prisons that are larger and more modern to meet this rising need for space (California Department of Corrections [CDC], 2001a). Indeed, according to the CDC, without the construction of penitentiaries, the growing convict population will greatly exceed the maximum-operating housing capacity by 2005.

A Novel Correctional Response to the Criminal Behavior of Women

California offers the innovative "**prisoner mother program**" that allows women in prison to care for their young children while incarcerated (CDC, 2001b). These programs are intended to build better parenting skills and relationships for the offender. As the CDC explains:

> While in the program, the mothers reestablish bonds with their children and prepare to return to the community as working, productive members. The homelike facilities provide a stable, caregiving environment. In specialized parenting classes, they learn how to talk and relate to their children and how to discipline effectively. Both mothers and children also may receive counseling. In preemployment training,

they gain practical information and tips about applying for, landing, and keeping a job.

Since the majority of the mothers have had some sort of chemical dependency in the past, they also attend drug education classes. The classes are geared to keeping them from returning to their old habits, making them aware of the dangers of drug addiction, and showing them how drugs impair both their lives and the lives of those around them, especially their children (http://www.corr.ca.communicationsoffice/publicsafetyps/plannedreentry.asp).

(To learn more about penitentiary programs similar to the prisoner mother program, see the section Assimilating Criminals Back into Society in this chapter.)

In order to appreciate the space dilemma in California, it is useful to compare it to other state jurisdictions. For example, in New York, 70 state correctional facilities housed approximately 70,000 inmates in 2001 (New York State Department of Correctional Services, 2001). However, for the same reporting year, convicts in California totaled 158,759, more than double the New York prison population. The 2001 operating budget for the CDC was $4.8 billion at an average yearly cost of $25,607 per offender and $2,636 per parolee (CDC, 2001a). Moreover, the CDC employs nearly 50,000 people, including 40,758 in correctional facilities, 3,172 working for parole, and 3,767 in administration. "While it [was] the largest in terms of staffing, [the] Corrections' operating budget [was] just 7.2 percent of the General Fund [of California] in the 2000–2001 Budget Act" (CDC, 2001a).

As of 2001, California had 33 state prisons and 41 minimum custody facilities located in wilderness areas known as "camps" (CDC, 2001a). In these camps, convicts are trained to fight wildfires—a tragic phenomenon that plagues the West Coast during the dry summer months. California also has 16 community correctional facilities and 8 prisoner mother facilities.

Prison Overcrowding

Prison overcrowding is a phenomenon that has plagued the criminal justice system in recent years. As Blumstein and Beck (1999) report:

> The United States over the past seventy-five years has experienced a dramatic change in its use of incarceration . . . Much of the [increase] was accounted for by two deviations: a rise [in the number of prisoners] toward the end of the Great Depression and a dip [in the number of prisoners] during World War II, when the nation had better uses for its young men. (pp. 17–18)

Between 1980 and 1996, incarceration rates for state and federal prisons significantly increased by over 200% (Platt, 2001; Ross & Richards, 2002a). This particular deviation can be attributed to law enforcement's emphasis on prosecuting drug offenses:

> In 1980 an estimated 23,900 people were in state and federal prisons for drug offenses, accounting for an incarceration rate of less than 15 inmates per 100,000 adults. By 1996, the drug incarceration rate had grown to 148 inmates per 100,000 adults, more than nine-fold, to a rate greater than that for the entire U.S. prison system in the fifty years [prior] to 1973. (Blumstein & Beck, 1999, pp. 17–18)

Explaining Overcrowded Prisons

How do we account for the swelling number of offenders housed in penal institutions? Prison overcrowding can be traced to society's fear of, and response to, crime (Reiman, 2001). Many legislators argue for longer sentences, mandatory prison time, and the abolition of parole in order to emphasize retribution for criminal behavior. Moreover, these policies are pursued under the guise of lowering recidivism among repeat offenders (Walker, 2001). "The sentencing of a convicted criminal lies at the very center of society's efforts to ensure public order. [Ideally,] the sentence serves the functions of both punishment and deterrence" (Wrightsman, Nietzel, & Fortune, 1998, p. 471). Thus, by adopting a "get tough on crime" approach through swift, severe, and certain punishments, the public's fears are allayed and the specter of crime reduction is promised. However, there are problems with this logic.

Many states have enacted determinate sentencing guidelines. As such, judges have little discretion and the possibility of parole does not exist. Given these realities, prisoners remain incarcerated longer with devastating consequences for the effective administration of confining offenders. For example, by the end of 2000, convicts who received determinate sentences took away space from 1 in every 109 men and 1 in every 1,695 women placed in state or federal prisons (Beck & Harrison, 2001). Furthermore, according to Stansky (1996), mandatory minimum sentences often mean first-time drug offenders take up precious prison space, creating a situation where correctional facilities are forced to release numerous, dangerous offenders back into society. (For more on the phenomenon of releasing ex-convicts back into society, see the last section of this chapter).

Not only does overcrowding create unfavorable conditions for overworked prison staff, but also prisoners themselves suffer, thus making rehabilitation an unreliable goal of incarceration. "Prisons in [the United States] have always been punitive and demeaning, but they reached a new low in the 1990's. Most institutions are now so hopelessly overcrowded that they are routinely in violation of court orders mandating basic rights" (Platt, 2001, p. 145). According to the U.S. Department of Justice (2001a), by the end of 2000, state prisons were operating between maximum capacity and 15% over capacity. Moreover, the same report found that federal prisons were overcrowded by 31% (U.S. Department of Justice, 2001b). When penitentiaries operate beyond their rated capacities, they face problems with understaffing, as well as inadequate resources (Beck & Mumola, 1999). In addition, conditions of overcrowding increase the potential for violence among convicts, as well as violence directed toward correctional officers (see chapter 5 regarding prison violence).

Prison Conditions

The revocation of public services during the 1980s created a serious health problem for state prisons and jails (Ross & Richards, 2002a). For example, as Platt (2001) explains, "By 1994, of the 3,200 prisoners in California's largest prison at Vacaville, 450 were HIV positive" (p. 145). Moreover, convicts with psychiatric problems flood the correctional system today more than ever before (Arrigo, 2000; Haney & Lynch, 1997). "[W]ith the closing of mental hospitals and community clinics, prisons and jails are turning into psychiatric facilities" (Platt, p. 145; see the section Prison Psychiatric Wards in this chapter). For example, some researchers estimate that as much as 25% of California's convict population is seriously mentally ill and in need of psychiatric care (Sward & Wallace, 1994). And there are further indications that prison conditions are suspect. Indeed, according to Elizabeth Olson, reporter for the *New York Times* (May 18, 2000):

> The deterioration of penal conditions was recently acknowledged by the United Nations Committee Against Torture, which cited the United States for violations of an international treaty against torture for its use of electroshock stun belts and restraint chairs against prisoners, sexual assaults of female prisoners, detention of juveniles, and revival of chain gangs in state prisons. (p. 11)

In addition to these questionable correctional facility conditions, the newest trend is to build **supermax prisons.** These expensive and massive facilities house the most violent and incorrigible convicts in **security housing units** (SHU). These are offenders who allegedly need to be separated from other prisoners for safety reasons (Elsner, 2001). This practice of separating convicts is also known as **solitary confinement,** penal isolation, or administrative segregation (Bullock & Arrigo, in press). According to the *Los Angeles Times* (March 11, 2001), supermax prisons are popular with politicians who want to appear tough on crime:

> Imagine being locked alone in a small, bare cell for 23 hours a day. Your meals are slid through a slot in a metal door. You cannot see or talk to another human being. You cannot see out the window. You cannot make telephone calls or have direct contact with visitors. When you briefly leave your cell for showers or solitary exercise, you must strip and permit a visual search of your body, including bending over and spreading your buttocks. Your legs are shackled, your arms are cuffed and you are led by two guards, one of whom presses an electric stun gun against your body at all times. Such conditions are typical in so-called "supermaximum" security prisons . . . which now house at least 20,000 inmates. (p. A.20)

A February 2000 report by Human Rights Watch reports that supermax prisons are, for the most part, inhumane and intolerable (Bullock & Arrigo, in press; Haney, 1993). As the organization explained:

> There is no way, of course, to measure the misery and suffering produced by prolonged supermax confinement. Inmates have described life in a supermax as akin to living in a tomb. At best, prisoners' days are marked by idleness, tedium, and tension. But for many, the absence of normal social interaction, of reasonable mental stimulus, of exposure to the natural world, of almost everything that makes life human and bearable, is emotionally, physically, and psychologically destructive. Prisoners subjected to prolonged isolation may experience depression, despair, anxiety, rage, claustrophobia, hallucinations, problems with impulse control, and/or an impaired ability to think, concentrate, or remember. As one federal judge noted, prolonged supermax confinement "may press the outer bounds of what most humans can psychologically tolerate." (Human Rights Watch, 2000, p. 2)

Concerns about supermax facilities and SHU confinement abound. For example, according to the *Los Angeles Times* (March 11, 2001), the Justice Department is investigating the suspicious deaths of two Connecticut men transferred to a Virginia supermax prison. One man committed suicide with just 7 months remaining on his sentence. The other man, a diabetic, went into convulsions after purportedly being deprived of his medication. In response to the convulsions, the guards fired their stun guns at him.

Currently, there is no set length of time a person can be housed in the SHU. As Cockburn (2001) indicates:

> Before 1999, the only way for a validated gang member to be released from a SHU was to be paroled, die, go insane or become an informant on other prisoners. Since a rule change, a prisoner now can be released to the general inmate population if prison investigators determine that he has been free from gang activity for six years. (p. A.20)

Clinically speaking, placement in the SHU presents a host of emotional problems for offenders. Indeed, it is not uncommon for many prisoners to experience debilitating psychological side effects (Bullock & Arrigo, in press; Haney & Lynch, 1997). According to Human Rights Watch (2000):

> Some inmates subjected to supermax confinement develop clinical symptoms usually associated with psychosis or severe affective disorders. For mentally ill prisoners, supermax confinement can be a living horror: the social isolation and restricted activities can aggravate their illness and immeasurably increase their pain and suffering. Moreover, few supermax facilities offer mentally ill inmates the full range of mental health services and treatment that their psychiatric conditions require. (p. 2)

Sensory-depriving prison conditions such as these create concerns on whether contemporary correctional strategies amount to anything more than retributive efforts at punishment and deterrence (Haney, 1993). Much like the previous subsections entertained in this section, the answer is not as easy as it appears.

For example, a recent a study conducted by Applegate (2001) suggests that the public may be inclined to value penal efforts at rehabilitation, especially if the need for such initiatives can be genuinely explained. Indeed, society at large looks more favorably on prison amenities than politicians do, and the "get-tough-on-prisoners" policies governmental officials recently have enacted. As Applegate (2001) therefore concluded:

> Retaining certain programs, services, and privileges in American prisons is unlikely to result in public outcry. Furthermore, if corrections professionals demonstrate the usefulness of amenities and provide the amenities in a way that does not give criminals an advantage over poor but free citizens, the public will support retention. (p. 266)

In order to achieve the goal of incapacitation and deterrence, politicians and lawmakers persuade the public that building more sensory-depriving facilities like supermax prisons is the best way to spend taxpayer dollars (Bullock & Arrigo, 2004). However, as Applegate (2001) noted, "[People] do not want luxurious prisons. Taxpayers want institutions [that] are humane and seek to improve inmates during their incarceration. Moreover, they are willing to provide the material resources necessary to reach these goals" (p. 266). Thus, once again, we see how the tension between retribution and rehabilitation drives correctional policy and programming as the system struggles to respond to criminal behavior.

Prison Psychiatric Wards

Prisons and jails provide mental health services to the growing number of incarcerated mentally disordered individuals. Jail mental health services must also deal with the high rates of drug addiction among convicts in need of psychiatric attention (Lurigio & Swartz, 2000). According to Chase Riveland, author of *Prison Management Trends, 1975–2025* (1999), correctional administrators routinely are challenged to provide such services for the mentally ill:

> The nationwide deinstitutionalization of mental hospitals in the late 1960's and 1970's, and the subsequent governmental failure to make treatment resources available in the community to treat the mentally ill, has resulted in many of those persons being handled by the criminal justice system. Many end up in prison. Issues of adequate mental health treatment feature in many federal lawsuits about prison conditions, making provision of those services a constant challenge for prison administrators. (p. 190)

What psychiatric services are mentally disordered offenders entitled to receive while incarcerated? According to the verdict issued in *Inmates v. Pierce* (1980), imprisoned individuals are entitled to adequate mental health treatment, provided the purpose of incarceration and the purpose of hospitalization regarding psychiatrically ill convicts remain distinguishable. As the Court in *Pierce* explained:

> The jail is not a mental health facility, nor do administrators intend that it become one. It must, however, be staffed and organized to meet emergency situations, to make appropriate referrals, and to carefully care for and protect those who must be housed in the jail for whatever reasons despite their mental illness. (p. 638)

Thus, the best jail-based psychiatric service programs do not attempt to duplicate community mental health services inside the facility. Instead, they focus on screening convicts for mental illness, conducting crisis intervention, stabilizing psychiatric symptoms, and referring mentally disordered offenders to other facilities or programs once the prisoners are released from custody (Cox, Landsberg, & Pavarati, 1989; Kimmel, 1987; Steadman, McCarty, & Morrissey, 1989).

Over the years, the quality of correctional treatment programs for psychiatrically disordered offenders has been abysmal and disgraceful at best (Arrigo, 2000, 2002; Lurigio & Swartz, 2000). Warner (1989) describes the conditions experienced by many mentally ill individuals incarcerated in jails:

> The conditions of detention for mentally ill offenders are, at best, barren and unstimulating, at worst degrading, dangerous, and inhumane. An entire floor of the ten-story Dade County Jail, for example, is given over to the detention of around 100 mentally ill inmates. The most floridly disturbed of these psychotic people are stripped naked and isolated; the feeding slits in the doors of their cells are sealed so that food cannot be hurled back at the corrections officers. Jail staff may be called to respond to half dozen or more suicide attempts in the jail on a single night. (p. 18)

Despite the large number of psychiatrically disordered individuals in prison, 20% of jails surveyed in a national study reported not having access to mental health services (Torrey et al., 1992). In addition, Steadman and Veysey (1997) found that larger jails were more likely than smaller jails to provide adequate mental health services, including screening and assessments, medications, and therapeutic segregation. They also found that very few jails provided case management services that worked to link released ex-convicts with community health care, housing, or addiction services. According to Torrey et al. (1992), almost 50% of the jails surveyed had no data on whether prisoners with serious mental illnesses released from custody had ever received any follow-up care.

State Psychiatric Facilities

Approximately 30 years ago, over 375,000 people with persistent and severe psychiatric disorders were treated in state psychiatric hospitals (Arrigo, 1996, 2002; Lurigio & Swartz, 2000). A marked decline occurred in the number of psychiatric patients being served by state hospitals between the years 1970 and 1990. Indeed, only 84,000 individuals were treated in state hospitals in 1990, and the numbers continue to drop (Witkin, Atay, & Manderscheid, 1996). However, as Cote, Lesage, Chawkey, and Loyer (1997) report, there are anywhere between 1.5 to 3 times as many mentally disordered offenders housed in state and federal prisons than there are psychiatric patients getting treatment in state psychiatric hospitals.

State psychiatric facilities often provide forensic mental health services for the criminal justice system. In Connecticut, for example, the Whiting Maximum Security Service (WMSS) facility treats patients who:

> . . . have a psychiatric disability and are a serious danger to themselves or others, including people who are found not guilty of a crime by reason of insanity, are not competent to stand trial, are convicted of a crime but whom the court sends to the division for pre-sentence evaluation, are in the custody of the Department of Corrections (DOC), but cannot be managed at DOC facilities, and people from the general psychiatric population at other mental health facilities who are dangerous to themselves or others. (Niesz, 2000, p. 1)

A similar trend can be identified in other state psychiatric facilities around the country. California is another case in point. For example, at Atascadero State Hospital in California, forensic mental health treatment is provided to patients held as Sexually Violent Predators under section 6600 of the Welfare and Institution Code. Atascadero (2002) also treats mentally disordered offenders committed to the state hospital as a condition of their parole.

Prison Subcultures

Historically, the study of prison subculture has centered on the debate between the deprivation and **importation models** (Arrigo & Williams, 2000). Bottoms (1999), describes the difference between the two sociological models as follows:

> The **deprivation model** argues, essentially, that inmates' adaptation to the prison, and the development of inmate subcultures, arises as a response to what Sykes (1958) called

"the pains of imprisonment"—the deprivation of liberty, goods, and services; personal autonomy; personal security; and heterosexual relationships. The "importation" model, by contrast, argues that prisoner adaptations and subcultures are primarily influenced by what the prisoner brings into the institution: personal history, informal links with particular social groups, formal affiliations with organized crime syndicates, and so on. (p. 245)

Notwithstanding these differences, scholars generally agree that both preprison socialization and the experience of incarceration, significantly influence the subcultural adaptation of a prisoner (Austin & Irwin, 2001; Ross & Richards, 2002). Moreover, there are "important extra-prison influences during one's prison stay (e.g., major events in a [convict's] family life)" (Bottoms, 1999, p. 246) that substantially contribute to the overall acculturation process.

Prison Subculture, Criminal Behavior, and Contemporary Challenges

What cultural challenges do contemporary penitentiaries face as they respond to criminal behavior? Two areas where cultural changes are particularly noteworthy include the presence of prison gangs and homosexuality. Interestingly, the most notorious subculture within the correctional system is the culture of gangs. One particularly large and violent prison gang calls itself, "La Eme" or "The Mexican Mafia." Membership in La Eme is estimated to be anywhere from 300 to 1,000 in 13 states and in Mexico (Valdez, 2000). "When experts are asked just how many murders [La Eme] has been responsible for in its 43-year history, the number of 1,000 plus is frequently given" (Valdez, 2000, p. 55).

Once inducted into the gang, a member is expected to live by certain rules of conduct. As Valdez (2000) explains,

> . . . by the early 1970's, a new member was . . . asked to take a blood oath for life. This was done to confirm complete unquestioned allegiance to the gang. The oath required that a member do whatever the gang asked, without question or comment. This membership was for life and was more important than your family. Any violation of this oath was punishable with death. Because of this philosophy the gang's rally cry became, "Blood in, Blood out." (p. 54)

(For more information on this phenomenon, see the sections in chapter 5 addressing prison violence and gang-related crime.)

Homosexuality is another subculture frequently found in prisons. According to Wooden and Parker's (1982) investigation of a California male prison, 65% of the study's sample acknowledged engaging in consensual homosexual activity. Nacci and Kane (1983) found that of the 211 male federal offenders surveyed, nearly 30% participated in homosexual activity. However, Saum, Surratt, Inciardi, and Bennett (1995) discovered that only 2% of their sample admitted to committing consensual homosexual acts while incarcerated.

Richmond (1978) conducted a study of convict attitudes toward homosexuality and found that prisoners' perceptions of the behavior principally were based on anxiety and uncertainty. Attitudes regarding homosexual conduct were also a function of whether homosexuality was accepted or ostracized in the correctional facility. According to Richmond, the subculture of homosexuality in prison was described hierarchically: "For example, 'punks' who took on the low status of the prison sexual hierarchy were ostracized as a 'despised caste'" (Richmond, 1978, p. 53). Moreover, as he reported:

> Wolves tended to escape such ostracism and labels because they often did not see themselves as homosexual. They often asserted their heterosexual status and masculinity in prison, either by establishing a relationship with a "fag" (an effeminate male) or by attacking punks to show their dominance and power. Finally, fags had medium to high status according to the degree to which they were aligned with wolves. (p. 435)

Observations such as these have led some researchers to conclude that perhaps the most important elements in the establishment of a prison subculture are "the characteristics of the inmates themselves" (Hensley, 2000, p. 440). Clearly, however, the subculture of prison gangs and homosexuality are important to understanding criminal behavior and the correctional system's response to it. In addition, given these compelling and contemporary subcultural challenges, the choices that administrators make as they establish programming and policy tell us a great deal about whether rehabilitation or retribution is at the heart of the prison system's response to criminal behavior.

Interestingly, some investigators maintain that previous research on prison subcultures and convict socialization needs updating (Ross & Richards, 2002; Tonry & Petersilia, 1999, p. 9). Indeed, as Tonry and Petersilia contend:

> Prisons have changed a great deal in the past thirty years, inmate and staff subcultures and interactions between them have changed, and the learning of older times may or may not be still valid but at least need augmentation. Compared with earlier times, many prisons are much larger, inmate populations and staffs are more disproportionately black and Hispanic, many more line and management staff are women, gangs are larger and their influence more pervasive, more prison staff are unionized, a large and growing fraction of prisons . . . [are] under private management, and the possibility of judicial oversight and intrusion is greater. (p. 9)

Given this perspective, researchers are now questioning how prisons are organized to accommodate these cultural influences and how they behave in light of these significant changes (Arrigo & Williams, 2000).

ASSIMILATING CRIMINALS BACK INTO SOCIETY

Introduction

There are many obstacles to successful community reentry following release from prison. Part of the difficulty is linked to the goals of punishment and the swelling number of persons incarcerated. Indeed, the prison population in the United States has grown to epidemic proportions over the last 20 years, "with the 1990s as the most punitive decade in United States history" (O'Brien, 2001, p. 287). In addition to rising incarceration rates, policies such as fixed or determinate sentencing laws (e.g., Three Strikes laws) have helped to create prison overcrowding. Overcrowding has often led to shortened sentences for some of society's most threatening criminals. Moreover, determinate sentencing also has meant automatic release; that is, "Offenders receive fixed terms when initially sentenced and are released at the end of their prison term, usually with credits for good time" (Petersilia, 2001, p. 36). Conditions such as these leave custody officials with the daunting task of preparing convicts for release into an often fearful and unforgiving society (Ross & Richards, 2002b).

Transitioning criminals back into society requires that prisoners be taught how to cope with the challenges of everyday life, without resorting to crime in order to survive (Maruna, 2001). Jails and prisons bear the responsibility of educating, training, and treating convicts while incarcerated. In doing so, the hope is that offenders will acquire the necessary skills that will keep them from recidivating. The final section of this chapter addresses several key concerns linked to offender reentry. In particular, the rise in the prison population is examined; the plight of female offenders is discussed; and political, substance abuse, and mental health issues are canvassed.

Rise in Prison Population

During the last decade, prisons had tremendous rate hikes in the number of incarcerated men and women throughout the country (Ross & Richards, 2002a, 2002b). According to **The Young Offender Initiative** (YOI), (a joint program report sponsored by the U.S. Department of Justice, the U.S. Department of Labor, and the U.S. Department of Health and Human Services, 2001d), "During the 90's . . . [the rate of incarcerated offenders] in state and federal prisons and local jails rose . . . from 292 inmates for every 100,000 residents in December 1990 to 481 inmates for every 100,000 residents in June 2000" (p. 2). The same report showed that the number of women convicts increased 110% over the last 10 years (1990–2000), making up 6.7% of the total offender population.

This large number of incarcerated individuals does not necessarily mean that society has successfully met the challenge of responding to criminal behavior (Maruna, 2001). On the contrary, "the long-term consequences of such unprecedented growth have implications for thousands of communities across the country, because most offenders complete their sentences and are released from prison, currently at a rate of 600,000 a year" (YOI, 2001, p. 3). Indeed, the swelling number of released convicts affects the public at large, mostly in negative ways. "A number of unfortunate collateral consequences are likely, including increases in child abuse, family violence, the spread of infectious diseases, homelessness, and community disorganization" (Petersilia, 2001, p. 33). Prisoners often become institutionalized and come to accept incarceration as a culture (Maruna, 2001; Richards & Ross, 2002b). When these individuals are released from prison, they often expect to violate the law as a matter of course. "[This] phenomenon may affect the socialization of young people, the power of prison sentences to deter, and the future trajectory of crime rates and crime victimization" (Petersilia, 2001, p. 33).

In 1998, felons sentenced to state correctional facilities received an average prison term of 5 years (but typically only served half of the sentence), whereas the average sentence to local jails was 6 months (U.S. Department of Justice, 2001b). In addition, over 15% of offenders released from federal prison between 1986 and 1994 returned to federal prison within 3 years of release. Of those criminals who recidivated between the years 1986 and 1997, 54% returned to prison within 1 year of being released. Offenders convicted of violent crimes had the highest recidivism rate among all offenders.

Women Prisoners: Unique Obstacles to Successful Reentry

The United States' attitude toward crime, especially drug use, has resulted in more than 2 million incarcerated individuals (Ross & Richards, 2002a). This figure represents 25% of the world's convict population (Ziedenberg & Schiraldi, 1999). However, the imprisonment binge has been particularly devastating for women. "By midyear 1999, there were 87,199 women incarcerated in State and Federal prison facilities in the United States, accounting for 6.5 percent of all inmates" (O'Brien, 2001, p. 287). According to Greenfield and Snell (1999), 250,000 children in the United States have mothers who are incarcerated. The incarceration rates for women are increasing more rapidly than those for men; consequently, the number of children with criminally confined mothers is also on the rise (Petersilia, 2001). "Maternal imprisonment affects future generations because children's psychological health and sense of family is damaged by the separation from their mothers" (O'Brien, 2001, p. 287). Thus, social life is tremendously affected and largely determined by the possibility of successful community reentry for incarcerated women.

What sort of problems do female ex-offenders confront once released from a correctional facility? "Mothers released from prison encounter difficulties finding housing, employment, and such services as childcare" (Petersilia, 2001, p. 39). Children, who are forced to adjust to their mother's arrest and eventual release from prison, endure an array of confusing and negative emotions. "The frequent outcome is school-related difficulties, low self-esteem, [and] aggressive behaviors . . . " (Petersilia, 2001, p. 39). Many prisons offer programs to help mothers with parenting issues, job skills, and child care. Initiatives such as these stress the importance of raising children capable of coping with the socially stigmatizing effects of the mother's criminal record, as well as valuing positive parental role models (Arrigo, 2000; see chapter 7 regarding parental responsibility). "If . . . parents are negative role models, children fail to develop [prosocial] attitudes toward work and responsibility" (Petersilia, 2001, p. 39). Moreover, the social consequence of imprisoning mothers is that their children are five times more likely to be arrested than are children whose parents have not served time (Petersilia, 2001).

How do female ex-offenders effectively resocialize? O'Brien (2001) examined the tactics utilized by women who successfully reentered the community upon release from prison. The study addressed the following challenge: " . . . [H]ow can we support women, consistent with our belief in empowerment practice, who are trying to beat the odds of recidivism to make it out in the communities to which they return after incarceration?"

(p. 288). The study found that successful reentry largely depended on the women developing a sense of self-efficacy and the strategic use of family, correctional, and community resources. Moreover, "the necessity [for] addressing the concrete realities of reconstructing families and lives after separation from home and community" (O'Brien, 2001, p. 294) were cited as main findings of the research. As a matter of correctional policy, then, prison programs for female offenders "must address both the psychological and the social aspects of women's lives upon release from prison . . . [coupled with] concrete assistance for acquiring safe and sufficient housing and employment that would enable them to support themselves and their children by legal means (O'Brien, 2001, p. 294; see also, Arrigo, 2000).

Political, Substance Abuse, and Mental Health Concerns Linked to Community Reentry

The dilemma of community reentry for ex-convicts is particularly troubling when considering the government's role in the process. Although lawmakers agreed to appropriate money to build new prisons in order to accommodate the growing convict population, they neglected to foresee the challenge of assimilating criminals back into society after their sentences expired. "[F]ewer dollars were directed to rehabilitative services for prisoners, such as job-skills training, mental health treatment, and substance abuse counseling" (YOI, 2001d, p. 3). Consequently, ex-offenders released into society have little money, often no place to live, and no new coping strategies to survive without returning to the criminal activities that got them confined in the first place (Ross & Richards, 2002b).

Ex-offenders find their way back into prison primarily because they are released into the community without adequate services that can assist them with reintegration (Maruna, 2001). "Studies of offenders making the transition to communities have found that the existence of multiple and organized services, combined with criminal justice supervision, can reduce the recidivism rate, which at its current level means nearly two thirds of ex-offenders fail to successfully reenter society" (YOI, 2001d, p. 3). Moreover, the YOI report suggests that there are many challenges to successful community reentry. These challenges include "reductions in personnel to supervise parolees; less funding for transitional support programs, including education programs and job-skills training; and high rates of substance abuse and undiagnosed and untreated mental illnesses" (p. 3).

There is little doubt that drug abuse and crime often go hand in hand. The U.S. Department of Justice (2000) released a study involving 35 cities and found that 68% of those arrested for all crimes tested positive for one or more illegal drugs. The same report indicated that arrested individuals 21 or older were very likely to test positive for drugs, and it was almost certain that arrestees between the ages of 31 and 35 would test positive for drugs. In a National Institute of Justice (1999) survey, the median rate of women arrestees who used drugs increased from 19% in 1998 to 22% in 1999. "Despite such evidence linking substance abuse with crime most prisons do not provide adequate treatment for inmates" (YOI, 2001d, p. 3). For instance, in a study conducted by the Department of Health and Human Services, Substance Abuse and Mental Health Services (SAMHSA; 1997), 60% of all correctional facilities nationwide failed to provide on-site substance abuse treatment to prisoners. Although treatment of offenders is most effective when they are segregated from the general prison population, only 16% of facilities that provide treatment did so (SAMHSA, 1997).

Without question, communities are concerned with safety when convicts with mental illness are released from prison. "Although protecting public safety and social order are paramount, significant investment also must be made in the successful reentry of the offender" (YOI, 2001d, p. 3). Assimilating the psychiatrically disordered offender into the community has its own set of challenges. Indeed, according to the YOI report:

> People who suffer with mental illness are greatly stigmatized, which hinders both their treatment and social adjustment. Likewise, there is a recognized stigma for individuals who have encountered the criminal justice system through arrest, detention, and incarceration. When someone has both a criminal record and mental illness, this stigma grows exponentially and becomes a way of excluding the offender from the social group. (p. 3)

Consequently, reentry programs must respond to these unique challenges in order to provide the psychiatrically disordered offender with a genuine opportunity to succeed in the community once released from prison.

> Without opportunities to be socially integrated and accepted, ex-offenders with mental illness will continue to be stigmatized . . . [and] in response to the feelings of shame and rejection associated with being stigmatized, the offender may become angry and defiant and end up again in the prison system." (p. 4)

(See Labeling Theory in chapter 4 for more on the problem of mental illness and stigma.)

According to the Bureau of Justice Statistics (BJS; U.S. Department of Justice, 2001a), 1,394 of the nation's 1,558 state public and private adult prisons reportedly provide mental health services to their convicts. "One in every 8 state prisoners was receiving

Community Reentry for Mental-Disordered Ex-Offenders

How do correctional facilities assist the psychiatrically ill ex-convict? One such program, called the New Support Treatment Advocacy Rehabilitation Team (New START) operates within the Fresno, California, County Detention Facility. New START provides over 100 mentally ill convicts with counseling, addressing such areas as anger management, substance abuse, daily living skills and recreation therapy. New START also helps ex-offenders understand the importance of medication compliance and management after they are released from jail.

Programs such as New START attempt to address the somber reality obstructing the ex-convict's ability to become a community asset once he/she is released from custody (Maruna, 2001). In other words, "people released from prison remain largely uneducated and unskilled and usually have little in the way of a solid family support system . . . [combined with] the unal-

terable fact of their prison record" (Petersilia, 2001, p. 37). These obstacles become detrimental to successful community reentry (Ross & Richards, 2002b). The New START prerelease discharge planning team assists mentally ill and dually diagnosed ex-offenders with housing, medication, follow-up mental health services, and reestablishment of financial support systems. According to Petersilia, (2001), parolees who are rearrested are typically back in custody within 6 months after release. Encouragingly, however, early statistics show that prisoners who spend at least 45 days in the New START program have only a 23% rate of recidivism after 12 months in the community[1] (J. Freitas, New START Clinical Supervisor, personal communication, December 6, 2001).

[1]Information concerning New START can be received by contacting program representatives at the Fresno County Detention Facility.

Prison Vocational Training and Community Reentry

Another initiative designed to effect successful community reentry for ex-convicts are work programs. Saylor and Gaes (1995) tested the efficacy of prison work experience and vocational training on an offender's behavior after reintegration into the community. The project was called Post-Release Employee Project (PREP). PREP was conceived as a longitudinal evaluation of recidivism among over 7,000 U.S. federal prisoners who worked or received vocational training between the years 1983 and 1987. After 1 year, only 6.6% of those prisoners who participated in work, vocational training, or apprenticeship programs were rearrested or had their supervised release taken away. However, in contrast, more than 10% of prisoners who did not participate in work programs during their sentences, recidivated. Even though "employers are in-

creasingly reluctant to hire ex-offenders" (Petersilia, 2001, p. 38), 72% of the working group compared with only 63% of the nonworking group found and maintained employment in the community.

In an 8-year follow-up of PREP, only 31.6% of men and 19.3% of women who participated in prison work programs recidivated after reentry into the community. This is remarkable when one considers that "the majority of inmates leave prison with no savings, no immediate entitlement to unemployment benefits, and few job prospects" (Petersilia, 2001, p. 38). The PREP findings suggest that, "The impact of in-prison employment in an industrial work setting and vocational or apprenticeship training can have both short- and long-term effects reducing the likelihood of recidivism . . ." (Saylor & Gaes, 1995, p. 4).

Faith-Based Rehabilitation Programs and Community Reentry

Another approach to assimilating offenders back into society involves the use of **faith-based rehabilitation programs.** "Common sense suggests that the more religious a person may be, the less likely he or she is to violate societal norms, values, and laws" (Johnson & Larson, 1998, p. 107). In Texas, Prison Fellowship International is a private Christian organization that attempts to transform convicts spiritually in order to keep them from committing crime once released into the community (Stream, 1998). "Patterned after the methods that have sharply reduced recidivism in Brazil and Ecuador, the program aims to reduce the 48% return rate of convicts to Texas prisons" (Stream, 1998, p. 89). However, due to the newness of the Fellowship program, there is little statistical evidence on its success. Supporters of these prison programs believe that statistics will show that offenders who undertake faith-based training while incarcerated will do better after reentry into the community than those who do not.

Religion opposes antisocial values; emphasizes responsibility and accountability; advances non-deviant behavior over socially deviant behavior; promotes reconciliation; seeks to mediate conflict; and champions social support and comfort for those in need. Holders of the latter tenets would suggest that religious commitment, in general, will be inversely related to deviant activity. (Johnson & Larson, 1998, p. 107)

Although spirituality can help ex-offenders think more humanely and socially, religious conviction alone cannot address deficits in housing, health care, money, and family. Moreover, such programs as these might even create self-loathing in an ex-convict who, upon release, inevitably will be forced to self-identify with a shameful label (e.g., a drug addict or sex offender). To be sure, a conflict of this sort might consume the person and, understandably, be psychologically devastating to successful community assimilation (see Labeling Theory in chapter 4 for more information).

some mental health therapy or counseling services . . . nearly 10% were receiving psychotropic medications" (p. 1). A high percentage of prisoners suffer from co-occurring mental illness and substance abuse disorders (YOI; U.S. Department of Justice, 2001d). "Untreated substance abuse and mental illness can make it almost impossible for an ex-offender to establish a full and productive life in the community" (p. 4). In an apparent response to this dilemma, 66% of state correctional facilities help released convicts obtain community mental health services (U.S. Department of Justice, 2001d).

Some Concluding Remarks on Community Reentry

Most prisoners will be released and will reenter society. California, along with many states, has budgeted money to build new prisons as a result of high recidivism rates. However, correctional programs that offer assistance to offenders who transition back into society may not only be cheaper in the long run but, in most instances, may even work (Maruna, 2001). Policymakers should pay attention. Indeed, as Petersilia (2001) cautions:

> Virtually no systematic, comprehensive attention has been paid by policymakers to dealing with people after release . . . Failure to address the issue may well backfire, and gains in crime reduction may erode if the cumulative impact of tens of thousands of returning felons on families, crime victims, and communities is not considered. (p. 33)

DISCUSSION QUESTIONS

1. What are some of the philosophical and practical tensions that exist between retribution and rehabilitation in the correctional context? From your perspective, which of the two is a more appropriate response to criminal and delinquent behavior?

2. Explain how such statutes as Three Strikes laws, 10–20–Life laws, and Megan's law promote the retributivist correctional philosophy?

3. What is parole and how does it work? What are some strengths and limits of parole?

4. Should mentally ill offenders be placed on parole? What is the relationship between sex offender registration and parole?

5. Explain some of the correctional challenges confronting federal and state prisons as they respond to criminal behavior.

6. What is the extent of prison overcrowding? How can this phenomenon be explained? Be specific.

7. Explain some of the prison conditions found in correctional facilities today. Do you believe that supermax units and solitary confinement are effective ways to address criminal behavior? What relationship do these practices have to the tension that exists between retribution and rehabilitation in corrections?

8. What types of psychiatric care are mentally disordered offenders entitled to while incarcerated? What relationship do state psychiatric facilities have in regard to correctional practice? What type of convicted offenders do state psychiatric facilities treat?

9. What is a prison subculture? Describe the differences between the deprivation and importation models. How do the culture of prison gangs and the culture of homosexuality influence prison subculture? Can you think of any other subculture challenges confronting correctional facilities that impact the system's response to criminal behavior?

10. What are some of the dilemmas to successful community reentry following release from prison? What are some of the difficulties female ex-offenders face as they return to their communities?

11. How do politics, substance abuse, and mental illness impact successful community reentry initiatives?

12. From your perspective, should community reintegration efforts for ex-convicts adopt a retributive or rehabilitative philosophy? Explain your response.

REFERENCES

Abadinsky, H. (2003). *Probation and parole: Theory and practice* (8th ed). Upper Saddle River, NJ: Prentice Hall.

Akers, J. R., Bohm, R. M., & Lanier, C. S. (1998). *America's experiment with capital punishment.* Durham, NC: Carolina Academic Press.

Applegate, B. K. (2001). Penal austerity: Perceived utility, desert, and public attitudes toward prison amenities. *American Journal of Criminal Justice, 25*(2), 253–268.

Arrigo, B. A. (1996). *The contours of psychiatric justice: A postmodern critique of mental illness, criminal insanity, and the law.* New York/London: Garland.

Arrigo, B. A. (2000). *Introduction to forensic psychology: Issues and controversies in crime and justice.* San Diego, CA: Academic Press.

Arrigo, B. A. (2002). *Punishing the mentally ill: A critical analysis of law and psychiatry.* Albany, NY: SUNY Press.

Arrigo, B. A., & Williams, C. R. (2000). Reading prisons: A metaphoric-organizational approach. *Sociology of Crime, Law, and Deviance, 2,* 191–231.

Atascadero State Hospital, Treatment and Rehabilitation. (2002). Retrieved January 14, 2002, from http://www.dmh.cahwnet.gov./Statehospitals/Atascadero/treatment.htm

Austin, J. (2001). Prisoner reentry: Current trends, practices, and issues. *Crime and Delinquency, 47,* 314–334.

Austin, J., & Irwin, J. (2001). *It's about time.* Belmont, CA: Wadsworth.

Bazemore, G. (1999). After shaming, whither reintegration: Restorative justice and relational rehabilitation. In G. Bazemore & L. Walgrave (Eds.), *Restorative juvenile justice: Repairing the harm of youth crime* (pp. 155–194). Monsey, NY: Criminal Justice Press.

Beck, A. J., & Harrison, P. M. (2001). *Prisoners in 2000* (Bureau of Justice Statistics Bulletin NCJ 188207). Washington DC: U.S. Department of Justice.

Beck, A. J., & Mumola, C. J. (1999). *Prisoners in 1998* (Bureau of Justice Statistics Bulletin NCJ 175687). Washington DC: U.S. Department of Justice.

Blumstein, A., & Beck, A. J. (1999). Population growth in U.S. prisons, 1980–1996. In M. Tonry & J. Petersilia (Eds.), *Prisons* (pp. 17–62). Chicago: University of Chicago Press.

Bottoms, A. E. (1999). Interpersonal violence and social order in prisons. In M. Tonry & J. Petersilia (Eds.), *Prisons* (pp. 205–282). Chicago: University of Chicago Press.

Bullock, J. L., & Arrigo, B. A. (in press). The psychological effects of solitary confinement on prisoners: Reviewing what we know and recommending what should change. In S. C. Richards (Ed.), *USP Marion.* Carbondale, IL: University Southern Illinois Press.

Bureau of Justice Statistics. (2001, August 28). *Probation and parole in the United States, 2000 press release (NCJ 188208)*. Washington DC: U.S. Department of Justice.

Cal. Penal Code 667 § 1170.12 (1999).

Cal. Wel. & Inst. Code § 6600 (2001).

California Department of Corrections. (2001a, Fourth Quarter). CDC facts. Retrieved January 13, 2002, from http://www.cdc.state.ca.us/factsht.htm

California Department of Corrections. (2001b). Mother infant program. Retrieved January 13, 2002, from http://www.cdc.state.ca.us/program/mother.htm

California Legislative Analyst's Office (CLAO). (2000). *Proposition 36: Drugs, probation and treatment program*. Report presented to Joint Hearing of the Senate Committees on Public Safety and Health and Human Services and the Assembly Committee on Public Safety, Sacramento, CA.

Cockburn, A. (2001, July 15). Commentary: Insane in the SHU box. *Los Angeles Times*, p. M.5.

Cote, G., Lesage, A., Chawkey, N., & Loyer, M. (1997). Clinical specificity of prison inmates with severe mental disorders. *British Journal of Psychiatry, 170*, 571–577.

Cox, J. F., Landsberg, G., & Pavarati, M. P. (1989). The essential components of a crisis intervention program for local jails: The New York forensic suicide prevention crisis model. *Psychiatric Quarterly, 60*, 103–118.

Cullen, F., & Gilbert, K. (1982). *Reaffirming rehabilitation*. Cincinnati, OH: Anderson Publishing.

Ditton, P. M. (1999). *Mental health and treatment and inmates and probationers* (NCJ 174463, July 1999). Washington DC: United States Department of Justice, Bureau of Justice Statistics.

Edwards, W., & Hensley, C. (2001). Contextualizing sex offender management legislation and policy: Evaluating the problem of latent consequences in community notification laws. *International Journal of Offender Therapy and Comparative Criminology, 45*(1), 83–101.

Elsner, A. (2001, March 11). U.S. supermax prisons incite human rights outcry. *Los Angeles Times*, p. A.20.

Fla. Stat. § 775.087 (2001).

Freeman-Longo, R. E., & Blanchard, G. T. (1998). *Sexual abuse in America: Epidemic of the 21st century*. Brandon, VT: Safer Society Press.

Greenfield, L. A., & Snell, T. L. (1999). *Women offenders* (NCJ 175688). Washington DC: U.S. Department of Justice, Bureau of Justice Statistics.

Haney, C. (1993). Infamous punishment: The psychological consequences of isolation. *National Prison Project Journal, 8*, 3–7, 21.

Haney, C., & Lynch, M. (1997). Regulating prisons of the future: A psychological analysis of Supermax and solitary confinement. *New York University Review of Law and Social Change, 23*, 477–570.

Hensley, C. (2000). Attitudes toward homosexuality in a male and female prison: An exploratory study. *Prison Journal, 80*(4), 434–441.

Hughes, T. A., Wilson, D. J., & Beck, A. J. (2001). *Special report: Trends in state parole, 1990–2000* (NCJ 184735). Washington DC: U.S. Department of Justice, Bureau of Justice Statistics.

Human Rights Watch. (2000). *Out of sight: Super-maximum security confinement in the United States, 12*(1)(G), 1–9.

Inmates v. Pierce, 489 F. Supp. 638 (1980).

Jacoby, S. (1983). *Wild justice: The evolution of revenge*. New York: Harper & Row.

Jett, K. P. (2001). Proposition 36: Issues and challenges. *Journal of Psychoactive Drugs, 33*(4), 321–328.

Johnson, B. R., & Larson, D. B. (1998). The faith factor. *Corrections Today, 60*(3), 106–110.

Kimmel, W. (1987). *Services for the mentally ill inmate: An exploratory inquiry*. Rockville, MD: U.S. Department of Health and Human Services, National Institute of Mental Health, Office of Policy Analysis and Coordination.

Logan, C. H., & Gaes, G. G. (1993). Meta-analysis and the rehabilitation of punishment. *Justice Quarterly, 10*, 245–263.

Lurigio, A. J., & Swartz, J. A. (2000). Changing the contours of the criminal justice system to meet the needs of persons with serious mental illness. *Criminal Justice, 3*, 45–108.

Macallair, D., & Miles, M. (1999). *Striking out: The failure of California's "three strikes and you're out" law*. San Francisco: Justice Policy Institute.

Martinson, R. (1974). What works? Questions and answers about prison reform. *Public Interest, 35*, 22–54.

Maruna, S. (2001). *Making good: How ex-convicts reform and rebuild their lives*. Washington DC: American Psychological Association.

Maruna, S., & LeBel, T. P. (2003). Welcome home? Examining the "reentry court" concept from a strength-based perspective. *Western Criminology Review, 4*, 91–107.

Menaster, A., & Ricciardulli, A. (1997). *3 strikes manual*. Woodland Hills, CA: Courtroom Compendiums.

Nacci, P., & Kane, T. R. (1983). The incidence of sex and sexual aggression in federal prisons. *Federal Probation, 47*(4), 31–36.

National Institute of Justice (1999). *Statistics on drugs and crime.* Retrieved March 18, 2003, from http://www.ojp.usdoj.gov/bjs/drugs.htm.

New York State Department of Correctional Services. (2001). Overview. Retrieved January 13, 2002, from http://www.docs.state.ny.us/

Niesz, H. (2000, August 2). Office of Legislative Research Report, 1-7. Retrieved January 14, 2002, from http://www.cga.state.ct.us/2000/rpt/olr/2000-r-0704.doc

O'Brien, P. (2001). "Just like baking a cake": Women describe the necessary ingredients for successful reentry after incarceration. *Families in Society: The Journal of Contemporary Human Services, 82*(3), 287–295.

Office of Justice Programs. (1999). *Reentry courts: Managing the transition from prison to community: A call for concept papers.* Washington DC: U.S. Department of Justice.

Olson, E. (2000, May 18). Geneva panel says U.S. prisoner restraints amount to torture. *New York Times,* p. 11.

Olson, T. M. (2000). Strike one, ready for more?: The consequences of plea bargaining "first strike" offenders under California's "Three Strikes" law. *California Western Law Review, 36,* 545.

Owens, K. C. (1995). California's "Three Strikes" debacle: A volatile mixture of fear, vengeance, and demagoguery will unravel the criminal justice system and bring California to its knees. *South West University Law Review, 25,* 129–153.

Partridge, E. (2001). The two faces of justice: The practice of criminal justice in the United States is based on two contradictory theories of human nature. *Free Inquiry in Creative Sociology, 21*(3), 43–44.

Pelletier, L. R. (1988). Psychiatric home care. *Journal of Psychosocial Nursing, 26*(3), 22–27.

Petersilia, J. (2001). When prisoners return to the community: Political, economic, and social consequences. *Corrections Forum, 10*(2), 33–43.

Platt, A. M. (2001). Social insecurity: The transformation of American criminal justice, 1965–2000. *Social Justice, 28*(1), 138–155.

Pratt, J. (2000). Sex crimes and the new punitiveness. *Behavioral Sciences and the Law, 18* (2/3), 35–51.

Pullen, S., & English, K. (1996). Law enforcement registration and community notification. In K. English, S. Pullen, & L. Jones (Eds.), *Managing adult sex offenders: A containment approach.* Lexington, KY: American Probation and Parole Association.

Quinsey, V. L., Harris, G. T., Rice, M. E., & Cormier, C. A. (1998). *Violent offenders: Appraising and managing risk.* Washington DC: American Psychological Association.

Reiman, J. (2001). *The rich get richer and the poor get prison* (6th ed.). Boston, MA: Allyn & Bacon.

Reynolds, M., & Kramer, J. (1999). Is the "three strikes and you're out" a useful sentencing policy? In J. Fuller & E. Hickey (Eds.), *Controversial issues in criminology* (pp. 240–258). Boston, MA: Allyn & Bacon.

Richmond, K. (1978). Fear of homosexuality and modes of rationalization in male prisons. *Australian and New Zealand Journal of Sociology, 14*(1), 51–57.

Riley, K. J., Ebener, P., Chiesa, J., Turner, S., & Ringel, J. (2000). *Drug offenders and the criminal justice system: Will Proposition 36 treat or create problems?* Santa Monica, CA: RAND.

Riveland, C. (1999). Prison management trends, 1975–2025. In M. Tonry & J. Petersilia (Eds.), *Prisons* (pp. 163–204). Chicago: University of Chicago Press.

Ross, J. I., & Richards, S. C. (2002a). *Convict criminology.* Belmont, CA: West/Wadsworth.

Ross, J. I., & Richards, S. C. (2002b). *Behind bars: Surviving prison.* Indianapolis, IN: Alpha.

Rothman, D. (1980). *Conscience and convenience: The asylum and its alternatives in progressive America.* Boston, MA: Little, Brown.

Rothwell, N. D., & Doniger, J. D. (1996). *The psychiatric halfway house.* Springfield, IL: Thomas.

Sabol, W. J., Adams, W. P., Parthasarathy, B., & Yuan, Y. (2000, September). *Offenders returning to Federal prison, 1986–97* (pp. 1–10). Washington DC: U.S. Department of Justice, Bureau of Justice Statistics.

Saum, C., Surratt, H., Inciardi, J., & Bennett, R. (1995). Sex in prison: Exploring the myths and realities. *Prison Journal, 75*(4), 413–430.

Saylor, W. G., & Gaes, G. G. (1995). *Long-term recidivism of U.S. federal prisoners: The effect of prison work experience, vocational and apprenticeship training* [Interim report]. Washington, DC: Federal Bureau of Prisons.

Sechrest, L. B., White, S. O., & Brown, E. (1979). *The rehabilitation of criminal offenders: Problems and prospects.* Washington, DC: National Academy of Sciences.

Shu, C., Lung, F-W., Lu, Y.-C., Chase, G. A., & Pan, P. (2001). Care of patients with chronic mental illness: Comparison of home and half-way house care. *International Journal of Social Psychology, 47*(2), 52–62.

Siegel, L. J. (1998). *Criminology* (4th ed.). St. Paul, MN: West.

Stansky, L. (1996). Age of innocence: More and more states are telling teens: If you do an adult crime, you'll serve adult time. *American Bar Association Journal, 82,* 60–70.

Steadman, H. J., McCarty, D. W., & Morrissey, J. P. (1989). *The mentally ill in jail: Planning for essential services.* New York: Guilford.

Steadman, H. J., & Veysey, B. M. (1997). *Providing services for jail inmates with mental disorders.* Research in Brief, NCJ 162207. Washington DC: U.S. Department of Justice, National Institute of Justice.

Stream, C. (1998). Unique prison program serves as a boot camp for heaven. *Christianity Today, 42*(2), 88–89.

Substance Abuse and Mental Health Services Administration. (1997). *Substance abuse treatment in adult and juvenile correctional facilities: Findings from the Uniform Facility Data Set 1997 survey of correctional facilities.* Retrieved November 27, 2001, from http://www.samhsa.gov/oas/ufds/correctionalfacilities97/index_m.htm

Sward, S., & Wallace, B. (1994, October 3, A-1). Health crisis behind bars: Inmates suffer from lack of care. *San Francisco Chronicle.*

Sykes, G. M. (1958). *The society of captives.* Princeton, NJ: Princeton University Press.

Teen who killed teacher sentenced to 28 years in prison. Retrieved February 10, 2002, from http://www.cnn.com/2001/LAW/07/27/brazill.sentencing/index.html

The Sentencing Project. (2002, January). Mentally ill offenders in the Criminal Justice System: An analysis and prescription. Retrieved March 8, 2002, from http://www.sentencingproject.org/policy/policy.htm

Tier, P., & Coy, K. (1997). Approaches to sexual predators: Community notification and civil commitment. *New England Journal of Criminal and Civil Confinement, 23*(2), 405–426.

Tonry, M., & Petersilia, J. (1999). American prisons at the beginning of the twenty-first century. In M. Tonry & J. Petersilia (Eds.), *Prisons* (pp. 1–16). Chicago: University of Chicago Press.

Torrey, E. F. (1997). *Out of the shadows: Confronting America's mental illness crisis.* New York: Wiley.

Torrey, E. F., Steiber, J., Ezekiel, J., Wolfe, S. M., Sharfstein, J., Noble, J. H., et al. (1992). *Criminalizing the seriously mentally ill.* Washington DC: Public Citizen's Health Research Group and the National Alliance for the Mentally Ill.

Travis, J. (2000). *But they all come back: Rethinking prisoner reentry, research in brief—Sentencing and corrections: Issues of the 21st century (NCJ 181413).* Washington DC: U.S. Department of Justice, National Institute of Justice.

Travis, J., & Petersilia, J. (2001). Reentry reconsidered: A new look at an old question. *Crime and Delinquency, 47,* 291–313.

United States Department of Justice, Bureau of Justice Statistics. (2001a). *Criminal sentencing statistics.* Retrieved October 18, 2001, from http://ojp.usdoj.gov/bjs/sent.htm

United States Department of Justice, Federal Bureau of Prisons. (2001b, August). National correctional population reaches new high, grows by 126,400 during 2000 to total 2.5 million adults (BJS 202/307-0784). Washington DC: U.S. Government Printing Office.

United States Department of Justice, Office of Justice Programs. (2000, June). *1999 Annual report on drug use among adult and juvenile arrestees* (pp. 1–16). Washington DC: U.S. Government Printing Office.

United States Department of Justice, Office of Justice Programs. (2001c, July). *Mental health treatment in state prisons, 2000* (pp. 1–8). Washington DC: U.S. Government Printing Office.

United States Department of Justice, United States Department of Health and Human Services, & United States Department of Labor. (2001d). *The young offender initiative: Reentry grant program* (pp. 1–64). Washington DC: U.S. Government Printing Office.

Valdez, A. (2000). The Mexican Mafia: The history of a powerful prison gang. *Police, 24,* 54–55.

Van Voorhis, P., Braswell, M., & Lester, D. (1999). *Correctional counseling and rehabilitation* (4th ed.). Cincinnati, OH: Anderson Publishing.

von Hirsch. (1976). *Doing justice: The choice of punishments.* New York: Hill and Wang.

Walker, S. (2001). *Sense and nonsense about crime and drugs: A policy guide* (5th ed.). Belmont, CA: West/Wadsworth.

Warner, R. (1989). Deinstitutionalization: How did we get where we are? *Journal of Social Issues, 45,* 17–30.

Witkin, M. H., Atay, J., & Manderscheid, R. W. (1996). Trends in state and county hospitals in the U.S. from 1970–1992. *Psychiatric Services, 47,* 1079–1081.

Wooden, W., & Parker, J. (1982). *Men behind bars: Sexual exploitation in prison.* New York: Plenum.

Wrightsman, L. S., Nietzel, M. T., & Fortune, W. H. (1998). *Psychology and the legal system* (4th ed.). Pacific Grove, CA: Brooks/Cole.

Ziedenberg, J., & Schiraldi, V. (1999). *Punishing decade: Prison and jail estimates at the millennium.* Washington DC: Justice Policy Institute.

chapter 12

Crime, Behavior, and Public Policy: Future Directions

OVERVIEW

The field of criminal behavior—from its conceptual underpinnings to its violent and nonviolent offenders to its police, court, and correctional responses—is evolving. Although we know more about the problems posed by crime and delinquency than ever before, the challenges that confront this domain of intellectual and practical inquiry are growing considerably. The evolution of the field raises a number of questions about the future of criminal behavior and the policy direction that must be in place in order for researchers, practitioners, advocates, educators, and other lay professionals to meaningfully address the discipline's substantial changes.

In this final chapter, a number of these more global themes are explored. In particular, existing and new educational models that facilitate the study of criminal behavior are reviewed, several emerging theories that reframe many of the debates in the field are examined, and some of the more novel strategies for prevention and intervention are discussed. Admittedly, it is difficult to say with precision what the systemic answers are to the presence of offender conduct in society and in our lives. Indeed, no one has a crystal ball; no one knows for sure what the future will be. However, educational, conceptual, and practical prospects for change in step with the challenges confronting the field are certainly one very useful place to begin. As long as this conviction is central to the debates encompassing the discipline, worthwhile policymaking will be possible and solutions to criminal behavior will be inevitable.

KEY TERMS

Clinical approach
Commonsense justice
Community penalties
Doctor of Philosophy
Doctor of Psychology
Forensic psychology
Juris Doctor
Law and psychology approach
Law–psychology–justice approach
Mental health courts

Preventive law
Procedural justice
Restorative justice
Revolving door "justice"
Therapeutic communities
Therapeutic jurisprudence
TJ preventive lawyers
Victim–offender mediation
Victim–offender reconciliation program
Voice effect

EDUCATIONAL MODELS

Introduction

There are many approaches or paradigms to the study of criminal behavior. The approach receiving the greatest attention today focuses on **forensic psychology** (Arrigo, 2000). Forensic psychology investigates issues and controversies at the intersection of criminal justice and mental health, informed by the disciplines of law and psychology (Arrigo, 2002a). Ultimately, forensic psychology is a template for understanding the links between offender conduct and individual harm and the systemic responses to both.

To be clear, there are many criminal justice and criminology programs offering undergraduate and graduate instruction in the realm of criminal behavior. Typically, however, the education is informed mostly by sociological theories and methods with psychological insights somewhat peripheral to the overall learning. In those instances where the discipline of psychology figures more prominently in the instruction, limited curricular coursework of this sort is made available to students. In large part, this is why the emergence of training in the field of forensics (read broadly to include police, legal, correctional, and criminal psychology), especially during the past 20 years, seems particularly well suited to explaining crime and interpreting behavior.

In this section, three graduate educational models in forensic psychology are reviewed. These models include (a) the **clinical approach,** (b) the law–psychology approach, and (c) the **law–psychology–justice approach.** In addition, the state of undergraduate academic instruction in this area is discussed, and several tentative observations regarding the future of forensic psychological education and training are presented. However, before these matters are addressed, some background information on the overall discipline is provided.

Background Information on Forensic Psychological Education and Training

Educational programs integrating psychology, crime, and the law can now be identified in a number of colleges and universities around the country (Arrigo, 2001). Interestingly, many professionals who practice in the field do not have a specialization in the area. Instead, these professionals attend weekend or 1-day seminars educating them about topics in forensic mental health, law, and crime (Bersoff et al., 1997). Although principally aimed at training clinical psychologists, other professionals such as lawyers, judges, social workers, nurses, criminologists, and pastoral counselors attend these training sessions as well.

As indicated earlier, there are three graduate models of instruction in forensic psychology. The degrees resulting from this education include the **Doctor of Philosophy** (PhD), the **Doctor of Psychology** (PsyD), or the joint **Juris Doctor** (JD) and psychology degree (either PsyD or PhD; Arrigo, 2002a). In addition to graduate instruction in the field, some colleges and universities now offer an undergraduate degree in forensic psychology. Similar to the graduate instruction, the training is designed to address issues and controversies at the intersection of criminal justice and mental health. The following subsection discusses graduate and undergraduate educational programs.

When considering a career in forensic psychology as a path by which to learn about criminal behavior, it is important to understand what the field encompasses. According to Wrightsman (2001), forensic psychology represents the "application of psychological knowledge or methods to [any] task faced by the legal system" (p. 2). Thus, for example, the field is broad and includes an investigation of such matters as child custody, jury selection, police burnout, competency evaluations, expert witness testimony, policy advising and development, dispute resolution, and research (Bersoff et al., 1997). In addition, those criminological issues linked to our regard for criminal behavior are also well within the scope of the discipline's expertise (Arrigo, 2000). As such, the topics examined throughout this textbook clearly are relevant to the field. Given the expanse of forensic psychology, it is not surprising that there is "little agreement about the primary focus of training" (Bersoff et al., 1997,

p. 1302). Consequently, it is imperative that the models of instruction, at the graduate and undergraduate levels, adequately account for the breadth (and growth) of the field. The three graduate educational approaches subsequently described uniquely address these matters.

The Clinical Approach

The clinical approach to forensic psychology offers two distinct graduate degrees: the PsyD and the PhD. In most instances, the curriculum that is developed resulting in the award of these degrees focuses on "the study of criminal and delinquent behavior" (Arrigo, 2001, p. 11). Employment opportunities that may arise for an individual seeking a degree in a clinically based forensic psychology program include police psychology, criminal psychology, and correctional psychology. In each of these occupations and settings, the forensic psychologist may be called on to use assessment instruments (i.e., intelligence tests, personality tests, and forensic evaluations) to diagnose clients or to conduct individual or group therapy with persons in forensic environments (e.g., correctional facilities, and psychiatric hospitals; Arrigo, 2001). Individuals trained clinically may also be expected to have an appropriate understanding of those assessment, diagnostic, and treatment issues related to juvenile offenders.

Clinically based forensic programs are typically found within universities that house departments of psychology. Most often, forensic training and experience is offered to students through dissertation supervision, independent study, ongoing mentoring, practicum training, and internship placement. Academic course work generally emphasizes clinical skills such as testing and assessment, ethical guidelines and procedures, research methods, and psychotherapy (Arrigo, 2001). However, there are a few graduate programs in the United States, Canada, Australia, and New Zealand that offer graduate programs exclusively in forensic instruction with a solid base in clinical psychology.

The three approaches to the study of forensic psychology also include relatively distinct client populations (Arrigo, 2002a). In the clinical orientation, the client is any member of society. Included within this group are offenders, the attorney who hires the psychologist to conduct an assessment, and prison units where correctional treatment is provided. The role of the clinically trained forensic psychologist is to engage in evaluation, diagnosis, therapy, courtroom testimony, and prevention (Arrigo, 2001). The principal tools of the clinical forensic psychologist include various assessment instruments. Examples of these instruments include the Wechsler Adult Intelligence Scale (WAIS), Rorschach Inkblots, Minnesota Multiphasic Personality Inventory (MMPI), and the MacArthur Competence Assessment Tool–Criminal Adjudication (MacCAT–CA).

Each educational approach to the study of forensic psychology possesses several strengths as well as several weaknesses (Arrigo, 2002a). Focusing on these matters is important, especially because developing appropriate training and instruction is key to meeting future challenges in the area of criminal behavior. The strengths of the clinical approach to forensic psychology include the depth in clinical instruction to which one is exposed. In addition, the accelerated level of training one receives in conducting assessments and providing psychotherapy is also noteworthy. Despite these advantages, the clinical approach has some limitations. In particular, the systematic focus on only one, though important, area of forensic psychology (assessment and treatment) is problematic. This emphasis leaves the forensic practitioner mostly ill equipped to handle non-clinically-based situations (Arrigo, 2001). Indeed, as the area of criminal behavior evolves, solutions to the problems posed by crime and delinquency will require more than a clinical perspective. However, for individuals interested exclusively in this approach to forensic psychology, this education model is appropriate. Having said this, although clinical training and instruction are useful in some facets of the field, they are not useful in all of them. Indeed, questions of criminal behavior that present themselves outside the clinical realm require different solutions. Thus, occupational challenges in policing, court administration, corrections, and juvenile justice necessitate that the clinically trained forensic psychologist recognize the limits of his or her areas of expertise.

The Law and Psychology Approach

The **law and psychology approach** to forensic psychology examines "individual behavior in civil and criminal settings where questions of professional and organizational practice are pivotal" (Arrigo, 2001, p. 12). The areas most commonly emphasized in the law and psychology approach are family law and mental health law. Individuals trained with this educational approach in mind receive training in two disciplines: psychology and law.

The forensic psychology degree that takes the longest to complete is the combined JD and PsyD, or the combined JD and PhD (Bersoff et al., 1997). Typically, these programs take 7 years to finish, including 1 year for internship. Joint-degree programs strive to provide an education that allows participants to "become legally informed clinicians" (Arrigo, 2001, p. 14). Individuals who choose to study forensic psychology from this unique perspective are expected not only to understand and study the link between psychology and the law but also to obtain a concrete understanding of each respective discipline. As such, graduate students enrolled in psychology and law programs not only receive training in mental health law, criminal behavior, and forensic assessment but also learn about psychology (i.e., history and systems and group psychotherapy) and law (i.e., wills and estates and corporate law; Arrigo, 2002a).

The client–practitioner relationship in the law and psychology approach to forensic psychology is similar to the association found in the clinical model. Accordingly, an individual who pursues the law and psychology approach is interested in addressing the client's legal and mental health issues but in relation to society. In this educational model, the client most frequently is the offender. The goal of treatment is to identify maladaptive behavior and to encourage the client to assume responsibility for his or her actions. This intervention approach assists the offender in future decision making. Moreover, the legally trained psychologist relies on the tools of psychology and the law to effect meaningful client outcomes (Hafemeister, Ogloff, & Small, 1990). These combined skills are particularly useful in the area of court proceedings. For example, court evaluations and expert testimony frequently require this level of expertise (Arrigo, 2001).

Forensic psychologists who pursue the law and psychology educational approach are expected to provide assessment, diagnosis, treatment, and expert testimony within the confines of their training and instruction. This represents somewhat of a limitation with this approach to forensic psychology. Indeed, in this regard, the standards governing the legal psychologist's professional practice work are restricted in the same way that clinically trained psychologists are restricted (Arrigo, 2002a). Moreover, similar to the clinical educational approach, functioning within the framework of legal psychology relegates the law–psychology practitioner to the position of an "outsider" (Arrigo, 2001). In other words, the person provides consulting services to the criminal justice system; however, he or she typically is not an employee of these systems. Finally, the law and psychology approach does not fully integrate the legal and psychological instruction. Linked to this is the time frame within which the degree is completed. To date, no proof exists that joint-degree programs are any more effective in preparing people for the rigors of forensic psychological practice work than are their single-degree counterparts (Bersoff et al., 1997).

Pursuing the joint-degree instructional model has benefits also. Clearly, these programs encourage individuals to assess issues and controversies at the crossroads of criminal justice and mental health from both a legal and a clinical standpoint. Moreover, this approach encourages the practitioner to have a more integrated and holistic perspective on mental health policy (Arrigo, 2001). Relatedly, when entering the workforce, legally trained clinicians are able to develop careers in more than just clinical settings. These nonclinical areas of forensic psychology are significant, especially as our understanding of criminal behavior develops and matures (Arrigo, 2000).

Overall, the law and psychology educational approach moves in the direction of broadening the discipline in ways that are consistent with the study of crime and behavior. Perhaps the only question is whether this movement is sufficient to address the expanding needs of forensic psychology as an evolving domain of intellectual and practical inquiry.

The Law–Psychology–Justice Approach

A third approach to graduate education in forensic psychology is the law–psychology–justice model. This model addresses several instructional aspects not contained in the other two educational approaches. In particular, these elements include an emphasis on both organizational and societal behavior in relation to crime and delinquency (Arrigo, 2001). Moreover, the law–psychology–justice model examines individual, group, and collective conduct. To be clear, this forensic psychological orientation does not emphasize the clinical aspects of the field; rather, it recognizes their importance in relation to several equally worthwhile disciplines that deepen our understanding of pressing issues at the crossroads of mental health and criminal justice (Arrigo, 2002a). As such, the contributions of sociology, political economy, organizational behavior, public administration, and legal theory also inform the training.

A graduate student who pursues this model of instruction can obtain either a PhD or a PsyD. Individuals enrolled in PhD programs "concentrate in criminal justice administration and management or law and public policy" (Arrigo, 2001, p. 15). Individuals who obtain the PsyD degree pursue professional licensure and forensic specializations (Arrigo).

The client–practitioner relationship in the law–psychology–justice approach distinguishes itself from the clinical and law–psychology models. Most frequently, the client is the organization itself responsible for housing or otherwise confining or detaining the offender. This is particularly the case in the criminal justice administration and management realm of forensic psychology. From a law and public policy perspective, the client is society itself. Indeed, society is the very reason for policy change in the first place, responding to individual and group needs while conforming to "institutional pressures" (Arrigo, 2001, p. 17).

For the PsyD practitioner supportive of the law–psychology–justice approach, therapeutic interventions are holistic and integrative. Accordingly, this forensic mental health professional examines the social, legal, psychological, political, and organizational facets of assessment, diagnosis, treatment, and prevention (Arrigo, 2002a). Adherents of this educational approach adopt "a more ecosystemic orientation in their professional practice work" (Arrigo, 2001, p. 19). With this perspective in mind, individuals who pursue the doctoral degree seek change and advocate for it, consistent with the interests of society.

There are advantages and disadvantages to this educational approach. One notable strength of the program is the acquisition of practical skills necessary for working within public- and private-sector criminal justice or related agencies. Indeed, given the diverse training experiences to which students are exposed, they are prepared to function as "insiders" familiar and comfortable with the world of policing, court administration, corrections, and juvenile justice. These skills extend to such areas as managerial tasks and policy work.

Despite these strengths, there are also limitations to this educational approach. For example, to date no law–psychology–justice program is accredited by the American Psychological Association. In addition, given the nonclinical nature of the coursework, there are only targeted employment opportunities (Arrigo, 2001). Indeed, graduates are best suited to securing employment within mental health and criminal justice agencies rather than working in private practice or in hospital settings. Then, too, the breadth of instruction and training (i.e., in psychology, sociology, law, and organizational theory) has yet to demonstrate that graduate students are any more prepared to meet the challenges within the field of forensic psychology (including the study of criminal behavior) than are clinically trained or law–psychology-trained graduate students.

Undergraduate Education in Forensic Psychology

Research examining the academic interests of undergraduate students suggests that there is quite a demand for education in forensic psychology (Arrigo, 2002a; Tomkins & Ogloff, 1990). Given this interest, the number of courses offered on college campuses integrating the study of psychology, crime, and the law has increased. However, as investigators note, the demand for this type of undergraduate instruction far exceeds the availability of the education (Bersoff et al., 1997). Moreover, despite the ground swell of enthusiasm for undergraduate course material on such cognate areas as criminal behavior, few, if any, general psychology textbooks used in introductory courses offer a chapter on forensic psychology, law and psychology, criminal psychology, or any combination pertaining to them. At best, there is some discussion of topical areas such as lie detection, repressed memory, and mental health defenses in a criminal court of law (Levine & Wallach, 2002). Thus, it is difficult to achieve a thorough or rigorous understanding of the very issues undergraduate students seek to know about if the extent of the textbook coverage is modest at best.

Most frequently, undergraduate students pursue classroom instruction in forensic psychology in advanced survey or upper-division courses (Bersoff et al., 1997; Tomkins & Ogloff, 1990). When students enroll in these sorts of courses, they benefit from a seminar-type classroom arrangement that specifically addresses the integration of law, psychology, and crime. Some undergraduate institutions offer a specialization in forensic psychology. In these instances, the undergraduate student completes coursework in basic principles of psychology, law and psychology research, police psychology, criminology, forensic psychology, and the integration of justice and the social sciences. The instruction also includes a practicum placement, supervised research, or the completion of an honors thesis (Bersoff et al., 1997). Unfortunately, professors who can teach these courses in a comprehensive and seamless fashion in their respective academic institutions are limited. Therefore, future instruction may entail videoconferencing or other distance learning techniques. Regrettably, despite the growing interest among undergraduate students for coursework in forensic psychology and criminal behavior, few educators and researchers have been willing or able to play a decisive role in developing and implementing curricula of this sort (Bersoff et al., 1997).

Implications of the Graduate and Undergraduate Educational Models

Without question, the academic discipline of law and the overall system of criminal justice affect human social behavior. Thus, educating people to become legally trained psychologists or criminal psychologists or even psychologically oriented criminologists meaningfully serves the interests of society (Weiner & Hess, 1987). This is why it is no longer sufficient to prepare individuals to engage in only the clinical pursuit of forensic psychology, or to apply these important skills to administrative and policy dynamics related to the field. The growth and breadth of forensic psychology necessitates much more. As such, different intellectual disciplines (and their corresponding assumptions) must be linked to the questions that make our understanding of criminal behavior so challenging today (Arrigo, 2002b). Indeed, prospects for policy reform, social change, and citizen justice demand it (Arrigo, 2003).

NEW AND FUTURE THEORIES OF CRIME, LAW, AND BEHAVIOR

Introduction

Educational models at the graduate and undergraduate level are related to new or emerging theories of psychology and criminal justice, and several appear to be rapidly developing. Moreover, as these more novel perspectives mature, they challenge our current understanding of criminal behavior. In this section, three of the more prominent theories receiving growing attention in the relevant applied literature in criminal justice and psychology are discussed. These perspectives include (a) **procedural justice,** (b) **commonsense justice,** and (c) **therapeutic jurisprudence.** Each of these theories is outlined and then integrated with some of the current research on criminal behavior.

Procedural Justice

According to some criminologists, crime, law, and justice are dependent in part on the way society defines or speaks about behavior (Arrigo, 1995). These abstract terms are not only perceived from this vantage but also anchored in personal experience. Models of procedural justice attempt to foster a just state of affairs in society by promoting a common or shared understanding about social life, relying on procedural mechanisms such as due process, fairness, equity, and reasonableness (Lind & Tyler, 1988). The meanings assigned to these procedural notions are linked to the recognition that inequality in a social and economic sense and personal harm in the wake of victimization are interrelated. Thus, the question is whether the *procedures* used to achieve a just state of affairs in specific societal contexts can be conceived and implemented in a fair and humane way. In response to this question, advocates of procedural justice seek to establish "a plan of justice based on treating like people equally with no [or little] regard for individual differences or circumstances" (Arrigo, 1999, p. 280).

Proponents of procedural justice tend to be more concerned with the fairness of judicial outcomes rather than with the actual outcome themselves (Mazerolle & Piquero, 1997). Indeed, people are generally in agreement with the law if it is perceived to be fair and just. Additionally, compliance with the law is emphasized when individuals have the opportunity to participate in legal decisions, such as jury decision making (Winick, 2001). Arguably, then, procedural safeguards help ensure a just state of affairs.

However, opponents of procedural justice contend that this perceived equality in modern law is itself a fiction, because biased forces such as the political economy, religion, and the media intervene to shape how procedures themselves are determined (Fox, 2001). Moreover, critics argue that procedural justice leads to inequalities by treating different people in similar circumstances identically (Young, 1990). As some investigators note, "liberal theories of redistributive and procedural justice fail to confront the realities of injustice and that procedural justice and criminal justice *contribute to, rather than ameliorate,* the problems of injustice rooted in inequality" (Barak & Henry, 1999, p. 152; emphasis added). The main limitation of procedural justice, then, is that it provides an illusion of justice (Fox) for all people when in reality it creates inequalities between different groups within society (e.g., inequality among social classes; Tyler, Boeckman, Smith, & Huo, 1997).

As a practical matter, one example of procedural justice is the Miranda rule (Wolfer & Friedrichs, 2001). The Miranda rule ensures that all alleged offenders are read the same rights on arrest. The treatment of all suspects in the same manner seemingly creates equality among citizen suspects. Miranda rules may differentiate slightly between jurisdictions; however, there is no differentiation in the manner in which they are read or the individuals to whom they are read. If the procedures of Miranda are not followed, the prosecution in the court of law cannot use any detrimental or incriminating admissions made by the alleged offender. The Miranda rights are as follows:

> (1) Suspects must be warned that they may remain silent, that anything they say may be used against them, that they have the right to have a lawyer present during questioning, and that a lawyer will be appointed if they cannot afford one; (2) If suspects waive their right to counsel and later change their minds, all questioning must stop until the lawyer arrives; (3) If suspects waive their right to an attorney and then confess, the prosecution must show that they knew what they were doing when they waived their rights. (Wrightsman, Neitzel, & Fortune, 1998, p. 227)

In this case, procedural justice protects the public as well as the police and the attorneys who try the case. However, the question is whether identical rights claiming applied to different citizens (the poor vs. the wealthy, straights vs. gays, Whites vs. Blacks, and men vs. women) uniquely embodies the life experiences of these various groups or even of members within these individual collectives (Arrigo, 2002b).

Procedural justice can also be identified in the courtroom during civil commitment hearings (Winick, 2001). Research indicates that an increase in a petitioner's participation during the hearing enables that person to be more accepting of the outcome and more apt to engage actively in the treatment plan. In addition, allowing the petitioner to participate in civil commitment hearings produces a "**voice effect.**" When the mentally ill are encouraged to disclose their stories, this produces an increase in "perceptions of fairness, respect, and dignity in the process, with a resulting increase in [the patient's] receptivity to treatment" (Winick, 2001, p. 295).

Procedural Justice and Criminal Behavior: Does It Always Work?

Procedural justice has numerous limits, especially when the crime in question is a violent offense. When adhering to the tenets of procedural justice, violent offenders may be placed back into the community, endangering the lives of many innocent people. Recently, Jackall (2000) aptly described this particular dilemma as follows:

> A gang member named Pasqualito, that is, Little Easter, one of the men whom Tebbens had arrested for the 1989 Double [homicide], was released on bail pending trial because the Bronx District Attorney's Office could not produce the witnesses to the shooting. While on bail, Pasqualito went to Brooklyn with Lenny Sepulveda and shot one of the witnesses to the Quad in the face. Police arrested Pasqualito for that assault, but even though he was on bail for the Double, and even though the Brooklyn assault aimed to silence a witness to the Quad,

he was released on $25,000 bail that he posted in five minutes. The Brooklyn night court district attorney and judge surely knew about Pasqualito's pending trial for the Double, but, given his bail on that charge in lieu of available witnesses, could not hold him for that as yet unproved offense. Further, Pasqualito was not accused of participating in the Quad. Therefore the Brooklyn assault, though an attack on a witness to a slaughter, was seen and treated as just another serious assault, not as part of a pattern of criminal activity. Even Pasqualito was surprised when he received bail. By the grace of the system, he went on to commit several other violent crimes, including at least one murder. The rationality of the law and the rational bureaucracy of the criminal justice system here produced irrationality. Procedural justice, here followed to the letter, differs from justice considered from some substantive standpoint. (p. 861)

Commonsense Justice

Linked to procedural justice is the notion of commonsense justice. In opposition to the written law that most people are familiar with, commonsense justice reflects what people in society perceive as just and fair (Finkel & Sales, 1997). Commonsense justice is perhaps best reflected in the decision making engaged in by juries. When a jury trial occurs, some members place more value in convicting a guilty defendant than they do in acquitting an innocent defendant. As a result, the values of jurors are in conflict with the values of the legal system, potentially undermining the judicial process and the administration of justice (Horowitz, 1997).

According to Finkel (1995), commonsense justice provides ordinary individuals with a practical theory about human perceptions, emotions, and behaviors. This knowledge enables people (i.e., jurors) to determine if the actions of the accused are punishable by law. The use of commonsense justice among juries is very prevalent. As such, it should not be ignored during legal and criminal processes (Finkel, 2000; Finkel & Sales, 1997).

There are also occasions where commonsense justice can be wrongly applied in specific contexts. Essentially, errors occur when personal or community interests are privileged over the rights of defendants and offenders. Three examples on the misuse of commonsense justice in relation to the actions of jurors include (a) reaching a decision based on an assessment of the facts that results in a wrongful conviction (jury nullification, notwithstanding), (b) dismissing the law thereby endangering the "common ground" by which laws themselves are conceived, and (c) applying "community sentiment" standards without concerns for constitutional protections (e.g., the penalty phase of a capital trial where personal or communal biases raise questions about the qualifications of a juror to make fair and impartial decisions concerning execution; Finkel, 1996).

The effect of commonsense justice on law and policy is also significant. When policies are created, community sentiment informs these decisions. Legislators and policymakers are aware of community sentiment; however, this does not imply that such input should govern the formulation of laws. Moreover, when community standards are emphasized, commonsense justice typically is not. This is because commonsense justice considers what is best practically for victims and offenders, not what is best for them based on some prejudicial standard based chiefly on personal beliefs and communal preferences (Finkel 1995).

Commonsense Justice and Criminal Behavior

Overall, the downside to commonsense justice is troubling and appears to outweigh its more practical intent. So, the question is whether it is a useful approach by which to respond to criminal behavior now and in the future. If you were an offender being tried by a jury of your peers, would you want the logic and reasoning of commonsense justice to determine your fate? If offenders were educated on the benefits and consequences of commonsense justice, would they still be committing crimes at such a prevalent rate? What if an offender knew that the decision of "guilty" or "not guilty" was based solely on the jury's practical opinion or interpretation of the facts rather than on the written law and legal guidelines given by the judge? These issues go to the heart of commonsense justice, criminal behavior, and courtroom practices.

As a future perspective by which to address the problems posed by criminal behavior, commonsense justice can be viewed either positively or negatively. Clearly, commonsense justice provides its own twist on the law and legal decision making. In particular, it encourages people to be in touch with the practical dimensions of how they understand and respond to the complexities of antisocial behavior and criminal conduct, empowering them to promote the administration of justice as they deem most appropriate. However, commonsense justice is threatened by misinformation and biased decision making. The more selfish attributes and flawed capabilities of jurors can affect the reasoned, fair, and prudent outcome of a commonsense decision. In addition, when legislators and policymakers rely on commonsense justice, their appreciation for criminal behavior may be tainted by the media, politics, and community sentiment (Finkel, 1997), forces that potentially erode the rights of citizens.

Jury instructions are an extremely significant factor in a courtroom finding of guilt or innocence, and commonsense justice may have an important role in this process. Jury instructions provide empaneled members with a foundation for their decision making including reasonable doubt standards, legal definitions, and verdict options. However, explanations concerning these essential guidelines can be misrepresented and interpretations of them can be misunderstood. Thus, the question is whether commonsense justice when applied in criminal matters can improve how jury instructions are presented by judges and used by juries.

One area where commonsense justice may be particularly helpful in relation to a jury trial is with the defense of criminal insanity (Finkel, 2000). Indeed, one controversial instance where commonsense justice underscored courtroom decision making was the M'Naghten case of 1843. M'Naghten was accused of the murder and assassination of Mr. Edward Drummond, the secretary for Prime Minister Peel of England. He was found not guilty by reason of insanity (NGRI). Critics of the NGRI defense state that it is difficult for society to categorize murderers, more specifically assassins, in a group other than individuals acting on pure "madness." Thus, despite jury instructions in a case such as M'Naghten, members rely on their own personal opinion of insanity and psychiatric disorder rather than on the instructions provided by the judge (Finkel, 2000). In this case, and in others like it, investigators query whether commonsense justice is "common, sensical, or just" (Finkel, p. 601). Indeed, when a NGRI verdict is issued, it is likely that the "blame the jurors" phenomenon is co-occurring. Thus, future research in the area of jury instructions, crime, and behavior would do well to assess where and how the logic of commonsense justice may help to avoid questionable outcomes linked to the insanity defense and elsewhere where personal prejudices replace practical reason.

Therapeutic Jurisprudence

Therapeutic jurisprudence (TJ) is broadly defined by Wexler (2001) as "the study of the role of the law as a therapeutic agent" (p. 279). Under such an all-encompassing definition, TJ is associated with or otherwise impacts a wide array of legal and criminal phenomena that, on their surface, do not appear related or reconcilable (Winick, 1997). Some examples include possible trauma effects caused by the criminal justice system on the victims of sexual abuse; the ethics of advocacy for persons with mental illness (Arrigo & Williams, 2001); sex offender laws and their therapeutic and antitherapeutic consequences (Winick, 1998); and stalking legislation and community peacemaking efforts (Vitello, 2004).

Current research on therapeutic jurisprudence is attempting to identify linkages between related perspectives, such as procedural justice (explained previously) and **restorative justice** (explained in the following; Wexler, 2001). In addition, TJ concentrates its efforts on reforming practice rather than law. In other words, therapeutic jurisprudence considers how the content of legal rules and practices can be concretely applied in a therapeutic manner.

Can TJ find a meaningful place in "real-world" applications or is it nothing more than an interesting academic notion? This question remains undecided. For example, although judges gravitate toward the concept, practicing attorneys do not. Moreover, although judicial interest in therapeutic jurisprudence is increasingly found in courts of first impression such as juvenile and family court (O'Neil & Schneider, 1999), drug treatment court (Wexler & Winick, 1991), and domestic violence court (Tsai, 2000), attorneys, in comparison, regard their reliance on therapeutic jurisprudence as akin to the practice of social work (Murdoch, 2001). If a therapeutic experience is to occur with a litigator, it will most likely take place in a client consultation context rather than in a judicial setting. Moreover, if therapeutic jurisprudence is to occur with attorneys, clients must be persuaded to seek out counsel for consultation purposes, even though presently this is not a common occurrence (Wexler, 2001). In addition, litigators must be prepared to practice from the perspective of therapeutic lawyering (Murdoch, 2001). This is a psychologically minded approach to addressing disputes in civil and criminal law, enhanced by empathy and a desire to resolve client problems. However, it remains to be seen whether attorneys will see the value in this perspective.

In order for therapeutic jurisprudence to function as a viable basis for resolving legal disputes and for assessing criminal behavior, it needs to be integrated with **preventive law** (Stolle, 1997). Preventive law is comprised of client interviewing and counseling, along with legal planning to avoid discord within the court system. Thus, its focus is "the prevention of litigation, with the aim of minimizing exposure to liability in the future rather than merely defending litigation when it occurs" (Murdoch, 2001, p. 484). The integration of therapeutic jurisprudence with preventive law enables researchers and practitioners to examine "psycholegal soft spots" (Patry, 1998). In other words, the integration targets legal procedures that foster needless anxiety, depression, distress, and resentment (Wexler, 2001). As Wexler (2001) explains:

> Preventive law gives therapeutic jurisprudence a set of practical procedures whereby lawyers may counsel clients to deal with legal problems in a more therapeutic manner; therapeutic jurisprudence gives to preventive law a humanistic, psychological dimension, while adding structure and substance to the lawyer's role as counselor. (p. 285)

Attorneys who practice law from this perspective are more commonly known as "**TJ preventive lawyers.**" TJ preventive lawyers are sought out when the practice of law is both psychologically minded and legally based.

One area in which TJ is commonly found is in civil commitment cases. Although not directly linked to criminal behavior, commentary in chapter 8 of this textbook examines involuntary hospitalization in relation to the competence-related abilities of defendants. Thus, there is some room to apply TJ to civil commitment determinations.

Many civil commitment cases have the result of being antitherapeutic. This is because persons with mental illness can be confined in psychiatric hospitals for extended periods of time (see chapter 11 on prisons and state psychiatric facilities). Consequently, it is useful to understand how the actions and decisions of attorneys, judges, and psychologists affect the emotional well-being of the defendant, and not simply the case's eventual outcome. As previously stated, an important aspect of TJ is whether the application of the law, and the effects of involuntarily confining or not confining a person, is sensitively interpreted by all decision brokers in the civil commitment hearing room (i.e., judges, psychologists, and attorneys). Given the general way in which the mentally ill are marginalized in the process, some investigators have argued that the entire process of involuntary hospitalization ought to be restructured (Arrigo, 1993a, 1993b). This is because the voice of and way of knowing for psychiatrically disordered patients are typically not valued in psycholegal decision making, resulting, instead, in their punishment (Arrigo, 2002c).

An important case with respect to TJ in a civil commitment context was *Lessard v. Schmidt* (1972). This case questioned whether it was constitutional to involuntarily hospitalize a person without a trial if the hearing court determined that the person was mentally ill. At the time of *Lessard,* civil commitment was not well defined; therefore, an individual subjected to involuntary hospitalization was unaware of the length of detainment. As a result, several due process rights for persons with mental illness were violated, reflecting the antitherapeutic effects of the law.

This same logic applies to mentally ill persons awaiting execution who refuse treatment. If a death row prisoner becomes legally incompetent during his or her confinement, the person cannot be executed under the cruel and unusual punishment clause of the Eighth Amendment (Arrigo & Tasca, 1999). Here, the question is whether competency restoration for purposes of capital punishment (especially when over objection) serves any therapeutic effects for the convict and for the administration of justice. Most researchers acknowledge that it does not. Indeed, before mandating drug treatment for purposes of competency restoration resulting in execution, it is necessary to determine the impact of this practice on the medical profession, on physicians who administer said treatment to psychiatrically disordered death row convicts, and on the prisoner awaiting execution (Arrigo & Tasca, 1999).

Therapeutic jurisprudence can also be applied to offenders of sex crimes (Edwards & Hensley, 2001; Winick, 1998). For example, therapeutic jurisprudence questions whether chemical castration can be justified as a correctional technique understood to be in the best interest of the offender. Investigators note that TJ does not deem medical punishment an objective of the law (Winick, 1998). Moreover, most sex offenders are not psychiatrically disordered (Palermo & Farkus, 2001). As such, mandating chemical castration seems unnecessary. Thus, without the application of TJ logic, sex offenders would be labeled mentally ill, would wrongly succumb to stigma, and would be denied their constitutional rights (Edwards & Hensley, 2001).

Overall, the establishment of therapeutic jurisprudence as a basis by which to assess the rights of civilly committed patients, mentally ill death row prisoners, and sex offenders represents a very practical approach to crime and delinquency and to the appropriate administration of justice in society. Moreover, TJ challenges the very nature of criminal behavior and our collective response to it. Clearly, these matters require additional reflection and research if the future problems posed by illicit conduct are to be realistically addressed.

COMMUNITY PREVENTION AND INTERVENTION PROGRAMS

Introduction

In addition to new or emerging educational initiatives and provocative or novel theoretical insights, innovative prevention or intervention solutions must be considered if society is to establish public policy that meaningfully addresses the problems posed by crime and delinquency. In this final section, four cutting-edge approaches to criminal behavior are described. These include **mental health courts, therapeutic communities** in prisons, restorative justice initiatives, and victim–offender mediation programs. Where appropriate, some comments on the relevant applied research in each of these areas are presented.

Mental Health Courts

Mental health courts provide an alternative to traditional courts. They are designed to offer nonpunitive options to psychiatrically disordered offenders based largely on the unique conditions that play a part in their alleged crimes (Hasselbrack, 2001). The traditional legal system does not provide the appropriate resources needed to address treatment issues that would otherwise limit or reduce the high re-arrest rates that offenders with persistent and severe mental illness confront (Arrigo, 1996). "These defendants frequently have a history of being arrested for behavior that is driven by their mental disability, and of being evaluated, briefly treated, released, and arrested again and again" (Lerner-Wren & Appel, 2001, p. 453). Indeed, these persons are arrested more often for being ill than for being criminal (Patch & Arrigo, 1999), and "this revolving door benefits no one—not the defendant, not the state, and certainly not the public. **Revolving door 'justice'** is expensive, ineffective, and unjust" (Lerner-Wren & Appel, 2001, p. 453).

According to Lerner-Wren and Appel (2001), the injustice caused by the legal system's revolving-door approach to psychiatric illness and crime is the driving force behind the creation of mental health court. As they note:

> As a consequence of the tendency to arrest and incarcerate individuals for exhibiting signs of their mental illness in public, and the lack of expeditious evaluation of those so arrested, the county courts were seeing large numbers of defendants who languished in jail without evaluation or treatment, and whose charges, even if proven, warranted no more incarceration than time already served. Without the ability to intervene to ensure that those who needed treatment but were not dangerous and thus not committable actually obtained treatment, the county courts were becoming revolving doors for a significant number of individuals whose real problems were psychiatric and not criminal. (p. 454)

Mental health courts are diversion-based interventions that exist for offenders "who could benefit from a proactive approach involving assessment, medication, housing, training and employment, versus a strictly punitive approach [exemplified by the traditional legal system] with little or no access to medical care" (Hasselbrack, 2001, p. 4). Incarceration rarely leads to appropriate care for persons with psychiatric disorders (Arrigo, 2002c), and "crowded conditions [of jails and prisons] cause additional stress for mentally ill offenders" (Hasselbrack, 2001, p. 4). Thus, mental health courts represent a reasonable intervention strategy in which they attempt to balance "an individual defendant's rights and his or her options for treatment, [against] the public's safety" (Hasselbrack, 2001, p. 4, 25). In order to effectively strike this balance, the philosophical orientation of the legal system has had to shift from an adversarial model to a model more accepting of therapeutic jurisprudence (Wexler, 1992; Wexler & Winick, 1991; Wincik, 1997; for more on therapeutic jurisprudence see the previous section in this chapter).

The first mental health court in the United States began operation in June 1997 in Broward County, Florida. As Lerner-Wren and Appel (2001) explain, the intensions of this court were to:

1. Ensure legal advocacy for defendants with mental illness
2. Ensure that defendants with mental illness do not languish in jail because of their mental illness
3. Balance the rights of the defendant and the safety of the public by recommending the least restrictive, most appropriate, and most workable disposition
4. Provide for the expeditious evaluation and treatment of individuals with a mental disability
5. Provide a means of ensuring needed follow-up for those defendants released into the community
6. Provide expedient, humane resolution of the defendant's criminal problem in an environment in which the defendant with a mental disorder can effectively participate in the process. (p. 454)

Three other state and city jurisdictions initiated mental health courts shortly after Broward County. These included Anchorage, Alaska (July 1998); Seattle, Washington (February 1999); and San Benardino, Cailfornia (February 1999) (Hasselbrack, 2001).

States with mental health courts give defendants the option to have their cases heard before a traditional tribunal or in the mental health court setting. Persons who waive their right to a conventional trial agree to follow a court-mandated treatment plan, "which may be in conjunction with a deferred or reduced sentence. Those who choose this alternative . . . are then expected to follow a plan that is created to meet their individual circumstances" (Hasselbrack, 2001, p. 25). If a person who chooses the mental health court alternative does not follow it, or if the individual refuses to cooperate with treatment providers, the offender is referred back to the traditional court. Although targeted exclusively to psychiatrically disordered offenders, the mental health court represents a provocative approach to criminal behavior. The long-term appeal of this diversion-oriented initiative will largely depend on whether it is successful in controlling and reducing crime for persons with mental illness.

Therapeutic Communities in Prison

The therapeutic community is a collection of individuals in treatment "assembled for the purpose of healing" (Jones, 1973, p. 17). According to Maxwell Jones (1973), "The therapeutic community is *distinctive* [italics in original] among other comparable treatment centers in the way the institution's total resources, both staff and patients, are self-consciously pooled in furthering treatment" (p. 17; see also, Arrigo, 1997a, 1997b). In the case of prisons, convicts collaborate with staff in order to become active participants in the treatment of other prisoners. In addition, offenders are active participants "in other aspects of overall [correctional] work—in contrast to their more passive, recipient role in conventional treatment regimes" (Jones, 1973, p. 17).

The idea that treatment can be facilitated by establishing mutual trust and cooperation among individuals living together is not new. However, what is new "is the attempt to develop this kind of community among individuals [such as prisoners] who have a variety of interpersonal and intrapersonal problems" (Filstead & Rossi, 1973, p. 4). According to Kiger (1973), the daily community meeting is the core of all therapeutic communities.

> . . . [The community meeting] is the place [for either convicts or patients] to bring up interpersonal problems that they are experiencing or have seen other patients struggling with, instead of refusing, out of false loyalty, to "tell tales" about their fellow patients [or offenders]. Only when they learn to identify appropriately with one another and understand one another's real problems can they help themselves and others. (p. 289)

In a therapeutic environment, prison staff must learn to give the convicts "considerable responsibility [wherein] they themselves [the prison treatment staff] can learn to feel secure in abandoning authoritarianism in favor of genuine democracy" (Kiger, 1973, p. 289).

A therapeutic community is one that becomes a problem-solving group whereby it continually "explores, accepts, modifies, or rejects ideas in efforts to develop better ways of functioning" (Kiger, 1973, p. 289). When effectively implemented, these entities discuss "everything that pertains to [an offender], a ward [or cellblock], or a unit-wide problem. Role relationships are considered, processes examined, therapeutic goals for individuals debated" (Kiger, 1973, pp. 289–290). Prisoners can be a very potent group in a therapeutic community (Arrigo, 1997a). Indeed, as Kiger describes, commenting on the psychopath in prison and his participation in a therapeutic community:

> . . . The psychopath is a master at wrong-doing and manipulating and is therefore sharp at spotting another's manipulating techniques. Although he may use poor judgment in examining his own behavior, he is usually quick to detect the same behavior in others. Many potential culprits have been "converted," and several planned escapades have been nipped in the bud by the psychopath's zealousness to protect his own comfort and hard-earned privileges. (p. 291)

Therapeutic Communities and Crime

Establishing a well-executed, therapeutic community is no small undertaking. This challenge exists as much in prisons as it does in nonpenal environments. One example of creating a therapeutic community for ex-convicts and other marginalized social groups (e.g., the homeless, the poor, and persons with psychiatric disabilities) occurred in Pittsburgh, Pennsylvania, through the Wood Street Commons (WSC) initiative.

WSC emphasized peer support, residential empowerment, affordable housing, and group decision making in its efforts to establish a sense of community for people living in a single-room-occupancy (SRO) housing facility. The facility provided single-room sleeping accommodations and basic dwelling amenities (e.g., congregate living room and congregate kitchen) for up to 259 adult men and women. The purpose of the SRO was to grow and sustain a culture where residents felt empowered to chart the direction of their community in responsible and reasonable ways.

Research on WSC indicates that when people are given a genuine opportunity to co-shape their environment and the organizational, political, and economic events or forces that impact it, they are less likely to act deviantly or criminally (Arrigo, 1994). This is particularly the case when the values of residents become part of the social fabric for the emerging community (Arrigo, 1997a). Admittedly, this strategy may produce some local or situational ambivalence, uncertainty, and disorder (Arrigo, 1997b); however, over time, residents in WSC actively reconstituted their identities and enthusiastically reclaimed their right to define the identity of their neighborhood in ways that mattered to them. Arguably, this same logic is relevant to establishing additional therapeutic communities where criminal behavior takes place or is otherwise problematic.

As a whole, prisoners in a therapeutic community place great value on privileges earned by carrying out responsibilities, displaying good behavior, and not tolerating misconduct (Kiger, 1973).

When convicts take an active part in the treatment of other offenders, the morals and biases of prison staff are less threatening to the therapeutic setting (Jones, 1973; Ross & Richards, 2002). In addition, "staff generally find it more difficult to understand and sympathize with [e.g., psychopaths and borderline-personality-disordered prisoners] whose behavior lacks manifest cause. The tendency is rather to see them as 'bad,' or 'antisocial,' and shun, avoid or become angry with them" (Jones, 1973, p. 18). Therefore, prisoners helping other prisoners can provide a less hostile or menacing environment in which genuine therapy and personal growth can occur. Therapeutic communities succeed to the extent that prisoners and staff believe in its methods, values, and objectives (Arrigo, 1997a; Filstead & Rossi, 1973). In the final analysis, it is up to everyone in the correctional setting to "study in more detail some of the cultural concepts which emerge when, as in [any] therapeutic community, people begin to examine their ideas, values, beliefs, etc., and self-consciously attempt to modify or reorganize them for a therapeutic purpose" (Jones, 1973, p. 24; Maruna, 2001). Future investigations of criminal behavior and society's response to its many violent and nonviolent forms would do well to consider the likely contributions therapeutic communities can make to transforming the correctional culture in which offenders are confined and punished, treated and rehabilitated, and released and reintegrated.

Restorative Justice

In order to become productive citizens in a community, offenders and ex-offenders need to "develop a coherent, prosocial identity for themselves" (Maruna, 2001, p. 7). In order for offenders to "change" their behavior, they must undergo a long-term process of personal growth and transformation. However, experiencing this process of change and renewal typically is not facilitated in jails or prisons (Ross & Richards, 2002). Incarcerating offenders and shipping them off to unfamiliar and faraway locations does not maximize prospects for personal growth (Sullivan & Tifft, 2001). Instead, change is created through the cohesion of the community and the building of relationships within and between groups and individual members within a community (Maruna, 2001).

Restorative justice promotes the goal of repairing harm and reconstructing relationships among offenders, victims, and the community of which both are a part (Bazemore & Schiff, 2001; Van Ness & Strong, 1997). Restorative justice is opposed to retributive models of intervention where the offender receives a punishment proportionate to the pain he or she inflicted on the victim or on the community. This is because restorative justice aims to repair harm, restore relationships, and reclaim compassion and forgiveness for all parties in the aftermath of criminal wrongdoing (Arrigo & Williams, 2004; Pepinsky, 1998). These pro-social ends are accomplished through a number of mediation techniques such as dialog and negotiation, victim empowerment, and dispute resolution (Levrant, Cullen, Fulton, & Wozniak, 1999).

Restoring victims and the community does not refer exclusively to the return of monetary losses. Restoration involves "making victims whole again" (Levrant et al., 1999, p. 10), reintegrating offenders with the community, and making community bonds stronger (Sullivan & Tifft, 2001). Several methods are employed to achieve restoration. The benefit of restoration for the victim can be noteworthy; however, in order to ensure that the process is meaningful rather than detrimental, it is necessary to offer mediation with competently trained individuals (Van Ness & Strong, 1997). If the mediation process does not employ the appropriate techniques and skills, the goals of restoration can be seriously compromised if not altogether undermined (Bazemore & Schiff, 2001).

Restorative justice techniques also attempt to facilitate the growth of offenders and reintegrate them into the community (Maruna, 2001). The restoration of offenders occurs through corrective methods that help offenders understand right from wrong. However, the restorative approach does not always address the role of rehabilitation within its corrective techniques (Maruna, 2004). Moreover, there are some concerns about whether the dialog entertained during **victim–offender mediation** sessions reduces the relationships to predetermined roles, resulting in staged and contrived restitution agreements (e.g., Arrigo & Schehr, 1998; Schehr & Milovanovic, 1999). Failure to genuinely address both of these matters can greatly erode the effectiveness of restorative interventions for the offender and may further damage the community efforts at reintegration and healing (Arrigo & Williams, 2004; Levrant et al., 1999).

Restorative justice is also responsive to neighborhoods. It attempts to strengthen community bonds in order to reduce the fear of crime and to reinforce the perceptions of informal, though empowering, social control (i.e., neighborhood responsibility for and ownership of making peace with crime). Projects that attempt to restore neighborhoods include community service initiatives engaged in by offenders and grassroots organizations designed to combat crime (Bazemore & Schiff, 2001; Sullivan & Tifft, 2001). Although these measures are effective, they hardly achieve full restoration within the community. Indeed, as some have suggested, the complete restoration of a neighborhood subjected to victimization may be no more than a "utopian" ideal (Levrant et al., 1999).

In order for restorative justice programs to be effective and beneficial, the community must be willing to accept and forgive the offender (Maruna, 2004). A main premise of restoration is reconciliation; however, this principle takes considerable time to achieve. Thus, neighborhoods must become patient, people must reflect on their experience of victimization or criminal wrongdoing, and all participants in the dispute must take the necessary time so that their deep, emotional wounds can heal (Arrigo & Schehr, 1998; Arrigo & Williams, 2004). If making peace with crime and restoring justice to society are the ultimate goals, then, following restorative justice, we can ill afford to postpone this worthwhile agenda (Rigby, 2001). As such, researchers would do well to further assess whether and how this strategy may represent a viable response to criminal behavior.

Can Restorative Justice Promote Greater Punishment for Offenders?

Although the intent of restorative justice appears to center on healing all parties victimized by crime, some question whether it is an entirely benevolent practice. For example, Levrant et al. (1999) contend that rather than achieving its progressive goals, restorative justice may in fact increase the severity of criminal punishment. To substantiate this claim, these investigators identified six factors relevant to any examination of restorative justice and its effects.

First, a system of restorative justice lacks the procedural safeguards that offenders are afforded in a more formal system of justice. This loss of rights can result in the criminal receiving a punishment harsher than what the person would have received had procedural justice safeguards been in place. Second, in some sentencing jurisdictions, judges and attorneys can assess whether an offender refused to participate in a restorative form of justice. If the criminal refused such an offer in these locales, the penalty could be greater than if the person had participated in the restorative plan in the first place. Third, restorative justice measures may enforce more control in the lives of less serious offenders who normally would be sanctioned with punishments such as probation, parole, or electronic monitoring. In a system of procedural justice, minor violators may receive little

to no formal criminal supervision; however, in the restorative justice system, the person may be surveilled through numerous means. Fourth, research indicates that offenders sanctioned through restorative justice often receive not only reparative conditions but also probation supervision. The offender who is penalized through a restorative justice standpoint may be at greater risk for additional punishments than what he or she would have received had other, more formal methods of justice been utilized. Fifth, restorative justice measures increase the likelihood that a criminal will not meet probation conditions. If noncompliance occurs, the offender may be sent back to prison for a probation violation. Therefore, relying on restorative justice measures may have an adverse (and unintended) effect in that more offenders may be likely to reoffend and, thus, may be at greater risk for returning to prison. Sixth, the punishment of criminal wrongdoing may increase in severity if restorative justice techniques are unable to successfully reintegrate offenders into the community. In other words, if an offender does not comply with the restorative justice plan and the community does not support and accept the ex-convict, the person may be subjected to a harsher punishment because of the ineffectiveness of restorative justice.

Victim–Offender Mediation Programs

As the previous subsection discloses, restorative justice is an emerging social trend within the arena of crime, law, and human behavior (Braithwaite, 1998). Bazemore and Umbreit (1995) describe restorative justice as a social reform movement that

> . . . emphasizes the need for active involvement of victims, the community, and offenders in a process focused on denunciation of the offense, offender acceptance of responsibility (accountability), and reparation, followed by resolution of conflict resulting from the criminal act and offender reintegration. (p. 302)

Thus, restorative justice initiatives are novel approaches to illicit conduct that regard crime as a breach of "human relationships rather than laws" (Maruna, 2001; Viano, 2000, p. 134).

One of the predecessors of restorative justice was the **victim–offender reconciliation program** (VORP), originating in Kitchener, Ontario, in 1974 (Van Ness & Strong, 1997). VORP "promoted mediation as a way to handle everything from divorce proceedings to business disputes, as well as [support for] the victims' rights movement" (Smith-Cunnien & Parilla, 2001, p. 387). Victim–offender mediation (often referred to as VOM) programs are based on restorative justice models as well (Van Ness & Strong, 1997; Wright, 1991; Zehr, 1990). VOM is a guided, face-to-face meeting between the victim of a crime and the person responsible for its commission (Galaway, 1988; Umbreit, 1993, 1995).

The goal of victim–offender mediation is to supply "a safe environment in which a genuine dialogue can take place between the involved parties so that emotional and informational needs are met and a plan for the offender to make things right, as much as possible, can be developed" (Nugent, Umbreit, Wiinamki, & Paddock, 2001, p. 6). According to Marshall (1998), the objectives of restorative justice programs, based on victim–offender mediation principles, include the following:

- To fully attend to the needs of the victim, survivors and others impacted by the crime
- To consider victims, communities and offenders as "customers" that are active participants in the system, rather than passive recipients of services or of interventions that might be unwanted, inappropriate, or ineffective
- To reintegrate offenders into the community so they do not reoffend
- To encourage and enable offenders to assume active responsibility for the harm they inflicted
- To create a community that actively supports the rehabilitation of victims and offenders and crime prevention
- To provide an alternative to the escalating costs and delays typically associated with the justice system as we know it (p. 134)

As Nugent et al. (2001) indicate, victim–offender mediation programs generally entail interaction between victims and perpetrators of juvenile property offenses, as well as minor assaults. However, there is a push to broaden the scope of these programs to include severely violent criminals and their victims (Flaten, 1996; Umbreit, 1994). According to Umbreit and Greenwood (1998), during the last 20 years, the number of victim–offender mediation programs has increased dramatically from a few in 1978 to over 300 as recently as 1998.

Are VOM programs successful? In response to this question, Nugent et al. (2001) conducted a statistical replication of four empirical studies reviewing the effect of involvement in victim–offender mediation programs. In particular, the researchers assessed the rate of reoffense for those criminals who participated. Their analysis combined samples of 1,298 juveniles. The results yielded a favorable replication of the four studies. Indeed, the investigators found that for those juveniles who participated in victim–offender mediation programs, they reoffended 32% less frequently than those who did not participate. This study suggests that VOM programs work to reduce the reoccurrence of criminal behavior in juveniles. Similar studies have produced comparable results. Consequently, future investigations regarding the use of victim–offender mediation would do well to consider where and how this approach could be employed to prevent future acts of crime and delinquency (Maruna, 2001).

Other Community Penalties

Another community-oriented response to offender behavior is **community penalties.** These are punishments applied to the offender in his or her neighborhood rather than in a penal setting. As Vass (1996) explains it,

> In conceptual terms, community penalties can refer to a wide assortment of tasks, sentences and dispositions . . . [and] can include many diverse activities in the criminal justice system: not just sentencing options following conviction, but also pre-trial decisions and even broader policies of preventing risk groups, such as juveniles, from experiencing formal justice and control. (p. 157)

Examples of community penalties vary and include the following:

> . . . fines and fixed penalties; electronic monitoring; intermediate treatment projects for juveniles; probation orders (with or without conditions or requirements); supervision orders; suspended sentences of imprisonment; parole; deferred sentences; compensation orders; binding over . . . [and] community service orders . . . [etc.]. (p. 157)

Community penalties have been varyingly described as community-based penal measures, community justice programs, decarceration, supervision in the community, punishment in the community, and community sentencing, among others. Vass (1996) attempts to give a definition to this rather ambiguous concept: "In general terms, what [such descriptions of community penalty] seem to have in common is that they denote almost anything which involves crime prevention, punishment or control outside custodial institutions" (p. 158). Although certainly less novel in many respects than victim-offender mediation programs, community penalties value intervention that occurs outside the confines of correctional environments.

DISCUSSION QUESTIONS

1. What is forensic psychology and what is its relationship to criminal behavior?
2. What are the strengths and limits of the clinical approach to forensic psychology? What are the strengths and limits of the law–psychology approach to forensic psychology? What are the strengths and limits of the law–psychology–justice approach to forensic psychology?
3. At the undergraduate level, what are some of the educational challenges that confront the field of forensic psychology as it prepares students to address the problems posed by crime and delinquency?
4. What is procedural justice and what is its relationship to the study of criminal behavior?
5. What is commonsense justice and what is its relationship to the study of criminal behavior?
6. What is therapeutic jurisprudence and what is its relationship to the study of criminal behavior?
7. What is restorative justice and what is its relationship to the study of criminal behavior?
8. How does victim–offender mediation (VOM) offer a future direction by which to promote social and individual change, especially as a response to the problems posed by crime and delinquency?
9. How do mental health courts work? As a policy matter, do you believe they are an effective solution to the problems posed by psychiatrically disordered offenders and revolving-door criminal justice treatment?
10. What are therapeutic communities and how do they function? As a policy matter, do you believe therapeutic communities are a useful direction by which to address the problems posed by criminal behavior?

REFERENCES

Arrigo, B. A. (1993a). *Madness, language, and law.* Albany, NY: Harrow and Heston.

Arrigo, B. A. (1993b). Paternalism, civil commitment, and illness politics: Assessing the current debate and outlining a future direction. *Journal of Law and Health, 7*(2), 131–168.

Arrigo, B. A. (1994). Rooms for the misbegotten: On social design and social deviance. *Journal of Sociology and Social Welfare, 21,* 95–113.

Arrigo, B. A. (1995). The peripheral core of law and criminology: On postmodern social theory and conceptual integration. *Justice Quarterly, 12*(3), 447–472.

Arrigo, B. A. (1996). *The contours of psychiatric justice: A postmodern critique of mental illness, criminal insanity, and the law.* New York: Garland.

Arrigo, B. A. (1997a). Recommunalizing drug offenders: The drug peace agenda. *Journal of Offender Rehabilitation, 14,* 53–73.

Arrigo, B. A. (1997b). Dimensions of social justice in a single room occupancy (SRO): Contributions from chaos theory, policy, and practice. In D. Milovanovic (Ed.), *Chaos, criminology and social justice* (pp. 179–194). New York: Praeger.

Arrigo, B. A. (Ed.). (1999). *Social justice/criminal justice: The maturation of critical theory in law, crime, and deviance.* Belmont, CA: West/Wadsworth.

Arrigo, B. A. (2000). *Introduction to forensic psychology: Issues and controversies in crime and justice.* San Diego, CA: Academic Press.

Arrigo, B. A. (2001). Reviewing graduate training models in forensic psychology: Implications for practice. *Journal of Forensic Psychology Practice, 1*(1), 9–31.

Arrigo, B. A. (2002a). Forensic psychology. In D. Levinson (Ed.), *The encyclopedia of crime and punishment* (Vol. II, pp. 1295–1301). Thousand Oaks, CA: Sage.

Arrigo, B. A. (2002b). The critical perspective in psychological jurisprudence: Theoretical advances and epistemological assumptions. *International Journal of Law and Psychiatry, 25,* 151–172.

Arrigo, B. A. (2002c). *Punishing the mentally ill: A critical analysis of law and psychiatry.* Albany, NY: SUNY Press.

Arrigo, B. A. (2003). Psychology and the law: The critical agenda for citizen justice and radical social change. *Justice Quarterly, 20*(2), 399–444.

Arrigo, B. A., & Schehr, R. C. (1998). Restoring justice for juveniles: A critical analysis of victim offender mediation. *Justice Quarterly, 15*(4), 629–666.

Arrigo, B. A., & Tasca, J. J. (1999). Right to refuse treatment, competency to be executed, and therapeutic jurisprudence: Toward a systematic analysis. *Law and Psychology Review, 23*(1), 1–47.

Arrigo, B. A., & Williams, C. R. (2001). The ethics of advocacy for the mentally ill: Philosophic and ethnographic considerations. *Seattle University Law Review, 24*, 245–295.

Arrigo, B. A., & Williams, C. R. (2003). Victim vices, victim voices, and impact statements: On the place of emotion and the role of restorative justice. *Crime and Delinquency, 49*(4), 603–626.

Barak, G., & Henry, S. (1999). An integrative-constitutive theory of crime, law, and social justice. In B. A. Arrigo (Ed.), *Social justice/criminal justice: The maturation of critical theory in law, crime, and deviance* (pp. 152–175). Belmont, CA: West/Wadsworth.

Bazemore, G., & Schiff, M. (Eds.). (2001). *Restorative community justice: Repairing harm and transforming communities*. Cincinnati, OH: Anderson.

Bazemore, G., & Umbreit, M. S. (1995). Rethinking the sanctioning function in juvenile court: Retributive or restorative responses in youth crime. *Crime and Delinquency, 41*, 296–316.

Bersoff, D. N., Goodman-Delahunty, J., Grisso, J. T., Hans, V. P., Poythress, N. G., Jr., & Roesch, R. G. (1997). Training in law and psychology: Models from the Villanova conference. *American Psychologist, 52*(12), 1301–1310.

Braithwaite, J. (1998). Restorative justice. In M. Tonry (Ed.), *The handbook of crime and punishment* (pp. 323–344). New York: Oxford University Press.

Edwards, W., & Hensley, C. (2001). Restructuring sex offender sentencing: A therapeutic jurisprudence approach to the criminal justice process. *International Journal of Offender Therapy and Comparative Criminology, 45*, 646–662.

Filstead, W. J., & Rossi, J. J. (1973). Therapeutic milieu, therapeutic community, and milieu therapy: Some conceptual and definitional distinctions. In J. J. Rossi & W. J. Filstead (Eds.), *The therapeutic community* (pp. 285–300). New York: Behavioral Publications.

Finkel, N. J. (1995). *Commonsense justice*. Cambridge, MA: Harvard University Press.

Finkel, N. J. (1996). Culpability and commonsense justice: Lessons learned betwixt murder and madness. *Notre Dame Journal of Law, Ethics and Public Policy, 10*, 11–39.

Finkel, N. J. (2000). Commonsense justice and jury instructions: Instructive and reciprocating connections. *Psychology, Public Policy and Law, 6*, 591–628.

Finkel, N. J., & Sales, B. D. (1997). Commonsense justice: Old roots, germinant ground, and new shoots. *Psychology, Public Policy and Law, 3*, 227–241.

Flaten, C. (1996). Victim offender mediation: Application with serious offenses committed by juveniles. In B. Galaway & J. Hudson (Eds.), *Restorative justice: International perspectives* (pp. 387–402). Monsey, NY: Criminal Justice Press.

Fox, D. R. (2001). A critical-psychology approach to law's legitimacy. *Legal Studies Forum, 225*, 519–538.

Galaway, B. (1988). Crime victim and offender mediation as a social work strategy. *Social Service Review, 62*, 668–683.

Hafemeister, T. L., Ogloff, J. R. P., & Small, M. A. (1990). Training and careers in law and psychology: The perspective of students and graduates of dual degree programs. *Behavioral Sciences and the Law, 8*, 263–283.

Hasselbrack, A. M. (2001). Opting to mental health courts. *Corrections Compendium, 26*(10), 4, 25.

Horowitz, I. A. (1997). Reasonable doubt instructions: Commonsense justice and standard of proof. *Psychology, Public Policy and Law, 3*, 285–302.

Jackall, R. (2000). Investigating criminal violence. *Social Research, 67*(3), 849–875.

Jones, M. (1973). Towards a clarification of the "therapeutic community" concept. In J. J. Rossi & W. J. Filstead (Eds.), *The therapeutic community* (pp. 17–27). New York: Behavioral Publications.

Kiger, R. S. (1973). Treating the psychopathic patient in a therapeutic community. In J. J. Rossi & W. J. Filstead (Eds.), *The therapeutic community* (pp. 285–300). New York: Behavioral Publications.

Lerner-Wren, G., & Appel, A. R. (2001). A court for the non-violent defendant with a mental disability. *Psychiatric Annals, 31*, 453–458.

Lessard v. Schmidt, 349 F. Supp. 1084 (E.D. Wisc. 1972).

Levine, M., & Wallach, L. (2002). *Psychological problems, social issues, and law*. Boston, MA: Allyn & Bacon.

Levrant, S., Cullen, F. T., Fulton, B., & Wozniak, J. F. (1999). Reconsidering restorative justice: The corruption of benevolence revisited? *Crime and Delinquency, 45*(1), 3–27.

Lind, E. A., & Tyler, T. R. (1988). *The social psychology of procedural justice*. New York: Plenum.

Marshall, T. (1998). *Restorative justice: An overview*. London: Restorative Justice Consortium.

Maruna, S. (2001). *Making good: How ex-convicts reform and rebuild their lives*. Washington DC: American Psychological Association.

Maruna, S. (2004). Is rationalization good for the soul: Resisting "responsibilization" in corrections and courts. In B. A. Arrigo (Ed.), *Psychological jurisprudence: Critical explorations in law, crime, and society*. Albany, NY: SUNY Press.

Mazerolle, P., & Piquero, A. (1997). Violent responses to strain: An examination of conditioning influences. *Violence and Victims, 12,* 323–343.

Murdoch, L. L. (2001). Psychological consequences of adopting a therapeutic lawyering approach: Pitfalls and protective strategies. *Seattle University Law Review, 24,* 483–498.

Nugent, W. R., Umbreit, M. S., Wiinamki, L., & Paddock, J. (2001). Participation in victim-offender mediation and reoffense: Successful Replications? *Research on Social Work Practice, 11*(1), 5–23.

O'Neil, W. J., & Schneider, B. C. (1999). Recommendations of the committee to study family law issues in the Arizona Superior Court: A family court system. *Family and Conciliation Courts Review, 37,* 179–193.

Palermo, G. B., & Farkus, M. (2001). *The dilemma of the sexual offender.* Springfield, IL: Thomas.

Patch, P. C., & Arrigo, B. A. (1999). Police officer attitudes and the use of discretion in situations involving the mentally ill: The need to narrow the focus. *International Journal of Law and Psychiatry, 22,* 23–55.

Patry, M. W. (1998). Better legal counseling through empirical research: Identifying psycholegal soft spots and strategies. *California Western Law Review, 34,* 439–467.

Pepinsky, H. (1998). Empathy works, obedience doesn't. *Criminal Justice Policy Review, 9,* 141–167.

Rigby, A. (2001). *Justice and reconciliation: After the violence.* Boulder: Lynne Rienner Publishers.

Ross, J. I., & Richards, S. C. (2002). *Behind bars: Surviving prison.* Indianapolis, IN: Alpha.

Schehr, R. C., & Milovanovic, D. (1999). Conflict mediation and the postmodern: Chaos, catastrophe, and psychoanalytic semiotics. *Social Justice, 26*(1), 208–232.

Siegel, L. J. (1992). *Criminology* (4th ed.). St. Paul, MN: West.

Smith-Cunnien, S. L., & Parilla, P. F. (2001). Restorative justice in the criminal justice curriculum. *Journal of Criminal Justice Education, 12*(2), 385–403.

Stolle, D. P. (1997). Integrating preventive law and therapeutic jurisprudence: A law and psychology based approach to lawyering. *California Western Law Review, 35,* 17–43.

Sullivan, D., & Tifft, L. (2001). *Restorative justice: Healing the foundations of our everyday lives.* Monsey, NY: Willow Tree Press.

Tomkins, A. J., & Ogloff, J. R. P. (1990). Training and career options in psychology and law. *Behavioral Sciences and the Law, 8,* 205–216.

Tsai, B. (2000). The trend toward specialized domestic violence courts: Improvements on an effective innovation. *Fordham Law Review, 68,* 1285–1307.

Tyler, T. R., Boeckman, R. J., Smith, H. J., & Huo, Y. J. (1997). *Social justice in a diverse society.* Boulder, CO: Westview Press.

Umbreit, M. S. (1993). Crime victims and offenders in mediation: An emerging area of social work practice. *Social Work, 38,* 69–73.

Umbreit, M. S. (1994). Mediating homicide cases: A journey of the heart through dialogue and mutual aid. *Victim-Offender Mediation, 5,* 1–4.

Umbreit, M. S. (1995). The development and impact of victim-offender mediation in the United States. *Mediation Quarterly, 21,* 263–276.

Umbreit, M. S., & Greenwood, J. (1998). *National survey of victim offender mediation programs in the United States.* Washington DC: U.S. Department of Justice, Office for Victims of Crime.

Van Ness, D., & Strong, K. (1997). *Restoring Justice.* Cincinnati, OH: Anderson.

Vass, A. A. (1996). Community penalties: The politics of punishment. In T. May & A. A. Vass (Eds.), *Working with offenders: Issues, contexts and outcomes* (pp. 157–184). London: Sage.

Viano, E. C. (2000). Restorative justice for victims and offenders: A return to American traditions. *Corrections Today, 62*(4), 132–135.

Weiner, I. B., & Hess, A. K. (Eds.). (1987). *Handbook of forensic psychology.* New York: Wiley.

Wexler, D. B. (1992). Putting mental health into mental health law: Therapeutic jurisprudence. *Law and Human Behavior, 16,* 27–38.

Wexler, D. B. (2001). The development of therapeutic jurisprudence: From theory to practice. In L. E. Frost & R. J. Bonnie (Eds.), *The evolution of mental health law* (pp. 279–289). Washington DC: American Psychological Association.

Wexler, D. B., & Winick, B. J. (1991). *Essays in therapeutic jurisprudence.* Durham, NC: Carolina Academic Press.

Winick, B. J. (1997). The jurisprudence of therapeutic jurisprudence. *Psychology, Public Policy, and Law, 3,* 184–206.

Winick, B. J. (1998). Sex offender law in the 1990s: A therapeutic jurisprudence analysis. *Psychology, Public Policy and Law, 4,* 505–570.

Winick, B. J. (2001). The civil commitment hearing: Applying the law therapeutically. In L. E. Frost
    & R. J. Bonnie (Eds.), *The evolution of mental health law* (pp. 291–308). Washington DC: Ameri-
    can Psychological Association.

Wolfer, L., & Friedrichs, D. O. (2001). A commitment to justice at a Jesuit university: A comparison
    of criminal justice majors to non-majors. *Journal of Criminal Justice Education, 12*(2), 319–336.

Wright, M. (1991). *Justice for victims and offenders.* Philadelphia: Open University Press.

Wrightsman, L. S. (2001). *Forensic psychology.* Belmont, CA: Wadsworth.

Wrightsman, L. S., Nietzel, M. T., & Fortune, W. H. (1998). *Psychology and the legal system* (4th ed.).
    Pacific Grove, CA: Brooks/Cole.

Young, I. (1990). *Justice and the politics of difference.* Princeton, NJ: Princeton University Press.

Zehr, H. (1990). *Changing lenses: A new focus for crime and justice.* Scottsdale, PA: Herald.

Glossary

10–20–Life law   A retributive form of legislation designed in Florida to punish anyone who uses a gun to commit a crime by enforcing harsh mandatory sentencing; under this law persons convicted of carrying a gun during the commission of a crime face 10 years in prison; those who fire a gun during the commission of a crime receive 20 years in prison; and those who harm or kill someone by firing a gun during the commission of a crime can receive 25 years to life without parole and without time deducted for good behavior.

Acquaintance rape   A subcategory of forcible rape, also termed *date rape,* defined as an act in which the female victim is assaulted by someone known to her, ranging from a man she has just met, to a close friend, boyfriend, or husband.

Alcohol intoxication   The presence of clinically significant maladaptive behavioral or psychological changes that develop during, or shortly after, the ingestion of alcohol.

Anomie   Social instability resulting from a breakdown of standards and values; a weakening of the normative order in society or societal normlessness (Durkheim); cultural chaos produced when social organization fails to respond to nonconformity of its members (Merton).

Anomie theory (Durkheim)   A theory recognizing that social structure functions to provide opportunities to attain desired goals and functions to place limits on cultural necessities; rapid modernization within organic societies, where different social groups depend on each other in a highly organized division of labor, works to foster a state of disharmony among its people, moving the society toward a state of normlessness (anomie) making the production of crime more likely; criminal behavior increases during large-scale phases of social change; anomie at a societal level results in strain at the individual level, leading to anger and frustration, and then leading to possibly suicide or other violent acts.

Anomie theory (Merton)   A theory claiming that the interaction of a society's culture and structure resulted in a tendency for social norms to lose their regulatory force, and that these strains and pressures create high rates of crime and deviance; when means and ends are unbalanced within a society emphasizing beneficial economic outcomes, psychopathological personalities, antisocial conduct, or revolutionary activities may follow; when anomie occurs, individuals pursue illegal means (criminal behavior) in order to obtain desired ends (money) because of an insufficient ability to gain economic success legally, because of the perceived efficiency of implementing illegal means rather than legal means, and because of the lack of appropriate guidelines providing a behavioral basis for success in a market economy; strain at the individual level leads to anomie at a societal level.

Anthropophagy   A sadistic paraphilia associated with lust murder, implicating an intense desire to eat the flesh or body parts of another.

Antisocial personality disorder   A pervasive pattern of disregard for, and violation of, the rights of others that begins in childhood or early adolescence and continues into adulthood. The symptoms of such include a failure to conform to social norms with respect to lawful behaviors, deceitfulness, impulsivity, irritability and aggressiveness, reckless disregard for the safety of the self or others, consistent irresponsibility, and a lack of remorse.

Appellate process   The process whereby, after an individual has been found guilty within the legal system, he or she has the opportunity to appeal the conviction; this process is designed to ensure that constitutional rights are protected and that persons convicted unjustly have an avenue to pursue a new trial.

Arousal theory   A biosocial theory, which hypothesizes that delinquents engage in criminal behavior for the thrill of the crime.

Arson   The willful and malicious burning of property.

Atavism (criminal atavism)   A biological trait theory developed by Cesare Lombroso (1835–1909), which states that delinquents possess irregular physical characteristics, making them more similar, both biologically and physiologically, to primitive humans.

Axis I mental disorders   Psychiatric conditions that may be a focus of clinical attention, excluding personality disorders and mental retardation.

Axis II mental disorders   Psychiatric conditions including all personality disorders.

Bankruptcy fraud   An offense popular within some organized crime circles, whereby a legitimate business owner acquires solid credit, and then large orders are placed for merchandise yet payments on the goods are not submitted; the merchandise is then fenced out the back door without the knowledge of the bank or the lending institution; the organized crime syndicates escape with the merchandise and the money, while bankruptcy is filed on the part of the legitimate business.

Battered woman syndrome   A controversial psychiatric condition that women who have been constant recipients of physical, verbal, and emotional abuse, threats, and intimidation by their husbands or significant others are susceptible to; a unique legal defense that can be used as justification for either a self-defense or an insanity defense.

Behavior potential   According to Rotter and her expansion of Dollard and Miller's social learning theory, behavior potential refers to the range of actions a person may choose to express in a certain situation in order to attain a particular outcome.

Behaviorist approach   A perspective included in the developmental theory of personality, maintaining the view that the environment acts as the main determinant of personality.

Bidirectional approach   An approach to substance abuse contending that drugs and crime are causes and effects of one another; this approach suggests that appropriate intervention methods include the establishment of therapeutic communities.

Biocriminology   An interdisciplinary theory of criminal behavior, emphasizing an integration and interaction of biology, psychology, and sociology; basically states that the individual is a product of the interaction between his or her genetics and the environment.

Biological personality theories   Theories that use physiological variables as indicators of personality types.

Biosocial theories   Theories embracing the notion that the environment can alter an individual's tendency to engage in criminal behavior, integrating biology and sociology; focusing on biochemical reactions, neurological dysfunction, genetic influences, or the evolutionary theory.

Bipolar disorder   A life-threatening psychiatric condition highly correlated with antisocial behavior; symptoms include delusions, flat affect, incoherence, and hallucinations, which can lead to suicidal behavior.

Bipolar I disorder   The most common subtype of bipolar disorder, involving both full manic (manic episodes) and full depressive symptoms.

Bipolar II disorder   A subtype of bipolar disorder, involving full depressive symptoms in conjunction with hypomanic episodes.

Bipolar disorder not otherwise specified (NOS)   A subtype of bipolar disorder, including disorders with bipolar features, yet do not meet the formal criteria for bipolar disorder I or II.

Black rage defense   A legal defense asserting that Black people who are constantly subjected to actions that are perceived by them to be unfair and oppressive become angry, despite an appearance of external calm.

Bookmaking   An organized form of gambling, consisting of taking bets and manufacturing point spreads and odds on sporting events.

Boot camp   An intermediate sanction program designed for young, inexperienced, and nonviolent offenders; participants are usually sentenced for 3 to 4 months, and upon release remain on probation for the remainder of their sentence.

Borderline personality disorder   A personality disorder where the individual is somewhere between the Freudian-defined states of "neurosis" and "psychosis"; a pervasive pattern of instability of interpersonal relationships, self-image, affects, and a marked impulsivity beginning by early adulthood which is present in a variety of contexts; these individuals make frantic efforts to avoid real or imagined abandonment and display recurrent suicidal behavior, gestures, threats, or self-mutilating behavior.

Burglary   The unlawful entry of a structure to commit a felony or theft.

California Psychological Inventory (CPI)   A psychometric instrument that is designed to predict interpersonally consequential behavior and to identify individuals describable in important and differentiating ways by knowledgeable observers; an assessment tool that lends support to the notion that criminals think differently from noncriminals.

Child abuse   The violent abuse of a child, falling into one of four categories: physical abuse, emotional abuse, sexual abuse, or general neglect.

Child pornography   Any visual depiction, including any photograph, film, video, picture, or computer-generated image or picture of sexually explicit conduct of a minor.

Civil commitment   The process by which an individual is detained in a psychiatric facility because the person is mentally ill, is dangerous to self or others, and engages in behaviors suggestive of the nature and quality of one's psychiatric disorder.

Classroom avenger   As described by McGee and DeBernardo, the "classroom avenger" is the potentially dangerous student who perpetrates violence at school when they experience discipline by parents or authorities, or rejection by peers, boyfriends, or girlfriends; the motive is vengeance, and the action is a premeditated shooting spree with parents, fellow students, and faculty as target victims.

Commonsense justice   A criminal justice perspective that provides ordinary individuals with a practical theory about human perceptions, emotions, and behaviors, representing what people in society perceive as just as fair; commonsense justice strives to achieve what is best practically for victims and offenders, not what is best for them based on some prejudicial standard, based chiefly on personal beliefs and communal preferences.

Community policing   A form of policing where officers, in addition to their regular duties, are expected to establish more direct and intimate relationships with people in the community they serve in order to deter crime and raise the quality of life within lower income neighborhoods.

Competency to be executed   A two-prong test indicating that a prisoner cannot be executed by the state if he or she is mentally incompetent; to be found incompetent for execution the person must be unable to understand (a) the death penalty and (b) the reason's for execution in one's particular case.

Competency to stand trial   A person's ability to understand the nature and purpose of the court proceedings, and is applicable at every stage of the criminal justice process, from interrogations and pretrial hearings to trials and sentencing hearings; the Dutsky standard for competency to stand trial includes the accused's (a) present ability to sufficiently consult with one's attorney with a reasonable degree of understanding, and (b) a rational as well as a factual comprehension of the proceedings against the defendant.

Conduct disorder   A personality disorder found in children and adolescents, which displays a repetitive and persistent pattern of behavior in which the basic rights of others or major age-appropriate societal norms or rules are violated; these behaviors can be aggressive conduct that causes or threatens physical harm to other people or animals, nonaggressive conduct that causes property loss or damage, deceitfulness or theft, or serious violations of rules; characteristics include a lack of empathy, manipulative charm, and deceit.

Conflict theory   A theory stating that the occurrence of crime is a result of conflicting interests and values among members of a community; groups with less voice in a society are at risk for being treated as criminal when they behave according to their own interests, especially when these interests conflict with those in power.

Conflict model   A model of society assuming that at every point a society is subject to change, that society displays at every point conflict and disagreement, that every element of society contributes to change, and that society is based on the coercion of some of its members by others; according to the conflict model, society is held together by force and constraint and is characterized by ubiquitous conflicts that result in continuous change.

Consensus model   A model of society contrasting with the conflict theory of society; stating that society is a relatively stable structure; society is well integrated; every element of society has a function that helps to stabilize the system; and that society is a functioning, cohesive structure based on a consensus of values.

Contextual discrimination   A form of racial profiling within the courtroom whereby harsher sentences are imposed on racial minorities who victimize Whites, and more lenient sentences are imposed on racial minorities who victimize members of their own racial or ethnic group.

Control theories   Social–psychological perspectives that address crime, including social control theory and the learning or differential association theory.

Conviction appeal   An appeal that requests the higher court to overturn a guilty verdict.

Criminal profiling   The process of inferring distinctive personality characteristics of individuals responsible for committing criminal acts based on offender and victim data; often referred to as psychological or investigative profiling.

Criminal thinking errors   A theory developed by Yochelson and Samenow stating that criminals adopt thinking and reasoning patterns that are contrary to the thinking and reasoning of law-abiding individuals.

Critical theories   Theories exploring the idea of what justice is and for whom justice is served; theories suggesting that those who create and enforce laws also manipulate them, and these laws function to benefit the needs and interests of those who govern and to oppress and pacify those who are governed; includes Marxist or radical theories, peacemaking theories, postmodern criminology, the anarchist theory, the chaos theory, psychoanalytic semiotics, critical race theory, and integrative criminology.

Cue   As outlined by Dollard and Miller in their social learning theory, a motivator that determines when, where, and how an individual will react to a stimulus.

Cult   A group or movement that (a) exhibits excessive devotion to some person, idea or thing; (b) uses a thought–reform program to persuade, control, and socialize members; (c) systematically includes states of psychological dependency in members; and (d) exploits members to advance their leadership goals and causes psychological harm to members, their families, and the community.

Cyberstalking   The use of the Internet as a medium for harassment and stalking behaviors.

Cycle of violence   The three-phase cycle of spousal abuse, including the tension-building phase, the battering incident, and then the honeymoon phase, which then cycles back to the tension-building phase again.

Defense mechanisms   Mental actions operating on an unconscious level, distorting reality so as to protect the person from real or perceived mental harm.

Delinquent lifestyle   A criminal lifestyle including these four behavioral characteristics: irresponsibility, self-indulgence, interpersonal intrusiveness, and social rule breaking.

Denial   An ego defense mechanism occurring when a person refuses to accept the fact that something unpleasant or troubling has happened.

Deterrence   One of four important goals inherent in the criminal justice system's philosophical approach to crime and punishment; deterrence is designed to impose a sentence that would inhibit the offender from engaging in similar criminal behavior (specific deterrence), and to send a message to society that such actions will not be tolerated in the future (general deterrence).

Developmental theory   A personality theory including psychoanalytic, behavioral, humanistic and sociocultural and biosocial perspectives.

Diathesis   A biological or genetic condition (or predisposition) that makes an individual vulnerable to stress.

Diathesis–stress model   A theory suggesting that stress works to activate a diathesis, which transforms one's predisposition for violent or aggressive action into the presence of criminal behavior or psychopathology; psychosocial stressors precipitate disorders, but biology determines the form of the disorder.

Differential association   A term used in Sutherland and Akers' social learning theory, stating that the patterns of interaction with others who are the source of definitions that are either favorable or unfavorable to violating the law.

Differential reinforcement   A term utilized by Akers in his social learning theory, referring to the real or anticipated effects of a particular behavior.

Diminished responsibility   A legal defense used by persons suffering from a psychiatric disorder deeming themselves not criminally responsible because their mental defect did not allow them to formulate the requisite intent to commit the crime; the results of utilizing this defense often result in a reduction in punishment, or being considered as a mitigating factor at the defendant's sentencing; persons with conditions that cause psychoses, delusions, and impaired reality testing as well as cognitive, brain, organic, medical, or neurological disorders are more likely to meet the criteria for the diminished criminal responsibility standard.

Disciple killer   As defined by Holmes and Holmes, a unique type of mass murderer who is told to kill by a leader whom they follow.

Disgruntled worker   As defined by Holmes and Holmes, a unique type of mass murderer who kills in order to seek revenge against his or her place of employment.

Displacement   An ego defense mechanism where the individual substitutes an anxiety-producing goal with one that does not produce anxiety.

Diversion programs   A form of alternative sentencing, typically used for first-time offenders, younger persons, minor law violators, and individuals who pose little societal risk which is intended to prevent the assigning of stigmatizing labels to adolescents for petty acts; these programs are often community-based initiatives offering alternatives to prosecuting persons formally charged with criminal offenses.

Domestic terrorism   Terrorist acts of force or coercion that occur within the borders of a nation against whom the terrorist group or person is targeting.

Domestic violence (abuse)   Violence within the family or home; broken into the three main categories of child abuse, spousal abuse, and elder abuse.

Drive   As outlined by Dollard and Miller in their social learning theory, any strong stimulus that results in a response, either internally (primal drives) or externally.

D.A.R.E. (Drug Abuse Resistance Education)   A police intervention-oriented initiative designed to educate children about the dangers and risks of drug and alcohol use and abuse in order to prevent violence and the use of tobacco, alcohol, marijuana, and inhalants.

Dual diagnosis   A term applied to individuals who meet the criteria for a diagnosis of a severe mental illness and an alcohol- or drug-related disorder; otherwise known as "co-occurring disorders".

Dumpster diving   A method of obtaining another individual's identity, where the offender sorts through trash cans looking for data, such as credit card receipts, checks, names, addresses, and phone numbers, all of which assist the offender in assuming a new identity.

Ego   One of three interactive systems that, according to Freud, result in an individuals personality; the ego mediates between one's primal needs and society's demands.

Elder abuse   The physical abuse, emotional abuse, sexual abuse, general neglect, medical neglect, abandonment, isolation, fraud, or financial exploitation of a person age 65 or older by a caretaker.

Electrocution   A method of execution available in 11 of the 38 states that have the death penalty; the process of electrocution allows the force of electricity to surge through the body until the condemned's heart has stopped beating.

Electronically generated child pornography   Pornographic images that look exactly like children engaging in sexual conduct, but are merely images created by computers, without using real children.

Embezzlement   The theft of goods that one had been entrusted with by another.

Emotional abuse   A form of child abuse where any type of mental or psychological damage is inflicted on a minor by one's parents or caretakers.

Epiphenomenal approach   An approach to substance abuse contending that drugs are not the cause of crime, and crime is not the result of drugs; this approach suggests that appropriate intervention methods include psychoanalytic and behavioral therapy techniques.

Equipotentiality   The view that all people are equal at birth and are thereafter influenced by their environment; a view vastly rejected by biological trait theorists.

Erotomantic Stalker   A type of stalking offender, much like the love obsessional stalker, except that the delusional thought patterns of the offender here escalate to the point where the person truly believes that he or she is loved by the victim; the perpetrators here are typically females and the victims are men of considerable socioeconomic status or well-known celebrities.

Erotophonophilia   The acting out of deviant sexual behavior by means of brutally and sadistically killing the victim to achieve ultimate sexual satisfaction; located on the extreme end of the paraphilic continuum, commonly referred to as lust murder.

Evolutionary theory   A biosocial theory hypothesizing that aggression and violent behavior exist as positive adaptive behaviors for human evolution, and that these aggressive and violent traits allow their bearers to reproduce disproportionately, therefore affecting the entirety of the gene pool.

Expectancy   According to Rotter and her expansion of Dollard and Miller's social learning theory, expectancy refers to the probability that certain reinforcements will occur if a specific behavior is selected.

False consciousness   A Marxist term, referring to a social and psychological condition in which people accept existing economic relations in society because they are believed to be the result of natural and inevitable forces.

Family annihilator   As defined by Holmes and Holmes, a unique type of mass murderer who kills multiple family members, typically in their own home.

Firing squad   A method of execution available in 3 of the 38 states that have the death penalty; here the prisoner is strapped to a chair and a hood is placed over the convict's head and five shooters armed with .30-caliber weapons aim at the white cloth target placed over the person's heart.

Flagellationism   A sadistic paraphilia associated with lust murder, implicating an intense desire to beat, whip, or club someone.

Flat affect   A symptom found in individuals with schizophrenia and bipolar disorder, which includes restrictions in the range and intensity of emotional expression.

Forcible rape   The carnal knowledge of a female, forcibly against her will; inclusive of sexual assault and attempts to commit rape by either threat or force.

Foreign terrorism   Terrorist acts taking place outside of the country in conflict with the group's political, religious, or ideological belief, targeting citizens of that nation abroad; also called transnational terrorism.

Forensic psychology   A unique paradigm to the study of criminal behavior that investigates issues and controversies at the intersection of criminal justice and mental health, informed by the disciplines of law and psychology; forensic psychology works as a template both to understand the link between offender conduct and individual harm, and to understand systematic responses to both.

Fraud   The act of deceiving or misrepresenting.

Free association   A Freudian concept referring to a psychoanalytic process in which the patient says whatever comes to his or her mind in relation to that person's fantasies, memories, dreams, or conflicts, helping the patient to analyze his or her thoughts, beliefs, attitudes, and feelings.

Gangs   A gathering of men or women in order to maintain a sense of purpose, camaraderie, psychological and emotional support, entertainment, and economic well-being; gangs can exist on response to racial identity and pride or as a profit-seeking entity within a particular neighborhood.

Gang bangers   An extremely violent cadre of youth organized around a particular neighborhood, who forcefully defend their community against the threat of outside invasion.

Gas chamber   A method of execution available in 4 of the 38 states that have the death penalty; here crystals of sodium cyanide are released, causing a chemical reaction that discharges hydrogen cyanide gas; and after breathing in several times, the condemned eventually dies of hypoxia.

General strain theory   A strain theory developed by Robert Agnew focusing on an individual social–psychological level of strains; when individuals are treated in ways they do not appreciate, negative affects occur, most commonly characterized by anger and frustration which can pressure adolescents into delinquency if other coping strategies are not present.

Genetic theory   A theory proposing that an individual's chromosomal characteristics result from the genes received by the person from his or her parents; criminal behaviors according to this theory then are the result of an inheritance of criminal genes.

Group conflict theory   A theory proposing that once a new law is passed, the group who opposed the law in the legislature are more likely to violate that law, and those who supported the law are more likely to obey and follow it and demand police enforcement of the law against violators.

Guilty But Mentally Ill (GBMI)   A defense strategy that acknowledges that persons with psychiatric disorders are mentally fit enough to be found guilty of a criminal act; defendant is held responsible for the crime, but the presence of a mental disorder is recognized.

Habeas corpus writs (petitions)   A request to release a detained person, usually used in death penalty cases; these petitions challenge the constitutionality of imprisonment because it unjustly violates one's personal liberties.

Halfway houses   Community-based psychiatric home-care facilities, designed to protect patients from the debilitating effects of institutionalization, maintain patients in the community as long as possible, and assist patients in leading relatively normal and independent lives.

Hanging   A method of execution available in 3 of the 38 states that have the death penalty; the convict is placed on top of a chair and a noose is placed around his or her neck, then the chair is removed and the condemned is unable to breath or the neck snaps in the hanging process, resulting in death.

Hate crime   An act of intimidation, harassment, physical force, or threat of physical force, against a person, property, family, or supporter motivated in whole or in part by prejudice due to a person's race, color, religion, ethnicity, gender, disability, sexual orientation, or national origin.

Hedonistic killer   As defined by Holmes and DeBurger, a unique type of serial murderer who kills for the exhilarating thrill of it.

Heredity theory   A theory developed by Charles Goring stating that criminal behavior is an inherited trait, similar to physical traits and features.

Home confinement   An intermediate sanction program that requires offenders to remain at their residences for specific periods of the day; this is enforced by probation officers who call the individual randomly, making home visits, and electronic monitoring.

Hostile work environment sexual harassment   A type of sexual harassment, representing a situation in which an employee is the victim of severe or pervasive sexual conduct that she or he did not welcome.

Hypoglycemia   A medical condition caused by the body's inability to utilize sugar effectively, causing low blood sugar.

Hypomania   One of three distinct manic states; less severe than pure mania, yet characterized by a distinct period of persistently elevated, expansive, or irritable mood, lasting at least 4 days; and clearly distinguishable from the usual nondepressed mood.

Hypomanic episode   A severe mood disturbance, absent of psychotic features, found in individuals with bipolar disorder II; a less severe form of mania that is not sufficiently severe enough to cause marked impairment in social or occupational functioning.

Humanistic approach   A perspective included in the developmental theory of personality, stating that an individual's personality develops as a result of parent–child interactions.

Id   One of three interactive systems that, according to Freud, results in an individual's personality; the id represents unconscious and instinctual desires.

Identity theft (fraud)   Crimes in which a person wrongfully acquires and uses another individual's personal information in a manner that involves fraud or deception, usually for economic gain.

Imitation   A term utilized by Akers in his social learning theory, referring to when individuals participate in the observed behaviors of other people.

Incapacitation   One of four important goals inherent in the criminal justice system's philosophical approach to crime and punishment; incapacitation is designed to isolate the offender, preventing the possibility that similar criminal actions will occur.

Insanity   A legal defense, referring to the ability of the defendant to understand and appreciate the wrongfulness of his or her act, at the time the alleged criminal offense occurred; distinguishable from the term "competency".

Insider trading   A Securities and Exchange Commission (SEC) violation, whereby information or material that is not made public is used for personal profit by those individuals within an organization who own more than 10% of any equity class of securities that must have decision-making authority that affects the entire organization.

Integration   One of three essential activities involved in the money-laundering process, whereby the illicit funds are reintroduced into the legitimate financial economy, allowing the individual to spend or invest the laundered money.

Integrative conflict model   A three-tier model of the criminal law and the processes by which it is formed, proposed by McGarrell and Castellano, dealing with the structural foundations of crime and conflict in societies, the enforcement of criminal laws, and the enactment of criminal laws.

Intensive Supervision Probation (ISP)   An intermediate sanction program designed for high-risk offenders; participants have more contact with probation officers, perform community service, are under some form of house arrest, and are frequently drug tested.

Intermediate sanctions   An alternative sentencing option consisting of a combination of probation and incarceration; some examples include boot camp, home confinement, and ISP.

Internet fraud   The act of deceiving another individual(s) or business(es) through means of the Internet; five general types include auction and retail schemes, business opportunity schemes, identity theft and fraud, investment schemes, and credit card schemes.

Interpersonal triviality   A behavioral characteristic of the juvenile drug lifestyle, occurring when a person downplays the importance of close, interpersonal relationships with family, friends, or other loved ones.

Involuntary civil commitment   Forced psychiatric treatment for individuals who have been found to be incompetent to stand trial, in attempts to restore these individuals to competency.

Irresistible impulse test   A standard that must be met to use the criminal defense of not guilty by reason of insanity (NGRI); this test requires that the accused, as a result of mental disease or defect, lacks the substantial capacity to appreciate the criminality or wrongfulness of his or her conduct or to conform the conduct to the requirements of the law.

Jockers A subculture of rapists within prisons who forcefully penetrate other prisoners in order to further their masculinity and sense of control; these individuals tend to consider themselves heterosexual.

Judicial waivers A type of waiver that assists in determining whether a juvenile should be tried as an adult; a waiver that gives discretionary power to the judges who can waive juveniles into the adult system on their authorization; the decision of which is determined by the offenders age, the offense committed by the juvenile, the youth's past record, the weapon(s) used during the crime, the severity of harm inflicted on the victim(s), the gender of the juvenile, and the race of the offender.

Juvenile drug lifestyle A criminal lifestyle including these four behavioral characteristics: irresponsibility or pseudoresponsibility, stress–coping imbalance, interpersonal triviality, and social rule breaking or bending.

Labeling theory A criminal theory maintaining that societal institutions categorize and define persons as "criminal" or "mentally ill," such that these labels become part of the persons identity, and the individuals then embrace those criminal or stigmatizing characteristics society has assigned to them.

Labor racketeering The illegal infiltration into labor unions by organized crime syndicates for personal profit.

Larceny or Theft The unlawful taking, leading, or riding away of property from the possession or constructive possession of another.

Layering One of three essential activities involved in the money-laundering process, whereby the illicit funds are moved through worldwide financial accounts in an attempt to conceal them.

Legislative waivers (direct file waivers) A type of waiver that assists in determining whether a juvenile should be tried as an adult; waivers designed to elicit a stronger response to serious juvenile crime than the response elicited by the process of judicial waivers; these waivers take into account the level of criminal sophistication demonstrated by the youth, the possibility of rehabilitation for the youth, previous delinquent history of the youth, the success or failure of previous rehabilitation attempts, and the severity of the offense and the circumstances in which the crime occurred.

Less-than-lethal weapons Extremely forceful and immobilizing weapons used by law enforcement that rarely kill, maim, or produce lasting harm in individuals; some examples include pepper spray, rubber bullets, and beanbag guns.

Lethal injection A method of execution available in 34 of the 38 states that have the death penalty; death by lethal injection results from an anesthetic that is administered in order to paralyze the entire muscular system of the condemned, and to stop the person's breathing, which results in respiratory and cardiac arrest.

Life-course-persistent theory of offenders A theory developed by Terrie Moffit stating that life-course-persistent impulsive criminal behavior is a result of early neuropsychological damage caused by early-life shortcomings or prenatal deficiencies.

Loan sharking An organized form of gambling, where a bookie will lend a bettor or gambler a set amount of money, under the condition that the loan or debt will be repaid at a specific date and with a sizable interest rate attached.

Love obsessional stalker A type of stalking offender, where the victim and offender have had no prior relationship with one another; the stalking victims here tend to be high-profile celebrities; the stalking behavior emerges from some sort of delusional thought pattern allowing the stalker to believe that if they met the famous object of their affection, then they would fall in love and have a long-lasting relationship; when the stalker receives no response or acknowledgment from their victim, he or she then relies on threats of physical harm to convey his or her sentiments.

M'Naghten Standard The standard that must be met (in most jurisdictions) to use the criminal defense of not guilty by reason of insanity (NGRI); this test requires that as a result of mental disorder or defect the defendant did not know the nature and quality of the conduct, or that he or she did not know that the act was wrong.

Mandatory minimum sentencing   A form of determinate sentencing specifically designed to support the goal of deterrence and incapacitation by limiting the discretion of judges and parole boards; these laws require a minimum term of incarceration for an offender who commits a particular offense.

Manic episode   A severe mood disturbance, possibly with psychotic features, found in individuals with bipolar disorder I, which causes marked impairment in occupational, social, or relationship functioning; typically these episodes last at least 1 week, or for any duration if the episode requires hospitalization.

Marxist or radical criminology   A branch of criminology, where the goal is to promote social justice by changing or eliminating the political and economic systems that produce inequalities.

Marxist or radical theories   Theories stating that societies are structured in order to criminalize and marginalize those who cannot play by the rules imposed on them by the powerful rule makers.

Mass arsonist   The offender who sets three or more fires at the same location within a limited amount of time.

Mass murder   A phenomenon when an individual kills multiple people over the course of a few minutes or hours, and in the same general area.

Megan's law   A sex offender registration law designed in New Jersey requiring sex offenders to register with local law enforcement upon release from incarceration; this law is designed to assist police and corrections departments in tracking the location of sex offenders released from prison.

Mental health courts   An alternative court that is designed to offer nonpunitive options to psychiatrically disordered offenders based largely on the unique conditions that play a part in their alleged crimes; mental health courts attempt to balance an individual defendant's rights and his or her options for treatment against the public's safety.

Mission-oriented killer   As defined by Holmes and DeBurger, a unique type of serial murderer who kills to rid the world of a certain type of people whose presence they feel is negative for society; they tend to be in touch with reality and aware of their actions.

Mixed mania   One of three distinct manic states; a combination of depressive and manic thoughts; although manic symptoms are present, the content of the individuals thoughts are depressive in nature.

Modeling   As outlined by Akers in an expansion of his social learning theory, modeling contends that people learn deviance by observing the behaviors of others and by evaluating the consequences that those behaviors have for other people.

Money laundering   The process whereby proceeds, reasonably believed to have been derived from criminal activity, are transported, transferred, transformed, converted, or intermingled with legitimate funds, for the purpose of concealing or disguising the true nature, source, disposition, movement, or ownership of those proceeds; the goal of the money-laundering process is to make funds derived from, or associated with, illicit activity appear legitimate.

Moral anxiety   A Freudian-defined form of anxiety that is produced when an inherent moral code or value is about to be violated.

Murder or nonnegligent homicide   The willful (nonnegligent) killing of one human being by another.

Narcissistic Personality Disorder (NPD)   A personality disorder whereby the individual demonstrates a grandiose sense of self-importance and is preoccupied with fantasies of power, brilliance, beauty, and ideal love; individuals with this disorder require excessive amounts of admiration and are interpersonally exploitative.

Necrosadism   A sadistic paraphilia associated with lust murder, implicating sexual contact with a dead body.

Negative emotionality   An increased likelihood of experiencing such feelings of anger and irritability; the theory proposes that individuals with higher levels of negative emotionality have more difficulty regulating their impulses and so are more prone to engaging in criminal behavior.

Neglect A form of child abuse ranging from being unable to care for a child's basic needs to abandoning a youth.

Neighborhood watch Proactive police initiatives, developed to prevent crime by stressing security education, commonsense reporting techniques to reduce the likelihood of becoming victims, and community integration with police presence; otherwise known as community Block Watch programs.

Nets (portable vehicle—Arresting Barriers) A nonlethal device that stops a moving vehicle, thereby confining the vehicle's occupants.

Neurosis A Freudian-defined emotional disorder in which psychic functioning is relatively intact and contact with reality is sound; the result of a conflict between the ego and its id.

Neurotic anxiety A Freudian-defined form of anxiety that is produced when the ego feels it is being taken over by the id and feels these idlike impulses are beyond the ego's control.

Not Guilty by Reason of Insanity (NGRI) A defense strategy that requires a defendant to show that he or she was mentally ill at the time the illicit act occurred; available in most jurisdictions under the standard of M'Naghten.

Numbers running An organized form of gambling, whereby the person manipulating the project (the "controller") employs "runners" who take bets from people in a given area, who then run back to the banker; when it is time for payout, the runners do the distributing and collecting for the banker who holds all of the money.

Objective anxiety A Freudian-defined form of anxiety that is produced out of an awareness of an obvious conscious threat such as impending physical harm.

Obsessional following A clinical definition of stalking, meaning an abnormal or long-term pattern of threat or harassment directed toward a specific individual.

Organized crime All sophisticated networks engaged in a variety of criminal activities, both violent and nonviolent alike.

Paraphilias Sexually deviant or aberrant behaviors, mostly associated crimes that are sexual in nature; they tend to exist on a continuum and vary in severity, with some indexed as criminal in nature (such as pedophilia) and others as seemingly harmless (such as voyeurism); from a clinical perspective, paraphilias are a group of persistent sexual behavioral patterns in which unusual objects, fetishes, rituals, or situations are required for full sexual satisfaction.

Parental responsibility laws Statutes or codes that make parents legally responsible for the intentional damage and injuries inflicted by their children; these laws hold parents accountable for the antisocial behavior of their children and can require them to pay fines, attend court, frequent parenting classes, do community service, and attend school with their children.

Parole The planned release and community management of incarcerated offenders before the actual termination of their prison sentences; a rehabilitative effort.

Peacemaking criminology A branch of criminology, stating that open and frank dialog during the recovery process with criminal offenders, their victims, and with the larger community of which both are a part is essential to restoring societal justice.

Peacemaking theories Theories stating that in order to restore true justice to society, people have to make peace with crime; in addition, theories embracing the belief that individuals must look past the delinquent or criminal behaviors of people and realize that these actions do not define who they are, and that these people resort to criminal conduct because they are in pain, afraid, and in need of compassion.

Pedophilia Recurrent, intense sexually arousing fantasies, sexual urges, or behaviors involving sexual activity with a prepubescent child or children.

Personality A complex set of emotional and behavioral attributes that tend to remain relatively constant as the individual moves from situation to situation.

Personality disorder An enduring pattern of inner experience and behavior that deviates markedly from the expectations of the individual's culture, is pervasive and inflexible, has an onset in adolescence or early adulthood, is stable over time, and leads to distress or impairment.

Personality tests Measures such as the Rorschach Inkblot Test, the Minnesota Multiphasic Personality Inventory-2 (MMPI-2), the Millon Clinical Multiaxial Inventory-III (MCMI-III), and the Thematic Apperception Test (TAT) that assess levels of antisocial behavior in addition to a multitude of other personality factors.

Personality theories Theories assuming that criminal behavior originates in the complex web of emotional and behavioral characteristics of the individual, rather than in biological or environmental factors.

Physical abuse A form of child abuse where bodily injury is inflicted on anyone who is 17 years old or younger by a parent or caretaker.

Piquerism A sadistic paraphilia associated with lust murder, implicating an intense desire to stab, wound, or cut the flesh of another person.

Placement One of three essential activities involved in the money-laundering process, whereby the bulk of the money derived from illicit activities is changed into a less conspicuous form, which is then placed into a legitimate financial system.

Plea bargaining A defendant's agreement to plead guilty to a criminal charge with the reasonable expectation of receiving some sentencing consideration from the state.

Postmodern criminology A branch of criminology, theorizing that language shapes reality and human behavior, and that there is no universal way in which to interpret behavior or serve justice; in addition criminal justice language represents the interests of those in authority, and therefore this language victimizes, alienates, and oppresses its people.

Posttraumatic Stress Disorder (PTSD) A psychological or psychiatric condition affecting individuals who have suffered severe emotional trauma, resulting in sleep disturbance, flashbacks, anxiety, fatigue, and depression.

Power- or control-oriented killers As defined by Holmes and DeBurger, a unique type of serial murderer who kills in order to dominate their victims; they are motivated by the lust for power and control.

Prefrontal dysfunction A condition where the frontal lobe, which controls such functions as judgment, social functioning, and ethical behaviors, has been damaged, possibly resulting in chaotic, disorganized, asocial, and criminal behavior.

Preventive law Integrated with the practice of therapeutic jurisprudence, preventive law is comprised of client interviewing and counseling, along with legal planning to avoid discord within the court system, focusing on the prevention litigation in order to minimize exposure to liability in the future with the ultimate goal being to prevent clients from suffering needless anxiety, depression, distress or resentment.

Primal drives As outlined by Dollard and Miller in their social learning theory, any innate stimuli such as hunger, pain, or sexual urges that give way to acquiring and learning secondary drives.

Probation (community release) The supervised release of offenders; a rehabilitative model of punishment, allowing the defendant's sentence to be suspended as long as the defendant meets all the requirements set forth by probation, such as attendance in treatment programs, travel restriction, drug testing, and work release.

Procedural justice A perspective of crime, law, and behavior that endeavors to foster a just state of affairs in society through a common or shared understanding about social life; procedural mechanisms such as due process, fairness, equity, and reasonableness are emphasized; here the question is whether the procedures used to achieve a just state of affairs in specific societal contexts can be conceived and implemented in a fair and humane way.

Projection An ego defense mechanism occurring when an alternative way to deal with possible anxiety-producing thoughts is attributed to another person.

Property crimes Inclusive of the offenses of burglary, larceny-theft, motor vehicle theft, and arson.

Prostitute   A person who exchanges sex or sexual favors for money, drugs, or other desirable commodities.

Protective factors   Biological variables that may help an individual compensate for high levels of stress or risk factors, possibly safeguarding one against antisocial conduct.

Pseudoresponsibility   A behavioral characteristic of the juvenile drug lifestyle, meaning the failure to meet personal or family obligations while maintaining individual appearances.

Psychoanalytic approach   A perspective included in the developmental theory of personality, stating that unconscious and repressed forces, along with unexamined feelings and situations, impact how one's personality is formed.

Psychoanalytic or psychodynamic theory   A psychological theory developed by Sigmund Freud, rooted in the belief that mental life functions on both conscious and unconscious levels.

Psychoanalysis   The treatment of patients based on the psychological theory developed by Sigmund Freud, rooted in the belief that mental life functions on both conscious and unconscious levels.

Psychodynamic theory of juvenile delinquency   A theory developed by August Aichhorn and his reliance on Freudian psychoanalysis, stating that juvenile offenders possess underdeveloped superegos and therefore have a psychological predisposition toward criminal behavior.

Psychopathy   A severe personality disorder characterized by antisocial thought and behavior; characteristics constituting one a psychopath include glibness, superficial charm, grandiose sense of self-worth, pathological lying, conning or manipulative, lack of remorse, lack of empathy, shallow affect, impulsivity, and failure to accept responsibility for one's own actions.

Psychosis   A Freudian-defined disorder in which the individual is unable to maintain a stable integration of the concept of self or others; the result of a disturbance between the ego and the external world.

Pseudocommando (barricaded sniper)   As defined by Holmes and Holmes, a unique type of mass murderer who kills in order to lash out against society, or to seek revenge against specific individuals, typically occurring within a public setting.

Punks   A subculture of rape victims within prisons who, despite their heterosexuality, are gang raped and sexually enslaved by other convicts; these individuals tend to be nonviolent offenders with smaller physiques.

Pure mania   One of three distinct manic states; a classic acute mania characterized by euphoria and grandiosity, common in persons with bipolar disorder I.

Queens   A subculture of rape victims within prisons who engage in homosexual activity before and after incarceration; these individuals tend to endure brutal physical harm from guards and inmates, despite efforts from the prison system to isolate and protect them.

***Quid pro quo* sexual harassment**   A type of sexual harassment, involving an act in which a supervisor demands sexual favors in exchange for tangible job benefits.

Racial profiling   A form of criminal profiling whereby an individual is stopped by a police officer or security guard because of one's skin color in which there is a fleeting suspicion that the person is engaging in criminal behavior.

Racketeering   Organized criminal activity that includes, but is not limited to, murder, kidnapping, gambling, arson, robbery, bribery, extortion, embezzlement, and dealing in narcotics; a person needs only to belong to or be a co-conspirator with the organization that is committing these unlawful acts.

Rapist (or displaced anger murderer)   A type of sexual homicide offender who kills their victims after raping them, primarily as a means of escaping detection; these offenders do not become sexually satisfied from the rape.

Rationalization   An ego defense mechanism occurring when a person relies on excessive logic to account for one's anxiety-producing situation.

Reaction formation   An ego defense mechanism occurring when the person does the direct opposite of what is indicated by the anxiety-inducing thought, feeling, or impulse.

Rehabilitation One of four important goals inherent in the criminal justice system's philosophical approach to crime and punishment; rehabilitation is designed to reform, treat, or otherwise cure the criminal through therapeutic interventions in a jail, prison, or community setting.

Reinforcement As outlined by Dollard and Miller in their social learning theory, any occurrence that strengthens the tendency for a response to stimulus to be repeated, also known as drive reduction.

Reinforcement value According to Rotter and her expansion of Dollard and Miller's social learning theory, reinforcement value refers to the degree of preference one has for a particular outcome when all outcomes are equal.

Repression An ego defense mechanism occurring when a person is unable to bring to consciousness threatening thoughts, feelings, ideas, or memories.

Restorative justice A criminal justice perspective that promotes the goal of repairing harm and reconstructing relationships among offenders, victims, and the community of which both are a part.

Retribution One of four important goals inherent in the criminal justice system's philosophical approach to crime and punishment; retribution is designed to punish the offender with a sentence that would be proportionate to the crime committed, making the criminal pay their debt to society through incarceration.

Sadistic murderer (or lust murderer) A type of sexual homicide offender who acts out of deviant sexual behavior by means of brutally and sadistically killing the victim to achieve ultimate sexual satisfaction; they tend to mutilate their victims and to repeat their offenses, making them serial in disposition.

Schizophrenia A psychiatric condition highly correlated with antisocial behavior; a disorder that lasts for at least 6 months and includes at least 1 month with two or more of the following symptoms: delusions, hallucinations, disorganized speech, grossly disorganized, or catatonic behavior.

Secondary deviance A term outlined by Lemert describing the process when an individual has incorporated the criminal "label" into their self-image, which this person then allows this criminal designation to become the driving force in his or her interaction with others.

Secondary drives As outlined by Dollard and Miller in their social learning theory, expansions of primary drives, serving as a façade behind which the functions of the underlying primary drives are hidden.

Securities fraud A Securities and Exchange Commission (SEC) violation, involving the fraudulent activities such as the sale, transfer, or purchase of securities or of money interests in the business activities of others.

Self-control theory A theory stemming from Hirschi's social control theory, stating that individuals who had less self-control are more likely to engage in deviant behavior than those with high levels of self-control.

Sentence appeal A request to appeal the sentence due to its severity.

Sentencing The phase in courtroom processing that occurs only after a person has been convicted of a crime; a judge or jury determines how the guilty person should be punished.

Serial arsonist The offender who engages in three or more separate fire-setting incidents with an emotional cooling-off period in between each fire.

Serial murder Holmes and Holmes offer the most general and accepted definition of serial murder as the killing of three or more people over a period of more than 30 days, with a significant cooling-off period between the killings.

Set and run killer As defined by Holmes and Holmes, a unique type of mass murderer who, unlike other mass murderers, seeks to remain anonymous.

Sexual abuse A form of child abuse where a minor is fondled, molested, or penetrated by a parent, caretaker, or other individual above the age of consent.

Sexual abuse cycle A cycle of abuse, beginning when the juvenile responds to a triggering event, giving him a negative outlook toward the future (negative anticipation); feeling hopeless, the juvenile then attempts to avoid the issue altogether; when avoidance is unsuccessful, the juvenile becomes resentful and angry and endeavors to exert power over others in nonsexual ways; as this nonsexual power is displayed, the juvenile fantasizes about other controlling and gratifying behaviors, such as sex; this control and power is eventually expressed outwardly in a sexual manner; the juvenile then attempts to deal with the offense and the fear of being apprehended (fugitive thinking); finally through the use of thinking errors the juvenile assimilates the behavior, and the cycle begins anew.

Sexual harassment Unwanted sexual advances, requests for sexual favors, and other verbal or physical conduct of a sexual nature.

Sexually abusive behavior Any sexual interaction with person(s) of any age that is perpetrated (a) against the victim's will; (b) without consent; or (c) in an aggressive, exploitative, manipulative, or threatening manner.

Shoulder surfing A method of obtaining another individual's identity, where the offender observes an individual using an ATM card or calling card in order to determine pin numbers.

Simple obsessional stalker A type of stalking offender, where the victim and offender have had some sort of prior relationship with one another; the stalking behavior typically emerges in the aftermath of a failed relationship in an attempt for the offender to sustain that relationship.

Skimming An offense popular within some organized crime circles, where money is taken "off the top" of any cash transaction.

Social bonds As defined by Travis Hirschi in his social control theory, social bonds to society such as emotional attachment to other people, commitment to conforming to conventional society, frequent involvement in conventional activities, and a strong belief in the rules of society that work to prevent deviant and criminal behavior.

Social control theory A criminal theory maintaining that the motivations for delinquent behavior are constant across all individuals and that deviant acts are not learned but expressions of natural tendencies for fulfilling the needs and desires that all people possess; a theory originally developed by Travis Hirschi, which stated that different levels of deviance are triggered by the strengths of one's bonds to conventional societal values, because strong social bonds do not reinforce deviant behavior, despite negative or positive peer associations.

Social learning theory A theory originally developed by Dollard and Miller, which focused on the impact that the learning process and reinforcement has on personality development; the theory according to Burgess and Akers maintains that criminal behavior is learned by both the positive and the negative the reinforcements provided by one's environment as well as by members of one's social group; the theory according to Sutherland (also called differential association theory) recognizes that criminal behavior is learned when interacting with intimates, and the individual is exposed to an excess of definitions favorable to law violation over definitions unfavorable to law violation; the theory according to Akers states that both general definitions (moral code and belief system) and specific definitions (the application of selected meanings to a particular behavior) are involved in the learning and meaning-making process.

Social rule breaking A behavioral characteristic of the juvenile drug lifestyle, occurring when an individual engages in dishonest acts with the intention of avoiding conventional rules because they are perceived as unjust or otherwise unfair.

Sociocultural or biosocial approach A perspective included in the developmental theory of personality, stating that social and cultural influences outside of the individual work to develop one's personality.

Somatotype (school of thought) A biological trait theory hypothesizing that delinquents display distinctive body physiques or "types" that increase their susceptibility to certain kinds of criminal behavior.

Spousal abuse The emotional abuse, financial abuse, or physical battering of one's partner.

Spree arsonist   The offender who sets three or more fires at separate occasions, but does not have an emotional cooling-off period between each incident.

Spree murder   A series of murders connected to one event committed over a time period of hours to days without a break or cooling-off period, and may be a subset of either mass or serial murder.

Statutory rape   The carnal knowledge of a female with or without her consent; any male who engages in sexual intercourse with a female minor (as defined by the state).

Strain theory   A theory similar to the anomie theory, developed primarily by Robert Merton, hypothesizing that the greater the perceived discrepancy between aspirations and expectations, the higher the probability of deviant behavior; aspects of social culture and social learning contribute to the creation of criminal behavior and attitudes.

Stalking   The act of willfully, maliciously, and repeatedly following or harassing another person, and therefore making a credible threat, or a threat implied by a pattern of conduct or combination of verbal, written, or electronically communicated statements and conduct made with the intent to place that person in reasonable fear of death or grave bodily injury.

Status offenses   Acts that are illegal for minors only; in most jurisdictions minors are those under the age of 18, with the exception of underage drinking violations, deeming one a minor if under the age of 21.

Stranger rape   A subcategory of forcible rape, defined as an act in which the female victim is assaulted by someone unknown to her, and where the offender is not motivated by sexual forces; three subcategories include the anger, the power, and the sadistic rapist.

Stress   External sources of negative feelings accompanied by physiological arousal; the events or event occurring in close proximity to the appearance of psychopathology.

Stress–coping imbalance   A behavioral characteristic of the juvenile drug lifestyle, meaning that an individual's approach to accommodating tension contributes to long-term stress, even though short-term discomfort might be reduced.

Structural or process theories   Theories of crime stating that higher rates of crime are related to specific environmental situations and influences rather than to individual differences including theories such as differential association theory, conflict theory, strain theory, and developmental theory.

Subcultural theories   Theories of crime stating that the values, norms, and expectations pertaining to an understanding of crime and delinquency produce illicit conduct more so than the actual social conditions in which these ideas are fostered; learned values and norms work together with societal conditions that are transmitted in group settings to produce gang delinquency and crime.

Subcultural theory of gangs   A theory developed by Cohen stating that a separate culture from the dominant culture is formed by male youth rebelling against middle-class values, instating a different set of values in order to achieve a sense of high social status within the subcultural group; a theory developed by Cloward and Ohlin stating that delinquency is a learned behavior performed in an attempt to achieve social status and money.

Subcultural theory of violence   A theory developed by Wolfgang stating that violent subcultures accept behaviors that the dominant culture considers criminal and antisocial; violence within this subculture is normalized and socially tolerated, and an integrated part of the subculture's belief system.

Sublimation   A form of the defense mechanism displacement, occurring when a person identifies and utilizes socially acceptable outlets for their otherwise nonsocially acceptable thoughts, feelings, impulses, and ideas.

Substance abuse   A maladaptive pattern of substance use manifested by recurrent and significant adverse consequences related to the repeated use of substances.

Substance dependence   A pattern of repeated self-administration that can result in tolerance, withdrawal, and compulsive drug-taking behavior.

Superego   One of three interactive systems that, according to Freud, results in an individual's personality; the superego acts as the moral regulator or the conscience overseeing the individual's behaviors and choices.

Techniques of neutralization   Methods individuals may incorporate in order to desta-bilize the criminal "label" that has been attached to them (as described in Labeling Theory in chapter 4) so as to deny responsibility for their behavior as well as to maintain a non-criminal self-image.

Telemarketing fraud   False and misleading statements, representations, and promises made to people, in which goods and services are offered, investments are requested, or donations for charitable causes are asked for.

Terrorism   According to the State Department, terrorism is a violent attack on an inter-nationally protected person or on the liberty of such person; an assassination; the use of, or a threat, attempt, or conspiracy to use any biological agent, chemical agent, or nuclear weapon or device or explosive or firearm with the intent to endanger, directly or indi-rectly, the safety of one or more individuals or to cause substantial damage to property; the objective of a terrorist is to instill terror in a population to further a political, reli-gious, or ideological objective.

Therapeutic community   A collection of individuals in treatment who assemble for the purpose of healing; therapeutic communities in prisons consist of convicts collaborat-ing with the prison staff in order to become active participants in the treatment of other prisoners.

Therapeutic jurisprudence (TJ)   The study of the role of the law as a therapeutic agent; associated with or otherwise impacts a wide array of legal and criminal phenomena such as trauma effects caused by the criminal justice system on victims of sexual abuse, ethics of advocacy for persons with mental illness, the therapeutic and antitherapeutic conse-quences of sex offender registration laws, as well as stalking legislation and community peacemaking efforts.

Thinking errors   Different thought processes (than law-abiding citizens) that result in criminal behavior.

Three Strikes legislation   A form of retributive mandatory minimum sentencing de-signed to incarcerate repeat offenders for long periods of time; California's Three Strikes law mandates that an offender with two prior convictions for serious or violent felonies must be sentenced to at least 25 years to life in prison on the third offense that qualifies as a felony.

Unidirectional approach   An approach to substance abuse contending that crime causes substance abuse and substance abuse causes crime; this approach suggests that appro-priate intervention methods include the use of 12-step programs.

Visionary killer   As defined by Holmes and DeBurger, a unique type of serial murderer who commits murder because of some inner voice commanding him or her to kill; they tend to be psychotic and constantly out of touch with reality.

Waiver (transfer)   The process whereby a juvenile is transferred from juvenile court to the criminal court system; inclusive of legislative and judicial waivers.

White-collar crime   As defined by Edwin Sutherland in 1939, a crime committed by a person of respectability and high social status in the course of his occupation; as defined by Donald Gibbons in 1977, a violation of business rules and occupational practices, but only insofar as those offenses were committed to benefit legitimate enterprises or organ-izations; as defined by Clinnard and Quinney in 1980, as nonviolent infractions of legal codes within an otherwise legitimate occupation or enterprise; as defined by the U.S. Congressional Subcommittees on Crime, an illegal act or series of illegal acts committed by nonphysical means and by concealment or guile, to obtain money or property, or to obtain personal or business advantage.

XYY syndrome   A biosocial or heredity theory hypothesizing that males possessing an ex-tra Y chromosome are predisposed to behave in violent and criminal manners

Index